THE GUINNESS

BOOK OF RECORDS

International Standard Book Number ISBN 0-9652383-9-3

Managing Editor
Nic Kynaston

Editor
Rhonda Carrier

Assistant Editors
Hephzibah Anderson and Georgie Naumann

Picture Editor
Gregory King

Consultant Editor
Elizabeth Wyse

Proof Reader
Debra Clapson

Index
Sue Harper

Designers
Lesley Horowitz and Dominic Sinesio at Office, NYC

Assistant Designers
Garry Waller and Robert Hackett

Mac Operator
Tamsin Pender

Cover
Ron Callow at Design 23 and Office, NYC

Page Production
Catherine Bonifassi

Pre Production Manager
Patricia Langton

Fulfilment
Mary Hill and Cathryn Harker

Director of Records Research
Mark Young

Keeper of the Records
Clive Carpenter

Research
Jane Bolton, Shelley Flacks, John Hansen, Della Howes, Stewart Newport, Antonia Short, Kim Stram

Correspondence
Amanda Brooks

Production Director
Chris Lingard

Colour Origination
Rival Colour

Printing and Binding
Printer Industria Grafica, S.A., Barcelona

Paper
Printed on woodfree, chlorine free and acid free paper

Publishing Director
Ian Castello-Cortes

Managing Director
Christopher Irwin

Abbreviations and measurements

The Guinness Book of Records uses imperial measurements. The only exception to this rule is for some scientific data, where metric measurements only are universally accepted, and for some sports data.

All currency values are shown in dollars. Where a specific date is given the exchange rate is calculated according to the currency values that were in operation at the time. Where only a year date is given the exchange rate is calculated from December of that year.

Accreditation

Guinness Publishing Ltd has a very thorough accreditation system for records verification. However, whilst every effort is made to ensure accuracy, Guinness Publishing Ltd cannot be held responsible for any errors contained in this work. Feedback from our readers on any points of accuracy is always welcomed.

General Warning

Attempting to break records or set new records can be dangerous. Appropriate advice should be taken first and all record attempts are undertaken entirely at the participant's risk. In no circumstances will Guinness Publishing Ltd have any liability for death or injury suffered in any record attempts. Guinness Publishing Ltd has complete discretion over whether or not to include any particular records in the book.

THE GUINNESS

BOOK OF RECORDS

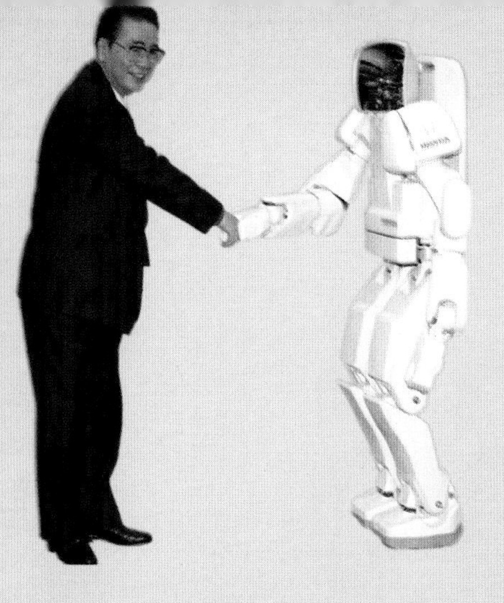

introduction

The Guinness Book of Records that you have in your hands is part of a global phenomenon. Many countries including Brazil, the Czech Republic, Denmark, Finland, France, Germany, Greece, Hungary, Italy, the Netherlands, Norway, Poland, Romania, Russia, Sweden and much of Latin America, as well as the United Kingdom and the United States, have contributed to what we believe is the most exciting *Guinness Book of Records* ever.

Our transatlantic research teams, based in London and Stamford, Connecticut, have brought you not only the latest records, but also whole new categories that reflect the true state of the record-breaking world in 1999. We have even more hi-tech and computer records than last year. There are new music and fashion sections and lots more on stars and celebrities. We also celebrate the achievements of the unique Guinness record-breakers in our section 'Extraordinary People', which features many new records and personalities but also some old favorites surpassing their own extraordinary standards.

Most of you are keen sports fans, and we hope you will like our new Sports Reference section, which begins on page 304. This lists important world records in a quick-access format. You will find the traditional sports section between pages 250 and 303. We are particularly thrilled to have added paralympics records on pages 266 and 267; the sheer determination and excellence of the achievers in this section really captures that special *Guinness Book of Records* spirit.

The records that really stand out this year? As ever it is hard to chose, but Richard Noble's breaking of the land speed record (page 158), the amazing success of the film *Titanic* (page 209) and the winning of an eighth gold medal at the Nagano Olympic Games by Nordic skier Bjørn Dæhlie (page 276), making him the most successful individual in the history of the Winter Olympics, really did amaze everyone.

Finally, remember that we are always in search of new record-breakers. See pages 334 and 335 on how to compete for a record and how you too could become an accredited Guinness record-holder. You never know – you may even see yourself in *The Guinness Book of Records* one day!

contents

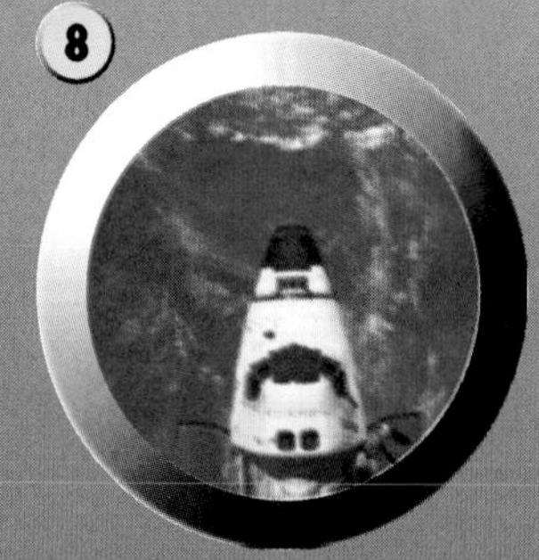

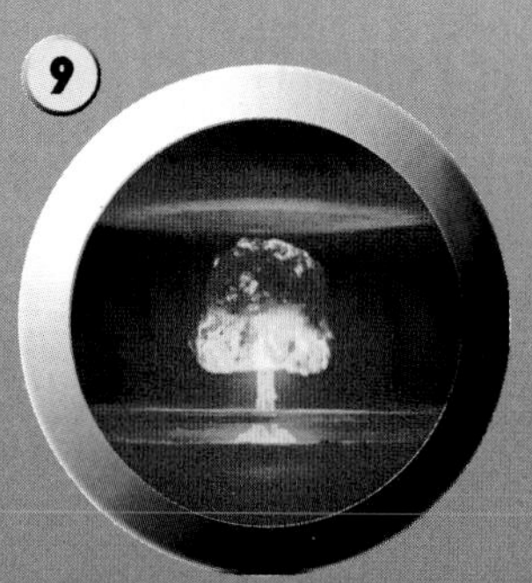

4
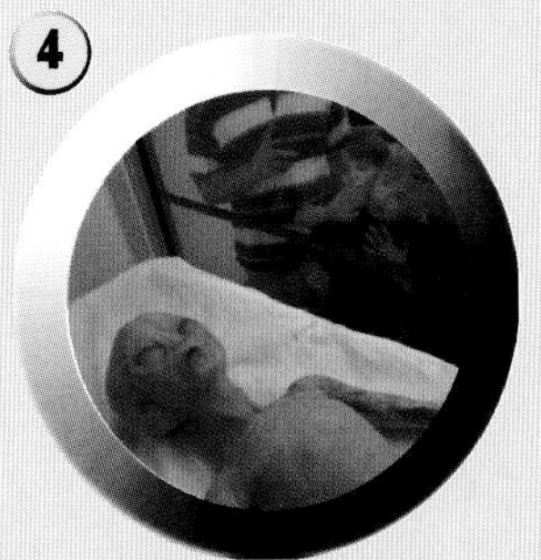

5
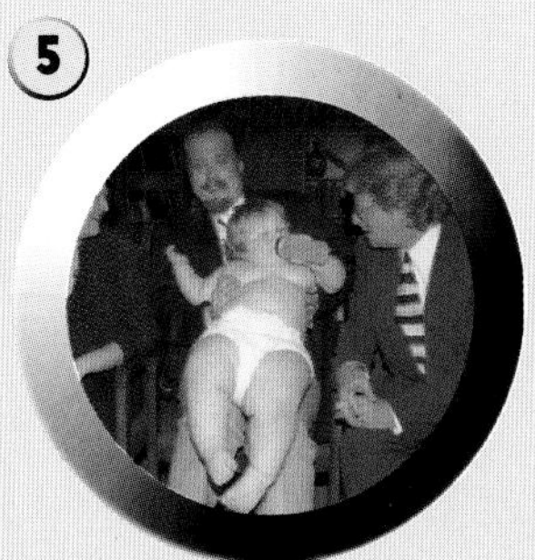

6

10

11

12

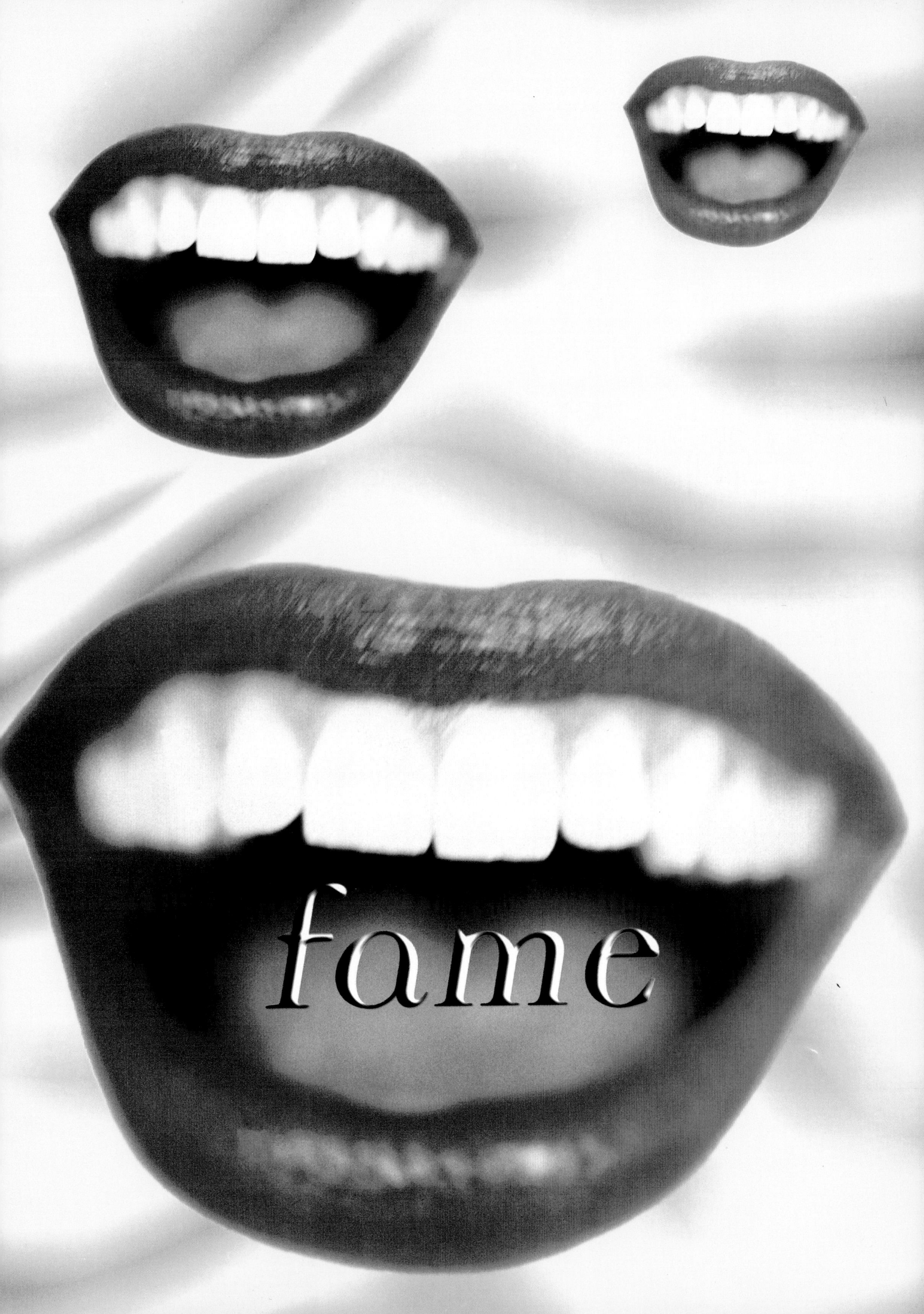
fame

hollywood

RICHEST HOLLYWOOD SCHOOL
Beverly Hills High School is the wealthiest school in Hollywood. The school is set in a 26-acre site on Lasky Drive. Established in 1928, the school's revenue from its own oil wells has underwritten its lavish sports facilities, which include the famous gym-over-a-swimming-pool featured in the Frank Capra movie *It's a Wonderful Life* (1946). The school is used by many Hollywood parents, and famous former pupils have included Richard Dreyfuss, Carrie Fisher, Nicolas Cage and Richard Chamberlain. The school depicted in the TV series *Beverly Hills 90210* is not the real Beverly Hills High School.

MOST MARRIED HOLLYWOOD STARS
Actors Stan Laurel, Mickey Rooney, Lana Turner, Georgia Holt and Zsa Zsa Gabor have all been married a total of eight times. Elizabeth Taylor has also married eight times to date, but has only had seven different husbands: she married Richard Burton twice.

MOST JAILED HOLLYWOOD STAR
Errol Flynn, the star of *The Adventures of Robin Hood* (1938) and *They Died with Their Boots On* (1941) was jailed more often than any other Hollywood star. In the 1920s, he was sentenced to two weeks in prison in New Guinea for hitting a man who had addressed him by his surname without the title "Mr." In 1929, he was charged with murder, but he was acquitted when the prosecution failed to produce a body. He was jailed in 1933 in Somaliland (now Somalia) for hitting a customs officer, and a few years later he stamped on the instep of a policeman who had forced his car off the road in New York and demanded his autograph in an allegedly menacing manner. Flynn was thrown into a cell for the night.

BIGGEST HOLLYWOOD RIVALRY
Peter Sellers and Orson Welles disliked each other so intensely that when they had to play a major scene together at the gaming table in *Casino Royale* (GB, 1967) they acted the scene on different days, each performing to a double.

MOST VALUABLE HOLLYWOOD LEGS
Actress Cyd Charisse, who starred in *Brigadoon* (1954) and *Singin' in the Rain* (1952), had an insurance policy for the sum of $5 million taken out on her legs. This outdid Betty Grable, who had been dubbed "the Girl with the Million Dollar Legs" when she insured hers for the sum of $1.25 million c. 1940.

MOST FAMILY MEMBERS TO LEAVE MARK ON HOLLYWOOD BOULEVARD
Kirk Douglas, the star of *The Vikings* (1958) and *Spartacus* (1960), became the first member of his family to leave his mark on Hollywood Boulevard, Los Angeles, when his footprints were set in stone in 1962. His son Michael, who has starred in *Fatal Attraction* (1987) and *Basic Instinct* (1992), was invited to leave his mark in September 1997. Their hand- and footprints now sit side by side, making the Douglases the first ever family to have two generations of prints in cement. Between them, Kirk and Michael have starred in more than 100 films.

MOST ENDURING HOLLYWOOD STAR
Lillian Gish made her acting debut in *An Unseen Enemy* (1912), and her last film, *The Whales of August* (1987), was made 75 years later.

BIGGEST HOLLYWOOD CEMETERY
Forest Lawn Memorial Park in Glendale, Hollywood covers 300 acres and has three churches. Its celebrity graves include those of Walt Disney, Errol Flynn, Nat King Cole, Clark Gable and Jean Harlow.

MOST EXPENSIVE HOLLYWOOD HOTEL
The Beverly Hills Hotel on Sunset Boulevard, nicknamed "The Pink Palace," is the most expensive hotel in Hollywood and one of the most expensive hotels in the world. A visual and social landmark in Hollywood, it was the location for many of the scenes in *Pretty Woman* (1990), which starred Richard Gere and Julia Roberts. Its best suites cost $3,300 a night.

MOST *LIFE* COVERS
Elizabeth Taylor has been on the cover of *Life* magazine a total of 11 times, more than any other Hollywood star. Taylor began her film career at the age of 10 in 1942, with *There's One Born Every Minute*. She won two Oscars, for *Butterfield 8* (1960) and *Who's Afraid of Virginia Woolf* (1966), and was the first actress to earn $1 million for a movie, for *Cleopatra* in 1963.

LARGEST HOLLYWOOD HOME

The Manor on Mapleton Drive, Hollywood was built for Aaron Spelling. The largest home in Hollywood, it occupies 36,500 square feet on a 65,000-square-foot plot of land. The estate includes a doll museum, four bars, three kitchens, a gymnasium, a theater, eight two-car garages, an Olympic-size swimming pool, a bowling alley, a skating rink, six formal gardens, 12 fountains and a room in which to wrap gifts. Spelling is the producer of a number of TV series, including *Beverly Hills 90210,* which stars his daughter Tori (pictured right, third from left).

HOLLYWOOD STREET WITH THE MOST CELEBRITY HOMES

Mulholland Drive, the long thoroughfare that forms the dividing line between the San Fernando valley and Los Angeles, is lined with expensive houses. The stretch where the drive passes the edge of Beverly Hills and Bel-Air has been nicknamed "Bad Boy Drive," because it housed the estates of Jack Nicholson, Warren Beatty and Marlon Brando.

RICHEST HOLLYWOOD PET

Screen legend Ava Gardner's beloved corgi Morgan Gardner was left a monthly salary and his own limousine and maid when the star passed away in 1990. He lived off his inheritance for seven years in a Hollywood mansion before passing away at the age of 15 in March 1997. Morgan, who had been given to Ava by her third husband Frank Sinatra, was buried in the backyard of the actress' friend Gregory Peck.

MOST POPULAR HOLLYWOOD DIET DESIGNERS

PhD nutritionist Tony Perrone has customized diets for stars such as Demi Moore, Denzel Washington and Robin Williams, while Carrie Latt Wiatt of Diet Designs delivers low-fat meals to the doors of Jennifer Aniston, Ben Stiler and Neve Campbell. David Kelmenson and Steven Kates of the Brentwood training studios have been known to race their motorcycles to the Ivy and Spago restaurants to assist clients in ordering meals. Rob Parr, another diet guru, invented a pregnancy workout that has helped reshape stars such as Demi Moore and Tatum O'Neal.

MOST HOLLYWOOD MARRIAGES

Born in Hungary in either 1917, 1918 or 1919 (the real date remains a mystery), Zsa Zsa Gabor has had roles in a number of movies and is famous for her succession of wealthy husbands. Her first marriage, reputedly when she was 13, was to Burhan Belge, a Turkish diplomat. After fleeing to the US, she married, in swift succession, Texan hotel magnate Conrad Hilton, British actor George Sanders (who later married Zsa Zsa's sister Magda), businessmen Herbert Hunter and Joshua Cosden Jr, and Barbie Doll creator Jack Ryan. Her seventh husband was the lawyer Michael O'Hara, who had dealt with her divorce from Ryan. In 1982, Zsa Zsa claimed that her eight-day marriage to Felipe De Alba, whom she wed at sea, was invalid because she was still technically married to O'Hara. Her longest marriage to date was to official husband No. 8, Prince Frederick von Anhalt, whom she married in 1986 and divorced in 1998. Zsa Zsa, whose movie career highlights have included *Moulin Rouge* (1952), *The Girl in the Kremlin* (1957), in which she was bald, and *A Nightmare on Elm Street 3: Dream Warriors* (1987), has also been romantically linked with John F. Kennedy, Henry Kissinger, Mario Lanza, Sean Connery, Richard Burton and Frank Sinatra.

movie stars

TOP-EARNING FRENCH MOVIE STAR

Gerard Depardieu, who received an Oscar nomination for *Cyrano de Bergerac* (France, 1990) and has won 10 Césars, is the highest-earning French film actor today. In 1992 he earned $1.89 million for his role as Christopher Columbus in the film *1492: Conquest of Paradise*. He also earned a total of $1.32 million for two advertisements made for the Italian pasta company Barilla.

MOST DEVOTED METHOD ACTORS

Daniel Day Lewis is said to have spent many nights without sleep in a mock jail cell in order to prepare for his role in *In the Name of the Father* (1993), while for *Last of the Mohicans* (1992) he went to a survival camp, where he learned to track and kill animals and make canoes from trees.

Nicolas Cage had two teeth removed without painkillers for his part in *Vampire's Kiss* (1988). He also ate six live cockroaches to make the scene "really shock."

MOST WEIGHT GAINED FOR A FILM APPEARANCE

Robert De Niro gained a total of 60 pounds for his role as the heavyweight boxer Jake La Motta in the classic movie *Raging Bull* (1980).

MOST WEIGHT LOST FOR FILM APPEARANCES

Gary Oldman's efforts to lose weight to play the punk star Sid Vicious in *Sid and Nancy* (1986) were so successful that the British actor ended up in the hospital, where he was treated for malnutrition.

Jennifer Jason Leigh slimmed down to 86 pounds for her role as an anorexic teenager in the TV movie *The Best Little Girl in the World* (1981).

GREATEST AGE SPAN PORTRAYED BY AN ACTOR IN ONE FILM

Dustin Hoffman was 33 years old when he played the title role in *Little Big Man* (1970). His character aged from 17 to 121.

MOST SOCIALLY CONCERNED CONTRACT

Comic actor Robin Williams is famous for demanding the most socially concerned film contracts on record: each one prohibits commercial tie-ins connected with alcohol, tobacco, weapons, toys of violence, soft drinks and junk food.

MOST COSTLY LATE ATTENDANCE

Eddie Murphy's habitual lateness allegedly cost the producers of *Boomerang* (1992) more than $1 million.

HIGHEST INSURANCE QUOTE

Robert Downey Jr. reputedly worked uninsured on *The Gingerbread Man* (1998). The premium would have cost $1.4 million on a movie with a budget of less than $42 million.

MOST LEADING ROLES

John Wayne was in 153 films from *The Drop Kick* (1927) to *The Shootist* (1976). In all but 11, he played the lead.

MOST SUCCESSFUL ACTOR-TURNED-POLITICIAN

Ronald Reagan, who starred in *Bedtime for Bonzo* in 1951, was elected governor of California in 1966 and 1970. He was elected to the first of his two terms as president of the United States in 1980.

LONGEST SCREEN CAREER

Curt Bois made his debut in *Der Fidele Bauer* (Germany, 1908) at the age of eight and his final film appearance in Wim Wenders' *Wings of Desire* (Germany, 1988).

LONGEST SCREEN PARTNERSHIPS

Indian superstars Prem Nazir and Sheela had played opposite each other in 130 movies by 1975.

The longest Hollywood partnership (excluding performers billed together solely in "series" films) was 15 films, by husband-and-wife team Charles Bronson and Jill Ireland from 1968 to 1986.

MOST GENERATIONS OF SCREEN ACTORS

There have been four generations of screen actors in the Redgrave family, from Roy Redgrave, who made his screen debut in 1911, through Sir Michael Redgrave and his daughters Vanessa and Lynn and son Corin, to Vanessa's daughters Joely and Natasha and Corin's daughter Jemma.

YOUNGEST NO. 1 BOX-OFFICE STAR

Shirley Temple was seven years old when she became the No. 1 star at the box office in 1935.

HIGHEST-PAID CHILD PERFORMER

Macaulay Culkin was paid $1 million for *My Girl* (1991), when he was 11 years old. He was subsequently paid $5 million plus 5% gross for *Home Alone II: Lost in New York* (1992) and a reported $8 million for *Richie Rich* (1994).

YOUNGEST OSCAR-WINNERS

Tatum O'Neal was 10 years old when she was voted Best Supporting Actress for *Paper Moon* (1973).

In 1934, at the age of just five, actress Shirley Temple was awarded an honorary Oscar for her achievements.

OLDEST OSCAR-WINNER

Jessica Tandy won the Best Actress award for *Driving Miss Daisy* in 1990, at the age of 80.

MOST BEST ACTOR AWARDS

Jack Nicholson, who has won Best Actor Academy Awards for *One Flew Over the Cuckoo's Nest* (1975) and *As Good as It Gets* (1997), is one of seven actors who have won the award twice. In 1998, ABC News ranked the star, who dropped out of school and grew up believing his grandmother was his mother and his mother was his sister, as one of the most powerful people in Hollywood today. In total, he has received 11 Oscar nominations for Best Actor and Best Supporting Actor. The other actors who have won the Best Actor award twice are Spencer Tracy for *Captain Courageous* (1937) and *Boys Town* (1938), Fredric March for *Dr. Jekyll and Mr. Hyde* (1932) and *The Best Years of Our Lives* (1946), Gary Cooper for *Sergeant York* (1941) and *High Noon* (1952), Marlon Brando for *On the Waterfront* (1954) and *The Godfather* (1972), Dustin Hoffman for *Kramer vs. Kramer* (1979) and *Rain Man* (1988) and Tom Hanks for *Philadelphia* (1993) and *Forrest Gump* (1994).

MOST BEST ACTRESS AWARDS
Katharine Hepburn won four Oscars, for *Morning Glory* (1933), *Guess Who's Coming to Dinner* (1967), *The Lion in Winter* (GB, 1968) and *On Golden Pond* (1981).

MOST OSCAR NOMINATIONS WITHOUT AN AWARD
Richard Burton received six nominations, for *My Cousin Rachel* (1952), *The Robe* (1953), *The Spy Who Came In from the Cold* (GB, 1965), *Who's Afraid of Virginia Woolf* (1966), *Anne of the Thousand Days* (GB, 1970) and *Equus* (GB, 1977), but never won.

MOST APPEARANCES AS HOST AT THE OSCARS
Bob Hope hosted the Academy Awards a record 13 times: in 1940 (the second half of the show), 1945, 1946, 1953, 1955, 1958, 1959, 1960, 1966, 1967, 1968, 1975 and 1978.

HIGHEST CAREER GROSS (ACTOR)
The all-time North American box office champion is Harrison Ford. Including the opening weekend for his 1998 movie *Six Days, Seven Nights*, Ford's films have grossed $2,103,094,065.

HIGHEST CAREER GROSS (ACTRESS)
The highest gross in North America for any actress is $1,018,845,113 by Julia Roberts.

MOST CONSECUTIVE $100-MILLION-GROSSING MOVIES
The longest run of consecutive $100-million-grossing movies is five, by Tom Cruise. The actor's last five releases all topped the magic $100 million blockbuster mark: *A Few Good Men* (1992), *The Firm* (1993), *Interview With the Vampire* (1994), *Mission Impossible* (1996), and *Jerry Maguire* (1996).

MOST $100-MILLION MOVIES (ACTOR)
All-time box office champion Harrison Ford has starred in nine movies that have grossed over $100 million in North American theaters. Ford's blockbusters are: *Star Wars* (1977, including 1997 re-release), *The Empire Strikes Back* (1980, including re-release), *Raiders of the Lost Ark* (1981), *Return of the Jedi* (1983, including re-release), *Indiana Jones and the Temple of Doom* (1984), *Indiana Jones and the Last Crusade* (1989), *The Fugitive* (1993), *Clear and Present Danger* (1994), and *Air Force One* (1997).

MOST $100-MILLION MOVIES (ACTRESS)
Julia Roberts leads actresses in the category of most $100-million movies. Her five blockbusters are: *Pretty Woman* (1990), *Sleeping With the Enemy* (1991), *Hook* (1991), *The Pelican Brief* (1993), and *My Best Friend's Wedding* (1997).

HIGHEST SALARY
Following Leonardo Di Caprio's successes in *William Shakespeare's Romeo and Juliet* (1996) and *Titanic* (1997), it is reported that his representatives are seeking a $21 million salary for his next movie.

HIGHEST-PAID ACTRESSES
With a current asking price of $12.5 million per movie, Demi Moore is one of the most highly paid actresses in the world today. Born Demetria Guynes in 1962, Moore began her acting career at the age of 20, when she became a regular on the soap opera *General Hospital*. She now has 26 films under her belt. In 1987, she married fellow movie star Bruce Willis.

BIGGEST BREACH OF CONTRACT AWARD
In 1991, Kim Basinger pulled out of the movie *Boxing Helena* four weeks before the start of filming, a move that resulted in her bankruptcy in 1993, when a jury ordered her to pay $8.1 million to the movie's producer for breach of contract. A court of appeals subsequently threw out that ruling. In a subsequent compromise, Basinger paid an undisclosed amount to the producer.

tv stars

MOST POPULAR CULT TV STAR
Gillian Anderson, who stars as Agent Dana Scully in *The X-Files*, is one of the most popular TV stars of the 1990s. Pictured left with her co-star, David Duchovny, Anderson was voted the world's sexiest woman in 1996 by more than 10,000 readers of the British magazine *FHM*. She earns $58,000 per episode and signed a $6.6-million deal to star in the movie spinoff *The X-Files* (1998).

MOST WATCHED TELEVISION STAR IN FRANCE
News presenter Patrick Poivre d'Arvor is watched by more viewers than any other French television personality. On December 2, 1997, his news show *TF1 20 hrs* had a record 15.02 million viewers across the country. The star receives extensive press attention, and in April 1996 he was the victim of *L'entarteur* – the Belgian "Pieman," Noel Godin – who also pelted Bill Gates with custard pies in February 1998.

HIGHEST-PAID TV ACTOR
Jerry Seinfeld, the star of *Seinfeld*, is the most highly-paid television star in the world, with an estimated total worth of $94 million. His 1997 earnings were estimated at $66 million.

HIGHEST-PAID TV COOK
The British cook Delia Smith is reputed to have amassed a $38.4-million fortune, making her the highest-paid TV cook. She has hosted six hit British television series and written more than 13 accompanying books.

MOST WATCHED MALE TV STAR
George Clooney, who plays pediatrician Doug Ross in the popular hospital drama *ER*, is the most watched male television star in the world. He is reputed to earn $147,200 for each episode of the show, which had an average of 20.78 million viewers per episode in the United States and 3.45 million viewers in the United Kingdom in the 1996/97 season. Clooney has also made his mark in the film world, alongside Quentin Tarantino, Harvey Keitel and Juliette Lewis in *From Dusk Til Dawn* (1996), with Michelle Pfeiffer in *One Fine Day* (1996) and with Uma Thurman and Alicia Silverstone in *Batman and Robin* (1997).

MOST WATCHED TELEVISION PRESENTER IN GERMANY
Thomas Gottschalk currently hosts Germany's top-rating show *Wetten Daß* (*I Bet That...*), in which guest celebrities are asked to bet on whether the contestants will succeed in record attempts. Viewing figures exceeded 71 million in 1997 and the program receives 23% of the total audience share. Gottschalk, Germany's most popular personality, has also appeared in many other TV shows and a great number of national advertising campaigns.

MOST POPULAR TV STAR IN THE NETHERLANDS
Henny Huisman holds the largest audience share in the Netherlands with the show *SurpriseShowFin*. The show tries to make people's dreams come true. Huisman began his career as a DJ, and got his break in TV with *The Playback Show*, where candidates impersonated their favorite stars.

MOST WATCHED FEMALE PRESENTER IN THE UNITED KINGDOM
Cilla Black, who hosts the popular British dating show *Blind Date*, is currently the most viewed television presenter in the United Kingdom. The show, which has been running since 1984, had an average of 9.1 million viewers per show in the 1997/98 season. In 1997, Black was awarded an OBE (Order of the British Empire) from Queen Elizabeth II for her services to British entertainment.

MOST WATCHED MALE PRESENTER IN THE UNITED KINGDOM
Michael Aspel's *This Is Your Life*, which celebrates the careers of celebrities, won an average audience of 10 million viewers in the United Kingdom for the 1998 series.

HIGHEST-PAID FEMALE TV STAR
Talk show host Oprah Winfrey, who earned $104 million in 1997, is the richest television entertainer in the world, with an estimated total worth of $201 million, according to *Forbes* magazine. She is due to receive $130 million for her talk show alone – which has been rated the No.1 television talk show for 11 seasons in a row and been awarded 30 Emmys – for the TV season 1999/2000. Oprah, who is now 44 years old, landed her first broadcasting job at the age of 19 in 1973. In 1976, she was hired to host Baltimore's WJZ-TV talk show, *People Are Talking*, and in 1984 she moved to Chicago to host *A.M. Chicago*. In 1985, she starred in Steven Spielberg's *The Color Purple*, for which she received an Oscar nomination for Best Supporting Actress. *A.M. Chicago*, now called *The Oprah Winfrey Show*, was relaunched in 1986, and Oprah, having established Harpo Productions, went on to buy the program outright from Capital Cities/ABC. In 1998, a group of Texas cattlemen filed suit against the star, claiming that she had defamed the beef industry by making comments about "mad cow disease" on her show. Oprah won the case.

FASTEST TELEVISION DEAL
On June 20, 1997, production company King World signed actress/comedienne Roseanne — the star of the hit series *Roseanne* from 1988 to 1997 — for a new talk show. Five days later, the show had been cleared for air by five major television stations, and the next day it had been accepted by a further two stations. The enthusiasm for the show was said to be "unprecedented in television history."

MOST WATCHED TELEVISION PRESENTER IN JAPAN
George Tokoro, who currently appears in two of Japan's top shows, *Ichiokuninn no Daihitsumon* and *Tokoro-san no Kaitaishinasho*, is the nation's most popular television star. *Ichiokuninn no Daihitsumon* is a road show in which Tokoro and his guests taste famous local dishes from different villages all over the country, while *Tokoro-san no Kaitaishinasho* deals with thematic historical issues. Tokoro is also a comedian and singer and has appeared in a number of national TV ads.

MOST WATCHED TELEVISION STAR IN RUSSIA
Valdis Pelsh, the star of the music show *Uguday Melodiyu* (*Guess the Melody*), is Russia's most popular television personality. The show, which is shown six times a week (three original broadcasts and three morning repeats) receives up to 56% of the total audience share in Russia.

MOST WATCHED TV STAR IN BRAZIL
Regina Duarte, who has been appearing on Brazilian television for more than 33 years and has appeared in many Brazilian soap operas (*telenovelas*), is Brazil's most popular and prolific TV star. She is nicknamed "Namoradinha do Brasil" ("Brazil's Girlfriend").

MOST MONEY REFUSED
In December 1997, comedian Jerry Seinfeld turned down the largest personal contract in television history. NBC had offered the star $5 million per episode to continue *Seinfeld*, one of the most popular shows in the United States. A third of the US population of 263 million tuned in to watch the final episode, which was aired in May 1998, and all-day and all-night Seinfeld parties took place across the country. One-minute commercials during the 75-minute episode cost advertisers more than $1.66 million.

sports superstars

FASTEST $1 MILLION BY GOLFER

In 1996, Tiger Woods broke Ernie Els' record for the fewest events played to earn $1 million. Woods, a 20-year-old, needed only nine pro starts. By the end of his rookie season, he had won five tournaments and earned more than $2 million. He was the second highest-paid endorser in sports in 1997, collecting $2.1 million in prize money and $24 million in endorsements. Also in 1997, Woods signed a $40-million contract with Nike, which planned to bring out a new Woods apparel line in spring 1998. Other contracts include American Express, Rolex and japanese company Asahi.

LARGEST SPORTS SPONSORSHIP
Michael Jordan of the Chicago Bulls reportedly earns $12 million a year from his deal with sports manufacturer Nike and is said to have been paid more than $100 million in total by Nike during his career.

LARGEST SPORTS CONTRACTS
In 1997, NBA stars Shaquille O'Neal, Alonzo Mourning and Juwan Howard all signed deals worth more than $100 million – the first nine-figure contracts in sports history.

HIGHEST EARNINGS IN A YEAR
In 1996, boxer Mike Tyson earned a record $75 million from three fights. In doing so, he made more money in one year than any other athlete in history. In 1986, Tyson had become the youngest boxing heavyweight world champion of all time when he beat fellow US boxer Trevor Berbick to win the WBC version in Las Vegas, Nevada at the age of 20 years 144 days. He added the WBA title to his achievements with his victory over James "Bonecrusher" Smith on March 7, 1987, at the age of 20 years 249 days, and he became undisputed champion on August 2, 1987, when he beat Tony Tucker (US) for the IBF title.

HIGHEST CAREER EARNINGS BY A SPORTSMAN
Michael Jordan has earned more money during his eight-year basketball career than any other sportsman in history. Now aged 34, Jordan earned a total of $30 million in 1997, plus a further $47 million in endorsements, making him the highest-paid sportsman for the fifth time in six years. By 1998, his career earnings had exceeded $300 million.

HIGHEST CAREER EARNINGS BY SPORTSWOMEN
In April 1998, tennis player Martina Navrátilová continued to hold the record for the highest career earnings of any sportswoman, despite having retired from her 14-year career on the tennis circuit in 1994. She had earned $20.34 million in prize money alone, and had won a world record 167 singles tournaments and 165 doubles titles. German tennis star Steffi Graf had earned a total of $20.18 million in prize money by April 1998. It is estimated that by the end of the 1998 season, she will have exceeded Navrátilová's career earnings. However, Navrátilová will continue to hold the record if endorsements and sponsorship deals are included in total career earnings.

HIGHEST-EARNING TENNIS PLAYER
By April 1998, US tennis player Pete Sampras' career earnings from prize money alone totaled $32.3 million. In 1997, he was paid $8 million for his biggest endorsement deals, with Nike and Wilson. Sampras also holds the men's record for earnings in a season, at $6.5 million in 1997.

HIGHEST-EARNING FORMULA 1 DRIVER
In 1996, German driver Michael Schumacher was paid a record $25 million to drive for Ferrari's

HIGHEST-EARNING SOCCER STAR

Brazilian soccer star Ronaldo Luis Nazario de Lima, known simply as Ronaldo, was traded for a record $28.8-million from Spain's Barcelona to Internazionale Milano (Inter Milan) of Italy at the age of just 20 in 1997, and now earns more than $160,000 a week, making him the world's richest soccer player. He is seen here during the unveiling of a Pirelli advertising campaign, which shows the Brazilian star with his arms outstretched over the Rio de Janeiro landscape. Ronaldo had been a member of the winning Brazilian squad in the 1994 World Cup and won a bronze medal with the Brazilian Olympic team in 1996. When he joined Inter Milan, the team's season ticket sales rose by 40%. In 1998, Inter Milan won the UEFA Cup, with Ronaldo scoring the third goal in a 3–0 victory over Lazio of Rome.

Formula 1 team. This is the highest salary in the history of Formula 1. Schumacher's total earnings in 1997 have been estimated at $35 million, including salary and winnings, as well as endorsements.

HIGHEST-EARNING GOLFERS
The highest all-time career earnings on the PGA Tour is $11.91 million, by Australia's Greg Norman, 1976–97.

The season's record on the PGA tour is $2.1 million, by Tiger Woods in 1997.

Hale Irwin won a record-breaking $2.34 million on the Senior PGA Tour in 1997.

Nick Faldo (Great Britain) won a record total of $2.74 million worldwide in 1992.

The record career earnings for a woman golfer is $5.97 million, by Betsy King from 1977 to 1997.

The record season's earnings by a woman golfer is $1.24 million, by Annika Sorenstam of Sweden in 1997.

Colin Montgomerie (Great Britain) won a season's record of $1.37 million in European Order of Merit tournaments in 1996.

On November 1, 1992, Jason Bohn (US) won $1 million when he made a hole in one in a charity contest. He aced the 136-yard second hole at the Harry S. Pritchett Golf Course, Tuscaloosa, Alabama using a 9-iron.

OLDEST HIGH-EARNING SPORTSMAN
In 1997, 68-year-old golf legend Arnold Palmer earned a total of $16.1 million from salary, winnings and endorsements, making him the 12th highest earner in sport. Palmer, who was the first golfer ever to win more than $1 million on the PGA Tour, still plays on the PGA Senior Tour.

MOST SUCCESSFUL MUSICAL CAREER BY A SPORTSMAN
Shaquille O'Neal, center for the Los Angeles Lakers, also has a highly successful music career. He released his debut album, *Shaq Diesel* (1993), when he was 21, and in 1997 his record label Twism (The World is Mine) formed a joint venture with A&M Records with the aim of producing a fourth album.

YOUNGEST SPORTSWOMAN TO EARN $1 MILLION
In 1997, at 16 years of age, Swiss tennis star Martina Hingis became the youngest sportswoman ever to earn $1 million. By April 1997, the No. 1 player had earned $3 million, and by September of that year, in the space of six months, she had achieved 37 successive victories. The only woman in the history of the Open era to have started a year on better form was Steffi Graf (Germany), who had 45 successive wins in 1987. Hingis became the first woman to surpass $4 million in earnings over the course of a single season. In addition to prize money, her sponsorship deals are worth an estimated $5 million a year. In 1997, she set a season's winnings record of $3.4 million.

MOST MAGAZINE COVERS
Six-time NBA Finals MVP Michael Jordan appeared on the cover of *Sports Illustrated* for the 42nd time on February 16, 1998. The previous record was 34, by boxer Muhammad Ali.

pop stars

MOST FAN CLUBS
There are more than 480 active Elvis Presley fan clubs worldwide – more than for any other star. This is particularly astonishing in view of the fact that Elvis did not record in other languages, except for a few soundtrack songs, and only once performed in concert outside the United States (in Canada in 1957).

HIGHEST-EARNING POP GROUP
The Beatles are the wealthiest musical entertainers of all time. In 1997, their earnings were estimated at £41.5 million ($68 million). The Beatles formed in 1960 and had their first hit with "Love Me Do" in 1962. After disbanding in 1970, the Fab Four – Paul McCartney, John Lennon, Ringo Starr and George Harrison – all pursued solo careers.

MOST VALUABLE POP STAR ON THE STOCK MARKET
David Bowie commands an estimated fortune of £150 million ($250 million). In 1997, Bowie raised £33 million ($55 million) through the issue of bonds, which he sold to Prudential Insurance. Other stars allegedly following suit include members of the Rolling Stones.

MOST SHOPAHOLIC POP STAR
The star who confesses to the biggest shopping sprees is Elton John, whose average monthly credit card bill is about $413,000. His most memorable bills have included $63,000 for a month's purchases from the florist's department of Bloomingdale's, New York City, and $330,000 for a single visit to jeweler Theo Fennell in London, England.

LARGEST PRIZE DONATIONS TO A CHARITY BY POP STARS
In 1996, Pulp, fronted by Jarvis Cocker, won the Mercury Prize for music over the favorite, Oasis, and donated their £25,000 ($41,000) check to the War Child charity. Other Mercury prizewinners who have made sizeable donations to charity include Suede in 1993, M People in 1994 and 1997 winner Roni Size, who gave most of his prize money to a community project in Bristol, England.

MOST PROMOTIONS FOR AN ALBUM BY A POP STAR
Promotions for Michael Jackson's album *HIStory* (1995) included a 30-foot-high inflated statue of the star on top of Tower Records in Hollywood, California; a huge sign in Times Square, New York City; and another statue floated on a barge down the River Thames in London, England. Jackson's record company Sony spent $40 million on the launch of the album in the United States, the United Kingdom, Italy, Australia, Japan, South Africa and the Netherlands.

BIGGEST LEGAL BATTLE OVER A RECORD CONTRACT
George Michael fought a nine-month court battle during 1993 and 1994 in an attempt to end his contract with Sony Music. He lost the case, which cost him an estimated $1.96 million, and the contract was bought out by David Geffen's Dreamworks label.

MOST PRODUCT ENDORSEMENTS BY A POP GROUP IN A YEAR
The Spice Girls hold the record for the greatest number of promotions by a group in any one year, with 10 different advertisers in 1997. They included Sony PlayStation, Mercedes, and a $1-million deal with Pepsi, which involved 40,000 Pepsi drinkers being flown to Istanbul, Turkey for a Spice Girls concert and after-show party.

MOST PAID TO A POP GROUP FOR ADVERTISING RIGHTS
Microsoft paid the Rolling Stones $8 million to feature their hit "Start me Up" in its Windows '95 ad campaign.

BIGGEST ADVERTISING DEAL TO BE TURNED DOWN
The record for the largest sum of money ever rejected by a pop star for an advertising deal is $12 million, by Bruce Springsteen in 1987. The money had been offered by Chrysler for the use of Springsteen's "Born in the USA" in a car commercial.

MOST APPEARANCES ON THE COVER OF *ROLLING STONE*
Rolling Stones frontman Mick Jagger has appeared on the cover of *Rolling Stone* a total of 15 times. He first featured on the cover of the 50th issue on August 10, 1968, and his most recent appearance was with Keith Richards on December 11, 1997 (issue 775).

MOST CAMEOS IN A POP MOVIE
The Spice Girls' movie *Spiceworld – the Movie* (UK, 1997) featured a larger cameo cast than any other pop film, with appearances by Meat Loaf, Roger Moore, Stephen Fry, Michael Barrymore, Richard Briers and Elvis Costello.

MOST MONEY RAISED IN A SECOND-HAND CLOTHING SALE
Elton John's infamous wardrobe has had to be cleared many times because of its overwhelming size. The star's last two sales made a total of £530,000 ($875,000) for the Elton John AIDS Foundation, and he once had to rent a shop to sell off more than 10,000 outfits, which were estimated to have originally cost £2.5 million ($4.13 million). The Stage Costume and Memorabilia section of Elton's 1988 sale at Sotheby's, London, which included personal possessions as well as clothes, raised £421,185 ($758,133) at auction.

HIGHEST PRICES PAID FOR POP STAR CLOTHING
The most expensive item of clothing formerly owned by John Lennon is an afghan coat that he wore on the cover of the Beatles' *Magical Mystery Tour* album in 1967. It was bought for £34,999 ($57,750) in 1997 on behalf of the star's son, Julian Lennon.

STAR COUPLE
Whitney Houston and Bobby Brown are one of the world's most successful pop star couples. Houston, the daughter of gospel/soul singer Cissy Houston, spent her early teens modeling for *Vogue* and *Glamour* and was signed to the Arista label at the age of 19. In 1992, she achieved popular acclaim for her role in *The Bodyguard* alongside Kevin Costner, as well as for her best-selling soundtrack to the film. Her cover of Dolly Parton's "I Will Always Love You" for the album stayed at the top of the US singles chart for an unprecedented 14 weeks. In the same year, Houston married Bobby Brown, an R&B star who first achieved pop success with "Don't Be Cruel" and "My Prerogative" in 1988, the latter giving him his first No. 1. During 1988 and 1989, he had five singles in the US Top 10. The couple have had one child, and Houston has received the Outstanding Career Achievement award at the Soul Train Music Awards.

The most ever paid for an item of clothing belonging to Madonna is £12,100 ($19,360), for a corset designed by Jean Paul Gaultier and sold at Christie's, London in May 1994.

The most expensive item of clothing to have belonged to ♀ (The Artist formerly known as Prince) is a complete stage costume that sold for £12,100 ($20,570) at Christie's, London in December 1991.

The most expensive piece of Michael Jackson clothing is a white rhinestone that sold for £16,500 ($28,050) in December 1991.

MOST VALUABLE SONG LYRICS

Paul McCartney's hand-written lyrics for the Beatles' "Getting Better" sold for £161,000 ($257,600) in September 1995.

MOST GRAMMYS WON IN A YEAR
The most Grammy awards won in a single year is eight, by Michael Jackson in 1984. Jackson was born on August 29, 1958 in Gary, Indiana, and began his career as a child star in his older brothers' band, the Jackson Five. He launched his solo career in 1972 with *Got To Be There*, and 10 years later released *Thriller*, which sold more than 48 million copies worldwide.

MADONNA
Born Madonna Louise Ciccone in Rochester, Michigan on August 26, 1958, the self-styled "queen of controversy" has sold 100 million records worldwide and had almost 50 hit records. Madonna's major breakthrough came in 1984 with *Like A Virgin*. She has also enjoyed box-office success as an actress, most memorably in *Desperately Seeking Susan* (1985) and *Evita* (1996).

super models

BIGGEST SUPERMODEL
Sophie Dahl, the granddaughter of British author Roald Dahl, was discovered by fashion editor Isabella Blow, who thought the size-14 beauty — whose measurements are 40-30-40 — looked like a *Playboy* bunny. Dahl has worked with top photographers such as David Bailey, appeared in *Vanity Fair* and modeled at big shows such as Nina Ricci. Her agency, Storm, has asked her not to lose any weight.

MOST MAGAZINE COVERS
German model Claudia Schiffer was spotted in a disco in her native country when she was 17 and has not stopped working since. She has appeared on a record 550 magazine covers, including *Vanity Fair*, despite the latter's editorial line against featuring models on its covers.

BIGGEST COSMETICS CONTRACT
In 1993, Claudia Schiffer signed the biggest ever cosmetics contract when she was offered $6 million to become the face of Revlon. Schiffer has done campaigns for all the big fashion houses and is a particular favorite of Karl Lagerfeld. She has produced her own fitness video, and made her movie debut in 1998 with *The Blackout*. She co-owns the Fashion Cafe chain with fellow supermodels Naomi Campbell and Christy Turlington.

LONGEST CONTRACT
Christy Turlington has represented Calvin Klein for almost 10 years — a record in the industry. The groundbreaking model has twice clinched big deals without signing exclusivity contracts. She gave up the international catwalks in 1995 and now works for Max Mara and Calvin Klein, among others.

TOP-PAYING CATWALK SHOWS
One of the main forces behind the supermodel phenomenon was the late Italian designer Gianni Versace, who is reputed to have paid the top models as much as $50,000 for a half-hour show in the late 1980s and early 1990s on the proviso that they would only appear in his show that season. This is said to have created the elite group of women — Christy Turlington, Naomi Campbell and Linda Evangelista — who dominated fashion magazines in the early 1990s.

YOUNGEST SUPERMODEL TO WIN A MAJOR COSMETICS CONTRACT
Nikki Taylor was 13 when she won $500,000 in a "Fresh Faces" contest in 1989 — the most money won in a contest of this kind by a girl who has gone on to become a supermodel. She went on to sign a deal with L'Oreal for Cover Girl, making her the youngest girl to win a major cosmetics contract.

SHORTEST SUPERMODEL
Kate Moss was discovered by Storm's Sarah Doukas at John F. Kennedy Airport in New York City in 1990. At just over 5 ft. 6 in. tall, the then British schoolgirl seemed an unlikely model, but Moss went on to revolutionize the modeling world, making way for a new type of model and a new trend called the "waif look."

HIGHEST HEELS
British supermodel Naomi Campbell was discovered by Elite scout Beth Boldt while she was shopping in Covent Garden, London. Her career was launched by her appearance on the cover of French *Vogue* in 1990. She is now one of the most successful models in the world and has been featured on numerous magazine covers. In 1993, Campbell hit the headlines when she fell off her 12-inch-high platform shoes and twisted her ankle at the Vivienne Westwood "Anglomania" catwalk show (pictured below). The mock snakeskin lace-ups that she wore are now on show in a specially-made glass case at the Victoria and Albert Museum, London. Campbell's numerous high-profile boyfriends have reportedly included actors Robert de Niro and Sylvester Stallone, boxer Mike Tyson, bassist Adam Clayton of rock group U2, and flamenco dancer Joaquín Cortés. Now an international celebrity, she has released an album, *Baby Woman*, and published a novel, *Swan*. She has also appeared in the movies *Miami Rhapsody*, *Invasion of Privacy* and *Girl Six*, and co-owns the Fashion Cafe in London. In November 1993, Campbell left her agency, Elite New York, and was subsequently signed up by Ford.

At 16, she became a self-made millionaire with her own company, Nikki Inc., and now has her own lawyer, accountant, manager and publicist.

TALLEST SUPERMODEL
Australian-born supermodel Elle MacPherson is 6 ft. 1 in. tall and is known as "the Body" because her measurements — 36-24-35 — are regarded as perfect. MacPherson, who made her screen debut in *Sirens* (1994), is now pursuing an acting career. She also owns one of Australia's most popular lingerie lines, which has an estimated annual turnover of $30 million.

MOST DRAMATIC CAREER CHANGE
Before being booked by Select Agency, Jayne Windsor was a 21-year-old single mother of two working in a factory in Newcastle, England. She now earns $200 an hour working for major fashion magazines, including *Elle* and *Vogue*.

LONGEST-LEGGED SUPERMODEL
Of all the supermodels, German model Nadja Auerman has the longest legs, at 45 inches. She shot to fame in 1993, when the fashion world rejected grunge in favor of glamour. By 1994 she had begun to appear on the cover of *Harper's Bazaar* and US and British *Vogue* and worked for prestigious fashion houses such as Versace and Prada.

OLDEST CATWALK SUPERMODEL
At 34, Canadian model Linda Evangelista is the world's oldest catwalk supermodel. According to her agency, Elite, she is still offered many assignments. Evangelista's success may be partly due to her famed ability to transform herself: in 1990, she claimed that she spent all of her free time coloring her hair. Evangelista is also responsible for the most famous supermodel quote: "We don't get out of bed for less than $10,000 a day."

YOUNGEST CURRENT SUPERMODEL
Model Karen Elson has taken the fashion world by storm since being discovered by a scout in Manchester, England at the age of 15. Now 18, she is the youngest supermodel working today, and has been the star of many prestigious campaigns, including Christian Lacroix, Hermes and Comme des Garçons.

LONGEST SUPERMODEL CAREER
Christy Turlington has been modeling for a longer period of time than any other supermodel since being spotted at the age of 13 during a school vacation. Turlington began modeling full-time at the age of 17, in 1987. By 1988, she was the face of Eternity perfume and had secured a deal with Maybelline worth $800,000 for just 12 days' work.

MOST SUCCESSFUL AGENCIES
Elite Agency has a record 35 supermodels on its books, including Claudia Schiffer, Cindy Crawford, Christy Turlington and Amber Valetta, and bills more than $100 million in modeling fees every year. Set up by John Casablanca in Paris, France in 1971, Elite now has offices in a further 23 cities worldwide, including New York, Milan, Munich, London and Tokyo.

Ford, which is run by Eileen Ford, has had more supermodels on its books for longer periods of time than any other agency. Its greatest successes have included Christy Turlington and Jerry Hall.

HIGHEST-PAID SUPERMODEL
Supermodel Cindy Crawford began modeling at age 17 and now earns an estimated $12 million a year from modeling assignments — more than any other model. Following her success as the host of MTV's *House of Style*, Crawford diversified her career. Her first fitness video sold 2 million copies within a month of its release.

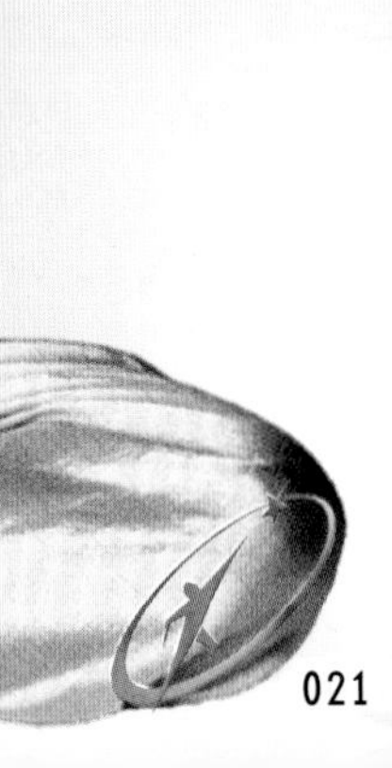

diana and royalty

MOST WATCHED WEDDING

On July 29, 1981, approximately 750 million people in 74 countries tuned in to a live broadcast of Diana and Prince Charles' wedding at St. Paul's Cathedral, London. The estimated earnings from mementos relating to the wedding exceeded $1 billion. The wedding dress, designed by Elizabeth and David Emmanuel, is displayed at the exhibition commemorating Diana in Althorp, England.

DIANA CHARITIES

In 1998, the Diana Scratchcard was launched in the UK for the Princess of Wales memorial fund. Money raised by the lottery goes to Diana's favorite charitable causes, which include AIDS, the fight against cancer, and homelessness. An estimated 250,000 cards were sold on their first day, with 20p (33¢) of the £1 ($1.66) ticket going to the memorial fund. The top prize was £25,000 ($41,600).

BIGGEST TV AUDIENCE

More people watched the funeral of Diana, Princess of Wales on September 6, 1997 than any other TV broadcast. The global audience was estimated at 2.5 billion.

MOST PHOTOGRAPHED WOMAN OF THE 1990S

It is impossible to know exactly how many photographs were taken of Diana during her life, but she was undoubtedly the most photographed woman of the last 15 years. Not even Grace Kelly or Jackie Kennedy caught the media's attention to the same extent. Photos taken of Diana and Dodi Al Fayed on vacation off the island of Sardinia shortly before their deaths sold for up to $210,000 , and photographer Mario Brenna stood to make up to $3 million worldwide from their sale.

BIGGEST-SELLING SINGLE

"Candle In The Wind," a song originally about Marilyn Monroe composed by Elton John and Bernie Taupin in 1973, was rewritten as a tribute to Diana. It was performed by John at her funeral and recorded later that day. On December 19, 1997 the singer was presented with a disc commemorating 33 million sales of "Candle in The Wind 1997/ Something About the Way You Look Tonight." The first single to top the chart in almost every country, it had earned more than 140 platinum discs around the world and became the biggest- and fastest-selling single in many countries by the end of 1997.

MOST EXPENSIVE LYRICS

In February 1998, the autographed lyrics to "Candle In The Wind 1997" sold for $400,000 to the Lund Foundation for Children, which was founded by Walt Disney's daughter, Sharon Disney-Lund. Consisting of three handwritten pages and a printed version, they are the world's most valuable contemporary lyrics.

MOST EXPENSIVE DRESSES SOLD AT AUCTION

The record for the most valuable auctioned dress is $200,000, for a blue silk and velvet gown owned by Diana and sold at Christie's, New York on June 26, 1997. The dress, one of a selection sold by Diana to raise money for British and US AIDS charities, was the one she wore when she danced with John Travolta at the White House in 1985. The previous record for a garment sold at auction was $145,000, for the white suit worn by Travolta in *Saturday Night Fever* (1977).

At a charity auction in Boston, Massachusetts in September 1997, an anonymous buyer paid $200,000 for a black velvet gown worn by Diana to a London premiere in 1985. It had originally sold for $36,000 at the auction of Diana's dresses at Christie's, New York City the previous June.

MOST EXPENSIVE 20TH-CENTURY PRINTED BOOK SOLD AT AUCTION

Christie's leather-bound limited edition of the catalog of Diana's dresses sold for £50,000 ($83,000) to Firoz Kassam, head of the Holiday Inn hotel chain in Asia, at the Grosvenor House Hotel, Mayfair, London, England on October 4, 1997.

BIGGEST FLORAL SHRINE

Between September 1 and September 8, 1997, an estimated 5 million bouquets of flowers weighing 10,000–15,000 tons were laid in memory of Diana at Buckingham Palace, St. James's Palace and Diana's home, Kensington Palace (seen left), in London, England, forming the world's biggest floral shrine. Diana, together with her friend Dodi Al Fayed and their driver Henri Paul, died after a car crash at the Pont de l'Alma in Paris, France on August 31, 1997, and her body was sent back to London 16 hours after the accident. Mourners began to lay flowers at the palaces as soon as news of the tragic event broke, and a total of 43 books were filled with messages of condolence from the public at St. James's Palace alone, with hundreds more filled around the world, although it had initially been thought that four books would suffice. On September 9, three days after her funeral, Diana's brother, Earl Spencer, and the rest of her family made an appeal to the public to stop laying flowers at her ancestral home, Althorp Park in Northamptonshire, and to contribute the money that they would have spent on blooms to some of Diana's favorite charities. Most of the flowers that were laid at the gates of Althorp were eventually taken by boat to the island in the park's grounds where Diana was buried, and were placed around her grave. The others were given to hospitals.

LANDMINE AWARENESS

In January 1997, Diana made a high-profile visit to Huambo in central Angola, one of the most densely-mined areas in a country with one of the worst landmine problems in the world. Diana was briefed by the British minesweeping organization Halo Trust. On September 18, 1997 a ban on antipersonnel landmines was signed in Oslo, Norway by more than 100 countries. Notable exceptions were the United States, China and Russia.

BIGGEST MEMORABILIA INDUSTRY

By December 1997, the Diana memorabilia industry was worth $240 million worldwide. An estimated 25,000 products, official and unofficial, bear Diana's image or signature, including ashtrays, rose bushes and dolls (above). There are some 36,000 Internet sites linked to Diana memorabilia, and her estate receives up to 200 applications a day from prospective manufacturers.

MOST VALUABLE PLAYING CARD

A Queen of Hearts card signed by Diana in 1995 for flight attendant Sheila Berkley-White was due to fetch up to $83,215 at auction in New York City on June 4, 1998 but was sold before the auction. It is thought to have fetched the expected price.

MOST CONDOLENCES EXPRESSED VIA THE INTERNET

A record 350,000 people left messages of condolence for Diana at the official memorial Web site of the British monarchy. The latter is also the most popular royal Web site: in the month after Diana's death, about 14 million people visited it.

GREATEST NUMBER OF ROYALS KILLED IN AN ACCIDENT

Seven members of the royal family of Hesse (Ernst Ludwig, the last Grand Duke of Hesse, and his wife, son, daughter-in-law and three grandchildren) died in an air crash at Ostende, Belgium, on November 16, 1937.

GREATEST NUMBER OF ROYALS KILLED IN A REVOLUTION

Between 1918 and 1919, a record 15 members of the Russian imperial family were killed by the Bolsheviks during the Russian Revolution, including Czar Nicholas II, Czarina Alexandra, their five children and seven other members of the family. There are continuing claims that at least one of the czar's children escaped the massacre of the immediate imperial family at Yekaterinburg.

MOST STATE ROLES HELD BY A MODERN ROYAL

King Norodom Sihanouk of Cambodia was king from 1941 to 1955, prime minister from 1955 to 1966, head of state and regent from 1960 to 1970, head of the government-in-exile in 1970, president in 1976, president-in-exile from 1982 to 1988, head of the government-in-exile from 1989 to 1991, president of the National Council in 1991 and head of state from 1991 to 1993. In 1993 he was restored as king.

OLDEST ROYAL FAMILY

The present Japanese imperial family is descended from Jimmu, who is said to have ascended the throne on February 11, 660 BC.

RICHEST ROYAL FAMILY

Saudi Arabia's Saudi dynasty is the richest royal family. In 1998, King Fahd and the Saudi princes had an estimated personal wealth of $32.2 billion.

QUEEN OF HEARTS

On July 1, 1997, her 36th birthday, Diana attended a centennial gala honoring the Tate Gallery in London. It was the first time Diana had socialized with members of the royal family since her divorce. She was dressed in a black Jacques Azagury beaded evening gown, with the Queen Mary diamond and emerald necklace that she famously once wore as a headband to dance with her ex-husband, Prince Charles.

BIGGEST ROYAL FAMILY

There are more than 4,200 royal princes and more than 40,000 other relatives in the Saudi royal family.

MOST ROYAL SIBLINGS

King Mswati III of Swaziland has 600 siblings; his father, King Sobhuza II, had 112 wives.

MOST POP HITS BY A ROYAL

Princess Stephanie of Monaco has had several pop records in the charts around the world. Her biggest hit was "Comme un Ouragan" (1985). She has also been a designer and model.

LONGEST ROYAL JOURNEY

In 1985 Prince Abdul aziz al-Saud, a nephew of King Fahd of Saudi Arabia, flew more than 1.8 million miles on *Discovery STS 51G*. His space trip lasted 7 days 1 hr. 48 min.

celebrity icons

MOST VISITED GRAVE SITE
Graceland, the former home and final resting place of Elvis Presley, receives over 700,000 visitors annually from all over the world – more than any other grave site. The record for the greatest number of visitors to Graceland in one year is 753,962, in 1995.

MOST MOURNERS TO ATTEND AN OPEN CASKET IN ONE DAY
On August 17, 1977, about 75,000 mourning fans attempted to visit Elvis's open casket and an estimated 10,000 to 20,000 people actually made it inside the foyer of Graceland. On the same day, a total of 3,166 floral wreaths were sent to Graceland by fans and celebrities.

MOST INEPT ROBBERY OF A CELEBRITY GRAVE
In March 1978, the body of the silent movie star Charlie Chaplin was stolen from its grave in Vevey, Switzerland. The graverobbers, Roman Wardas and Gantcho Ganev, demanded a $133,240 ransom for Chaplin's body, but were arrested a short distance away from the cemetery.

MOST ROCK STARS KILLED IN A SINGLE DISASTER
Rock stars Ritchie Valens, Buddy Holly and "The Big Bopper" Richardson were flying in the same airplane when it crashed on February 3, 1959, killing all three. The stars had chartered the plane in order to avoid the weather conditions that were making ground travel difficult. Valens reportedly obtained a seat on the plane by the toss of a coin.

ROCK CONTROVERSY
In the most controversial music documentary of recent times, *Kurt and Courtney*, the suicide of Kurt Cobain came under question. Award-winning journalist Nick Broomfield unveiled new witnesses claiming to have been offered money to kill Cobain. The star's widow, Courtney Love, who appeared in the documentary, took legal action to stop the film from being shown, but this only increased the media's interest.

MOST POSTERS OF A MALE ICON SOLD
James Dean, the star of *East of Eden* (1955) and *Rebel Without a Cause* (1955), died in a car accident at the age of 24 in 1955, but his legend lives on. In the last six years alone, Cartell International has sold more than 17,500 posters of Dean.

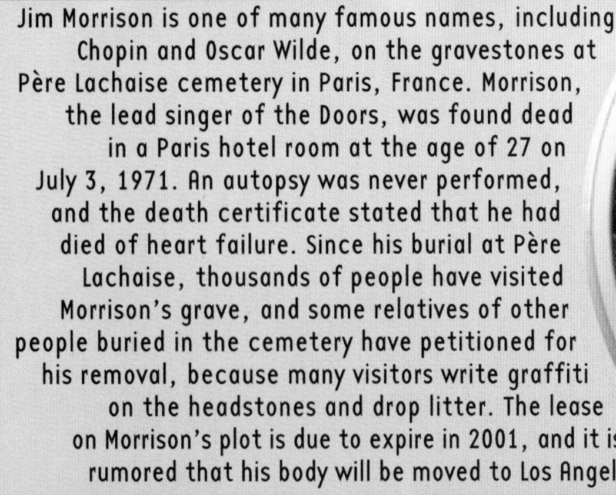

BIGGEST GAP BETWEEN ARTIST'S DEATH AND A NO. 1 HIT
"Words of Love" by Buddy Holly (& The Crickets) set the record for the longest interval between an artist's death and a No. 1 hit when it reached the top of the UK album chart in February 1993, 34 years after Holly's death.

MOST ALBUMS SOLD IN A DAY
On August 17, 1977, the day after his death, Elvis sold in excess of 20 million albums – more than any other artist in a single day.

MOST POSTHUMOUS NO. 1s IN SUCCESSION
Former Beatle John Lennon, who was shot dead in New York City on December 8, 1980, had three No. 1 hit singles in the following two months. "(Just Like) Starting Over" was the first on December 20, followed by "Imagine" on January 10 and "Woman" on February 7.

CELEBRITY CEMETERY
Jim Morrison is one of many famous names, including Chopin and Oscar Wilde, on the gravestones at Père Lachaise cemetery in Paris, France. Morrison, the lead singer of the Doors, was found dead in a Paris hotel room at the age of 27 on July 3, 1971. An autopsy was never performed, and the death certificate stated that he had died of heart failure. Since his burial at Père Lachaise, thousands of people have visited Morrison's grave, and some relatives of other people buried in the cemetery have petitioned for his removal, because many visitors write graffiti on the headstones and drop litter. The lease on Morrison's plot is due to expire in 2001, and it is rumored that his body will be moved to Los Angeles.

LONGEST SPANS IN THE U.K. AND U.S. ALBUM CHARTS
Following his death on May 14, 1998, Frank Sinatra's album *My Way* reentered the British chart. This was 40 years after his *Come Fly with Me* featured on the first ever British chart, in November 1958. "The Voice" also holds the record for the longest Top 20 album career

in the United States: his first chart entry in the rock era was *In The Wee Small Hours*, which entered on May 28, 1955, and, prior to his death, his most recent was *Duets II*, on December 30, 1994. Mourners at Sinatra's funeral included his ex-wife Mia Farrow, former First Lady Nancy Reagan, singers Bob Dylan, Tony Bennett and Liza Minnelli, actors Jack Lemmon, Jack Nicholson and Sophia Loren, and a host of other celebrities.

MOST CONSPIRACY THEORIES

The assassination of President John F. Kennedy has sparked numerous conspiracy theories, spawning movies, books and endless debate. The report of the Warren Commission, the official investigation by the US government, famously declared that Lee Harvey Oswald acted alone in killing the president in Dallas on November 22, 1963. Among those accused of being involved in plotting the assassination are the CIA, the Mafia, Fidel Castro, the KGB and even Lyndon B. Johnson, the vice-president who succeeded Kennedy after his untimely death.

MOST POSTERS OF A FEMALE ICON SOLD

Marilyn Monroe has featured on a record number of posters: since 1992, Cartell International has sold more than 37,500 posters of the star worldwide. Marilyn will also be among the first stars to have her DNA extracted, if California-based company Stargene has its way. It plans to extract the DNA of famous Americans, including George Washington.

BIGGEST AUSTRALIAN ROCK ICON

Michael Hutchence, lead singer of INXS, died in a hotel room in Sydney, Australia, on November 21, 1997, at age 37. After an accident in 1992 robbed him of his senses of taste and smell, he was reportedly prone to periods of depression, and it was this tendency that was later blamed by some for the resulting verdict of suicide. INXS had been preparing to embark on their 20th anniversary tour.

world leaders

HIGHEST-PAID WORLD LEADER
Ryutaro Hashimoto, who was the prime minister of Japan until 1998, had an annual salary of $343,000, including monthly allowances and bonuses.

MOST PRESIDENTIAL PALACES
Saddam Hussein, who has been the president of Iraq since 1979, has eight main palaces containing a total of 1,058 buildings, as well as a number of other minor residences throughout Iraq. His palace in Babylon, 55 miles south of Baghdad, is built alongside the remains of the palace of Nebuchadnezzar II (630–562 BC), and every brick is stamped with the legend "The Leader, Saddam Hussein, Victor of Allah." Additional palaces are currently under construction in Baghdad and in Saddam's home town of Tikrit.

MOST EXPENSIVE PRESIDENTIAL INAUGURATION
The inauguration of the president of the United States, including all gala balls and other celebrations, is the most expensive in the world. The most expensive ceremony ever is believed to be the inauguration of George Bush in 1989, at a reported cost of $30 million.

BIGGEST GATHERING OF WORLD LEADERS
A Special Commemorative Meeting of the General Assembly was held at United Nations Headquarters, New York City, October 22–24, 1995 to celebrate the 50th anniversary of the UN. It was addressed by 128 heads of state and heads of government.

PRESIDENT WHO HAS SPENT THE LEAST TIME IN HIS COUNTRY
Valdus Adamkus, who became president of Lithuania in 1998, returned to the republic in 1997 after living in Chicago, Illinois for more than 50 years, where he was Midwest chief of the Environmental Protection Agency (EPA). His opponents say he speaks Lithuanian with an American accent.

MOST RELUCTANT PRESIDENT
Kim Jong-Il has been head of state of the Democratic People's Republic of Korea (North Korea) since the death of his father in 1994. As of June 1998, Kim had not formally taken the title of president, although he had assumed the most powerful post in the land: leader of the Korean Workers' Party.

MOST ACCESSIBLE PRIME MINISTER
With the exception of the leaders of some "micro-states," the most accessible head of government is the Danish premier Poul Nyrup Rasmussen, whose home phone number is in the public domain. Rasmussen often personally answers telephone calls from citizens. Openness in government in Denmark extends to the sovereign — any citizen may request a personal audience with Queen Margrethe II.

BIGGEST SOCIAL CLIMB TO THE PRESIDENCY
Kocheril Raman Narayanan was inaugurated as president of India in July 1997, despite having been born an "untouchable" (the lowest social caste in India) and suffering extreme poverty. Caste discrimination was made illegal in 1947 but has not disappeared from Indian society.

MOST LITERARY PRESIDENT
The leader with the greatest literary reputation is Vaclav Havel, a Czech playwright and poet whose works were banned for 20 years after the 1968 Soviet invasion. Havel became president of Czechoslovakia in 1989 and president of the Czech Republic in 1993.

PRESIDENT WITH MOST FAMILY MEMBERS IN POWER
Until 1995, Barzan Ibrahim, a half-brother of Iraqi president Saddam Hussein, was ambassador to the UN and controlled much of the family fortune. Another of Saddam's half-brothers, Watban Ibrahim, was minister of the interior, and a third half-brother, Sabaoni Ibrahim, was chief of general security. Saddam's son-in-law Saddam Kamal Hussein was commander of the presidential guard until he fled to Jordan in 1995, and his sons, Udday and Qusay, hold various state and other offices. The latter was head of security services but was replaced by one of Saddam's in-laws.

HIGHEST PERSONAL MAJORITIES
The highest personal majority for a politician was 4.73 million, for Boris Yeltsin, the people's deputy candidate for Moscow, in the parliamentary elections in the Soviet Union in March 1989. He received 5.12 million votes out of the 5.72 million cast in the Moscow constituency. His closest rival received 392,633 votes.

Benazir Bhutto achieved 98.48% of the poll in the Larkana-III constituency in the 1990 general election in

MOST "SUBSTANTIAL" WORLD LEADER
Helmut Kohl, left of picture, has been the Federal German chancellor since 1982. At 6 ft. 4 in. in height and with an average weight of almost 266 pounds, he is the most "substantial" world leader. Kohl's weight fluctuates considerably and he has been known to weigh considerably more than 266 pounds at times. His healthy appetite is renowned, and his wife, Hannelore, has published a book called *A Culinary Voyage Through Germany*, which features some of the Chancellor's favorite food, including many hearty meat and cream dishes but also some low-calorie platters such as Paderborn Carrot Salad. Kohl is pictured here with Tony Blair, who became the first British prime minister to give a live video interview over the internet on April 29, 1998. Interviewer Sir David Frost chose from more than 700 questions sent in to the 10 Downing Street Web site before the interview. Tony Blair said he believed information technology had the potential to give people more control over the way their country is run.

Pakistan, with 94,462 votes. The next highest candidate obtained 718 votes.

LONGEST TIME IN POWER
Fidel Castro became prime minister of Cuba in July 1959 and has been president of Cuba and head of state and head of government since December 3, 1976.

LONGEST SPEECH BY A POLITICIAN
Chief Mangosuthu Buthelezi, the leader of the Inkatha Freedom Party and South African home affairs minister, spoke for an average of 2½ hours on 11 of the 18 days of the KwaZulu legislative assembly in 1993.

YOUNGEST PRESIDENT
The youngest republican head of state is Lt. Yaya Jammeh, who became president of the provisional council and head of state of the Gambia at the age of 29 on July 26, 1994 and was elected president at the age of 31 on September 27, 1996.

YOUNGEST PRIME MINISTER
The youngest head of government is Dr. Mario Frick, who became prime minister of Liechtenstein at age 28 on December 15, 1993.

OLDEST PRESIDENT
Rafael Caldera became president of Venezuela at the age of 76 in 1993. He had previously served as president from 1969 to 1974. When he leaves office in February 1999, the oldest republican head of state will be 82-year-old Kiro Gligorov, president of the former Yugoslav Republic of Macedonia.

OLDEST PRIME MINISTER
Sirimavo Bandaranaike became the Sri Lankan prime minister at the age of 78 in 1994. When she first became premier in 1960, she was the world's first woman prime minister. Her daughter, Chandrika Bandaranaike Kumaratunga, is the republic's president.

BIGGEST PRESIDENTIAL STAFF
The republican head of state with the biggest staff is the president of the United States, Bill Clinton, seen here with the highest-paid world leader, Japanese prime minister Ryutaro Hashimoto. There are more than 1,000 employees at the White House, including domestic staff, caterers, groundspeople, security personnel and interns. Some of this number also work for Hillary Rodham Clinton.

MOST HOSPITALIZED PRESIDENT
Boris Yeltsin, the president of the Russian Federation since 1991, has had nine known hospital stays, some of them emergency admissions, during his term of office, but has surpassed the average age attained by Russian males, 58, by more than nine years.

benefits, charities and parties

MOST SECURITY AT A HOLLYWOOD WEDDING

Elizabeth Taylor's eighth wedding ceremony was expected to attract about 1,000 journalists to Michael Jackson's Neverland estate in California in 1991. As a result, the 2,700-acre site was guarded by some of the tightest security the world has ever seen. Eighty security guards worked with mounted police and secret service bodyguards to watch for intruders, and red and white balloons were floated 540 feet above the estate to keep helicopters from filming. Despite all the security, a parachutist with a video camera managed to land at the wedding, but was immediately arrested. Taylor married former construction worker Larry Fortensky. She wore a yellow chiffon Valentino dress that reportedly cost $20,000. The official wedding photographs were taken by Herb Ritts and sold exclusively to the British magazine *Hello!*. In 1996, Taylor filed for divorce.

NEURO-SPINAL RESEARCH

On February 1, 1998, Christopher Reeve (seen above with his wife and son) hosted Hollywood's biggest fundraiser in aid of neuro-spinal research. The event raised $256,000, and was attended by more than 1,000 guests, including Robin Williams, Jane Seymour and Glenn Close. In May 1995, Reeve, the star of *Superman* (1978), was injured in a riding accident that left him wheelchair-bound.

MOST MONEY RAISED BY A BIRTHDAY FUNDRAISER

Elizabeth Taylor's 65th birthday party, which was held in Hollywood on February 15, 1997, raised a total of $1 million for AIDS causes. The record-breaking party was attended by a host of celebrities, including Michael Jackson, Dennis Hopper, Shirley MacLaine, Cher, Roseanne, Patti LaBelle and Madonna.

BIGGEST TELETHON

The Jerry Lewis "Stars Across America" Muscular Dystrophy Association Labor Day Telethon reached 27.6 million US homes and 75 million US viewers in 1997. The $21\frac{1}{2}$-hour live extravaganza is broadcast from CBS Television City in Hollywood and carried by about 200 "Love Network" TV stations. Hosted by actor and producer Jerry Lewis, it was first broadcast by a station in New York in 1966 and was the first televised fundraising event of its kind to raise more than $1 million. In 1997, it raised a record $50.47 million in pledges and contributions.

The most money raised by a British TV fundraiser is $27.87 million, by Comic Relief in 1997. Comic Relief is held every year in aid of a variety of charitable causes and has raised a total of $233 million over six years.

MOST MONEY RAISED BY A WAR RELIEF BENEFIT

Luciano Pavarotti's two concerts for the War Child charity, which supports child victims of war around the world, raised $863,915. Held in Modena, Italy on September 12, 1995 and June 20, 1996, the concerts also included artists such as Eric Clapton, Brian Eno and Sheryl Crow. U2's Bono wrote "Miss Sarajevo" for the 1995 show.

BIGGEST ROCK BENEFIT

Live Aid was the first ever simultaneous rock concert with satellite links between two countries. The 17-hour concert took place at Wembley Stadium, London, England and JFK Stadium, Philadelphia, Pennsylvania on July 13, 1985 and was attended by 150,000 people (80,000 people in Philadelphia and 70,000 in London). More than 1.6 billion people around the world watched satellite broadcasts of the event. Organized by the British charity Band Aid, which was masterminded by musicians Bob Geldof (seen center left, with Pete Townsend and Paul McCartney) and Midge Ure, it raised $80 million for the Ethiopian Famine Relief Fund and has raised more than $60 million since then. Included in the star-studded lineup were Queen, U2, Elvis Costello, INXS, Sting, Phil Collins, the Beach Boys, Elton John, Mick Jagger and Tina Turner. In the finale, all the musicians got on the stage and sang "Do They Know It's Christmas," the song that reached No. 1 in the United Kingdom at Christmas 1984, selling 6 million copies and raising about $8 million for famine relief.

BIGGEST ANNUAL PARTIES AT BUCKINGHAM PALACE
The garden parties held by the British Royal Family are attended by more than 30,000 people a year. At least three have been held every year since the 1860s, and each party is attended by approximately 8,000 people. At a typical garden party, which is attended by the Queen, the Duke of Edinburgh and other members of the Royal Family, about 27,000 cups of tea, 20,000 sandwiches and 20,000 slices of cake are consumed.

BIGGEST REGULAR SIT-DOWN DINNER AT BUCKINGHAM PALACE
On the occasion of an incoming state visit – such as the visit of the Emperor of Japan in June 1998 – Queen Elizabeth II holds a state banquet in honor of the visitor. The dinners, which are generally attended by up to 140 people, usually take place twice a year and are the biggest formal dinners regularly held at the palace. The annual gathering of the ambassadors from all countries that are accredited by the Court of St. James has a guest list of 1,500 people, and is the biggest reception held at Buckingham Palace.

BIGGEST WHITE HOUSE EVENT
The annual Easter Egg Roll on the front lawn of the White House is the biggest celebration held at the presidential dwelling. On March 31, 1997, it was attended by a record 29,000 people.

BIGGEST PARTY IN LAS VEGAS
The first annual Frank Sinatra Las Vegas Celebrity Golf Classic was held in Las Vegas, Nevada from May 28 to May 31, 1998, as a tribute to Sinatra, who had died on May 15. The proceeds went to Opportunity Village, Las Vegas, and the Barbara Sinatra Children's Center in Rancho Mirage, California, which was founded to counsel abused children. The tribute was the biggest party ever held in Las Vegas, with the golf tournament alone attracting an estimated 10,000 spectators. Guests at the black-tie gala included Gregory Peck, Robert de Niro, Leslie Nielsen, Jack Lemmon, and Dina Merrill. Among the Honorary Chairs of the tournament were Bruce Springsteen, Brooke Shields, Andre Agassi, and the Aga Khan.

MOST SUCCESSFUL FUND-RAISER FOR EJAF
A musical event held on February 8, 1997 raised $900,000 for the Elton John Aids Foundation (EJAF). Elton John gave a concert with Jessye Norman and Luciano Pavarotti, and an auction was held with prizes including dinner with Cindy Crawford and tennis lessons with Andre Agassi. Billy Joel and Whoopi Goldberg were among the guests.

MOST LAVISH BIRTHDAY PARTY
On July 13, 1996, Sir Muda Hassanal Bolkiah Mu'izzaddin Waddaulah, the Sultan of Brunei and one of the richest men in the world, put on the world's most lavish ever party. The attractions included an amusement park, which was later donated to the people of Brunei. The party cost a total of $27.2 million, $16 million of which was spent on three concerts by Michael Jackson.

BIGGEST ROCK BENEFIT FOR AIDS
A concert held in memory of Freddie Mercury (left), the rock star who died of AIDS in November 1991, was held at Wembley Stadium, London, England on April 20, 1992. The event was attended by approximately 75,000 people and was estimated to have reached close to 1 billion people in more than 70 countries. It was the biggest ever rock benefit for AIDS causes, and raised a total of $25 million. Artists including U2, Elton John, Guns 'N' Roses and Liza Minnelli all featured in the concert. Freddie Mercury was the lead singer of the rock group Queen.

money
& big business

wealth

RICHEST MAN
Bill Gates, the 42-year-old chairman and co-founder of Microsoft Corporation, has a net worth of $39.8 billion. His wealth now exceeds that of the Sultan of Brunei, whose fortune is estimated to be $38 billion.

RICHEST WOMAN
Liliane Bettencourt is the daughter of L'Oreal's founder. As an heiress to the fortune of the cosmetics empire, Bettencourt has a net worth of $8.4 billion.

YOUNGEST MULTI-BILLIONAIRE
Athina Onassis Roussel, the granddaughter of shipping magnate Aristotle Onassis, inherited an estimated $5-billion empire and the Greek island of Skorpios in 1988, at age three. She will have control of the fortune in 2003 when she is 18.

HIGHEST PERSONAL TAX LEVY
The highest recorded personal tax levy is one of $336 million on 70% of the estate of Howard Hughes.

LARGEST DOWRY
In 1929, Bolivian tin millionaire Simón Iturbi Patiño bestowed $39 million on his daughter, Elena Patiño. His total fortune was estimated to be worth $607.5 million.

MOST EXPENSIVE HOUSES
In 1997, Wong Kwan, chairman of Pearl Oriental Holdings, bought two properties in the Skyhigh development, Hong Kong for $70.2 million

MOST EXPENSIVE LUXURY LINER
The world's most expensive luxury liner, *The World of ResidenSea*, is due to be launched in the year 2000. Of its 250 ocean-going apartments, which are currently on sale for $1.3–5.8 million, the most covetable will be the 2,152-square-foot, three-bedroom, three-bathroom penthouses. The 1,000-foot ship, which is being produced by a German shipyard, is expected to cost $529.7 million, and will be the most luxurious ever built: there will be 500 staff to cater to guests' whims, as well as seven restaurants, bars, a movie theater, a casino, a nightclub, a Roman spa, a house of worship, a library, museums, a business service center with secretaries, and a licensed stock and bond broker. On the top three of the 15 decks there will be shops, a supermarket, a swimming pool, a retractable marina for water sports, a golf academy with driving ranges and putting greens, a tennis court and a helipad. *The World of ResidenSea* will follow the sun so that it will always be summer on board. Passengers will stop off at major events such as the Sydney 2000 Olympics and the Monaco Grand Prix, and will celebrate the millennium with a two-day stop on the International Date Line.

RICHEST MEN
The richest man for many years was the Sultan of Brunei (seen above, center). In 1998 his fortune was exceeded by that of Bill Gates, but Gates' wealth fluctuates according to the value of Microsoft shares, and the gap between their fortunes is at times minimal.

and $48.9 million. Another property was reported to have sold for $98.88 million. At $2,863 per square foot, it was then the world's most expensive house.

Bill Gates' house in Seattle, Washington was appraised by King County assessors at $53,392,000, but Gates claims that it is worth "only" $30.3 million.

MOST EXPENSIVE ISLANDS
The 40,000-acre island of Niihau, Hawaii is the largest privately owned island in the United States and has been valued at $100 million. The island is owned by the Robinson family.

The most expensive island currently on the market is D'Arros in the Seychelles. The atoll, which covers 600 acres and has a private lagoon, an airstrip and three homes, can be bought for $21 million.

MOST LUXURIOUS PRIVATE JET
The $35-million *Gulfstream V*, the highest-flying passenger aircraft after Concorde and the fastest long-range executive jet, can fly 6,500 nautical miles at almost the speed of sound. If fitted with customized extras, the jet's value increases to $40 million.

MOST EXPENSIVE YACHT
The *Prince Abdul Aziz*, which belongs to the Saudi Arabian royal family and was built in 1984 at a cost of $109 million, is believed to be the world's most expensive yacht. It is also the world's largest yacht, with a crew of 60, a complex underwater surveillance system and a swimming pool that converts into a dance floor.

GREATEST PHILANTHROPIST
New Jersey businessman Charles "Chuck" Feeney has given away almost all of his $4.1 billion fortune. He owns neither a car nor a house and wears a $16 wristwatch. The 66-year-old's wealth comes from the duty-free empire that he co-founded and sold to Moet & Chandon. Most of his money has gone into education and research in Ireland, with $5 million put aside for personal living expenses.

LARGEST BEQUESTS
In 1997, CNN founder Ted Turner pledged $1 billion to United Nations causes, including anti-landmine and refugee aid programs.

In 1991, publishing tycoon Walter Annenberg announced his intention to leave his $1 billion collection of artworks to the Metropolitan Museum of Art in New York City.

BIGGEST DIVORCE SETTLEMENTS
The world's largest ever publicly declared divorce settlement amounted to £500 million ($874 million) plus property. It was secured in 1982 by the lawyers of Soraya Khashoggi from her husband Adnan, a Saudi entrepreneur and property owner.

In 1997, US mobile phone pioneer Craig McCaw gave his ex-wife Wendy *c.*$463 million in stock plus $19 million in real estate. The settlement was so large that the US Securities and Exchange Commission was notified of the stock transfers.

LARGEST ROCK INHERITANCE
Lisa Marie Presley, Elvis' daughter, seen here with her former husband Michael Jackson, has inherited $130 million. She received $38 million on her 30th birthday in 1997, and will get the rest in installments. When Elvis died, his estate faced liquidation, but it has since been turned into one of the world's most successful merchandising enterprises.

valuable stuff

MOST VALUABLE JEWELRY The largest jewelry auction was the sale of the Duchess of Windsor's collection at Sotheby's, Geneva, Switzerland on April 3, 1987. It fetched a total of $53 million.

The most expensive ring was a 13.49-carat Fancy Deep Blue diamond ring bought for $7.5 million by an Asian buyer at Christie's, New York in April 1995. It was the highest price per carat ever paid for a blue diamond.

The costliest diamond per carat was a 0.95-carat fancy purplish-red stone sold at Christie's, New York in 1987. It fetched $926,315.79.

The highest price paid for a diamond was $16.55 million, for a 100.10-carat pear-shaped "D" Flawless diamond sold at Sotheby's, Geneva, Switzerland, on May 17, 1995. It was purchased by Sheikh Ahmed Fitaihi for his chain of jewelry stores in Saudi Arabia.

The highest known price paid for a rough diamond was $9.8 million, for a 255.10-carat stone from Guinea, bought by the William Goldberg Diamond Corporation with the Chow Tai Fook Jewelry Co. Ltd. in 1989.

The highest price paid for a ruby is $4.6 million, for a 32.08-carat ruby and diamond ring made by Chaumet in Paris, France, and sold at Sotheby's, New York in 1989.

The highest-priced ruby per carat is $227,300, for a ring with a stone weighing 15.97 carats sold at Sotheby's, New York on October 18, 1988.

The highest price paid for a single emerald is $2.1 million, for a 19.77-carat emerald and diamond ring made by Cartier in 1958. The ring was sold at Sotheby's, Geneva, Switzerland in April 1987.

The top price paid for a sapphire is $2.8 million, for a 62.02-carat step-cut stone sold as a sapphire and diamond ring at Sotheby's, St. Moritz, Switzerland on February 20, 1988.

The world's highest-priced pearl is the egg-shaped 15.13-g (302 7/10-grain) La Régente. Formerly part of the French crown jewels, it sold for a record-breaking $864,280 at Christie's, Geneva, Switzerland on May 12, 1988.

The record price paid per carat for an emerald is $107,569, for the 19.77-carat diamond and emerald ring that sold for $2.13 million at Sotheby's, Geneva, Switzerland, on April 2, 1987.

MOST EXPENSIVE BOX
A Cartier jeweled vanity case set with a fragment of ancient Egyptian steel was sold at Christie's, New York for the record sum of $189,000 in November 1993.

MOST VALUABLE FABERGÉ EGG
Fabergé, jeweler to the Russian Imperial family, created about 56 Imperial eggs between 1885 and 1917. The most valuable is the Imperial Winter Egg, made of solid rock crystal and embellished with more than 3,000 diamonds. In November 1994, it sold at Christie's, Geneva, Switzerland for $5,587,308. The most valuable Easter egg (above) sold at Sotheby's, New York for $2,141,563 in 1985.

MOST EXPENSIVE CUE
A cue incorporating an 18-diamond tube mounted in 14-carat gold was designed by Joe Gold Cognoscenti Cues and is worth $22,000. It was produced over nine months during 1997. The cue is the most elaborate ever designed by Joe Gold, and was delivered to a Mr. Keith Walton when it was finished.

MOST EXPENSIVE BILLIARD TABLE
The Golden Fleece has been valued at $100,000, making it the most expensive billiard table on sale in the world. The carved table, which is covered in 23-carat gold leaf and protected with a special aged varnish, is the only one of its kind. It was designed and built by husband and wife team Andee and Gil Atkisson, who own one of the world's leading billiard table companies.

MOST VALUABLE MISSING ART TREASURE
The Amber Room, which consisted of intricately carved amber panels and richly decorated chairs, tables and amber ornaments, was presented to Catherine the Great of Russia by Frederick William I of Prussia in 1716 and installed in the Catherine Palace at Tsarskoye Selo near St. Petersburg, Russia. Described as "the eighth wonder of the world," it was at the top of Hitler's trophy list during World War II. Before the German invasion, he carefully plotted the dismantling of the room, but was thwarted by the Russians, who buried the delicate panels in the palace garden. However, Hitler seconded hundreds of troops to dig them up and had them shipped to Königsberg castle in East Prussia (now Kaliningrad, Russia). In 1945, the room was put into storage because the Russian army was advancing, and it subsequently disappeared. A single panel surfaced in Germany in 1997, fostering hopes of rebuilding the room. Meanwhile, 22 Russian craftsmen are painstakingly recreating the room from photographs taken before the war. A total of 66 tons of amber are being used, at a cost of $164 million. Work began in 1982 and will not be complete for at least 15 years.

MOST EXPENSIVE WATCHES
The most paid for a watch is $3.15 million, for a Patek Philippe Calibre '89 with 1,728 separate parts, at Habsburg Feldman, Geneva, Switzerland on April 9, 1989.

The highest price ever paid for a wristwatch is $1.78 million, for a Patek Philippe Calatrava 1939 that was auctioned at Antiquorum, Geneva, Switzerland on April 20, 1996.

The most expensive wristwatches currently on sale are Abraham-Louis Breguet 18-carat-gold watches, with tourbillon, perpetual calendar, minute-repeater and retrograde date. Only 10 of the watches have been made, and each one costs $450,000.

The most expensive Rolex in the world is an extremely rare Oyster Perpetual that was sold for the sum of $83,220 by Antiquorum in Geneva, Switzerland, in April 1997. The 18-carat yellow gold and diamond gentleman's wristwatch is waterproof and self-winding.

MOST EXPENSIVE LUGGAGE
A complete set of Louis Vuitton luggage, which includes an armoire trunk, a wardrobe trunk, a steamer trunk, four matching suitcases, a hat box, a cruiser bag and a jewelry case, costs a total of $601,340, making it the world's most expensive luggage.

MOST EXPENSIVE SHOES
Emperor Field Marshall Jean Feeder Bokassa of the Central African Empire (now Republic) commissioned a pair of pearl-studded shoes costing a record $85,000 from the House of Berluti, Paris, France, for his self-coronation in 1977.

MOST EXPENSIVE WEDDING DRESS
A wedding outfit created by Hélène Gainville with jewels by Alexander Reza is estimated to be worth $7,301,587. The dress, which is embroidered with diamonds and mounted on platinum, was unveiled in Paris, France on March 23, 1989.

MOST EXPENSIVE CIGARS
On November 16, 1997 an Asian buyer paid a record $16,560 each for 25 Trinidad cigars made by the Cuban National Factory. The sale took place at Christie's, London.

MOST EXPENSIVE SURGICAL INSTRUMENT
A 19th-century German mechanical chainsaw sold for $34,848 at Christie's, London in August 1993, making it the most expensive surgical instrument ever sold.

MOST EXPENSIVE SKULL
The skull of the Swedish philosopher and theologian Emanuel Swedenborg was purchased in London, England by the Royal Swedish Academy of Sciences for $10,668 on March 6, 1978.

MOST EXPENSIVE MONOPOLY SET
An exclusive $2-million Monopoly set was created by jeweler Sidney Mobell of San Francisco, California in 1988. The board is made from 23-carat gold and the dice have 42 full cut diamonds for spots.

MOST EXPENSIVE PHONE CARD
The highest price known to have been paid for a telephone card is $49,462, for the first card ever issued in Japan, which was sold in January 1992.

MOST EXPENSIVE FOUNTAIN PEN
A Japanese collector paid a record sum of $218,007 in February 1988 for the 'Anémone' fountain pen, which was made by French company Réden. The pen was encrusted with a total of 600 precious stones, including emeralds, amethysts, rubies, sapphires and onyx, and took a team of skilled craftsmen more than a year to complete.

MOST EXPENSIVE LETTER SIGNED BY A LIVING PERSON
The record sum of $12,500 was paid at the Hamilton Galleries in New York City on January 22, 1981 for a two-page signed letter from former president Ronald Reagan. The letter, which was undated, praised the singer and actor Frank Sinatra. It is the most expensive letter to have been signed by a person who is still alive today.

MOST EXPENSIVE TAPES
In 1997, the government paid $28 million to the estate of former president Richard Nixon for the Watergate tape recordings, which forced him out of office in 1974 by proving that he had plotted to cover up the bugging of the Democratic Party headquarters. The tapes are now in the US National Archives.

MOST EXPENSIVE FILM SCRIPT
Clark Gable's script for *Gone With The Wind* (1939) sold for $244,500 in December 1996 at Christie's, New York.

MOST EXPENSIVE OSCAR
Clark Gable's Academy Award for *It Happened One Night* (1934) sold for $607,500 at Christie's, New York in December 1996.

MOST EXPENSIVE SLICE OF CAKE
In February 1998, a piece of cake left over from the wedding of the Duke and Duchess of Windsor sold at Sotheby's, New York for $29,900 to Californian entrepreneur Benjamin Yim and his wife Amanda. The cake, which was part of the Windsor collection auction, had only been expected to fetch a maximum of $1,000 at the sale.

going, going, gone

MOST EXPENSIVE MOVIE POSTER
The poster from Universal Studios' 1932 film *The Mummy* sold for a record $453,000 at Sotheby's, New York in March 1997. The poster, which features the film's star, Boris Karloff, went for more than twice the previous record of $198,000. There are only two known copies of *The Mummy* poster in existence.

MOST VALUABLE PIECES OF OTHER PLANETS
A tiny piece of Martian meteorite fetched $7,333 – more than 1,000 times its weight in gold – at Phillips, New York in May 1998. The rock, which measures 7/100 x 7/100 x 3/20 inch and weighs 9/1,000 ounce, was found in Brazil in 1958 and was expected to sell for $1,600–3,200. Known as the Governador Valadares, it is the most valuable of the 12 Martian meteorites discovered on Earth.

Sotheby's sold 1/100 ounce, or less than two carats, of rock from the Moon for $442,000 in 1996. A total of 800 pounds of lunar rock exists on Earth, compared with 90 pounds of Martian rock.

MOST IMPORTANT SCIENTIFIC THEORY SOLD AT AUCTION
Albert Einstein's *Theory of Relativity*, which was written in 1913 in collaboration with Michele Besso and proposed to account for the constant speed of light, sold for $398,500 at Christie's, New York in 1996. The 51-page manuscript of the most important document in modern science had an asking price of $250,000–350,000. Einstein went on to formulate his general theory of relativity in 1919.

MOST EXPENSIVE TOBACCO TIN
The tobacco tin in which John Lennon kept his cigarette papers fetched $8,453 at a sale of Beatles memorabilia at Christie's, London in September 1995. The 11-inch-high leather-covered pot, which was bought by a British fan, had been expected to fetch between $475 and $635. Cynthia Lennon, the star's first wife, provided the items for the sale.

MOST EXPENSIVE BIRTH CERTIFICATE
Sir Paul McCartney's birth certificate sold for $84,146 in a Bonhams auction conducted simultaneously in Tokyo, Japan and London, England in March 1997. The pre-sale estimate was $13,000. The certificate, which was originally sold by McCartney's stepmother after the death of his father, was put on the market by a Californian record collector and bought by an anonymous London buyer.

MOST EXPENSIVE TELEGRAM
The highest price ever paid for a telegram is $68,500, for a telegram sent by Soviet premier Nikita Khrushchev to Yuri Gagarin on April 12, 1961, congratulating him on becoming the first man in space. It was bought by Alberto Bolaffi of Turin, Italy at Sotheby's, New York on December 11, 1993.

MOST PAID FOR PRESIDENTIAL UNDERWEAR
Two pairs of John F. Kennedy's long johns were bought for $3,450 by Richard Wilson (left) at Guernsey's, New York City in March 1998. Wilson runs a mail order business selling unusual celebrity memorabilia. He plans to display the former president's underwear alongside Marilyn Monroe's slip and panties. Many of the items in the auction were part of Robert White's 100,000-piece Kennedy collection, left to him in 1995 by Kennedy's secretary, Evelyn Lincoln, who saved almost everything to do with Kennedy or his family. The sunglasses that Kennedy was wearing on the day he was shot went for $46,000 and a plastic comb that probably cost about $0.25 sold for $1,265.

MOST EXPENSIVE SHOES SOLD AT AUCTION
The red slippers worn by Judy Garland when she played Dorothy in *The Wizard of Oz* (1939) sold for $165,000 at Christie's, New York on June 2, 1988. The shoes belonged to Roberta Baumann, who had won them in a competition in 1940, and were bought by Anthony Landini. At the time, it was a record price for any item worn in a movie.

MOST EXPENSIVE WINE COLLECTION
Andrew Lloyd Webber's collection of 18,000 bottles of wine sold for a total of $6,056,783 (an average price of about $336 per bottle) at Sotheby's, London, May 20–21, 1997.

MOST EXPENSIVE PLAYING CARDS
The highest price for a deck of playing cards is $143,352, paid by the Metropolitan Museum of Art, New York City at Sotheby's, London on December 6, 1983. The cards, dating from *c.* 1470–85, constituted the oldest known complete hand-painted set.

MOST EXPENSIVE RACING CAR MEMORABILIA
A pair of overalls worn by Brazilian racing driver Ayrton Senna, who died in a high-speed crash at the 1994 San Marino Grand Prix, sold at Sotheby's, London in December 1996 for $42,140. Senna had worn the overalls in his first Formula 1 race for the Toleman team in Monaco in 1984. A pair of gloves worn by Senna during the 1987 season were sold for $4,048 and a race helmet he wore in 1982 fetched $46,000. The latter was bought by British fan Peter Radcliffe, the overalls and gloves by anonymous bidders.

MOST EXPENSIVE WORLD CUP REPLICA
A World Cup "decoy" trophy fetched 12 times the estimated price, selling for $407,200 at Sotheby's, London in July 1997. The gold-painted trophy, a replica of the one won by England in 1966, was ordered by the Football Association after the real cup was stolen in 1966. For two years, it was passed off as the genuine Jules Rimet trophy and was protected by security guards to keep up the pretense for the public. The original was later found in London by a dog named Pickles.

MOST EXPENSIVE GUN
An 1873 .45 caliber Colt single-action army revolver, Serial No. 1, was sold for $242,000 at Christie's, New York on May 14, 1987.

MOST PAID FOR A BARK PAINTING
An Aboriginal bark painting from the late 1960s sold for a record $18,400 to an art collector in Sydney, Australia in 1996. The artist, Yarawala, who died in 1970, was admired by Picasso.

MOST PAID FOR AN ABORIGINAL SCULPTURE
A large Tiwi figure carved by Aurangamirri sold for $20,700 in Sydney, Australia in 1996 to an Australian collector.

MOST EXPENSIVE TEDDY BEAR
A 1904 Steiff bear called Teddy Girl was sold to Japanese businessman Yoshihiro Sekiguchi for $171,523 at Christie's, London in December 1994. The teddy bear is now in a Japanese museum. The previous record was $86,589 for a Steiff brown bear, *c.* 1920, at Sotheby's, London in September 1989.

MOST EXPENSIVE STUFFED DOG
The stuffed body of Toto the dog, who starred alongside Judy Garland in *The Wizard of Oz* (1939), sold for $3,680 at auction in 1996.

MOST VALUABLE FILM PROP
A statuette used in *The Maltese Falcon* (1941) sold for $398,500 at Christie's, New York in 1994.

MOST EXPENSIVE CARTOON POSTER
A poster for Walt Disney's film short *Alice's Day At Sea* (1924) sold for the record sum of $34,273 at Christie's, London in April 1994.

MOST PAID FOR A FILM COSTUME
The white polyester suit worn by John Travolta in *Saturday Night Fever* (1977) was sold for $145,500 in June 1995. The pre-sale estimate was between $30,000 and $50,000.

BOXING MEMORABILIA
The calf-length white robe worn by Muhammad Ali when he beat George Foreman in their "Rumble In the Jungle" world heavyweight title fight in Zaire (now Congo) in 1974 sold for $140,000 – a record for boxing memorabilia – at Christie's, Los Angeles in October 1997. A pair of gloves (below) worn by Ali for a fight against Zora Folley in 1967 sold for a record $29,900. The buyers were anonymous.

gambling

BIGGEST POKER TOURNAMENT
The World Poker Series, which was won by Stu Unger (above right) in 1997, is the largest poker tournament in the world. The annual event began in 1970 at Binion's Horseshoe, Las Vegas, Nevada, and the total prize money won since then exceeds $117 million. The tournament offers a $1-million prize for the winner as well as a $10,000 buy-in.

BIGGEST LOTTERY JACKPOT
The biggest individual gambling jackpot was $195 million, won by Frank and Shirley Capaci of Streamwood, Illinois in the Powerball lottery draw on May 20, 1998. The retired electrician and his wife, who had a friend buy their ticket in Pell Lake, Wisconsin, elected to take a lump-sum payment of $104, 269,458, the largest U.S. single lump-sum lottery payoff.

BIGGEST MEGABUCKS JACKPOT
The Nevada Megabucks progressive slot jackpot passed the $15-million mark in April 1998 and will be the largest slot jackpot in history when it is hit. The current record stands at $12.51 million, which was won by Suzanne Henley in Las Vegas in April 1997.

BIGGEST VIDEO POKER JACKPOT
In April 1998, a grandmother from San Antonio, Texas hit a jackpot of $839,306.92 on the Five Duck Frenzy™ at the Las Vegas Club, Las Vegas, Nevada.

BIGGEST GAMBLERS
Australia has a greater number of gamblers than any other country, and on average an Australian bets in excess of $2,700 a year – three times more than a US citizen.

BIGGEST HIGH ROLLER
The world's biggest high roller or "whale" (the term for people who bet huge amounts at casinos) is Australian media tycoon Kerry Packer, who has an estimated personal fortune of $1.5 billion. Packer is guaranteed an instant $20-million line of credit at any casino that is prepared to admit him. In 1997, he

BIGGEST SLOT MACHINE JACKPOT
The largest amount ever won on a "one-armed bandit" is $12,510,550, by Suzanne Henley on a Megabucks machine at the New York–New York Hotel and Casino, Las Vegas on April 14, 1997. Henley, who was 46 at the time, said she "just had a feeling" about the poker machine, which for major prizes is linked to 746 others. She waited for more than an hour to play it.

BIGGEST LOTTERY
Spain's government-run lottery, El Gordo ("The Fat One"), is the biggest in the world, awarding more prize money and offering 800% better odds of winning (one in six) than any other lottery. Winning ticket holders are seen here celebrating after their numbers came up. El Gordo awarded $1.2 billion in December 1997, with a grand prize of $270 million. Its largest ever cash jackpot was $236 million. The next biggest lotteries in terms of average pool size are the Florida state lottery, at $14 million, the Australian government lottery, at $10 million, the German state lottery, at $6.5 million, and the New York State Lottery and the French national lottery, both at $6 million. Of these, the biggest jackpot prize has been $7 million, on the Florida state lottery. The United Kingdom's National Lottery is one of the world's newest: it began in 1994 – 168 years after the last lottery was allowed in the country. The typical jackpot prize is $3.33 million and the chance of winning the jackpot is one in 14 million.

U.S. GAMBLING
Gambling is a $40-billion-a-year industry in the United States, and there is some form of legalized gambling in every state except Hawaii and Utah. The most popular forms of gambling are lotteries, racetrack betting, bingo and charity benefits. Casinos are allowed in 23 states, often on Native American reservations, and are popular attractions along with high-stakes bingo.

purchased his own casino in Australia after two Las Vegas casinos lost $22 million to him. He also won the sum of $26 million in seven hands of blackjack at the MGM Grand Casino, Las Vegas. His favorite bet is $1 million.

BIGGEST CASINO
Foxwoods Resort Casino in Ledyard, Connecticut is the largest in the world, with a gaming area covering 193,000 square feet and a total of 3,854 slot machines, 234 gaming tables and 3,500 bingo seats.

HIGHEST CASINO
The Stratosphere Hotel Casino in Las Vegas is the highest casino in the world. The 1,149-foot-high, 100-story tower, which opened in April 1996 at a cost of about $550 million, is the tallest free-standing observation tower in the United States. It is 156 feet taller than the Eiffel Tower in Paris, France. The casino covers 100,000 square feet and has more than 2,000 slot and video poker machines.

BIGGEST POT IN POKER
In 1996, Huck Seed, a poker professional from Las Vegas, won a pot of $2.3 million from Dr. Bruce Van Horn of Ada, Oklahoma — the largest in the history of the game. Seed went on to win the World Series Poker Title.

BIGGEST HOUSE IN BINGO
The largest ever house in bingo sessions was 15,756, at the Canadian National Exhibition, Toronto, on August 19, 1983. The competition was staged by the Variety Club of Ontario Tent Number 28, offered total prize money of $203,252 with a record one-game payout of $81,300.

BIGGEST BOOKMAKER
The world's largest bookmaker is Ladbrokes, which has more than 2,460 off-track betting units in the United Kingdom, 74 in the Republic of Ireland, 474 in Belgium, six in the United States, and seven in Argentina.

LONGEST ODDS EVER OFFERED
In 1996, bookmaker William Hill offered odds of 15 million to one on Screaming Lord Sutch of the Monster Raving Loony Party becoming British prime minister — longer odds than they offer for Elvis Presley crashing a UFO into the Loch Ness Monster (14 million to one). Lord Sutch has been a familiar face on the political scene since 1963 and is the UK's longest-serving political leader.

BIGGEST HORSE RACING PAYOUT
The largest horse racing payout, after tax, was $1,627,084, to Anthony Speelman and Nicholas Cowan (both Great Britain) on a $64 9-horse accumulator at Santa Anita Racetrack, Arcadia, California on April 19, 1987.

MOST NEON LIGHTS
Las Vegas is world famous for its 24-hour-a-day legal gambling. Casinos and other gaming units line the "Strip," and the hotels and nightclubs have made Las Vegas a major year-round tourist destination. It is also a favorite for weddings — Elvis Presley and Priscilla Beaulieu, Demi Moore and Bruce Willis, and Cindy Crawford and Richard Gere all got married here. Sadly, all these couples separated.

shopping

BIGGEST DEPARTMENT STORE
At 2.15 million square feet, the largest department store by area is Macy's. The shop's 11-story building occupies an entire block in Herald Square, New York City. Macy's also has a chain of department stores across the US and was one of the first major retailers to place stores in shopping malls. The firm's red star trademark derives from a tattoo borne by its founder, Rowland Macy.

MOST MALLS IN ONE COUNTRY
The United States has more shopping malls (defined as enclosed, climate-controlled environments typically anchored by at least one major full-line department store with an area of more than 400,000 square feet) than any other country, with a total of 1,897 to date. If they are added to the number of grocery-, drug- or discount-store-anchored centers, the total number of shopping centers is 42,048.

LONGEST MALL
The shopping mall located inside the $64-million shopping centre in Milton Keynes, England is 2,360 feet in length, making it the world's longest shopping mall.

BIGGEST RETAIL SPACE
The Del Amo Fashion Center in Torrance, California is the biggest retail center in the world in terms of floor area, covering a total of 3 million square feet.

BIGGEST OPEN-AIR SHOPPING CENTER
Ala Moana Center in Honolulu, Hawaii has more than 200 stores over a 50-acre site, making it the world's largest open-air shopping center. It is visited by more than 56 million shoppers every year.

BIGGEST UNDERGROUND SHOPPING COMPLEX
The Toronto Underground in Canada has more than 6 miles of shopping arcades and a total of 1,100 shops and restaurants, making it the world's biggest subterranean shopping complex.

BIGGEST WHOLESALER
The world's biggest wholesale merchandise mart is the Dallas Market Center in Texas, which has a floor area of almost 6.9 million square feet and houses about 2,580 permanent showrooms displaying the merchandise of more than 50,000 manufacturers.

BIGGEST RETAILING FIRM
Wal-Mart Stores, Inc., which was founded by Sam Walton in Bentonville, Arkansas in 1962, had a net income of $2.74 billion as of January 31, 1996. By June 1998, it had had total sales of $117.9 billion and 3,487 retail locations worldwide. Wal-Mart employs 800,000 people.

FIRST SUPERMARKET ART GALLERY
From December 9, 1997 to January 10, 1998, the Leclerc supermarket at Le Cannet, near Cannes on the French Riviera, installed an art gallery in its aisles in an effort to boost a local art market that had been in decline for a considerable time. A total of 17 artists from the region had their work on display and received all profits from the sales. The supermarket did not take any commission. Some of the artists were present in the "art gallery" to explain their works to potential buyers. During the trial period, visitors to the supermarket could fill their shopping carts with paintings, sculptures and lithographs, all of which were shrinkwrapped and labeled for price scanners. The 1,700 pieces of art ranged in price from $14 to $4,167 and were aimed at the supermarket's wealthier customers. By the end of the five weeks, the supermarket had sold 185 pieces for a total of $5,553. Yvon Guidez, one of the artists and a promoter of the program, said that art should be open to everyone and treated in the same way as consumer items such as laundry detergent or soft drinks. One of his works, a bronze sculpture entitled *Octave Auguste*, was bought by a French shopper for $2,500.

MOST SHOPS
On January 28, 1996, the Woolworth Corporation had 8,178 retail stores worldwide — the most that any company has ever had. The company's founder, Frank Winfield Woolworth, opened his first shop, The Great Five Cent Store, in Utica, New York in 1879.

MOST SHOPPERS AT ONE DEPARTMENT STORE
The most visitors to a single department store on one day is an estimated 1.07 million, to the Nextage Shanghai, China, on December 20, 1995.

BIGGEST SHOPPING CENTER
The West Edmonton Mall in Alberta, Canada was opened in 1981 and completed four years later. The mall covers an area of 5.2 million square feet on a 121-acre site, and houses more than 800 stores and services, as well as 11 major department stores. It serves approximately 20 million customers annually and provides parking for 20,000 vehicles. A water park, golf course, ice rink and chapel can all be found inside the mall.

BIGGEST DUTY FREE SHOP
The world's biggest duty free shop will be opened by the Indonesian tourist operator PT Sona Topas in Bali in late 1998. It will bring the total number of duty free shops on the island to 22. PT Sona Topas currently accounts for 60% of Indonesia's duty free market and has prime locations in every major international airport worldwide.

BIGGEST DUTY FREE CENTER
Heathrow Airport, London, England is currently the biggest duty free center in the world in terms of revenue, which amounted to $585.2 million in 1996. Honolulu Airport is second, with $425.8 million, followed by Hong Kong, China, with $380 million. It is predicted that the new Chek Lap Kok Airport in Hong Kong will overtake all three of these airports to become the most lucrative duty free shopping area in the world.

BIGGEST TOY STORE CHAIN
Toys 'R' Us, which has its headquarters in Paramus, New Jersey, has a total of 1,000 stores and 43 million square feet of retail space worldwide. The largest single Toys 'R' Us store is the branch in Birmingham, England, at 65,000 square feet.

GREATEST SALES PER UNIT AREA
The record for the greatest sales based on sales floor area is held by Richer Sounds plc, the stereo retail chain. Its sales at London Bridge Walk, London, England reached a peak of $26,380 per square foot for the year ending January 31, 1994.

MOST EXPENSIVE STORE RENTAL
Oxford Street in London, England is the most expensive place in the world in which to rent store space. The price of renting the equivalent floor area of a wastepaper basket there has jumped by 25% to £500 ($800).

BIGGEST RUMMAGE SALES
The record for the greatest amount of money raised at a one-day sale is $214,085.99, at the 62nd one-day rummage sale organized by the Winnetka Congregational Church, Winnetka, Illinois, in May 1994.

The White Elephant Sale at the Cleveland Convention Center, Ohio raised $427,935.21 over two days from October 18 to October 19, 1983.

HIGHEST CHARGE CARD TRANSACTION
In 1995, Eli Broad, an art collector from Los Angeles, California, purchased Roy Lichtenstein's painting *I...I'm Sorry* (1965–66) for the sum of $2.5 million, paying for it by American Express. The highest Amex transaction to date, it earned Broad a total of 2.5 million air miles.

MOST CREDIT CARDS
Walter Cavanagh of Santa Clara, California has a total of 1,397 different credit cards, which together are worth more than $1.65 million in credit. He keeps his collection in the world's longest wallet, which is 250 feet in length and weighs 38 lb. 8 oz.

BIGGEST PURCHASER OF HAUTE-COUTURE
Mouna al-Ayoub, the ex-wife of Nasser al-Rashid, the consultant to the Saudi royal family, spends more money on haute-couture than anybody else in the world. Al-Ayoub's most expensive purchase to date was a $160,000 gold embroidered dress from Chanel.

brand names

MOST VALUABLE BRAND NAME
The most valuable brand name in the world today is Coca-Cola, which was worth $48 billion in 1997. Coca-Cola is also considered by many people to be the most famous brand name in the world and the brand name with the strongest global advertising image. Its share value has increased from $4 billion in 1981 to more than $150 billion today.

MOST POPULAR SPORTS BRAND
Nike is the top sporting goods group, with a global market share of 35%, and the biggest shoe manufacturer in the world. It is worth $6.16 billion. In 1998, it signed an eight-year sponsorship deal with the US Soccer Federation worth $120 million. It has also put up $1 billion to sponsor leading athletes and teams around the world, in a marketing battle with its rival Adidas. Tiger Woods, Michael Jordan and Pete Sampras are some of its sponsored celebrities. The Nike "swoosh," now so recognizable that sports stars do not need to wear anything else on their clothes to identify their sponsor, was created by a designer in Oregon for $35 in 1971.

MOST EXPENSIVE RE-BRANDING OF AN AIRLINE
In 1997, British Airways, the biggest international carrier in the world, underwent a $98-million facelift in the biggest ever relaunch of its kind. British Airways' previous symbol, the Union Jack flag, was replaced by African paintings of jackals, Japanese wave designs and other internationally inspired works of art. Payment to artists, lawyers and design consultancies accounted for about $3.2 million of the total sum, and a similar amount was spent on a satellite broadcast to 63 countries of the unveiling ceremony at Heathrow airport, London. Numerous other launch events were organized including a flotilla of barges in Thailand, with sails displaying the new images.

BIGGEST BRAND CONSULTANCY
In 1997, Interbrand, which branded the antidepressant drug Prozac, merged with design business Newell and Sorrell, who had overhauled British Airways' image, to create the world's biggest brand consultancy. The combined business, which has an annual turnover of $33.2 million, is owned by the US advertising agency Omnicom and employs a total of 600 people worldwide.

MOST SUCCESSFUL BRAND AGENCY
Set up in 1981, Dentsu Young and Rubicam is the world's largest advertising resource. In 1996 it was worth $1,930 million. An alliance between Dentsu, the largest agency in Japan, and Young and Rubicam, the biggest US agency, Dentsu Young and Rubicam has 19 offices in 12 countries in Asia and 341 offices worldwide. Its main accounts include AT&T, Cadbury Schweppes, Kraft Foods, Colgate–Palmolive, Ericsson, Fuji–Xerox, Nike, Philip Morris, Sony and United Airlines.

BIGGEST BRAND SPONSORSHIP DEAL
In 1996, Nike signed a record $400-million deal with the Brazilian national soccer team. It gives Nike the right to arrange a series of international soccer fixtures over 10 years with the team as part of the group's expansion into sports sponsorship.

MOST VALUABLE COLLECTIBLE BRANDS
Old Nike, Puma and Adidas shoes are being included for the first

TOP SOFT DRINK BRAND
The world's most popular soft drink brand by volume sales is Coca-Cola, which had a 43.9% share of the $54.7-billion United States carbonated drinks market in 1997. Its closest rival, Pepsi, has 30.9% of the market. Coca-Cola sales in the United States in 1996 indicate a consumption of 54 gallons per person.

BIGGEST BRAND FORGERY
Financial losses created by counterfeiting operations amount to 5–7% of world trade, or $250–$350 billion. From 1990 to 1995, world trade grew by 47% and the counterfeiting trade grew by 150%, and in 1995–96 British customs officers seized a total of 81 counterfeit consignments, compared with just 12 the previous year. The world's top producer of counterfeit products is Turkey, followed by China, Thailand, Italy and Colombia. According to the Service de Statistiques Industrielles, 60% of the world's counterfeited goods end up for sale in the European Union, with France receiving 25% of them. In the United States, the most common form of piracy, according to the Motion Picture Association of America (MPAA), is the "back to back" copying of videos, but the industry is more affected by organized and sophisticated duplication facilities that have the ability to produce hundreds of thousands of copies a year. Worldwide video piracy currently costs US motion picture companies $2.5 billion a year in lost revenues. The music industry also loses vast sums each year through piracy. At left, a consignment of pirated videos is crushed by a steamroller in Bangkok, Thailand.

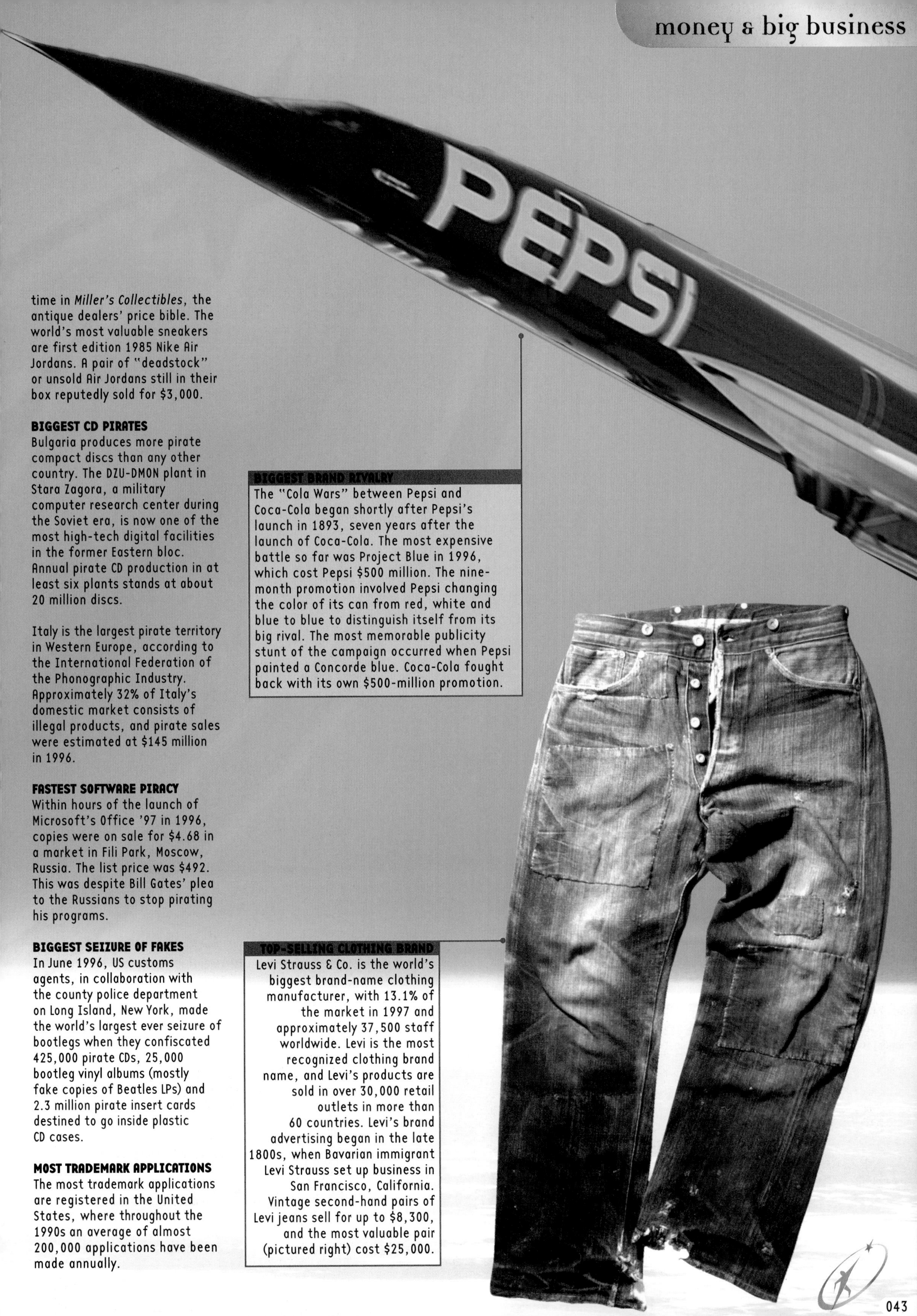

time in *Miller's Collectibles*, the antique dealers' price bible. The world's most valuable sneakers are first edition 1985 Nike Air Jordans. A pair of "deadstock" or unsold Air Jordans still in their box reputedly sold for $3,000.

BIGGEST CD PIRATES
Bulgaria produces more pirate compact discs than any other country. The DZU-DMON plant in Stara Zagora, a military computer research center during the Soviet era, is now one of the most high-tech digital facilities in the former Eastern bloc. Annual pirate CD production in at least six plants stands at about 20 million discs.

Italy is the largest pirate territory in Western Europe, according to the International Federation of the Phonographic Industry. Approximately 32% of Italy's domestic market consists of illegal products, and pirate sales were estimated at $145 million in 1996.

FASTEST SOFTWARE PIRACY
Within hours of the launch of Microsoft's Office '97 in 1996, copies were on sale for $4.68 in a market in Fili Park, Moscow, Russia. The list price was $492. This was despite Bill Gates' plea to the Russians to stop pirating his programs.

BIGGEST SEIZURE OF FAKES
In June 1996, US customs agents, in collaboration with the county police department on Long Island, New York, made the world's largest ever seizure of bootlegs when they confiscated 425,000 pirate CDs, 25,000 bootleg vinyl albums (mostly fake copies of Beatles LPs) and 2.3 million pirate insert cards destined to go inside plastic CD cases.

MOST TRADEMARK APPLICATIONS
The most trademark applications are registered in the United States, where throughout the 1990s an average of almost 200,000 applications have been made annually.

BIGGEST BRAND RIVALRY
The "Cola Wars" between Pepsi and Coca-Cola began shortly after Pepsi's launch in 1893, seven years after the launch of Coca-Cola. The most expensive battle so far was Project Blue in 1996, which cost Pepsi $500 million. The nine-month promotion involved Pepsi changing the color of its can from red, white and blue to blue to distinguish itself from its big rival. The most memorable publicity stunt of the campaign occurred when Pepsi painted a Concorde blue. Coca-Cola fought back with its own $500-million promotion.

TOP-SELLING CLOTHING BRAND
Levi Strauss & Co. is the world's biggest brand-name clothing manufacturer, with 13.1% of the market in 1997 and approximately 37,500 staff worldwide. Levi is the most recognized clothing brand name, and Levi's products are sold in over 30,000 retail outlets in more than 60 countries. Levi's brand advertising began in the late 1800s, when Bavarian immigrant Levi Strauss set up business in San Francisco, California. Vintage second-hand pairs of Levi jeans sell for up to $8,300, and the most valuable pair (pictured right) cost $25,000.

advertising

MOST EXPENSIVE TV AD
A commercial for computer manufacturer Apple Macintosh cost a total of $600,000 to produce and $1 million to air. Produced by Ridley Scott, the director of *Blade Runner* (1982), the advertisement's impact was so great and the recall among viewers so high that it is believed to be one of the most cost-effective commercials ever made. Based on the novel *1984* by George Orwell, the ad was shown only once, in 1984.

FASTEST PRODUCTION OF AN AD
A television ad for Reebok's InstaPUMP shoes was created, filmed and aired during Super Bowl XXVII at the Atlanta Georgia Dome on January 31, 1993. Filming took place up to the beginning of the fourth quarter of play, editing began in the middle of the third quarter and the finished product was aired during the break at the two-minute warning of the fourth quarter. The 30-second commercial starred Emmitt Smith of the Dallas Cowboys.

SHORTEST AD
A commercial lasting four frames (there are 30 frames in a second) was aired on KING-TV's *Evening Magazine* on November 29, 1993. The ad, which was for Bon Marché's Frango sweets, cost $3,780.

MOST EXPENSIVE COMMERCIAL BREAK
NBC charged $2 million for some 30-second spots during the final episode of *Seinfeld* on May 14, 1998. The sitcom was regularly No. 1 in the Nielsen ratings, with audiences of about 20 million, but it was estimated that there were more than 40 million viewers for the last show. Half-minute spots during regular episodes cost $575,000 in 1998 – $15,000 more than *Seinfeld*'s closest rival, *ER*.

LONGEST ADVERTISING MESSAGE
The British Yellow Pages created the world's longest advertising message on a London Underground train in February 1997. The train was painted with brightly-colored images on the outside to reflect the different services covered by the directory, while the interior was refurbished with Yellow Pages upholstery. The ad cost $1.6 million.

MOST CELEBRITIES IN AN AD
Reebok's 90-second ad "Field of Dreams," which ran on British TV in 1996, starred 22 celebrities, including singer Tom Jones, movie director Richard Attenborough, opera singer José Carreras and ex-soccer star George Best. The stars had to imagine they were Ryan Giggs, the British soccer star sponsored by Reebok.

MOST LUCRATIVE AD CONTRACT
In April 1997, Tiger Woods landed the most lucrative advertising and sponsorship contract in history after winning the Masters at the age of 21. Nike signed up the new star for a $40-million, five-year deal involving product endorsement and appearances in ads. Experts estimate that Woods will be able to generate around $1 billion in other endorsement deals, making him the most valuable human billboard ever.

TOP-SELLING SINGLE FROM AN AD
In December 1995, Levi's "Planet," a European TV ad promoting Women's Fit 501 jeans, used "Spaceman" by British band Babylon Zoo, which had been released in September 1995 but failed to chart. The remix for the commercial was released in January 1996 and went straight to No. 1 in the UK charts. It stayed there for five weeks, selling 420,000 copies in its first week.

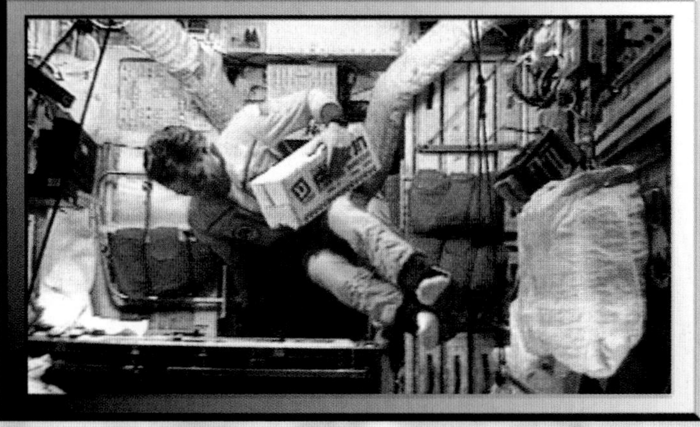

RUSSIAN SPACE ADVERTISING
"Milk in Space," a commercial advertising a brand of Israeli milk, was filmed aboard the Russian orbiting station *Mir* on July 25, 1997 and portrays a cosmonaut who longs for the taste of fresh milk while in space. The ad, which shows the space station commander Vasily Tsibliyev swallowing floating milk bubbles squeezed out of a Hebrew-lettered carton and singing the praises of the product in Russian, was shot one month after an accident on board involving Alexander Lazutkin, *Mir*'s flight engineer. The milk was delivered into orbit by the space shuttle *Progress*. The Russians reportedly charged the Israeli GITAM/BBDO advertising agency $450,000 for the 90-second ad, which was shown on Israeli television for the first time on August 20, 1997. It was the second advertisement filmed on a Russian spaceflight: in 1996, two *Mir* cosmonauts were filmed with an oversize replica of a Pepsi can during a spacewalk.

MOST INNOVATIVE AD DEAL
In August 1995, Microsoft tied up a ground-breaking deal with British newspaper *The Times* to promote its new operating software package, Windows '95. For the first time in its 210-year history, the paper was given away for free, at Microsoft's expense. In exchange for sponsoring the edition and matching its cover price revenue, Microsoft had a near monopoly on all premium advertising space and distributed a 28-page supplement for free with the paper's increased 1.5 million print run.

MOST COMMERCIALS MADE BY A CELEBRITY FOR ONE ADVERTISER
Between May 1994 and December 1996, British actor Bob Hoskins made 55 TV commercials, rising to 94 different cutdowns and adaptations, for British telecommunications giant BT. His slogan, "It's good to talk," reached No. 1 in Adwatch, the weekly survey on advertising recall carried out for the British trade magazine *Marketing*, soon after the campaign broke, and remained unchallenged in the top spot for 14 months.

MOST AWARDS WON BY AN INTERNATIONAL COMMERCIAL
The Levi 501 jeans "Drugstore" TV ad won 33 awards in 1995.

MOST ADS IN ONE EVENING
All 17 versions of a Castlemaine XXXX beer commercial were shown on Granada Sky Broadcasting in the UK on October 1, 1996.

BIGGEST ADVERTISER
Procter & Gamble, which manufactures global brands such as Pampers, Clearasil and Pringles, was the leading national advertiser in the US in 1996, spending $2.62 billion. It is also the leading TV advertiser in a number of Western European countries (including Germany, the Netherlands and Scandinavia), and spent $2.56 billion on non-US advertising in 1995.

BIGGEST AD CAMPAIGN BY A COMPANY
The 1996 campaign for AT&T telephone services cost AT&T Corporation $474 million.

LARGEST ADVERTISING NATION
In 1996, the United States spent more than $63.81 billion on advertising and promotion. Japan, in second place, has an annual advertising expenditure just one-third that of the US.

FASTEST-GROWING AD MARKET
Russia had a record-breaking 94% year-on-year increase in 1996, according to *World Advertising Trends 1998*. The survey, which examines advertising expenditure from 86 countries, found that seven of the world's highest-growing markets are in Eastern Europe.

BIGGEST CAST IN AN AD
Saatchi and Saatchi's 60-second ad "Global," for British Airways, was filmed in Utah in October 1989 and starred 6,300 people in colored jogging suits. Shot from the air, the cast assembled in different configurations to create giant images of an ear, an eye, a pair of lips and finally a whole face and a globe. It took 350 people to create the lips, 410 to make the ear and about 2,000 to make the face.

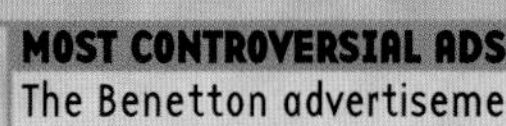

MOST CONTROVERSIAL ADS
The Benetton advertisement featuring a newborn baby, which was run in the UK in 1991, prompted more than 800 complaints to the Advertising Standards Authority. Also in the UK, the series of Wonderbra advertisements starring the model Eva Herzigova (pictured left) was the subject of 100 complaints and was even reported to be distracting male drivers and causing car crashes.

world markets

MOST RURAL ECONOMY
Somalia has the most rural economy in the world, with an estimated 65% of its GDP generated by agriculture. Its two major crops are bananas and sugar cane. About two-thirds of the labor force are either nomadic herdsmen or subsistence farmers. Much of Somalia's infrastructure has been destroyed by a civil war that began in 1991, and famine has been widespread, although it has been partially alleviated by $47.1 million worth of international aid.

OLDEST STOCK EXCHANGE
The Stock Exchange in Amsterdam, Netherlands was founded in the Oude Zijds Kapel in 1602 for dealings in printed shares of the United East India Company of the Netherlands.

BIGGEST TRADING LOSSES
In 1996, Sumitomo Corporation of Japan revealed that they had suffered losses of $2.6 billion due to unauthorized dealings over 10 years on the London Metal Exchange by one of their top traders.

BIGGEST PERSONAL LOSS OF STOCKS IN ONE DAY
The highest known personal paper losses on stock values were incurred by Ray Kroc, the former chairman of McDonald's Corporation, on July 8, 1974. They amounted to $65 million.

HIGHEST SHARE VALUE
On April 22, 1992, a single share in Moeara Enim Petroleum Corporation was worth a record-breaking $89,032.

BIGGEST FLOTATION
The privatization of Japan's Nippon Telegraph and Telephones in 1986 had an initial public offering of $12.4 billion, making it the biggest ever flotation.

BIGGEST BROKERAGES
In 1997, Merrill Lynch and Company had an annual revenue of $31,731 million. The Institutional Network of Instinet Corp., which began operating in 1969, became the world's largest computerized brokerage when it was purchased by Reuters in 1987. In 1997, it had a volume of over 110 million shares per day trading via more than 55,000 terminals.

BIGGEST FINANCIAL SECTORS
Singapore and the United Kingdom have the largest financial sectors of any nations, representing 27% of their gross domestic product.

RICHEST COUNTRIES
According to OECD (Organization for Economic and Commercial Development), the country with the highest gross domestic product (GDP) per capita in 1996 was Switzerland, with $43,233. Luxembourg came second with $42,298 and Japan was third with $40,726.

BIGGEST GNP
The country with the largest gross national product (GNP) in the world is the United States, with an estimated $7,300.2 billion for 1997.

BIGGEST BALANCE OF PAYMENTS SURPLUS
Japan had a $131.5-billion surplus in 1993.

BIGGEST BALANCE OF PAYMENTS DEFICIT
The United States reported a record deficit of $167.1 billion for the 1987 calendar year.

MOST INDUSTRIAL ECONOMY
Belarus has the most industrial economy, with a total of 45% of its GDP coming from manufacturing industries.

HIGHEST TAXATION
The highest rate of income tax in Denmark is 68%, but a net wealth tax of 1% can result in a tax of more than 100% on income in extreme situations.

LOWEST TAXATION
The sovereign countries with the lowest income tax are Bahrain and Qatar, where the rate is zero, regardless of income.

BIGGEST STOCK EXCHANGE
At the end of December 1996, more than 2,900 companies had stock listed on the New York Stock Exchange (NYSE), and more than 180 billion shares worth a total of $9.2 trillion were available for trading on the exchange, giving Wall Street the world's biggest market capitalization. The NYSE also holds the record for the largest ever trading volume, at $3.1 trillion in 1995. This compares with $1,640 billion for London and $1,400 billion for the Federation of Germany Stock Exchanges. The NYSE has its origins in a meeting of 24 men beneath a tree on what is now Wall Street in 1792. It was formalized as the New York Stock and Exchange Board in 1817 and took its present name in 1863. It is now threatened with a "bug" that has the potential to paralyze trading: when New York's Dow Jones Industrial average reaches 10,000, which it is predicted to do in the near future, it will be illegible to much of the software used to monitor share activity, and in a similar manner to the millennium bug, the figure 10,000 will be read as 1,000 or 0,000. This could cause electronic trading systems to dump stock, which may result in a global stock market crash.

HIGHEST INFLATION
The world's worst inflation occurred in Hungary in June 1946, when the 1931 gold pengó was valued at 130 million trillion (1.3×10^{20}) paper pengós. Notes were issued for 'Egymillárd billió' (1,000 trillion or 10^{21}) pengós on June 3 and withdrawn on July 11. Vouchers for 1 billion trillion (10^{27}) pengós were issued for taxation payment only.

On November 6, 1923, there were 400,338,326,350,700,000,000 German marks in circulation – taking the level of inflation to 755,700 million times the level of 1913.

LOWEST MODERN INFLATION
The Seychelles had deflation in 1995, when the CPI (consumer price index) fell by 1.28%.

MOST WORTHLESS CURRENCY
In May 1998, there were 257,128 Angolan kwanza to the US dollar.

BIGGEST FOREIGN AID DONOR
The largest foreign aid donor in 1996, in terms of Official Development Assistance, was Japan, with aid amounting to $14.489 billion.

Denmark has the highest ratio of Official Development Assistance to GNP, at 0.96% in 1996.

HIGHEST EDUCATION BUDGET
Canada and Finland spend 7.3% of their GDP on education (public and private expenditure).

LOWEST EDUCATION BUDGET
The OECD country spending the least on education is Turkey, which allocates 3.3% of its GDP.

FASTEST EXPANSION AND DECLINE
The GNP of Thailand grew by an average of 9.8% a year in the decade ending 1995, making it the most rapidly expanding economy in the world in the early 1990s. By 1998, it was decreasing by 0.4% a year, and the fastest-growing country was Uganda, with a 10% growth rate. In the decade up to 1995, Armenia's GNP decreased by a record average of 12.9% a year.

HIGHEST HEALTH BUDGET
The United States is the country with the highest health expenditure as a percentage of GDP. In 1995, the last year for which figures are available, health expenditure totaled 14.2% of GDP.

BIGGEST GOLD RESERVES
The US Treasury had approximately 262 million fine ounces of gold in 1996, which would have been worth $100 billion at the June 1996 price of $382 per fine ounce. The US Bullion Depository at Fort Knox, 30 miles southwest of Louisville, Kentucky, has been the principal federal depository of US gold since December 1936, and 147 million fine ounces are currently stored there. Gold's peak price was $850 on January 21, 1980.

BIGGEST MINT
The largest mint in the world is the US Treasury, which was built on Independence Mall, Philadelphia, Pennsylvania between 1965 and 1969 and covers an area of 11.5 acres. The Treasury used to have an annual production capacity of 15 billion coins and now produces 12 billion coins a year. One high-speed stamping machine called Graebner Press is capable of producing coins at a rate of 42,000 per hour. The highest-ever production was 19,519,253,440 coins, in the fiscal year 1995. The Denver Mint also set a record for coin production by a single facility, with more than 10.3 billion coins in the fiscal year 1995.

POOREST COUNTRIES
Pictured right, a woman from Mozambique carries water on her head. For most of the 1990s, Mozambique and Rwanda had the lowest GDP per capita in the world, according to the World Bank. In 1996, GDP per capita in Rwanda was less than $80, which represented a decrease on the previous year. Mozambique is now experiencing economic growth and in 1996 had a GDP per capita of $133.

SMALLEST MINT
The smallest issuing mint in the world belongs to the Sovereign Military Order of Malta, in the City of Rome. Its single-press mint is housed in one small room.

company power

BIGGEST MEDIA CORPORATION
Walt Disney had $40 to his name when he began his company in 1923. His first commission, about a little girl named Alice, was the start of what is now the world's largest entertainment empire. The Walt Disney Company had total assets of $37.77 billion in 1997 and a turnover of $22.473 billion. In comparison,Viacom, the world's second largest media corporation, had a turnover of $13.2 billion that year. *Steamboat Willie* (1928), Disney's first movie with a soundtrack, was an immediate success, and since then, 35 feature films have been released. Disney also has a host of theme parks, the latest addition being Animal Kingdom in Florida.

MOST EXPENSIVE COMPANY BUILDING
The headquarters of the Hong Kong Shanghai Bank is the world's most expensive building. Built from 1982 to 1985, it cost $645.4 million to construct, while the land that it was built on cost $387 million. The 52-story, 586-foot-tall building has a total of 23 express elevators and 63 escalators (the most escalators in any building in the world). Its air-conditioning and flushing water systems use pumped-in seawater.

MOST EXPENSIVE OFFICE LOCATIONS
The highest-ever office rents were in central Tokyo, Japan, in June 1991. Prime spaces there were at a peak of $219 per square foot.

Rents for prime space in the central business district of Bombay (Mumbai), India, in January 1997 were $143 per square foot per year. Total costs (including property taxes and service charges) were $156 per square foot for a three-year lease. These costs were 31% higher than in Hong Kong, which was then the world's second most expensive location.

BIGGEST ANNUAL PROFIT
The largest ever net profit by a corporation in 12 months was $7.6 billion, by American Telephone and Telegraph Company (now AT&T Corporation) from October 1, 1981 to September 30, 1982.

BIGGEST ANNUAL SALES
In 1995, General Motors Corporation of Detroit, Michigan had record annual sales of $168.8 billion.

BIGGEST COMPANY REVENUES
In 1996, the Japanese trading company Mitsubishi Corporation had revenues of $184,365.2 million.

HIGHEST MARKET VALUE OF A COMPANY
General Electric of Fairfield, Connecticut has the highest aggregate market value of any corporation in the world. In May 1995, it was valued at $152.3 billion.

BIGGEST RAILROAD COMPANY
The East Japan Railroad Company had revenues of $25.63 billion in 1996, making it the world's largest railroad company. The Japanese railroad network, which began in 1872, is believed to be one of the safest and most efficient in the world. It has more than 12,500 miles of track and runs an average of 25,000 trains a day. In 1964 certain main lines, amounting to just under 15% of the entire Japanese rail system, were revolutionized by the introduction of the *Shinkansen* or bullet train, which has been known to reach a speed of 275 mph. Here, an ASAMA bullet train is seen crossing a bridge over the Chikuma River in Ueda City, Nagano prefecture, in October 1997. It was part of a brand new train service linking Nagano, the location of the 1998 Winter Olympics, and Tokyo.

BIGGEST RESTAURANT CHAIN
The largest global food service retailer is McDonald's, which opened its first fast food outlet in Des Plaines, Illinois in 1955. By the end of 1997, McDonald's operated more than 21,000 restaurants in 101 countries around the world. Global revenue in 1997 exceeded $10.7 billion. Here, two workers install a sign at a new McDonald's in Beijing, China.

HIGHEST AGM ATTENDANCE
A total of 20,109 shareholders attended the Annual General Meeting of American Telephone and Telegraph Company (now AT&T Corporation) in April 1961.

BIGGEST MERGER
The biggest ever industrial merger was between the motor companies Daimler-Benz and Chrysler. Announced in May 1998, it created a company worth $92 billion.

BIGGEST TAKEOVER BID
The highest bid in a corporate takeover was $21 billion, for the tobacco, food and beverage company RJR Nabisco Inc. by Wall Street leveraged-buyout firm Kohlberg Kravis Roberts. The latter offered $90 a share on October 24, 1988. By December 1, the shares had reached $109, making an aggregate of $25 billion.

BIGGEST SINGLE CASH BEQUEST
The Ford Foundation of New York City announced a bequest of $500 million to a total of 4,157 educational and other institutions in December 1995.

BIGGEST CORPORATE BANKRUPTCY
The world's biggest ever corporate bankruptcy in terms of assets amounted to $35.9 billion. The bankruptcy was filed by the petroleum company Texaco in 1987.

BIGGEST COMPANIES
The Ford Motor Company, the multinational automobile manufacturer, is the biggest company in the world in terms of assets. In 1997, its total assets were valued at $222.14 billion.

The biggest company in terms of the number of employees is the United States Postal Service, which employed more than 887,600 people in 1997.

The world's biggest company in terms of profits is the Royal Dutch Shell Group, a jointly-owned Anglo-Dutch petroleum refining company. In 1997 it had profits of $8.89 billion.

The biggest manufacturing company in terms of revenues and employees is the General Motors Corporation, which has a global workforce of 647,000. In 1997, the company's revenues were $168.39 billion and it had assets of $222.14 billion. The company announced a profit of $4.96 billion for the year.

BIGGEST BANKS
The biggest bank in the world today in terms of the number of branches is the State Bank of India, which had a record-breaking 12,947 outlets and total assets of $42 billion as of March 31, 1996.

The largest bank by equity is the British-based HSBC Holdings. In 1996, it had $25.8 billion of equity.

The world's biggest commercial bank by assets is the Bank of Tokyo-Mitsubishi, Japan. In July 1997, it had assets of $692.3 billion.

The biggest international investment bank is Morgan Stanley, Dean Witter, Discover & Co., which has a market capitalization of $21 billion.

The biggest multilateral development bank in the world is the International Bank for Reconstruction and Development, known as the World Bank. Based in Washington, DC, the bank had total assets of $168.7 billion for the 1995 fiscal year.

BIGGEST EMPLOYER
The largest commercial or utility employer in the world is Indian Railways, which had more than 1 million regular employees in 1997.

BIGGEST PUBLISHING COMPANY
The largest publishing and printing company in the world is Bertelsmann AG of Germany. In 1997, the company's total revenue was $14.73 billion.

BIGGEST PC COMPANY
Compaq Computer Corp. of Houston, Texas is the world's biggest manufacturer of personal computers. In 1997, its revenues rose by more than 30% to $24.6 billion and its profits climbed 36% to $1.9 billion.

BIGGEST TELECOMMUNICATIONS COMPANY
Nippon Telegraph and Telephone Corporation of Japan had revenues of $78.32 billion in 1997.

BIGGEST PETROLEUM COMPANY
The largest petroleum company is Anglo-Dutch Royal Dutch Shell Group, based in the Netherlands. In 1997, it had a total revenue of $128.17 billion.

BIGGEST AEROSPACE GROUP
McDonnell Douglas Corp., the world's biggest military aircraft maker, and Boeing Co., the world's biggest commercial aircraft maker, merged in 1996 to form the largest aerospace group in the world. The group's total annual revenues are approximately $35 billion.

BIGGEST AIRLINE
AMR Corporation of Fort Worth, Texas, whose major subsidiary is American Airlines, had a total revenue of $17.75 billion for the year 1997, making it the largest airline in the world today.

BIGGEST BEVERAGE COMPANY
The Coca-Cola Company had revenues of $18,018 million in 1996, making it the biggest beverage company in the world. The picture above shows spectators gathering to see the world's largest replica Coca-Cola bottle surrounded by fireworks at the Showcase Mall on the Strip, Las Vegas, Nevada in July 1997. The display was part of the opening of the Coca-Cola Museum.

BIGGEST FOOD COMPANY
Unilever N.V./Unilever Plc is the biggest food company in the world. It is also the world's biggest ice cream maker, with more than 50% of the ice cream market in several European countries. Its brands include Cornetto, Viennetta and Magnum. The company is also the world leader in prestige fragrances, including Calvin Klein perfume.

BIGGEST DAIRY FARM
Al Safi dairy farm near Al Kharj, Saudi Arabia covers 8,600 acres.

BIGGEST BREWER
The world's biggest brewing organization is Anheuser-Busch Inc. of St. Louis, Missouri. In 1995, it sold 2.78 billion gallons of beer.

business tycoons

MOST POWERFUL MEDIA TYCOON

Rupert Murdoch (pictured with his eldest son Lachlan) is one of the world's most powerful businessmen and successful entrepreneurs. The son of Sir Keith Murdoch, the late editor of the Australian newspaper the *Melbourne Herald*, Murdoch was born in 1931 and was running his first newspaper, the *Adelaide Herald*, by the age of 23. An Oxford graduate, he expanded into the United Kingdom with the daily newspapers the *Sun* and *The Times*. Today he is chairman of News Corporation Ltd. and Fox Broadcasting Company, which he took over in 1985. His communications empire, News Corporation, is worth about $26 billion. Murdoch's net worth is estimated at $5.3 billion. In 1985, Murdoch renounced his Australian citizenship and became a US citizen in order to comply with US laws that prohibit non-citizens from owning US television stations. He is now the largest owner of TV stations in the United States, and in terms of his global reach and the diversity of his interests, he is the most powerful media tycoon in history.

GREATEST EVER TYCOON

The legendary oilman John D. Rockefeller founded the Standard Oil Company of Ohio with his brother William in 1870. By the time of his death in 1937, Rockefeller had amassed a $1.4-billion fortune at a time when the GNP of the United States was just $90 billion. This makes him the richest US citizen ever, with a wealth amounting to $1/65$th of the wealth of the entire country. As a comparison, Bill Gates' fortune only amounts to $1/213$th of the United States' GNP today. On this basis, Rockefeller can be seen as the greatest tycoon in the history of the world.

RICHEST BUSINESSMAN

Bill Gates, the chairman and CEO of Microsoft Corporation, is the richest man in the world, according to *Forbes* magazine, with an estimated fortune of $51 billion. The *New York Times* predicts that if Microsoft's value continues to grow at its current rate, Bill Gates will become the world's first dollar trillionaire by the age of 48. In 1997, his net worth grew by an average of $300 million a week, and his personal holdings are now worth twice the gross domestic product of Sri Lanka. His wealth increased by $15 billion in 1997. In a single morning in 1996, a jump in the price of Microsoft stock increased Gates' worth by $2 billion.

RICHEST BUSINESSWOMAN

Nina Wang of Hong Kong is the richest businesswoman in the world. *Forbes* magazine estimates Wang's fortune at $6 billion as of July 6, 1998. Wang's husband was kidnapped in 1990, and subsequently she inherited his vast real estate holdings. Wang's father-in-law is currently challenging her control of the holdings in court.

The richest businesswoman in the United States is Martha Ingram, who commands a fortune estimated at $4.5 billion. Ingram's business empire includes computer, video wholesale and retail distribution operations.

RICHEST SELF-MADE WOMAN IN THE UNITED STATES

Pam Lopker, the founder of the software company QAD, is worth an estimated $425 million.

RICHEST BUSINESS FAMILY

According to *Forbes*, the richest business family in the world today is the Walton family of the United States. The empire's founder, Sam Walton, opened his first "small-town discount store" in Arkansas in 1962. Today, Wal-Mart is the largest US retailer, with 2,750 stores. It also has a further 250 stores in six other countries. Wal-Mart Corporation is said to be a huge spender on information technology, with storage capacity second only to the US government's. Sam Walton's widow Helen and their three sons and one daughter have a combined fortune of $48 billion.

RICHEST BUSINESSMAN IN CANADA

Kenneth Thomson's fortune is estimated at $14.4 billion. His business interests include publishing and a variety of other enterprises.

RICHEST BUSINESSMAN IN GERMANY

As owners of Europe's top discount food retailer, Karl and Theo Albrecht, together with their family, are worth $11.7 billion.

BIGGEST CHARITABLE DONOR, UK

John Paul Getty II, the oil heir and reclusive son of the late John Paul Getty (once the richest man in the world), has distributed at least $192 million of his estimated $1.6-billion personal fortune to a number of British causes, making him the country's single biggest charitable donor. During the 1980s, Getty gave a $31.14-million donation to the British Film Institute, ensuring that thousands of old movies were saved from certain destruction. Among other notable gifts, he bestowed $77.85 million on the National Gallery, London, England, and has helped to keep several rare works of art in Britain, including pieces that were destined to be sold to his father's museum in California. In 1986, the 65-year-old billionaire philanthropist was awarded an honorary KBE for his charitable efforts, and in 1997 he was granted British citizenship. Sir Paul, as he is now known, took up residence the United Kingdom in 1972 following the death of his second wife.

RICHEST BUSINESSMAN IN FRANCE

With various holdings in the retail industry, Gerard Mulliez, together with his family, is worth $10.3 billion.

RICHEST BUSINESSMAN IN JAPAN

Yoshiaki Tsutsumi, with holdings in real estate, equities, hotels and railways, is worth $5.7 billion. Tsutsumi was formerly the world's richest person.

RICHEST BUSINESSMAN IN HONG KONG

Lee Shan Kee, with holdings in real estate, energy and banking, is worth $12.7 billion.

RICHEST BUSINESSMAN IN TAIWAN

Taiwan's richest businessman is the construction and insurance services broker Tsai Wan-lin, who, with his family, is worth $8.5 billion.

RICHEST BUSINESSMAN IN SOUTH KOREA

Businessman Chung Ju Yung made his money from diversified enterprises, and together with his family is worth $1.5 billion.

BIGGEST EUROPEAN BANKRUPTCY

In 1991, Robert Maxwell died in mysterious circumstances soon after it was discovered that he had taken assets from the Maxwell Communications Works Pension Scheme. His company, Maxwell Communications, became the subject of Europe's largest ever bankruptcy when it collapsed in December 1992. It had previously had assets of $6.35 billion.

MOST RECLUSIVE TYCOON

Considered the most reclusive tycoon ever, film director and aviator Howard Hughes died on a flight to Houston, Texas, in 1976. Obsessively secretive, Hughes was once contracted by the CIA to build a giant spy station on the ocean bed. In the 1970s, he received the largest cash settlement ever paid to an individual when he received $546 million for his holdings in the airline TWA.

BIGGEST CHARITABLE DONATIONS BY BUSINESSMEN

John D. Rockefeller gave away $500 million, equivalent to $14.1 billion in today's terms, by the time of his death in 1937.

During his lifetime and through legacies made in his will, Andrew Carnegie, the Scottish-born steel magnate, gave away the equivalent of $3.5 billion in today's money. Among the causes to benefit from his interest were libraries, the Carnegie Peace Fund, and Carnegie Hall, New York City.

David Packard, co-founder of the technology giant Hewlett-Packard, gave away more than $5 billion – most of his life earnings – before he died on March 26, 1996.

BIGGEST PRIVATE MODERN ART COLLECTOR IN THE UNITED KINGDOM

Charles Saatchi is widely considered to be the biggest private modern art collector in the United Kingdom today, with a collection believed to number more than 800 works. Only an estimated 5% of Saatchi's collection, which includes works by Damien Hirst, has been shown in public; the rest is stockpiled unseen in a warehouse. Saatchi has been buying modern art over a period of almost 30 years.

SPORTSMAN BILLIONAIRE

America's Cup-winning captain Ted Turner is one of the world's wealthiest sports owners, with a fortune of $4.8 billion. His interests include baseball's Atlanta Braves and the NBA's Atlanta Hawks. In 1985, Turner founded the Goodwill Games as a means to promote world peace through sports. The 1998 Goodwill Games were staged in New York City.

high earners

VIRGIN EMPIRE

Richard Branson was the 14th richest man in the United Kingdom in 1998, according to the *Sunday Times*, with a fortune estimated at $2.8 billion. He left school at 16 to launch a student magazine, and founded a record label, Virgin Records, in 1973. Today, Branson's Virgin empire includes an airline, a rail service, jeans, cola, pensions and even a bridal company.

HIGHEST-EARNING CHIEF EXECUTIVES

In 1997, Millard Drexler, the chief executive officer of the clothing company Gap, earned $104.8 million.

Stephen C. Hilbert, the chief executive of Conesco, earned $277 million over the five-year period 1992–96. Hilbert founded the construction company in 1979 with a loan of $10,000, and it is now worth $7 billion.

HIGHEST-EARNING BANK HEAD

John Reed of Citicorp earned $46 million in 1996, and $70 million in total over the last five years.

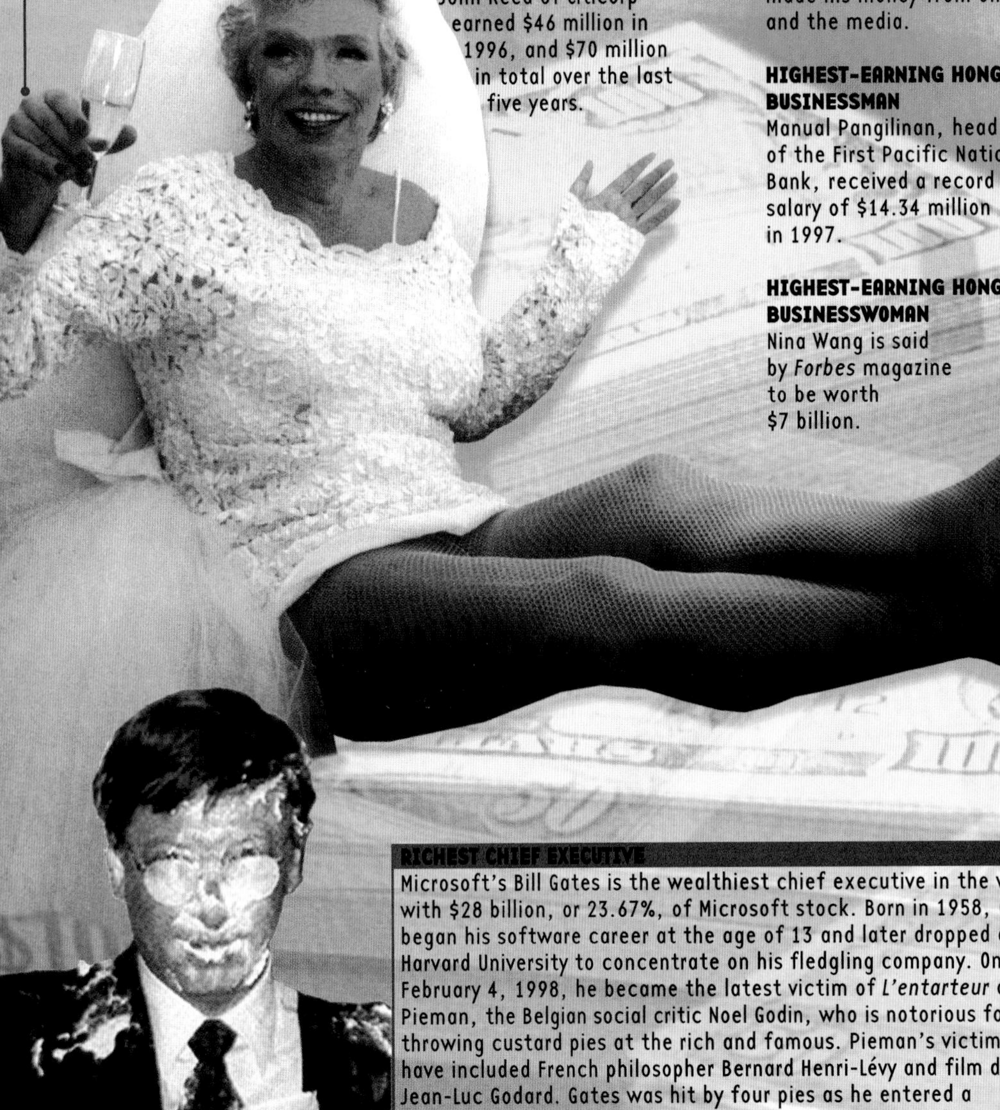

HIGHEST-EARNING LAWYER

In 1995, when *Forbes* magazine published its most recent survey of the best-paid lawyers, William Lerach earned a record $7 million. At the time, he was running the office of Melvyn Weiss' firm in San Diego, California, specializing in shareholder class-action suits.

HIGHEST-EARNING POLITICIAN

Boris Berezovsky, deputy chief of the Russian security council, is worth $4.05 billion. A wealthy businessman before he became a politician, he claims to have made his money from oil, cars and the media.

HIGHEST-EARNING HONG KONG BUSINESSMAN

Manual Pangilinan, head of the First Pacific National Bank, received a record salary of $14.34 million in 1997.

HIGHEST-EARNING HONG KONG BUSINESSWOMAN

Nina Wang is said by *Forbes* magazine to be worth $7 billion. She took over the Chinachem real estate empire, considered the largest private landholder in Hong Kong, after her husband was kidnapped and disappeared, and is now widely regarded as Asia's most powerful businesswoman. The Chinachem Group's 108-story "Nina Tower" in Hong Kong, one of the world's tallest buildings, is named after her.

HIGHEST-EARNING JAPANESE BUSINESSMAN

Yoshiaki Tsutsumi, a real estate and transport mogul, is worth an estimated $8 billion. Once the world's richest businessman, he owns over 40 golf courses in Japan and was a major force behind the country's successful bid for the 1998 Winter Olympics.

HIGHEST-EARNING PUBLISHING EXECUTIVE

Australian-born media baron Rupert Murdoch is currently worth $2.8 billion. His media holdings include 20th Century Fox, the Fox television network, and numerous newspapers around the world. In the United Kingdom alone, Murdoch owns 36% of the national press.

HIGHEST-EARNING FILM EXECUTIVE

Michael Eisner, the chairman and CEO of the Walt Disney Company, earned $8.65 million in 1996. He is the third highest-paid chief executive of the last five years, with total earnings of $236 million.

HIGHEST-EARNING TV EXECUTIVE

Ted Turner, founder of Cable News Network (CNN) and Vice Chairman of Time Warner Inc., is worth about $3.2 billion.

HIGHEST-PAID SCREENWRITERS

Shane Black sold the script for *The Long Kiss Goodnight* (1996) to New Line Cinema for $4 million. His girlfriend came up with the idea, and he gave her a check for $20,000 before starting to write.

RICHEST CHIEF EXECUTIVE

Microsoft's Bill Gates is the wealthiest chief executive in the world, with $28 billion, or 23.67%, of Microsoft stock. Born in 1958, Gates began his software career at the age of 13 and later dropped out of Harvard University to concentrate on his fledgling company. On February 4, 1998, he became the latest victim of *L'entarteur* or Pieman, the Belgian social critic Noel Godin, who is notorious for throwing custard pies at the rich and famous. Pieman's victims have included French philosopher Bernard Henri-Lévy and film director Jean-Luc Godard. Gates was hit by four pies as he entered a government building in Brussels, Belgium to give a speech on education. Pieman escaped, but his two apprentices were held in custody. He eventually came forward to confess to his crime, but Gates did not press charges.

Hungarian-born Joe Eszterhas has written 13 screenplays, including *Flashdance* (1983), *Basic Instinct* (1992) and *Showgirls* (1995). He is Hollywood's highest-paid screenwriter, and his scripts now sell for at least $1 million.

Michael Crichton, the co-writer of *Jurassic Park* (1993) and originator of TV series *ER*, earned $65 million in 1997.

HIGHEST-EARNING DIRECTOR
Steven Spielberg, director of such films as *E.T.: the Extra-Terrestrial* (1982) and *Amistad* (1997) earned $283 million in 1997, making him the world's highest-earning director. George Lucas, the director of *Star Wars* (1977), follows with $249 million.

BIGGEST BONUS
Lawrence Coss, the CEO of Green Tree Financial Corporation, which finances mobile homes, reaped a bonus of $102 million in 1996, the highest ever reported in *Forbes'* annual executive pay surveys. The bonus was almost a quarter of the size of his salary, and took his total earnings over the last five years to $216 million, of which $95 million was in stock.

HIGHEST-EARNING COMEDIAN
Forbes magazine estimated that the highest-earning comedian in 1997 was Robin Williams, with $53 million. Much of Williams' earnings come from his film company, Blue Wolf Productions, which made $431 million from *Mrs. Doubtfire* (1993).

HIGHEST-EARNING WRITER
Mary Higgins Clark began writing to support her five children. Her first suspense novel, *Where Are the Children?* (1992), brought her $100,000 in royalties. In 1996, she signed a contract with Simon and Schuster giving her $12 million for each of three novels — almost double the amount paid to John Grisham and Stephen King.

HIGHEST-EARNING ARTIST
LeRoy Neiman is famous for painting athletes, jetsetters and celebrities, including Michael Jordan, Frank Sinatra, Liza Minnelli, Robert Kennedy Jr. and Princess Grace of Monaco. He produces about 1,000 pieces a year and his original paintings sell for between $20,000 and $500,000.

HIGHEST-EARNING OPERA STAR
Italian opera superstar Luciano Pavarotti is said to earn $16 million a year.

HIGHEST-EARNING MAGICIAN
Illusionist David Copperfield is the world's most successful magician today, earning $45 million in 1997.

MOST SUCCESSFUL INVESTOR
Warren Buffett, founder of Berkshire Hathaway, is widely regarded as the most successful stock market analyst. His stock portfolios have netted him an estimated $23.2 billion.

HIGHEST OPTION GAIN
In 1997, Andrew Grove of Intel had the highest option gain of any chief executive, at $95 million.

BIGGEST GOLDEN HANDSHAKE
A record golden handshake of $53.8 million was given to F. Ross Johnson when he stepped down as chairman of RJR Nabisco in February 1989.

HIGHEST SALARY
Hungarian-born George Soros earned at least $1.1 billion in 1993, according to *Financial World*'s list of the highest-paid individuals on Wall Street. His company, Soros Fund Management, is principal advisor to the Quantum Group, which includes Quantum Fund N.V., the fund with the best performance record in the world.

HIGHEST FEES
Harry D. Schultz, an investment consultant who owns houses in Monte Carlo, Monaco and Zürich, Switzerland, charges $2,400 for a standard one-hour consultation on weekdays and $3,400 on weekends.

HIGHEST LECTURE FEES
In June 1986, Dr. Ronald Dante was paid $3.08 million for lecturing students on hypnotherapy at a two-day course in Chicago, Illinois.

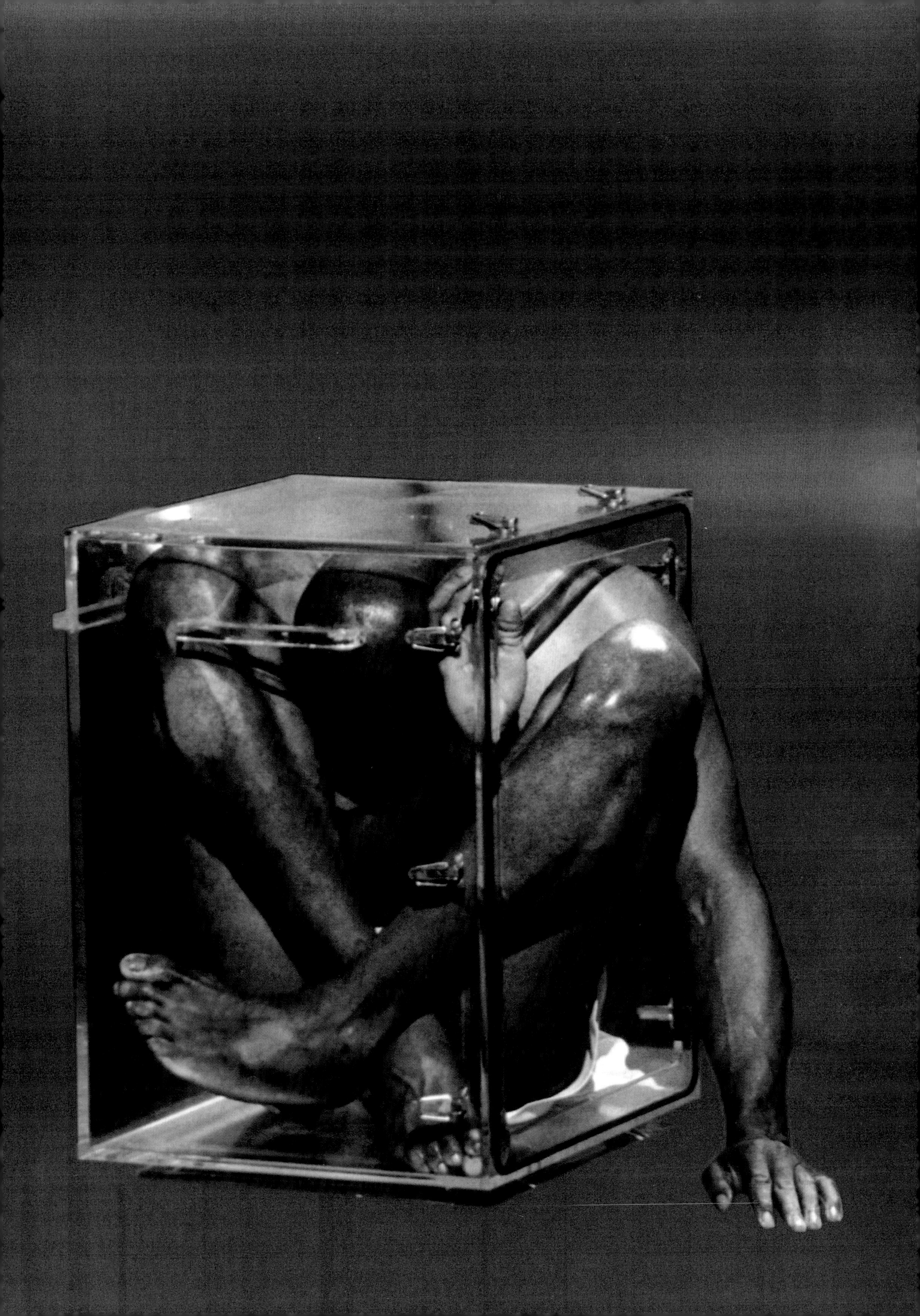

extraordinary people

collections

BIGGEST MOUSETRAP COLLECTION
Reinhard Hellwig of Meerbusch, North Rhine Westphalia, Germany, has collected 2,334 mousetraps from a total of 66 countries since he first became interested in them in 1964. The most unusual mousetrap in his collection is currently a replica of a 5,000-year-old trap crafted from clay – one of the earliest known examples. As well as being an avid collector, Hellwig has also managed to acquire more than 6,300 patents on mousetraps over the years.

BIGGEST FAMOUS HAIR COLLECTION
John Reznikoff of Stamford, Connecticut, collects the hair of long-dead celebrities. Some of the most famous hair in his 100-strong collection, which is insured for $1 million, belonged to Abraham Lincoln, John F. Kennedy, Marilyn Monroe, and Elvis Presley.

BIGGEST GOLF BALL COLLECTION
Ted J. Hoz of Baton Rouge, Louisiana, has a collection of 43,824 different logo golf balls. Hoz estimates that there are 100,000 logo balls in existence, and his storage cabinets have space for another 31,886 balls.

BIGGEST UNDERWEAR COLLECTIONS
Imelda Marcos, the former First Lady of the Philippines, had 500 black bras (one of which was bulletproof), 200 girdles, and 1,000 packets of unopened pantyhose in her palace wardrobe, as well as about 3,000 pairs of shoes.

Robert Corlett and Mary Ann King of Glasgow, Scotland, started collecting 1970s nylon underpants after finding a signed pair of Engelbert Humperdinck's underpants in an Engelbert Humperdinck record cover two years ago. They now have more than 200 pairs, including 30 psychedelic pairs. They have received underpants from all around Europe since displaying their collection in their shop, Mr. Ben Vintage Clothing.

BIGGEST SHOE COLLECTION
Sonja Bata of Toronto, Canada, has collected 10,000 pairs of shoes over a period of 50 years. While her family firm, Bata, sold low-cost footwear, Sonja bought the shoes that their customers discarded. She has set up a museum in Toronto to house her collection, which includes Queen Victoria's dancing slippers, John Lennon's Beatle boots, and Napoleon's socks.

BIGGEST COLLECTION OF SWATCH WATCHES
Fiorenzo Barindelli of Cesano Maderno in Milan, Italy, has amassed 3,562 Swatch watches since he started his collection in 1983. It includes every watch documented in the Swatch catalog, as well as some prototypes and special edition pieces. He plans to open a Swatch museum in the year 2000.

BIGGEST BARBIE DOLL COLLECTION
Tony Mattia of Brighton, England, has about half of all the Barbie doll models produced since 1959 and many versions of Barbie's boyfriend, Ken. He changes the dolls' costumes once a month and spends hours brushing their hair. The collection has grown so large that Mattia has had to move to a larger home.

BIGGEST COLLECTION OF GNOMES AND PIXIES
Since 1978, Anne Atkin of North Devon, England, has collected a record 2,010 gnomes and pixies, all of whom live on her 4-acre Gnome Reserve. Atkin's collection has been seen by more than 25,000 visitors over the past 18 years.

BIGGEST LIGHTBULB COLLECTION
Collector Hugh Hicks has amassed 60,000 different lightbulbs since childhood. Included in his collection is the world's largest lightbulb, which is 4 feet in height, and the smallest lightbulb, a pinpoint used to inspect missile parts.

BIGGEST COLLECTION OF CHAMBER POTS
Manfred Klauda (Germany) has collected a total of 9,400

BIGGEST JET FIGHTER COLLECTION
Michel Pont, a winemaker and collector who lives in Savigny-Les-Beaune, Burgundy, France, has a personal collection of 100 jet fighters, ranging from British *Vampires* to Russian *MiGs*. Pont first started collecting jet fighters in 1986, having collected motorbikes since 1958 and cars since 1970. By January 1998, the 66-year-old had accumulated 70 different jet fighters, 500 motorcycles, and a series of crimson *Abarth* race cars. His rarest jet is a Dassault *Mirage 4*, the aircraft that carries French nuclear weapons, with the oldest being a 1949 Dassault *Ouragan*. Although the planes' exteriors are in perfect condition and are cleaned twice a year, some are no longer in working order. Pont, who has never flown a plane and has given up motorcycling, opened his collection to the public by setting up a museum at his home, the 14th-century Château de Savigny-Les-Beaune that he bought 20 years ago. As well as viewing the collection, the estimated 30,000 visitors a year can also sample the Burgundy wines of which Pont produces around 275,000 bottles a year.

BIGGEST BANKNOTE COLLECTION
Israel Gerber of Ashdod, Israel, began collecting banknotes in 1962 and now has notes from 215 different countries and territories. There are an estimated 4,000 banknote collectors worldwide. In 1993, the second £1 note ever issued in the United Kingdom fetched a record $78,078 at auction. It is not only old notes that are valuable: a note with an error, such as an image that has been printed backwards, may also command a high price.

BIGGEST MARBLE COLLECTION
Over the past 45 years, printer Sam McCarthy-Fox of Worthing, England, has built up a collection of 40,000 marbles. His record-breaking collection includes antique marbles as well as modern glass and fiber-optic marbles made from semi-precious stones. McCarthy-Fox, who is now 53 years old, spends much of his free time polishing his marbles in his attic. He also helps organize international marble-playing championships.

chamber pots, the earliest of which dates back to the 16th century. His record-breaking collection can be viewed at the Zentrum für Aussergewöhnliche Museum in Munich, Germany.

BIGGEST COLLECTION OF AIRSICKNESS BAGS
Niek Vermeulen of Wormerveer, Netherlands, has built up a record-breaking collection of 2,112 different airsickness bags from a total of 470 airlines.

BIGGEST BANDAGE COLLECTION
Brian Viner of London, England, has collected 3,750 unused adhesive bandages of many different colors, styles, shapes, and sizes.

BIGGEST FRIDGE MAGNET COLLECTION
Louise J. Greenfarb of Henderson, NV, has collected 21,500 refrigerator magnets.

BIGGEST PEN COLLECTION
Angelika Unverhau of Dinslaken, Germany, has a collection of 108,500 different ballpoint pens.

BIGGEST COLLECTION OF PARKING METERS
In 1989, Lotta Sjölin of Solna, Sweden began collecting different disused parking meters from local authorities all over the world. Her collection now contains a record 292 meters.

BIGGEST CLOVER COLLECTION
Over five months in 1995, George Kaminski single-handedly collected a total of 13,382 four-leaf clovers during his recreation time in the prison yard at the Pennsylvania State Correctional Institution. He also found 1,336 five-leaf, 78 six-leaf and six seven-leaf clovers in the same 5-acre area. The collection had to be sent home to Kaminski's sister, since the Bureau of Corrections has a policy stating that no inmate is allowed to collect anything for any reason whatsoever.

BIGGEST BUBBLEGUM COLLECTION
Thomas and Volker Martins of Freiburg, Germany have collected 1,712 packs of bubblegum since 1992.

BIGGEST PIGGY BANK COLLECTION
Ove Nordstrom of Spanga, Sweden, has collected 3,575 different money holders in pig form over the past 40 years.

BIGGEST NUTCRACKER COLLECTION
Jürgen Löschner of Neuhausen, Germany, has collected 2,200 nutcrackers since 1966.

fans and followers

BIGGEST SCI-FI FOLLOWING
Star Trek premiered in 1966 and now has an unprecedented following. The TV series can be seen in more than 100 countries, and a "Trekker" convention takes place somewhere almost every weekend. There are more than 350 *Star Trek* sites on the Net and about 500 fan publications. After more than 400,000 requests from fans, NASA named one of its space shuttles *Enterprise*.

MOST ARDENT MOVIE WATCHERS
Sal Piro, the president of the *Rocky Horror Show* fan club, has seen *The Rocky Horror Picture Show* (GB, 1975) about 1,000 times. *The Rocky Horror Show*, the stage show on which the movie is based, was written by Richard O'Brien and opened at the Royal Court Theater, London, England, in 1973. It rapidly crossed from cult status to the mainstream, and today has played in the US and all the major European countries as well as Australia and the Far East. The movie is still showing in more than 100 movie theaters across the US. Many of its fans dress up as their favorite characters when they watch the movie.

Gwilym Hughes of Gwynedd, Wales saw his first movie in 1953, while he was in the hospital. He keeps a diary of the movies he has seen and had logged a total of 22,990 by February 1997. Most of the movies he now watches are on video.

MOST POPULAR DOLL
On May 13, 1998, a group of Barbie fans hit the streets of Westchester, Los Angeles, in a campaign to have their idol depicted on a stamp as part of the US Postal Service's 20th Century Commemorative Stamp Program. In April 1998, it had been announced that "Barbie Steps Out" was among 30 subjects that would compete by popular vote to appear on stamps depicting the 1960s. Barbie, whose full name is Barbara Millicent Roberts, was "born" on March 9, 1958, and since then has become one of the world's most talked-about women. In the US, it has been estimated that a typical girl between the ages of three and 10 owns an average of 10 Barbie dolls. The world's love affair with the doll, which is made by Mattel, has spawned thousands of fan clubs, and a number of Barbie conventions take place across the globe every year. In 1995, the first Internet Barbie Collector's convention, Cybervention, was held in Seattle. In 1976, during the US Bicentennial celebrations, some Barbie dolls were placed in sealed time capsules to be opened in 2076.

MOST ARDENT THEATER-GOERS
Dr. H. Howard Hughes, Prof. Emeritus of Texas Wesleyan College, Fort Worth, Texas, attended a record 6,136 shows from 1956 to 1987.

Edward Sutro saw a record 3,000 first-night productions in his native United Kingdom from 1916 to 1956 and possibly more than 5,000 shows in his 60 years of theater-going.

TOP TRAINSPOTTER
Bill Curtis of Clacton-on-Sea, England, is the world champion trainspotter, or "gricer" (after Richard Grice, the first champion, who held the title from 1896 to 1931). Curtis' sightings include about 60,000 locomotives, 11,200 electric units, and 8,300 diesel units over 40 years in a number of different countries.

TOP BIRD-WATCHERS
Phoebe Snetsinger of Webster Groves, Missouri, has spotted 8,040 of the 9,700 known bird species since 1965. She has now seen 82% of the world's species, all of the families on the official list and more than 90% of the genera.

The greatest number of bird species spotted in a 24-hour period is 342, by Kenyan spotters Terry Stevenson, John Fanshawe and Andy Roberts on the second day of Birdwatch Kenya '86, which took place on November 29–30, 1986.

MOST BIRDS RINGED
Óskar J. Sigurósson, principal bird-ringer of the Icelandic Institute of Natural History and lighthouse keeper at Stórhöfôi on Heimay in the Westmann Islands, has ringed 65,243 birds since 1953.

MOST AERIALS PHOTOGRAPHED
David Neal of Kent, England, has spent 10 years photographing aerials in his native country. By January 1998, the 22-year-old had taken more than 3,000 photos of 524 different types of aerial. His ambition is to photograph every aerial mast in the United Kingdom — approximately 10,000 in total. Neal used to record his sightings of electricity pylons, but now finds aerials more "majestic."

MOST PUBS VISITED
Bruce Masters of Flitwick, England, has visited 29,203 pubs and 1,568 other drinking establishments since 1960, drinking local beer wherever it was available.

MOST IMPERSONATED ICON
There are estimated to be more than 48,000 Elvis impersonators worldwide. In 1988, the First Presleyterian Church of Elvis the Divine was formed in the United States. In London, England, Paul Chan entertains customers at his Gracelands Palace restaurant with his Elvis impressions. Known as "the Chinese Elvis," Chan has even changed his middle name to his hero's. Seen here are two impersonators at an Elvis convention in the United States.

MOST RESTAURANTS DINED IN
Fred Magel of Chicago, Illinois, dined out a record 46,000 times in 60 countries during his 50 years as a restaurant grader. Magel claimed that the restaurant that served the largest helpings was Zehnder's Hotel, Frankenmuth, Michigan. His all-time favorite dishes were South African rock lobster and mousse of fresh English strawberries.

MOST CHRISTMAS CARDS SENT
The record for the greatest number of personal Christmas cards ever sent out is believed to be 62,824, by Werner Erhard of San Francisco, California in December 1975.

MOST LETTERS WRITTEN
Uichi Noda, the former deputy minister of the treasury and minister of construction in Japan, wrote 1,307 letters to his bedridden wife Mitsu during his overseas trips from July 1961 until her death in March 1985. They have been published in 25 volumes totaling 12,404 pages and more than 5 million characters.

MOST LETTERS TO AN EDITOR
David Green had his 143rd letter printed in the correspondence columns of *The Times* (of London) on April 21, 1998. This is the most letters published in a national newspaper.

LONGEST-KEPT DIARY
Col. Ernest Loftus from Harare, Zimbabwe, began writing his daily diary at the age of 12 on May 4, 1896, and continued it until his death aged 103 years 178 days on July 7, 1987.

GREATEST *STAR WARS* TRIBUTE
In 1998, a group of friends from California made a 10-minute film depicting scenes that are only mentioned in *Star Wars* (1977). *Troops*, which was directed by Kevin Rubio, shows the death of Luke Skywalker's Aunt Beru and Uncle Owen, which inspired his mission to save the galaxy. It has its own Web site (www.theforce.net), and fans are said to include *Stars Wars* director George Lucas and Mark Hamill, who played Luke.

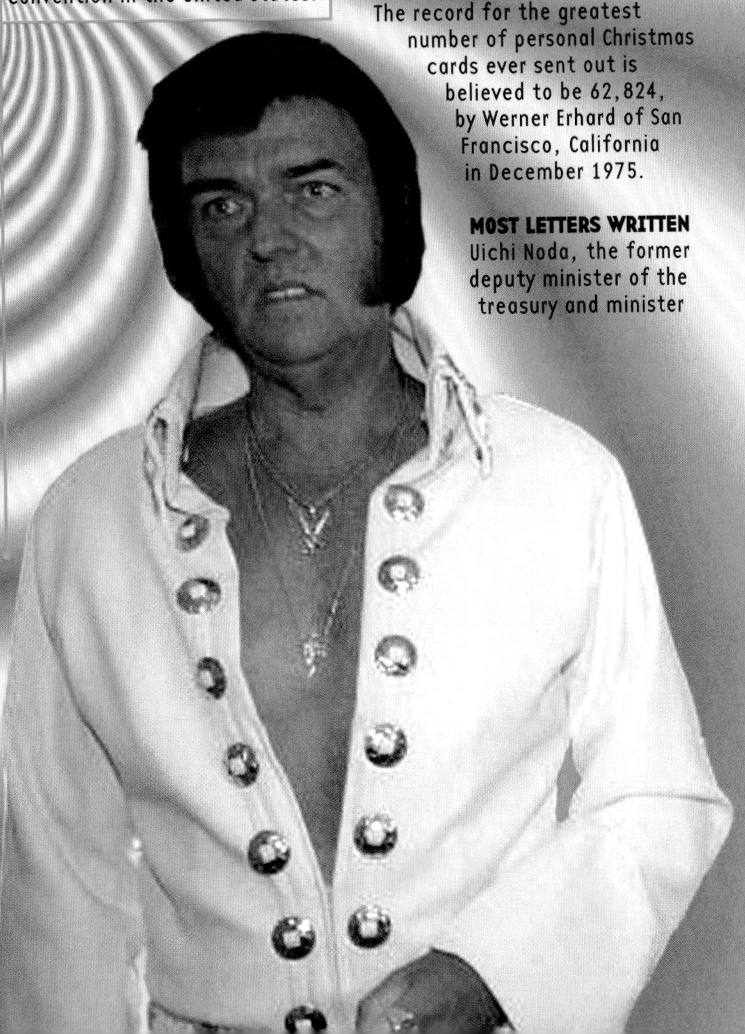

food and drink I

HEALTH WARNING
The following gluttony records are historical and should not be attempted today. Guinness Publishing Ltd. in no way condones these records and will not accept any further claims to them. Potential record-breakers should also note that attempts to break or set any new records for eating and drinking can be dangerous, and medical advice should always be taken before attempting a record. Under no circumstances will Guinness Publishing Ltd. accept any liability for death or injury suffered in record attempts.

FASTEST YARD OF ALE
Peter Dowdeswell (Great Britain) drank a yard of ale (1.42 liters or 3 US pints) in five seconds in May 1975.

BIGGEST WINE TASTING
In 1986, about 4,000 tasters consumed 9,360 bottles of wine at a tasting sponsored by California TV station KQED.

MOST MEAT EATEN AT A BARBECUE
In 1996, 23.87 tons of meat and 24.2 tons of chicken were cooked and eaten in eight hours at the Lancaster, Pennsylvania, Sertoma Club's Chicken Bar-B-Que.

HEARTIEST EATER
In 1963, Edward Miller ate 28 pullets, weighing 2 pounds each, in one sitting at Trader Vic's restaurant, San Francisco, California.

FASTEST EGG EATERS
In 1984, Peter Dowdeswell ate 13 raw eggs in one second.

In 1987, John Kenmuir ate 14 cooked eggs in 14.42 seconds.

FASTEST KIPPER EATER
Reg Morris fileted and ate 27 kippers in 16 min. 52.66 sec. in Walsall, England, in 1988.

FASTEST HOT DOG EATER
Reg Morris ate 30 hot dogs in 64 seconds in Burntwood, England, in December 1986.

FASTEST SAUSAGE MEAT EATER
Reg Morris ate 6 pounds of sausage meat in 3 min. 10 sec. in Walsall, England, in 1986.

FASTEST SPAGHETTI EATER
In 1986, Peter Dowdeswell ate 100 yards of spaghetti in just 12.02 seconds in Halesowen, England.

FASTEST PICKLED ONION EATER
Pat Donahue ate 91 pickled onions in 1 min. 8 sec. in Victoria, British Columbia, Canada, in 1978.

FASTEST BANANA EATER
Dr Ronald Alkana ate 17 bananas, each with an edible weight of at least $4^{1}/_{2}$ ounces, in two minutes at the University of California, Irvine, in 1973.

FASTEST LEMON EATER
In 1979, Bobby Kempf of Virginia ate three lemons, including skin and seeds, in 15.3 seconds.

FASTEST GRAPE EATER
Jim Ellis of Montrose, Michigan, ate 3 lb. 1 oz. of grapes in 34.6 seconds in 1976.

FASTEST ICE CREAM EATER
Tony Dowdeswell ate 3 lb. 6 oz. of unmelted ice cream in 31.67 seconds in New York City in July 1986.

FASTEST NOODLE MAKER
Simon Sang Koon Sung made 8,192 strings from one piece of dough in 59.29 seconds at the Singapore Food Festival in 1994.

FASTEST ONION PEELERS
In July 1980, Alan St. Jean peeled 50 pounds of onions in 3 min. 18 sec. in Connecticut.

In October 1980, under new rules stipulating that a minimum of 50 onions have to be peeled, Alfonso Salvo of Pennsylvania peeled 50 pounds of onions (52 onions) in 5 min. 23 sec.

FASTEST OYSTER OPENER
Mike Racz opened 100 oysters in 2 min. 20.07 sec. in Invercargill, New Zealand, on July 16, 1990.

FASTEST PANCAKE TOSSER
Ralf Laue (Germany) tossed a pancake 416 times in 2 minutes in Linz, Austria, in 1997.

BIGGEST HAMBURGER
In 1989, a 5,520-pound, 21-foot-diameter hamburger was made at Outagamie County Fairgrounds in Wisconsin.

LONGEST KEBAB
A 2,889-ft.-3-in.-long kebab was made by the West Yorkshire Family Service Units, the Trade Association of Asian Restaurant Owners and National Power in Bradford, England, June 19, 1994.

LONGEST SALAMI
In 1992 a record-breaking 68-ft.-9-in.-long salami was made by A/S Svindlands in Pølsefabrikk, Norway.

LONGEST SAUSAGE
A 28-mile-1,354-yd.-long continuous sausage was made by M & M Meat Shops and J. M. Schneider Inc. in Kitchener, Ontario, Canada, in April 1995.

LONGEST BRATWURST
A 1-mile-1,630-yd.-long bratwurst was made in Jena, Thuringia, Germany in 1994.

BIGGEST LASAGNA
A 70-by-7-foot lasagna was made by the Food Bank for Monterey County in Salinas, California in 1993.

BIGGEST PIZZA
A pizza measuring 122 ft. 8 in. in diameter was made at Norwood Hypermarket in South Africa on December 8, 1990.

BIGGEST QUICHE LORRAINE
The world's biggest ever quiche Lorraine was baked in Paris, France in November 1997 by chef Alain Marcotullio and a team of 30 cooks. Its preparation took more than 16 hours. The 16-foot-wide quiche contained, among other ingredients, 1,298 eggs, 156 pounds of bacon and 31 gallons of milk. A standard-size quiche Lorraine requires just three eggs, eight slices of bacon and half a cup of milk. Here Claude Dejean, dressed as an 18th-century custodian, beats a drum to celebrate the completion of the quiche.

BIGGEST FOOD FAIR
Gudrun and Lena, promoters of the "Green Week" fair in Berlin, Germany, bite into a giant pretzel in front of the Brandenburg Gate. The fair is the biggest food and agriculture fair in the world today. In 1998, it was attended by exhibitors from more than 60 countries. Germany also produced the biggest apple strudel and the longest bratwurst.

BIGGEST PAELLA
Juan Carlos Galbis and a team of helpers made a paella measuring 65 ft. 7 in. in diameter in Valencia, Spain in March 1992. It was eaten by 100,000 people.

BIGGEST OMELET
In 1994 representatives of Swatch cooked a 1,383-square-foot omelet containing a total of 160,000 eggs in Yokohama, Japan.

BIGGEST CHINESE DUMPLING
In 1997, the Hong Kong Union of Chinese Food and Culture Ltd. and the Southern District Committee made a Chinese dumpling weighing 1,058 lb. 6¼ oz. for the celebration of Hong Kong's return to China.

BIGGEST CREPE
A 3.3-ton crepe with a diameter of 49 ft. 3 in. was flipped in Manchester, England, in August 1994 during celebrations to mark the 150th anniversary of the Cooperative movement.

TALLEST CAKE
In August 1997, Network Television Marketing Ltd. created a 105-foot-tall, 105-tier cake in Faisalabad, Pakistan.

LONGEST APPLE STRUDEL
A 1-mile-2,211-yd. apple strudel was made on May 26, 1994 in Karlsruhe, Germany.

BIGGEST PIE
In 1989, a pecan pie weighing 40,266 pounds and measuring 40 feet in diameter was baked in Okmulgee, Oklahoma.

BIGGEST CANDY
In 1997, a 2.54-ton Turkish delight was made by Bahattin, Bulent and Ediz Pektuzun at Real Turkish Delight of Australia.

BIGGEST COCKTAIL
A 6,859-gallon Juicy Duce was made at the Buderim Tavern, Queensland, Australia, in 1996. It contained 26 gallons each of rum, scotch, gin, bourbon, ouzo and brandy, 1,040 gallons of vodka, 468 gallons of orange juice, 4.4 tons of ice, 400 watermelons, 400 oranges and 400 lemons.

BIGGEST MILK SHAKE
A 4,333-gallon strawberry shake was made by Age Concern East Cheshire and Lancashire Dairies in Macclesfield, England, in 1996.

food and drink II

MOST EXPENSIVE MEAL PER HEAD
In September 1997, three diners at Le Gavroche, London, England spent £13,091.20 ($20,945.92) on one meal. Only £216.20 ($345.60) went on food: cigars and liquor accounted for £845 ($1,384) and the remaining £12,030 ($19,248) went on six bottles of wine. The most expensive bottle, a 1985 Romanee Conti costing £4,950 ($7,920), proved "a bit young" so they gave it to the restaurant staff. The diners began with a 1949 Krug champagne at £560 ($896) and followed it with fine clarets and burgundies: a 1985 DRC Montrachet at £1,400 ($2,240), a 1954 Haut Brion at £2,100 ($3,360), a 1967 Château D'Yquem at £1,070 ($1,712) and a 1961 Château Latour at £1,950 ($3,120).

MOST EXPENSIVE BOTTLE OF WINE
In December 1985, £105,000 ($136,248) was paid for a bottle of 1787 Château Lafite claret at Christie's, London. It was engraved with the initials of Thomas Jefferson. In 1986, its cork, dried out by exhibition lights, slipped, spoiling the wine.

MOST EXPENSIVE GLASS OF WINE
A record $1,453 was paid for the first glass of Beaujolais Nouveau 1993 released in Beaune (from Maison Jaffelin), Burgundy, France. It was bought by Robert Denby at Pickwick's, a British pub in Beaune, on November 18, 1993.

MOST EXPENSIVE LIQUOR
The most expensive liquor is Springbank 1919 Malt Whisky, a bottle of which costs £6,750 including tax ($10,800) at Fortnum & Mason, London, England.

The highest price paid for liquor at auction was $79,552 for a bottle of 50-year-old Glenfiddich whisky. It was sold to an anonymous Italian businessman at a charity auction in Milan, Italy in 1992.

MOST EXPENSIVE STEAK
The most expensive steak comes from Wagyu cattle, which have been bred around the Japanese city of Kobe for centuries. The herds have a remarkable genetic purity and the cows are treated like royalty, regularly rubbed down with saké and fed huge amounts of beer. They are extremely docile animals and their stress-free life is said to explain the quality of their flesh. Since the Japanese will not export any cattle for breeding, Kobe beef is rarely available, and costs about $160 per pound.

MOST EXPENSIVE FISH
Sushi chefs pay phenomenal prices for giant bluefin tuna. In January 1992, a 715-pound bluefin sold for the sum of $83,500 – almost $117 per pound – in Tokyo, Japan. The tuna was reduced to 2,400 servings of sushi for wealthy diners at $75 per serving. The estimated income from this one fish was $180,000.

MOST EXPENSIVE CAVIAR
The most expensive caviar in the world is Almas caviar, the yellow eggs from an albino beluga sturgeon, which sells for $1,000 per 50 g ($1\frac{3}{4}$ ounces).

MOST EXPENSIVE MUSSELS
The world's most expensive mussel is the Percebes barnacle, at $176 per pound. Known as the "truffle of the seas," the barnacles need a lot of oxygen to survive and so attach themselves to rocks where waves are most violent and the water is very aerated. They live in the uninhabited Sisargas Islands off Spain, where fishermen risk their lives to catch them. Deaths and casualties are commonplace. Once the shellfish reach a restaurant, they are boiled alive and served up with a garlic sauce. They are so highly prized that a festival, the Fiesta de Los Percebes, is held in their honor.

MOST EXPENSIVE SPICES
Prices for wild ginseng (the root of *Panax quinquefolium*) from China's Chan Pak mountain area were as high as $23,000 per ounce in Hong Kong in November 1979. Total annual shipments of the spice – which is thought by many to be an aphrodisiac – from Jilin Province do not exceed 9 pounds.

MOST EXPENSIVE TRUFFLE
Guy Monier, the owner of the Truffle House in Paris, France, displays a giant 2.5-pound black truffle. Found by a dog in Tricastin, southern France, in December 1997, it was worth an estimated $1,500. The world's most expensive truffle is *Tuber magmatum pico*, a rare white truffle found in Alba, Italy, which sells for $8,820 per pound. The fungus cannot be cultivated and can only be found by trained pigs or dogs.

The most expensive widely-used spice is saffron, made from the dried stigmas of *Crocus sativus*. It costs $4 for $^{11}/_{500}$ ounce.

HOTTEST SPICE
A single dried gram ($^{3}/_{100}$ ounce) of Red "Savina" Habanero (1994 special), developed by GNS Spices of Walnut, California, can produce detectable heat in 1,272 pounds of bland sauce.

MOST EXPENSIVE CHILI PEPPER
The most expensive chili pepper is served by Chasen's of West Hollywood, California, at $16.75 for $^{1}/_{2}$ pound. Elizabeth Taylor had some flown to her when she was filming *Cleopatra* (1963).

MOST METAL EATEN
Michel Lotito of Grenoble, France is known as Monsieur Mangetout ("Mr. Eat-everything") and has been eating metal and glass since 1959. Gastroenterologists who have x-rayed his stomach have described his ability to consume up to 2 pounds of metal a day as unique. Mangetout's diet since 1966 has included 18 bicycles, 15 supermarket carts, seven TV sets, six chandeliers, two beds, a pair of skis, a Cessna light aircraft, a computer and a coffin (including handles). He cuts up the objects with a power saw to make bite-size chunks, and instead of chewing the pieces of "food," swallows the metal like a pill – something that would normally prove fatal and should never be attempted. He first became aware of his ability one day when a glass from which he was drinking broke. He started chewing the fragments, found that he could swallow them, and began eating glass and metal as a party trick. Now he makes a living from his act. By October 1997, the 47-year-old had eaten nearly 9 tons of metal. Mangetout says that bananas and hard-boiled eggs make him sick.

MOST EXPENSIVE FRUIT
In 1977, restaurateur Leslie Cooke paid £530 ($906) for 1 pound of strawberries at an auction in Dublin, Ireland.

MOST EXPENSIVE COFFEE
The Indonesian coffee Kopi Luwak sells for $75 per quarter-pound, partly because of its rarity but also because of the way it is processed: the beans from which it is made are ingested by a small tree-dwelling animal called the *Paradoxurus* before being extracted from the excreta of the animals and made into Kopi Luwak.

BIGGEST RESTAURANT
Mang Gorn Luang (The Royal Dragon) in Bangkok, Thailand has 1,200 staff and can seat 5,000 customers. The 541 waiters wear rollerskates to serve up to 3,000 dishes an hour in the 4-acre service area.

LONGEST LUNCH TABLE
In March 1998, a team of caterers set places for more than 15,000 guests to eat at the longest continuous table. The table stretched over 3 miles along the newly-built Vasco da Gama bridge in Lisbon, Portugal – Europe's longest bridge, at 11 miles. The organizers of the event had to rent 200 buses to transport the diners to their seats.

BIGGEST PUB
Germany is renowned for its production and consumption of beer, most notably at the Oktoberfest held each year in Munich. Munich is also home to the Mathäser, the world's biggest pub, which sells 12,480 gallons of beer every day.

achievers I

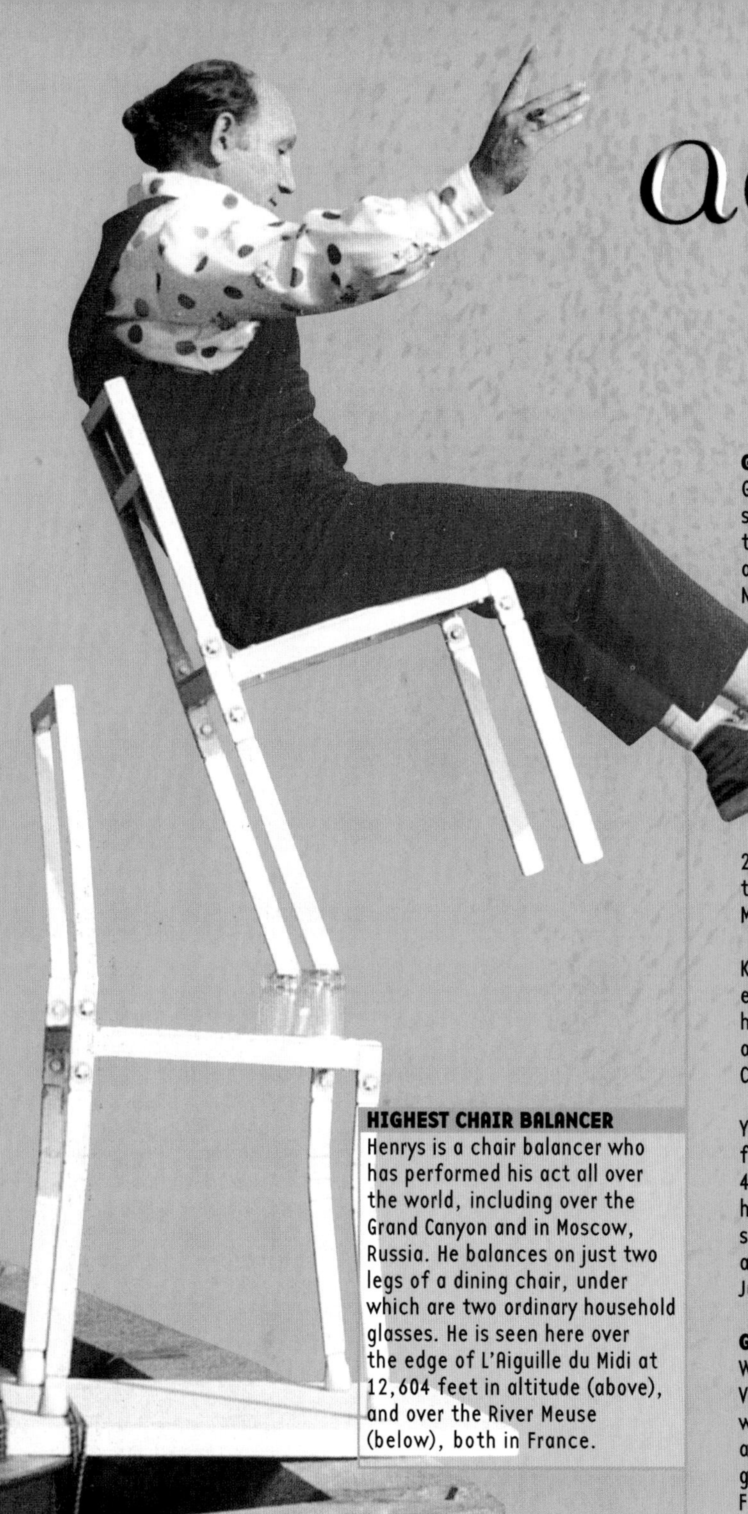

HIGHEST CHAIR BALANCER
Henrys is a chair balancer who has performed his act all over the world, including over the Grand Canyon and in Moscow, Russia. He balances on just two legs of a dining chair, under which are two ordinary household glasses. He is seen here over the edge of L'Aiguille du Midi at 12,604 feet in altitude (above), and over the River Meuse (below), both in France.

GREATEST DISPLAYS OF STRENGTH
Grant Edwards of Sydney, Australia single-handedly pulled a 221-ton train a distance of 120 ft. 9 in. along a railroad track at the New South Wales Rail Transport Museum, Thirlmere, Australia on April 4, 1996.

Juraj Barbaric single-handedly pulled a 396-ton train a record distance of 25 ft. 3 in. along a railroad track in Kosice, Slovakia, on May 25, 1996.

Khalil Oghaby (Iran) lifted an elephant off the ground using a harness and platform weighing approximately 2.2 tons at Gerry Cottle's Circus in the UK in 1975.

Yuri Scherbina, a powerjuggler from Ukraine, threw a 35-lb.-4½-oz. weightball from hand to hand 100 times on the eastern summit of Mount Elbrus (at an altitude of 13,800 feet) in July 1995.

GREATEST LIFT USING TEETH
Walter Arfeuille of Ieper-Vlamertinge, Belgium lifted weights totaling 620 lb. 10 oz. a distance of 6¾ inches off the ground with his teeth in Paris, France on March 31, 1990.

GREATEST PULL USING TEETH
Robert Galstyan of Masis, Armenia, pulled two railroad cars a distance of 23 feet along a railroad track with his teeth in Shcherbinka, Moscow, Russia on July 21, 1992. The cars were coupled together and had a total combined weight of 483,198 pounds.

PULLING FEATS
David Huxley single-handedly pulled a 305.7-ton Qantas Boeing 747-400 a distance of 298 ft. 6 in. across the tarmac at Sydney Airport, Australia on October 15, 1997, beating his previous record of 179 ft. 6 in. Huxley has also pulled the 115.5-ton Concorde for a distance of 469 ft. 2 in., and the 425.7-ton HMAV *Bounty* for a distance of 82 feet.

GREATEST DISPLAY OF LUNG POWER
On September 26, 1994, Nicholas Mason of Cheadle, Greater Manchester, England inflated a standard 35-ounce meteorological balloon to a diameter of 8 feet in a time of 45 min. 2.5 sec. for BBC TV's *Record Breakers* show.

FASTEST BEER KEG LIFTER
Tom Gaskin lifted a keg of beer above his head a total of 902 times in six hours at Liska House, Newry, Northern Ireland on October 26, 1996. The keg weighed 137 lb. 8 oz.

FASTEST INVERTED SPRINTER
On February 19, 1994, Mark Kenny of Norwood, Massachusetts completed a 164-foot sprint on his hands in a record time of 16.93 seconds.

FASTEST YODELER
Thomas Scholl (Germany) achieved 22 tones (15 falsetto) in one second on February 9, 1992.

FASTEST DRUMMER
Rory Blackwell (Great Britain) played a total of 400 separate drums in a time of 16.2 seconds on May 29, 1995.

FASTEST SHAVERS

The record for the most people shaved with a straight razor in 60 minutes is 278, by Tom Rodden (Great Britain) on November 10, 1993 for BBC TV's *Record Breakers* show. Averaging 12.9 seconds per face, he drew blood seven times.

The record for the greatest number of people shaved with a safety razor in 60 minutes is 1,994, by Denny Rowe in Herne Bay, England on June 19, 1988. Rowe took an average of 1.8 seconds per volunteer and drew blood four times.

FASTEST HAIRCUTTER

The most haircuts given in an hour is 18, by Trevor Mitchell at the Wembley Conference Center, London, England on October 27, 1996, meeting guidelines set down by the Organisation Artistique Internationale de la Coiffure. During this attempt he completed one haircut in a record time of 2 min. 20 sec.

FASTEST SHEEP SHEARERS

The record for hand shearing is 390 lambs in eight hours, by Deanne Sarre of Pingrup in Yealering, Western Australia on October 1, 1989.

The men's record for hand shearing is 353 lambs in nine hours, by Peter Casserly of Christchurch, New Zealand, on February 13, 1976.

The highest ever speed for solo machine-shearing in one working day (nine hours) is 805 lambs, by Alan MacDonald in Waitnaguru, New Zealand on December 20, 1990. This works out to an average of 89.4 sheep per hour.

FASTEST TREE TOPPER

Guy German ascended a 100-foot-tall spar pole and sawed off the top, which had a circumference of 3 ft. 4 in., in a record time of 53.35 seconds in Albany, Oregon on July 3, 1989.

FASTEST WIFE-CARRIER

Jouni Jussila carried his wife Tiina over the World Wife-Carrying Championship course — a 771-foot-long obstacle course that includes chest-high water and two wooden stiles — in a record time of 1 min. 5 sec. in 1997. It was the Jussilas' fifth success in the annual contest, which is held in Sonkajärvi, Finland. The winner takes home liters of beer equivalent to the weight of his partner, who need not be his wife but must be over the age of 17 and wear a crash helmet.

FASTEST COCONUT TREE CLIMBER

The annual Coconut Tree Climbing Competition held at Sukana Park, Fiji is a local tradition that has become an international event, and organizers have had to standardize the length of the climb. The fastest time in which a 9-meter-tall (29-ft.-6-in.) coconut tree has been climbed barefoot is 4.88 seconds, by Fuatai Solo of Western Samoa (now Samoa) in Sukana Park on August 22, 1980. After being declared the winner for the third time in a row, Fuatai climbed the tree again, holding the prize money of $100 in his mouth.

FASTEST TALKERS

The world's fastest talkers are Steve Woodmore (Great Britain), Sean Shannon (Canada; pictured right) and Steve Briers (Great Britain). Woodmore spoke 595 words in 56.01 seconds (equal to 637.4 words per minute) on British TV show *Motor Mouth* on September 22, 1990. He trains by choosing a passage from a book and reciting it over and over again until it becomes second nature. He usually only practices the evening before a speaking event, but if his record is broken he trains for up to six weeks to win it back. Shannon recited Hamlet's soliloquy, "To be or not to be" (260 words), in a time of 23.8 seconds (equal to 655 words per minute) in Edinburgh, Scotland on August 30, 1995. He realized that he had a talent while he was still a child, when people would ask him to slow down because they could not understand what he was saying. Now he only practices for a few minutes a day: if he does more, the speech becomes impossible to keep together. Briers recited the lyrics of Queen's album *A Night at the Opera* backwards in 9 min. 58.44 sec. on February 6, 1990. The world's fastest backwards talker, he locks himself in his room until he has learned his speeches, sometimes training for four hours a day.

achievers II

MOST PLATES FLASHED
Albert Lucas flashed eight plates in 1993. He also juggled eight plates in 1997, equaling the record that was reputedly set by Enrico Rastelli (Italy) in the 1920s. "Flashed" means that the number of catches made at least equals the number of objects, while "juggled" requires double the number of catches.

LONGEST BUBBLE
Alan McKay of Wellington, New Zealand created a 105-foot-long bubble on August 9, 1996. He used a bubble wand, dishwashing liquid, glycerine and water.

BIGGEST BUBBLE-GUM BUBBLE
The greatest reported diameter of a bubble-gum bubble is 23 inches. It was blown by Susan Montgomery Williams of Fresno, California at the ABC TV studios in New York City on July 19, 1994.

LARGEST BUBBLE WALL
Fan-Yang of Mississauga, Ontario, Canada, created a 156-foot bubble wall with an area of about 4,000 square feet at the Kingdome Pavilion, Seattle, Washington on August 11, 1997. The bubble stayed up continuously for between 5 and 10 seconds.

MOST MOSQUITOES KILLED
The most mosquitoes ever killed in the five-minute world mosquito killing championships held yearly in Finland is 21, by Henri Pellonpää in 1995.

LONGEST EGG THROW
Johnny Dell Foley threw a fresh hen's egg 323 ft. 2 in. without breaking it, on November 12, 1978 in Jewett, Texas. The egg was caught by Keith Thomas.

LONGEST FLYING DISC THROWS
The World Flying Disc Federation distance record for men is 656 ft. 2 in., by Scott Stokely (US) on May 14, 1995 in Fort Collins, Colorado.

The official Flying Disc distance record for women is 447 ft. 3 in., by Anni Kreml (US) in Fort Collins, Colorado on August 21, 1994.

LONGEST GUMBOOT THROWS
A size 8½ Challenger Dunlop boot was thrown a record 209 ft. 9 in. by Teppo Luoma in Hämeenlinna, Finland, on October 12, 1996.

The women's record for throwing a size 8½ Challenger Dunlop boot is 134 ft. 1 in., by Sari Tirkkonen in Turku, Finland, on April 19, 1996.

LONGEST COW PAT THROW
The greatest distance that a cow pat has been thrown under the "non-sphericalization and 100% organic" rule is 266 feet, by Steve Urner at the Mountain Festival, Tehachapi, California on August 14, 1981.

LONGEST SPEAR THROW
The furthest that a spear has been thrown using an atlatl, a hand-held device that fits onto it, is 848 ft. 6½ in., by David Engvall in Aurora, Colorado on July 15, 1995.

LONGEST SPITS
The greatest recorded distance that a cherry stone has been spat is 95 ft. 1 in., by Horst Ortmann in Langenthal, Germany, on August 27, 1994.

David O'Dell of Apple Valley, California spat a tobacco wad a record distance of 49 ft. 5½ in. at the 19th World Tobacco Spitting Championships at Calico Ghost Town, California in March 1994.

The greatest distance that a watermelon seed has been spat is 75 ft. 2 in., by Jason Schayot in De Leon, Texas on August 12, 1995.

GREATEST GRAPE CATCH
The greatest ever distance at which a grape thrown from level ground has been caught in the mouth is 327 ft. 6 in., by Paul Tavilla in East Boston, Massachusetts on May 27, 1991. The grape was thrown by James Deady.

LONGEST CRAWLS
Over the 15 months up to March 9, 1985, Jagdish Chander crawled a distance of 870 miles from Aligarh to Jamma, India, in order to appease his revered Hindu goddess, Mata.

The longest ever continuous voluntary crawl, keeping at least one knee in unbroken contact with the ground, was 31 miles 880 yd. by Peter McKinlay and John Murrie, from March 28 to March 29, 1992. They completed 115 laps of a running track in Falkirk, Scotland.

LONGEST DANCE
The greatest distance ever danced by one person is 23 miles 385 yd., by David Meenan, who tap-danced for 6 hr. 12 min. 53 sec. in Red Bank, New Jersey on June 30, 1996.

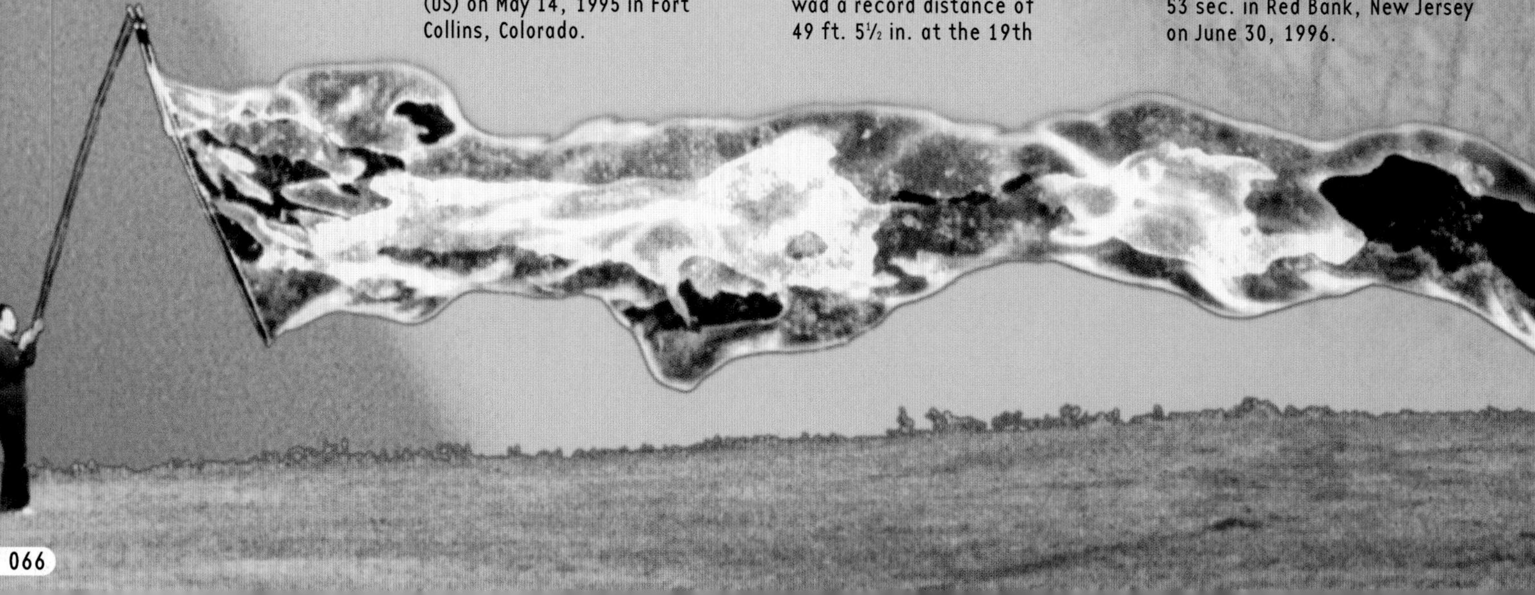

LONGEST TIME SPENT BALANCING ON ONE FOOT
Amresh Kumar Jha balanced on one foot for a record time of 71 hr. 40 min. in Bihar, India, September 13–16, 1995. He did not rest his disengaged foot on the standing foot or use any object for support or balance at any point.

LONGEST PERIOD WITHOUT MOVING
Radhey Shyam Prajapati (India) stood motionless for a record 18 hr. 5 min. 50 sec. at Gandhi Bhawan, Bhopal, India, January 25–26, 1996.

LONGEST STATIC WALL SIT
Rajkumar Chakraborty (India) stayed in an unsupported sitting position against a wall for a time of 11 hr. 5 min. at Panposh Sports Hostel, Rourkela, India on April 22, 1994.

LONGEST TIME CAMPING OUT
The silent Indian *fakir* Mastram Bapu ("contented father") remained on the same spot by the roadside in the village of Chitra for a total of 22 years from 1960 to 1982.

LONGEST TIME SPENT IN A TREE
Bungkas went up a palm tree in the Indonesian village of Bengkes in 1970 and has been there ever since, living in a nest that he made from branches and leaves. Repeated efforts to persuade him to come down have failed.

CHINESE CIRCUS
Balancing and juggling acts date back to the Middle Ages in Europe, Asia and Africa, but Chinese circus in particular is renowned for its balancing acts. The Chinese State Circus, which was put together by Philip Gandey, is an animal-free circus which has dazzled audiences worldwide with its daring high wire and trapeze acts, massive human pyramids, plate balancing and acrobatics.

LONGEST RIDE IN ARMOR
The longest known ride while wearing armor is 208 miles, by Dick Brown, from Edinburgh to Dumfries, Scotland in 1989. His total riding time was 35 hr. 25 min.

LONGEST BACKWARDS UNICYCLE
Ashrita Furman (US) rode backwards for a distance of 53 miles 299 yd, at Forest Park, Queens, New York on September 16, 1994.

MOST BOOMERANGS CAUGHT
Lawrence West of Basingstoke, England threw, and caught, a boomerang 20 times in one minute at the Indoor Boomerang Throwing Competition held on BBC TV's *Tomorrow's World* on March 20, 1998.

MOST GLASSES BALANCED
Ashrita Furman balanced a vertical stack of 62 pint glasses on his chin for 10 seconds on June 18, 1998. Furman set his record on the set of the Fox television series *Guinness World Records™: Primetime*.

MOST EGGS BALANCED
The most eggs simultaneously balanced on end on a flat surface by one person is 210, by Kenneth Epperson of Monroe, Georgia on September 23, 1990. The most eggs simultaneously balanced by a group is 467, by a class at Bayfield School in Colorado on March 20, 1986, the vernal equinox. The picture at left shows eight-year-old Malik Shabazz Pizzarro and urban park ranger June Yoo balancing eggs on a wall in Central Park, New York City, as part of a vernal equinox celebration in March 1997. It had long been thought that it is possible to balance raw eggs on their end on the first day of spring, although astronomers argued that there was no reason for this. In 1996 they were proved right by Science Alliance, which demonstrated that if an egg balances on an equinox day, it will balance on any other day.

MOST FLAMING TORCHES JUGGLED
Anthony Gatto (US) juggled seven flaming torches in 1989.

MOST DOMINOES STACKED
Ralf Laue of Leipzig, Germany successfully stacked 529 dominoes on a single supporting domino on June 26, 1997 at the Ramada Hotel, Linz, Austria.

FASTEST BED MAKER
The fastest time for one person to make a bed is 28.2 seconds, by Wendy Wall of Sydney, Australia, on November 30, 1978.

teamwork

BIGGEST DANCE
An estimated 72,000 people took part in a Chicken Dance during the Canfield (Ohio) Fair on September 1, 1996.

BIGGEST TAP DANCE
A record-breaking 6,654 people tap-danced outside Macy's department store in New York City on August 18, 1996.

BIGGEST LINE DANCE
On January 25, 1997, a total of 5,502 people took part in a country line dance held in Tamworth, Australia. They danced to Brooks & Dunn's extended play version of "Boot Scootin' Boogie," which is 6 min. 28 sec. long.

LONGEST CONGA LINE
On March 13, 1988, the Miami Super Conga, held in conjunction with Calle Ocho — a Cuban-American celebration of life held in Miami, Florida — consisted of 119,986 people.

LONGEST DANCING DRAGON
On November 3, 1996, a team of 2,431 people brought a dancing dragon to life measuring 1 mile 317 yd. from the end of its nose to the tip of its tail. The dragon danced for more than a minute at the Grandstand Forecourt, Shatin Racecourse, Hong Kong.

BIGGEST HUMAN CENTIPEDE
On September 2, 1996, a "human centipede" made up of 1,665 students from the University of Guelph, Canada, with their ankles firmly tied together, moved 98 ft. 5 in. without any of them falling over.

BIGGEST SIMULTANEOUS SIGNING
The most people to have signed simultaneously is 250, signing "Somewhere Over The Rainbow" during a performance of the *Wizard of Oz* at the Swan Theater, High Wycombe, England on August 9, 1996.

MOST KISSING COUPLES
The greatest number of couples to have kissed in the same place at the same time was 1,420, at the University of Maine at Orono, Maine on February 14, 1996.

FASTEST HUMAN DEMOLITION
On May 11, 1996, 15 members of the Aurora Karate Do demolished a 10-room house in Prince Albert, Saskatchewan, Canada with their feet and hands in 3 hr. 6 min. 50 sec.

FASTEST BRIDGE BUILDERS
On November 3, 1995, a team of British soldiers from 21 Engineer Regiment, based in Nienburg, Germany, constructed a bridge across a 26-ft.-3-in. gap using a five-bay single-story medium girder bridge at Hameln, Germany, in a time of 8 min. 44 sec.

FASTEST CAR WASHERS
The record for the greatest number of cars to have been washed in eight hours at one location is 2,169, by a team of people led by police officers from Walsall at Aldridge Airport, England on June 9, 1996.

FASTEST BEDMAKERS
The fastest time in which two people have made a bed with one blanket, two sheets, an undersheet, an uncased pillow, a bedspread and "hospital" corners is 14 seconds, by Sharon Stringer and Michelle Benkel of the Royal Masonic Hospital, London, England, November 26, 1993.

FASTEST SHOE SHINERS
The most shoes shined by a team of four people in eight hours is 14,975, by four teenagers from the London Church of Christ at Leicester Square, London, England on June 15, 1996.

FASTEST CLOTHES MAKERS
On September 3, 1986, a team of eight people at the International Wool Secretariat Development Center in Ilkley, England sheared a sheep and made a sweater from its wool in 2 hr. 28 min. 32 sec. using commercial machinery.

The record for the fastest production of a three-piece suit from sheep to finished article is 1 hr. 34 min. 33.42 sec., by 65 members of the Melbourne College of Textiles, Victoria, Australia on June 24, 1982. Catching and fleecing took 2 min. 21 sec., and carding, spinning, weaving and tailoring occupied the remaining time.

FASTEST COAL SHOVELERS
Brian McArdle and Rodney Spark

BIGGEST ALUMINUM CAN REPLICA
In December 1997, about 40 volunteers, mostly retired construction workers, constructed a scale version of St. Peter's Basilica, Rome, Italy from more than 10 million empty aluminum cans. The model, which was one-fifth the size of the original and built mainly from Coca-Cola cans, was created in aid of AIDO and AVIS, the Italian blood and organ donation charities. It was 316 feet long, 160 feet wide and 97 feet high, with a 67-foot-wide dome, and remained in place on the outskirts of Rome for two months. The aluminum was then auctioned off, with the proceeds going to the charities, whose previous projects included can replicas of Rome's Colosseum, Verona's Roman arena and St. Anthony's Basilica in Padua, Italy. The world's biggest can pyramids consisted of 6,201 empty cans built by two teams of 10 people in 30 minutes at Tamokutekihiroba Ouike Park, Tokai, Japan on September 1, 1996.

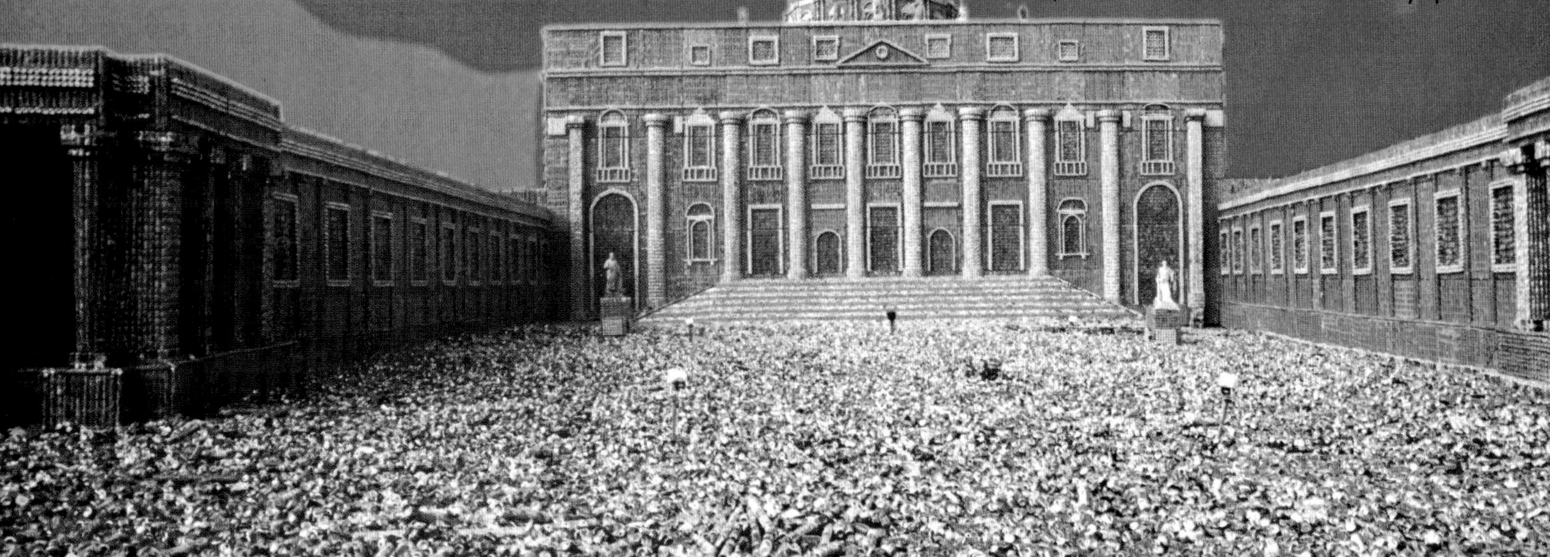

BIGGEST ORCHESTRA

In April 1998, the record for the world's largest orchestra was broken by the 2,049-strong Pittsburgh Symphony Youth Orchestra at the Civic Arena, Pittsburgh, Pennsylvania. It consisted of 961 string players, 458 woodwind instrument players, a 410-person brass section and 220 percussionists, recruited from more than 5,000 young hopefuls who applied through their schools and youth orchestras, or auditioned individually. The players, who were conducted by Pittsburgh Symphony Orchestra Music Director Mariss Janson, performed the world premiere of *Music Forever* by local composer Michael Moricz. The ambitious event was part of a community outreach and education program by the Pittsburgh Symphony. The record was previously held by the Wolverhampton (England) Orchestra, with a total of 2,023 players.

of Middlemount, Queensland, Australia, filled a 1,100-pound coal hopper in 15.01 seconds, the record by a team of two, at the Fingal Valley Festival, Tasmania, Australia, March 5, 1994.

FASTEST LADDER CLIMBERS
A team of 10 firefighters from the Pietermaritzburg Msunduzi Fire Services, South Africa climbed a vertical height of 56 miles 401 yd. up a standard fire ladder in 24 hours, June 14–15, 1996.

MOST LITTER COLLECTORS
The greatest number of volunteers to have collected litter in one place on one day is 50,405, along the coastline of California on October 2, 1993. The record was set in conjunction with International Coastal Cleanup.

LONGEST BUCKET CHAIN
On August 5, 1997, 6,569 boys representing Boy Scouts of America made a bucket chain that stretched for 2 miles 59 yd. at the National Scout Jamboree, Fort A. P. Hills, Virginia. They started with 164 gallons and finished with 149 gallons.

BIGGEST UNSUPPORTED CIRCLE
The greatest number of people seated without a chair in an unsupported circle was 10,323, all employees of the Nissan Motor Co., at Komazawa Stadium, Tokyo, Japan on October 23, 1982.

MOST DOMINOES TOPPLED
On January 2, 1988, 30 students at Delft, Eindhoven and Twente Technical Universities in the Netherlands set up 1.5 million dominoes. Of these, 1,138,101 were toppled by one push and only 117,889 remained standing.

BIGGEST ROPE PULLED
A 564-ft.-4-in.-long rice straw rope — the biggest made from natural materials — was pulled at the Giant Tug-of-War at the annual Naha City Festival, Okinawa, Japan, in 1995.

TALLEST SCARECROW
A 103-ft.-6¼-in.-tall scarecrow called "Stretch II" was constructed by the Speers family and 15 helpers at the Paris Fall Fair, Ontario, Canada, on September 2, 1989.

LONGEST DAISY CHAIN
On May 27, 1985, the villagers of Good Easter, Chelmsford, England constructed a 1-mile-3-ft.-long daisy chain over seven hours.

BIGGEST ORIGAMI MODEL
A paper crane with a record wingspan of 117 ft. 2 in. was folded by residents of the district of Gunma at Maebashi, Japan, on October 28, 1995. The 52-ft.-6-in. crane took six hours to make.

LONGEST STUFFED TOY
A 556-yard-long Asian dragon was created at the National Stadium, Singapore, on September 28, 1997 to mark the 50th anniversary of Singapore Airlines (SIA). The body of the dragon, which was made by volunteers from SIA and MINDS (Movement for the Intellectually Disabled of Singapore), was stuffed with foam rubber by representatives of both organizations in front of 20,000 spectators after a charity walk-a-jog that raised a total of $121,294 for MINDS.

TALLEST SANDCASTLE
A record-breaking 21-ft.-6-in.-tall sandcastle was constructed by a team led by Joe Maize, George Pennock and Ted Siebert in Harrison Hot Springs, British Columbia, Canada on September 26, 1993. The team used only their hands, buckets and shovels.

LONGEST KISS

Mark and Roberta Griswold of Allen Park, Michigan kissed continuously for a record 29 hours at the "Breathsavers Longest Kiss Challenge" at the Harley Davidson Cafe, New York City, March 24–25, 1998. They remained standing without rest breaks throughout their attempt. The Griswolds captured the record and the Grand Prize, a trip to Paris.

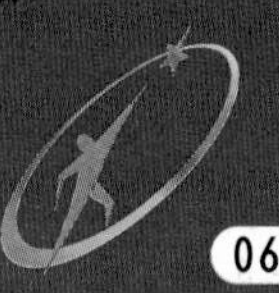

early starters

YOUNGEST DIRECTOR, WRITER AND PRODUCER

The thriller *Lex the Wonderdog* (1972) was written, produced and directed by Sydney Ling at the age of just 13, making him the youngest-ever director of a professionally made, feature-length movie.

YOUNGEST HOLLYWOOD MOVIE PRODUCER

Steven Paul wrote, produced, directed and appeared in the romantic comedy *Falling In Love Again* (1980) – which starred Eliott Gould, Susannah York and Michelle Pfeiffer – at the age of 20, making him the youngest Hollywood producer.

YOUNGEST TO HAVE A NO. 1 HIT

Jordy (Jordy Lemoine) was four and a half years old when he reached No. 1 in the French charts with "Dur Dur d'Etre Bébé (It's Tough To Be A Baby)." The song later entered the US chart. In February 1994, France's main TV channel, TF1, and RTL, the country's largest radio station, banned Jordy, saying that his parents, Claude Lemoine, a songwriter, and Patricia Lemoine, a singer, were exploiting him.

YOUNGEST PERFORMER TO RECEIVE STAR BILLING

Leroy Overacker, whose screen name was Baby Leroy, starred opposite Maurice Chevalier in *Bedtime Story* (1933) at the age of six months.

YOUNGEST PERSON TO BE INCLUDED IN *WHO'S WHO*

The youngest ever entrant in *Who's Who* (excluding people who qualify for inclusion because of their hereditary title) was the concert violinist Yehudi Menuhin (now Lord Menuhin), a child prodigy who first appeared in the 1932 edition of the book at the age of 15.

YOUNGEST GRADUATE

Michael Kearney began studying for an Associate of Science degree at Santa Rosa Junior College in California at the age of 6 years 7 months in September 1990. He became the youngest graduate in June 1994, at the age of 10 years 4 months, when he obtained his BA in anthropology from the University of South Alabama.

YOUNGEST NOBEL PRIZE WINNERS

Theodore W. Richards won the 1914 Chemistry Prize for work done when he was 23, as did Professor Sir Lawrence Bragg, the winner of the 1915 Nobel Prize for Physics.

YOUNGEST PEOPLE TO RECEIVE BRAVERY AWARDS

Kristina Stragauskaite of Skirmantiskes, Lithuania was awarded a medal "For Courage in Fire" when she was just 4 years 252 days old, after saving the lives of her younger brother and sister in a fire that broke out at their home while their parents were out in April 1989.

YOUNGEST CHESS GRANDMASTER

On March 22, 1997, Etienne Bacrot of France became the youngest person to qualify as an International Grand Master, winning the masters tournament at Enghien-les-Bains, near Paris, France, at the age of 14 years 59 days. Etienne, who began playing chess at the age of four, beat the previous record set by Hungarian Peter Leko, who won the title of Grand Master at the age of 14 years six months in 1994.

The youngest person to receive an official gallantry award was Julius Rosenberg of Winnipeg, Canada, who was awarded the Medal of Bravery in March 1994 for stopping a black bear that attacked his three-year-old sister in September 1992. He was five at the time of the incident.

YOUNGEST PERSON TO VISIT BOTH POLES

British boy Robert Schumann (seen left) went to the North Pole at the age of 10 on April 6, 1992 and the South Pole at the age of 11 on December 29, 1993. On the first trip he arrived and left by air, while on the second he arrived by mountain bike (having flown to within a short distance of the pole) and left by air. On May 1, 1997, eight-year-old Alicia Hempleman-Adams of Swindon, England became the youngest person ever to visit the North Pole. Alicia flew to the pole to meet her father David, who, after a 600-mile, 57-day journey across ice, had become the first person to complete the grand slam – all four poles: magnetic and geographic, north and south – and climb the highest peak in every continent. The challenge took him 18 years to complete, and it was his third attempt at the North Pole following unsuccessful trips in 1983 and 1997.

YOUNGEST PERSON TO MAKE A SOLO CIRCUMNAVIGATION

David Dicks of Australia was 18 years 41 days old when he completed his circumnavigation of the globe in 264 days 16 hr. 49 min. on November 16, 1996.

YOUNGEST PERSON TO MAKE A SOLO TRANSATLANTIC CROSSING

David Sanderman was 17 years 176 days old when he made a 43-day crossing in 1976.

YOUNGEST WORLD RECORD-BREAKERS

The youngest person to have ever broken a nonmechanical world record was swimmer Gertrude Ederle, who was 12 years

298 days old when she set a record for the women's 880-yd freestyle in Indianapolis, Indiana on August 17, 1919. Her time was 13 min. 19 sec.

YOUNGEST WORLD CHAMPIONS
The youngest ever successful competitor in a world title event was a French boy — whose name is not recorded — who coxed the Netherlands' Olympic rowing pair in Paris, France on August 26, 1900. The boy was not more than 10 years of age and may have been as young as seven.

Fu Mingxia (China) won the women's world title for platform diving at Perth, Australia on January 4, 1991, at the age of 12 years 141 days.

YOUNGEST INTERNATIONAL
Tennis player Joy Foster was eight years old when she represented Jamaica in the West Indies Championships at Port of Spain, Trinidad in August 1958, making her the world's youngest ever international.

YOUNGEST PERSON TO PERFORM QUADRUPLE SOMERSAULTS
The youngest person to have achieved a quadruple somersault was 15-year-old Pak Yong Suk of North Korea's Pyongyang Circus troupe, during the Monte Carlo Circus Festival in Monaco in February 1997.

YOUNGEST CONSCRIPTS
In March 1976, President Francisco Macías Nguema of Equatorial Guinea decreed compulsory military service for all boys aged between seven and 14. Any parents refusing to hand over their son would be "imprisoned or shot."

YOUNGEST SOLDIERS
The Brazilian military hero and statesman Luís Alves de Lima e Silva, Marshall Duke of Caxias, entered his infantry regiment at the age of five in 1808.

Fernando Inchauste Montalvo, the son of a major in the Bolivian air force, went to the front with his father on his fifth birthday during the war between Bolivia and Paraguay from 1932 to 1935. Montalvo had received military training and was subject to military discipline.

YOUNGEST JUDGE
John Payton took office as Justice of the Peace in Plano, Texas at the age of 18 years 11 months in January 1991.

YOUNGEST MARRIED COUPLE
In 1986, it was reported that an 11-month-old boy had been married to a three-month-old girl in Aminpur, Bangladesh. The marriage had been arranged in order to end a 20-year feud between two families.

YOUNGEST AUTOBIOGRAPHER
Drew Barrymore, a member of the famous Barrymore family, was born on February 22, 1975 and co-wrote her autobiography *Little Girl Lost* in 1989, at the age of 14, making her the world's youngest published autobiographer. The star had dropped out of school and entered a rehabilitation clinic at the age of 13, after the pressures of her celebrity childhood became too much. Barrymore made her screen debut at the age of 11 months in a television commercial for Puppy Choice Dog Food, made her TV movie debut in *Suddenly Love* (1978) and achieved international stardom at the age of seven, when she starred in *E.T.: the Extra Terrestrial* (1982), the sci-fi blockbuster directed by her godfather Steven Spielberg. By the time she was 21, the actress had posed nude for an *Interview* cover and for *Playboy*, played Amy Fisher in *The Amy Fisher Story* (1993), and married and then divorced after less than two months. In 1996, she appeared in a cameo role in Wes Craven's *Scream*, the top-grossing horror movie of all time. By May 1998, she had appeared in a total of 37 films for television and the big screen, and was seen most recently in *The Wedding Singer* (1998).

golden oldies

OLDEST PERSON TO HAVE A NO. 1
What a Wonderful World gave jazz trumpeter and singer Louis Armstrong a No. 1 hit in the UK in 1968 and was No. 1 in several countries as late as 1970, when he was 69. Armstrong, whose nickname was Satchmo, was almost 63 when he had his first No. 1, with *Hello Dolly!* in 1964. He had made a name for himself in the 1920s with his Chicago recordings with the Hot Five and the Hot Seven.

OLDEST PARACHUTISTS
Hildegarde Ferrera became the oldest ever parachutist when she made a tandem parachute jump at age 99 in Mokuleia, Hawaii on February 17, 1996.

The world's oldest ever male parachutist was Edward Royds-Jones, who parachuted in tandem at the age of 95 years 170 days in Dunkeswell, Devon, England on July 2, 1994.

Sylvia Brett became the oldest female solo parachutist at the age of 80 years 166 days. She made a jump in Cranfield, England on August 23, 1986.

OLDEST CRESTA RUN RIDER
Prince Constantin of Liechtenstein rode the Cresta Run tobogganing course at the age of 85 on February 11, 1997.

OLDEST TIGHTROPE WALKER
William Ivy Baldwin became the world's oldest ever tightrope walker when he crossed the South Boulder Canyon, Colorado on a 320-foot high wire with a 125-foot drop on his 82nd birthday on July 31, 1948.

OLDEST HOT-AIR BALLOONIST
Florence Laine of New Zealand flew in a balloon at the age of 102 in Cust, New Zealand, on September 26, 1996.

OLDEST BOARDSAILER
Charles Ruijter (Netherlands) took up boardsailing in 1978 at the age of 63 and still sails in the lakes around Eindhoven, Netherlands at the age of 83.

OLDEST OLYMPIC MEDALLIST
Oscar Swahn from Sweden was in the winning Running Deer shooting team at the age of 64 in 1912 and was a silver medalist in the same event in 1920, at the age of 72.

OLDEST PERSON TO HAVE VISITED BOTH POLES
Major Will Lacy from the United Kingdom travelled to the North Pole on April 9, 1990 at the age of 82 and to the South Pole on December 20, 1991 at the age of 84. On both trips he arrived and left by light aircraft.

OLDEST PEOPLE TO HAVE CLIMBED MT EVEREST
Spanish guitar- and violin-maker Ramón Blanco, who has lived in Venezuela since 1970, became the oldest person ever to reach the summit of Mt. Everest on October 7, 1993, at the age of 60 years 160 days.

The oldest woman to climb Mt. Everest was Yasuko Namba of Japan, at the age of 47 in 1996.

OLDEST PERSON TO FLY
Charlotte Hughes of Redcar, England was given a flight on Concorde from London, England to New York City as a 110th birthday present in 1987. She flew again in 1992, aged 115.

OLDEST PILOTS
Burnet Patten of Victoria, Australia obtained his flying license on May 2, 1997 at the age of 80, making him the oldest person ever to qualify as a pilot.

LONGEST MARRIAGE IN THE UNITED STATES
Paul and Mary Onesi, who are now 101 and 93 years old respectively, are seen (top) at their wedding in Clymer, Pennsylvania in 1917. In January 1998, they celebrated their 80th anniversary (bottom), becoming the longest-married couple in the United States. For the past 51 years, the couple, who never celebrate Valentine's Day, have lived in Niagara Falls, America's "honeymoon capital."

OLDEST PERSON IN SPACE
Senator John Glenn is set to become the oldest person ever to visit space when he takes part in the space shuttle mission in October 1998. Glenn, who was born in 1921, first achieved fame in February 1962, when he became the first US astronaut to orbit Earth. A former marine pilot who had served in both World War II and the Korean War, he entered politics in the 1970s and was elected Democratic senator for Ohio in 1974. Glenn is pictured here outside the Levette research laboratory, addressing the media in his space shuttle suit, shortly before beginning NASA space shuttle training at Brooks Air Force Base Research Laboratory's centrifuge in February 1998. The centrifuge is used by NASA space shuttle astronauts to simulate the *g*-forces that are experienced by astronauts during a shuttle launch, and Glenn's training there will help to prepare him for the shuttle mission.

Clarence Cornish of Indianapolis, Indiana flew aircraft until he was 97. He died 18 days after his last flight on December 4, 1995.

OLDEST WALL-OF-DEATH RIDER
The oldest rider to regularly perform in public is 71-year-old Jerry De Roye, who rides a 1927 Indian Type 101 "Scout".

OLDEST GROOM
Harry Stevens was 103 years old when he married 84-year-old Thelma Lucas at the Caravilla Retirement Home, Beloit, Wisconsin on December 3, 1984.

OLDEST BRIDE
Minnie Munro became the world's oldest known bride when she married Dudley Reid at the age of 102 in Point Clare, New South Wales, Australia, on May 31, 1991. The groom was 83.

OLDEST DIVORCED COUPLE
The highest combined age of a divorcing couple is 188, by Ida Stern (91) and her husband Simon (97) of Milwaukee, Wisconsin in February 1984.

LONGEST MARRIAGES
Cousins Sir Temulji Bhicaji Nariman and Lady Nariman from India were married when they were both five years old in 1853. Their marriage lasted 86 years, until Sir Temulji's death at age 91 years 11 months in 1940.

Records show Lazarus Rowe and Molly Webber, who were both born in 1725, to have married in 1743. Molly died in June 1829 in Limington, Maine after 86 years of marriage.

LONGEST ENGAGEMENT
Octavio Guillén and Adriana Martínez from Mexico finally got married in June 1969, after a 67-year engagement. Both were 82 years old when they wed.

LONGEST CAREERS
Shigechiyo Izumi, who lived to a greater age than any other man on record, began working with draft animals at a sugar mill at Isen, Tokunoshima, Japan in 1872 and retired as a sugar-cane farmer in 1970, 98 years later, when he was 105 years old. He died at age 120 in 1986.

Johann Heinrich Karl Thieme, the sexton of Aldenburg, Germany, was a gravedigger for a record 50 years, during which time he dug 23,311 graves. In 1826, his understudy dug his grave.

NATIONAL TREASURES
Kin ("Gold") and Gin ("Silver") Kanie became Japan's most famous twins in 1992 when they celebrated their 100th birthday, prompting the mayor of their town, Nagoya, to call a press conference reminding people of the need to respect the elderly. Since then, the twins have made a number of television appearances and advertisements and have been interviewed many times. Now 105 years old, they remain in very good health.

players and games

FASTEST BARROW RACERS
The fastest time in a 1-mile wheelbarrow race is 4 min. 48.51 sec., by Piet Pitzer and Jaco Erasmus at Transvalia High School, Vanderbijlpark, South Africa on October 3, 1987.

FASTEST BED RACERS
The fastest time in the 2-mile-56-yd. Knaresborough (England) Bed Race is 12 min. 9 sec., by the Vibroplant team in June 1990.

FASTEST PANCAKE RACE
The fastest time in the annual 420-yard pancake race held in Melbourne, Australia is 59.5 seconds, by Jan Stickland on February 19, 1985.

FASTEST SNAIL
The all-time record-holder at the annual World Snail Racing Championships, held in Congham, England, is Archie, trained by Carl Banham. His best time over the 13-inch circular course was 2 min. 20 sec.

FASTEST COAL CARRIER
David Jones carried a 110-pound bag over the 3,321-foot course in Gawthorpe, England in a record-breaking 4 min. 6 sec. in April 1991.

BEST LOG ROLLER
The most International Championships won is 10, by Jubiel Wickheim of Shawnigan Lake, British Columbia, Canada, between 1956 and 1969.

FASTEST BOG SNORKELER
Steve Madeline has won the annual World Bog Snorkeling Championship at Llanwrtyd Wells, Wales on a record two occasions, in 1989 and 1994. Contestants swim two lengths of a 60-m (196-ft.-10-in.) bog filled with weeds, leeches and salamanders.

MOST GAMES OF HOPSCOTCH
The greatest number of hopscotch games successfully completed in 24 hours is 434, by Ashrita Furman (US), at the Westin Regina Hotel, Cancun, Mexico, January 12–13, 1998.

BIGGEST GAME OF MUSICAL CHAIRS
The biggest game of musical chairs involved 8,238 people at the Anglo-Chinese School, Singapore on August 5, 1989.

BIGGEST GAME OF PASS THE PARCEL
The largest game of pass the parcel involved 3,464 people removing 2,000 wrappers from a 5 x 3 x 3-foot parcel in two hours at Alton Towers, England on November 8, 1992. The event was organized by Parcelforce International, and the gift, an electronic keyboard, was won by Sylvia Wilshaw.

LONGEST GIANT TOP SPIN
A team of 25 people from the Mizushima Plant of Kawasaki Steel Works in Okayama, Japan, spun a giant top 6 ft. 6 3/4 in. in height, 8 ft. 6 1/4 in. in diameter and 793 lb. 10 oz. in weight for 1 hr. 21 min. 35 sec. on November 3, 1986.

MOST YO-YO LOOPS
Eddy McDonald (Canada) completed 21,663 loops with a yo-yo in three hours in Boston, Massachusetts on October 14, 1990. He had set a one-hour record of 8,437 loops in 1990.

BIGGEST YO-YO
A yo-yo with a diameter of 10 ft. 4 in. and a weight of 897 pounds was devised by J. N. Nichols (Vimto) Ltd. and constructed by engineering students at Stockport College, England. It was launched by crane from 187 feet in Wythenshawe, England on August 1, 1993 and yo-yoed about four times.

BIGGEST JIGSAW PUZZLES
The world's largest jigsaw puzzle measured 51,484 square feet and consisted of 43,924 pieces. Assembled on July 8, 1992, it was devised by Centre Socio-Culturel d'Endoume in Marseille, France.

A jigsaw puzzle consisting of a record 204,484 pieces was made by BCF Holland b.v. of Almelo, Netherlands, and assembled by students from the local Gravenvoorde School from May 25 to June 1, 1991. The completed puzzle measured 1,036 square feet.

TALLEST TOY BRICK STRUCTURE
An 82-ft.-2-in. toy brick pyramid was built by a team of 800 people to commemorate the inauguration of Taiwanese president Lee Teng-hui. The tower burned down almost immediately after it was constructed in Taipei, Taiwan in May 1996.

MOST WORLD TIDDLYWINKS TITLES
Larry Kahn (US) won the singles title 16 times from 1983 to 1997 and the pairs title nine times between 1978 and 1997.

Geoff Myers and Andy Purvis won seven consecutive pairs titles from 1991 to 1995.

HIGHEST TIDDLYWINK JUMP
The high-jump record is 11 ft. 5 in., by Adrian Jones, David Smith and Ed Wynn of Cambridge University Tiddlywinks Club, England, all on October 21, 1989.

LONGEST TIDDLYWINK JUMP
A 31-ft.-3-in. jump was made by Ben Soares (St. Andrews Tiddlywinks Society) in January 1995.

CRICKET SPITTING
Every year, thousands of people visit the annual Bug Bowl at Purdue University in West Lafayette, Indiana. The three-day insect celebration includes a cricket-spitting contest and cockroach racing. The Bug Bowl was founded by the university's professor of entomology Tom Turpin in 1990 as a way to stir up campus interest in entomology. Word spread and the event went public, attracting 1,500 bug-cravers in its first year. The following year, the Bug Bowl was formalized, and in 1997 it was attended by more than 12,000 people. In April 1997, 11-year-old Matt Criswell, seen left, competed in the first cricket-spitting contest, in which contestants had to spit dead crickets as far as possible. On June 26, 1998, Danny Capps set a new indoor cricket spitting record of 32 ft. 1/2 in. on the Fox television series *Guinness World Records™: Primetime.*

MOST TIDDLYWINKS POTTED
The record for potting winks in relay is 41 in three minutes, by Patrick Barrie, Nick Inglis, Geoff Myers and Andy Purvis of the Cambridge University Tiddlywinks Club, on October 21, 1989 and January 14, 1995.

FASTEST GAME OF SOLITAIRE
Stephen Twigge played a game of solitaire lasting 10 seconds at Scissett Baths, England on August 2, 1991.

HIGHEST SCRABBLE SCORES
The highest competitive single turn score recorded is 392, by Dr. Saladin Karl Khoshnaw in Manchester, England in April 1982. He laid down "CAZIQUES," which means "native chiefs of West Indian aborigines."

The highest score achieved on the opening move is 124, by Sam Kantimathi in Portland, Oregon in July 1993. He laid "BEZIQUE," which is a card game.

MOST WORLD CHECKERS TITLES
Walter Hellman (US) won a record-breaking eight world titles during his tenure as World Champion from 1948 to 1975.

MOST WORLD CHESS TITLES
The USSR won the biennial men's team title (Olympiad) a record 18 times between 1952 and 1990 and the women's team title a record 11 times between 1957 and 1986.

FEWEST GAMES LOST BY A WORLD CHESS CHAMPION
José Raúl Capablanca (Cuba) lost only 34 games out of 571 in his adult career from 1909 to 1939. He was unbeaten from February 10, 1916 to March 21, 1924 (63 games) and was World Champion from 1921 to 1927.

YOUNGEST WORLD CHESS CHAMPIONS
Gary Kasparov (USSR, now Russia) won the title on November 9, 1985 at the age of 22 years 210 days.

Maya Grigoryevna Chiburdanidze (USSR, now Georgia) won the women's title at age 17 in 1978.

SLOWEST CHESS MOVES
The slowest move played since time clocks were introduced was 2 hr. 20 min., by Francisco Torres Trois on his seventh move against Luis Santos in Vigo, Spain in 1980.

The slowest reported move in an official event before the use of time clocks is reputed to have been made by Louis Paulsen (Germany) against Paul Morphy (US) at the first American Chess Congress, New York, October 29, 1857. The game ended in a draw on move 56 after 15 hours of play, of which Paulsen used about 11 hours.

The most moves known in a Master game was 269, in the tie between Ivan Nikolic and Goran Arsovic in Belgrade, Yugoslavia in February 1989. The game lasted 20 hr. 15 min.

FASTEST BATHTUB RACERS
Above, a replica bathtub is raced off the coast of Vancouver, Canada. The record for a 36-mile bathtub race over water is 1 hr. 22 min. 27 sec., by Greg Mutton at the Grafton Jacaranda Festival in New South Wales, Australia on November 8, 1987. Tubs must be no longer than 75 inches and must have 6-hp motors. The World Championship Bathtub Races are held every July. Competitors race from Nanaimo on Vancouver Island across the strait to Vancouver, Canada.

The highest competitive game score is 1,049, by Phil Appleby in June 1989. His opponent scored 253, giving Appleby a record 796-point margin of victory.

The highest score in an Open tournament is 770, by Mark Landsberg (US) in Pasadena, California on June 13, 1993.

MOST CHECKERS OPPONENTS
Ronald "Suki" King (Barbados) played 385 simultaneous games, and won all of them, at the Houston International Festival in Texas, on April 26, 1998. King's attempt lasted for 3 hr. 44 min.

LONGEST-HELD CHESS TITLES
The record for the longest ever undisputed tenure as World Chess Champion was 26 years 337 days, by Dr. Emanuel Lasker of Germany, who held the title from 1894 to 1921.

The record for the longest-held women's World Chess Championship title was set by Vera Francevna Stevenson-Menchik of Czechoslovakia (later Great Britain), whose tenure lasted from 1927 until her death in 1944. She successfully defended the title a record-breaking seven times.

MOST CHESS OPPONENTS
The most consecutive games played is 686 with 16 defeats, by Gert Jan Ludden (Netherlands) over 29½ hours in Gouda, Netherlands, October 24–25, 1997.

The record for the greatest number of games to have been played simultaneously is 310, with just two defeats, by Ulf Andersson (Sweden) in Alvsjö, Sweden, from January 6 to January 7, 1996.

driving and riding

HEAVIEST VOLUME OF TRAFFIC
The most heavily traveled road is Interstate 405 (San Diego Freeway) in Orange County, California, which carries 331,000 vehicles a day. The 1,584-yard stretch between Garden Grove Freeway and Seal Beach Boulevard has a peak-hour volume of 25,500 vehicles. The road runs through a built-up area of West Los Angeles to the beach. California has 19 million licensed drivers.

HIGHEST AUTO FLIGHT
In February 1998, stunt driver Brian Carson of Tarzana, California broke his own 298-foot "auto flight" record with a 314-foot flight in a specially-constructed sedan, at a speed of 93 mph. The stunt took place at the Orleans Hotel and Casino in Las Vegas, Nevada.

FASTEST REVERSE DRIVE
The highest average speed achieved in a nonstop reverse drive exceeding 500 miles was 36.30 mph, by John Smith, who drove a 1983 Chevrolet Caprice Classic 501 miles in 13 hr. 48 min. at the I-94 Speedway, Fergus Falls, Minnesota on August 11, 1996.

FASTEST SPEED REACHED ON TWO SIDE WHEELS
Göran Eliason (Sweden) achieved a record speed of 112.62 mph over a 100-m (328-foot) flying start on the two wheels of a Volvo 850 Turbo. The record was set in Såtenäs, Sweden on April 19, 1997 and Eliason set a world speed record of 98.90 mph for the flying kilometer on the same occasion.

LONGEST DRIVE ON TWO SIDE WHEELS
Bengt Norberg of Äppelbo, Sweden drove a Mitsubishi Colt GTi-16V on two side wheels nonstop for 192.873 miles in a time of 7 hr. 15 min. 50 sec. He also drove 27.842 miles in one hour at Rattvik Horse Track, Sweden on May 24, 1989.

LONGEST RAMP JUMP IN A CAR
The longest ever ramp jump in a car, with the car landing on its wheels and being driven on, is 232 feet, by Jacqueline De Creed in a 1967 Ford Mustang at Santa Pod Raceway, Bedfordshire, England on April 3, 1983.

LONGEST RAMP JUMPS ON MOTORCYCLES
The longest distance jumped by a rider on a motorcycle is 251 feet, by Doug Danger (US) on a 1991 Honda CR500 in Loudon, New Hampshire in 1991.

The longest distance ever jumped by a woman on a motorcycle is 190 ft. 2 in., over 12 trucks, by Fiona Beale of Derby, England on August 14, 1997. She was riding a Kawasaki KX500.

LONGEST WALL OF DEATH FEAT
The greatest ever endurance feat on a wall of death was 7 hr. 0 min. 13 sec., by Martin Blume in Berlin, Germany, on April 16, 1983. He rode a Yamaha XS 400 over 12,000 laps on a wall with a diameter of 33 feet, averaging 30 mph over the 181 miles 880 yd.

MOST PEOPLE ON ONE MOTORBIKE
The most people ever on one machine was 47, by the Army Corps of Brasília, Brazil, on a 1200cc Harley Davidson in December 1995.

BIGGEST MOTORCYCLE PYRAMID
The "Dare Devils" team from the Signals Corps of the Indian army created a pyramid of 140 men on 11 motorcycles, without using straps, harnesses or any other aids, and traveled a distance of 218 yards in Jabalpur, India on February 14, 1996.

FASTEST MOTORCYCLE WHEELIE
The highest speed attained on a back wheel of a motorcycle is 167.8 mph, by Patrik Furstehoff (Sweden) on a Suzuki GSXR 1100 at Bruntingthorpe Proving Ground, Leicester, England on April 26, 1994.

FURTHEST DISTANCE TRAVELLED ON A MOTORCYCLE WHEELIE
Yasuyuki Kudo covered 205 miles 1,232 yd. nonstop on the rear wheel of his Honda TLM220R motorcycle at the Japan Automobile Research Institute proving ground on May 5, 1991.

LONGEST BICYCLE WHEELIE
The longest ever bicycle wheelie lasted for 10 hr. 40 min. 8 sec. It was achieved by Leandro Henrique Basseto in Madaguari, Brazil on December 2, 1995.

FASTEST CAMPER TOW
The record speed for a camper tow is 126.77 mph, for a

Roadstar camper towed by a 1990 Ford EA Falcon sedan driven by Charlie Kovacs, at Mangalore Airfield, Seymour, Victoria, Australia on April 18, 1991.

LONGEST TAXI RIDE
The longest taxi ride on record covered 21,691 miles from London, England to Cape Town, South Africa and back, at a cost of £40,210 ($62,908). It was made by Jeremy Levine, Mark Aylett and Carlos Arrese from June 3 to October 17, 1994.

LONGEST SKID MARKS
The skid marks made by the jet-powered *Spirit of America*, driven by Craig Breedlove, when the car went out of control at Bonneville Salt Flats, Utah on October 15, 1964, were almost 6 miles long.

WORST ROAD ACCIDENT
At least 176 people died when a gasoline tanker exploded in the Salang Tunnel, Afghanistan in November 1982. Unconfirmed estimates put the death toll at *c.* 1,100.

MOST ROAD DEATHS
Latvia is the country with the highest fatality rate in road accidents, with 34.7 deaths per 100,000 of the population.

LONGEST TRAFFIC JAMS
The longest known traffic jam stretched 109 miles from Lyon towards Paris, France on February 16, 1980.

A traffic jam with a record 1.5 million cars was reported on the East–West German border on April 12, 1990.

LONGEST JOURNEY BY CAR
Since October 16, 1984, Emil and Liliana Schmidt (Germany) have traveled a record 280,609 miles through a total of 117 countries in a Toyota Landcruiser.

FASTEST DRIVE OVER SIX CONTINENTS
The fastest drive over six continents, with a total traveled distance of more than an equator's length (24,901 miles), lasted 39 days 7 hr. 55 min. It was achieved by Navin Kapila, Man Bahadur and Vijay Raman, who left New Delhi, India in their Hindustan "Contessa Classic" on November 22, 1992 and returned on December 31, 1992.

OLDEST DRIVER
Layne Hall of Silver Creek, New York was issued a driving license on June 15, 1989, when, according to the date on the license, he was 109 years old. He died the following year, but his death certificate gave his age as 105.

MOTORCYCLE JUMPING
Robbie Knievel, the son of legendary stunt man Evel Knievel, soared more than 230 feet over 30 limousines at the Tropicana Hotel, Las Vegas, Nevada in February 1998, reaching a speed of almost 100 mph. The stunt was part of a two-hour television special. The 35-year-old gained fame in 1989, when he jumped the 160-foot fountains at Caesar's Palace, Las Vegas — a feat that nearly killed his father. Robbie is now said to be planning jumps over the reflecting pool in front of the Washington Monument and across the Grand Canyon. He followed in his father's footsteps from an early age: as a nine-year-old he mounted a Harley Davidson 10cc motorcycle, and while his father watched, jumped 5 feet from ramp to ramp at a practice field.

CIRCUMNAVIGATION BY CAR
The record for the first and fastest circumnavigation of the world by car, under the applicable rules in 1989 and 1991, embracing more than an equator's length of driving (24,901.41 road miles), is held by Mohammed Salahuddin Choudhury and his wife Neena of Calcutta, India. The first circumnavigation took 69 days 19 hr. 5 min., from September 9 to November 17. The Choudhurys drove a 1989 Hindustan Contessa Classic, starting and finishing in Delhi, India.

epic journeys I

FASTEST TRANSATLANTIC ROW
New Zealanders Phil Stubbs and Robert Hamill raise their national flag to celebrate breaking the transatlantic rowing record by a wide margin. They reached Port St. Charles, Barbados on November 22, 1997, after setting out from Tenerife 41 days before. The previous record for rowing across the Atlantic was 73 days, by Britons Sean Crowley and Mike Nestor in 1986.

LONGEST NONSTOP FLIGHT
The longest ever unrefueled nonstop flight was by Robert Ferry (US), who flew a Hughes YOH-6A 2,213 miles 132 yd. from Culver City, California to Ormond Beach, Florida in April 1966.

LONGEST JOURNEYS MADE BY SCHEDULED FLIGHT
The fastest round-the-world journey taking in antipodal points was by former Scottish rugby union captain David Sole, who travelled 25,917 miles in a time of 64 hr 2 min. from May 2 to May 5, 1995.

Brother Michael Bartlett of Sandy, England flew around the world on scheduled flights in 58 hr. 44 min. in 1995, taking in the airports closest to antipodal points and covering 25,816 miles.

The fastest circumnavigation using scheduled flights under Fédération Aéronautique Internationale regulations was 44 hr. 6 min., by David J. Springbett (GB). He traveled 23,068 miles from January 8 to January 10, 1980.

FASTEST HELICOPTER CIRCUMNAVIGATION
Ron Bower and John Williams (both US) flew around the world in a Bell helicopter in 17 days 6 hr. 14 min. 25 sec. in 1996.

HIGHEST ALTITUDE REACHED IN A HOT-AIR BALLOON
Per Lindstrand (GB) reached 64,997 feet in a Colt 600 over Texas in 1988.

GREATEST DISTANCE BY BALLOON
In January 1997, Steve Fossett (US) flew a record 10,406 miles from St. Louis, Missouri to Sultanpur, India as part of an aborted attempt to fly around the world. Fossett ascended to 24,000 feet, exceeded speeds of 100 mph and endured storms and subzero temperatures in his $300,000 balloon *Free Spirit*.

FASTEST ATLANTIC CROSSING
The record for the fastest ever crossing of the Atlantic is 58 hr. 34 min., by the 222-foot powerboat *Destriero* in 1992.

FASTEST PACIFIC CROSSING
The fastest ever crossing from Yokohama, Japan to Long Beach, California, (a total distance of 4,840 nautical miles) was 6 days 1 hr. 27 min., by the 50,315-ton container ship *Sea-Land Commerce* in 1973. Its average speed during the trip was 33.27 knots.

FASTEST TRANSATLANTIC SAILS
The record for the fastest west–east crewed sail is 6 days 13 hr. 3 min. 32 sec., by the 75-foot catamaran sloop *Jet Services 5* between Ambrose Light Tower and Lizard Point, Cornwall, England from June 2 to June 9, 1990. The skipper was Serge Madec (France).

The fastest west–east solo sail was 7 days 2 hr. 34 min. 42 sec., by the 60-foot trimaran *Primagaz* between Ambrose Light Tower and Lizard Point, Cornwall, England from June 27 to July 4, 1994. The skipper was Laurent Bourgnon (France).

The record for the fastest ever east–west crewed sail is 9 days 8 hr. 58 min. 20 sec., by the trimaran *Primagaz* between Plymouth, Devon, England and Newport, Rhode Island, from June 5 to June 14, 1994. The skippers were Laurent Bourgnon (France) and Cam Lewis (US).

The fastest ever east–west solo sail was 10 days 9 hr., by the

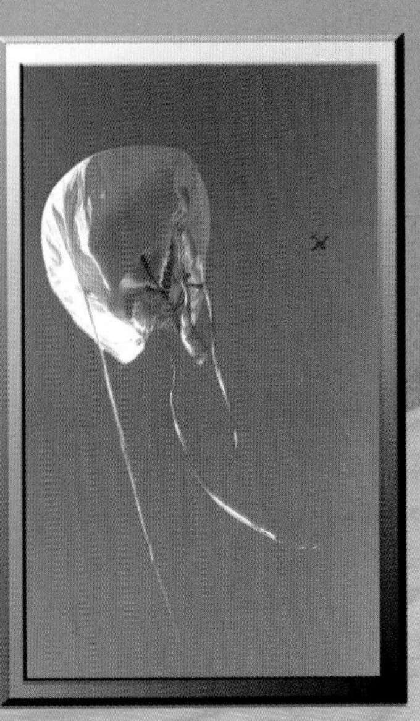

BALLOON CIRCUMNAVIGATION
Since January 1997, there have been eight attempts to circumnavigate the world nonstop by hot-air balloon. All the teams failed to capture aviation's final "Holy Grail," but their daring and courage captured the world's attention.

In January 1997, American businessman and adventurer Steve Fossett set the distance record for balloon flight, traveling 10,406 miles from St. Louis, Missouri to Sultanpur, India.

In the same year, British businessman Richard Branson announced his plan to make the journey in 18 days with two other crew members. Branson held records for flying the Atlantic and the Pacific, but his 1997 attempt ended dramatically less than 48 hours into the journey. Undaunted, Branson prepared an attempt for December 1997, but bad luck plagued his team again; their balloon was blown from its moorings and irreparably damaged by a freak gust of wind.

Another record was set in February 1998, when the three-man crew of the *Breitling Orbiter II*, led by Dr. Bertrand Piccard, achieved a flight duration record of 9 days 17 hr. 15 min.

FIRST UNAIDED SOLO TREK
In January 1997, explorer Boerge Ousland (Norway) became the first person ever to cross Antarctica alone and unsupported. His 64-day trek began at Berkner Island and ended at Scott Base, a New Zealand station in Antarctica. During the trip, Ousland towed a 400-pound sled loaded with his supplies and used skis and a sail to take advantage of wind currents.

60-foot trimaran *Fleury Michon (IX)* between Plymouth, England and Newport, Rhode Island, June 5–15, 1988. The skipper was Philippe Poupon (France).

FASTEST TRANSPACIFIC SAILS
The fastest crewed sail was 16 days 17 hr. 21 min. 19 sec., by the 60-foot trimaran *Lakota* from Yokohama, Japan to San Francisco, August 14–31, 1995. It was sailed by Steve Fossett and three crew (US).

The fastest solo sail was 20 days 9 hr. 52 min. 59 sec., by the *Lakota*, skippered by Steve Fossett between Yokohama, Japan and San Francisco, August 5–24, 1996.

FASTEST CIRCUMNAVIGATIONS
The fastest crewed nonstop marine circumnavigation was 74 days 22 hr. 17 min., by the 92-foot catamaran *Enza*, which was sailed by Peter Blake (NZ) and Robin Knox-Johnston (GB) from Ushant, France, between January 16 and April 1, 1994.

The fastest solo nonstop marine circumnavigation was 109 days 8 hr. 48 min., by the 60-foot monohull *Ecureuil d'Aquitaine II*, sailed by Titouan Lamazou (France) from Les Sables d'Olonne, France between November 1989 and March 1990.

DEEPEST DIVES
The deepest ever breath-held dive was 428 feet, by Francisco "Pipín" Ferreras (Cuba) off Cabo San Lucas, Mexico, on March 10, 1996. He was underwater for 2 min. 11 sec.

The deepest ever dive with scuba gear was 925 feet, by Jim Bowden (US) in the Zacaton cave, Mexico in April 1994.

GREATEST OCEAN DESCENT
In January 1960, the Swiss-built US Navy bathyscaphe *Trieste,* which was manned by Dr. Jacques Piccard (Switzerland) and Lt. Donald Walsh (US), reached a record depth of 35,797 feet in the Challenger Deep of the Mariana Trench in the Pacific Ocean.

LONGEST POLAR SLED JOURNEY
The six-member International Trans-Antarctica Expedition covered a record distance of 3,750 miles from Seal Nunataks to Mirnyy in 220 days from July 27, 1989 to March 3, 1990.

MOTORCYCLE CIRCUMNAVIGATION
British adventurer Nick Sanders completed a 19,930-mile circumnavigation in a record riding time of 31 days 20 hours between April 18 and June 9, 1997. Starting and finishing in Calais, France, Sanders' trip took him through Europe, India, Southeast Asia, Australia, New Zealand and North America.

LONGEST MOTORCYCLE RIDE
Emilio Scotto (Argentina) covered more than 457,000 miles by motorcycle in 214 countries from 1985 to 1995.

LONGEST BICYCLE JOURNEYS
Heinz Stucke (Germany) has traveled 226,800 miles and visited 211 countries since November 1962.

Walter Stolle (Germany) cycled more than 402,000 miles and visited 159 countries from 1959 to 1976.

John W. Hathaway (Canada) cycled a total of 50,600 miles from November 10, 1974 to October 6, 1976, visiting every continent including Antarctica.

Laura Geoghegan and Mark Tong rode 20,155 miles by tandem from London, England to Sydney, Australia, from May 21, 1994 to November 11, 1995.

Thomas Godwin (UK) covered 75,065 miles in 365 days in 1939. He then rode 100,000 miles in 500 days by May 1940.

Jay Aldous and Matt DeWaal (US) cycled 14,290 miles in 106 days on a round-the-world trip from This is the Place Monument, Salt Lake City, Utah in 1984.

Tal Burt (Israel) circumnavigated the world from Place du Trocadéro, Paris, France, in 77 days 14 hr. in 1992. He covered 13,253 road miles.

epic journeys II

LONGEST SNOWMOBILE JOURNEY
John Outzen and Carl, Denis and Andre Boucher drove snowmobiles from Anchorage, Alaska to Dartmouth, Nova Scotia between January 2 and March 3, 1992, covering a record distance of 10,252 miles 528 yd. in a total of 56 riding days. Their crossing of the continent was undertaken in celebration of the 500th anniversary of Christopher Columbus' landing in North America. It was the first such journey to be made entirely on snow.

BEST-TRAVELLED PERSON
The most traveled man in the world is John D. Clouse, a lawyer from Evansville, Indiana, who has visited all of the sovereign countries and all but three of the nonsovereign or other territories that existed in early 1998. His most recent trip was to the disputed Spratly Islands in 1997. John's son George began traveling at the age of 10 weeks and had accompanied his father to 104 countries by his fifth birthday.

LONGEST WALKS
Arthur Blessitt of North Fort Myers, Florida has walked a total distance of 32,202 miles in more than 27 years since 1969. Carrying a 12-foot cross and preaching throughout his walk, Blessitt has been to all seven continents, including Antarctica.

Steven Newman of Bethel, Ohio spent four years (April 1, 1983 to April 1, 1987) walking 15,509 miles around the world solo, at a faster rate than Blessitt. Newman covered 20 countries and five continents.

LONGEST BACKWARDS WALK
Plennie L. Wingo, then of Abilene, Texas, made an 8,000-mile transcontinental walk from Santa Monica, California to Istanbul, Turkey from April 15, 1931 to October 24, 1932.

LONGEST BACKWARDS RUN
Arvind Pandya of India ran backwards across the United States (from Los Angeles to New York) in a time of 107 days between August 18 and December 3, 1984, covering more than 3,100 miles. He also ran backwards from John o'Groat's, Scotland to Land's End, England in 26 days 7 hr. from April 6 to May 2, 1990, covering a distance of 940 miles.

LONGEST WHEELCHAIR JOURNEY
Rick Hansen (Canada), who has been paralyzed from the waist down since a car crash in 1973, traveled a record distance of 24,901 miles 960 yd. by wheelchair over four continents and through 34 countries. He started his journey in Vancouver, Canada on March 21, 1985 and arrived back in Vancouver on May 22, 1987.

GREATEST DISTANCE HITCHHIKED
Since 1972, hitchhiker Stephan Schlei of Ratingen, Germany has obtained free rides over a total distance of 501,750 miles.

LONGEST HORSE-DRAWN JOURNEY
The Grant family from the United Kingdom covered a distance of more than 17,200 miles during a round-the-world trip in a horse-drawn caravan. They began their journey in Vierhouten, Netherlands on October 25, 1990 and returned to the UK early in 1998, after traveling through Belgium, France, Italy, Austria, northern Yugoslavia (which became Slovenia while they were there), Hungary, Russia, the Ukraine, Kazakhstan, Mongolia, China, Japan, the United States and Canada. They sold their house to finance the trip, which cost them £60,000 ($96,000) over seven years.

LONGEST UNICYCLE RIDE
Akira Matsushima (Japan) unicycled 3,261 miles across the United States from Newport, Oregon to Washington, DC between July 10 and August 22, 1992.

LONGEST LAWNMOWER RIDE
In the summer of 1997, 12-year-old Ryan Tripp made a 3,366-mile journey by lawnmower across the United States, raising $10,400 for a sick baby in his town. Beginning in Salt Lake City, Utah, Ryan rode the Walker 25-hp mower along secondary roads approved by police, following a lead car driven in turn by a family friend, an aunt and uncle, and his grandparents. Ryan's father Todd followed in a pickup truck with an equipment trailer. The mower was fitted with road tires and had extra springs and seat padding to make the trip comfortable for Ryan, who slept in rooms donated by hotels along the route. Nineteen states and 42 days later, he arrived at the US Capitol building in Washington, DC, where he was welcomed by Utah senator Orrin Hatch. Soon afterwards, he was asked to appear on David Letterman's *Late Show* (right). Ryan's next ambition is to make the high school basketball team.

MICROLIGHTING
Britons Brian Milton (right) and his co-pilot Keith Reynolds pose for photographers in London, England in January 1998, just prior to setting out on their attempt to make the first ever circumnavigation of the globe by microlight aircraft. The pair hoped to make the journey in their GT Global flyer in 80 days, over a route that included Europe, the Middle East, India, Japan and the United States.

LONGEST STILT-WALKS
The record for the greatest distance ever covered on stilts is 3,008 miles, by Joe Bowen, from Los Angeles, California to Bowen, Kentucky, from February 20 to July 26, 1980.

In 1891, Sylvain Dornon walked from Paris, France to Moscow, Russia on stilts in either 50 or 58 stages, covering a distance of 1,830 miles. He walked at a much higher speed than Joe Bowen.

LONGEST WALK ON HANDS
The greatest distance ever covered by a person walking on their hands is 870 miles, by Johann Hurlinger (Austria) in 1900. He walked from Vienna, Austria to Paris, France in a total of 55 daily 10-hour stints, averaging 1.58 mph.

LONGEST WALK ON WATER
Rémy Bricka of Paris, France walked across the Atlantic Ocean on 13-ft.-9-in.-long skis. He left Tenerife, Canary Islands on April 2, 1988 and arrived in Trinidad in the Caribbean on May 31, 1988, after covering 3,502 miles.

LONGEST LAND-ROW
Rob Bryant of Fort Worth, Texas covered 3,280 miles on a land-rowing machine. He left Los Angeles, California on April 2, 1990 and reached Washington, DC on July 30.

LONGEST LEAPFROG
The record for the greatest distance covered while leapfrogging is 996 miles 352 yards, by 14 students from Stanford University, California They began on May 16, 1991 and stopped 244 hr. 43 min. later, on May 26.

LONGEST PEDAL-BOAT JOURNEY
Kenichi Horie of Kobe, Japan set a pedal-boating distance record of 4,660 miles. He left Honolulu, Hawaii on October 30, 1992 and arrived in Naha, Okinawa, Japan on February 17, 1993.

MOST COUNTRIES TRAVELLED THROUGH IN 24 HOURS
The most countries traveled through entirely by train in 24 hours is 11, by Alison Bailey, Ian Bailey, John English and David Kellie, May 1–2, 1993. They started in Hungary and continued through Slovakia, the Czech Republic, Austria, Germany, Liechtenstein, Switzerland, France, Luxembourg and Belgium, and arrived in the Netherlands 22 hr. 10 min. after setting off.

FURTHEST PIZZA DELIVERY
Eagle Boys Dial-a-Pizza in Christchurch, New Zealand regularly delivers pizzas to Scott Base, Antarctica for the New Zealand Antarctic Program team. The pizzas are cooked, packed and shipped to a military air field, where they are loaded onto a C130 Hercules. They arrive at the base nine hours later, with reheating instructions.

extraordinary lives

crime

HIGHEST MURDER RATES

The country with the greatest number of murders is the United States, which has around 25,000 cases of homicide per year.

The country with the highest murder rate in proportion to its population varies from year to year, but Colombia has had a consistently high rate of 77.5 per 100,000 for the last 10 years (more than eight times higher than the United States rate). It has more than 27,000 murder victims a year.

The city with the highest murder rate in proportion to its population is the Colombian capital Bogotá, where violence is the leading cause of death for individuals aged between 10 and 60. The city has about 8,600 murders per year — an average of 23 per day.

MOST PROLIFIC MURDERERS

Behram, a member of the Thuggee cult, strangled at least 931 victims with his yellow and white cloth strip or *ruhmal* in the Oudh district of India between 1790 and 1840.

The most prolific murderer of all time in the western world, and the most prolific ever female murderer, was Elizabeth Bathori. The niece of Stephen Bathori, who became King of Poland in 1575, she is alleged to have killed more than 600 girls and young women in order to drink and bathe in their blood, ostensibly to preserve her youth. When the murders were discovered, the countess was walled up in her home, Csej Castle in Transylvania (now in Romania), from 1610 until her death in 1614.

The most prolific murderer of the 20th century was the bandit leader Teófilo "Sparks" Rojas, who is said to have killed between 592 and 3,500 people from 1945 to his death in an ambush near Armenia, Colombia, on January 22, 1963.

The most prolific known serial killer of recent times was Pedro Lopez, who killed a total of 300 young girls in Colombia, Peru and Ecuador. Known as the "Monster of the Andes," Lopez was charged on 57 counts of murder in Ecuador in 1980 and sentenced to life imprisonment.

Mexican sisters Delfina and Maria de Jesus Gonzales, who abducted girls to work in brothels, formed the world's most prolific ever murder partnership. Known to have murdered at least 90 of their victims but suspected to have killed many more, Delfina and Maria were sentenced to 40 years' imprisonment in 1964.

The world's biggest ever mass killing carried out by one person took place in April 1982, when policeman Wou Bom-kon went on a drunken eight-hour rampage in the Kyong Sang-namdo province of South Korea. He killed a total of 57 people and wounded another 35 with 176 rounds of rifle ammunition and hand grenades, before blowing himself up with a grenade.

The world's most prolific ever murderer by poison was nurse Jane Toppan of Massachusetts, who killed between 30 and 100 patients with morphine or atropine over a period of 20 years. In 1902, Toppan confessed to a total of 30 murders but claimed that they had been acts of mercy. She was committed to a mental institution.

MOST ASSASSINATION ATTEMPTS

Charles de Gaulle, who was president of France from 1958 to 1969, was the target of the greatest number of failed assassination attempts on any head of state in modern times. He is reputed to have survived a total of 31 plots against his life between 1944 and 1966.

BIGGEST CRIMINAL ORGANIZATION

The Six Great Triads of China form the largest organized crime association in the world today, with an estimated 100,000-plus members worldwide. The five Triads with headquarters in Taiwan and Hong Kong have recently been joined by the Great Circle Triad, which is based in Shanghai, China.

MOST BANKS CONTROLLED BY A CRIMINAL ORGANIZATION

The Russian *Mafiya*, which has extended into Europe and North America, controls an estimated 400 banks. The organization has annual profits of about $250 billion, derived from drug trafficking, which the banks are used to launder.

BIGGEST MAFIA TRIALS

In 1986, a total of 474 Mafia suspects were formally charged in Palermo, Italy. Of these, 121 had fled and had to be charged *in absentia*.

The most publicized Mafia trial in the world took place in Caltanisetta, Italy in May 1995, when Salvatore "Toto" Riina, the reputed head of the Sicilian Mafia and the most wanted person in Italy, went on trial with 40 other alleged mob bosses. Riina was charged with drug trafficking, extortion and 50 murders.

BIGGEST DRUGS HAUL

On September 28, 1989, cocaine with an estimated street value

BIGGEST PURPORTED THEFT FROM A NATION

In 1986, the Filipino government claimed that $860.8 million had been salted away by the country's former president Ferdinand Marcos and his wife Imelda. The total national loss from November 1965 was believed to be $5–$10 billion. The presidential couple were renowned for their extravagant lifestyle: when Corazon Aquino, Marcos' successor, opened the Malancanang Palace, she found 3,000 pairs of shoes, 2,000 ball gowns, 1,000 unopened packets of tights, 200 girdles and 500 bras that had belonged to the former First Lady. When they were toppled by "People Power" in 1986, Ferdinand and Imelda fled to Hawaii, where Ferdinand died in exile in 1989. Imelda was allowed back into the Philippines in 1991, and the following year she returned again with her husband's body, which was buried there. Imelda was found guilty of corruption in 1998, shortly after an unsuccessful bid for the presidency. The conviction is subject to appeal.

of $6–7 billion was seized in a raid on a warehouse in Los Angeles, California. The 22-ton haul was prompted by a tipoff from a local resident who had complained about heavy truck traffic and people leaving the warehouse "at odd hours and in a suspicious manner."

BIGGEST ROBBERIES
The robbery of the Reichsbank following the collapse of Germany during April and May 1945 was the world's biggest ever bank robbery. The book *Nazi Gold* estimated that the total haul would have been worth $3.34 billion at 1984 values.

During the extreme civil disorder that took place in Beirut, Lebanon in 1976, a guerrilla force blasted the vaults of the British Bank of the Middle East in Bab Idriss and cleared out safe-deposit boxes with contents valued by the former finance minister Lucien Dahdah at $50 million and by another source at an "absolute minimum" of $20 million.

The biggest ever jewel robbery on record took place in August 1994, when gems with an estimated value of $46 million were stolen from the jewelry shop at the Carlton Hotel in Cannes, France by a three-man gang. A security guard was seriously injured in the raid.

The largest object ever stolen by one person was the 10,639-dwt *SS Orient Trader*, which was slashed free from Wolfe's Cove, St. Lawrence Seaway, Canada by N. William Kennedy on June 5, 1966. The vessel drifted to a waiting blacked-out tug, thus evading a ban on shipping movements during a violent wildcat waterfront strike. It then set sail for Spain.

VIOLENT CRIME
Despite a decline in violent crime since 1994, the United States still has the highest incidence of armed robbery in the world. More than 620,000 cases of robbery are officially recorded each year, with firearms being used in around 30% of these crimes. Firearms are used in more than 1.28 million cases of murder, rape, robbery and aggravated assault in the United States each year.

BIGGEST RANSOMS
A hall full of gold and silver worth $1.6 billion at today's values was paid to the Spanish conquistador Francisco Pizarro at Cajamarca, Peru for the release of Atahualpa, the last Inca emperor, in the 16th century. Pizarro murdered Atahualpa instead of returning him.

In 1975, $57.7 million was paid to the left-wing urban guerrilla group Montoneros for the release of brothers Jorge and Juan Born, of the family firm Bunge and Born, in Buenos Aires, Argentina.

BIGGEST BANK FRAUD
In 1989, the Banca Nazionale del Lavoro, Italy admitted that it had been defrauded of a huge amount of money when its branch in Atlanta, Georgia made unauthorized loan commitments to Iraq. The loss was subsequently estimated to be about $5 billion.

BIGGEST BANKNOTE FORGERY
The German Third Reich's forging operation during World War II involved more than $216 million in counterfeit British notes, produced by 140 prisoners at Sachsenhausen concentration camp.

BIGGEST WHITE-COLLAR CRIME
In February 1997, copper trader Yasuo Hamanaka pleaded guilty to fraud and forgery in connection with illicit trading. It cost Sumitomo, the largest trading company in Japan, an estimated $2.6 billion over a 10-year period of unauthorized transactions, making it the biggest known white-collar crime in history.

punishment

CAPITAL PUNISHMENT
The electric chair as a method of execution was the brainchild of Dr. Albert Southwick in 1881. Southwick, an American dentist, believed that it would be a painless and humane method of killing criminals, and told a senator friend of his, who thought that it would be a good replacement for hanging. The state of New York was the first to introduce electrocution, in 1888, and the following year the world's first Electrical Execution law was passed. The first person to be killed in the electric chair was William Lelmer, who had murdered his lover Matilda with an ax. Between 1891 and 1963, a further 614 inmates were executed in the Sing Sing electric chair. The death penalty has now been abolished in half of the countries of the world: 97 countries in total still employ it.

LARGEST PRISONS
The largest known prison in modern times was the State Prison of Southern Michigan, which had a peak maximum capacity of 6,500 inmates.

Kresty Prison in St. Petersburg, Russia houses between 6,000 and 6,500 inmates.

MOST EXPENSIVE PRISONS
The most expensive civil prison to maintain was Alcatraz in San Francisco Bay, California. Nicknamed "the Rock," it became a federal maximum security prison in 1933 and was closed by the government in 1963, when the annual cost of running and maintaining it had risen to double that of any other prison in the United States.

The most expensive prisons on record today (figures are not kept in all countries) are US maximum security prisons, where the "cost per bed" exceeds $155,000 a year or $425 a day.

MOST PRISONERS
Some human-rights organizations have estimated that there are currently approximately 20 million prisoners in China (1,658 per 100,000 people), but this figure has never been officially acknowledged.

The highest prison population per capita among countries for which statistics are available is in the United States, which has 1.75 million prisoners (or one prisoner out of every 147 people).

FEWEST PRISONERS
Slovenia has less than 500 prisoners in a population of almost 2 million. Few offenders are jailed: community service, probation and similar programs are employed where possible.

MOST OVERCROWDED PRISONS
The most overcrowded prisons today are in the former Soviet republic of Turkmenistan, where several prisoners died of suffocation in overcrowded cells in 1996 and 1997.

The number of people detained in the Central African state of Rwanda is so great that many prisoners are held in tents and former warehouses.

MOST RAPID MODERN INCREASE IN PRISON POPULATION
The number of convicted detainees in Italy doubled to 55,000 between 1990 and 1995.

MOST PRISONERS AWAITING TRIAL
In 1997, more than 35,000 people were awaiting trial in Nigerian jails. Some had been detained for more than 10 years.

MOST EXECUTIONS
China exercises the death penalty more than any other country: in 1996, about 2,200 of the 2,930-plus executions worldwide took place in China.

MOST PEOPLE HANGED
The record for the most people hanged from one gallows was set by William Duly, who executed 38 members of the Sioux tribe outside Mankato, Minnesota in December 1862.

A Nazi *feldkommandant* simultaneously hanged a total of 50 Greek resistance men as a reprisal measure in Athens, Greece on July 22, 1944.

MOST LEGAL HANGINGS SURVIVED
Joseph Samuel was sentenced to death for murder in Sydney, Australia in 1803, and survived three attempts to execute him. The first attempt failed when the rope broke, the second attempt misfired when the replacement rope stretched so much that Samuel's feet touched the ground, and the third attempt was aborted when the second replacement rope broke. Samuel was reprieved.

John Lee escaped execution three times in Exeter, England in 1885: the trap door failed to open on each attempt.

MOST FAMOUS POLITICAL PRISONER
Nelson Mandela and Bill Clinton are seen in the cell on Robben Island where Mandela spent more than 27 years in prison. In the 1980s, Mandela was often described as "the world's most famous political prisoner." He was, however, one of many national leaders who have been political prisoners. Kim Dae Jung, president of South Korea, was detained by a previous military regime, as was Argentine president Carlos Menem. Among the East European leaders detained during the Communist era are presidents Vaclav Havel (of the Czech Republic) and Arpad Goncz (of Hungary).

MOST WITCHES BURNED
At least 1,500 alleged witches were burned at the stake in less than a decade in the towns of Wurzburg and Bamberg, Germany, in the mid-17th century.

A total of 133 people were burned as witches in one day in Quedlinburg, near Leipzig, Germany in 1589.

MOST PRISONERS ON DEATH ROW
In 1996, there were more than 3,150 prisoners on death row in the 39 US states in which the death penalty is exercised.

LONGEST TIME ON DEATH ROW
Sadamichi Hirasawa from Japan was convicted of poisoning bank employees with potassium cyanide in order to steal $370 in 1948. He died in Sendai Prison, Japan, aged 94, after 39 years on death row.

LONGEST SENTENCES
Chamoy Thipyaso and seven of her associates were each jailed for 141,078 years by the Bangkok Criminal Court, Thailand in July 1989. They were found guilty of swindling the public.

A 384,912-year sentence was demanded at the prosecution of Gabriel March Grandos at Palma de Majorca, Spain on March 11, 1972. The former mailman had failed to deliver 42,768 letters.

The longest sentence ever imposed on a mass murderer was 21 consecutive life sentences and 12 death sentences, for John Wayne Gacy, who killed 33 boys and young men between 1972 and 1978. He was sentenced by a jury in Chicago, Illinois in March 1980 and executed in May 1994.

LONGEST TIME SERVED
Paul Geidel was convicted of second-degree murder at the age of 17 in September 1911 and released from the Fishkill Correctional Facility, Beacon, New York at the age of 85, in 1980. Geidel, who first refused parole in 1974, had served 68 years 245 days.

LONGEST-SERVING PRISONER OF CONSCIENCE
Kim Sung-myun served 43 years 10 months in Seoul, South Korea, after being arrested in 1951 for supporting North Korea.

OLDEST PRISONER
Bill Wallace spent the last 63 years of his life in Aradale Psychiatric Hospital in Ararat, Victoria, Australia, after shooting a man dead in December 1925. He died in 1989, aged 107.

BIGGEST JAILBREAK
On February 11, 1979, approximately 11,000 inmates of Gasr prison, Tehran, Iran took advantage of an attempt to rescue two US prisoners and the Islamic revolution to make history's largest ever jailbreak.

LONGEST ESCAPE BY A RECAPTURED PRISONER
In 1923, Leonard Fristoe escaped from the Nevada State Prison, where he had been jailed for killing two sheriff's deputies in 1920. He was turned in by his son at the age of 77 in 1969, after almost 46 years of freedom.

MOST ARRESTS
Tommy Johns of Queensland, Australia was convicted of drunkenness almost 3,000 times between 1957 and 1988.

BIGGEST ARREST
The biggest known mass arrest in a democratic country occurred when 15,617 demonstrators were rounded up by South Korean police in July 1988 to ensure security prior to the Olympic Games in Seoul.

BIGGEST FINE
A fine of $650 million was imposed on the US securities house Drexel Burnham Lambert in 1988 for insider trading. Of this, $300 million was direct fines; the balance was to be put into an account to satisfy claims of parties that could prove they were defrauded by Drexel's actions.

HIGHEST FINE ON ONE PERSON
The highest fine imposed on an individual was $200 million in settlement of a criminal racketeering and securities fraud suit brought by the United States government against Michael Milken in 1990. Originally, 98 counts were filed against Milken, but 92 were dropped in exchange for Milken's plea of guilty. Milken also agreed to settle civil charges filed by the Securities and Exchange Commission. He was released from a 10-year prison sentence in January 1993. In addition, he received three years' probation and 5,400 hours of community service.

hoaxes and confidence tricks

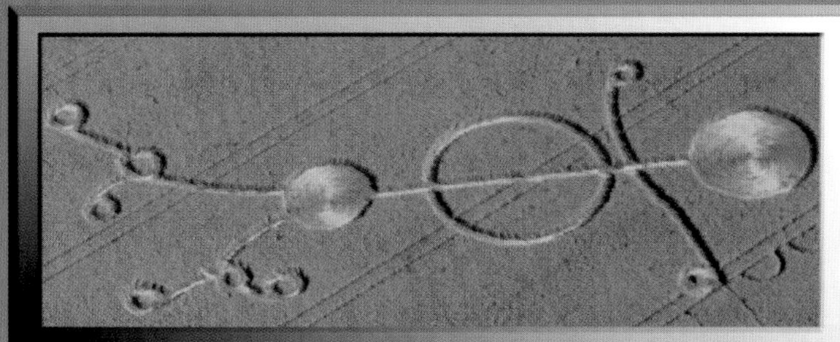

CROP CIRCLES
The depressions in fields known as crop circles were first widely reported in the 1970s, and more than 9,000 have now been sighted, mostly in the UK, the US and Germany. Some people claim that they are caused by alien spacecraft or vortexes; others believe they are hoaxes or the result of unusual weather conditions. In 1991, two British men claimed to have been producing circles since 1978.

BIGGEST PANIC CAUSED BY A RADIO PLAY
Orson Welles' radio play *War of the Worlds*, based on H. G. Wells' novel chronicling a Martian invasion of Earth, caused unintentional mass hysteria in the United States when it was broadcast on October 30, 1938. Several million listeners who tuned in late missed the introduction and caught what they believed were a series of special radio bulletins describing the alien events. Some listeners, mostly from New York and New Jersey, panicked and fled their homes. The public reaction sparked research into the phenomenon of mass hysteria.

LONGEST HOAXES
Huge footprints discovered on a beach in Clearwater, Florida in 1948 were believed to belong to a giant penguin until 1988, when a reporter at the St. Petersburg *Times* managed to get the hoaxer to confess. The latter still owned the three-toed feet made out of concrete.

In 1912, the reported discovery of a half-human, half-primate skull in the village of Piltdown, England caused worldwide controversy. Scientists thought that Piltdown Man might be a million-year-old "missing link" between ape and man. In 1952, it emerged that a 200-year old human skull had been joined to an orangutan's jaw. *Sherlock Holmes* creator Sir Arthur Conan Doyle was one of those accused of the hoax.

MOST FAMOUS SUSPECTED HOAXES
Bigfoot, a giant ape-like creature purported to walk on its hind legs and live in dense forested regions of the United States, is said to be 6–10 feet tall and weigh 700–2,500 pounds. On October 20, 1967, Roger Patterson shot a film that apparently shows Bigfoot at Bluff Creek, northern California, but skeptics believe that it was a man in a gorilla suit. There have been hundreds of sightings and several photographs have been taken, but their authenticity is still doubted. Along with crop circles and the Roswell Incident, Bigfoot is the most famous suspected hoax.

BIGGEST POLITICAL HOAX
In 1967, the book *Report From Iron Mountain* – supposedly a secret US government document examining the drawbacks of world peace – caused worldwide controversy by claiming that war creates vital social and economic controls. It suggested deliberate environmental pollution, modern forms of slavery and birth control and the addition of drugs to food and water supplies to maintain control if peace broke out. Author Leonard Lewin admitted that it was a hoax in 1972, after it had been translated into 15 languages and had fooled many prominent intellectuals.

In 1972 it was claimed that a primitive tribe, the Tasadays, had been discovered in the Mindanao rainforest of the Philippines. The tribe was said to be on the verge of extinction and to have had no previous contact with the modern world. Anthropologists later discovered that Filipino cultural minister Manuel Elizalde had hired a group of local people to pose as the tribe in order to boost the government's claim to be protecting minorities.

BIGGEST INTERNET HOAX
The original Good Times virus hoax started in November 1994 and is still circulating on the Internet. It relies on people to pass it along rather than spreading from one computer to another by itself. The hoax claims that the virus is sent via e-mail and erases hard drives, and the hoaxers falsely allege that the Federal Communications Commission has released a warning about it.

BIGGEST JOURNALISTIC HOAX
The Great Moon Hoax of 1835 is the most famous and enduring newspaper hoax. A series of articles describing the discovery of life on the moon was printed in the New York *Sun* starting on

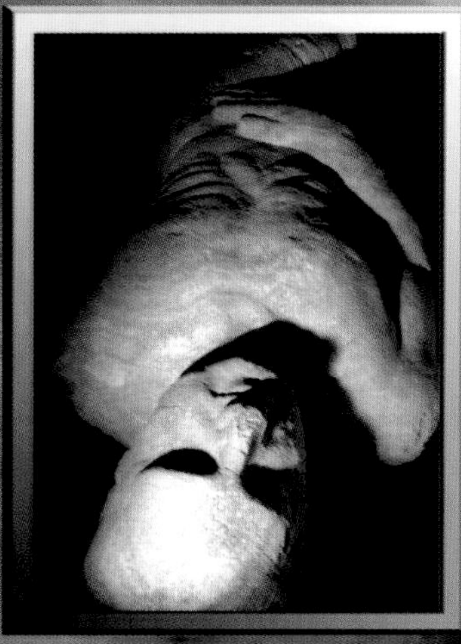

BIGGEST LAWSUIT OVER A HOAX
In 1868, archaeologist George Hull of Binghamton, New York had a giant carved from gypsum shipped from Chicago to Cardiff, New York and buried on his cousin's farm. He had been planning the elaborate hoax for two years. Hull had the Giant's carved as if he had suffered great pain during death, and the end result was slightly twisted in agony, with the giant's right hand clutching his stomach. The giant was carved down to the finest of details: it had toenails, nostrils and genitals, and even realistic looking skin pores that were created with a needlepoint mallet. A year later, on October 15, 1869, workers "discovered" it and it became an instant tourist attraction. It was believed to be either a real fossilized giant or an ancient statue. Circus founder P. T. Barnum offered to buy it from its new owner for $50,000 but was turned down, so he built his own and claimed that he had bought the original. A lawsuit ensued, with each owner claiming the other's giant was a fake. It came to an end when Hull confessed that the Cardiff Giant was a hoax, too.

August 25. Details included the existence of furry, winged men resembling bats and a temple built from sapphires and gold. The articles, supposedly written by eminent British astronomer Sir John Herschel, so intrigued the public that the *Sun* claimed what was then the world's largest newspaper circulation of 19,360. Rival editors were panicked into reprinting the articles and Edgar Allan Poe stopped work on *The Strange Adventures of Hans Pfaall* because he felt he had been outdone. On September 16, the hoax was revealed.

BIGGEST DIARY HOAX
In 1983, British newspaper *The S. Times* fell victim to the biggest hoax in post-war newspaper history when it published the "Hitler Diaries." The German magazine *Stern* and the US magazine *Newsweek* were also deceived and published the forgeries. It was later discovered that the diaries were the work of German hoaxer Konrad Kujau, who had also faked some Hitler poetry. The first person to declare the diaries a fraud was the British journalist and historian David Irving, but he changed his mind and claimed that they were authentic, days before they were proved fake.

MOST SUCCESSFUL ART HOAXES
In 1936, little-known Dutch artist Han van Meegeren began painting forgeries with the aim of proving the ignorance of art critics. Seven others followed, all passed off as the works of Vermeer and de Hooch, and they sold for more than $2.25 million. Van Meegeren lived a lavish lifestyle and had bought a mansion in France and 50 houses by the time of his eventual arrest. In October 1947, he was sentenced to a year in prison after being convicted of forging signatures rather than paintings, but he died in December 1947.

BIGGEST FILM HOAX
Forgotten Silver (New Zealand, 1995) was allegedly a documentary about a forgotten pioneer of cinema, Colin McKenzie. Its director, Peter Jackson, who also made the successful film *Heavenly Creatures* (New Zealand, 1994) created the hoax as a satire on the number of historical documentaries made for the centenary of cinema. The story chronicles how McKenzie invented a motion picture camera in 1900 when he was 12, produced his own film stock from raw eggs, discovered how to make color film stock from a type of berry in 1911, and finally filmed his own death in 1937. The film sparked complaints from deceived viewers when shown on New Zealand TV in 1995.

BIGGEST PHOTOGRAPHIC HOAX
In July 1917, 15-year-old Elsie Wright took photographs of her cousin Frances with a group of fairies dancing in front of her in woodland near Cottingley, England. Photographic experts could not explain how such images had been taken by the girls. On March 17, 1983 – 66 years later – Frances confessed that the fairies had been cut out and painted by Elsie, then held in place by hatpins.

BIGGEST BIZARRE PHENOMENA HOAX
In 1974, Ronald DeFeo murdered his mother, father, two brothers and two sisters at their home in Amityville, New York. The house's subsequent owners, George and Kathy Lutz, soon claimed that ghosts drove them away, and in 1977 a book was published based on their accounts of bizarre phenomena corresponding to the slaughter. A film was made in 1979. The Lutzes' story was soon exposed as a hoax, but a further seven novels and films based on the "Amityville Horror" were released.

BIGGEST PARANORMAL HOAX
From 1983 to 1987, thousands of people believed that they saw a 200–1,000-foot-long, boomerang-shaped UFO covered in multicolored lights in Hudson Valley, New York. In 1987 the phenomenon was exposed as a giant hoax by a science magazine: a group of pilots known as the Stormville Flyers had been flying in formation and attached lights to their craft, making them look like a huge UFO. When they switched the lights off, the "ship" seemed to disappear.

THE ROSWELL INCIDENT
In 1947, an officer at Roswell Army Air Field, New Mexico issued an unauthorized press release stating that the army had gained possession of a flying disc. This was later denied by the Air Force. Years of controversy over whether aliens landed has followed. A 1997 report by the US military stated the "bodies" found were dummies from a test aircraft. Roswell now has a museum devoted to UFOs; shown here is a model of an alien from the museum.

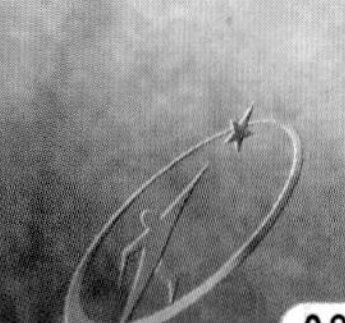

religions rites and cults

BIGGEST SUICIDE BY POISONING
The biggest ever mass suicide in peacetime took place on November 18, 1978, when 913 members of the People's Temple cult died after drinking Kool-Aid mixed with cyanide at Jonestown near Port Kaituma, Guyana. The leader of the cult, Jim Jones, had fled San Francisco together with 900 followers after accusations of financial irregularities. Jones was found to have died of a gunshot wound.

LONGEST PERIOD OF STIGMATISM
Padre Pio (Francesco Forguione), a devout Italian Capuchin friar, bore the stigmata (the wounds received by Christ on the Cross) from 1918 until his death in 1968. They were seen by thousands of pilgrims.

FURTHEST REINCARNATION OF A BUDDHIST LAMA
Following the death of lama Thubten Teshe, the leader of the Buddhists of Mongolia, in 1984, his reincarnated successor, Osel Hita Torres, was found more than 5,000 miles away in Spain. Torres, who was born in 1985, is the son of Catholic converts to Buddhism.

LONGEST SIEGE INVOLVING A RELIGIOUS CULT
The armed standoff at Mount Carmel Center, Waco, Texas by US Federal agents lasted from February 23 to April 19, 1993. The compound was the headquarters of the Branch Davidians, led by self-styled messiah David Koresh. The cult was stockpiling arms and ammunition. Four agents were shot dead during an initial gun battle, leading the Federal forces to lay siege to the compound. On April 19, the buildings went up in flames, and about 80 cult members died, including Koresh. Some of the corpses had gunshot wounds. It is not known how the fire started or whether the deaths were the result of a suicide pact or mass murder.

MOST MURDEROUS RELIGIOUS SECT
Members of India's Thuggee cult, a secret society devoted to Kali, the Hindu goddess of death and destruction, are estimated to have ritually strangled more than 2 million people in 300 years. The cult was wiped out during the British Raj in the 19th century, when more than 4,000 members were put on trial. Most were hanged or jailed.

MOST HUMAN SACRIFICES IN A RELIGIOUS CEREMONY
The most human sacrifices made at a single ceremony is believed to have been the 20,000 people killed by Aztec priests at the dedication of the Great Temple (Teocalli) at Tenochtitlan (now Mexico City) to the war god Huitzilpochtli in 1486.

MOST WITNESSES TO A MODERN-DAY RELIGIOUS APPARITION
About 70,000 people saw the sun "dance" in the sky during the sixth and last apparition of the Virgin Mary to three children in Fatima, Portugal, on October 13, 1915. The globe seemed to fall and rise in a circular motion. The Fatima apparitions have been officially recognized by the Roman Catholic Church.

MOST RECENT RECOGNIZED APPARITION OF THE VIRGIN MARY
An apparition at the cave of Betania, Cau, Venezuela has been seen by Maria Esperanza Medrano Bianchini at intervals since March 1976, and has also been witnessed by hundreds of other people. It was recognized by the Roman Catholic Church in 1987.

MOST RECENTLY DISCOVERED RELIC OF THE BUDDHA
In 1981, a box containing ashes of the Buddha was found in Yunju, 47 miles from Beijing, China. The ashes were divided into eight parts on the Buddha's death c.483 BC in Kusinārā (now Kasia), India, and sent to different parts of Asia for safekeeping.

MOST INACCESSIBLE RELIC
A relic believed by the Ethiopian Orthodox Church to be the Ark of the Covenant is guarded by one priest in a chapel in Axum, Ethiopia. The guardian, the only person allowed to see the relic or be in its presence, cannot leave the chapel area ever again, and must appoint a successor before his death.

MOST HINDU PILGRIMS
Every three years, millions of people gather at India's Kumbha Mela, the largest Hindu festival in the world. According to myth, the son of the Hindu god Indra was chased by demons for a pot of ambrosia (the food of the gods) and spilled the nectar at four sites – Nasiik, Ujjain, Haridwar and Prayag. The 1½-month-long Kumbha Mela is held at the four sites in rotation, but the biggest event takes place at Prayag ("place of purification") every 12 years. On January 30, 1995, during a "half" Kumbha Mela in Prayag, a record 20 million pilgrims bathed in the cold waters at the confluence of the Ganges and Jumna rivers – a ritual which they believe will absolve them of all sins. An estimated 200,000 people an hour had entered Prayag the day before the festival. The pilgrims began bathing soon after midnight, and by 10am an estimated 15 million people had been in the water and another 5 million were waiting their turn. The next Kumbha Mela will take place in 2001.

MOST FEMALE-DOMINATED RELIGIOUS SECT
Dianic Wicca, a neopagan movement, worships a monotheistic goddess and has female-only covens. The feminist witchcraft sect was founded in California in the 1920s.

MOST MALE-DOMINATED SOCIETY
Mount Athos, a 129-square-mile autonomous republic within Greece, bars all females, including domestic animals and birds, and women are not allowed to approach its shores by boat. The republic is occupied by 20 Orthodox monasteries and their dependencies.

MOST COMPLETE MODERN PURDAH
Since the Taliban movement took the capital of Afghanistan, Kabul, in 1996, Afghan women have to wear a loose garment hiding their body and face, with a cotton grille covering the eyes.

MOST THREATENED MAJOR RELIGION
Parseism, a religion of the Indian subcontinent, encourages neither intermarriage nor conversion. Its dwindling numbers are now estimated at no more than 120,000.

BIGGEST WEDDING CEREMONIES
Blessing '97 saw 30,000 couples rededicate their marriages at RFK Stadium, Washington, DC in November 1997. The ceremony was carried out by the Holy Spirit Association for the Unification of World Christianity, founded by the Reverend Sun Myung Moon and his wife Dr. Hak Ja Han Moon. In 1995, Moon married a record 35,000 couples in the Olympic Stadium in Seoul, South Korea, and a further 325,000 via a satellite link.

FASTEST-GROWING CHURCH TODAY
The Kimbanguist Church was founded in the Democratic Republic of Congo (ex-Zaire) by Baptist student Simon Kimbangu in 1959. By 1996, the Church, which is a member of the World Council of Churches, had more than 6.5 million members.

BIGGEST RADIO AUDIENCE FOR A REGULAR RELIGIOUS BROADCAST
Decision Hour, a religious radio show that has been broadcast regularly since 1957 by evangelist Billy Graham, attracts an average audience of 20 million people.

BIGGEST RELIGION WITHOUT ANY RITES
The Baha'i faith, which is practiced by approximately 6 million people in more than 70 countries worldwide, has no ceremonies, no sacraments and no clergy. The religion, which emphasizes the importance of all religion and the spiritual unity of humanity, developed through the teaching of two Iranian visionaries in the 19th century.

SMALLEST CHRISTIAN SECT
The Sabbathday Lake community of Shakers in Maine currently has seven members, making it the smallest surviving Christian sect. The Shakers, formally known as the United Society of Believers in Christ's Second Appearing, were founded in England in 1747 and taken to the New World by Ann Lee, known as Mother Ann, in 1774. The followers of the religion, who formed the first communistic settlement in the United States, claimed they had been "commissioned by Almighty God to preach the everlasting Gospel to America."

MOST PROLIFIC CRYING STATUE
In April 1998, a statue brought from the Marian shrine of Medjugorje, Bosnia was thought to be weeping blood at Sant Marti church, Mora, Catalonia, Spain, but was declared a hoax by local Roman Catholic authorities. The most prolific crying religious statue was a 15-inch-high plaster of the Virgin Mary brought from the same shrine by a curate from Civitavecchia, Italy in 1994. The statue appeared to cry tears of blood on 14 days between February 2 and March 17, 1995. One manifestation was witnessed by the diocesan bishop.

MOST CHRISTIAN PILGRIMS
The House of the Virgin Mary in Loretto, Italy and the basilica of St. Antony in Padua, Italy both receive about 3.5 million pilgrims a year — more than three times the number who visit Lourdes, France each year.

MOST MUSLIM PILGRIMS
The annual Muslim pilgrimage (*hajj*) to Mecca, Saudi Arabia, attracts an average of 2 million people a year.

great escapes

MOST LABOR CAMP ESCAPES
Tatyana Mikhailovna Russanova, a former Soviet citizen who now lives in Haifa, Israel, escaped from Stalin's forced labor camps, or gulags, in the former USSR a total of 15 times between 1943 and 1954. She was recaptured and resentenced 14 times. All of the escapes are judicially recognized by independent Russian lawyers, but only nine of them are recognized by Soviet Supreme Court officials.

LONGEST FALL SURVIVED WITHOUT A PARACHUTE
On January 26, 1972, Vesna Vulovic, a flight attendant from what was then Yugoslavia, survived a fall from a record-breaking height of 6 miles 551 yd. when the DC-9 in which she was traveling blew up over Srbska Kamenice, Czechoslovakia (now Czech Republic).

LONGEST UPWARDS FALL SURVIVED
In May 1993, Didier Dahran, who was making his third parachute jump at Boulac, France, was sucked into a freak cyclone current. The reading on his altimeter shot up from 1,000 feet to 25,000 feet before jamming at its maximum. Two hours after the jump, at the kind of altitude that is usually only reached by jet airliners, Dahran's rectangular parachute collapsed in the thin atmosphere, sending him hurtling towards the ground. He launched his emergency parachute and passed out, landing 30 miles from where he had jumped.

HIGHEST WAVE RIDDEN
On April 3, 1868, a Hawaiian man named Holua was forced to ride a tsunami "perhaps 50 feet" high in order to save his life when the wave struck Minole, Hawaii.

MOST LIGHTNING STRIKES SURVIVED
The only person to have been struck by lightning seven times was Roy Sullivan, a former park ranger from Virginia. In 1942, Sullivan lost a big toe nail after being struck; in 1969, he lost his eyebrows; in July 1970, his left shoulder was seared; in April 1972, his hair caught fire; in August 1973, his hair caught fire again and his legs were seared; in June 1976, his ankle was injured; and in June 1977, he received chest and stomach burns. Sullivan committed suicide in September 1983.

LONGEST TIME SURVIVED IN FREEZER ROOM
In January 1997, Dale Powitsky of Dayton, Ohio was loading sides of beef into a cold room when the heavy steel door slammed behind him, trapping him inside for two days. To lessen the danger of freezing to death, Powitsky collected the labels from the animal carcasses and set fire to them with his cigarette lighter. He then cut pieces of fat off the carcasses and melted them before dripping the liquid fat onto a pad made from asbestos lagging from the freezer pipes. This allowed him to generate just enough heat to keep himself alive.

LONGEST DESERT SURVIVAL
A Mexican man survived for a record eight days in the desert in temperatures of 102°F. Equipped with only 2 gallons of water, he traveled 35 miles on horseback until his horse died, and then walked 100 miles to reach help. When he was finally found, he had gone blind and deaf and lost 25% of his body weight, and his hair had turned completely gray.

DEEPEST UNDERWATER ESCAPES
The record for the deepest underwater rescue is 1,575 feet, by Roger Chapman and Roger Mallinson, who were trapped in *Pisces III* for 76 hours when it sank 150 miles southeast of Cork, Ireland on August 29, 1973. The vessel was hauled to the surface by the cable ship *John Cabot* after work by *Pisces V*, *Pisces II* and the remote-control recovery vessel *Curv* (Controlled Underwater Recovery Vehicle) on September 1.

The greatest depth from which an escape has been made without any kind of equipment is 225 feet, by Richard Slater from the rammed submersible *Nekton Beta*, off Catalina Island, California on September 28, 1970.

The record for the deepest escape with equipment is 601 feet, by Norman Cooke and Hamish Jones from the submarine *HMS Otus* in Bjørnefjorden, off Bergen, Norway, during a naval exercise on July 22, 1987. The men were wearing standard suits with built-in lifejackets, which allow air expanding during the ascent to pass into a hood over the escapee's head.

LONGEST SURVIVAL UNDERWATER WITHOUT EQUIPMENT
In 1991, Michael Proudfoot was investigating a sunken naval cruiser around Baja California, Mexico when he smashed his scuba regulator and lost all air. Unable to make it back to the ship's hull, Proudfoot found a big bubble of air trapped in the ship's galley and a tea-urn almost full of fresh water. By rationing the water, breathing shallowly and eating sea urchins, he stayed alive for two days until he was rescued.

YOUNGEST SURVIVOR OF THE *TITANIC*
Millvina Dean was eight weeks old when the *Titanic* struck an iceberg and sank on April 14, 1912. Although she was traveling third class, Millvina survived, along with her mother and her 18-month-old brother. Her father, Bert, was among the 1,517 passengers who were never seen again.

LOWEST AIRPLANE RESCUE
On April 9, 1998, a *Cessna 150* became entangled in power lines and was left hanging by one wheel when its pilot aborted landing and veered sharply about 200 yards from the control tower at Boeing Field near Seattle. Authorities immediately cut off electricity to the power lines. The pilot, 47-year-old crane operator Mike Warren, remained in the cockpit – which was hanging upside down halfway between two power poles about 60 feet above a main road – for four hours before he was rescued by firefighters. The rescuers gave the uninjured pilot a harness through a window of the plane. He put it on, released his seatbelt and exited from the cockpit window feet first. He then slid down the underside of the plane's left wing into the bucket of a cherrypicker. The plane, which had only suffered a bent propeller, was then lowered to the ground in a harness.

BIGGEST RESCUE WITHOUT LOSS OF LIFE
All 2,689 people aboard the *Susan B. Anthony* survived when the ship sank off Normandy, France, on June 7, 1944.

LONGEST PERIODS SURVIVED ON RAFTS
The longest known survival by one person on a raft is 133 days, by Poon Lim of the British Merchant Navy after his ship, the *SS Ben Lomond*, was torpedoed in the Atlantic 565 miles west of St. Paul's Rocks at 11.45 am on November 23, 1942. He was picked up by a fishing boat off Salinópolis, Brazil on April 5, 1943, and was able to walk ashore.

The record for the longest known survival by two people on a raft is 177 days, by fishermen Tabwai Mikaie and Arenta Tebeitabu from the island of Nikunau in Kiribati. The pair, together with another man, were caught in a cyclone shortly after setting out on a trip in their 13-foot-long open dinghy on November 17, 1991, and were found washed ashore in Western Samoa (now Samoa) – 1,100 miles away – on May 11, 1992. The third man died a few days before they reached safety.

ANDES CRASH
In 1972, a plane flying from Uruguay to Chile crashed into the Andes, killing 16 of the 45 passengers. For 10 days the survivors starved in temperatures as low as –40°F, finally having to resort to eating the flesh of the dead. A further 13 people died, either from their injuries or in an avalanche. Rescue came 72 days later, when two of the survivors traveled more than 50 miles in eight days to find help.

LEAST SUCCESSFUL SUICIDE PACT
In March 1996, Taiwanese newlyweds Huang Pin-jen and Chang Shu-mei made a suicide pact when their parents refused to sanction their marriage, but went on to survive four suicide attempts, including hanging, driving their car off a cliff and leaping from the top of a 12-story building. They stopped trying when their parents agreed to reconsider their position.

MOST PEOPLE RESCUED BY A DOG
The most famous canine rescuer of all time is Barry, a St. Bernard who saved more than 40 people during his 12-year career in the Swiss Alps. His best known rescue was that of a boy who lay half frozen under an avalanche in which his mother had died. Barry spread himself across the boy's body to warm him and licked the child's face to wake him up, before carrying him back to the nearest house.

LONGEST PERIOD SURVIVED IN AN UNDERGROUND CAVERN
Bats are generally seen as sinister creatures, but speleologist George Du Prisne owes his life to them. In 1983, he was exploring a cave in Wisconsin when he fell into an underground river and was sucked down a water siphon into a cavern. Rescuers abandoned their search after four days, but Du Prisne was alive, surviving on fish and algae scraped from the walls. Determined to escape, he unraveled orange yarn from his sweater and tied it to the legs of a dozen bats. Residents of a nearby town saw the bats, and he was saved 13 days later.

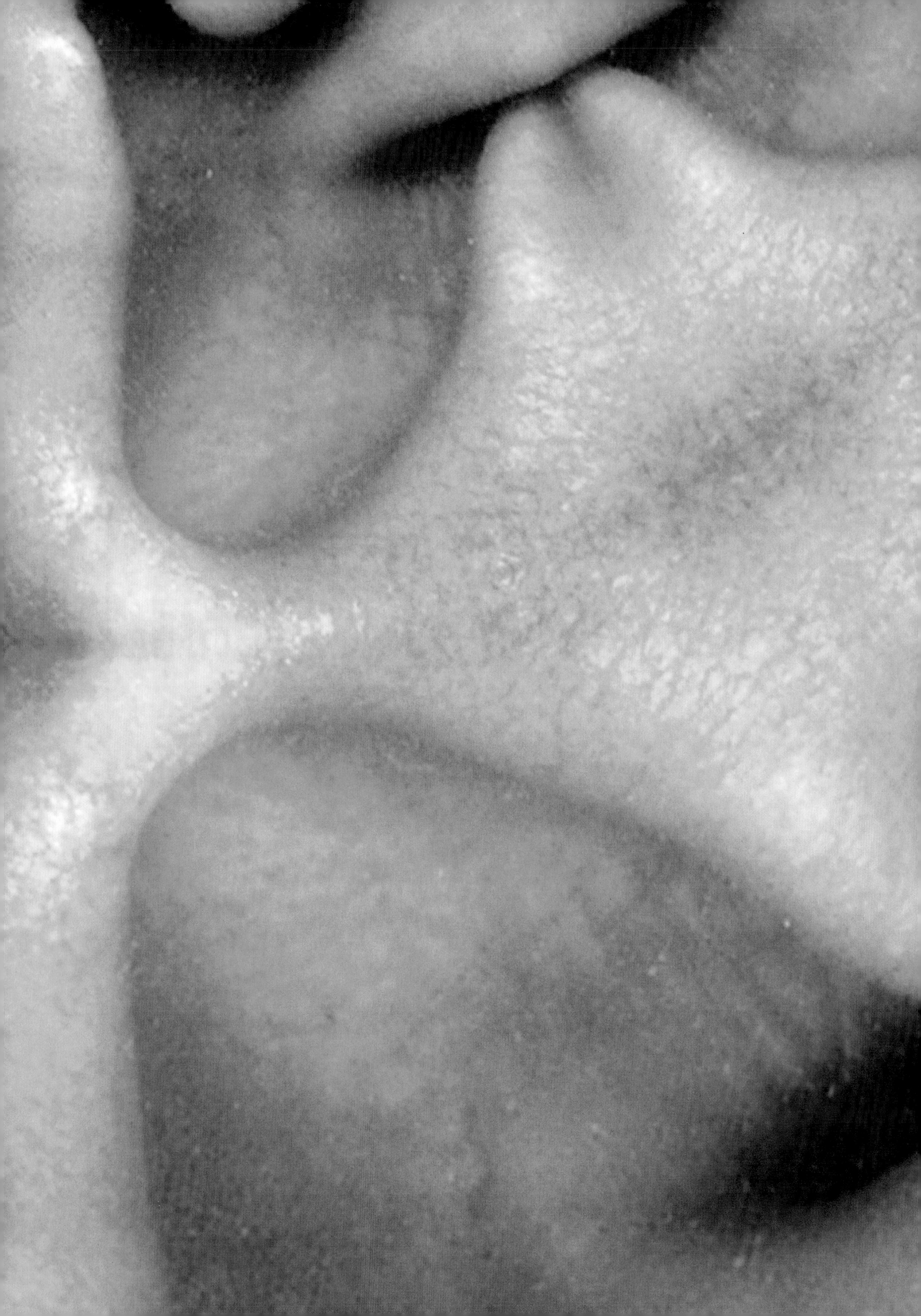

the body

big and small

TALLEST TRIBE
The world's tallest major tribe is the Tutsi (also known as the Watussi) of Rwanda and Burundi, Central Africa. Young men average 6 feet.

SMALLEST TRIBE
The smallest pygmies are the Mbutsi of Congo (ex-Zaïre), who have an average height of 4 ft. 6 in. for men and 4 ft. 5 in. for women. Some groups average only 4 ft. 4 in. for men and 4 ft. 1 in. for women. Pygmy children are generally not significantly shorter than other children, but they do not grow in adolescence because they produce a limited amount of the hormone IGF (insulin-like growth factor).

TALLEST PEOPLE
The tallest ever person for whom there is irrefutable evidence was Robert Wadlow (US), who was 8 ft. 11$\frac{1}{10}$ in. tall with an arm-span of 9 ft. 5$\frac{3}{4}$ in. when he was last measured in 1940, shortly before his death. He would probably have just exceeded 9 feet in height had he survived for another year.

The tallest living American man is Manute Bol, who is 7 ft .6$\frac{3}{4}$ in. tall and was born in 1962 in Sudan. He is a naturalized US citizen, and played professional basketball for the Philadelphia 76ers and other teams.

The tallest living British man is Christopher Greener, who is 7 ft. 6$\frac{1}{4}$ in. tall.

The tallest woman ever was Zeng Jinlian of Yujiang village in the Bright Moon Commune, Hunan Province, China. Zeng Jinlian's height was recorded at 8 ft. 1$\frac{3}{4}$ in. when she died in 1982, (assuming normal spinal curvature: she had severe curvature of the spine).

The tallest living woman is Sandy Allen (US), who is currently 7 ft. 7$\frac{1}{4}$ in. in height. Her abnormal growth began soon after birth, and by the age of 10 she stood 6 ft. 3 in. tall.

The tallest married couple were Anna Hanen Swan of Nova Scotia, Canada and Martin van Buren Bates of Kentucky, who stood 7 ft. 5$\frac{1}{2}$ in. and 7 ft. 2$\frac{1}{2}$ in. respectively when they married in 1871.

The tallest male twins in the world are Michael and James Lanier of Troy, Michigan, who were born in 1969 and are both 7 ft. 4 in. tall.

The tallest female twins are Heather and Heidi Burge of Palos Verdes, California. Born in 1971, they are 6 ft. 4$\frac{3}{4}$ in. tall.

SHORTEST PEOPLE
The shortest female was Pauline Musters, who measured 1 foot long when she was born in Ossendrecht, Netherlands, in 1876, and at the age of nine was 1 ft. 9$\frac{3}{4}$ in. tall. A postmortem examination after her death from pneumonia with meningitis at the age of 19 in New York City showed her to be exactly 2 feet in height (there was some elongation after death).

The shortest living female is Madge Bester of Johannesburg, South Africa, at 2 ft. 1$\frac{1}{2}$ in. She suffers from osteogenesis imperfecta, which results in brittle bones and other deformities of the skeleton.

The shortest twins were Matyus and Béla Matina of Budapest, Hungary (later the United States), who were both 2 ft. 6 in. tall.

The shortest living twins are John and Greg Rice of West Palm Beach, Florida, who are both 2 ft. 10 in. tall.

MOST VARIABLE STATURE
Adam Rainer (Austria) was 3 ft. 10$\frac{1}{2}$ in. tall at the age of 21, but started growing at a rapid rate and by the age of 32 was 7 ft. 1$\frac{3}{4}$ in. He became so weak as a result that he was bedridden for the rest of his life. At his death at age 51 in 1950, he was 7 ft. 8 in. tall.

MOST DISSIMILAR COUPLE
When 3-ft.-1-in. Natalie Lucius married 6-ft.-2-in. Fabien Pretou at Seyssinet-Pariset, France in 1990, there was a record height difference of 3 ft. 1 in. between bride and groom.

HEAVIEST PEOPLE
The heaviest person in medical history was Jon Minnoch of Bainbridge Island, Washington, who was 6 ft. 1 in. tall and weighed more than 1,403 pounds when he was rushed to the hospital suffering from heart and respiratory failure in 1978.

The heaviest ever woman is Rosalie Bradford (US), who is reported to have registered a peak weight of 1,202.24 pounds in January 1987. Bradford started a strict diet after developing congestive heart failure.

The world's heaviest twins were Billy and Benny McCrary, alias the McGuires, from Hendersonville, North Carolina. Normal in size until they were six years old, Billy and Benny

FATTEST MAN CONTEST

"Big is Beautiful" is a motto dear to the males of Sudan's Dinka tribe, who compete each year to earn the title of "fattest man." With an unstable future and no other material way of showing their wealth, obesity is a status symbol for the Dinka – it proves that a tribesman has enough money to keep a large herd of cattle and as a result is able to fatten up on their milk.

Not only does a larger physical size set Dinka men above their peers and command their respect, it also makes the men more attractive to the opposite sex: Dinka women choose their husbands according to their size.

The Dinka are not only famous for their traditions: one of the most successful supermodels in the world was born to this tribe. Alek Wek was brought up in a mud hut before embarking on her career in London, England. She has now appeared on a number of magazine covers, including *Elle*, and earns an average of $16,600 a day.

weighed in at 744.77 pounds and 724.88 pounds respectively in November 1978, when each had a waist measurement of 7 feet. As professional tag wrestling performers, they were billed at weights of up to 770 pounds.

GREATEST WEIGHT LOSS
The greatest recorded slimming feat by a man was that of Jon Minnoch (see HEAVIEST PEOPLE), who had reduced to 476 pounds by July 1979, a weight loss of at least 920 pounds in 16 months.

Rosalie Bradford went from a weight of 1,202.24 pounds in January 1987 to 283 pounds in February 1994, a women's record loss of 917 pounds.

LIGHTEST PERSON
Lucia Xarate, a $26\frac{1}{2}$-inch dwarf from San Carlos, Mexico, weighed just 4.7 pounds at the age of 17. She had increased to 13 pounds by her 20th birthday.

SMALLEST WAISTS
The smallest waist of a person of normal height was 13 inches, for Ethel Granger of Peterborough, England. She reduced from a natural 22 inches between 1929 and 1939.

The 19th-century French actress Mlle. Polaire (Emile Marie Bouchand) also claimed a waist measurement of 13 inches.

HEAVIEST SINGLE BIRTH
Anna Bates (Canada) gave birth to a 23-lb.-12-oz. boy in Seville, Ohio in 1879.

LIGHTEST SINGLE BIRTHS
A premature baby girl weighing $9\frac{9}{10}$ ounces is reported to have been born at Loyola University Medical Center, Maywood, Illinois on June 27, 1989.

The lowest definite birthweight recorded for a surviving infant is 10 ounces, for Marian Taggart (née Chapman), who was born six weeks premature in Tyne & Wear, England in 1938. The 12-inch-long child was nursed by Dr. D. A. Shearer, who fed her hourly for the first 30 hours with brandy, glucose and water through a fountain-pen filler.

SHORTEST TWINS
John and Greg Rice are the world's shortest living twins. Being just 2 ft. 10 in. tall has not stopped them from becoming successful businessmen. They made their fortunes in real estate in Florida in the 1970s, and now own a multimillion-dollar motivational speaking company called Think Big, which organizes seminars on creative problem solving. In addition, the twins produce, write and even star in commercials for their clients. The Rices are seen here in scenes broadcast on the Fox TV series *Guinness World Records™: Primetime*.

SHORTEST PERSON
The shortest ever mature human of whom there is independent evidence was Gul Mohammed of New Delhi, India. In 1990, he was 1 ft. $10\frac{1}{2}$ in. in height and weighed $37\frac{1}{2}$ pounds. He died at age 36 in 1997 of a heart attack, after a long struggle with asthma and bronchitis. Mohammed had a lifelong dislike of children, who sometimes bullied and robbed him. He also had a great fear of cats and dogs because of his size.

LARGEST WAIST
Walter Hudson (US) had a 9-ft.-11-in. waist in 1987. His typical daily snack intake was 12 doughnuts, 10 bags of potato chips, two giant pizzas or eight Chinese carryouts, and half a cake.

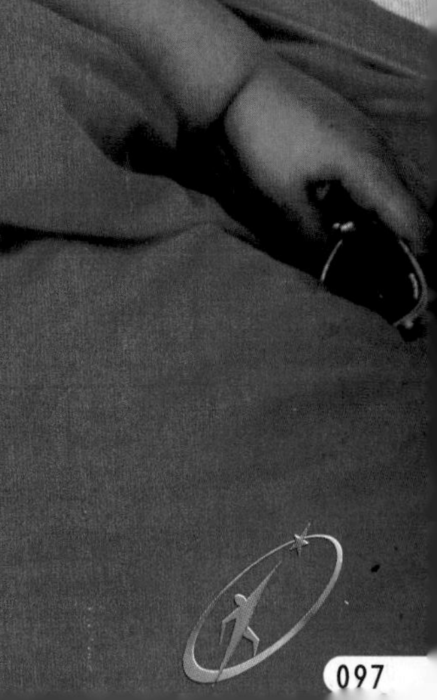

body parts

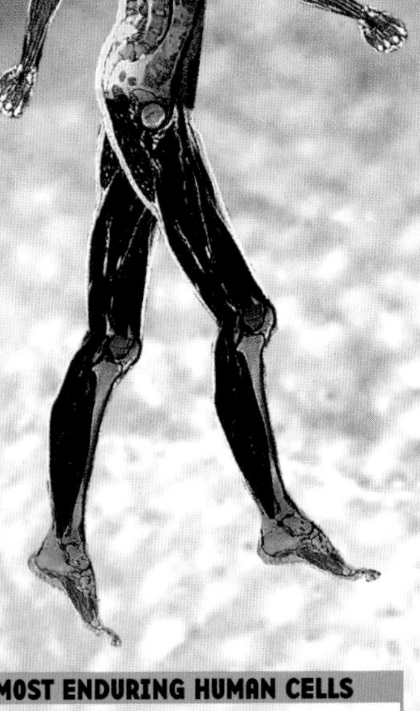

MOST ENDURING HUMAN CELLS

Cells taken from the body of Henrietta Lacks were missing a particular chromosome, which means they can live indefinitely, and are still alive in laboratories more than 40 years after Lacks' death. Scientists hope these cells may one day help in the search for a cure for cancer.

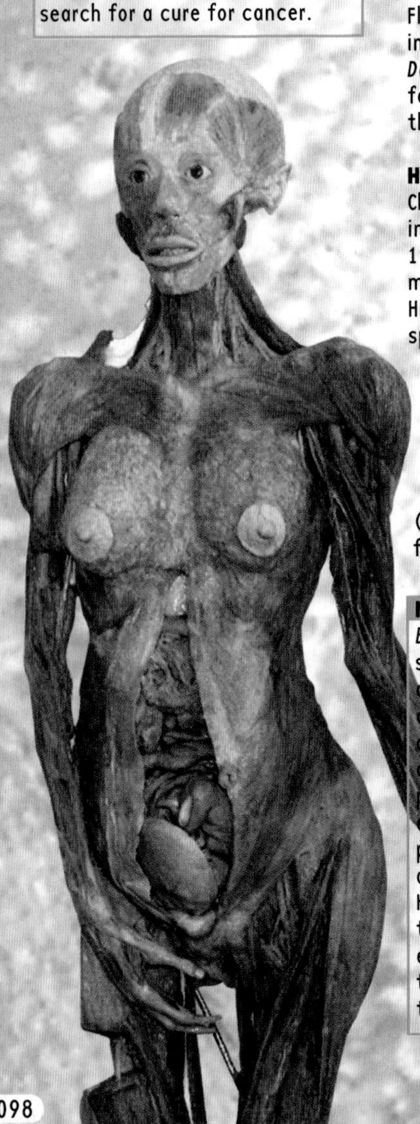

HIGHEST-INSURED BODY

British glamour model Suzanne Mizzi's 34-24-34 figure has been insured by a fashion firm for the sum of $16.6 million. This includes $8.3 million for her face, $1.66 million for her arms, $1.66 million for her behind, $1.66 million for her legs and $3.32 million for her breasts. The premiums cost a total $58,100 a year. One of the conditions of the policy is that Mizzi must not get pregnant for a period of three years. Among other restrictions imposed by the policy, Mizzi is barred from going hot-air ballooning, standing on soccer terraces, and indulging in "immoral behavior."

HIGHEST-INSURED LEGS

Former *Riverdance* star Michael Flatley, who is now performing in the hit show *Lord of the Dance*, has had his legs insured for $40 million. He is currently the world's highest-paid dancer.

HIGHEST-INSURED FEET

Charlie Chaplin had his feet insured for $150,000 in the 1920s. Charlie Chaplin was the most popular comedian of Hollywood's silent era, and a splay-legged walk was the trademark of his character the Tramp.

HIGHEST-INSURED HANDS

Rolling Stones guitarist Keith Richards has had his left (guitar-playing) hand insured for $1.6 million.

British boxer Nigel Benn, the former super middleweight world champion nicknamed the "Dark Destroyer," had his fists insured for $16.6 million in the 1990s.

In 1939, Fleischer Studios in Hollywood took out an insurance policy for $185,000 with Lloyd's of London to cover the hands of the 116 animators employed to work on the full-length cartoon *Mr. Bug Goes To Town* (1941).

HIGHEST-INSURED FACES

Hollywood screen stars Rudolph Valentino, Douglas Fairbanks and Mary Pickford all had their faces insured in the early 1920s, the latter for $1 million. The actors were all taking advantage of the "scarred face" policy that had recently been introduced by Los Angeles underwriter Arthur Stebbins.

Silent screen star John Bunny insured his comical face for $100,000 in 1911. Bunny made a total of 260 short films known as "Bunnygraphs," "Bunnyfinches" and "Bunnyfinchgraphs" between 1910 and 1914.

HIGHEST-INSURED NECK

Hollywood star Kathleen Key, whose 19 films included *College Days* (1926) and *North of Hudson Bay* (1923), had her neck insured for $25,000 in the mid-1920s.

MOST CONTROVERSIAL MEDICAL EXHIBITION

Body World: A Look into the Human Body, an exhibition of dissected, skinless human bodies, opened at the State Museum for Technology and Labor in Mannheim, Germany in October 1997. Despite causing controversy among many local people, who thought that the display of human limbs and organs – which included lungs infected by cancer – was undignified, the show was an enormous success, with people waiting in line for up to three hours to get in. It has been estimated that more than 200,000 people saw the show, which was put on by Professor Gunther Von Hagens of the University of Heidelberg and first shown in Japan in 1996, where it attracted a million visitors. Hagens is responsible for developing the "Plastination technique," the process by which dead bodies are put into cold acetone to extract water, which is replaced by molten plastics. The plastic then turns hard, making the bodies and body parts shine. The bodies were those of people who had donated their remains to science.

HIGHEST-INSURED EYES

In the 1920s, Ben Turpin, the cross-eyed Hollywood movie and vaudeville actor whose 114 films included early Keystone Cops comedies, paid the sum of $100,000 to insure against his eyes ever uncrossing.

In 1918, at the peak of her career, the actress Clara Kimball Young, often described as the most beautiful woman in the world, insured her large eyes for $150,000.

HIGHEST-INSURED TEETH

British entertainer Ken Dodd has insured his trademark buckteeth for $6.6 million. The insurers prohibit him from eating hard candy and riding a motorbike, and insist that he brushes his teeth at least three times a day. They have also said they would not pay out a claim for an accident occurring in a bar fight. The entertainer's buckteeth are the result of a childhood bicycling accident.

HIGHEST-INSURED NOSE

Jimmy Durante, who starred in *It's A Mad Mad Mad Mad World* (1963) and *Billy Rose's Jumbo* (1962), had the most famous nose in Hollywood. Nicknamed "Da Schnozz," he had it insured for $100,000 in the mid-1930s.

HIGHEST-INSURED VOICES

The members of pop group En Vogue, one of the most successful all-girl groups ever, have insured their voices for a total of $6.4 million.

Rock star Bruce Springsteen, whose multiplatinum album *Born in the USA* (1984) is one of the biggest-selling records in history, has insured his voice for $5.6 million.

MOST VALUABLE PENIS

Napoleon Bonaparte's penis was removed at autopsy by a team of French and Belgian doctors and first put up for auction at Christie's in 1972. About 1 inch long and listed as "a small dried- up object," it failed to get the reserve price. It was purchased five years later by an American urologist for $3,800.

MOST VALUABLE HAIR
In 1988, a lock of Horatio Nelson's hair sold for $9,475 to a bookseller in Cirencester, England.

In 1994, two collectors paid Sotheby's, London the sum of $6,000 for a 4-inch lock of Beethoven's hair, said to have been cut off by the composer's father in 1827. The buyers wanted to have it DNA-tested to confirm reports that the composer had African blood and suffered from syphilis.

MOST EXPENSIVE BEARD HAIRS
Hairs pulled from the beard of Henri IV of France when his tomb was desecrated in 1793 were sold for $122 in Paris, France in 1994.

MOST VALUABLE TOOTH
In 1816, a tooth belonging to Sir Isaac Newton sold for $3,785 in London, England. It was purchased by a nobleman who had it set in a ring.

STRANGEST BODY PART KEPT AS A KEEPSAKE
Joni Mabe of Athens, Georgia owns one of Elvis Presley's warts as part of her collection of Elvis memorabilia.

HEAVIEST AND LIGHTEST BRAINS
The world's heaviest known brain weighed 5 lb. $1^{1}/_{10}$ oz. and belonged to a 30-year-old man. It was reported by Dr. T. Mandybur and Karen Carney of the Department of Pathology and Laboratory Medicine at the University of Cincinnati in December 1992. The lightest normal or non-atrophied brain on record weighed 1 lb. 8 oz. It belonged to Daniel Lyon, who died at the age of 46 in New York in 1907. He was just over 5 feet tall and weighed 145 pounds.

MOST BIZARRE USE FOR A BODY PART
King Charles I's fourth cervical vertebra was stolen by a surgeon during an autopsy and fashioned into a salt cellar. The novelist Sir Walter Scott used it at dinner parties for 30 years until Queen Victoria found out and demanded its return to St. George's Chapel in Windsor, England.

MOST ARTIFICIAL JOINTS
Norma Wickwire, who has rheumatoid arthritis, had eight of her 10 major joints replaced from 1976 to 1989.

BIGGEST FEET
Excluding cases of elephantiasis, the biggest known feet of any living person are those of Matthew McGrory of Westchester, Pennsylvania, seen here with his mother Maureen McGrory-Lacey in scenes broadcast on the Fox TV series *Guinness World Records™: Primetime.* McGrory is 25 years old and stands 7 ft. 6 in. tall. He wears size $28^{1}/_{2}$ shoes specially made for him by Converse, and his socks are knitted by his mother.

BIGGEST GALLBLADDER
The world's biggest gallbladder weighed 23 pounds and was removed from a 69-year-old woman by Professor Bimal C. Ghosh at the National Naval Medical Center in Bethesda, Maryland on March 15, 1989. The patient recovered and left the hospital 10 days later.

bodily phenomena

OLDEST CONJOINED TWINS
Chang and Eng Bunker, the famous conjoined twins from Siam (now Thailand), were born on May 11, 1811, married sisters Sarah and Adelaide Yates of Wilkes County, North Carolina, and fathered 22 children between them. They died within three hours of each other at age 63 on January 17, 1874. The pair, who were never separated because it was thought that to do so would endanger both their lives, earned their living in the US as a circus attraction in the Barnum and Bailey Circus.

Millie and Christine McCoy were born into slavery in North Carolina on July 11, 1851, and sold several times. They were very successful in show business under the title of "Two-Headed Nightingale" or "Two-Headed Lady." In 1900, the pair, who were never separated, retired. They died aged 61 in 1912.

MOST SUCCESSFUL CONJOINED TWIN OF MODERN TIMES
Andy Garcia, the actor who has starred in movies such as *The Godfather, Part 3* (1994) and *Things to Do in Denver When You're Dead* (1995), was born with his twin attached to his shoulder in Cuba in 1956. The twin was no bigger than a tennis ball and was removed by surgeons minutes after birth.

LONGEST UNDISCOVERED TWIN
In July 1997, a fetus was discovered in the abdomen of 16-year-old Hisham Ragab of Egypt, who had been complaining of stomach pains. A swollen sac found pressing against his kidneys turned out to be Hisham's 7-inch-long, 4-lb.-6-oz. identical twin. The fetus, which had been growing inside him, had lived to the age of 32 or 33 weeks.

LONGEST HUMAN TAIL
In 1889, *Scientific American* described a 12-year-old Moi boy from Thailand who had a soft tail almost 1 foot in length. In ancient literature there are many reports of adult men and women with 6–7-inch tails. Today they are removed at birth.

FASTEST-GROWING HUMAN TAIL
In 1901, Ross Granville Harrison of Johns Hopkins University, Maryland described a child whose tail grew at an alarming rate. By the time the boy was six months old, his tail, which was covered by normal skin with muscular strands but without a bone, was 3 inches long. When he sneezed or coughed, his tail would wag or contract.

LONGEST-LIVING TWO-HEADED PERSON
The Two-Headed Boy of Bengal was born in 1783 and died of a cobra bite at the age of four. His two heads, each of which had its own brain, were the same size and were covered with black hair at their junction. When the boy cried or smiled the features of the upper head were not always affected and their movements were thought to be reflexive.

HAIRIEST WOMAN
Julia Pastrana, who was born into an Indian tribe in Mexico in 1834, was covered in hair except for her eyes. She was exhibited to the public in the US, Canada, and Europe in the 1850s and mummified on her death in 1860. In 1964, Marco Ferreri made *La Donna Scimmia* (*The Ape Woman*) based on her life. Pastrana's mummy was exhibited in Norway and Denmark in the 1970s before mysteriously vanishing. It was found in 1990.

CONJOINED TWINS
Twins with the condition called dicephales tetrabrachius dipus have two heads, four arms and two legs. The only documented case is that of Masha and Dasha Krivoshlyapovy (below), born in the USSR in 1950. They had three legs (one vestigial) at birth. The first successful separation of conjoined twins was performed on xiphopagous (joined at the sternum) girls by Dr. Jac S. Geller in Ohio in 1952.

LONGEST BEARDS
Hans Langseth had a record-breaking $17\frac{1}{2}$-foot-long beard at the time of his death in Kensett, Iowa, in 1927. The beard was presented to the Smithsonian Institute in Washington, DC, in 1967.

Janice Deveree of Bracken County, Kentucky, had a 14-inch beard in 1884 — the longest of any "bearded lady."

LONGEST MOUSTACHE
Kalyan Ramji Sain of India began growing a moustache in 1976. In July 1993 it had a total span of 11 ft 11 in.

MOST FINGERS AND TOES
A baby boy was found to have 14 fingers and 15 toes at an inquest in London in September 1921.

FEWEST TOES
Some members of the Wadomo tribe of Zimbabwe and the Kalanga tribe of Botswana have only two toes.

MOST BREASTS
The greatest number of distinct breasts is believed to have been 10. Between 1878 and 1898, a total of 930 cases of multiple breasts were reported.

MOST SETS OF TEETH
In 1896, "Lison's case," describing a woman who grew a fourth set of teeth, was published in France.

MOST EXTREMES CASES OF COMPULSIVE SWALLOWING
In 1927, a 42-year-old woman complaining of "slight abdominal pain" was found by doctors at Ontario Hospital, Canada to have 2,533 objects, including 947 bent pins, in her stomach.

The heaviest object to have been extracted from a human stomach is a 5-lb.-3-oz. hairball, from a 20-year-old British woman on March 30, 1895.

MOST EXTREME CASE OF MUNCHAUSEN'S SYNDROME
William McIlroy (Great Britain) had the most extreme known case of Munchausen's syndrome, an incurable condition characterized by a constant desire for medical treatment. In 50 years, McIlroy had 400 operations and stayed at 100 hospitals under 22 aliases. The estimated cost of his treatment up to 1979, when he moved into a retirement home, was $5.3 million.

MOST FAMOUS WIND BREAKER
Joseph Pujol, better known as Le Petomane, was born in France in 1857 and discovered at an early age that he had an amazing talent for breaking wind. He perfected his skill and eventually put on shows in which he played tunes and imitated noises by breaking wind. When he died in 1945, the Sorbonne offered his family $4,940 to examine his body. The family refused.

LONGEST FINGERNAILS
Frances Redmond, pictured right, has the longest fingernails in the United States. They have grown to 17¼ inches in 12 years. The world's longest fingernails are those of Shridhar Chillal of India, who last cut his fingernails in 1952. At the end of March 1997, the nails of his left hand, from the thumb to the little finger, were 55 inches, 43 inches, 46 inches, 49 inches, and 48 inches long.

LONGEST HAIR
Hu Saelao, pictured above, second from left, an 85-year-old tribesman from Chiang Mai province, Thailand, is one of several people claiming to have the world's longest hair. It is a tradition in this particular part of Thailand for men to grow their hair very long. Saelao claims that he has not cut his hair for more than 70 years and it now measures 16 ft. 10 in. long.

life

OLDEST PEOPLE
The greatest fully authenticated age to which a human being has ever lived is 122 years 164 days, by Jeanne Calment (France). She died on August 4, 1997.

The greatest age to which any man has lived is 120 years 237 days, by Shigechiyo Izumi of Isen, Tokunoshima, Japan. He was recorded as a six-year-old in Japan's first census of 1871 and worked until he was 105. He died of pneumonia in 1986.

The oldest ever twins were Eli Shadrack and John Meshak Phipps, who were born on February 14, 1803 in Affington, Virginia. Eli died first, at age 108, in 1911.

The longest-lived triplets were Faith, Hope and Charity Cardwell, who were born on May 18, 1899 in Elm Mott, Texas. Faith died at age 95 years 137 days in 1994.

MOST DESCENDANTS
Samuel S. Mast of Fryburg, Pennsylvania had 824 living descendants (11 children, 97 grandchildren, 634 great-grandchildren and 82 great-great-grandchildren) when he died at the age of 96 on October 15, 1992.

MOST LIVING ASCENDANTS
Megan Austin of Bar Harbor, Maine had a complete set of grandparents and great-grandparents and five great-great-grandparents (a total of 19 direct ascendants) when she was born in 1982 .

LONGEST LINEAGE
The written lineage of K'ung Chia (the great-great-great-great-grandfather of Confucius) extends from the eighth century BC to the present. Seven of K'ung Chia's 86th lineal descendants are alive today.

In January 1997, Chief Rabbi Lau of Israel and the Jerusalem Institute of Jewish Genealogy concluded that the Lurie (or Luria) family is directly descended from the royal house of the biblical King David and can trace its genealogy back to the 10th century BC. The Lurie family tree includes such distinguished members as the prophet Isaiah (8th century BC), the Rashi (1040–1105), Hillel Hanasi ("the Elder"; 30 BC–1st century AD), Felix Mendelssohn, Karl Marx, Sigmund Freud, Salvador Luria, Yehudi Menuhin, Sir Immanuel Jakobovitz, and Ranan Lurie.

MOST LIVING GENERATIONS OF ONE FAMILY
Augusta Bunge of Wisconsin became a great-great-great-great-grandmother on January 21, 1989, when her great-great-great-granddaughter gave birth to a son, Christopher Bollig. Augusta was born in 1879.

YOUNGEST LIVING GREAT-GREAT-GREAT GRANDMOTHER
Harriet Holmes of Newfoundland, Canada was a record 88 years 50 days old when she became a great-great-great-grandmother on March 8, 1987.

OLDEST MOTHERS
Arceli Keh of Highland, California gave birth to a daughter, Cynthia, at age 63 years 9 mo. on November 7, 1996, at Loma Linda University Medical Center. News of the birth was made public on April 23, 1997.

MOST PROLIFIC MOTHERS
The greatest officially recorded number of children born to one mother is 69, to the wife of Feodor Vassilyev, a peasant from Shuya, Russia. In a total of 27 confinements between 1725 and 1765, she gave birth to 16 pairs of twins, seven sets of triplets and four sets of quadruplets (the greatest number of multiple births in one family). Only two of the children failed to survive their infancy.

The world's most prolific living mother is believed to be Leontina Albina from San Antonio, Chile, who produced her 55th and last child in 1981. Her husband states that they were married in Argentina in 1943 and had five

OLDEST PEOPLE

The title of world's oldest person may be one of the most coveted of all, but the many claims to it are usually fraught with difficulty and controversy. Amm Atwa Moussa, a former fisherman from Egypt, claims to be 150. In evidence, Moussa (pictured being bathed by one of his 39 grandchildren) states that he was married to his first wife for 60 years prior to a further four marriages, and says that he can recall fleeing with his family in 1869 to avoid being forced to work on the Suez Canal.

However, *The Guinness Book of Records* requires at least one of the following forms of evidence: a birth certificate, together with proof that it is that of the individual concerned rather than that of a relative; evidence from a census; or proof of the person's age at a major event in their life. People who live to be 100 are called centenarians, while those who live to 110 are supercentenarians. Of the former, there are approximately 20,000 in the United States alone, and according to demographers, the number of people who live to at least 100 is increasing all the time. Perhaps the most famous supercentenarian of all was Frenchwoman Jeanne Calment, who died at age 122 in 1997.

sets of triplets (all boys) before moving to Chile.

MOST CONFINEMENTS
Elizabeth Greenhille of Abbots Langley, Hertfordshire, England is reported to have had a total of 39 children (32 daughters and seven sons) in a record 38 confinements. She died in 1681.

LARGEST PREGNANCY
In 1971, Dr. Gennaro Montanino of Rome, Italy claimed to have removed the fetuses of 10 girls and five boys from the womb of a 35-year-old woman after four months of the pregnancy. A fertility drug was responsible for this unique instance of quindecaplets.

MOST CHILDREN PRODUCED IN A SINGLE BIRTH
A record 10 children (two males and eight females) are reported to have been born at Bacacai, Brazil, on April 22, 1946. Reports of 10 children in one birth were also received from Spain in 1924 and China in 1936.

The record for the greatest fully authenticated number of children ever produced in one birth is nine, to Geraldine Brodrick at the Royal Hospital for Women, Sydney, Australia on June 13, 1971. None of the five boys and four girls lived for more than six days. The birth of nine children was also reported in Philadelphia, Pennsylvania in 1971 and in Bagerhat, Bangladesh, in 1977. No children survived in either case.

LONGEST INTERVAL BETWEEN THE BIRTH OF TWINS
Peggy Lynn of Huntingdon, Pennsylvania gave birth to a baby girl, Hanna, at the Geisinger Medical Center, Danville, Pennsylvania on November 11, 1995. She gave birth to Hanna's twin Eric 84 days later, on February 2, 1996.

WORLD'S BIGGEST BABIES
In September 1996, 17-month-old Zack Strenkert, one of the largest babies in the world, made an appearance on *The Jerry Springer Show* with his parents, Chris and Laurie, from Goshen, New York. Zack weighed in at an astonishing 70.17 pounds — the weight usually reached by boys at any age between six and 14. Zack's elder brother Andrew weighed 121.55 pounds at the age of seven.

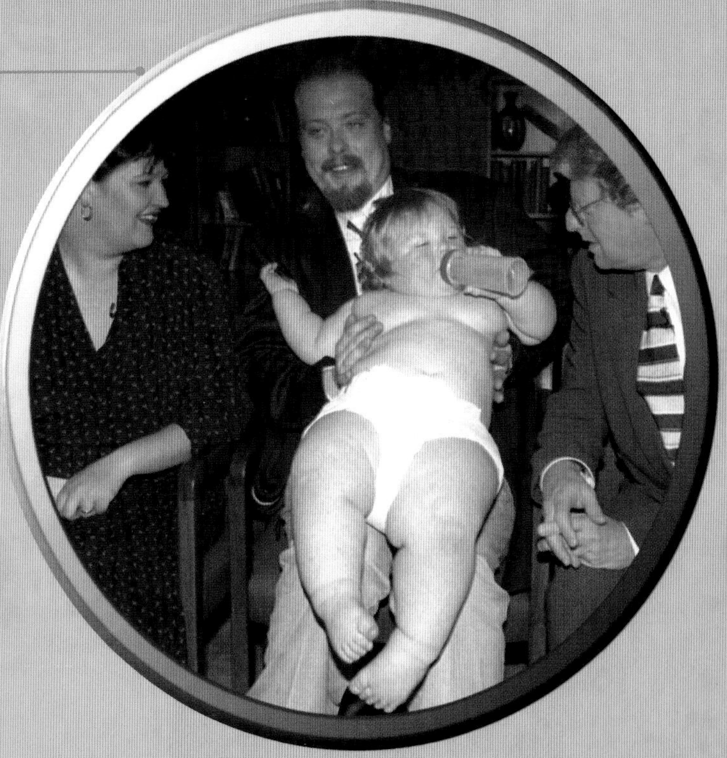

SHORTEST INTERVAL BETWEEN THE BIRTH OF TWO CHILDREN
The record for the shortest interval between the birth of two children in separate confinements is 209 days, to Margaret Blake of Luton, England, who gave birth to Conor on March 27, 1995 and Bunty on October 23, 1995.

LONGEST INTERVAL BETWEEN THE BIRTH OF TWO CHILDREN
The longest interval between the birth of two children to one mother is 41 years, by Elizabeth Buttle of Carmarthenshire, Wales, who gave birth to a daughter, Belinda, in 1956, and a son, Joseph, on November 20, 1997, when she was 60.

MOST PREMATURE BABY
James Gill was born 128 days premature to Brenda and James Gill in Ottawa, Ontario, Canada, on May 20, 1987. He weighed 1 lb. 6 oz. — about the same as a dozen eggs.

OLDEST LIVING PERSON
The greatest fully authenticated age of any person alive today is 119, by Sarah Knauss, seen here with her great-great-great grandson. She was born on September 24, 1880 in Hollywood, a small mining village which is now part of Hazelton, Pennsylvania, and now lives in a nursing home in Allentown, Pennsylvania. Six generations of her family celebrated her 119th birthday with her.

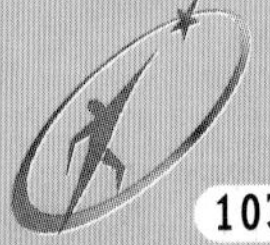

death and disease

BIGGEST KILLER OF WOMEN
Tuberculosis (TB) has now become the single biggest killer of women globally. It has been estimated that a third of all women in Asia are infected with it.

MOST DEVASTATING PANDEMIC
The pneumonic form of plague (bacterial infection) killed about 25% of the population of Europe and approximately 75 million people worldwide during the Black Death of 1347–51. Between one-eighth and two-thirds of infected people are estimated to have died of the disease.

MOST HIV INFECTIONS
Above, the HIV virus (in red) is shown attacking a T-cell. According to the UN AIDS Report of November 25, 1997, India holds the record for the country most affected by the disease, with between 3 and 5 million HIV-positive people. The World Health Organization calculates that 20 million people – more than the total population of Australia and New Zealand – are infected with HIV worldwide.

DEADLIEST BUG
The bacterium *Yersinia pestis* caused the death of 25 million people in 14th-century Europe. Transmitted by fleas and rats, it causes bubonic plague, the symptoms of which include fever, headache and chills.

DEADLIEST DISEASES
The AIDS virus (Acquired Immune Deficiency Syndrome) and rabies encephalitis, a viral infection of the central nervous system, are universally considered to be fatal.

Lassa fever, a condition caused by a rare West African virus, has a mortality rate of more than 50%. Marburg fever and Ebola fever also have very high death rates.

Cholera has killed approximately 20 million people in India since 1900. Death rates can be up to 50% in untreated outbreaks.

Yellow fever is an increasingly rare mosquito-borne infection prevalent in the Caribbean, Brazil and the west coast of Africa. Some reports suggest yellow fever kills as many as 90% of those infected.

MOST URGENT HEALTH PROBLEM
According to a 1996 report by the WHO, tuberculosis (TB) is spreading rapidly and will kill more than 30 million people worldwide between 1996 and 2005 if this spread continues at the present rate. One-third of people with HIV die from TB.

MOST KILLED BY INFLUENZA
A record 21,640,000 people worldwide died of influenza between 1918 and 1919.

DEADLIEST MALARIAL INFECTION
Plasmodium falciparum causes malignant tertian malaria, which can affect the brain. It causes seizures, coma or even sudden death.

MOST KILLED BY INFECTION
The West African island-republic of Sao Tome and Principe has a record 241 deaths per annum from infectious diseases for every 100,000 people.

NEWEST INFECTIOUS DISEASE
The most recently discovered disease that infects humans is

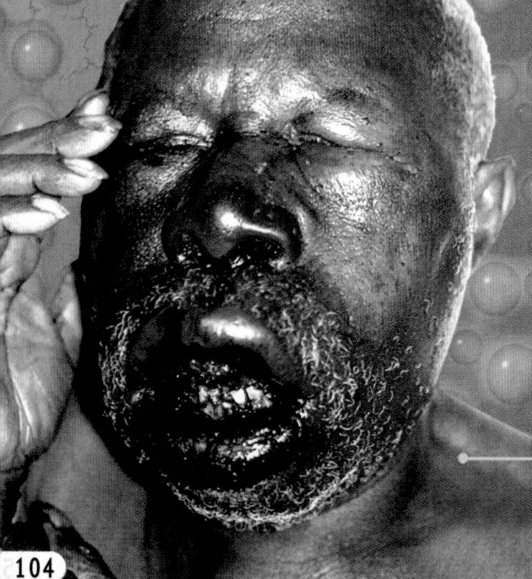

WORST FLESH-EATING BACTERIA
Necrotizing fasciitis, the extremely rare disease dubbed the "flesh-eating bug" by the British press in May 1994 after a number of outbreaks, has been known since World War I and is the world's most dangerous flesh-destroying disease. It is caused by Streptococcus A bacteria multiplying under a person's skin to form a mixture of toxins that attacks the tissue and leaves gangrene in its wake. The only cure is surgical removal of the damaged area. Sufferers report wounds that gush cloudy, bloody-orange fluid, fevers of up to 104° F, delirium, oozing pus, purple skin, open sores up to 6 inches deep and flesh that comes off in pieces in their hands. Those with a weakened immune system are thought to be most at risk, but it is possible for a healthy person to contract the disease. However, new research has shown that injections of a blood product containing immunoglobulins pooled from many people seems to reduce deaths from the disease.

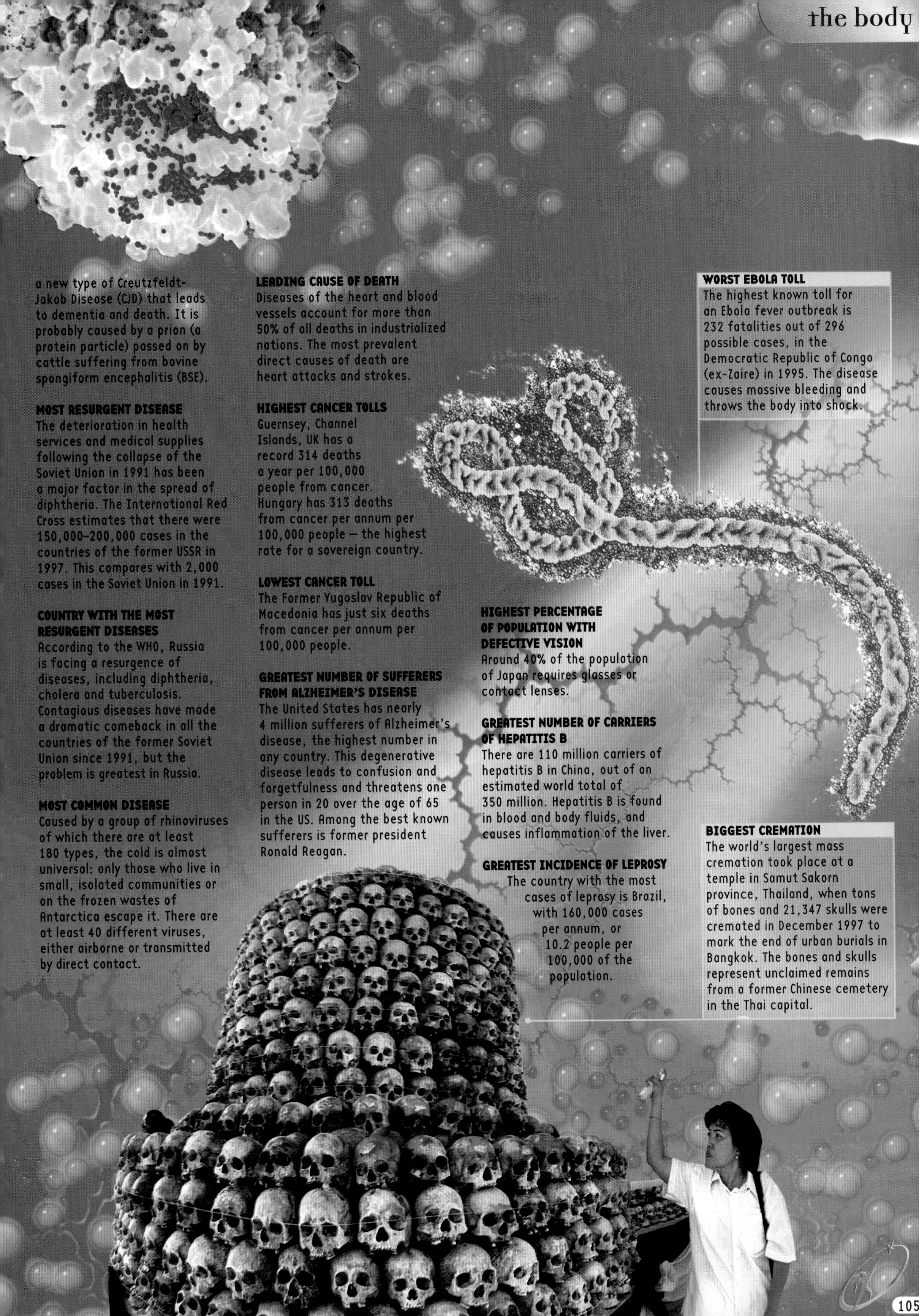

a new type of Creutzfeldt-Jakob Disease (CJD) that leads to dementia and death. It is probably caused by a prion (a protein particle) passed on by cattle suffering from bovine spongiform encephalitis (BSE).

MOST RESURGENT DISEASE
The deterioration in health services and medical supplies following the collapse of the Soviet Union in 1991 has been a major factor in the spread of diphtheria. The International Red Cross estimates that there were 150,000–200,000 cases in the countries of the former USSR in 1997. This compares with 2,000 cases in the Soviet Union in 1991.

COUNTRY WITH THE MOST RESURGENT DISEASES
According to the WHO, Russia is facing a resurgence of diseases, including diphtheria, cholera and tuberculosis. Contagious diseases have made a dramatic comeback in all the countries of the former Soviet Union since 1991, but the problem is greatest in Russia.

MOST COMMON DISEASE
Caused by a group of rhinoviruses of which there are at least 180 types, the cold is almost universal: only those who live in small, isolated communities or on the frozen wastes of Antarctica escape it. There are at least 40 different viruses, either airborne or transmitted by direct contact.

LEADING CAUSE OF DEATH
Diseases of the heart and blood vessels account for more than 50% of all deaths in industrialized nations. The most prevalent direct causes of death are heart attacks and strokes.

HIGHEST CANCER TOLLS
Guernsey, Channel Islands, UK has a record 314 deaths a year per 100,000 people from cancer. Hungary has 313 deaths from cancer per annum per 100,000 people – the highest rate for a sovereign country.

LOWEST CANCER TOLL
The Former Yugoslav Republic of Macedonia has just six deaths from cancer per annum per 100,000 people.

GREATEST NUMBER OF SUFFERERS FROM ALZHEIMER'S DISEASE
The United States has nearly 4 million sufferers of Alzheimer's disease, the highest number in any country. This degenerative disease leads to confusion and forgetfulness and threatens one person in 20 over the age of 65 in the US. Among the best known sufferers is former president Ronald Reagan.

HIGHEST PERCENTAGE OF POPULATION WITH DEFECTIVE VISION
Around 40% of the population of Japan requires glasses or contact lenses.

GREATEST NUMBER OF CARRIERS OF HEPATITIS B
There are 110 million carriers of hepatitis B in China, out of an estimated world total of 350 million. Hepatitis B is found in blood and body fluids, and causes inflammation of the liver.

GREATEST INCIDENCE OF LEPROSY
The country with the most cases of leprosy is Brazil, with 160,000 cases per annum, or 10.2 people per 100,000 of the population.

WORST EBOLA TOLL
The highest known toll for an Ebola fever outbreak is 232 fatalities out of 296 possible cases, in the Democratic Republic of Congo (ex-Zaire) in 1995. The disease causes massive bleeding and throws the body into shock.

BIGGEST CREMATION
The world's largest mass cremation took place at a temple in Samut Sakorn province, Thailand, when tons of bones and 21,347 skulls were cremated in December 1997 to mark the end of urban burials in Bangkok. The bones and skulls represent unclaimed remains from a former Chinese cemetery in the Thai capital.

medical extremes

MOST PILLS TAKEN
The record for the greatest number of pills known to have been taken by one patient is 565,939, by C. H. A. Kilner of Bindura, Zimbabwe, between June 9, 1967 and June 19, 1988. This works out at an average of 73 pills per day. It is estimated that if all the pills he had taken were laid out end to end, they would form an unbroken line 2 miles 186 yd. long.

LONGEST COMA
Elaine Esposito of Tarpon Springs, Florida went into a coma at the age of six, after an appendectomy on August 6, 1941. She died at age 43 on November 25, 1978, having been comatose for 37 years 111 days.

LATEST POST-MORTEM BIRTH
On July 5, 1983, a baby girl was delivered from a woman who had been brain-dead for 84 days in Roanoke, Virginia.

LONGEST TIME SPENT IN AN IRON LUNG
Jane Firwell of Chichester, England has been using a negative pressure respirator since May 1946.

John Prestwich of Kings Langley, England was put on a respirator on November 24, 1955, and has been dependent on it ever since.

LONGEST-LASTING TRACHEOTOMY
Winifred Campbell of London, England breathed through a silver tube in her throat for 86 years. She died in 1992.

LONGEST CARDIAC ARREST
On December 7, 1987 fisherman Jan Egil Refsdahl went into cardiac arrest for a record four hours after falling overboard in the freezing waters off Bergen, Norway. Refsdahl was rushed to Haukeland hospital when his body temperature fell to 75°F and his heart stopped beating, but he went on to make a complete recovery after being hooked up to a heart-lung machine.

OLDEST PERSON TO UNDERGO AN OPERATION
The oldest person ever to have been operated on was James Henry Brett Jr., who underwent a hip operation in Houston, Texas at the age of 111 years 105 days on November 7, 1960.

BIGGEST BLOOD TRANSFUSION
Warren Jyrich, a 50-year-old hemophiliac, required a record 2,400 donor units of blood – the equivalent of 280⁸⁄₁₀ gallons – during open-heart surgery at the Michael Reese Hospital, Chicago, Illinois in December 1970.

HIGHEST BLOOD SUGAR LEVEL
On October 27, 1995 James LeRoy Flinchbaugh of Kalispell, Montana was admitted to Aurora Presbyterian Hospital, Aurora, Colorado with a blood sugar level of 2,048 mg/dl. He was still conscious.

HIGHEST BODY TEMPERATURE
On July 10, 1980, 52-year-old Willie Jones was admitted to Grady Memorial Hospital, Atlanta, Georgia with heatstroke and found to have a body temperature of 115.7°F – the highest on record. He was discharged after 24 days.

LOWEST BODY TEMPERATURE
The lowest authenticated body temperature was 57.5°F, registered by two-year-old Karlee Kosolofski of Regina, Saskatchewan, Canada on February 23, 1994. Karlee, who had been accidentally locked outside her home for six hours in a temperature of -8°F, suffered frostbite and had to have her left leg amputated above the knee, but made a full recovery. Some people have died of hypothermia with body temperatures of 95°F.

LONGEST HICCUPPING FIT
Charles Osborne of Anthon, Iowa began hiccupping in 1922, while he was trying to weigh a hog before slaughtering it, and continued until February 1990. He was unable to find a cure, but managed to lead a normal life, marrying twice and fathering eight children.

LONGEST SNEEZING FIT
Donna Griffiths of Pershore, England started sneezing at age 12 on January 13, 1981 and sneezed an estimated 1 million times in the following year. She did not have a sneeze-free day until September 16, 1983.

OLDEST KIDNEY DONOR AND RECIPIENT
In December 1995, 78-year-old Victoria Whybrew became the oldest kidney donor on record when she donated one of her kidneys to her 77-year-old husband Robert, who is now the oldest kidney recipient on record with the US United Network for Organ Sharing. The couple, pictured left, had been married for 49 years when the exchange took place at the San Francisco Medical Center. In May 1998, two couples took part in a medical first by swapping kidneys at the Beilinson Hospital in Petach Tikva, outside Tel Aviv, Israel. Yosef Chillag needed a new kidney but his wife Victoria was not a good match. Victoria did match Suham Hamash, a woman from a village in northern Israel, and Suham's husband Youssef turned out to be the right match for Yosef. In operations lasting six hours, doctors removed the kidneys from the spouses and transplanted them into the other two. The Chillags, who are in their sixties, and the Hamashes, who are in their fifties, were the first people to take part in the computerized kidney cross-swap program at Beilinson Hospital. The program is aimed at reducing the three- to four-year wait for kidney transplants in Israel.

LOUDEST SNORER
Kåre Walkert of Kumala, Sweden, who suffers from the breathing disorder apnea, recorded peak noise levels of 93 dBA while sleeping at the Örebro Regional Hospital in Sweden in May 1993.

LONGEST DREAM
The longest known period of REM sleep (the dream sleep characterized by rapid eye movements) was 3 hours 8 min., by David Powell at the Puget Sound Sleep Disorder Center, Seattle, Washington on April 29, 1994.

HIGHEST G FORCES BORNE
On July 13, 1977, British race car driver David Purley survived a deceleration from 108 mph to zero within a distance of 2 ft. 2 in. in a crash at Silverstone racetrack in England. Purley endured 179.8 *g* and suffered 29 fractures and three dislocations, and his heart stopped beating six times after the accident.

The highest voluntarily endured *g* force was 82.6 *g*, for 0.04 seconds, by Eli Beeding Jr. on a water-braked rocket sled at Holloman Air Force Base, New Mexico on May 16, 1958. Beeding was subsequently hospitalized for three days.

LONGEST PERIOD SURVIVED UNDERWATER
In 1986, two-year-old Michelle Funk of Salt Lake City, Utah made a full recovery after spending 1 hr. 6 min. underwater. She had fallen into a creek.

HIGHEST DRY-AIR TEMPERATURES BORNE
In US Air Force experiments carried out in 1960, the highest dry-air temperature endured by naked men was 400°F, while heavily clothed men could bear temperatures of up to 500°F. By comparison, a bearable temperature in a sauna is about 284°F.

LONGEST PERIOD SURVIVED WITHOUT FOOD AND WATER
Andreas Mihavecz of Bregenz, Austria lived for a record-breaking 18 days without food and water after being put into a holding cell in a local government building in Höchst by the police on April 1, 1979 and then forgotten. The 18-year-old, who had been a passenger in a crashed car, was found close to death on April 18, 1979.

MOST INJECTIONS RECEIVED
Samuel Davidson of Glasgow, Scotland has had at least 78,900 insulin injections since the age of 11 in 1923. Insulin lets the body absorb sugar and is taken by people with diabetes, which develops when the body does not produce enough insulin or utilize it properly. It was discovered by Canadian Frederick Banting and first used on humans in 1922. Before insulin, diabetes was usually fatal.

LARGEST TUMOR
A tumor weighing 302¾ pounds and measuring 3 feet in diameter was removed intact from a 34-year-old woman's abdomen in October 1991. It had been growing for eight years, according to Dr. Kate O'Hanlan of Stanford University. She is seen here preparing to remove it in a clip from the hit TV show, *Guinness World Records™: Primetime.*

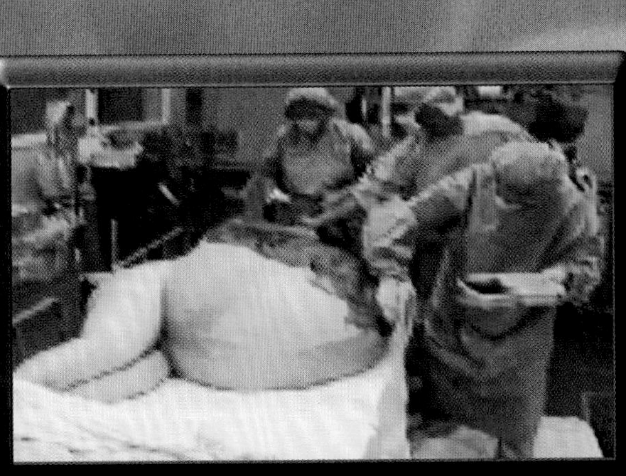

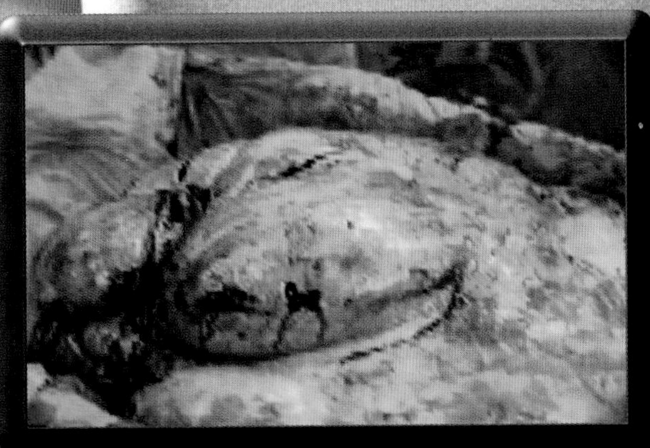

body transformation I

MOST PLASTIC SURGERY FOR ART
Since May 1990, Orlan, a French performance artist whose most recent work is herself, has undergone a series of plastic surgical operations to transform herself into a new being, *The Reincarnation of Saint Orlan*, modeled on Venus, Diana, Europa, Psyche and Mona Lisa. Orlan has been exhibited worldwide and is supported by the French Ministry of Culture. Her video *New York Omnipresence* shows implants being sewn into her temples.

MOST WEIGHT GAINED
Doris James of San Francisco, California is alleged to have gained 325 pounds in the 12 months before her death in August 1965, aged 38, when she weighed 675 pounds. She was 5 ft. 2 in. tall.

The greatest weight gain by a man was 196 pounds in seven days, by Jon Minnoch (US), the heaviest person in medical history, in October 1981.

Arthur Knorr (US) gained 294 pounds in the six months prior to his death in 1960.

MOST WEIGHT LOST
Jon Minnoch reduced from 1,400 pounds to 476 pounds in the 16 months up to July 1979.

The greatest weight loss by a woman is 917 pounds, by Rosalie Bradford (US), the heaviest ever woman, when she reduced from 1,202.24 pounds in January 1987 to 283 pounds in February 1994.

In 1984, Ron Allen sweated off $21\frac{1}{2}$ pounds of his weight of 239 pounds in 24 hours in Nashville, Tennessee.

MOST PLASTIC SURGERY
Cindy Jackson has spent $99,600 on 27 operations over a period of nine years. Born on a pig farm in Ohio, 42-year-old Jackson has had three full facelifts, two nose operations, knee, abdomen and jawline surgery, thigh liposuction, breast reduction and augmentation, and semi-permanent makeup. Her look is based on Leonardo da Vinci's theory of a classically proportioned face. Dubbed the "human Barbie Doll," Cindy is now the director of the London-based Cosmetic Surgery Network.

MOST DOUBLES CREATED BY PLASTIC SURGERY
The Russian dictator Stalin was reportedly so paranoid that he employed several doubles to lessen the likelihood of being assassinated. The lookalikes, who had plastic surgery to resemble him, are said to have attended most state funerals, and Stalin's own guards often could not tell the difference.

MOST PLASTIC SURGERY UNDERGONE BY A CRIMINAL
Drug baron Richie Ramos had an extra 16 months of freedom from the FBI after plastic surgery. The 27-year-old boss of an immense drug empire in Philadelphia, Ramos had five bullet-wound scars removed and the skin on his fingertips changed, in addition to work on his "bull-like chest, flabby waist and fleshy face." The operations cost a total of $74,900. Ramos is now serving a 30-year prison sentence.

LONGEST NECKS
The women of the Padaung or Kareni tribe of Myanmar (Burma) extend their necks by putting copper coils around them. The maximum recorded length is $15\frac{3}{4}$ inches, and a Padaung woman of marriageable age will have had her neck extended by an average of $9\frac{4}{5}$ inches. Worn in an increasing number from age five or six, the coils can reach a weight of 20 pounds.

MOST DRAMATIC CHANGE UNDERGONE FOR ART
Former British photographer Della Grace has undergone a self-transformation through the use of male hormone injections. Now Del La Grace, she has a beard and a deep husky voice. The procedure is irreversible.

MOST FAMOUS SEX CHANGE
In 1953, Christine Jorgensen, a former male GI from the Bronx, New York City, made headlines when she had a sex change. Part of it was done in Casablanca, Morocco — then the sex change capital of the world — and part of it was carried out in Denmark. Christine's 1967 autobiography inspired other transsexuals.

OLDEST SEX CHANGE
The greatest age at which a person is known to have had sex change surgery is 74. According to the American Educational Gender Information Service, it is common for individuals to change gender roles at retirement age.

YOUNGEST SEX CHANGE
Neonates are frequently born with ambiguous genitalia, and doctors often decide whether they are to be raised as boys or girls. Sometimes their genitals are operated on in infancy to match the doctors' selections. The most famous instance of this was the John/Joan case in which John, one of a pair of identical twin boys, suffered an accident during circumcision at the age of about six months and was raised as a girl, Joan. Joan was never very happy as a girl, and in her late teen years, when she discovered what had happened to her, became John again.

HEAVIEST BREASTS

Eve Lolo Ferrari of Grasse, Alpes-Maritimes, France, has one of the world's biggest chests. She has undergone a total of 18 operations – five for her face and 13 for the rest of her body – and currently takes a size 57F bra. Each of her breasts weighs 6 lb. 2 oz. "Lolo," who lives in Cannes, France, starred in *Camping Cosmos* (Belgium, 1996).

MOST SEX CHANGES

It is estimated that there are 12,000 surgeons in the United States who carry out sex change operations, making it the sex change capital of the world. (It has been suggested that Thailand leads the field, and there is great demand for operations in Asia, but no figures are available.)

BIGGEST COMPENSATION PAYOUT FOR BREAST IMPLANT CLAIMS

In August 1997, the Dow Corning Corporation offered $2.4 billion to 200,000 women who claimed that their health had been ruined by breast implants. The women blamed leaking silicone for a flu-like syndrome, pain, and fatigue.

MOST EXPENSIVE WIG

The toupee worn by Sean Connery in the James Bond movie *Never Say Never Again* (GB, 1983) cost Warner Bros. $52,000. The film company decided that a full head of hair was necessary for the portrayal of Bond as envisaged by Ian Fleming, the character's creator.

MOST BEAUTY QUEENS PRODUCED

Venezuela is seen as the beauty queen factory of the world – over the last 20 years, Venezuelan women have won a total of 10 top international beauty contests, a record unmatched by any other country, and of the last 18 Miss Universes, four have been from Venezuela. Aspiring beauty queens attend schools such as the Miss Venezuela Academy, where they work out in the gym, answer pageant questions, practice catwalk modeling for a grueling 16 hours a day and sometimes undergo plastic surgery over a period of six months. The most successful beauty school in the world is the Miss Venezuela Organization, which also attracts potential beauty queens from Brazil, Colombia, Bolivia and the Dominican Republic. The average cost of training a beauty queen in Venezuela, where poverty affects 70–80% of the population, is $60,000, but the beauty contests are as popular with the public as important sporting events, with 90% of the Venezuelan population – approximately 21 million people – tuning in. The shows themselves cost $7–8 million to produce.

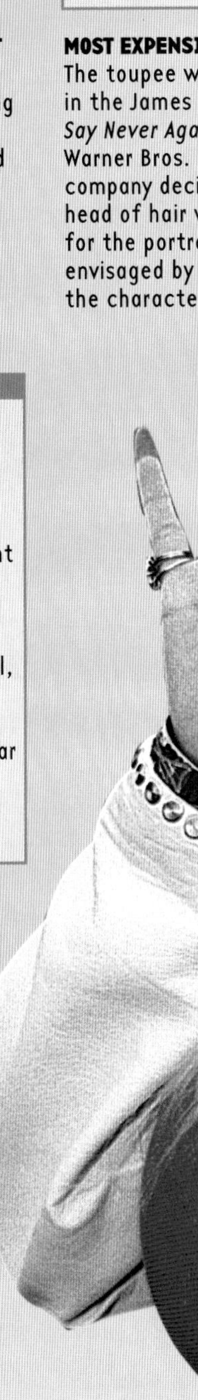

MOST EXPENSIVE HAIRCUT

In 1993, President Bill Clinton went under the scissors of Monsieur Christophe, a top Beverly Hills stylist, while sitting aboard Air Force One on the tarmac at Los Angeles Airport. The full cost of his "runway trim," taking into account delays to other aircraft, was estimated at more than $83,000.

MOST TEETH BLEACHED

Dr. Ronald Goldstein and colleagues at his practice have bleached more than 100,000 teeth in the United States over the last 40 years. One of the first dentists ever to bleach teeth, Goldstein wrote a book, *Change Your Smile*, that has been read by more people than any other book on cosmetic dentistry, and has been translated into six languages.

body transformation II

BIGGEST BICEPS

The right biceps of Denis Sester of Bloomington, Minnesota measure $30\frac{5}{8}$ inches when cold. Sester began building his biceps when he started wrestling pigs on his parents' farm as a teenager.

GREATEST STRONGMEN

Iceland's Magnus Ver Magnusson won the World's Strongest Man contest four times, in 1991, 1994, 1995 and 1996, becoming only the second man (after Bill Kazmaier [US]) to win three years in a row. He began powerlifting in 1984 and won senior titles in Europe in 1989 and 1990. He also won the World Muscle Power Championship in 1995. Born in 1963, he is 6 ft. 2 in. tall, weighs 287 pounds, and has a chest measurement of 51 inches. He now owns Magnus' Gym, Reykjavik, Iceland.

Jon Pall Sigmarsson from Iceland also won the World's Strongest Man contest four times, in 1984, 1986, 1988 and 1990. Sigmarsson, who weighed 294 pounds and had a 57-inch chest, dominated the WSM competition in the mid and late 1980s and won five World Muscle Power titles. He died of a heart attack while weightlifting in 1993.

MOST MR. OLYMPIA TITLES

Lee Haney (US) won the Mr Olympia contest eight times from 1984 to 1991.

MOST CONSECUTIVE MR. OLYMPIA TITLES

Dorian Yates (GB) won five Mr. Olympia contests in a row from 1992 to 1997.

MOST IFBB PRO WINS

Vince Taylor of Pembroke Pines, Florida has had a record 19 wins from competitions all over the world recognized by the International Federation of Body Building (IFBB). He won the Masters Olympia for those aged 40 and over in 1996 and 1997.

MOST ARNOLD CLASSICS (FORMERLY MEN'S PRO WORLD) TITLES

Ken "Flex" Wheeler, nicknamed the "Sultan of Symmetry," won the "triple crown" (the Ironman, the Arnold Classic and the San Jose Classic) in 1997 and the Arnold Classic in 1993, 1997 and 1998. He has been training since the age of 15.

MOST SUCCESSFUL FORMER BODYBUILDERS

Along with Arnold Schwarzenegger, Lou Ferrigno — the only man in history to win the Mr. Universe title two years in succession — is the most successful former bodybuilder. Ferrigno starred in *The Incredible Hulk* from 1978 to 1982 and has since appeared in a succession of TV shows, plays and films, including *Hercules* (1983) and *The Adventures of Hercules* (1985). He is 6 ft. 5 in. tall and weighs 300 pounds.

MOST SUCCESSFUL PERSONAL TRAINERS

Jake Steinfeld has trained Steven Spielberg, Harrison Ford and Priscilla Presley and heads a multimillion-dollar fitness empire which includes a cable television network FiT TV — the world's only 24-hour fitness channel — a national magazine, home videos and branded equipment and merchandise. Over a period of three years, Los Angeles-based Body by Jake Enterprises sold more than $250 million in licensed products through infomercials.

Radu Teodorescu, known as the "Grand Master" of exercise, has been a personal trainer for more than 20 years, and his clientele has included Candice Bergen, John Kennedy Jr. and Matthew Broderick. Voted "Toughest Trainer In Town" by *New York* magazine, Radu has featured in more than 400 magazine articles and created Cindy Crawford's multimillion-selling fitness video *Shape Your Body Workout.*

Ray Kybartas of Chicago, Illinois began as a fitness consultant to entertainment attorneys in the 1970s and has since worked with Tatum O'Neal and Sean Penn, who asked him to help him gain

BODYBUILDING MECCA

Venice Beach, the beachfront between the *Baywatch* sands at Santa Monica and Marina del Rey, California, attracts up to 175,000 visitors every weekend. One of its most famous spots is Muscle Beach, an open-air gym where bodybuilders pump iron (left). The original Muscle Beach in Santa Monica was closed in 1959. A small group of weightlifters was working out at a facility known as "The Pen" in neighboring Venice, and this became the new Muscle Beach in the 1960s. It is now the world's most famous bodybuilding venue. The most successful bodybuilding empire is the Weider Corporation, a group of companies that sell more than 100 bodybuilding and fitness products. It is run by Canadian brothers Joe and Ben Weider, often seen as the pioneers of bodybuilding. In the 1960s, Ben established the International Federation of Bodybuilding, which has 150 member countries and promotes Mr. Olympia. Their magazine *Muscle & Fitness* has 1.7 million readers, and they also publish *Shape, Men's Fitness* and *Flex*, which, together with vitamin and food supplements, have sales of almost $1 billion in 60 countries.

MOST FAMOUS FORMER BODYBUILDER
Austrian-born Arnold Schwarzenegger, who is pictured here with Lou Ferrigno, has won 13 world titles (seven Mr. Olympia titles, five Mr. Universe titles, and one Mr. World title). He has been producing bodybuilding contests for 20 years, and in 1989 set up the Arnold Classic. During the administration of President Bush, Schwarzenegger was Chairman of the President's Council on Fitness and Sports. Since 1979, he has been International Weight Training Coach for the Special Olympics. He is one of the world's biggest box office draws, with movies such as *Conan the Barbarian* (1981), *The Terminator* (1984), *The Running Man* (1987), *Terminator 2: Judgment Day* (1991), *Total Recall* (1990), *Kindergarten Cop* (1990), *True Lies* (1994), and *Batman and Robin* (1997) under his belt.

30 pounds in three months for *At Close Range* (1985). This led Kybartas to a job with Madonna, and he is now one of Hollywood's most sought-after trainers.

BIGGEST-SELLING FITNESS VIDEO
Supermodel Cindy Crawford was the star and executive producer of the *Cindy Crawford/Shape Your Body Workout*, which topped the Billboard Health and Fitness chart for several years after its release in October 1992 and has sold more than 10 million copies worldwide to date.

BIGGEST CHAIN OF GYMS
Gold's Gym opened in Venice, California in 1965 and became internationally famous when it featured in *Pumping Iron* (1975), with up-and-coming stars Arnold Schwarzenegger and Lou Ferrigno. It is now the world's biggest international gym chain, with more than 500 centers. It has many star clients, including Charlie Sheen, Richard Dreyfuss, Janet Jackson, Carrie Fisher, Jodie Foster and Hulk Hogan, and boasts its own Motion Picture and TV Division.

BIGGEST CHEST
Isaac Nesser (pictured below) of Greensburg, Pennsylvania has a record muscular chest measurement of 6 ft. 2 $^{1}/_{16}$ in. He has been lifting weights since he was eight years old, and has worked out every day for the past 20 years. His routine includes bench-pressing 560 pounds in a series of repetitions and curling 300-pound barbells in a similar series.

MS. OLYMPIA
Right, a contestant flexes her muscles for the Ms. Olympia contest, which began in 1980. Bodybuilder Cory Everson (US) won the competition a record six times from 1984 to 1989. She is now the star of her own TV show, *Gotta Sweat*, and has produced successful fitness books and videos. The most consecutive titles is five, by Lenda Murray (US) between 1990 and 1994.

body art

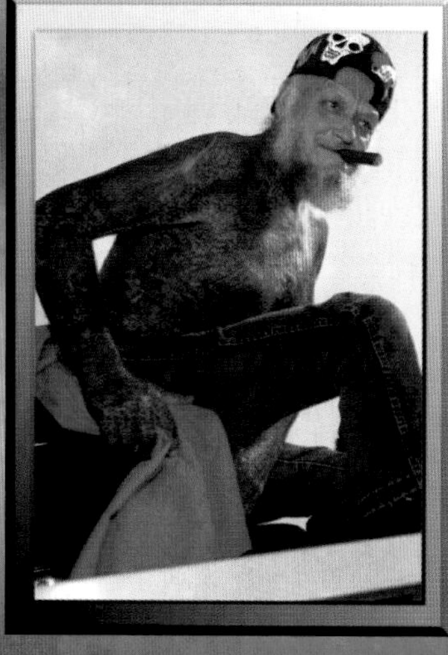

MOST INDIVIDUAL TATTOOS
Bernie Moeller of Pennsylvania has had his body covered with a record total of 14,006 individual tattoos. Moeller's tattoos have made him a popular guest at various outdoor events, and he has made several television appearances. In 1996, he was interviewed by Ron Reagan Jr., son of former president Ronald Reagan, and he was also present at the world's biggest tattoo and piercing contest, at the Astroland Amusement Park in New York.

MOST PIERCED MAN
Alex Lambrecht has acquired a total of 137 piercings with a combined weight of approximately 1 lb. 2 oz. over a period of 40 years, making him the most pierced man in the world. At an average of $83 each, Lambrecht's piercings would have cost him $11,400 had he not done them himself. Most of them are on his face, but more than 50 are intimate.

MOST TATTOOED WOMAN
The world's most tattooed woman is the strip artiste "Krystyne Kolorful" of Alberta, Canada. Krystyne's "suit" of tattoos covers 95% of her body and took a total of 10 years to complete.

OLDEST TATTOOS
Ötzi, the world's oldest accidentally preserved human body, has 15 tattoos. He was found in a glacier in the Ötztal Alps in 1991 and is believed to be 5,300 years old. Ötzi has a series of blue parallel lines covering his lower spine, as well as stripes across his right ankle and a tattoo of a cross behind his right knee.

Two Egyptian mummies dating back to 2160–1994 BC have abstract patterns of dots and dashes on their bodies. The tattoos were probably believed to offer protection from evil spirits.

MOST INFLUENTIAL BODY ARTIST
Body artist Fakir Mustafar of Aberdeen, South Dakota is known for his 50 years of research into primitive body decoration and his exploration of modern body modifications. The 68-year-old's work has been featured in a number of films, television programs and books, and has been a major catalyst in the recent revival of body piercing, branding and body sculpting. Mustafar co-developed the body piercing techniques that are used today and is the director of Fakir Body Piercing & Branding Intensives, which are licensed by the state of California and are the only courses of their kind in the world.

MOST DECORATED BODY ARTISTS
Enigma, an American circus star from Jim Rose's circus, has had his entire body covered in jigsaw-puzzle tattoos. He also has horns, a tail and porcupine quills, which were implanted into his body using coral. Real bone is growing around the implants, and the horns on his head are growing at the rate of 1½ inches per year. Enigma achieved TV stardom in 1995, when he appeared in an episode of *The X-Files* with David Duchovny and Gillian Anderson.

Michael Wilson, who died in 1996, was known as the "Illustrated Man" because of the tattoos that covered 90% of his body. In the 1980s, Wilson left his native California after tattooists there refused to color his face. He moved to New York and made a living exhibiting himself as the "Illustrated Man" at the famous Coney Island Circus Sideshow, where he became one of the most popular attractions. Wilson gradually covered almost his entire body with tattoos.

MOST BODY PARTS ADDED FOR ART
Stelarc, a performance artist based in Australia, has a third robotic hand which is operated by muscle stimulation from his real arm. Stelarc's work, which is based on the belief that the human body has become obsolete, explores the concept of the body and its relationship with technology. His latest project involves the grafting of an extra ear next to his existing right ear. It will be constructed by stretching his skin over an ear-shaped plastic scaffold. The second ear will not be able to hear, but the artist will be able to make it talk electronically using a sound chip – he wants to make it "whisper sweet nothings into the other ear."

MOST COMMON FORM OF BODY ART
Tattooing is an ancient form of body art that is found all over the world, including among the native peoples of Borneo, Polynesia, Thailand, New Zealand, Burma and parts of Asia and Africa. The Gauls and the

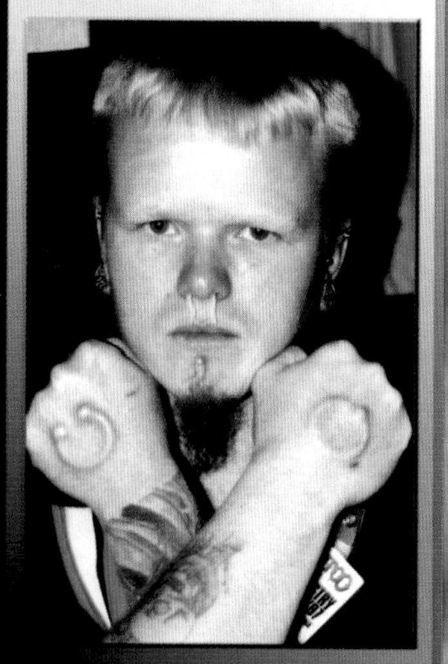

MOST SUCCESSFUL THREE-DIMENSIONAL BODY ARTIST
Steve Haworth, who is based at Haworth Tech Company Body Adornments of Phoenix, Arizona, is widely acknowledged as the world's leading 3-D artist working in the medium of human flesh. Haworth specializes in subdermal and transdermal implants and practices piercing, laser-cautery branding and near-surgical art. Haworth first started designing medical equipment at the age of 18, and in 1989 he began producing body jewelry. Examples of his work include the implantation of 11 rows of beads that look like vertebrae into a friend's forearm and the placing of a Mohawk made of steel spikes into a man's forehead.The artist has performed between 150 and 175 bead implants – which are generally easier to remove than they are to insert – on approximately 130 individuals. Haworth also creates subcutaneous horns for foreheads for about $600 and has worked on the famous circus star Enigma. He is apprehensive about doing work on the back of the hand (left) because of a possible loss of sensation in some of the tissue, but has completed eight pieces without any problems.

Teutonic peoples practiced tattooing, as did the Greeks, the Romans and the Iberians, who preceded the Celts in the British Isles. One of the world's most beautiful and complex forms of tattooing was practiced by the ancient Horis from Japan, whose decorations were made to look almost three-dimensional through design, color and the use of shade and light.

LONGEST EARS
The men and women from the Suya tribe in Africa wear large discs of wood in their ears in order to elongate them. When they take the discs out, they wrap their dangling ear lobes around their ears.

MOST POINTED HEADS
Head shaping was practiced by the Greeks, the Romans, Native Americans and Africans, as well as by certain groups in Europe during prehistoric times. The head-shaping process began in a person's infancy, when the head is still soft and malleable enough to be changed. Either the skull was tightly bound with a piece of cloth or the baby was placed into a cradle that had a specially shaped wooden headboard. The elongated head that resulted from these processes was deemed both beautiful and refined.

FLATTEST NOSES
In New Guinea people often insert feathers, small shells and tusks through a hole in their noses in order to flatten them out and render them more attractive. Certain Polynesian groups go so far as to break their noses in order to make them flatter.

SMALLEST FEET
The Chinese custom of foot binding dates back to the Sung dynasty (960–976 BC), when it arose in imitation of an imperial concubine who was required to dance with her feet bound. By the 12th century, when a girl turned three, eight of her toes were broken and her feet were bound with cloth strips to prevent them from growing any larger than 3 3/10 inches. The custom of foot binding ceased in the 20th century with the end of the imperial dynasties and the influence of western fashion. Studies showed that it caused severe, permanent disabilities for millions of Chinese women.

GREATEST COVERAGE BY TATTOOS
Tom Leppard, a retired soldier who lives alone on the Isle of Skye, UK, has had a record 99.9% of his body tattooed with a leopard skin design. His body is now covered with dark spots; the skin between them is tattooed saffron yellow. The only parts of Leppard's body that remain free of tattoos are the insides of his ears and the skin between his toes.

MOST PIERCED WOMAN
By January 31, 1998, just one year after getting her first piercing, Grace Martin of Edinburgh, Scotland had 290 piercings over her entire body.

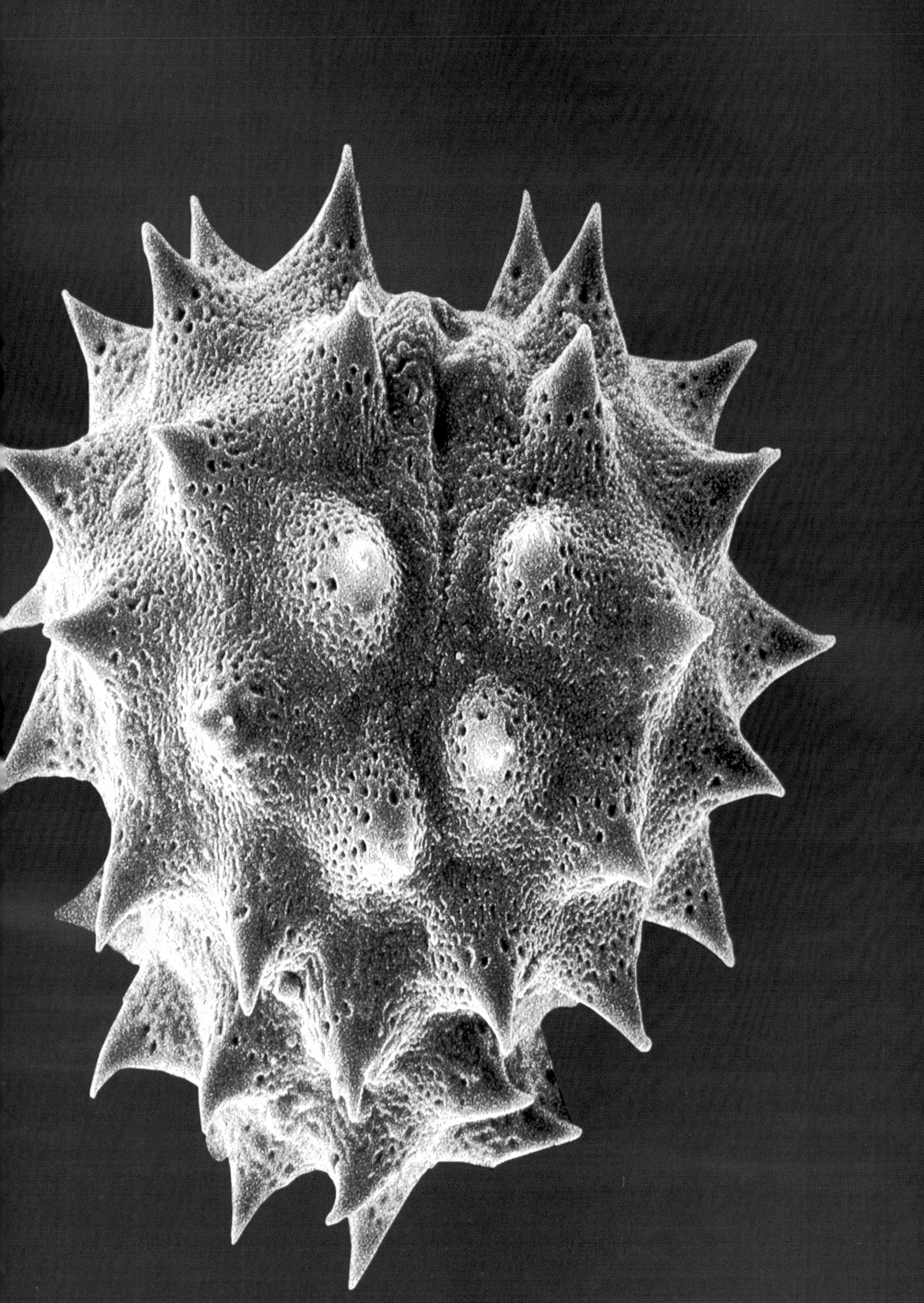

the natural world

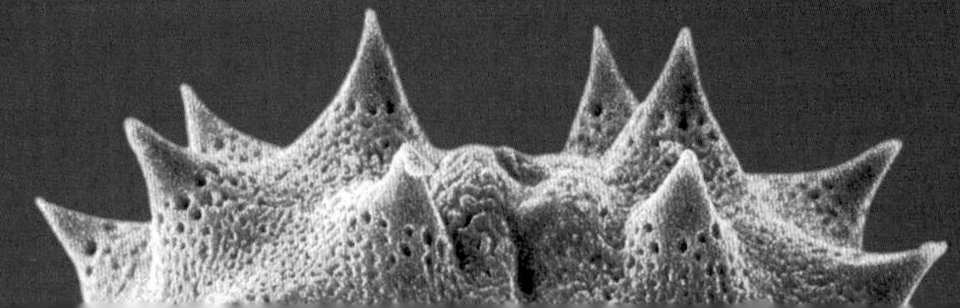

largest and smallest mammals

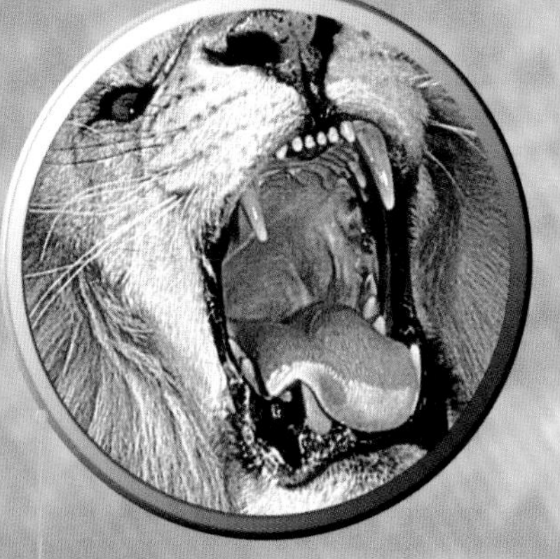

HEAVIEST LION
Confined mostly to sub-Saharan Africa, lions feed on large herbivores such as wildebeest, zebra and antelope, with most of the hunting carried out by female lions on a cooperative basis. The heaviest wild African lion (*Panthera leo*) on record weighed 690 pounds. It was shot near Hectorspruit, Transvaal, South Africa in 1936.

LARGEST ANIMAL
The blue whale (*Balaenoptera musculus*) begins life as an ovum weighing a fraction of a milligram and grows to an average weight of 28 tons by the age of 12 months. Newborn calves weigh up to 3.3 tons.

HEAVIEST MAMMAL
A 209-ton, 90-ft.-6-in.-long female blue whale was caught in the Southern Ocean in 1947.

LARGEST LAND MAMMAL
The male African bush elephant (*Loxodonta africana africana*) is 9 ft. 10 in.–12 ft. 2 in. tall at the shoulder and can weigh between 4.4 and 7.7 tons. The largest specimen on record was a bull shot in Mucosso, Angola in 1974. The creature had an estimated standing height of about 13 feet and is thought to have weighed 13.5 tons.

HEAVIEST CARNIVORE
A polar bear weighing an estimated 2,000 pounds was shot in the Chukchi Sea, Alaska in 1960, and is the heaviest known land mammal in the world. It was said to measure 11 ft. 3 in. from nose to tail over its body contours, 4 ft. 10 in. around the body and 1 ft. 5 in. around the paws.

LARGEST CARNIVOROUS MAMMAL
Adult male polar bears (*Ursus maritimus*) often weigh 880–1,320 pounds and have a nose-to-tail length of 7 ft. 11 in.–8 ft. 6 in. Male Kodiak bears (*Ursus arctos middendorffi*) are usually shorter but more robustly built.

LONGEST MAMMAL
A 110-ft.-$2\frac{1}{2}$-in.-long female blue whale was landed at Grytviken, South Georgia in the South Atlantic in 1909.

LARGEST TOOTHED MAMMAL
The 16-ft.-5-in. lower jaw of a male sperm whale (*Physeter macrocephalus*) estimated to have been almost 84 feet long is on display in the Natural History Museum in London, England. The longest officially measured specimen was a 67-ft.-11-in. male captured off the Kurile Islands in the northwest Pacific in 1950.

LARGEST RODENT
The capybara (*Hydrochoerus hydrochaeris*) of northern South America has a head-and-body length of $3\frac{1}{4}$–$4\frac{1}{2}$ feet and can weigh up to 174 pounds. One cage-fat specimen weighed 250 pounds.

LARGEST MARSUPIAL
The male red kangaroo (*Macropus rufus*) of Australia is up to 5 ft. 11 in. tall and 9 ft. 4 in. long (including the tail). Exceptional specimens have weighed 198 pounds.

TALLEST PRIMATE
The tallest wild gorilla on record was a mountain bull that was shot in the eastern Congo (ex-Zaïre) in 1938. It measured 6 ft. 5 in. from the top of the crest to the heel.

HEAVIEST PRIMATE
The heaviest gorilla kept in captivity was a male of the N'gagi mountain subspecies who died in San Diego Zoo, California in 1944. Weighing 683 pounds at its heaviest in 1943, it was 5 ft. $7\frac{3}{4}$ in. tall and boasted a record chest measurement of 6 ft. 6 in.

LARGEST PINNIPED
Male southern elephant seals (*Mirounga leonina*) from the sub-Antarctic islands average 16 ft. 6 in. in length from the tip of the inflated snout to the tips of the outstretched tail flippers, have a maximum girth of 12 feet and weigh 4,400–7,720 pounds. The largest accurately measured specimen was a bull weighing at least 4.4 tons. Measuring 21 ft. 4 in. after the blubber had been stripped off its skin, it had an estimated original length of 22 ft. 6 in. It was killed in the South Atlantic at Possession Bay, South Georgia in 1913.

SMALLEST MAMMAL
The bumblebee or Kitti's hog-nosed bat (*Craseonycteris thonglongyai*), which is confined to about 21 limestone caves on the Kwae Noi River, Kanchanaburi Province, southwest Thailand, has a body no bigger than that of a large bumblebee, a head-and-body length of $1\frac{7}{50}$–$1\frac{3}{10}$ inches and a wingspan of about $5\frac{1}{10}$–$5\frac{7}{10}$ inches. It weighs $\frac{3}{5}$–$\frac{7}{10}$ ounce.

SMALLEST NON-FLYING MAMMAL
Savi's white-toothed pygmy shrew (*Suncus etruscus*), also called the Etruscan shrew, has a head-and-body length of $1\frac{2}{5}$–$1\frac{4}{5}$ inches, a tail length of $\frac{49}{50}$–$1\frac{17}{100}$ inches and weighs $\frac{13}{25}$–$\frac{22}{25}$ ounce.

SMALLEST FELINE CARNIVORE
The rusty-spotted cat (*Prionailurus rubiginosus*), which lives in southern India and Sri Lanka, has a head-and-body length of $13\frac{2}{5}$–$18\frac{9}{10}$ inches and a tail length of $5\frac{9}{10}$–$9\frac{4}{5}$ inches. The average weight of a female is 2 lb. 7 oz.

LARGEST FELINE
The male Siberian tiger (*Panthera tigris altaica*) averages 10 ft. 4 in. in length from the nose to the tip of the extended tail, stands 3 ft. 3 in.–3 ft. 6 in. at the shoulder and weighs about 585 pounds. The world's largest feline, it faces a bleak future: compared with the 100,000 tigers alive a century ago, there are only 400 Siberian tigers, 3,000 Bengal tigers, 1,000 Indo-Chinese tigers and around 20 Sumatran tigers today. The latter are expected to become extinct in the near future, following the Bali tiger, which became the first tiger to die out in 1940, and the Caspian tiger, which disappeared in the 1970s. Tigers are endangered by hunting and by loss of their natural habitat. Despite classification as an endangered species by the World Conservation Union (IUCN) and protection by the Convention on International Trade in Endangered Species, 180 tigers were killed between 1991 and 1996. This led to the formation of several conservation groups, including the Tiger Trust, and Tuskforce in the United Kingdom. Together with the World Wide Fund for Nature, these groups have helped to slow the killing of tigers.

SMALLEST RODENT
The northern pygmy mouse (*Baiomys taylori*) from Arizona, Texas and Mexico, and the Baluchistan pygmy jerboa (*Salpingotulus michaelis*) from Pakistan are probably the world's smallest rodents. Both have a head-and-body length of as little as $1\frac{2}{5}$ inches and a tail length of $2\frac{4}{5}$ inches.

SMALLEST MARSUPIAL
The two main contenders for the title of smallest marsupial are the rare long-tailed planigale (*Planigale ingrami*) of northern Australia and the pilbara ningaui (*Ningaui timealeyi*) of northwestern Australia. The first has a head-and-body length of $2\frac{17}{100}$-$2\frac{12}{25}$ inches and a tail length of $2\frac{1}{4}$–$2\frac{9}{25}$ inches, and weighs $2\frac{1}{5}$–$2\frac{1}{2}$ dram. The ninguai has a head-and-body length of $1\frac{4}{5}$–$2\frac{1}{4}$ inches and a tail length of $2\frac{1}{3}$–$3\frac{1}{10}$ inches, and weighs $\frac{7}{100}$–$\frac{1}{3}$ ounce.

SMALLEST PRIMATE
The smallest true primate (excluding tree shrews, which are normally classified separately) is the pygmy mouse lemur (*Microcebus myoxinus*) from Madagascar. Its head-and-body length is about $2\frac{2}{5}$ inches, its tail is $5\frac{3}{5}$ inches long, and it weighs around $1\frac{1}{10}$ ounces.

SMALLEST PINNIPED
Female Galapagos fur seals (*Arctocephalus galapagoensis*) average 3 ft. 11 in. in length and weigh about 60 pounds.

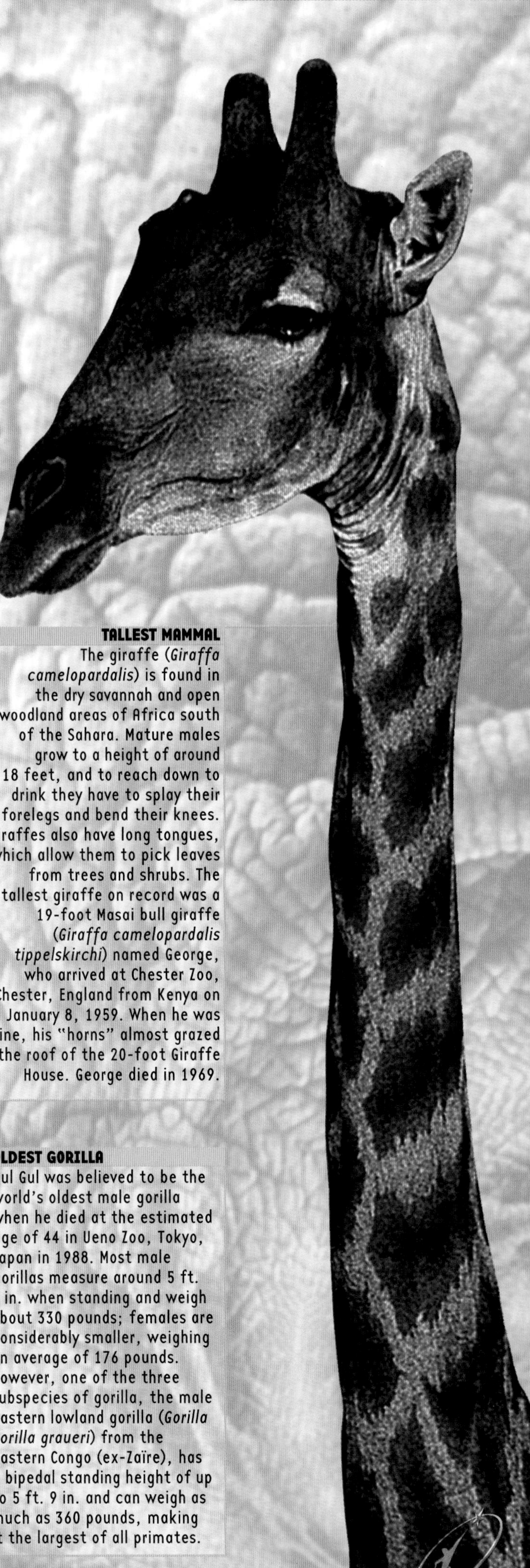

TALLEST MAMMAL
The giraffe (*Giraffa camelopardalis*) is found in the dry savannah and open woodland areas of Africa south of the Sahara. Mature males grow to a height of around 18 feet, and to reach down to drink they have to splay their forelegs and bend their knees. Giraffes also have long tongues, which allow them to pick leaves from trees and shrubs. The tallest giraffe on record was a 19-foot Masai bull giraffe (*Giraffa camelopardalis tippelskirchi*) named George, who arrived at Chester Zoo, Chester, England from Kenya on January 8, 1959. When he was nine, his "horns" almost grazed the roof of the 20-foot Giraffe House. George died in 1969.

OLDEST GORILLA
Gul Gul was believed to be the world's oldest male gorilla when he died at the estimated age of 44 in Ueno Zoo, Tokyo, Japan in 1988. Most male gorillas measure around 5 ft. 7 in. when standing and weigh about 330 pounds; females are considerably smaller, weighing an average of 176 pounds. However, one of the three subspecies of gorilla, the male eastern lowland gorilla (*Gorilla gorilla graueri*) from the eastern Congo (ex-Zaïre), has a bipedal standing height of up to 5 ft. 9 in. and can weigh as much as 360 pounds, making it the largest of all primates.

mammal lifestyle

FATTIEST DIET
In spring and early summer, the diet of the polar bear (*Ursus maritimus*) consists largely of recently weaned ringed seal pups, which have a fat content of up to 50%. When the seals are in plentiful supply, the bears feed only on the fat below the skin, leaving the rest of the carcass untouched.

FASTEST LAND MAMMALS
Over a short distance (up to 600 yards) on level ground, the cheetah (*Acinonyx jubatus*) has a probable maximum speed of about 60 mph.

The pronghorn antelope (*Antilocapra americana*) can sustain a speed of 35 mph for 4 miles, 42 mph for 1 mile and 55 mph for ½ mile, and is the fastest land animal over long distances.

FASTEST MARINE MAMMALS
In 1958, a bull killer whale (*Orcinus orca*) estimated to be 20–25 feet in length was timed swimming at a speed of 34½ mph in the eastern North Pacific. Similar speeds have been reported for Dall's porpoise (*Phocoenoides dalli*) during short bursts.

SLOWEST MAMMAL
The slowest mammal is the three-toed sloth (*Bradypus tridactylus*) from tropical South America, which has an average ground speed of between 6 and 8 feet per minute, or 7/100–1/10 mph. In the trees, it can accelerate to 15 feet per minute, or 17/100 mph.

DEEPEST DIVES
In 1969, a bull sperm whale (*Physeter macrocephalus*) surfaced from a 1-hr.-52-min. dive 100 miles south of Durban, South Africa, where the water is known to exceed a depth of 10,470 feet within a radius of 30–40 miles. Inside the sperm whale's stomach were two small sharks of a type found only on the sea floor. The sharks had been swallowed about an hour earlier, which suggests that sperm whales can descend more than 9,800 feet when seeking food and that they are limited by time rather than water pressure.

The deepest authenticated dive was 6,500 feet and lasted for 1 hr. 13 min. It was made by a bull sperm whale off the coast of Dominica in the Caribbean in 1991.

MOST DANGEROUS LOVE LIFE
The male brown antechinus (*Antechinus stuartii*), a marsupial mouse native to eastern Australia, has an insatiable sexual appetite. Every year the entire adult male population of the species goes on a rampage for two weeks in a bid to mate with as many females as possible. The mice are so busy chasing females and fighting off rivals that they do not have time to eat, and they die within days from starvation, ulcers or infection.

BIGGEST EYES
The tarsier (below) is one of the smallest primates, and lives in the forests of Borneo, Sumatra and the Philippines. Tarsiers have a maximum body length of 6⅓ inches and a 10½-inch tail. Their eyes are so large that they would be equivalent to grapefruit-sized eyes in a human being. Tarsiers, along with animals from the genus *Galago*, are the only primates able to turn their heads through 180° in each direction. Galagos, known as bush babies, also share the tarsiers' large eye-to-body ratio. They can be found in sub-Saharan African forests.

MOST SUCCESSFUL NON-NATIVE MAMMAL
The brown rat (*Rattus norvegicus*) has spread from its original habitat in Mongolia and Kazakhstan and can now be found almost everywhere. It is estimated that the number of rats in the world today is roughly equal to the number of humans (approximately 5.3 billion) but will increase more rapidly in the future. One 1993 British survey estimates that rat infestations in large towns have increased by 43% in 20 years. Rats spread a number of serious diseases, including bubonic plague and leptospirosis, but control of the creatures is difficult for several reasons, especially their staggering rate of reproduction: the female common rat (*Rattus rattus*) starts to mate when she is just two or three months old and can reproduce all year round, giving birth to litters of 10–12 babies. Rats are also extremely adaptable and can live off anything, from fast food to feces. When an epidemic of the pneumonic plague broke out in India in 1994, killing at least 60 people, thousands of dead rats from Bombay and surrounding areas were brought in daily to the Haffkine Institute and about 150 dissected and tested for the disease. Here a government employee is pictured inspecting part of the day's collection of rats.

SLEEPIEST MAMMALS
Certain species of armadillo (*Dasypodidae*), together with opossums (Didelphidae) and sloths (Bradypodidae and Megalonychidae) are the world's sleepiest mammals. They can spend as much as 80% of their lives sleeping or dozing. This efficient use of energy is due to their rather low body temperatures, their slow metabolic rates and their low-quality plant diet. As a result, they move slowly, have small territories and seldom venture far. Armadillos inhabit much of South and Central America and parts of the southern US and the West Indies.

MOST FERTILE MAMMAL
The field mouse (genus *Apodemus*) can produce up to seven litters of 4–12 young (occasionally more) a year in favorable conditions. The mice would overrun entire continents within decades were it not for disease, predators and lack of food, which kill most of them within a few months.

MOST STERILE MAMMAL
In a colony of sand or naked mole rats (*Heterocephalus glaber*) every male can breed, but all the females except the "queen" are sterile workers whose job is to care for the young and dig tunnels.

MOST VULNERABLE YOUNG
The smaller dasyurids (Australian carnivorous marsupials) have a precarious start to life because the females have six nipples but give birth to 12 or more young. Once the first six babies have reached the nipples, they hang on, and the rest of the litter dies.

EARLIEST PREGNANCY
The female true lemming (*Lemmus lemmus*) can get pregnant at the age of just 14 days, and give birth 16–23 days later. One lemming couple was reported to have produced eight litters in 167 days.

MOST DOMINANT FEMALES
Female hyenas of the family *Hyaenide* and female common squirrel monkeys (*Saimiri sciureus*) are larger and more aggressive than their mates.

BRAVEST MAMMAL
The ratel or honey badger (*Mellivora capensis*) will defend itself against animals of any size. Its tough skin is impervious to bee stings, porcupine quills and most snakebites. It is also so loose that if the creature is held by the scruff of the neck, it can turn inside its skin and bite the attacker until it lets go.

MOST TIME SPENT EATING
Apart from ungulates such as cattle, the mammals that spend the most time eating are probably weasels (genus *Mustela*). Their long, thin bodies lose a great deal of heat, so they have to consume protein- and fat-rich food ceaselessly. They require 100 times more energy per gram of body weight than an elephant.

FUSSIEST EATER
The koala (*Phascolarctos cinereus*) of eastern Australia feeds almost exclusively on eucalyptus leaves. It browses regularly on about six of the 500 species and selects certain individual trees and leaves in preference to others, sometimes sifting through up to 20 pounds of leaves a day to find the 1¼ pounds that it needs.

MOST MEAGER DIET
The dromedary or Arabian camel (*Camelus dromedarius*) can lose up to a quarter of its body fluid without suffering dehydration or overheating and can survive on the most meager diet, drawing upon a large fat reserve in its hump for sustenance.

SHARPEST HEARING
Ultrasonic echolocation gives bats the most acute hearing of any terrestrial animal. Some can hear frequencies as high as 120–250 kHz (the human limit is 20 kHz).

LOUDEST SOUND
Low-frequency pulses made by fin whales (*Balaenoptera physalus*) and blue whales (*B. musculus*) to communicate with each other have been measured at up to 188 decibels – the loudest sound by a living source.

LARGEST COLONY
A colony of black-tailed prairie dogs (*Cynomys ludovicianus*) found in 1901 contained about 400 million individuals and was estimated to cover 24,000 square miles – almost the size of Ireland.

HIGHEST RODENT DENSITY
A colony of house mice (*Mus musculus*) discovered in the dry bed of Buena Vista Lake, Kern County, California in 1926 and 1927 contained a total of 83,000 creatures per acre.

BEST BUILDER
The North American beaver (*Castor canadensis*) is the best mammalian builder (as opposed to excavator), constructing dams that are typically 16–96 feet long.

MOST EXPERT TOOL USER
Chimpanzees (*Pan troglodytes*) have developed tool use and simple tool-making to a higher level than any other mammal except humans: they use straw and twigs to extract termites; branches to investigate out-of-reach objects; stones to hammer open hard-shelled nuts; pointed sticks to pry pieces of nut from shells; and leaves as cloths to remove dirt from their bodies and as sponges to obtain water.

BIGGEST METHANE PRODUCER
Domestic cows emit about 105 pounds of methane a year, and annual bovine emissions of the gas exceed 136,000 million pounds. As a result, the level of methane in the atmosphere is increasing eight times faster than carbon dioxide levels.

fish

BIGGEST PREDATORY FISH
Adult rare great white sharks (*Carcharodon carcharias*) average 14–15 feet in length and weigh approximately 1,150–1,700 pounds. There has been circumstantial evidence to suggest that some specimens grow to more than 20 feet in length.

Arapaima gigas of South America is reported to grow to 14 ft. 9 in. in length but weighs only 440 pounds.

In the 19th century, there were several reports of 15-foot, 720-pound European catfish or wels (*Silurus glanis*) found in Russia. Today, any specimen

SMALLEST FRESHWATER FISH
The shortest and lightest freshwater fish in the world is the dwarf pygmy goby (*Pandaka pygmaea*), an almost transparent species found in the streams and lakes of Luzon, Philippines. Males are 1/3–2/5 inch long and weigh 3/50–2/25 grain.

SMALLEST COMMERCIAL FISH
Male specimens of the endangered sinarapan (*Mistichthys luzonensis*), a goby found only in Lake Buhi on Luzon in the Philippines, are just 39/100–51/100 inch long. One dried 1-pound fishcake would contain about 70,000 of them.

LIGHTEST FISH
The lightest vertebrate is the dwarf goby (*Schindleria praematurus*), which weighs only 3/100 grain and is 1/2–3/4 inch in length.

FASTEST FISH
The cosmopolitan sailfish (*Istiophorus platypterus*) is considered to be the fastest fish over short distances. In speed trials that were carried out at the Long Key Fishing Camp in Florida, one sailfish took out 300 feet of line in a time of 3 seconds. This is equivalent to a speed of 68 mph.

SLOWEST FISH
There are about 30 species of sea horse (family Syngnathidae), and all are very slow swimmers. The only parts which can be moved rapidly are the pectoral fins on either side of the back of the head, and the dorsal fin along the back. The fish propels itself forward in an erect posture by waving its dorsal fin. In still water, some of the smaller species, such as the dwarf sea horse (*Hippocampus zosterae*), probably never exceed 0.001 mph. Sea horses are incapable of swimming against the current and cling to plants to avoid being swept away.

LONGEST MIGRATION
The longest known straight-line distance covered by a fish is 5,800 miles, by a bluefin tuna (*Thunnus thynnus*) dart-tagged off Baja California, Mexico in 1958. It was caught 300 miles south of Tokyo, Japan in 1963. Its weight had increased from 35 pounds to 267 pounds.

LONGEST JOURNEY BY A FRESHWATER FISH
The European eel (*Anguilla anguilla*) spends between seven and 15 years in fresh water before setting out for the species' spawning grounds in the Sargasso Sea, a journey that may take it overland from landlocked waters to the Atlantic. The journey covers 3,000–4,000 miles and takes about six months.

DEEPEST-LIVING FISH
The deepest-living vertebrates are believed to be ophidiids of the genus *Bassogigas*. A specimen was recovered from a depth of 27,230 feet in the Puerto Rico Trench in the Atlantic in 1970.

HIGHEST-LIVING FISH
The Tibetan loach (Cobitidae) is found at an altitude of 17,056 feet in the Himalayas — higher than any other fish.

OLDEST FISH
A female European eel (*Anguilla anguilla*) named Putte was reported to be 88 years old when it died in the aquarium of Hälsingborg Museum in Sweden in 1948. It was believed to have been born in 1860 in the Sargasso Sea, North Atlantic, and was caught in a river as a three-year-old elver.

GENDER DIFFERENCE
A dwarf male anglerfish is seen permanently attached to the female. The dwarf anglerfish is one of four out of the 210 anglerfish species in which the male is unusually small. What is extraordinary about these four species is that the male attaches himself, by biting, to the female. The male's mouth fuses to the skin of his mate, and the bloodstreams of the two fish become connected.The male is then totally dependent upon the female for nourishment.

BIGGEST FRESHWATER FISH
The rare pla buk or pa beuk (*Pangasianodon gigas*), which lives mainly in the Mekong River basin, and *Pangasius sanitwongse*, which is generally found in the Chao Phraya River basin, are said to grow to 9 ft. 10 in. in length and attain a weight of 670 pounds.

over 6 feet long and 200 pounds in weight is considered large.

SMALLEST FISH
The dwarf goby (*Trimmatom nanus*) of the Indo-Pacific is the shortest known vertebrate. The average length of a male specimen is 34/100 inch.

BIGGEST FISH
The rare plankton-feeding whale shark (*Rhincodon typus*), which is found in warmer areas of the Atlantic, Pacific and Indian oceans, is the largest fish in the world. The first specimen to have been scientifically examined was harpooned in Table Bay, South Africa in 1828. Since then, many have been sighted but few have been examined. The largest on scientific record was captured off Baba Island, near Karachi, Pakistan, in November 1949. It was 41 ft. 6 in. long and 23 feet around the thickest part of the body and weighed an estimated 16–23 tons. Despite its size, the whale shark poses very little risk to humans, although some specimens have been known to ram boats that they have mistaken for rival sharks. The whale shark's diet consists of plankton and small fish, which it strains from the upper waters of tropical and subtropical seas.

SHORTEST-LIVED FISH
Some killifish species of the family Cyprinodontidae, found in Africa, the Americas, Asia and warmer parts of Europe, normally live for about eight months.

MOST ELECTRIC FISH
The electric eel or paroque (*Electrophorus electricus*), which is related to the piranha, can be up to 6 feet long and lives in Brazil and the Guianas. Live from head to tail, its electrical apparatus consists of two pairs of longitudinal organs which can release a shock of up to 650 volts. This force, which is used to immobilize prey, is strong enough to stun an adult human.

LONGEST FIN
All three species of thresher shark (family Alopiidae) have a huge scythe-shaped caudal fin (tail fin) which is roughly as long as the body itself. The largest and commonest species, *Alopias vulpinus*, found worldwide in temperate and tropical seas, may grow to a length of 19 ft. 8 in., of which almost 9 ft. 10 in. consists of the upper tail fin. It is thought that the tail is used to herd and stun schools of fish, which can then be eaten.

LARGEST EGG
The largest whale shark (*Rhincodon typhus*) egg on record measured 12 by 5½ by 3½ inches and contained a live 13⁴⁄₅-inch embryo. The specimen, which was found in 1953 in the Gulf of Mexico, may have been aborted.

MOST EGGS
The ocean sunfish (*Mola mola*) produces up to 30 million eggs, each about 1/20 inch in diameter, at a single spawning.

FEWEST EGGS
The mouth-brooding cichlid *Tropheus moorii* of Lake Tanganyika, East Africa produces a maximum of seven eggs during normal reproduction.

MOST VALUABLE FISH
A 2,706-pound female Russian sturgeon (*Huso huso*) caught in the River Tikhaya Sosna in 1924 yielded 540 pounds of top-quality caviar, which would be worth $315,135 on today's market.

A prizewinning ginrin showa koi from Japan sold for about $87,445 in 1982. In 1986, it was acquired for an undisclosed sum by the Kent Koi Center in England, where it died five months later. It has since been stuffed and mounted.

MOST ABUNDANT FISH
The 2½-inch-long deep-sea bristlemouth (*Cyclothone microdon*) has an almost worldwide distribution.

NEWEST LAND-LIVING FISH
Phreatobius walkeri, a wormlike species of trichomycterid catfish, was found in Brazil in the mid-1980s. It lives a fully terrestrial life among leaf litter on river banks; when it is placed into water, it jumps back out again.

LONGEST SURVIVAL OUT OF WATER
The six species of lung fish (Lepidosirenidae, Protopteride and Ceratodidae families) live in freshwater swamps that can dry out for months or even years at a time. Two of the four species found in Africa can live for up to four years in dormant positions in burrows in the ground, abandoning gill breathing in favor of their air-breathing lungs, and secreting a mucus to form a moisture-saving cocoon around their bodies.

FISH TEETH
The fangtooth anoplogaster bares its sharp fangs, which, like the teeth of all fish, are used not for chewing, but primarily for the capture of prey or the collection of plant food. The larger members of the shark subclasses Selachii and Elasmobranchii have the biggest teeth.

water creatures

BIGGEST ANIMAL STRUCTURE
The Great Barrier Reef off Queensland, Australia is the world's largest structure built by living creatures. It measures 1,260 miles long, and covers an area of about 80,000 square miles. Made up of billions of dead and living stony corals, the reef is estimated to have taken a total of 600 million years to accrete.

BIGGEST ANIMAL EYE
The world's largest invertebrate, the Atlantic giant squid, has the largest eye of any animal, living or extinct. A record-breaking specimen found in Thimble Tickle Bay, Newfoundland, Canada in 1878 had eyes estimated to have been 20 inches in diameter.

BIGGEST AMPHIBIAN
The world's largest amphibian is the Chinese giant salamander (*Andrias davidianus*), which lives in northeastern, central and southern China. The largest was found in Hunan Province, and was 5 ft. 11 in. long and weighed 143 pounds.

BIGGEST FROG
The African goliath frog (*Conraua goliath*) is the largest known frog. A specimen captured on the River Sanaga, Cameroon in 1989 had a snout-to-vent length of 1 ft. 2½ in. and an overall length of 2 ft. 10½ in. with its legs extended. It weighed 8 lb. 1 oz.

LONGEST FROG LEAP
The longest triple jump by a frog is 33 ft. 5½ in., made by a South African sharp-nosed frog (*Ptychadena oxyrhynchus*) called Santjie at a frog derby at Lurula Natal Spa, KwaZulu-Natal, South Africa in 1977.

SMALLEST AMPHIBIAN
The Cuban frog *Eleutherodactylus limbatus* is the world's smallest amphibian. When fully grown, it is 17/50–½ inch long from snout to vent.

BIGGEST TOAD
The cane or marine toad (*Bufo marinus*) of tropical South America and Queensland, Australia normally weighs about a pound. The largest specimen on record was called Prinsen and was owned by Håkan Forsberg of Sweden. In 1991, it weighed 5 lb. 13½ oz. and was 1 ft. 9¼ in. long when fully extended.

SMALLEST TOAD
The largest specimen of the African sub-species *Bufo taitanus beiranus* was just 15/16 inch long.

SMALLEST NEWT/SALAMANDER
The lungless salamander from Mexico (*Bolitoglossa mexicana*) has a maximum length of about an inch, including its tail.

BIGGEST CRUSTACEAN
The largest crustacean in the world is the taka-ashi-gani or giant spider crab (*Macrocheira kaempferi*). One specimen had a claw-span of 12 ft. 1½ in. and weighed 41 pounds.

HEAVIEST MARINE CRUSTACEAN
An American or North Atlantic lobster (*Homarus americanus*) weighing 44 lb. 6 oz. and measuring 3 ft. 6 in. from the end of the tail-fan to the tip of the largest claw was caught off Nova Scotia, Canada in 1977. It was later sold to a restaurant in New York City.

BIGGEST FRESHWATER CRUSTACEAN
The crayfish *Astacopsis gouldi*, found in the streams of Tasmania, Australia, can be up to 2 feet long and weigh as much as 9 pounds. One specimen caught in Bridport in 1934 was reported to weigh 14 pounds and was 29 inches long.

BIGGEST CRUSTACEAN SWARM
A swarm of krill (*Euphausia superba*) estimated to weigh up to 11 million tons was tracked by US scientists off Antarctica in March 1981. It was the largest concentration of crustaceans ever seen.

BIGGEST JELLYFISH
In 1870, an Arctic giant jellyfish (*Cyanea capillata arctica*) was washed up in Massachusetts Bay from the northwestern Atlantic. It had a bell diameter of 7 ft. 6 in. and tentacles 120 feet long.

BIGGEST CLAM
The marine giant clam *Tridacna gigas*, found off the

FROG SIZE
The green leaf frog belongs to the family Hylidae, the second largest frog family. There are 2,660 species of frog, ranging in length from ⅓ inch for *Eleutherodactylus limbatus* to 14½ inches for *Conraua goliath*, the African goliath frog.

GIANT CRABS
The annual Crabfest at Chandlers Restaurant in Seattle, Washington runs for six weeks between March and May, and offers crab-lovers a choice of 35 dishes, from chilled crabs and crab quiche to crab ice cream. Prior to the feast, four chefs scour the world for the finest crabs, including 35-pound giant Tasmanian crabs from Australia with claws as big as human arms, and Arkansas king crabs, which are reputed to be the tastiest in the world. The prized giant Tasmanian crabs cost $36.95 per pound. The restaurant, which normally sells 1,600 pounds of crab in six weeks, serves up about 10,000 pounds a week during the Crabfest and makes an extra $30,000–47,000. In 1998, a team of celebrities cracked and judged the first crabs for taste, texture and quality.

Indo-Pacific coral reefs, has the largest bivalve shell. A 3-ft.- 9¼-in.-long, 734-pound specimen was found off Ishigaki Island, Okinawa, Japan in 1956. It probably weighed just over 750 pounds when it was alive.

BIGGEST MARINE GASTROPOD
A trumpet or baler conch (*Syrinx aruanus*) found off Australia in 1979 had a 30⅖-inch-long shell and a girth of up to 39¾ inches. It weighed nearly 40 pounds when alive.

BIGGEST OYSTER
A common oyster (*Ostrea goulis*) found at Arisaig, Scotland in 1997 weighed 1 lb. 13 oz. and had a maximum width of 6½–6¾ inches.

BIGGEST SPONGE
Some sponges of the class Demospongiae reach giant proportions in cold waters. In 1996, specimens that exceeded 10 feet in height and were large enough for a diver to get inside, were found in Antarctic waters.

HEAVIEST SPONGE
A wool sponge (*Hippospongia canaliculatta*) that was collected off the Bahamas in 1909 weighed between 80 and 90 pounds and measured 6 feet in circumference.

SMALLEST SPONGE
Leucosolenia blanca is just 11/100 inch tall when fully grown.

BIGGEST STARFISH
A specimen of the very fragile brisingid *Midgardia xandaros* found in the Gulf of Mexico in 1968 was 4 ft. 6 in. long from tip to tip. Its disc was only 11/50 inch in diameter.

SMALLEST STARFISH
The asterinid sea star *Patiriella parvivipara,* discovered on the west coast of the Eyre peninsula, South Australia in 1975, had a maximum radius of 9/50 inch and a diameter of less than 7/20 inch.

GREATEST SIZE DIFFERENCE
Females of the marine worm *Bonellia viridis* are between 4 and 40 inches long, including the extendable proboscis, while males are only around 1/25–3/25 inch long. The females are thus thousands of times heavier than their mates.

MOST PATERNAL AMPHIBIAN
The 3-inch-long male West European midwife toad *Alytes obstetricans* fertilizes the string of eggs that the female has laid – which can be up to 4 feet long – and winds it around his thighs. He carries the eggs around for up to four weeks until they are ready to hatch, at which point he swims into suitable water and releases the tadpoles.

GREATEST REGENERATION
The sponges (Porifera) are able to regrow from tiny fragments of their former selves, and even if one of them is forced through a fine-meshed silk gauze, the separate fragments can reform into a full-sized sponge.

DEEPEST-LIVING SPONGE
Some sponges of the class Hexactinellida have been recovered from depths of up to 29,000 feet.

DEEPEST-LIVING STARFISH
A specimen of the species *Porcellanaster ivanovi* was collected from a depth of 24,881 feet by the Soviet research ship *Vityaz* in the Mariana Trench in the western Pacific *c.* 1962.

LARGEST INVERTEBRATE
The Atlantic giant squid (*Architeuthis dux*) is the largest known invertebrate. The heaviest ever discovered was a 2.2-ton specimen that washed ashore in Thimble Tickle Bay, Newfoundland, Canada on November 2, 1878. It had a body length of 20 feet, and one tentacle was 35 feet long.

reptiles and dinosaurs

SNAKE ATTACK AND DEFENSE

Snakes evolved from lizard ancestors 120 million years ago and have become extremely successful hunters, suffocating or biting their prey to death or killing it with their venom. Snakes' heads are specially adapted for eating large animals: they have a number of extra joints that allow the jaw to dislocate so that the snake can swallow large prey whole. The prey can sometimes be several times the normal diameter of the snake's mouth. Here, a black timber rattlesnake devours a field mouse. Rattlesnakes use their "rattles" to try to warn off other animals instead of attacking them. The rattle is made of dead scales that brush against one another when the snake vibrates its tail.

BIGGEST REPTILE

The longest known estuarine or saltwater crocodile (*Crocodylus porosus*) measures 23 feet and lives in the Bhitarkanika Wildlife Sanctuary, Orissa, India. There are several reports of 33-foot-long specimens, but they are not substantiated.

SMALLEST CROCODILIAN

Female dwarf caimans (*Paleosuchus palpebrosus*) from northern South America rarely exceed 4 feet in length, and males are usually not more than 5 feet long.

LONGEST LIZARD

The Salvadori or Papuan monitor (*Varanus salvadorii*) from Papua New Guinea can attain a length of up to 15 ft. 7 in. Its tail accounts for almost 70% of this length.

SMALLEST LIZARD

Sphaerodactylus parthenopion, a gecko indigenous to Virgin Gorda, British Virgin Islands, West Indies, is known from just 15 specimens. The three largest among some pregnant females found in 1964 were 7/10 inch long from snout to vent.

LONGEST SNAKE

The reticulated python (*Python reticulatus*) of Southeast Asia often exceeds 20 ft. 6 in. in length. A specimen shot in 1912 in Celebes, Indonesia was recorded as measuring 32 ft. 9½ in. long.

SHORTEST SNAKES

The thread snake (*Leptotyphlops bilineata*) is extremely rare, and the longest known specimen was just 4¼ inches long. The snake's body could have fit into the lead hole in a standard pencil. Another snake, the Brahminy blindsnake (*Rhamphotyphlops braminus*), from the tropics, is less than 4¼ inches long.

BIGGEST CHELONIAN

The biggest chelonian, the leatherback turtle (*Dermochelys coriacea*), averages 6–7 feet from the tip of the beak to the end of the tail and about 7 feet across the front flippers, and weighs up to 1,000 pounds. The largest known was a male found dead on the beach at Harlech, Wales in 1988. It measured 9 ft. 5½ in. in total length over the carapace and 9 feet across the front flippers, and weighed 2,120 pounds.

BIGGEST TORTOISE

The largest living tortoise is a Galapagos tortoise (*Geochelone elephantopos elephantopos*) known as Goliath, which has lived at the Life Fellowship Bird Sanctuary, Sessner, Florida since 1960. Goliath is 53⅝ inches long and 40½ inches wide, and weighs 849 pounds.

SMALLEST CHELONIANS

The speckled Cape tortoise or speckled padloper (*Homopus signatus*) has a total shell length of just 2.3–3.7 inches.

SNAKE EATING

A vendor in Ho Chi Minh City, Vietnam tries to attract customers to buy a 16-foot-long python. Snake venom is believed to help fight cancer and snakes are considered a culinary delicacy in a number of Asian countries. In Indonesia, the government is now discouraging snake eating because it is endangering certain species.To make your own snake dish, try the recipe below, though if you can't find rattlesnake, chicken will do!

GRILLED RATTLESNAKE CHINESE STYLE

1 fresh rattlesnake
⅓ cup soy sauce
¼ cup fresh lime juice
⅓ cup mirin or 2 tbsp. sweet sherry

Combine the soy sauce, lime juice and mirin or sherry. Add the snake and marinate for at least two hours. Prepare a fire in a charcoal grill. Remove the snake from the marinade and keep the marinade. Thread the snake onto bamboo skewers and grill over medium or hot coals, basting frequently with the marinade for about five minutes or until tender.

MOST SUCCESSFUL REPTILES
Pictured left is an emerald swift lizard. Lizards are the most successful living group of reptiles, with 3,100 species, compared with snakes, which are the second most successful group, with 2,000 species. Lizards are also the most diverse group of living reptiles in terms of size and shape, and range in total body length from small lizards such as geckos, measuring about $1^1/_5$ inches, to monitor lizards of 15 feet. Different species move at different speeds, depending on where they live – those native to desert regions are generally the fastest, and all are able to accelerate rapidly.

The smallest marine turtle in the world is the Atlantic ridley (*Lepidochelys kempii*), which has a shell length of 20–28 inches and a maximum weight of 175 pounds.

OLDEST CHELONIAN
A Madagascar radiated tortoise (*Astrochelys radiata*) called Tui Malila was presented by Captain Cook to the Tonga royal family in either 1773 or 1777. It was at least 188 years old when it died in 1965.

DEEPEST CHELONIAN DIVE
In 1987, a leatherback turtle fitted with a pressure-sensitive recording device was reported to have reached a depth of 3,973 feet off the Virgin Islands, West Indies.

FASTEST REPTILES
The highest speed attained by a reptile in water is recorded as 22 mph, by a scared Pacific leatherback turtle.

The highest speed measured for a reptile on land is $21^7/_{10}$ mph, attained by a spiny-tailed iguana (*Ctenosaura*) from Costa Rica.

FASTEST SNAKE
The fastest land snake is thought to be the aggressive black mamba (*Dendroaspis polylepis*) of eastern tropical Africa, which is capable of speeds as high as 10–12 mph in short bursts over level ground.

FASTEST DINOSAURS
Dinosaur trackways discovered in Texas in the Morrison formation, which dates from the Late Jurassic period, indicate that a carnivorous dinosaur had been moving at 25 mph.

The large-brained, 220-pound *Dromiceiomimus* ("emu mimic lizard") of the Late Cretaceous period, found in Alberta, Canada, could probably outsprint an ostrich, which can move at more than 37 mph.

BIGGEST HERBIVOROUS DINOSAUR
The world's largest ever land animals were sauropod dinosaurs, a group of long-necked, long-tailed, four-legged plant eaters that lumbered around most of the world during the Jurassic and Cretaceous periods, 208–65 million years ago. The largest specimen was 131 feet long and would have weighed up to 110 tons.

SMALLEST DINOSAUR
Compsognathus (meaning "pretty jaw"), a chicken-sized dinosaur from southern Germany and southeastern France, was 23 inches long from the snout to the tip of the tail and weighed approximately 6 lb. 8 oz.

BIGGEST DINOSAUR FOOTPRINTS
In 1932, the $53^1/_2$-inch-long, 32-inch-wide footprints of a bipedal hadrosaurid (meaning "duckbilled") were discovered in Salt Lake City, Utah. Other reports from Colorado and Utah refer to 37- to 40-inch footprints. Prints attributed to the hind feet of the largest brachiosaurids are also up to 40 inches wide.

BIGGEST DINOSAUR CLAWS
The therizinosaurids ("scythe lizards"), which lived in the Nemegt Basin, Mongolia in the Late Cretaceous period, had the largest claws of any known animal. Claws of *Therizinosaurus cheloniformis* measured up to 36 inches along the outer curve.

BIGGEST DINOSAUR SKULL
The long-frilled *Torosaurus* ("piercing lizard"), a ceratopsid, had the largest skull of any known land animal. The 25-foot-long, 8.8-ton herbivore's skull was up to 9 ft. 10 in. long (including the fringe) and weighed as much as 2.2 tons.

SMALLEST-BRAINED DINOSAUR
Stegosaurus (meaning "plated lizard"), which roamed across Colorado, Oklahoma, Utah and Wyoming about 150 million years ago, was up to 30 feet long but had a walnut-sized brain weighing $2^1/_2$ ounces. This is equal to 0.002 of 1% of its estimated bodyweight of 3.6 tons (compared with 0.06 of 1% for an elephant and 1.88% for a human).

BIGGEST LIZARD
Male Komodo dragons (*Varanus komodoensis*) average 7 ft. 5 in. in length and weigh about 130 pounds. Voracious carnivores, they have been reported to kill adult water buffalo and human beings. The largest accurately measured specimen was a male presented to a US zoologist by the Sultan of Bima in 1928. In 1937, it was 10 ft. 2 in. long and weighed 365 pounds.

birds

SMALLEST BIRD
Male bee hummingbirds (*Mellisuga helenae*), which live in Cuba, weigh 0.056 ounces and are 2¼ inches in length. The bill and tail account for half of this length.

SMALLEST BIRDS OF PREY
The black-legged falconet (*Microhierax fringillarius*) of Southeast Asia and the white-fronted or Bornean falconet (*M. latifrons*) of northwestern Borneo both have an average length of 5½–6 inches, including a 2-inch tail, and weigh approximately 1¼ ounces.

TALLEST FLYING BIRDS
The largest cranes (family Gruidae) can be almost 6 ft. 6 in. tall.

HEAVIEST FLYING BIRDS
The Kori bustard or paauw (*Ardeotis kori*) of northeast and southern Africa and the great bustard (*Otis tarda*) of Europe and Asia weigh about 40–42 pounds. There is a report of a 46-lb.-4-oz. male great bustard shot in northeastern China. It was too heavy to fly.

HEAVIEST BIRDS OF PREY
Andean condors (*Vultur gryphus*) are the heaviest species of bird of prey. Males weigh 20–27 pounds and have a wingspan of at least 10 feet.

A male California condor (*Gymnogyps californianus*) preserved in the California Academy of Sciences is reported to weigh 31 pounds. It is rare for the species to exceed 23 pounds in weight.

LONGEST FEATHERS
The phoenix fowl or Yokohama chicken (a strain of the red junglefowl *Gallus gallus*) is bred in Japan for ornamental purposes. A rooster with a 34-ft.-9½-in tail covert was reported in 1972.

LONGEST BILLS
The bill of the Australian pelican (*Pelicanus conspicillatus*) is 13–18½ inches long.

The longest beak in relation to body length is that of the sword-billed hummingbird (*Ensifera ensifera*) of the Andes. At 4 inches, the beak is longer than the bird's body (excluding the tail).

BIGGEST EYES
The ostrich has the largest eyes of any land animal. Each eye can be up to 2 inches in diameter.

MOST AIRBORNE BIRD
The sooty tern (*Sterna fuscata*) leaves its nesting grounds as a youngster and remains aloft for 3–10 years, settling on water from time to time. It returns to land to breed as an adult.

LONGEST FLIGHT
A common tern (*Sterna hirundo*) that was banded in June 1996 in Finland was recaptured alive 16,250 miles away at Rotamah Island, Victoria, Australia in January 1997. It had traveled at a rate of 125 miles a day.

SLOWEST-FLYING BIRDS
The American woodcock (*Scolopax minor*) and the Eurasian woodcock (*S. rusticola*) have both been timed flying at 5 mph without stalling during courtship displays.

SLOWEST WINGBEAT
The slowest wingbeats recorded during true level flight averaged one per second. They were by several species of the New World vulture (family Cathartidae).

BIGGEST EVER WINGSPAN
The South American teratoron (*Argentavis magnificens*), which existed 6–8 million years ago, had an estimated wingspan of 25 feet.

FASTEST FLYING BIRD
The peregrine falcon (*Falco peregrinus*) is the fastest living creature, reaching speeds of at least 124 mph and possibly as much as 168 mph when swooping from great heights during territorial displays or while catching prey birds in midair.

FASTEST WINGBEAT
The horned sungem (*Heliactin cornuta*), a hummingbird from South America, beats its wings 90 times a second.

FASTEST LAND BIRD
Despite its bulk, the ostrich can run at speeds of up to 45 mph if necessary.

HIGHEST-FLYING BIRDS
A Ruppell's vulture (*Gyps rueppellii*) collided with a commercial aircraft over Abidjan, Ivory Coast, at an altitude of 37,000 feet in November 1973. The impact damaged one of the aircraft's engines, but the plane landed safely. The species is rarely seen above 20,000 feet.

In 1967, about 30 whooper swans (*Cygnus cygnus*) were spotted at an altitude of just over 27,000 feet by an airline pilot over the Western Isles, UK. They were flying from Iceland to Loch Foyle on the Northern Ireland/Republic of Ireland border. Their altitude was confirmed by air traffic control.

LONGEST STRIDE
The stride of an ostrich may exceed 23 feet in length when the bird is sprinting.

HIGHEST G-FORCE BORNE
The beak of the red-headed woodpecker (*Melanerpes erythrocephalus*) hits the bark of a tree with an impact velocity of 13 mph, subjecting the bird's brain to a deceleration of approximately 10 *g* when its head snaps back. Other woodpeckers may experience an even higher *g*-force.

MOST FOOD CONSUMED
Hummingbirds (family Trochilidae) require at least half their own body weight in food (mainly nectar and tiny insects) every

BIGGEST BIRD
The largest and strongest living bird is the North African ostrich (*Struthio camelus camelus*). Males can be up to 9 feet tall and weigh 345 pounds, and when fully grown they have one of the most advanced immune systems of any animal. South Africa was the first country to see the commercial potential of ostrich products — the creatures are prized not only for their large soft white feathers and their meat but also for their skins, which are made into the strongest commercially available leather in the world. Ostrich farming is believed to have begun in the Karoo and Eastern Cape *c.* 1863. By 1910 there were more than 20,000 domesticated ostriches in the country, and by 1913 ostrich feathers were the fourth most important South African export product. Demand began to dry up soon afterwards, but there was an ostrich revival in the 1920s when farmers started to produce *biltong* (dried strips of ostrich meat) commercially. Ostrich farming is now practiced in 50 countries and is especially popular in South Africa, Algeria, Australia, France and the United States. It has saved ostriches from becoming an endangered species: there are currently about 1.75 million worldwide.

single day. With the possible exception of shrews, they have the highest metabolic rate of any known animal.

STRANGEST DIET
An ostrich living at London Zoo, England was found to have swallowed an alarm clock, a roll of film, a handkerchief, a 3-foot-long piece of rope, a cycle valve, a pencil, three gloves, a comb, part of a gold necklace, a collar stud, a Belgian franc, four halfpennies and two farthings.

LONGEST FAST
The male emperor penguin (*Aptenodytes forsteri*) spends several months without feeding on the frozen wastes of the Antarctic sea ice. It travels overland from the sea to the breeding colony, courts the female, incubates the egg for 62–67 days, waits for the female to return and travels back to the open sea, going without food for up to 134 days.

LARGEST PREY
The largest wild animal known to have been killed and carried away by a bird was a 15-pound male red howler monkey killed by a harpy eagle (*Harpia harpyja*) in Manu National Park, Peru in 1990. The harpy eagle is considered the world's most powerful bird of prey, although it weighs only 20 pounds.

SHARPEST VISION
The peregrine falcon (*Falco peregrinus*) is believed to be able to spot a pigeon from a distance of more than 5 miles under ideal conditions.

BIGGEST NESTS
The incubation mounds built by the mallee fowl (*Leipoa ocellata*) of Australia are up to 15 feet tall and 35 feet wide. A nest site is estimated to weigh 330 tons.

A 9-ft.-6-in.-wide, 20-foot-deep nest was built by a pair of bald eagles (*Haliaeetus leucocephalus*), and possibly by their successors, close to St. Petersburg, Florida. When examined in 1963, the nest was estimated to weigh in excess of 2.2 tons.

SMALLEST NESTS
The vervain hummingbird (*Mellisuga minima*) builds a nest about half the size of a walnut shell. The deeper but narrower nest of the bee hummingbird (*M. helenae*) is thimble-sized.

BIGGEST EGGS
The extinct giant elephant bird (*Aepyornis maximus*) laid 1-foot-long eggs with a liquid capacity of 2¼ gallons — the equivalent of seven ostrich eggs and more than 12,000 hummingbird eggs.

The ostrich egg is 6–8 inches long, 4–6 inches in diameter and weighs 2 lb. 3 oz.–3 lb. 14 oz. It is equal in volume to 24 chicken eggs. The shell is 3/50 inch thick but can support the weight of an adult human. The largest on record was laid in 1988 by a two-year-old northern/southern hybrid (*Struthio c. camelus* x *S. c. australis*) at the Kibbutz Ha'on collective farm, Israel. It weighed 5 lb. 2 oz.

LARGE FLOCKS
Flamingoes, with their long necks and legs, have a height range of 3–5 feet and are the biggest bird to form large flocks. Of the four species, the lesser flamingo (*Phoeniconaias minor*) of eastern and southern Africa has been seen in flocks of several million birds, particularly in the Great Lakes of eastern Africa.

SMALLEST EGG
The smallest known bird's eggs were two vervain hummingbird (*Mellisuga minima*) eggs less than 39/100 inch long. They weighed 0.365 g (0.0128 oz) and 0.375 g (0.0132 oz).

MOST ABUNDANT BIRD
The red-billed quelea (*Quelea quelea*) of Africa has an estimated adult breeding population of 1.5 billion. The slaughter of at least 200 million of them each year has no impact on this number.

BOSSIEST BIRD
The kea (*Nestor notabilis*) from New Zealand is the only bird known to have a society in which the higher-status individuals force others to work for them.

SMELLIEST BIRD
The South American hoatzin (*Opisthocomus hoazin*) has an odor similar to cow manure. Colombians call it *pava hedionda* ("stinking pheasant"). The cause of the smell is believed to be a combination of its diet of green leaves and its specialized digestive system, which involves a kind of foregut fermentation.

LARGEST WINGSPAN
The wandering albatross (*Diomedea exulans*) has the largest wingspan of any living bird. As a result, it is an expert glider and is capable of remaining in the air without beating its wings for several hours at a time. The largest known specimen was an extremely old male with an 11-ft.-11-in. wingspan. It was caught in the Tasman Sea in September 1965.

spiders and scorpions

BIGGEST SPIDER
The goliath bird-eating spider (*Theraphosa leblondi*), which is found mostly in the coastal rainforests of Surinam, Guyana and French Guiana, is the world's largest known spider. A male specimen found in Venezuela in 1965 had a leg-span of 11 inches and was big enough to cover a dinner plate.

HEAVIEST SPIDER
Female bird-eating spiders are more heavily built than the males. A 4³/₁₀-ounce female specimen captured in Surinam in 1985 had a maximum leg-span of 10½ inches and 1-inch fangs.

SMALLEST SPIDER
Patu marplesi of the family Symphytognathidae from Samoa is the world's smallest known spider. A male found in 1965 was ¹⁷/₁₀₀₀ inch long overall — about the size of one of the periods on this page.

LONGEST SPIDER FANGS
The bird-eating spider *Theraphosa leblondi* has fangs that are up to half an inch long.

BIGGEST SIZE DIFFERENCE
In some species of the golden orb-web spider (genus *Nephila*), which are found all over the tropical and temperate world, females are almost 1,000 times heavier than their mates. The males are smaller than the females' normal prey in order to avoid being eaten by them.

FASTEST SPIDERS
The long-legged sun spiders (order Solifugae) of the arid semidesert regions of Africa and the Middle East can reach speeds of over 10 mph.

NOISIEST SPIDERS
In courtship the male European buzzing spider (*Anyphaena accentuata*) produces a buzzing sound audible to the human ear. Produced when the spider vibrates his abdomen rapidly against a leaf, the sound cannot be heard by the female; she can only detect it through vibrations.

The male *Lycosa gulosa*, once known as the purring spider, taps his palps and abdomen on leaves to make a purring sound.

MOST SOCIABLE SPIDER
Several thousand members of both sexes of the South African species *Anelosimus eximus* cohabit peaceably on webs that are more than 3 feet across.

MOST MATERNAL SPIDER
In many spider species the maternal relationship ends when the eggs are laid, and the mother never sees her young. *Theridion sisyphium* females, however, feed their young with liquid from their own mouths. When they are a few days old, the infants begin to share their mother's prey, and as they grow older they help her to hunt. The relationship comes to an end when the mother dies and is eaten by her offspring.

LARGEST WEBS
The golden silk spider is one of around 50 species of the genus *Nephila*, found in tropical areas all over the world. The first lines of the yellow silk webs of the genus are up to 10 feet long and can even stretch across small rivers.

BIGGEST SCORPION
Steve Kutcher, seen left with his pet tropical emperor scorpion and Chilean rose tarantula, is famous for providing various trained creatures for movies. He began by supplying the locusts for *The Exorcist 2* (1977) and went on to provide the spiders for *Arachnophobia* (1990) and a huge mosquito for *Jurassic Park* (1993). In order to get his creatures to behave exactly as he wants them to on set, Kutcher takes along tweezers, a fishing line and plastic cases full of waxes and glue. He sometimes also blasts his creatures with gusts of hot air and carbon dioxide to make them act in a certain way. Steve, who lives in Arcadia, California, studied biology and entomology after becoming fascinated by bugs and starting a firefly collection one summer in New York. He now devotes an entire room in his house to insects, which live in glass and wooden boxes piled from floor to ceiling. The tropical emperor scorpion is one of the world's largest species of scorpion, reaching a length of up to 7 inches, but is totally harmless and makes a good housepet.

OLDEST SPIDERS
The tropical bird-eaters (family Theraphosidae) can live for up to 25 years.

STRONGEST SPIDER WEBS
Achaearenea tepidariorum weaves a web strong enough to trap a small mouse, completely lifting it off the ground.

The webs of the genus *Nephila* can trap small birds and even hamper the movements of humans.

Nephila senegalenis from tropical Africa has a special "litter line" in its webs where the sucked-out remains of small birds may often be found.

LARGEST CONTINUOUS WEBS
The largest continuous areas of web in the world are built by spiders of the Indian genus *Stegodyphus*, which create three-dimensional, interwoven and overlapping webs. A single continuous silken mass can cover considerable areas of vegetation, and extend unbroken over whole hedgerows.

SIMPLEST WEBS
Spider species of the genus *Miagrammopes* weave a single-stranded web that stretches for up to 3 feet between two small branches.

The American bolas spider of the genus *Mastophora* uses a small single strand to attach itself to a branch and a second, much longer, strand as a "fishing line" to catch passing moths.

The South African bolas spider *Cladomelea akermani* uses a similar technique but rotates the "fishing line" continuously for about 15 minutes. If no prey is ensnared, the spider consumes the sticky globe on the end of the line and replaces it with a new one.

LARGEST SCORPION
Heterometrus swannerdami from southern India frequently attains a length of more than 7 inches from the tips of the pincers to the end of the sting. The longest specimen was found during World War II and had an overall length of 11½ inches.

The tropical emperor or imperial scorpion (*Pandinus imperator*) of West Africa can also be up to 7 inches long. The largest on record is a 9-inch male from Sierra Leone.

The tropical African species *Pandinus giganticus* may grow to almost 8 inches in length.

SMALLEST SCORPION
Microbothus pusillus, a species which is found on the Red Sea coast, is the smallest scorpion in the world, with an approximate total length of half an inch.

HEAVIEST SCORPION
The West African tropical emperor or imperial scorpion (*Pandinus imperator*) can weigh up to 2 ounces.

DEEPEST-LIVING SCORPION
Alacran tartarus, which lives in South America, has been found in caves more than 2,625 feet deep.

MOST SOCIABLE SCORPION
West African tropical emperor or imperial scorpion (*Pandinus imperator*) offspring may remain with the family group when they are adults, and families cooperate to capture prey.

STRONGEST SPIDER
When an intruder is trying to open its "trap door" (a silken structure covering the entrance to its underground burrow), the Californian trap-door spider *Bothriocyrtum californicum* is capable of resisting a force up to 38 times its own weight.

BIGGEST EYES
The net-casting spider (*Dinopis subrufa*) of the genus *Dinopis* has huge eyes that shine like headlights when staring at a bright light. The *Dinopis* genus has the biggest eyes of any spider; ogre-faced or gladiator spiders have the largest simple eyes of any arthropod. About ½ inch in width, they do not produce very clear images but have excellent light-gathering power for night work.

insects and creepy crawlies

LONGEST INSECT
Measuring 21½ inches, the legs of *Pharnacia kirbyi*, a stick insect from the rainforests of Borneo, are so long that they can get trapped when it sheds its skin. The largest known specimen had a body length of 12⁹⁄₁₀ inches.

LIGHTEST INSECTS
The male bloodsucking banded louse (*Enderleinellus zonatus*) and the parasitic wasp (*Caraphractus cinctus*) may each weigh as little as 0.005 mg. This is equal to 1.6 billion creatures per gram (5,670,000 per ounce).

LARGEST FLEA
Hystrichopsylla schefferi females are up to half an inch long. The species was described from one specimen found in the nest of a mountain beaver in Washington in 1913.

LARGEST WINGED COCKROACH
A preserved *Megaloblatta longipennis* female in the collection of Akira Yokokura of Japan is 3⅘ inches long and 1¾ inches wide. The species originates in Columbia.

LARGEST TERMITE
Queens of the African termite species *Macrotermes bellicosus* are up to 5½ inches long and 1⅖ inches wide. They can produce 30,000 eggs a day, barely move and spend their entire lives in a "royal cell" in the center of the colony.

GREATEST CONCENTRATION OF INSECTS
In July 1874 a swarm of Rocky Mountain locusts (*Melanoplus spretus*) covered an estimated 198,600-square-mile area as they flew over the state of Nebraska. The swarm

GREEDIEST ANIMAL
The larva of the polyphemus moth (*Antheraea polyphemus*) consumes 86,000 times its own birthweight in its first 56 days. This is equal to a 7-pound human baby taking in 300 tons of nourishment.

HEAVIEST INSECT
Goliath beetles (from the family Scarabaeidae) of equatorial Africa, especially *Goliathus regius*, *G. meleagris*, *G. goliathus* or *giganteus* and *G. druryi*, are the heaviest insects in the world. Males are up to 4⅓ inches long from the tip of the frontal horns to the end of the abdomen and weigh up to 3½ ounces.

MOST DESTRUCTIVE INSECT
The desert locust (*Schistocerca gregaria*) can eat its own weight in food every day. In a single day, a "small" swarm of about 50 million specimens can eat food that would sustain 500 people for a year.

contained 12.5 trillion (12.5×10^{12}) insects and weighed 27.5 million tons.

MOST FERTILE ANIMAL
With unlimited food and no predators, one cabbage aphid (*Brevicoryne brassicae*) could theoretically create an 906-million-ton mass of descendants every year – more than three times the weight of the world's human population.

FASTEST-FLYING INSECTS
The highest maintainable airspeed of any insect is 24 mph, by the deer bot-fly (*Cephenemyia pratti*), hawk moths (Sphingidae), horseflies (*Tabanus bovinus*) and some tropical butterflies (Hesperiidae).

The Australian dragonfly (*Austrophlebia costalis*) can reach a speed of 36 mph for short bursts.

LONGEST JUMP BY A FLEA
The cat flea (*Ctenocephalides felis*) can make single jumps of up to 13⅓ inches, and the common flea (*Pulex irritans*) is capable of similar feats. In a 1910 experiment, a common flea allowed to leap at will performed a long jump of 13 inches and a high jump of 7¾ inches.

HIGHEST G FORCE ON AN INSECT
When jackknifing into the air to escape predators, the click beetle (*Athous haemorrhoidalis*) endures a force of 400 *g*. One half-inch-long, 0.00014-ounce specimen jumped to a height of 11¾ inches, and was calculated to have endured a peak brain deceleration of 2,300 *g*.

LOUDEST INSECT
The tymbal organs of the male cicada (family Cicadidae) pulse 7,400 times a minute. The noise (which the US Department of Agriculture lists as "Tsh-ee-EEEE-e-ou") is detectable more than a quarter of a mile away.

SHORTEST-LIVED INSECTS
Mayflies (*Ephemeroptera*) can spend 2–3 years as nymphs at the bottom of lakes and streams and live for as little as an hour as winged adults.

MOST ACUTE SENSE OF SMELL
The male emperor moth (*Eudia pavonia*) can detect the sex attractant of the virgin female from a distance of 6⅘ miles. The chemoreceptors on the male moth's antennae can detect a single molecule of the attractant, of which the female carries less than 0.0001 mg.

BIGGEST COCKROACH
Macropanesthia rhinoceros is the biggest cockroach species without wings. It is 3 inches long and 2 inches wide, and weighs 1¼ ounces, about the same weight as two sparrows. The species is native to Queensland, Australia.

parasites

MOST BLOODTHIRSTY PARASITES
Blood-sucking hookworms inhabit about 700 million people worldwide and may be responsible for a daily blood loss of 12.3 million pints – equal to the blood of more than 1 million people.

Each specimen of the digenean liver fluke *Fasciola hepatica*, a common mammalian parasite, consumes about 0.2 ml (0.007 fl.oz) of blood per day.

LONGEST PARASITIC FASTS
The common bedbug *Cimex lectularius* is famously able to survive without feeding for more than a year, but the soft tick *Ornithodoros turicata* can live through a period of starvation lasting up to five years.

MOST FERTILE PARASITES
One female *Ascaris lumbricoides* can produce up to 200,000 eggs every day of her adult life, and has a total productive capacity of 26 million eggs.

Echinococcus granulosus, a canine tapeworm, can also infect the liver, lungs and brain of humans, producing cyst-like structures called hydatids. These can measure as much as 10 inches across and can seriously damage the organs containing them. A fertile hydatid contains an average of 2 million larvae, which can yield innumerable adult tapeworms.

FASTEST PARASITIC WORM
Specimens of the subcutaneous eyeworm *Loa loa*, which is up to 3 inches long, have been removed from all parts of patients' bodies. As adults, their maximum migration rate through the human body equals 1/2 inch per minute. The eyeworm is an endoparasite or internal parasite. The most common endoparasites are microparasites such as viruses.

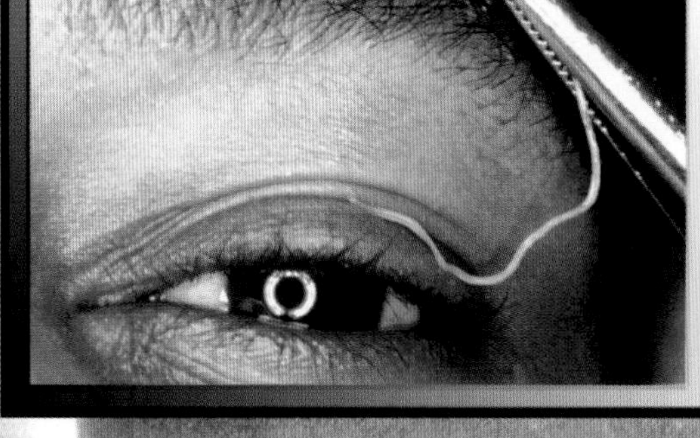

MOST COMMON HUMAN PARASITE
Ascaris lumbricoides, a roundworm that inhabits the small intestine and is up to 18 inches long, infects about 25% of the world's human population. Each host is usually infected with 10–20 specimens, but higher numbers have been recorded. The simultaneous migration of large numbers through the lungs can cause severe hemorrhagic pneumonia.

The body of the beef tapeworm *Taeniarhynchus saginatus* can consist of more than 1,000 segments, each of which contains about 80,000 eggs. A person infected with one specimen (which can live for up to 25 years) probably excretes about nine of its constantly-renewed segments, and therefore approximately 0.75 million eggs, each day.

LARGEST PARASITES
The broad or fish tapeworm *Diphyllobothrium latum*, which inhabits the small intestine of fish and sometimes humans, is usually 30–40 feet long, but it can grow to 60 feet. If a specimen survived for 10 years, it could possess a chain of segments almost 5 miles long, containing about 2 billion eggs.

Taeniarhynchus saginatus, the beef tapeworm, usually grows to 50 feet, but one specimen measured more than 75 feet – three times the length of the human intestine.

LARGEST PARASITIC FLUKE
A didymozoid digenean species found in the ocean sunfish *Mola mola* can reportedly grow to 20–30 feet in length.

MOST BENEFICIAL PARASITE TO HUMANS
The medicinal leech *Hirudo medicinalis*, which was used by doctors for bloodletting up to the 19th century, has made a surprising comeback now that physicians have begun to employ it for significant new purposes. Since 1990, the creatures have been used by a team of surgeons at Harper Hospital, Denver, Colorado to improve blood circulation in gunshot wounds and in severed limbs or fingers that are being reattached. In 1991, a team of Canadian surgeons used leeches to drain blood and prevent it from clotting under a patient's scalp, which had been sewn back on after a grizzly bear ripped it off. Leeches, which are both predatory and parasitic, are common in aquatic habitats and in moist situations on land. They have a very well developed sense of smell, which enables them to locate their prey, and suckers on both ends of their bodies with which to grasp their hosts. The saliva of parasitic leeches contains an anesthetic, which prevents the host from detecting the parasite's presence, and powerful anticoagulants, which ensure that the blood of the prey remains fluid and can be easily digested by the leech.

LARGEST ROUNDWORM IN HUMANS
The largest parasitic nematode (roundworm) of humans is probably the Guinea worm *Dracunculus medinensis*, a subcutaneous species with females up to 4 feet long.

LARGEST PARASITIC INSECT
The exceptionally large flea *Hystrichopsylla schefferi*, dubbed "super flea," can exceed 9/25 inch in length. Its only known host is *Aplodontia rufa*, a North American rodent.

LARGEST TICKS
Ticks are small arachnids that often live on the skin of warm-blooded animals. The largest belong to the suborder Ixodida and can be 2/5 inch long.

LARGEST LEECH
Haementeria ghilianii, an Amazonian species, is 1 foot long. A freshwater species, it has protruding mouth parts and no true jaws.

GREATEST SIZE DIFFERENCE
The biggest difference in size between the sexes of an animal associated with parasitism is in *Bonellia viridis*, a species of echiuroid or spoon worm. The adult female is around 3 feet long and is nonparasitic, while the adult male is no more than 1/20 inch long and lives as an endoparasite inside the female's brood pouch, where it fertilizes her eggs.

Female nematodes are typically larger than males, but this difference is extreme in *Trichosomoides crassicauda*, which inhabits the urinary bladder of rats. Compared with the female, the male – which lives as an endoparasite inside her uterus – is minute.

LONGEST-LIVING PARASITE
A lifespan of 27 years has been reliably recorded for a medicinal leech, *Hirudo medicinalis*.

MOST DANGEROUS MIGRATION
The far-flung migrations of the roundworm *Ascaris lumbricoides* can have severe and sometimes fatal consequences for its human host. These sizeable worms can block the bile and pancreatic ducts or penetrate the intestinal wall and cause peritonitis. There are even cases where, due to their sensitivity to anaesthetics, *Ascaris* worms have emerged out of the nose or mouth of a patient recovering from a surgical procedure.

MOST PARASITIZED HOST SPECIES
Stagnicola emarginata, a freshwater snail, is a host for the larvae of at least 35 species of parasitic fluke.

MOST WIDESPREAD PARASITE ACROSS SPECIES
The liver fluke *Fasciola hepatica* has been found as an adult in the liver, gallbladder and associated ducts of a range of mammalian species, including sheep, cattle, goats, pigs, horses, rabbits, squirrels, dogs and humans, and its larval stage has been discovered in a variety of different species of freshwater snail.

MOST CUNNING PARASITE
In Jan 1998 scientists at Vrije University, Amsterdam, Netherlands found that specimens of the freshwater snail *Lymnaea stagnalis* parasitized by the digenean fluke *Trichobilharzia ocellata* develop an aversion to sex. Instead, they grow more quickly, allowing their parasites to thrive. The parasite achieves this behavioral change in its host by directly affecting the latter's gene expression.

MOST DRASTIC PARASITIC EFFECTS
The larvae of parasitic flukes often inhibit the growth of their snail host's gonads, sometimes even causing castration. Consequently, parasitized snails often cannot reproduce.

Bees, homopteran bugs and other insects hosting infections of tiny endoparasitic insects known as stylopids or strepsipterans often experience noticeable alterations of their secondary sexual characteristics.

Scientific literature contains mystifying reports of weasels that have been observed performing strange circular "dances." Some scientists suggest that these are due to the action of parasitic flukes inhabiting the weasels' brains.

Brain-dwelling flukes have been held responsible by some researchers for mysterious occurrences in which whales appear to have stranded themselves deliberately on beaches, from where they were unable to return to the sea and eventually died.

MOST DRASTIC TRANSFORMATION OF A PARASITE
The larvae of the copepod crustacean *Sacculina carcini* are free-swimming and closely resemble those of typical, nonparasitic copepods, but as adults they bear no resemblance to any type of crustacean. Losing their limbs, gut and segmentation, their bodies transform into sac-like structures that pierce the body of a crab and send branches throughout the crab's body and limbs. The crab then often undergoes a degree of sex reversal due to the modification of its gonads and/or release of inhibiting compounds by the now strangely plantlike *Sacculina*.

MOST GROTESQUE EFFECTS
Extraordinary cases of frogs with six or more limbs may be the direct result of parasitic fluke activity. The bases of these extra limbs are packed with masses of metacercariae, an encysted larval stage in the lifecycle of various digenean parasitic flukes. These cysts may be disrupting the limb development of tadpoles, splitting the limb buds into several sections, each of which grows a limb.

MOST DANGEROUS PARASITES
The most dangerous multi-cellular parasite is the rat flea *Xenopsylla cheopsis*. The carrier of the bubonic plague (Black Death), it is believed to be to the cause of most of the world's catastrophic pandemics.

Malarial parasites of the genus *Plasmodium*, carried by *Anopheles* mosquitoes, are the most dangerous protozoan parasites. They are probably responsible for 50% of all human deaths (excluding those caused by wars and accidents) since the Stone Age. In sub-Saharan Africa, up to 2.8 million people die of malaria each year.

animal attack

MOST POISONOUS ANIMAL
Poison-arrow frogs (*Dendrobates* and *Phyllobates*) from South and Central America secrete some of the deadliest biological toxins in the world. The skin secretion of the golden poison-arrow frog (*Phyllobates terribilis*) of western Colombia is the most poisonous of all – scientists have to wear thick gloves when handling them.

MOST VENOMOUS SCORPION
The Tunisian fat-tailed scorpion (*Androctomus australis*) is responsible for 80% of stings and 90% of deaths from scorpion stings in North Africa.

MOST VENOMOUS SPIDER
The Brazilian huntsman (*Phoneutria fera*) has the most active neurotoxic venom of any spider. Large and highly aggressive, huntsmen often hide in clothing or shoes and bite furiously several times if disturbed. Hundreds of accidents involving the Brazilian huntsman and other Brazilian wandering spiders are reported annually, but an antivenin is now available. Most deaths that occur are of children under the age of seven.

MOST VENOMOUS SNAKE
The king cobra (*Ophiophagus hannah*) or hamadryad of Southeast Asia and India averages 12–15 feet in length and is both the deadliest and the longest venomous snake.

LONGEST SNAKE FANGS
The longest fangs of any snake are those of the highly venomous Gaboon viper (*Bitis gabonica*) of tropical Africa. In one 6-foot-long specimen they measured 2 inches.

MOST DANGEROUS LIZARDS
Unusually for lizards, the Gila monster (*Heloderma suspectum*) of Mexico and the southwestern United States and the Mexican beaded lizard (*Heloderma horridum*) from western coastal Mexico both have a venomous bite.

MOST DANGEROUS BIG CATS
Tigers seem to attack humans more than any other cats, probably because humans fall within the natural size range of a tiger's prey and are fairly easy to catch, particularly for old or injured tigers.

MOST DANGEROUS PRIMATE
Irate silverback gorillas are potentially the most dangerous of all primates. When defending their families, they rush toward intruders and emit roars. These displays are now known to be bluffs in most cases, although some end with the gorilla thumping or biting the intruder.

MOST DANGEROUS BEAR
The only species of bear that actively preys on humans is the polar bear (*Ursus maritimus*). Most attacks occur during the night and are made by hungry adolescent males that are probably inexperienced hunters, and therefore more likely to be driven from their usual prey by larger bears.

MOST DANGEROUS SMALL MAMMALS
The most dangerous small mammal to humans is the rat. More than 20 pathogens are carried by them, including the bacterium that causes bubonic plague (the "Black Death"). They also carry leptospirosis (Weil's disease), Lassa fever, rat-bite fever and murine typhus, all of which can be fatal.

The Cuban solenodon (*Solenodon cubanus*) and the Haitian solenodon (*Solenodon paradoxus*) from the Caribbean have saliva that is toxic to prey and potentially dangerous to human beings.

MOST POISONOUS FISH
The puffer fish (*Tetraodon*) of the Red Sea and Indo-Pacific region delivers a fatal toxin called tetrodoxin, one of the most powerful nonproteinous poisons. Less than 0.004 ounces of the poison – which is contained in the fish's ovaries, eggs, blood, liver, intestines and skin – is enough to kill an adult human in as little as 20 minutes.

MOST DANGEROUS BEE
The venom of the Africanized honey bee (*Apis mellifera scutellata*) is no more potent than that of other bees, but the number of stings that it inflicts can kill humans.

MOST DANGEROUS BIRDS
The only birds known to have attacked and killed humans in the wild are ostriches (*Struthio camelus camelus*), mute swans (*Cygnus olor*) and the three cassowary species (family Casuariidae).

STRONGEST BITE
The strongest animal bite ever measured is that of the dusky shark (*Carcharhinus obscurus*): a 6-ft.-6¾-in. specimen can exert a force of 132 pounds between its

STRANGEST DEFENSE MECHANISM
The Texas horned lizard (*Phrynosoma douglassi*) remains motionless if approached, but if it is picked up it will often attempt to confuse its attacker by puffing up its body and spraying blood from the corners of its eyes, sometimes for a considerable distance. Of the 14 species of the genus *Phrynosoma*, which is mainly found in the desert areas of North America and Mexico, only two or three can squirt blood from their eyes. They achieve this by increasing the blood pressure in their heads. The specimen pictured here was caught at the Chaparral Wildlife Management area in Artesia Wells, Texas in 1997.

jaws. This is equivalent to a pressure of 19.6 tons per square inch at the tips of the teeth. The bites of larger sharks, such as the great white shark (*Carcharodon carcharias*), may be stronger, but have never been measured.

BEST SENSE OF SMELL
Sharks have a better sense of smell and more highly developed scent organs than any other fish. Well known for their ability to smell blood from enormous distances, sharks can detect one part of mammalian blood in 100 million parts of water and are even believed to be able to pick up the scent of other fishes' fear.

MOST VENOMOUS FISH
The stonefish *Synanceia horrida*, found in the tropical waters of the Indo-Pacific, has the largest venom glands of any known fish. Direct contact with the spines of its fins, which contain a strong neurotoxic poison, can be fatal for humans.

MOST DANGEROUS SEA URCHIN
Toxin from the spines and pedicellaria (the small pincer-like organs) of the flower sea urchin (*Toxopneustes pileolus*) causes severe pain, respiratory problems and even paralysis in human beings.

MOST DANGEROUS HYDROID
The Pacific Portuguese man-of-war (*Physalia utriculus*) and the Atlantic Portuguese man-of-war (*P. physalus*) both carry a virulent poison and are the only hydrozoans known to endanger human life. Even when they are dead, the creatures can sting almost as effectively as when they were alive.

MOST VENOMOUS JELLYFISH
The cardiotoxic venom of the beautiful but deadly Australian sea wasp or box jellyfish (*Chironex fleckeri*) has caused the deaths of at least 70 people off the coast of Australia alone in the past century. If medical aid is unavailable, some victims die within four minutes. One effective defense is women's hosiery: Queensland lifesavers once wore oversized versions during surfing tournaments.

MOST VENOMOUS GASTROPOD
Cone shells of the genus *Conus* can all deliver a fast-acting neurotoxic venom. Several of these species are poisonous enough to kill human beings, but the geographer cone (*Conus geographus*) of the Indo-Pacific is considered to be one of the most dangerous.

MOST VENOMOUS MOLLUSK
Hapalochlaena maculosa and *H. lunulata*, the two closely-related species of blue-ringed octopus found around the coast of Australia and in parts of Southeast Asia, both carry a neurotoxic venom so potent that their relatively painless bite can kill human beings in a matter of minutes. It has been estimated that a single specimen carries enough venom to cause the paralysis or even death of 10 adult people. The mollusks, which have a radial spread of just 4–8 inches, are not aggressive and generally only bite when they are taken out of the water and provoked.

MOST DANGEROUS PINNIPED
The carnivorous leopard seal (*Hydrurga leptonyx*) is the only species that has a reputation for apparently unprovoked attacks on human beings: at least one diver has been attacked and several people have been chased across the ice for a distance of up to 325 feet. However, experts believe that most leopard seal attacks are caused by the animals mistaking humans for emperor penguins or are due to provocation.

MOST DANGEROUS CROCODILIAN
The saltwater crocodile (*Crocodylus porosus*) kills an estimated 2,000 people every year, although the majority of these deaths go unrecorded. The largest reputed death toll in a crocodile attack occurred during World War II, on the night of February 19–20, 1945. Allied troops invaded Ramree Island off the coast of Burma, trapping between 800 and 1,000 Japanese infantrymen in a coastal mangrove swamp. By the following morning only 20 men were still alive: the majority of the infantrymen are believed to have been eaten alive by crocodiles.

MOST FEROCIOUS FISH
Razor-toothed piranhas of the genera *Serrasalmus* and *Pygocentrus* will attack any creature that is injured or makes a commotion in the water, regardless of its size. In 1981, more than 300 people were said to have been eaten when an overloaded passenger-cargo boat capsized and sank while docking at Obidos, Brazil.

endangered and new species

MOST INFLUENTIAL RARE ANIMAL
Since becoming the symbol for the World Wildlife Fund in 1961, the giant panda (*Ailuropoda melanoleuca*) has attracted huge international support for the preservation of endangered species. There are around 700 giant pandas left in the world.

BIGGEST ELEPHANT RELOCATION PROJECT
In 1993, Care for the Wild International transported more than 500 elephants in family groups from Gonerauzou National Park, Zimbabwe to the Save Valley Conservancy 155 miles away.

MOST SUCCESSFUL RETURN TO THE WILD OF CAPTIVE-BRED ANIMALS
The sand gazelle (genus *Gazella*) was returned to the Empty Quarter on the borders of Saudi Arabia and Oman after an absence of 40 years. It was thought extinct in the late 1950s, but a few survivors, plus specimens from private collections, were involved in a 10-year breeding program run by London [England] Zoo and the Saudi National Commission for Wildlife Conservation and Development. There are now almost 600 sand gazelles in the Empty Quarter.

RAREST LARGE LAND MAMMAL
The Javan rhinoceros (*Rhinoceros sondaicus*) is known only from a maximum of 70 specimens on Java in Indonesia, and in Vietnam.

SNOW LEOPARDS
On August 30, 1997, two 8-day-old snow leopard cubs were presented to the press at Lille Zoo in France. Snow leopards (of the genus *Panthera*) are an endangered species: only 5,000 specimens are believed to survive in the wild, more than half of them in Mongolia and the rest in neighboring areas of Russia, China, Pakistan, India, Nepal, Afghanistan and Kazakhstan. There are a further 150 in zoos.

RAREST MARINE MAMMAL
The baiji or Yangtze River dolphin (*Lipotes vexillifer*) has an estimated population of 150, and the number is still falling.

RAREST WILD CAT
There are currently less than 100 specimens of the Iriomote cat (*Felis iriomotensis*), which is confined to Iriomote in the Ryukyu island chain, Japan.

MOST ENDANGERED BIRDS
Spix's macaw (*Cyanopsitta spixii*) is now known from one wild and about 30 captive specimens.

The Hawaiian songbird Kauai o-o (*Moho braccatus*) is known from just two wild pairs.

RAREST BIRDS OF PREY
There are approximately 70 captive Californian condors (*Gymnogyps californianus*) and about five wild specimens.

A single specimen of the Madagascan red owl (*Tyto soumagnei*) was recorded in 1994, the first since 1934.

RAREST INSECT
Still sought by entomologists, the giant earwig of Saint Helena (*Labidura herculeana*) was last recorded in 1965.

MOST ENDANGERED FISH
The 200–500 existing Devil's Hole pupfish (*Cyprindon diabolis*) are restricted to one section of a single pool in Nevada.

RAREST AMPHIBIAN
The last known sighting of the Costa Rican golden toad (*Bufo periglenes*) was in 1990, when 11 specimens were found.

LONELIEST CREATURES
Darwin, a 70-year-old Seychelles giant tortoise, is pictured with 4-year-old Darren Short at Blackpool Zoo in England. The species was believed to be extinct until the identification of Darwin. The world's loneliest creature is Lonesome George, an aged male Abingdon Island giant tortoise (*Geochelone elephantopus abingdoni*) who is the last known specimen of his species. Although it is possible that other specimens exist, there is little hope of finding another, so the subspecies is effectively extinct.

RAREST SNAKES
The burrowing boa (*Bolyeria multicarinata*) may already be extinct, and the keel-scaled boa (*Casarea dussumieri*) is currently being maintained in Jersey Zoo, UK. Both come from the tiny Round Island, Mauritius.

GREATEST CONCENTRATION OF NEW ANIMALS
Twelve large new species of land mammal have been discovered or rediscovered in Vietnam, Laos and Cambodia in the 1990s, including the Vietnamese warty pig (*Sus bucculentis*).

MOST "NEW" SPECIES FOUND IN ONE COUNTRY IN A YEAR
In 1997, biologists discovered more than 16,000 minute species in caves in Spain. These included numerous new species of crustacean belonging to a new class of animal.

"NEWEST" ECOSYSTEM
The Movile Cave mini-ecosystem in Romania is completely sealed off from sunlight. It was discovered in the 1980s and houses more than 30 previously unknown invertebrate species.

NEWEST ANIMAL PHYLUM
A new species of tiny multicellular invertebrate called *Symbion pandora* (phylum Cycliophora), which lives on the lips of North Sea lobsters, was discovered in 1995.

FUR TRADE
The fur industry has declined dramatically over the last 10–15 years as people have come to realize the immense suffering endured by the animals. However, the $648-million-a-year trade continues to claim the lives of about 3.5 million animals annually, 2.5 million of which are raised on fur farms. In the past, the fur trade contributed to the extinction of animal species, although fur farms, which are estimated to number 500 in the United States alone, have now eased the threat of extinction. The majority of clothing designers today do not use fur in their collections, and many of the world's top models, including Kate Moss, Tyra Banks, Cindy Crawford, Christy Turlington, Elle MacPherson and Claudia Schiffer, have been designated "models of compassion" by Peta, the world's largest animal rights movement. The latter has done much to convince the public that wearing fur is cruel through its powerful advertisement campaigns and publicity stunts. In London, England, there remain just 14 of the 85 fur shops that existed in 1985.

MOST SENSATIONAL COMEBACK
The colonial marine invertebrate *Cephalodiscus graptolitoides*, formally described in 1993, is believed by some zoologists to be a living species of graptolite, hitherto known only from fossils and believed to have been extinct for 300 million years.

BIGGEST "NEW" LAND MAMMAL
The Vu Quang ox (*Pseudoryx nghetinhensis*) of Vietnam is the largest species of land mammal discovered since 1936.

MOST ELUSIVE "NEW" MAMMAL
The holy goat or kting voar (*Pseudonovibos spiralis*) of Vietnam, which was scientifically named in 1994, is only known from its distinctive horns.

LARGEST "NEW" MARSUPIAL
The bondegezou or mbaiso tree kangaroo (*Dendrolagus mbaiso*), found in Irian Jaya, Indonesia in 1994, is 4 feet long.

"NEWEST" WHALE
Bahamonde's beaked whale (*Mesoplodan bahamondi*) was described in 1996 from a skull washed up on Robinson Crusoe Island, Chile.

MOST ELUSIVE "NEW" BIRD
The Nechisar nightjar (*Caprimulgus solala*) was named a new species in 1995 but is only known from a wing found on a road in Nechisar Plain National Park, Ethiopia.

MOST RECENTLY DISCOVERED "LIVING FOSSIL"
A Gulf snapping turtle that was discovered in Queensland, Australia in 1996 resembles Australian freshwater tortoises that became extinct 5,000–20,000 years ago.

"NEWEST" LIZARD
Codling's lizard was discovered in the Kalahari Desert, Botswana by Professor Charlemagne B'Nkobo of Durban University, South Africa, in 1996. Characterized by extremely blue eyes and a rippled brown skin, the species was named after Neil Codling, the keyboard player from British pop group Suede, of which Professor B'Nkobo is a fan.

"NEWEST" BIRD
The pink-legged graveteiro (*Acrobatornis fonsecai*), an ovenbird-related species from Brazil, is the most recently discovered bird. It was first sighted by a scientist in 1994.

MOST VOCALLY DISTINCTIVE "NEW" SPECIES
The electric frog (*Litoria electrica*), which was discovered in Queensland, Australia in 1990, has an extraordinary mating call that resembles the sound produced by a high-voltage, long-duration electric arc.

BLUE-EYED LEMURS
Six-month-old blue-eyed lemur Dern and her mother Bacall are seen on their arrival at Los Angeles Zoo in November 1997. They were accompanied by Dern's father, Cagney. The zoo is the fourth in the United States to display the Madagascan species (family Lemuridae), which is endangered.

pets

MOST GLAMOROUS PET WEDDING
In September 1996, two rare "diamond-eyed" cats, Phet and Ploy, were married at a lavish ceremony at Phoebus House, Thailand's biggest discotheque. It cost their owner, Wichan Jaratarcha, $16,241 plus a dowry of $23,202. The groom, Phet, arrived in a Rolls Royce. Ploy arrived by helicopter. Bride and groom wore matching pink satin outfits.

MOST VALUABLE SHOWBIZ ANIMAL
The original *Lassie* star, Pal, was the first of nine male dogs to play the canine heroine. His great-great-great-great-great grandson "Lassie IX," also known as Howard, is the most valuable animal in showbusiness history. He travels in his own airplane.

MOST FAMOUS ADVERTISING CAT
Morris was rescued from an animal shelter in Chicago by an animal trainer in 1968 and was chosen to promote Nine Lives cat food. He went on to appear in 40 advertisements over the next decade.

MOST "PATSYS" WON
Francis the mule was the first animal to be awarded first place at the PATSY awards, which were held annually from 1951 to 1987 to honor the Picture/Performing Animal Top Stars of the Year and promote the health and safety of showbiz animals. Francis, the star of *Francis the Talking Mule* (1949), received his award from actor James Stewart. He went on to win a further six PATSYs. The original film was so successful that five sequels were made in as many years.

MOST SUCCESSFUL SHOWBIZ PIG
Luise of Hanover, Germany rose to fame when she became the world's first drug-sniffing pig at the age of three weeks in 1984. She turned to acting in 1987 and starred in her first movie, *Blutrausch* (*Blood Frenzy*), in which she played a porcine detective. Luise subsequently made almost 70 television appearances and was celebrity guest at the Hanover Opera, in a non-singing role.

MOST SUCCESSFUL CANINE SUPERMODELS

English bulldog Rosie Lee starred in shoe designer Patrick Cox's 1996 spring campaign, posed for fashion photographer Bruce Weber for a Pepe Jeans ad and appeared in an IBM commercial. Rosie is 1 ft. 6 in. tall and weighs 48 pounds. She lives in New York City with her owner Nikki Perry, who runs Tea and Sympathy, a restaurant popular with human supermodels such as Naomi Campbell and Kate Moss.

Magic Star Francky, known as Francky, is a French fashion poodle who doesn't get out of his basket for less than $165 a day. At seven years old, Francky's vital statistics — 24½ inches tall and 53 pounds — have made him the favorite of photographers such as Patrick Demarchelier. He has starred in catwalk shows for Jean-Paul Gaultier alongside supermodel Karen Mulder and appeared in Robert Altman's *Ready To Wear* (1994).

HIGHEST-EARNING LITERARY DOG
In 1991, springer spaniel Mildred Kerr, Millie for short, brought in a salary more than four times bigger than that of her owner, President George Bush, when her "autobiography" sold 400,000 copies. "Dictated" to First Lady Barbara Bush, *Millie's Book* was described as "an under-the-table look at life in the Bush family." It made a total of $900,000.

HIGHEST-EARNING ANIMAL ARTIST
Ruby the elephant has been painting for eight years, since her keepers at Phoenix Zoo, Arizona saw her making patterns in the dirt with a stick clutched in her trunk and provided her with paints, brushes and an easel. Ruby's canvasses now sell for up to $3,500. The 23-year-old has her own office, and assistants who change her brushes and hold her palette while she mixes colors.

MOST EXPENSIVE CATS
Bullseye and Cucamonga, who are Californian spangled cats, were on sale in the Neiman-Marcus department store's 1986 Christmas catalog for $1,400 each. In 1987, one of them sold for $24,000, to a movie star who preferred to remain anonymous. Californian spangled cats were bred by Hollywood scriptwriter Paul Casey, who crossed various types to develop a new breed of domestic cat that resembles spotted wildcats. There are currently fewer than 200 specimens in the world.

BEST-TRAVELED CAT
Hamlet the cat escaped from his cage during a flight from Toronto, Canada and traveled more than 600,000 miles in the plane's cargo hold in just over seven weeks. He was caught in February 1984.

MOST PETTED DOG
Josh the Wonder Dog was petted by 478,802 people between 1989 and 1997. Josh, who belonged to author Richard Stack of Glen Burnie, Maryland, died on July 23, 1997.

MOST JET-SETTING DOGS
Pumpkin Matthews, a tiny champagne-colored toy poodle,

ANIMAL AEROBICS
Catflexing was invented by Stephanie Jackson, who began to include her cat Bad (pictured left with Jackson) in workout sessions when the latter started demanding her attention while she was pumping iron. Jackson picked up the cat and continued exercising with Bad's additional 8-pound weight, incorporating her into bicep curls and behind-the-neck curls. She soon adapted other exercises to include Bad, such as the Catbell Press, where she lies down and lifts the cat above her chest, the Upright Cat Row, where she lifts the cat up to her chest, Cat Crunches, Cat Twists and the Dead Cat Lift.
Cats are not the only animals involved in regular workouts. In 1996, the Total Dog Inc. fitness center opened on Santa Monica Boulevard in Los Angeles. There, canine fitness freaks regularly work out on the treadmill, swim in the pool and complete the outdoor agility course. The center also boasts therapists for massage and personal trainers to develop workout and weight-reduction programs.

used to commute by Concorde between her homes in New York City and St. Tropez, France in the 1980s. By the time she was 10 years old, she had visited Paris a total of 50 times. Her successor, Precious Pi, now travels as frequently as Pumpkin.

RICHEST DOG
The biggest legacy ever left to a dog was $15 million, bequeathed by Ella Wendel of New York City to her standard poodle Toby in 1931. Elsa was part of an eccentric family whose dogs were served prime lamb chops by personal butlers and slept in their own bedrooms in hand-carved miniature four-poster beds with silk sheets.

RICHEST CAT
Blackie, the last in a household of 15 cats, was left $15 million in the will of his millionaire owner, Ben Rea.

MOST PEOPLE AT A PET FUNERAL
In 1920, the funeral of Jimmy the canary, from New Jersey, was attended by 10,000 mourners. Jimmy's owner, cobbler Edidio Rusomanno, had his body placed in a white casket. The funeral cortege was followed by two coaches and a 15-piece band.

FATTEST CATS
Kato the cat from Sogndal, Norway, pictured above, is the fattest living cat in the world. In February 1998, he weighed in at 36 pounds and had a neck measurement of 14 inches. The fattest ever cat was Himmy, a tabby owned by Thomas Vyse of Cairns, Queensland, Australia. Himmy weighed 46 lb. 15 1/4 oz. and had a 33-inch waist when he died at the age of 10 years 4 months on March 12, 1986. He was so huge that he had to be transported in a wheelbarrow.

MOST TRICKS PERFORMED BY A DOG
Chanda-Leah, a champagne-colored toy poodle from Hamilton, Ontario, Canada, can perform a repertoire of more than 300 tricks. Chanda-Leah's owner, Sharon Robinson, has taught the four-year-old to play the piano, count and spell. The dog has appeared on numerous television shows, including *Live! With Regis and Kathy Lee* and *The Maury Povich Show*, and now has her own publicist.

UGLIEST DOG
Chi Chi, a rare African sand dog, has won the World Championship Ugly Dog Contest in Petaluma, California a total of five times, and took first place in the contest's "Ring of Champions," which pits the winners from the previous 25 years against one another. Chi Chi was described by the *National Enquirer* as a "space alien" and by his owner Doris Beezley as a "bow-legged, pig-like dog." He has made several television appearances and is the star of a comic strip called "The Ugliest Dog".

BIGGEST CHICKEN
The heaviest breed of chicken in the world is the White Sully, a hybrid of large Rhode Island Reds and other varieties. The largest on record, a rooster named Weirdo, reportedly weighed 22 pounds in January 1973. Weirdo's prodigious size was the result of cross-breeding and was accompanied by a vicious streak: he once ripped through a wire fence to maul another giant rooster, and on another occasion maimed a dog and killed two cats.

trees and plants

FASTEST-GROWING TREE
An *Albizzia falcata* planted in Sabah, Malaysia in 1974 was found to have grown 35 ft. 3 in. in 13 months – about 1 1/10 inches a day.

FASTEST-GROWING PLANT
Some species of bamboo grow at a rate of 3 feet per day, or 0.00002 mph.

FASTEST-GROWING AQUATIC WEED
The mat-forming water weed *Salvinia auriculata* was detected when Lake Kariba on the Zimbabwe–Zambia border was filled in 1959. In 13 months, the weed had choked a 200-square-mile area; by 1963, it had overtaken a 387-square-mile area.

LONGEST SEAWEED
Macrocystis pyrifera, the Pacific giant kelp, does not exceed 200 feet in length but can grow 18 inches in a day.

DEEPEST-LIVING PLANT
In 1984, algae was found at a depth of 884 feet off San Salvadore Island in the Bahamas, where 99.9995% of sunlight was filtered out.

TALLEST ORCHID
Galeola foliata, a saprophyte of the vanilla family, is known to have grown to a height of 49 feet in the rainforests of Queensland, Australia.

BIRD OF PARADISE
The bird of paradise flower (*Strelitzia reginae*), belonging to the South African genus *Strelitzia*, has a type of inflorescence known as a cincinnus. The flower is grown for its exotic colorings.

LARGEST INFLORESCENCE
The erect panicle of *Puya raimondii*, a rare member of the Bromeliaceae family from Bolivia, has a diameter of 8 feet and emerges to a height of 35 feet. Each can bear up to 8,000 white blooms.

LARGEST FUNGUS
A single living clonal growth of the underground fungus *Armillaria ostoyae* covers an area of about 1,500 acres in the forests of Washington state. Its size suggests that it is between 500 and 1,000 years old.

HEAVIEST FUNGUS
One living mass of *Armillaria bulbosa* covering about 37 acres of forest in Michigan weighed more than 110 tons – approximately the same as a blue whale. The entire mass probably started from a single fertilized spore at least 1,500 years ago.

LARGEST TREE FUNGUS
The bracket fungus *Rigidoporus ulmarius*, growing from dead elm wood in the grounds of the International Mycological Institute in Kew, England, measured 5 ft. 7 in. by 4 ft. 10 in. in 1996 and had a circumference of 16 ft. 2 in. In 1992, it was growing at an annual rate of 9 inches a year, but it has since slowed to about 1 1/5 inches a year.

LARGEST WEED
The giant hogweed (*Heracleum mantegazzianum*), originally from the Caucasus, can reach a height of 12 feet and has 3-foot-long leaves.

LARGEST WEED COLONY
A colony of wild box huckleberry (*Gaylussacia brachycera*) covering about 100 acres was found in 1920 near the Juniata River in Pennsylvania. It is estimated to be about 13,000 years old.

CLOVERS WITH THE MOST LEAVES
A 14-leaved white clover (*Trifolium repens*) was found by Randy Farland near Sioux Falls, South Dakota in 1975, and a 14-leaved red clover (*Trifolium pratense*) was reported by Paul Haizlip in Bellevue, Washington in 1987.

PLANT WITH THE GREATEST MASS
A network of quaking aspen trees (*Populus tremuloides*) growing from a single root system in the Wasatch Mountains of Utah covers 106 acres and weighs an estimated 6,600 tons. The clonal system is genetically uniform and acts as a single organism: all the trees in the network change color and shed their leaves in unison.

BIGGEST TREES
"Lindsey Creek Tree," a coast redwood (*Sequoia sempervirens*) with a minimum trunk volume of 90,000 cubic feet and a minimum total mass of 3,630 tons, had the greatest mass of any tree. It blew over in a storm in 1905.

The living tree with the greatest mass is "General Sherman," a giant sequoia (*Sequoiadendron*

OLDEST PLANT
King's holly (*Lomatia tasmanica*) was discovered at New Harbour in the southwestern wilderness of Tasmania, Australia by miner and amateur naturalist Denny King in 1934 and is the oldest known plant in the world. After being carbon dated from a fossil of an identical specimen found nearby at Melaleuca Inlet, it was estimated to be at least 43,000 years old. King's holly is extremely rare (it can only thrive naturally in a small area of the world), lacks genetic diversity (all individual specimens are genetically identical) and is a tripod – although it produces flowers, it has never produced fruit or seed and is therefore sterile, reproducing itself through vegetative means alone. The combination of these factors has resulted in its near extinction: there are currently only about 500 specimens in existence. In addition to these problems, the plant grows in areas that are extremely prone to disease and fire. It was therefore listed as endangered under the Threatened Species Protection Act 1995 and there have been many attempts to increase its chances of survival through fire and disease management planning.

giganteum) in Sequoia National Park, California. It is 274 ft. 11 in. tall with a 102-ft.-8-in. girth.

TALLEST TREES
The tallest tree standing today is the "Mendocino Tree," a coast redwood (*Sequoia sempervirens*) at Montgomery State Reserve in California. In 1996, it was 367 ft. 6 in. in height with a diameter of 10 ft. 4 in. It is estimated to be about 1,000 years old.

A *Eucalyptus regnans* found at Mt. Baw Baw, Victoria, Australia is believed to have been 470 feet tall when it was measured in 1885.

The tallest tree ever measured was an Australian eucalyptus at Watts River, Victoria, Australia. Reported by forester William Ferguson in 1872, the tree was 435 feet tall and had almost certainly measured more than 500 feet in height originally.

BIGGEST TREE CANOPY
The great banyan (*Ficus benghalensis*) in the Indian Botanical Garden, Calcutta has 1,775 prop or supporting roots and a circumference of 1,350 feet. It covers an area of approximately 3 acres and is the biggest known tree canopy.

LARGEST FLOWER
The blooms of the tropical mottled orange-brown and white parasite *Rafflesia arnoldi* are up to 3 feet across with petals ¾ inch thick. Each flower weighs up to 36 pounds. The plant is also known as the "stinking corpse lily" because its blossoms smell like rotten meat, attracting flies that act as pollinators. Local people have often attributed medicinal properties to the plant.

GREATEST TREE GIRTH
In the late 18th century, a European chestnut (*Castanea sativa*), known as the "Tree of the Hundred Horses," on Mt. Etna, Sicily, Italy was 190 feet in circumference. It has since separated into three parts.

REMOTEST TREE
A Norwegian spruce on Campbell Island, Antarctica is believed to be the most remote tree: its nearest companion is more than 120 nautical miles away on the Auckland Islands.

OLDEST TREE
"Eternal God," a 12,000-year-old redwood in Prairie Creek Redwoods State Park in California, is the oldest living tree on record. It is 238 feet tall and 19 ft. 7 in. in diameter.

LARGEST LEAVES
The raffia plant (*Raffia farinifera* or *R. ruffia*) of the Mascarene Islands in the Indian Ocean and the Amazonian bamboo palm (*Raffia taedigera*) of South America and Africa have the largest leaves of any plant. Their leaf blades may be up to 65 ft. 6 in. in length with 13-foot petioles.

LARGEST SEEDS
The giant fan palm *Lodoicea maldivica* (also called *L. callipyge* and *L. sechellarum*), commonly known as the double coconut or coco-de-mer, grows wild exclusively in the Seychelles. The palm produces single-seeded fruit that weigh up to 44 pounds and can take as long as 10 years to develop.

SMALLEST SEEDS
The epiphytic orchid has the smallest seeds of any plant in the world: it takes a total of 992.25 million seeds to make up 1 g (28,129.81 million/oz.).

DEEPEST TREE ROOTS
The greatest depth to which roots are known to have penetrated is 400 feet, by the roots of a wild fig tree at Echo Caves, situated near Ohrigstad, Transvaal, South Africa.

LONGEST PLANT ROOTS
A single winter rye plant (*Secale cereale*) can produce 387 miles of roots in 1⅕ cubic feet of earth.

LARGEST CACTUS
The world's largest cactus is the saguaro (*Cereus giganteus* or *Carnegiea gigantea*), native to Mexico, California and Arizona. The saguaro grows just ⅘ inch during its first 10 years, and does not flower before the age of 50, but it can live for up to 200 years and reach a height of 50 feet. One specimen discovered in the Maricopa Mountains, Arizona in 1988 has branches that rise to a height of 57 ft. 11¾ in.

dangerous and strange plantlife

MOST DAMAGING WEED
The weed that attacks the largest number of crops in the most countries is the purple nutgrass or nutsedge (*Cyperus rotundus*). The land weed is native to India but attacks 52 crops in 92 countries.

MOST THREATENING WATER WEED
The water hyacinth (*Eichhornia crassipes*), a native of South America, was introduced into Africa as an aquatic ornament and escaped into the River Nile in the 1950s. It spread rapidly in the absence of native predators and now seriously interferes with navigation in the Sudd region of Sudan and threatens to block the irrigation canals of the Gezira, the zone between the Blue Nile and the White Nile.

BIGGEST CARNIVOROUS PLANTS
Plants of the genus *Nepenthes* have vines that reach a length of up to 33 feet, making them the largest species of carnivorous plant. They capture some of the biggest prey of any plants, including creatures as large as frogs.

FASTEST-ACTING PLANT TRAP
The genus *Utricularia* has the fastest-acting trap of any plant. The underwater plant acts by sucking its prey into bladders in 1/30 of a second.

SMALLEST POISONOUS UNDERWATER PLANT
The toxins produced by the microscopic red tide algae are said to be among the most poisonous natural substances. The toxins have been known to poison humans, who ingest them when they eat shellfish.

MOST EXPENSIVE CACTUS
An *Arocarpus kotschubeyanus* cactus sold in France in 1832 for \$61 – more than its own weight in gold, and in today's terms the equivalent of \$2,353. Only three specimens were then known in cultivation.

ITCHIEST CACTUS
Opuntia, more commonly known as the prickly pear, has bristles barbed like bee stings. They are used to make the world's itchiest itching powder.

DEADLY FUNGI
The fly agaric (*Amanita muscaria*) is the best known of the *Amanita* genus of gill fungi. It is poisonous but rarely fatal, unlike its relatives the death cap (*Amanita phalloides*), destroying angel (*Amanita virosa*) and fool's mushroom (*Amanita verna*). The fly agaric earned its name in medieval times, when it was used as an insecticide. When crushed and mixed with sugar – which acts as an attractant – it was used as a poison for flies.

OLDEST SURVIVING CACTUS REMAINS
Dried cactus samples that were taken from the burrows of pack rats in Arizona have been dated back to about 24,000 BC by scientists.

MOST SOUTHERLY PLANTS
The most southerly point at which plants grow is 86°48'S, 145° 93'E, on top of Mt. Roland in the La Gorce Mountains of Antarctica. *Carbonea vorticosa* and *Lecidea cancriformis*, both forms of lichen, can be found growing there.

MOST SOUTHERLY FLOWERING PLANTS
Atlantic hair grass (*Deschampsia Antarctica*) and Antarctic pearlwort (*Colobanthus quitensis*) both flower on the Terra Firma Islands in the Southwest Antarctic Peninsula at 68° 42'S, 67° 32'W.

LOWEST TEMPERATURE AT WHICH PHOTOSYNTHESIS OCCURS
Although plants are capable of surviving for extensive periods without performing normal photosynthesis, they have to carry out this function in order to live and reproduce. The lowest temperature at which positive photosynthesis (carbon assimilation) has been recorded is 1°F, by the lichen *Umbilicaria aprina*.

LOWEST TEMPERATURE SURVIVED BY A PLANT
Experiments carried out by Otto Lange and Ludger Kappen as part of Antarctic Terrestrial Research put plants through prolonged periods of extreme temperatures. Several species of lichen managed to regain normal photosynthesis rates, surviving temperatures as low as –320°F. This is the lowest temperature known to have been borne by plants.

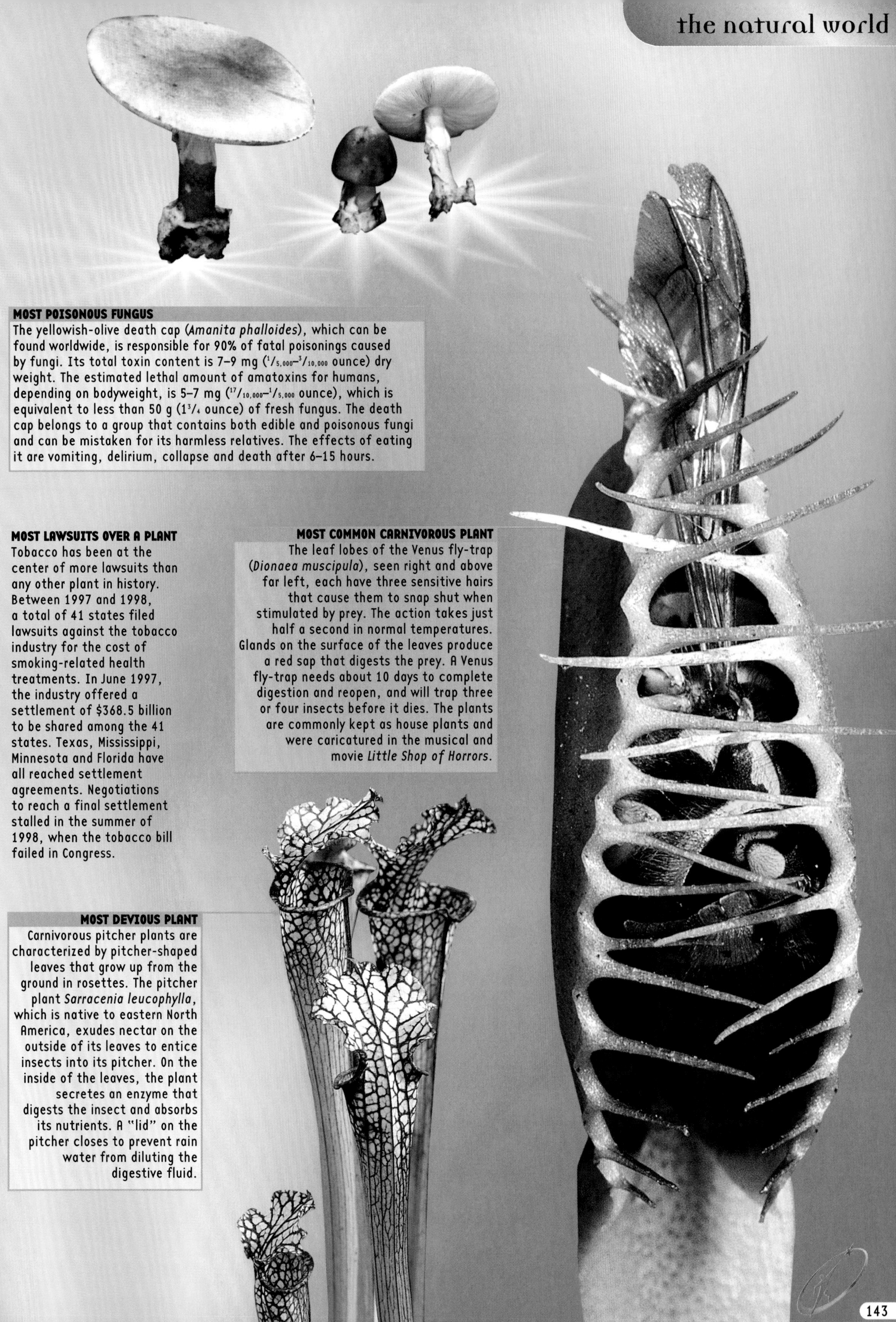

MOST POISONOUS FUNGUS

The yellowish-olive death cap (*Amanita phalloides*), which can be found worldwide, is responsible for 90% of fatal poisonings caused by fungi. Its total toxin content is 7–9 mg (1/5,000–3/10,000 ounce) dry weight. The estimated lethal amount of amatoxins for humans, depending on bodyweight, is 5–7 mg (17/10,000–1/5,000 ounce), which is equivalent to less than 50 g (1 3/4 ounce) of fresh fungus. The death cap belongs to a group that contains both edible and poisonous fungi and can be mistaken for its harmless relatives. The effects of eating it are vomiting, delirium, collapse and death after 6–15 hours.

MOST LAWSUITS OVER A PLANT

Tobacco has been at the center of more lawsuits than any other plant in history. Between 1997 and 1998, a total of 41 states filed lawsuits against the tobacco industry for the cost of smoking-related health treatments. In June 1997, the industry offered a settlement of $368.5 billion to be shared among the 41 states. Texas, Mississippi, Minnesota and Florida have all reached settlement agreements. Negotiations to reach a final settlement stalled in the summer of 1998, when the tobacco bill failed in Congress.

MOST COMMON CARNIVOROUS PLANT

The leaf lobes of the Venus fly-trap (*Dionaea muscipula*), seen right and above far left, each have three sensitive hairs that cause them to snap shut when stimulated by prey. The action takes just half a second in normal temperatures. Glands on the surface of the leaves produce a red sap that digests the prey. A Venus fly-trap needs about 10 days to complete digestion and reopen, and will trap three or four insects before it dies. The plants are commonly kept as house plants and were caricatured in the musical and movie *Little Shop of Horrors*.

MOST DEVIOUS PLANT

Carnivorous pitcher plants are characterized by pitcher-shaped leaves that grow up from the ground in rosettes. The pitcher plant *Sarracenia leucophylla*, which is native to eastern North America, exudes nectar on the outside of its leaves to entice insects into its pitcher. On the inside of the leaves, the plant secretes an enzyme that digests the insect and absorbs its nutrients. A "lid" on the pitcher closes to prevent rain water from diluting the digestive fluid.

genetics

FIRST CLONED PRIMATES
In March 1997, geneticists at the Primate Research Center in Oregon announced that they had cloned two monkeys from embryos. They stripped the DNA from monkey egg cells and replaced it with DNA taken from monkey embryos, creating nine altered egg cells in this way. After they implanted the egg cells into female monkeys, three monkeys became pregnant and two went on to produce live offspring.

FIRST DNA FINGERPRINT
In 1985, Sir Alec Jeffreys and fellow researchers at the University of Leicester, England made the first DNA fingerprint. Looking a little like a barcode, a DNA fingerprint is an image that shows the sequence of DNA unique to each living thing. It can be used to identify people and to establish how they are related. DNA was first used to identify a crime suspect in 1987.

FASTEST DNA FINGERPRINT
The LightCycler was developed by Idaho Technology and can produce a DNA fingerprint in less than 10 minutes. It uses the polymerase chain reaction (PCR), a standard method of amplifying DNA, to produce a fingerprint from a sample of blood, or from other material with a volume of only 10 millionths of a liter (2 millionths of a gallon).

OLDEST DNA USED TO MAKE A FINGERPRINT
In 1993, R. J. Cano and fellow paleontologists announced that they were able to extract and sequence DNA from a fossil that was 125–130 million years old. According to Cano, their partial-DNA fingerprint was from a weevil trapped in amber. The claim remains controversial, however. Other paleontologists have been unable to replicate Cano's experiment, and it has been suggested that the fossil may have been inadvertently contaminated – for instance, with fungal material from the air.

MOST NOTORIOUS CRIMINAL IDENTIFIED USING DNA
In 1992, forensic scientists confirmed that the bones of a man who had drowned in Embú, Brazil 13 years earlier belonged to Nazi war criminal Josef Mengele. They were able to determine this by comparing DNA extracted from the bones with that of Mengele's surviving son Rolf. Dubbed the "Angel of Death," Mengele was responsible for sending around 400,000 people to the gas chambers at the Nazi concentration camp in Auschwitz, Poland during World War II.

BIGGEST PATENTED ANIMAL
The Oncomouse, a strain of mouse that has been genetically engineered to have a high predisposition to developing cancer, was produced in 1984 by geneticists at Harvard University. Four years later, the US Patent Office granted the university a patent for this "invention." As early as 1972, a Supreme Court hearing ruled that a patent should be granted to Ananada Chakrabarty for bacteria that he had genetically engineered to break down crude oil.

BIGGEST CROSS-SPECIES TRANSPLANT
In August 1996, scientists from Imutran of Cambridge, England reported that they had transplanted the hearts of seven pigs into monkeys. The pigs, some of whose DNA had been replaced with DNA taken from human cells, were the first of their kind. The genetic modification that they had undergone enabled them to make a human protein that

HUMAN CLONING
In February 1998, Dr. Richard Seed, a physicist from Chicago, shocked the scientific community when he claimed that within 18 months he would develop the world's first human clone, using similar techniques to those used to produce Dolly the sheep. Seed's views were greeted with consternation by some geneticists, but he vowed to continue his work in Mexico if Congress obstructed it.

would lower the risk of human beings rejecting the pig hearts. The operations were the first successful example of organ xenotransplantation (transplantation from one species to another) where the donor contained human genes.

MOST INSECT-RESISTANT POTATO

Introduced in 1995 by Monsanto, the NewLeaf potato has been genetically engineered to protect itself against the Colorado potato beetle. Scientists genetically modified the NewLeaf potato to enable it to produce a protein that kills this beetle, which is the most damaging insect pest in potato crops.

COUNTRY WITH GREATEST NUMBER OF GENETICALLY-MODIFIED CROPS

More than 25% of cotton crops, 14% of soy crops and 10% of maize crops in the United States have been genetically modified. Genetic engineering by companies such as Monsanto and Calgene can provide these crops with resistance to herbicides and pests, or endow them with new or enhanced commercially useful properties, including extra strength and crispness.

MOST BENEFICIAL GENETICALLY-ENGINEERED DRUG

A synthetic version of insulin, the drug which is used to stabilize the disease diabetes, was first genetically engineered by the biotechnology firm Genetech in 1978. Genetech's synthetic insulin was engineered to be genetically close to the insulin that is produced by the human pancreas. Now called Humulin, it was first sold commercially by pharmaceutical giant Eli Lilly in 1982. Before then, all insulin came from animal glands, so demand might eventually have outstripped supply — it is estimated that more than 100 million people around the world have diabetes.

MOST GENETICALLY SOPHISTICATED TOMATO

On May 18, 1994, the Food and Drug Administration cleared the Flavr Savr tomato for sale to consumers, declaring it as safe as any traditionally-bred variety. It was the first such food to win approval. The Flavr Savr , which was developed by Calgene, takes far longer to soften than a conventional tomato, giving it a much longer shelf life. The flawt Sovr proved costly to produce, due to different regional growing conditions and the need for new picking equipment. By 1997, the advent of Israeli varieties grown in Mexico with a longer shelf life had lessened the need for a genetically engineered tomato.

BIGGEST GENETIC PROJECT

The Human Genome Project is a global effort to map the precise sequence of the 3 billion nucleotides that make up the human genome, the blueprint of human life. Scientists hope that the information will allow researchers to find the genetic causes and cures for many diseases. So far more than $10 billion has been spent on the project, which began in 1990 and should end in 2005. It has been estimated that it would take one researcher 30,000 years to complete.

FIRST AUTOMATIC GENE SEQUENCER

Produced by Applied Biosystems in 1982, the world's first ever gene sequencer enabled a single researcher to sequence about 18,000 genes per day. Before the advent of this ground-breaking machine, researchers had to sequence genes by hand, and they could complete only a few hundred sequences at the most in a working day. Without the automatic gene sequencer, it is unlikely that the Human Genome Project would have been viable.

FIRST MAMMAL CLONED FROM AN ADULT CELL

In January 1997, scientists from the Roslin Institute and PPL Therapeutics in Edinburgh, Scotland announced the birth of Dolly, a Welsh mountain ewe cloned from a single udder cell of an adult ewe. Dolly's DNA was injected into another sheep's egg that had been stripped of its DNA. They had attempted the cloning of more than 220 sheep before they produced one live, healthy lamb. Dolly is seen here with her daughter Bonnie, a Finn Dorset whose creation was completely natural. In February 1998, PPL Therapeutics revealed that they had cloned a calf. The 98-pound Holstein breed, named Mr. Jefferson, was born in Virginia on February 16. Unlike Dolly, who was produced from an adult cell line, Mr. Jefferson was produced by nuclear transfer from a fetal cell. PPL has also genetically engineered sheep to produce alpha-1-antitrypsin (AAT), a human protein used to treat cystic fibrosis, in their milk.

amazing earth

LONGEST RIVERS
The two longest rivers are the Nile and the Amazon – which is the longer is more a matter of definition than of measurement. The Amazon has several mouths, so the point where it ends is uncertain. If the Pará estuary (the most distant mouth) is counted, it is about 4,195 miles long. The Nile was 4,145 miles long before the loss of a few sections of meanders due to the formation of Lake Nasser behind the Aswan High Dam.

GREATEST RIVER FLOW
The greatest flow of any river is that of the Amazon, which discharges an average of 7.1 million cusec into the Atlantic Ocean. The flow increases to more than 12 million cusec when the river is in full flood.

HIGHEST WATERFALL
The Salto Angel in Venezuela has a total drop of 3,212 feet and a longest single drop of 2,648 feet.

LARGEST SWAMP
The Pantanal in Mato Grosso and Mato Grosso do Sul states in Brazil covers about 42,000 square miles.

LARGEST OCEAN
The Pacific makes up 45.9% of the world's oceans and covers an area of 64,186,300 square miles.

SMALLEST OCEAN
The total surface area of the Arctic Ocean is 5,105,700 square miles, making it the world's smallest ocean.

DEEPEST OCEAN
The Japanese probe *Kaiko* recorded a depth of 35,797 feet when it reached the bottom of the Mariana Trench in the Pacific Ocean in 1995.

THICKEST ICE
In 1975, ice measuring 2$\frac{7}{10}$-mile-thick was found 270 miles from the coast of Wilkes Land, Antarctica.

HIGHEST TSUNAMI
On July 9, 1958, a 100-mph wave washed a record 1,720 feet high along Lituya Bay in Alaska. The wave was caused by a landslip.

FREAK WEATHER
The Pacific Ocean current El Niño is as old as the ocean itself. El Niño is cyclical and flows every few years, but the recent phenomenon is set to have the most devastating economic and environmental effects ever recorded. The seesaw in atmospheric pressure over the Pacific began in July 1997 and by early 1998 was estimated to have cost $33 billion and caused the death of 5,000 people from floods, drought and the spread of disease, as well as malnutrition caused by crop damage. In Indonesia and Malaysia, the land became so dry that manmade fires spread rapidly, resulting in more than 1,000 blazes and causing widespread smog across Southeast Asia. At the same time, El Niño fanned even more extensive fires in the Amazon rainforest.

LONGEST REEF
The Great Barrier Reef off the coast of Australia consists of thousands of separate reefs and is 1,260 miles long.

TALLEST GEYSER
In 1903, the Waimangu geyser in New Zealand erupted every 30–36 hours to a height in excess of 1,500 feet. It has been inactive since 1904.

The tallest active geyser in the world is Steamboat Geyser in Yellowstone National Park, Wyoming. It erupts to a height of 380 feet.

LARGEST "BOILING RIVER"
The alkaline hot springs in Deildartunguhver, north of Reykjavik, Iceland, send out 64 gallons of boiling water a second.

HOTTEST PLACES
Between 1960 and 1966, the annual mean temperature in Dallol, Ethiopia was recorded at 94°F.

Temperatures of over 120°F were recorded in Death Valley, California on 43 consecutive days between July 6 and August 17, 1917.

Temperatures of 100°F or more were recorded in Marble Bar, Western Australia for 160 consecutive days between October 1923 and April 1924. The maximum was 120.5°F.

The temperature reached 90°F or more in Wyndham, in Western Australia, on 333 days during 1946.

COLDEST PLACES
A record low temperature of –128.6°F was registered in Vostok, Antarctica at an altitude of 11,220 feet on July 21, 1983.

The coldest permanently inhabited place is the village of Oymyakon (63°16'N, 143°15'E) at an altitude of 2,300 feet in Siberia, Russia. The temperature there descended to –90°F in 1933 and to an unofficial –98°F more recently.

Polyus Nedostupnosti in Antarctica (78°S, 96°E) has an extrapolated annual mean of –72°F.

The coldest measured mean is –70°F at Plateau Station, Antarctica.

MOST SUNSHINE
The annual average in Yuma, Arizona is 91% of the possible hours of sunshine (4,055 hours out of 4,456).

St. Petersburg, Florida had 768 consecutive sunny days from February 1967 to March 1969.

MOST RAINY DAYS
Mt. Wai-'ale-'ale, Kauai, Hawaii has up to 350 rainy days a year.

LONGEST DROUGHT
The Atacama Desert in northern Chile has almost no rain. Squalls strike small areas several times a century.

MOST TORNADOES IN 24 HOURS
A total of 148 tornadoes swept through the southern and midwestern United States on April 3–4, 1974.

FASTEST TORNADO
A tornado blew at 280 mph in Wichita Falls, Texas on April 2, 1958.

HEAVIEST HAILSTONES
Hailstones weighing up to 2 lb. 3 oz. are reported to have killed 92 people in Gopalganj, Bangladesh on April 14, 1986.

GREATEST VOLCANIC ERUPTIONS
The Taupo eruption in New Zealand c. AD 130 is estimated to have ejected 33 billion tons of pumice at 400 mph. It flattened a 6,200-square-mile area.

The total volume of matter discharged in the eruption of Tambora on Sumbawa, Indonesia from April 5 to April 10, 1815 was 36–43 cubic miles.

LARGEST ACTIVE VOLCANO
Mauna Loa on Hawaii is 75 miles long and 31 miles wide. Of its total volume, 84.2% is below sea level. Lava flows from Mauna Loa cover over 1,980 square miles of Hawaii.

LONGEST GLACIER
Icebergs are ice masses that have broken away from glaciers. The longest glacier, Lambert Glacier in the Antarctic, is at least 440 miles long.

the universe

BIGGEST PLANET
With an equatorial diameter of 88,846 miles and a polar diameter of 83,082 miles, Jupiter is the largest of the nine major planets. It also has the shortest period of rotation of any planet, resulting in a 9-hr.-55-min.-29.69-sec. day.

BIGGEST STRUCTURE
A cocoon-shaped shell of galaxies about 650 million light-years across is the largest structure found in the Universe to date. Its discovery by a team of French astronomers was announced in June 1994.

LARGEST GALAXY
The central galaxy of the Abell 2029 galaxy cluster, which is 1.07 billion light-years away in Virgo, has a major diameter of 5.6 million light-years – 80 times the diameter of the Milky Way. Its light output is equal to two trillion ($2x10^{12}$) Suns.

REMOTEST GALAXIES
In 1996 Esther M. Hu (US) and Richard G. McMahon (UK) detected two star-forming galaxies with red shifts of 4.55 (indicating a distance of 13.1billion light-years).

The most remote radio galaxy, 6C0140 + 326, has a red shift of 4.41. It was discovered in 1995 by a British team.

LARGEST STAR
The M-class supergiant Betelgeuse (*Alpha Orionis*), which is 430 light-years away from Earth, has a diameter of 610 million miles – 700 times greater than the diameter of the Sun.

SMALLEST STARS
Neutron stars, which may have a mass up to three times that of the Sun, are 6–19 miles in diameter.

SMALLEST AND COLDEST PLANET
Pluto has a diameter of 1,442 miles and a mass 0.0022 times that of Earth. Its surface temperature is believed to be similar to that of Neptune's moon Triton, which is –387°F — the lowest surface temperature observed on a natural body in our solar system.

HOTTEST PLANET
Measurements by the *Venera* (USSR) and *Pioneer* (US) probes indicate that Venus' surface temperature is 867°F.

MOST VOLCANIC BODY
The most volcanically active body in our solar system is Io, Jupiter's third largest moon. Its orange color is caused by the hundreds of vents on its surface, which eject sulfur.

FASTEST PLANET
Mercury orbits the Sun at a mean distance of 35,983,036 miles and has an orbital period of 87.9684 days. This gives it the highest average speed in orbit of 107,088 mph.

LONGEST ECLIPSE
The longest possible lunar eclipse is 1 hr. 47 min. This will occur on July 16, 2000.

LONGEST SOLAR ECLIPSE
The longest possible eclipse of the Sun is 7 min. 31 sec. The longest of recent date lasted 7 min. 8 sec, west of the Philippines in 1955. A 7-min.-29-sec. eclipse should occur in the mid-Atlantic Ocean in 2186.

LONGEST "EXTENDED" ECLIPSE
A total eclipse of the Sun was extended to 1 hr. 14 min. for passengers aboard a Concorde flight that took off from Toulouse, France, and stayed in the Moon's shadow over the Atlantic from 10:51 to 12:05 GMT on June 30, 1973.

MOST ECLIPSES IN ONE YEAR
Seven eclipses are possible in one year. This occurred in 1935 (five solar and two lunar eclipses) and 1982 (four solar and three lunar eclipses).

FEWEST ECLIPSES IN ONE YEAR
It is possible for only two eclipses to occur in a year, both solar. This was seen in 1944, 1969 and 1984.

MOST ECLIPSES AT A SINGLE LOCATION
The most recent case of three total solar eclipses at a single location was east of the Aral Sea, Kazakhstan (44°N, 67°E), in 1941, 1945 and 1952.

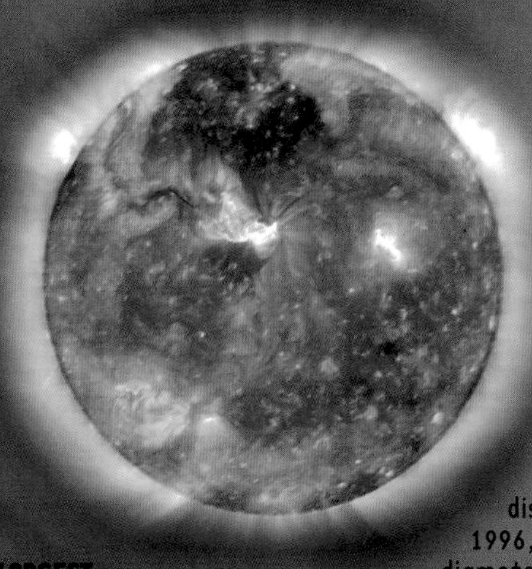

LARGEST ASTEROID
The first asteroid discovered, 1 Ceres, has an average diameter of 585 miles.

SMALLEST ASTEROID
Discovered in 1993, 1993KA² is about 16 feet in diameter.

CLOSEST ASTEROID APPROACH
The asteroid 1994XM, was discovered by James Scotti (US) on December 9, 1994, 14 hours before it came within 62,000 miles of the Earth. It is 33 feet in diameter.

LARGEST COMET
Centaur 2060 Chiron has a diameter of 113 miles.

BIGGEST KUIPER BELT OBJECT
The object 1996TO66, discovered in October 1996, has an estimated diameter of 500 miles.

LARGEST METEORITE
A 9-foot-by-8-foot block was found near Grootfontein, Namibia, in 1920.

LARGEST STONY METEORITE
The largest piece of stony meteorite ever recovered weighs 3,902 pounds. It was part of a 4.4-ton shower over Jilin, China in 1976.

GREATEST METEORITE EXPLOSION
In 1908, an explosion over the Podkamennaya Tunguska River basin in Russia devastated 1,500 square miles of land. It was equal to 10–15 megatons of high explosive.

GREATEST METEOR SHOWER
The Leonid meteors were calculated to have passed over Arizona at a rate of 2,300 per minute for 20 minutes on November 17, 1966.

LARGEST METEOR CRATER
The largest crater definitely formed by a meteorite is Coon Butte or Barringer Crater, Arizona. It is 4,150 feet in diameter and about 575 feet deep.

BRIGHTEST FIREBALL
The brightest known fireball passed over Sumava, Czechoslovakia (now the Czech Republic) in December 1974. For a few moments, it was 10,000 times brighter than a full moon.

LEAST DENSE PLANET
Made up of 70% water, Saturn has the lowest density of any planet. The image above was taken by *Voyager I*, one of the probes that showed that Saturn's "rings" actually consist of thousands of closely spaced ringlets.

BIGGEST SUNSPOT
An infrared image highlights sunspots. In 1947, a sunspot covering a record 7 billion square miles was seen.

BIGGEST CANYON
The largest canyon system is the Valles Marineris on Mars. It is at least 2,800 miles long and 370 miles wide, with a maximum depth of about 4 miles.

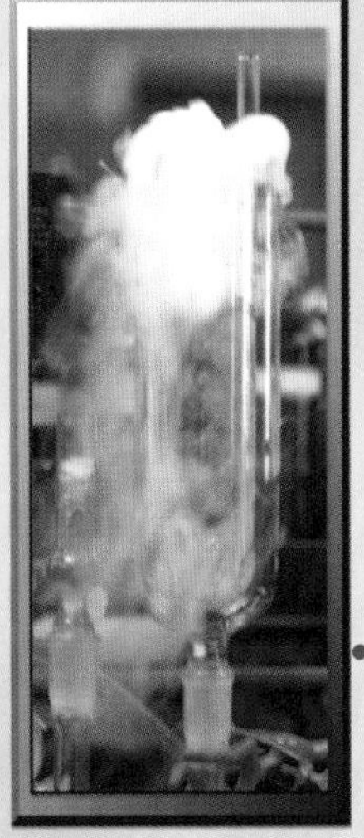

weird science

SMALLEST TEST TUBES
The smallest ever test tubes for containing a chemical reaction were made at the Ecole Polytechnique Fédérale de Lausanne in Switzerland in 1996. Each is 1 micron (1 millionth of a meter) long and has an internal diameter of less than 10 nanometers (10 billionths of a meter). The carbon nanotubes contained silver nitrate, which was heated until it formed chains of tiny silver beads.

STRANGEST SUBSTANCE
Scientifically speaking, water is the world's strangest substance. Where most substances shrink when they are cooled, water expands, and unlike most substances, water is less dense as a solid than as a liquid (ice floats). It needs 10 times as much energy to heat as solid iron and dissolves almost anything.

SALTIEST WATER
The lower layer of the Dead Sea has a salinity of 332 parts per thousand, making it the world's saltiest water. The dry heat of the Middle East has caused much of the sea to evaporate over the centuries, and as it has shrunk, its saline content has increased.

MOST COMMON SUBSTANCE
Hydrogen accounts for over 90% of all known matter in the universe and 70.68% by mass of the solar system.

MOST ABSORBENT SUBSTANCE
"H-span" or Super Slurper (which is 50% starch derivative and 25% each of acrylamide and acrylic acid) can, when treated with iron, retain 1,300 times its own weight in water.

MOST HEAT-RESISTANT SUBSTANCE
NFAAR, or Ultra Hightech Starlite, is able to temporarily resist plasma temperatures (10,000°C or 18,032°F).

SMELLIEST SUBSTANCES
Ethyl mercaptan (C_2H_5SH) and butyl seleno-mercaptan (C_4H_9SeH) are among the most evil of the 17,000 smells classified to date. Each smells like a combination of rotting cabbage, garlic, onions, burned toast and sewer gas.

BITTEREST SUBSTANCES
The world's bitterest substances are based on the denatonium cation and have been produced commercially as benzoate and saccharide. Taste detection levels are as low as one part in 500 million, and a dilution of one part in 100 million will leave a lingering taste in the mouth.

SWEETEST SUBSTANCE
Talin obtained from arils (appendages found on certain seeds) of the katemfe plant (*Thaumatococcus daniellii*), which grows in West Africa, is 6,150 times as sweet as a 1% sucrose solution.

DEADLIEST ARTIFICIAL CHEMICAL
The compound 2, 3, 7, 8-tetrachlorodibenzo-p-dioxin, or TCDD, is 150,000 times more deadly than cyanide.

MOST CARCINOGENIC CHEMICAL
The most carcinogenic substance ever tested is the compound 3-nitrobenzathrone, found in the exhaust fumes of diesel engines. In October 1997, it produced the highest score ever in an Ames test, a standard measure of the cancer-causing potential of toxic chemicals, carried out at Kyoto University, Tokyo, Japan.

MOST CHEMICALLY COMPLEX FOOD
Chocolate contains approximately 300 chemicals, including caffeine, phenylethylamine and N-acylethanolamines, which mimic the effects of some drugs.

MOST HARMFUL RADIATION
Gamma rays, the most harmful form of radiation, can only be stopped by thick lead or concrete. They travel at the speed of light.

LOWEST FRICTION
The lowest coefficient of static and dynamic friction of any solid is 0.03, for Hi-T-Lube with an MOS2 burnished (B) exterior. The 0.03 result was achieved by sliding Hi-T-Lube (B) against Hi-T-Lube (B). This material was developed for NASA in 1965 by General Magnaplate Corp., Linden, New Jersey.

Tufoil, manufactured by Fluoramics Inc. of Mahwah, New Jersey, is the lubricant with the lowest coefficient of friction, at .029.

STRONGEST SUPERACID
A 50% solution of antimony pentafluoride in hydrofluoric acid (fluoro-antimonic acid $HF:SbF_5$) is a record 10^{18} times stronger than concentrated sulfuric acid.

STRONGEST NATURAL FIBER
Silk is the strongest natural fiber. About 10,000 silk worms are needed to make a garment. To prevent the larvae from emerging as moths and breaking the cocoon filament, they are steamed alive.

STRONGEST PLASTIC
Kevlar, created in 1965, is the strongest plastic substance in the world. Fire resistant, flexible and light, it is extremely strong (five times stronger than steel) and becomes even stronger

NATURAL CHEMICALS
Unlike most amphibians, which are relatively defenseless, cane toads (*Bufo marinus*), along with a number of other toads, salamanders and the great crested newt (order Urodela), secrete potent poisons called bufotoxins from their head and skin. These hallucinogenic toxins, which affect the blood pressure, nerves and muscles of the animals' predators, are used by Amazonian Indians to tip their arrows. Several other animals are believed — often without any scientific evidence — to have chemical/medicinal properties: in Africa, rhinos are killed for their horns, which are used in medicines; in Southeast Asia, tigers are slaughtered for their bones for use in Chinese medicines; and bears are killed in Asia for their gallbladders, which are used in medicines and in food in Taiwan. The shooting, poisoning and trapping of these animals has endangered a great number of species, despite being illegal in many of the countries where it takes place.

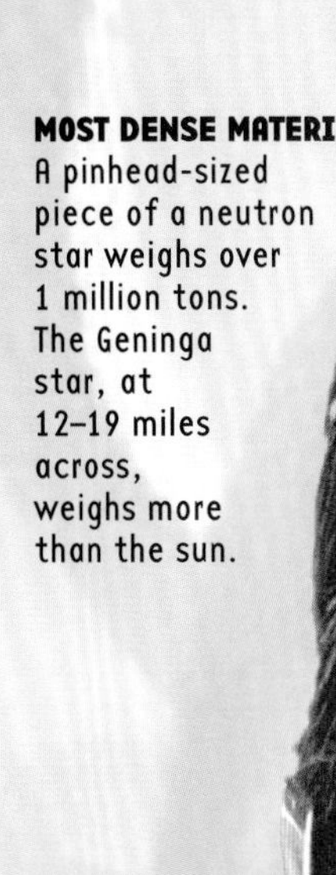

when it is spun into fiber and heat-treated. Kevlar is used in the manufacture of bulletproof vests, spacesuits and race cars.

MOST DUCTILE ELEMENT
One ounce of gold (Au) can be drawn to a length of 43 miles.

MOST REACTIVE ELEMENT
Fluorine, which is used in the production of Teflon (the material used in space vehicles, protective clothing and nonstick cooking utensils), is the most reactive of all the elements — steel wool bursts into flames in fluorine.

SHORTEST-LIVED ELEMENT
Only a few atoms of seaborgium, element 106, have ever been produced, and none of them lasted more than half a minute. They were produced by bombarding californium with oxygen in a cyclotron.

Crocus flowers are the most accurate natural thermometers in the world. The spring blooms can react to temperature differences of as little as 0.9°F by opening and closing as the temperature rises and falls. The seed-producing element of spring crocuses is under the ground to protect it from the cold. Crocuses have been cultivated since the 16th century, and wild crocuses were used by the Romans to scent theaters and public places.

HIGHEST TEMPERATURE
The highest temperature ever produced in a laboratory was 920,000,000°F — 30 times hotter than the center of the sun. It was created using a deuterium–tritium plasma mix at the Tokamak Fusion Test Reactor at the Princeton Plasma Physics Laboratory in New Jersey on May 27, 1994.

LOWEST TEMPERATURE
Absolute zero (0K on the Kelvin scale, or –459.67°F) is the point where all atomic and molecular thermal motion ceases. The lowest temperature ever produced in a laboratory is 280 picoKelvin (280 trillionths of a degree), in a nuclear demagnetization device at the Low Temperature Laboratory of the Helsinki University of Technology, Finland. It was announced in 1993.

HOTTEST FLAME
At a pressure of one atmosphere, carbon subnitride (C_4N_2) can generate a flame calculated to reach 4,988°C (9,010°F).

MOST DENSE MATERIAL
A pinhead-sized piece of a neutron star weighs over 1 million tons. The Geninga star, at 12–19 miles across, weighs more than the sun.

the
material
world

buildings and structures

TALLEST HOTEL
The 73-story Westin Stamford in Raffles City, Singapore is 742 feet in height from the street level of its main entrance. It cost $235 million to build in 1985 and had a $54-million facelift in 1990/91.

The Ryujyong Hotel in Pyongyang, North Korea is reportedly 105 stories high. It has been under construction for 20 years.

LARGEST HOTEL
The MGM Grand Hotel and Casino, which is situated in Las Vegas, Nevada, has four 30-story towers and covers 112 acres. The hotel has 5,005 rooms, a 15,200-seat arena and a 33-acre theme park.

LARGEST IGLOO
With a floor area of 3,888 square yards and the capacity to sleep up to 100 guests per night, the Ice Hotel in Jukkasjavi, Sweden is the world's largest igloo. Rebuilt every December for the past five years, the igloo gets bigger every year. It currently features ice sculptures, a movie theater, saunas, an ice bar and the world's only ice chapel.

TALLEST APARTMENT BUILDING
The John Hancock Center in Chicago, Illinois is 1,127 feet tall. The building has 100 stories, of which floors 44–92 are residential.

LARGEST PALACE
The Imperial Palace in Beijing, China has a total area of 178 acres.

LARGEST RESIDENTIAL PALACE
Istana Nurul Iman in Bandar Seri Begawan, Brunei belongs to the Sultan of Brunei and is the world's largest residence. Completed in 1984 at a reported cost of $400 million, it has 1,788 rooms, 257 bathrooms, and an underground garage housing 153 cars.

LARGEST AIR-SUPPORTED BUILDING
The 770-foot-long, 600-foot-wide Pontiac Silverdome Stadium in Detroit, Michigan has a 10-acre Fiberglas roof that reaches up to a height of 202 feet. The structure is supported by air pressure of five pounds per square foot.

MOST EXPENSIVE STADIUM
The $466-million Stade de France in Saint-Denis, France was built for the 1998 World Cup soccer tournament. The stadium is able to seat 80,000 spectators and has a massive roof that has little visible means of support, though it contains steelwork weighing as much as the Eiffel Tower.

TALLEST MONUMENT
The stainless steel Gateway to the West arch in St. Louis, Missouri spans 630 feet and rises to the same height. Commemorating westward expansion after the Louisiana Purchase of 1803, it was completed in 1965 and cost $29 million.

TALLEST BUILDING
The $63-million CN Tower in Toronto, Ontario was built from 1973 to 1975 and is 1,815 ft. 5 in. tall.

LONGEST FRESHWATER SWIMMING POOL
The Hyatt Regency Cerromar Beach Resort in Puerto Rico has a 1,755-foot-long swimming pool that covers 4½ acres and consists of five connected pools with water slides, a subterranean jacuzzi, tropical landscaping and 14 waterfalls. It takes 15 minutes to float from one end of the pool to the other.

TALLEST CEMETERY
The permanently illuminated Memorial Necrópole Ecumênica in Santos, Brazil is 10 stories high and covers 4⅘ acres. Construction began in March 1983 and the first burial took place in July 1984.

LARGEST CEMETERY
Ohlsdorf Cemetery in Hamburg, Germany covers 990 acres. In use since 1877, it had hosted 984,006 burials and 418,323 cremations by the end of 1997.

LARGEST CREMATORIUM
The Nikolo-Arkhangelskiy Crematorium in Moscow, Russia has seven British-designed twin cremators, the construction of which ended in 1972. It covers 519 acres and has six Halls of Farewell for atheists.

LARGEST CATHEDRAL
St. John the Divine, the cathedral of the Diocese of New York City, has a volume of 16,822,000 cubic feet and a floor area of 121,000 square feet. The building's cornerstone was laid in December 1892, but work on the building was stopped in 1941 and only restarted in earnest in July 1979.

LARGEST MOSQUE
The Shah Faisal Mosque near Islamabad, Pakistan has a total area of 46⁹⁄₁₀ acres. The prayer hall covers 1⅕ acres and together with the courtyard can accommodate 100,000 worshippers, while the adjacent grounds can accommodate a further 200,000 people.

LARGEST SYNAGOGUE
Temple Emanu-El in New York City was completed in September 1929 and has a frontage of 150 feet on Fifth Avenue and 253 feet on 65th Street. The main sanctuary can take up to 2,500 people and the adjoining Beth-El Chapel seats 350. When the temple's other three sanctuaries are in use, a total of 5,500 worshippers can be accommodated.

LARGEST TEMPLE
Angkor Wat ("City Temple") in Cambodia is the largest religious structure ever built, covering an area of 402 acres. The entire temple complex has a total area of 15 by 5 miles and consists of 72 major monuments, the construction of which began c. AD 900.

LARGEST BUDDHIST TEMPLE
The 8th-century Borobudur temple near Jogjakarta, Indonesia covers an area of 403 square feet and is 103 feet in height.

LONGEST BRIDGE
The Second Lake Pontchartrain Causeway, which joins Mandeville and Metairie, Louisiana, is the longest bridge in the world. Completed in 1969, it is 23 mi. 1,538 yd. long.

WIDEST BRIDGE
The widest long-span bridge in the world is the 1,650-foot-long Sydney Harbor Bridge in Sydney, Australia. Officially opened on March 19, 1932, the bridge is 160 feet wide and carries two electric overhead railroad tracks, a total of eight road lanes, and a bicycle track and pedestrian walkway.

LONGEST UNDERSEA TUNNEL
The $17-billion Channel Tunnel, running beneath the English Channel between Folkestone, England and Calais, France, was built between December 1987 and December 1990 and was officially opened by Queen Elizabeth II and President François Mitterrand of France on May 6, 1994. Each of the twin rail tunnels is 31 mi. 53 yd. long and has a diameter of 24 ft. 11 in.

LONGEST ROAD TUNNEL
The two-lane St. Gotthard tunnel, which runs between Göschenen and Airolo, Switzerland, is the longest road tunnel in the world, with a total length of 10 mi. 246 yd. It was opened to traffic on September 5, 1980. Building began in 1969 and cost the equivalent of $418 million in 1998 terms. The lives of 19 workers were lost during the construction of the tunnel.

TALLEST OFFICES
In 1996, the Petronas Towers in Malaysia became the tallest office building when 241-foot-tall pinnacles were placed on top of the 88-story towers, bringing their height to 1,482 ft. 8 in.

future buildings

BIGGEST PURPOSE-BUILT GALLERY

At 450 feet in length and 80 feet in width, the biggest gallery in the Guggenheim Museum Bilbao in Spain has been designed to hold some of the world's most spectacular 20th-century works of art. It presently houses *Snake*, which comprises three 100-foot-long, 13-foot-high plates of steel sculpted by Richard Serra. The $100-million museum was designed by Californian architect Frank Gehry.

MOST "INTELLIGENT" TOWN

With living space for 20,000 people, Celebration, Florida is a futuristic city designed by the Walt Disney Company. All 8,000 of the homes in this $350-million city have a high-speed ISDN link with cable TV, multimedia resources, video on demand and an internet connection. Celebration, under construction since 1996, had 1,000 residents by the summer of 1997.

MOST "INTELLIGENT" HOUSE

Bill Gates' house, which reportedly cost $55 million to build over seven years, uses state-of-the-art information technology to tailor itself to the preferences of its guests. Everyone who enters is given an electronic pin that can be detected by sensors located in each room, enabling the house to adapt the services and entertainments to suit their requirements. These sensors also control the lights and other appliances in the house, turning them off automatically as soon as someone leaves a room. Gates' hi-tech home is situated on the eastern shore of Lake Washington.

SELF-SUFFICIENT HOMES

Perfected by architect Michael Reynolds over the past 25 years, Earthships are self-sustaining structures that produce their own energy, catch their own water, recycle used water and gather their own heat. There are an estimated 1,000 such structures to date, all built from old tires and aluminum cans, which are compressed and filled with earth. They have been built all around the world in a wide variety of climates (the Earthship pictured here is in the desert in New Mexico). The most expensive one to date is a multimillion-dollar luxury Earthship belonging to the actor Dennis Weaver, in Ridgeway, Colorado.

MOST "INTELLIGENT" STRUCTURE

Thousands of optical fibers are embedded between the segments of concrete that make up the recently built Winooski One Hydroelectric Dam in Vermont. Sensors constantly monitor the light that these fibers receive for signs that the concrete structure is shifting. Intelligent structures like this can help engineers spot the early signs that a dam, skyscraper, bridge or other high-performance structure is about to fail.

MOST ENERGY-EFFICIENT HOUSE

The Autonomous House in Southwell, England produces more energy than it consumes. Photovoltaic panels provide electricity, and the 1,450 kWh produced by the house annually is sold back to the UK National Grid.

MOST EARTHQUAKE-PROOF AIRPORT

Built 3 miles offshore on an artificial island in Osaka Bay, Japan, Kansai International Airport was virtually unscathed by the earthquake that hit the nearby city of Kobe in January 1995. The sea acted as a natural defense for the airport, damping out some of the vibrations and enabling the airport to move freely with minimal damage.

BIGGEST BUILDING CONSTRUCTED ON BASE ISOLATORS

The six-story West Japan Building of the Ministry of Posts and Telecommunications, another survivor of the Kobe quake, sits on 120 vibration isolators, which act like shock absorbers. In an earthquake they compress, absorbing some of the energy of the quake and ensuring that as little as possible is transmitted to the building.

MOST EXPENSIVE COMPLETED GALLERY PROJECT

The Getty Center in Los Angeles, California cost $1 billion to build. The million-square-foot

complex was designed by Richard Meier and Partners. Along with countless other materials, 165,000 square feet of exterior glass, 295,000 pieces of Italian travertine, 8.1 million cubic feet of concrete and 4.4 million square feet of steel stud were used.

BIGGEST SELF-SHAPING CONCRETE CONSTRUCTION
The Mega-City-Pyramid TRY-2004, which is still being developed, is a 1-mile-440-yd. ultra-high-rise pyramid intended to relieve overcrowding in Tokyo, Japan. It will accommodate 1 million people but only take up 30,000 square feet. It will use the sun and wind as energy sources, and residents will move around it in circulatory cabins, some of which will be propelled by linear-induction motors.

BIGGEST FUTURE BUILDING
Construction work officially began on the Shanghai World Financial Center in China on August 27, 1997. Due for completion in 2001, this skyscraper will be 1,509 feet tall — higher than both the Sears Tower and Petronas Towers. It will include a glazed viewing area on the 94th floor and a high, open-air walkway known as the "bridge of world cooperation and friendship."

BIGGEST PLANNED FLOATING BUILDING
First designed in the 1980s for an artificial island off the coast of Japan, X-Seed 4000 is a proposed dwelling for 1 million people, based on an open steel construction. The designers of X-Seed 4000, the Taisei Corporation, intend it to be used for research and mountain sports such as skiing, as well as for accommodation. They have suggested magnetic elevators, which would carry 2,000 people to the top floor in 30 minutes.

BIGGEST T-UP BUILDING
The new headquarters of the Fuji Television Network in Tokyo Bay, Japan was designed and constructed by the Taisei Corporation, the designers of X-Seed 4000 and inventors of the T-Up construction process. The latter was developed as a quick and safe way to erect high-rise buildings automatically. After each floor of a T-Up building is built, it is raised so that the next floor can be built below it.

MOST ADVANCED CONCERT HALL
Symphony Hall, Birmingham, England opened in April 1991 and is famed for its acoustics, which can be modified in minutes by opening and closing large doors around its perimeter. The doors cover large chambers that increase the reverberation of the hall when they are revealed.

BIGGEST PUBLIC VENUE INSIDE A MOUNTAIN
Built for the 1994 Olympic Winter Games, Olympic Cavern Hall in Gjøvik, Norway is now used as an exhibition center, concert and sports venue and tourist attraction. Visitors venture 390 feet inside Mt. Hovdetoppen to reach the 200-foot-wide, 300-foot-long venue.

BIGGEST BUILDING PROJECT
Chinese authorities are trying to build a 21st-century financial and business center from scratch on the east bank of Shanghai, and architects and engineers are hard at work on everything from sewers to airports. Highlights include a subway system and the Shanghai World Financial Center (see below left). Pictured below is the Oriental Pearl TV tower.

FIRST UNDERWATER HOTEL
Situated 30 feet underwater in a mangrove lagoon in Key Largo, Florida, Jules' Undersea Lodge was opened as a hotel in 1986. It was formerly an aquatic research laboratory. Diving tuition and underwater natural history courses are the main attractions for guests.

BIGGEST UNDERGROUND HOUSE OF MODERN TIMES
Underhill in Holme, England has an interior area of 3,500 square feet. The home of architect Arthur Quarmby since 1976, it cannot be seen from the surrounding moorland.

MOST ECO-FRIENDLY SKYSCRAPER
The new Commerzbank HQ in Frankfurt, Germany, is a 849-foot-tall skyscraper designed by Sir Norman Foster and Partners. An atrium towers 524 feet through the core of the building, providing it with plenty of natural ventilation. Its spiraling sky gardens are places for occupants to meet and relax. The skyscraper has been designed to receive as much natural daylight as possible and has been positioned to minimize the amount of shadow it casts on nearby buildings.

cars

HIGHEST SPEEDS

The record for the highest speed attained in a rocket-engined car is 631.367 mph over the first 1,056 yards by *The Blue Flame*, a four-wheeled vehicle driven by Gary Gabelich on the Bonneville Salt Flats, Utah on October 23, 1970. He momentarily exceeded 650 mph. The car was powered by a liquid natural gas/ hydrogen peroxide rocket engine that could develop thrust up to 22,000 pounds.

The highest land speed by a woman is 524.016 mph, by Kitty Hambleton in the rocket-powered three-wheeled *SM1 Motivator* over the Alvard Desert, Oregon on December 6, 1976. Her official two-way record was 512.710 mph and it is likely that she touched 600 mph momentarily.

The highest speed reached in a wheel-driven car is 432.692 mph, by Al Teague (US) in *Speed-O-Motive/Spirit of 76* over the final 132 feet of a one-mile run at Bonneville Salt Flats, Utah on August 21, 1991. His speed over the mile was 425.230 mph.

FASTEST SPEED ON LAND

The official one-mile land speed record is 763.035 mph, by Andy Green (GB) in *Thrust SSC* over the Black Rock Desert, Nevada on October 15, 1997. *Thrust SSC* is powered by two Rolls-Royce Spey 205 jet engines, which generate a total of 50,000 pounds of thrust. It is the first car to have exceeded the speed of sound.

The highest ever speed reached by a diesel-engined car is 203.3 mph, by the prototype 3-liter Mercedes C 111/3 in tests conducted on the Nardo Circuit, Italy, from October 5 to October 15, 1978. A few months earlier, in April of the same year, the car attained an average speed of 195.4 mph for 12 hours over a record distance of 2,344 miles 1,232 yd.

The record for the highest speed achieved by an electric vehicle is 183.822 mph over a two-way flying kilometer (1,056 yards), by General Motors' *Impact*, driven by Clive Roberts (GB) at Fort Stockton Test Center in Texas on March 11, 1994.

Robert E. Barber broke the 79-year-old steam car world record when *Steamin' Demon*, built by the Barber-Nichols Engineering Company, attained a speed of 145.607 mph at Bonneville Salt Flats, Utah on August 19, 1985.

The record for the highest speed attained using solar/ battery power is 83.88 mph, by Star Micronics' solar car *Solar Star*. The speed was recorded at Richmond RAAF Base, New South Wales, Australia, on January 5, 1991, and the vehicle was driven by Manfred Hermann.

The record for the highest speed ever attained by a solely solar-powered land vehicle is 48.71 mph, by Molly Brennan in the General Motors' *Sunraycer* at Mesa, Arizona on June 24, 1988.

FASTEST ROAD CARS

The highest speed reached by a standard production car is 217.1 mph, by a Jaguar XJ220 driven by British Formula 1 race driver Martin Brundle at the Nardo test track in Italy, on June 21, 1992.

The highest road-tested acceleration on record is 0–60 mph in 3.07 seconds, by a Ford RS200 Evolution driven by Graham Hathaway at Millbrook Proving Ground, Bedfordshire, England in May 1994.

LOWEST GAS CONSUMPTION

In 1989, Stuart Bladon drove a Citroën AX 14DTR 112 miles 18 yd on one gallon of fuel on the M11 highway in England, in a test run arranged by Lucas Diesel Systems.

A vehicle designed by Team 1200 from Honda in Suzuka City, Japan achieved 9,426 mpg in the Pisaralla Pisimmälle mileage marathon at Nokia, Finland, on September 1, 1996.

BIGGEST PRODUCTION RUN

More than 21.3 million Volkswagen Beetles have been produced since 1937. The model was first developed in Germany in 1936, three years after Adolf Hitler asked Ferdinand Porsche for a blueprint for a "Volkswagen" or "people's car." The result, which was nicknamed the Beetle because it resembles the insect, went on to be produced in Nigeria, Belgium, Mexico and Brazil in addition to its native Germany. In 1994, a prototype for a new Beetle (left) was unveiled at the Detroit Auto Show and was rapturously received, causing the value of the company on the stock market to increase. The new car, which was launched in North America in 1998, is significantly larger than the original and is built out of completely different components. Volkswagen does not see the vehicle as an update of the first Beetle but as a completely new, futuristic car that should appeal both to people who loved the original and to young people who have little knowledge of it. Volkswagen expects that in the first year, between 100,000 and 200,000 will be produced.

MOST POWERFUL CAR
The most powerful current production car in the world is the McLaren F1 6.1, which develops in excess of 627 bhp. The F1 is also the most expensive list-price British standard car, costing £634,500 (over $1 million) including tax. It can accelerate to 60 mph in 3.2 seconds, and is capable of a top speed in excess of 230 mph.

LONGEST FUEL RANGE
The greatest distance travelled by a vehicle on the contents of a standard fuel tank is 1,338 miles 18 yd. by an Audi 100 TDI diesel car (capacity 80.1 liters). Stuart Bladon, with RAC observer Robert Proctor, drove from John o'Groat's to Land's End and returned to Scotland between July 26 and July 28, 1992.

HIGHEST CAR MILEAGE
"Old Faithful," a 1963 Volkswagen Beetle owned by Albert Klein of Pasadena, California, clocked up 1.6 million miles before it was totaled on March 29, 1997.

LARGEST ENGINE
The greatest ever engine capacity of a production car was 13.5 liters, by the US Pierce-Arrow 6–66 Raceabout (1912–18), the US Peerless 6–60 (1912–14) and the Fageol (1918).

LARGEST CAR
The largest car to have been produced for private use was the Bugatti "Royale" type 41, which was assembled in Molsheim, France by the Italian designer Ettore Bugatti. First built in 1927, it has an eight-cylinder engine with a capacity of 12.7 liters and is more than 22 feet long. The hood alone is 7 feet long.

LONGEST CAR
A 100-foot-long, 26-wheeled limousine designed by Jay Ohrberg of Burbank, California includes a swimming pool with a diving board and a king-sized waterbed among its many features. It can be driven as a rigid vehicle or altered to bend in the middle.

WIDEST CARS
The Koenig Competition:2417, built in 1989, and the Koenig Competition Evolution:2418, built in 1990, are both 86²/₅ inches wide.

HEAVIEST CAR
The Soviet-built Zil–41047 limousine is probably the heaviest car in recent production. It has a 12-ft.-9-in. wheel-base and weighs a total of 7,352 pounds. A "stretched" Zil was used by former Soviet president Mikhail Gorbachev until December 1991. It weighed 6.6 tons and had 3-inch-thick armor-plated steel for protection in key areas. The eight-cylinder, seven-liter engine guzzled fuel at the rate of 6 mpg.

SMALLEST CAR
The Peel P50, which was constructed by the Peel Engineering Company in Peel, Isle of Man, UK in 1962, was 53 inches in length, 39 inches in width and 53 inches in height. It weighed 132 pounds.

LIGHTEST CAR
The world's lightest ever car was built and driven by Louis Borsi of London, England and weighs 21 pounds. It has a 2.5-cc engine and can reach a maximum speed of 15 mph.

CHEAPEST CAR
The 1922 Red Bug Buckboard, built by Briggs & Stratton of Milwaukee, Wisconsin, sold for $125–$150, the equivalent of $1,130–$1,870 in 1998 terms. It had a 62-inch wheel-base and weighed 245 pounds. King Midget cars were made in the United States and sold in kit form for self-assembly. Early models of the vehicle could be bought for as little as $100 in 1948, the equivalent of $842 in 1998 terms.

LONGEST PRODUCTION RUN
The Morgan 4/4, built by the Morgan Motor Car Company of Malvern, Worcestershire, England, celebrated its 63rd birthday in December 1998. There is currently a waiting list of between six and eight years for the car.

MOST CARS PRODUCED IN A YEAR
In 1994, a record 49.97 million vehicles were constructed worldwide. Of this total, more than 36 million were cars, making 1994 a record-breaking year for car production.

LARGEST MANUFACTURER
The largest manufacturer of motor vehicles and parts in the world, and the largest manufacturing company, is the General Motors Corporation of Detroit, Michigan. The company has about 610,000 employees worldwide. In 1997, General Motors sold a total of 8.776 million units to its retailers worldwide.

LOWEST PETROL CONSUMPTION
The lowest gas consumption by a road-legal vehicle in the Shell Mileage Marathon is 568 mpg, by the diesel-powered Combidrive "Mouse," at Silverstone race track, Northamptonshire, England in 1996.

concept cars

MOST ECO-FRIENDLY HYBRID SOLD
On October 14, 1997, Toyota launched the Prius, a hybrid-powertrain vehicle combining a 1.5-liter gasoline engine with a generator that halves emissions, cuts smog chemicals by up to 90% and is able to go twice as far as a standard car on 1 liter ($^{13}/_{50}$ gallon) of fuel. During one Japanese test cycle, the Prius achieved a fuel consumption of 77 mpg. The car currently costs approximately $17,000 in Japan and is the most eco-friendly commercially available hybrid. Toyota had initially intended to produce 1,000 units a month but the car was so popular, with a total of 3,500 orders placed in the month after its launch, that they planned to double its production beginning in June 1998. The Prius is set to be launched outside Japan in 1999.

MOST ECO-FRIENDLY CAR
A team of scientists working at Washington University have succeeded in developing the world's most eco-friendly car. The vehicle has a revolutionary zero-emission engine and is powered by energy produced by pressure build-up caused when liquid nitrogen is beaten by ambient air. Nitrogen gas then turns an air motor, propelling the car forwards, before being pumped out as clean air. The prototype is said to be a great deal cleaner than any other zero-emission vehicle but is unlikely ever to be seen on the market because its fuel consumption works out at 0.2 mpg, with an estimated maximum of 3 mpg.

MOST ECO-FRIENDLY GASOLINE-POWERED CAR
The ZLEV (Zero Low Emission Vehicle), which was developed by the Japanese company Honda, has the lowest emission levels of any gasoline car. When tested on smoggy streets, the ZLEV's exhaust was cleaner in terms of hydrocarbon levels than the surrounding air. The car is not yet on the market.

MOST ECO-FRIENDLY CAR POWERED BY NATURAL GAS
The most eco-friendly natural gas vehicle in the world is the Civic GX, which was developed by Honda. Emissions of CO, HC and NO_x from the car have been reduced to almost zero, while CO_2 emissions have been reduced by about 20%. The car is currently available in Japan, and Honda plans to launch it worldwide in the near future.

MOST ECO-FRIENDLY CAR RENTAL COMPANY
Kobe Ecocar, an auto rental business offering only clean-running cars, opened in Kobe, Japan on April 4, 1998. The company, which is supplied by Pasona, Orix, Toyota, Nissan and Kansai Electric Power, initially offered customers a choice of 10 electric cars, but plans to build up a fleet of 60 cars, including electric and gas vehicles, by April 1999. It announced that it will purchase 40 RAV4L-V-EV electric vehicles from Toyota, with Nissan providing natural gas cars. Toyota's Prius model will function as a backup.

LONGEST DISTANCES COVERED ON A SINGLE CHARGE
Solectria Corporation's Geo Metro conversion set a single-charge distance record for a production motor vehicle of 249 miles in May 1997. The production category requires that at least five vehicles must have been sold. The record was set using Ovonic nickel-metal hybrid batteries at the Tour de Sol in Portland, Maine.

The greatest distance that a prototype electric vehicle has traveled on a single charge is 343 miles, by Solectria Corporation's prototype Sunrise at the 1996 Tour de Sol.

MOST "INTELLIGENT" CARS
The Concept 2096 car of the future was unveiled at the 1996 British Motor Show. The car is painted with "smart" colors that change according to the environment, and the glass has the ability to change from transparent to opaque. The car has no steering wheel or engine and is controlled by a computer navigation system into which the user can enter a destination and desired route.

The Hypercar, an ultralight hybrid-electric car three times more efficient and 10 times cleaner than a conventional car, was under development at the Rocky Mountain Institute in 1998. The car uses space-age materials, is rust-free, dent- and scratch-resistant and can absorb five times as much crash energy as steel. Its "smart" windows reflect solar rays, and special paints, a vented roof and solar-powered vent fans monitor heat absorption to the interior.

The HSR (Highly Sophisticated Research) V1, which is computer driven but also has an optional

RENAULT ZO
In March 1998, Renault launched the ZO concept three-seater roadster at the Geneva Auto Show, Switzerland, to celebrate its 100th anniversary. The car is an all-terrain vehicle inspired by motorcycle scramblers. Special 17-inch Michelin tires have been designed to use the inner side for road driving and the outside for off-road surfaces. Its three seats are in a row, with the driver's in the center and slightly further forward than the others. The ZO has no windshield or roof, but instead has an aperture directing the air over the passengers' heads. Powered by a new 2.0-liter engine with direct fuel injection, it has a four-speed automatic "intelligent" gearbox and a chassis with hydraulic pumps to allow the clearance height to change within a range of 6–11 inches. Although the ZO is unlikely to hit the mass market in its present state, the engine may be used in future Renault production cars.

WORLD SOLAR CHALLENGE WINNER

Honda's *Dream Solar* car is the current holder of the World Solar Challenge Race record. In 1996, it completed the 1,870-mile-669-yd. race from Darwin to Adelaide, Australia in a record time of 33.32 hours. The car reached a maximum speed of 87 mph and completed the race with an average speed of 53 mph. The *Dream Solar* is capable of travelling an estimated 56 miles on pure solar power, and a further 62 miles on energy collected from the solar cells and stored in a silver oxide zinc battery.

RINSPEED E-GO ROCKET

The Swiss car manufacturer Rinspeed unveiled its E-Go Rocket at the 1998 Geneva Auto Show in Switzerland. Powered by a V8 aluminum 410-hp engine, it has a top speed of 162 mph and claims 0–60 mph acceleration in 4.8 seconds. The E-Go Rocket is a single-seater, with a stonewashed denim seat cover. The angle of the windshield adjusts to the vehicle's speed.

steering wheel concealed in the dashboard, was launched by Mitsubishi at the Tokyo Car Show in Japan in 1997. The car's ignition is turned on using a personal identity medallion in place of a key.

MOST ADVANCED IN-CAR COMPUTER SYSTEM

In 1998, Microsoft launched the AutoPC system, a specially programmed version of *Windows CE2* that runs on a single DIN hardware unit in place of a conventional car stereo and is the most advanced in-car computer system. The computer is fitted into the dashboard and is capable of operating a CD player and radio, sending and receiving e-mail, and operating navigation and security systems. The Clarion unit, the first to adopt the system, can be used either directly or via remote control. The computer can also be voice-activated, responding to 200 commands.

FASTEST PRODUCTION OF A CAR

In 1997, Ford designed and developed its Puma, a small sports coupe, in 135 days, setting a world record in the automotive industry. The company used computer processing power unrivaled by any institution except the US government to design the Puma to approval stage in less than half the time it usually takes to turn a concept into reality.

MOST EXPENSIVE THREE-WHEELED CAR

The F300 Life-Jet, a vehicle that combines the safety of a car with the thrill of riding a motorcycle, was unveiled by Mercedes-Benz in 1998. The Life-Jet tips into turns rather than away from them — a sensation that is unavailable in a car because of Newton's law. If the Life-Jet makes it to production, it will be the most expensive three-wheeled car in the world.

MOST RECYCLABLE CAR

In 1998, Chrysler unveiled the CCV (Composite Compact Vehicle) ESX2, the most recyclable car in the world. The CCV is made out of plastic similar to that used for soda bottles and can be made in six and a half hours. At the end of its life, it can be melted down and recycled. With injection-molded plastic, the car could be built using only 1,100 parts instead of the standard 4,000 components.

planes and helicopters

The fastest experimental propeller-driven aircraft is the turboprop-powered Republic XF-84H US fighter, which flew in July 1955 and had a top design speed of 670 mph.

The fastest propeller-driven aircraft was the former Soviet Tu-95/142, which has four 11,033-kW (14,795-hp) engines driving eight-blade contra-rotating propellers and a maximum level speed of Mach 0.82 or 575 mph.

The top speed by a piston-engined aircraft is 528.33 mph over a 10-mile course, by the *Rare Bear*, a modified Grumman F8F Bearcat piloted by Lyle Shelton, in Las Vegas, Nevada in August 1989.

The fastest biplane was the Italian Fiat CR42B, which had a 753-kW (1,010-hp) Daimler-Benz DB601A engine. It travelled at 323 mph in 1941.

FASTEST HELICOPTER

Under FAI rules, the record for the highest helicopter speed in the world was set by John Trevor Eggington and his co-pilot Derek Clews in a Westland Lynx demonstrator. The pair averaged 249.09 mph over Glastonbury, England on August 11, 1986. It had taken a total of 10 years to design and develop the helicopter in order to achieve this speed.

FASTEST AIRCRAFT

The USAF Lockheed SR-71, a reconnaissance aircraft, was the world's fastest ever jet. First flown in its definitive form in 1964, the Lockheed was reportedly capable of attaining an altitude of about 100,000 feet. It was 107 ft. 5 in. long, had a wingspan of 55 ft. 7 in., and weighed 84.8 tons at takeoff. Its reported range at Mach 3 was 3,000 miles at 79,000 feet.

FASTEST FLYING BOAT

The Martin XP6M-1 SeaMaster, the four-jet-engined US Navy minelayer flown from 1955 to 1959, had a top speed of 646 mph.

FASTEST TRANSATLANTIC FLIGHTS

Major James Sullivan and Major Noel Widdifield flew a Lockheed SR-71A "Blackbird" eastbound in 1 hr. 54 min. 56.4 sec. in 1974. The average speed for the 3,461.53-mile New York–London stage was 1,806.96 mph. It was reduced by refuelling from a Boeing KC-135 tanker aircraft.

The solo record is 8 hr. 47 min. 32 sec. at an average speed of 265.1 mph, by Capt. John Smith in a Rockwell Commander 685 twin-turboprop in 1978. Smith flew from Gander, Newfoundland, Canada to Gatwick, England.

LONGEST CONTINUOUS FLIGHT

Robert Timm and John Cook flew for a total of 64 days 22 hr. 19 min. 5 sec. in a Cessna 172 "Hacienda" from December 1958 to February 1959. The distance was the equivalent of flying around the world six times.

BIGGEST AIRCRAFT

The jet airliner with the highest capacity is the Boeing 747-400, which entered service with Northwest Airlines in 1989. It has a wingspan of 213 feet and a range of 8,290 miles, and can carry up to 566 passengers.

The aircraft with the highest standard maximum takeoff weight is the 660-ton Antonov An-225 Mriya ("Dream"). One plane lifted a payload of 344,582 pounds to a height of 40,715 feet in March 1989. It covered 1,305 miles in 3 hours 47 min.

The airliner with the greatest volume is the Airbus Super Transporter A300-600ST Beluga, which has a 49,441-cubic-foot main cargo compartment, a maximum takeoff weight

HIGHEST AIRSPEED

Capt. Eldon W. Joersz and Major George T. Morgan Jr. attained a record speed of 2,193.17 mph in a Lockheed SR-71A "Blackbird" near Beale Air Force Base, California, over a 25-km (15-mile 940-yard) course on July 28, 1976. The Lockheed SR-71A achieved an unofficial average speed of 2,242 mph during a flight from St. Louis to Cincinnati in 1990.

of 165 tons, a 147-ft.-1-in. wingspan and an overall length of 184 ft. 3 in. The usable length of its cargo compartment is 123 ft. 8 in.

The production airliner with the greatest volume is the Ukrainian Antonov An-124 Ruslan, the cargo hold of which has a usable volume of 35,800 cubic feet and a maximum takeoff weight of 445 tons. The heavy-lift version of the An-124, the An-225 Mriya, has a stretched fuselage providing as much as 42,000 cubic feet of usable volume. Its cargo compartment includes an unobstructed 141-foot hold length and has a maximum width and height of 21 feet and 14 ft. 5 in. respectively.

LARGEST WINGSPANS

The $40-million Hughes H4 Hercules flying-boat, also known as the *Spruce Goose*, had the largest ever wingspan of any aircraft, at 319 ft. 11 in. The 213-ton, 218-ft.-8-in., eight-engined aircraft was raised 70 feet into the air in a 1,000-yard test run piloted by aviation tycoon Howard Hughes off Long Beach Harbor, California in 1947, but never flew again.

The record for the largest wingspan of a current aircraft is 240 ft. 5¾ in., for the Ukrainian Antonov An-124.

SMALLEST AIRCRAFT

The smallest monoplane ever flown is the *Baby Bird*, which was designed and built by Donald Stits. First flown in 1984, the plane is 11 feet in length and has a wingspan of 6 ft. 3 in. *Baby Bird* weighs just 252 pounds when empty and has a maximum speed of 110 mph.

The smallest biplane ever flown was *Bumble Bee Two*, which was designed and constructed by Robert Starr of Tempe, Arizona. Capable of carrying just one person, *Bumble Bee Two* was 8 ft. 10 in. in overall length and had a wingspan of 5 ft. 6 in. It weighed 396 pounds when empty. The highest speed it ever attained was 190 mph.

FASTEST AIRLINERS

The Tupolev Tu-144 (above left), first flown in 1968, was reported to have achieved Mach 2.4 (1,600 mph) but had a normal cruising speed of Mach 2.2. In May 1970, it became the first commercial transport to exceed Mach 2. The BAC/Aérospatiale Concorde (above) was first flown in 1969. It cruises at up to Mach 2.2 (1,450 mph) and is the fastest supersonic airliner.

In 1988 it crashed and was totally destroyed after having attained an altitude of 400 feet.

The world's smallest ever twin-engined aircraft is believed to be the Colombian MGI5 Cricri, which was first flown in 1973. The Cricri has a wingspan of 16 feet and an overall length of 12 ft. 10 in. It is powered by two 11.25-kW (15-hp) JPX PUL engines.

LARGEST HELICOPTER

The largest helicopter in production is the Russian Mil Mi-26, which is 131 feet in length and has a maximum takeoff weight of 61.6 tons. The eight-bladed main rotor is 105 feet in diameter and powered by two 11,240 static HP turbo shaft engines.

LARGEST ROTORCRAFT

The 343-foot-long, 111-foot-high, 149-foot-wide Piasecki Heli-Stat used four Sikorsky S-58 airframes attached to a surplus Goodyear ZPG-2 airship and was powered by four 1,525 hp piston engines. It first flew in October 1985 but was destroyed in a crash in July 1986.

SMALLEST HELICOPTER

The single-seat Seremet WS-8 ultra-light helicopter was built in Denmark in 1976 and had a 35-hp engine and an empty weight of 117 pounds. The rotor diameter was 14 ft. 9 in.

FUTURE AIRCRAFT

The A3XX jumbo airbus, now in its prototype stage, will be the largest airliner in the world. Its manufacturer, Airbus Industrie, intends it to be in service by 2003, and is being assisted in its efforts by representatives from 19 airlines. The four-engined double-decker aircraft will be able to carry a record 1,000 passengers and will be the first airliner with four aisles (two on the main deck and two on the top deck). It will help to cope with the increase in air travel, which is expected to triple over the next 20 years. The cost of developing the airbus is expected to reach $8 billion.

trains and boats

BIGGEST AIRCRAFT CARRIERS
The Nimitz class US Navy aircraft carriers USS *Nimitz*, *Dwight D. Eisenhower*, *Carl Vinson*, *Theodore Roosevelt*, *Abraham Lincoln*, *George Washington* and *John C. Stennis* (the last three of which displace 114,240 tons) have the biggest full-load displacement of any warships. They are 1,092 feet long with 4½ acres of flight deck. Driven by four nuclear-powered 260,000-shp geared steam turbines, they can reach speeds of more than 30 knots. Two more ships of this class, *Harry S. Truman* and *Ronald Reagan*, are under construction. The Nimitz has four C-13 Mod 1 catapults that propel aircraft off the flight deck. The "cats" can accelerate even the heaviest carrier-based aircraft to speeds of 170 mph from a standing start.

FASTEST RAIL SYSTEM
The highest speed recorded on any national rail system is 320.2 mph, by the SNCF TGV Atlantique between Courtalain and Tours, France on May 18, 1990. TGV Atlantique and Nord services now run at up to 186 mph, as does the Eurostar between Paris and Calais, France. Cruising 18 mph faster than the old TGV, Atlantique has eight rather than 12 motors, but can haul 10 trailer cars instead of eight, and can climb a 5% gradient at 12,000 hp without losing speed.

FASTEST TRAINS
The fastest point-to-point schedule in the world is between Hiroshima and Kokura in Japan on the Nozomi 500 and 503. The 119 miles are covered in 44 minutes – an average of 162.7 mph.

The fastest train in Europe is the French TGV that runs between Lille and Roissy, France. It covers the 126 miles 704 yd. in 48 minutes, traveling at an average of 158 mph.

LONGEST FREIGHT TRAINS
From August 26 to August 27, 1989, a record 660-wagon, (4½-mile) train with a tank car and a caboose made a 535-mile run on the 3-ft.-6-in.-gauge Sishen–Saldanha railway, South Africa, in a time of 22 hr. 40 min. The freight train was moved by a total of nine 50-kV electric and seven diesel-electric locomotives distributed along its length.

FASTEST DIESEL TRAIN
The record for the fastest ever speed by a diesel train is 148 mph, by an Intercity 125 train on a test run between Darlington and York, England on November 1, 1987. The train was one of a number of Intercity 125s used by British Rail for their HST (High Speed Train) daily service, which was inaugurated between London, Bristol and south Wales on August 4, 1976.

LONGEST PASSENGER TRAIN
On April 27, 1991, a 1-mile-135-yd., 3,064-ton passenger train took 1 hr. 11 min. 5 sec. to complete the 38-mile journey from Ghent to Ostend, Belgium. Run by the National Belgian Railway Company, the train had a total of 70 coaches pulled by a single electric locomotive.

BIGGEST SAILING SHIP
The largest vessel built in the era of sail was the 5,899-gross-ton *France II*, which was launched at Bordeaux, France, in 1911. The steel-hulled, five-masted barque had a 418-foot hull, and although principally designed as a sailing vessel with a stump top gallant rig, was also fitted with two auxiliary engines. The latter were removed in 1919, and the ship became a pure sailing vessel. *France II* was wrecked off New Caledonia in the South Pacific on July 12, 1922.

BIGGEST SAILING SHIP IN SERVICE
The biggest sailing ship now in service is the 357-foot *Sedov*, built in 1921 in Kiel, Germany, and now used by the Russian Navy. It is 48 ft wide, has a displacement of 6,300 tons, and a sail area of 45,123 square feet. *Sedov* can reach up to 17 knots, and carries a crew of 65 cadets and 120 officer trainees.

LONGEST SAILING SHIP
The 613-foot French-built *Club Med 1*, which has five aluminum masts and 30,100 square feet of computer-controlled polyester sails, operates as a Caribbean cruise vessel for 425 passengers for Club Med. With a small sail area and powerful engines, it is really a motor-sailer.

BIGGEST CARGO VESSEL
The oil tanker *Jahre Viking* (formerly known as the *Happy Giant* and the *Seawise Giant*), weighs 564,763 dwt. The tanker, which is 1,504 feet long overall, has a beam of 226 feet and a draft of 80 ft. 9 in. It was declared a total loss after being disabled during the Iran–Iraq war but underwent a $60-million renovation in Singapore and the United Arab Emirates and was relaunched under its new name in November 1991.

BIGGEST CONTAINER SHIP
The largest container vessel now in service is *Regina Maersk*, which was built at Odense, Denmark. Completed in January 1996, it has a gross tonnage of 81,488 and a capacity of 6,000 TEU (Twenty-foot Equivalent Units; the standard container is 20 feet long).

BIGGEST HYDROFOIL
The 212-foot-long naval hydrofoil *Plainview*, which weighs 345 tons with a full load, was launched by the Lockheed Shipbuilding and Construction Co. in Seattle, Washington on June 28, 1965, and has a service speed of 57.2 mph.

BIGGEST PASSENGER HYDROFOIL
Three 165-ton *Supramar PTS 150* Mk III hydrofoils, which can carry up to 250 passengers at a speed of 40 knots across the Ore Sound between Copenhagen, Denmark and Malmö, Sweden, were built by Westermoen Hydrofoil Ltd. of Mandal, Norway.

BIGGEST HOVERCRAFT
The 185-foot-long *SRN4* Mk III, a British-built civil hovercraft, weighs 341 tons and is large enough to accommodate a total of 418 passengers and 60 cars. Powered by four Bristol Siddeley Marine Proteus engines, the hovercraft has a maximum speed in excess of 65 knots, which is the scheduled permitted cross-Channel operating speed.

BIGGEST YACHT
The Saudi Arabian royal yacht *Abdul Aziz*, which was built in Denmark and completed at Vospers Yard, Southampton, England on June 22, 1984, is 482 feet long.

BIGGEST PRIVATE YACHT
The largest private (nonroyal) yacht in the world is the 407-foot *Savarona*, which was built for Turkish president Mustafa Ataturk in 1931 and privatized in 1992.

BIGGEST JUNK
The seagoing *Zheng He* had a displacement of 3,150 tons and an estimated length of up to 538 feet. The flagship of Admiral Zheng He's 62 treasure ships c. 1420, it is believed to have had nine masts.

BIGGEST LINER
P&O Princess Cruise Line's *Grand Princess* is seen here setting off on its maiden voyage in Istanbul, Turkey. The liner has a displacement of 109,000 gross registered tons. Operating between Istanbul and Barcelona, Spain during the summer months and in the Caribbean in the winter, it is 15 storeys high, has a crew of 1,150 and carries 2,600 passengers.

bikes and motorbikes

MINIATURE MOTORCYCLE RACING
The first Spanish Miniature Motorcycling Championships were held on February 1, 1998 at the racing circuit at Albacete, Spain. The sport is acquiring a global following, and international championships are planned for 1999. They will be held in the United States.

HIGHEST BICYCLE SPEEDS
The record for the highest speed ever achieved on a bicycle is 166.94 mph, by Fred Rompelberg (Netherlands) behind a windshield at Bonneville Salt Flats, Utah on October 3, 1995. The slipstreaming effect of the lead vehicle provided considerable assistance in the record attempt.

The 24-hour behind pace record is 1,216 miles 1,310 yd., by Michael Secrest at Phoenix International Raceway in Arizona in April 1990.

FASTEST UNICYCLE SPRINT
Peter Rosendahl set a 100-m sprint record of 12.11 seconds (18.47 mph) from a standing start in Las Vegas, Nevada on March 25, 1994.

FASTEST LAND SPEEDS BY HUMAN-POWERED VEHICLES
The world speed record by a single rider on a human-powered vehicle (HPV) over a 200-m flying start is 65.48 mph, by Fred Markham at Mono Lake, California on May 11, 1986.

The one-hour standing start record by a single rider was set by Pat Kinch, who averaged a speed of 46.96 mph riding *Kingcycle Bean* at Millbrook Proving Ground, Bedford, England on September 8, 1990.

HIGHEST MOTORCYCLE SPEEDS
On July 14, 1990, Dave Campos (US) set AMA and FIM records on the 23-foot-long streamliner *Easyriders*, powered by two 1,491-cc Ruxton Harley-Davidson engines, at Bonneville Salt Flats, Utah. Campos' overall average speed was 322.15 mph, and he completed the faster run at an average speed of 322.87 mph.

The fastest time for a single run over 440 yards is 6.19 seconds, by Tony Lang (US) riding a supercharged Suzuki in Gainesville, Florida in 1994.

The record for the highest terminal velocity at the end of a 440-yard run is 213.24 mph, by Elmer Trett (US) at Virginia Motorsports Park, Petersburg, Virginia in 1994.

BIGGEST BICYCLE
The world's biggest bicycle by wheel diameter is *Frankencycle*, which is 11 ft. 2 in. in height and has a wheel diameter of 10 feet. Built by Dave Moore of Rosemead, California, it was first ridden by Steve Gordon of Moorpark, California, on June 4, 1989.

BIGGEST TRICYCLE
The Dillon *Colossal*, designed by Arthur Dillon and constructed by Dave Moore in 1994, has a back wheel diameter of 11 feet and a front wheel diameter of 5 ft. 10 in.

BIGGEST MOTORCYCLE GATHERING
In March 1998, an estimated 500,000 bikers and motorcycle enthusiasts from all over the world attended Bike Week at Daytona Beach, Florida. The 10-day event has been held every winter for the last 57 years and has spawned a host of imitators across the United States, where a motorcycle event is held somewhere almost every weekend of the year. In conjunction with the gathering, the Daytona 200 and the Daytona Supercross are held at the Daytona International Speedway. When bike gangs first began to show up in Daytona in the 1940s, the scene was much wilder than it is today. This continued until the 1980s, when a new set of followers began to appear; local residents say that the event has been transformed from a gathering of outlaws to a well organized Mardi Gras with parades, displays and the chance to test drive the latest models.

LONGEST BICYCLE
The longest bicycle built without a third stabilizing wheel is 72 ft. 11½ in. in length and weighs 750 pounds. Designed and built by Terry Thessman of Pahiatua, New Zealand, it was ridden 807 feet by four riders on February 27, 1988.

SMALLEST BICYCLE
The wheels of the smallest wheeled rideable bicycle in the world are 19/25 inch in diameter. On March 25, 1988 the bike was ridden for 13 ft. 5½ in. by its constructor, Neville Patten of Gladstone, Queensland, Australia.

SMALLEST UNICYCLE
Peter Rosendahl (Sweden) rode an 8-inch tall unicycle with a wheel diameter of 71/100 inch a distance of 13 ft. 1½ in. at the University of Physical Education, Budapest, Hungary on July 28, 1996. No attachments or extensions were fitted to the cycle.

LONGEST MOTORCYCLE
In 1996, Douglas and Roger Bell of Perth, Western Australia designed and built a motorcycle with a record length of 24 ft. 11 in. It weighed almost 4,400 pounds.

SMALLEST MOTORCYCLE
In 1990, Simon Timperley and Clive Williams of Progressive Engineering Ltd., Manchester, England designed and constructed a motorcycle with a wheel-base of 4¼ inches, a seat height of 3¼ inches, a front wheel diameter of ¾ inch and a back wheel diameter of 19/20 inch. The motorcycle was ridden a distance of 3 ft. 2 in.

MOST EXPENSIVE MOTORCYCLE
The world's most expensive production motorbike is the Morbidelli 850 V8, which retailed for $98,400 in 1998.

MOST EXPENSIVE MOUNTAIN BIKE
The most expensive retail mountain bike in the world costs £7,244 ($12,025) – about the same as many small cars. Made by the British company Stif, it weighs just 20 pounds and is designed for off-road racing circuits. It has some of the world's most expensive components: the brakes, gears and pedals are made in Japan, the frame is from the United States, the forks and handlebar are British and the saddle is Italian.

SCOOTERS
The 125cc Vespa ET4 scooter was unveiled in Rome, Italy in September 1996, together with the 50cc ET2, in a ceremony marking the 50th anniversary of the manufacturer Piaggio. The then chairman of Piaggio, Giovanni Agnelli, is pictured here sitting on the ET4 during the launch. Piaggio's first Vespa scooter was launched more than 50 years ago, in the years following World War II, and has earned a reputation as an emblem of stylish two-wheeled transport in Europe and sold more than 15 million units. Despite 96 redesigns, the scooter – which was originally made from aircraft parts and is still the only scooter to be constructed from steel rather than plastic – has never moved away from its original image. Vespas have been used in worldwide advertising campaigns by IBM, Pepsi, and American Express. In a recent ad for the launch of the Fiat Seicento, a Vespa acted as a referee in a soccer game between yellow and blue Seicentos.

HARLEY DAVIDSON MOTORCYCLES
The Harley-Davidson Owners Group (HOG) is the world's largest company-sponsored motorcycle enthusiasts' group, with over 400,000 members in more than 1,000 branches worldwide. On June 13, 1998, 50,000 Harleys paraded through the streets of downtown Milwaukee, Wisconsin for almost four hours in the Harley-Davidson 95th Anniversary Parade.

hi-tech

computer games

MOST ADVANCED 3-D ANIMATION
MediEvil, developed by Sony Computer Entertainment Europe-Cambridge Studios, uses N-World, a modeling and painting package from Nichimen Graphics Inc., which has also been used to produce *Super Mario 64* and *Final Fantasy VII*.

BEST-SELLING COMPUTER GAMES
After its release in 1993, *Myst* sold 500,000 copies in its first year and has now topped sales of 4 million and made more than $100 million. It was the first CD-ROM entertainment to sell in excess of 2 million copies. *Myst* and its sequel *Riven* ranked first and second in computer games software in 1997. *Myst*, an interactive fantasy game that takes place on Myst Island, incorporates 3-D animation and advanced sound and music technology. It was developed by Cyan and launched through Broderbund.

Microsoft's *MS Flight Simulator* was released in April 1992 and had sold a total of 196,227 units by May 1998, taking in $99.2 million.

Resident Evil 2 from Capcom Entertainment sold more than 380,000 units in its debut weekend — more than 60% of its initial production. It made more than $19 million, surpassing the revenue of all but one Hollywood movie for the same weekend. The game was released on January 21, 1998 for the Sony PlayStation, and broke records set by some of the industry's biggest video games, including *Final Fantasy VII* and *Super Mario 64*. *Resident Evil 2* was supported by a $5-million advertising campaign.

FASTEST-SELLING GAMES
Final Fantasy VII from Squaresoft was released in November 1997 and has sold about 3 million units for Sony PlayStation.

Riven, the sequel to *Myst*, was developed by Cyan and released by Broderbund in December 1997. By May 1998, it had sold 1,003,414 units and taken $43.7 million. *Riven* contains five CD-ROMS with twice the number of images and three times the amount of animation of *Myst*.

MOST SUCCESSFUL GAMES IN TERMS OF MERCHANDISING
Mario, the character who first appeared in *Donkey Kong* in 1982 and subsequently starred in the *Mario Bros.* games, was more frequently recognized than Mickey Mouse in a poll of children carried out in 1991. Together with his brother Luigi, he has featured in three cartoon series, one major movie and a number of toys ranging from board games to water guns. Together the video games have spawned more merchandising than any other.

Resident Evil by Capcom Entertainment had generated more than $200 million worldwide by December 1997 and sold about 4 million units. Its success made it a popular licensing property and deals have been set for a feature movie, a line of action figures and a series of comic books.

Released in March 1996, *Resident Evil* established a new genre in the gaming industry and became one of Sony PlayStation's highest-selling third-party franchises ever.

BEST-SELLING GAMES CONSOLE
The Sony PlayStation had sold approximately 30 million units (10 million in North America) worldwide up to February 1998, making it the biggest-selling computer games console in the world. Sony Computer Entertainment Inc. has spent more than $300 million developing the PlayStation, which runs hit games such as *Tomb Raider* and *Final Fantasy VII*. Japan, North America and Europe have produced about 135 million units of PlayStation software so far.

BIGGEST CHAIN OF VIDEO GAME ARCADES
In 1996, DreamWorks announced a partnership with Sega and MCA to develop Sega GameWorks,

MOST ANTICIPATED GAME
Nintendo's *Diddy Kong Racing* had projected sales of 1.5 million copies between its launch on November 24 and Christmas 1997. In 14 days, it sold 800,000 units.

3-D SUPERHERO
Duke Nukem 3-D, the third chapter in the *Duke Nukem* series and the first to use 3-D perspective, was developed by Ritual Entertainment. Duke returns to 21st-century Earth to exterminate a race of aliens.

a number of 30,000–50,000-square-foot video entertainment super-centers featuring Sega titles and games designed by movie director Steven Spielberg. The first center opened in Seattle in 1997 and the company is planning a further 100 sites worldwide by 2002. Centers are already open in Pennsylvania, Texas and Ontario, and will soon open in Arizona and in Rio de Janeiro, Brazil.

MOST PLAYERS AT ONE TIME IN A GAME ON THE INTERNET
The multiplayer gaming engine *Ultima Online*, which was developed from *Ultima* — the best-selling role-playing series in the world — allows thousands of people to exist simultaneously in the same fantasy game world on the Internet. When *Ultima Online* was released in 1997, it sold far more copies than had been predicted. Servers overloaded as people flocked to play, and the game's manufacturer, Origin Systems Inc., had to add more servers and take on more employees in order to cope with the overwhelming number of players logging on.

MOST SUCCESSFUL STRATEGY WAR GAMES
The *Command & Conquer* line of strategy war games, which was developed by Westwood Studios, sold more than 5 million units between its release in 1995 and June 1997. The line includes the original *Command & Conquer* for MS-DOS, Windows 95, Macintosh, Sony PlayStation and Sega Saturn; *The Covert Operations*; and *Command & Conquer Red Alert* — the prequel to *Command & Conquer* and once the fastest-selling computer game in history.

BIGGEST COMPUTER GAME CULT
Quake took the games community by storm when it was released by Activision in 1996, and thousands of players are still blasting each other over the internet. Denis Fong (US), known as "Thresh," is the Internet's top *Quake* player. He has a sponsorship deal with Microsoft, and in 1997 became Intergraph's E3 *Quake* champion, winning $5,000, a computer system and a Ferrari.

MOST REALISTIC GRAPHICS
Video Reality, which was developed by the Australian company SouthPeak Interactive, uses video footage rather than computer-generated graphics, so that the background detail of games increases when seen close-up rather than losing sharpness. SouthPeak has used its Video Reality technology in its game *Temujin*, in which players navigate their way through a museum, deciphering puzzles and solving mysteries. The backgrounds were filmed in an on-site video production facility before being transferred to computer.

MOST INTELLECTUALLY CHALLENGING GAME
Jane's Combat Simulations' game *688(I) Hunter/Killer* is reportedly the most realistic submarine simulation developed for PCs. The game was developed by defense contractors who design submarine simulators for the US Navy, and a knowledge of flight dynamics is an advantage for players, who have to master sonar and weapons systems, develop real target solutions and outfit a boat with the latest weaponry.

BIGGEST COMPUTER GAME MANUFACTURER
During the third quarter of 1997 Electronic Arts of California reported sales of more than $391 million and profits of $58 million. The company develops, publishes and distributes software for PCs and entertainment systems such as Sony PlayStation and Nintendo 64.

BEST-SELLING VIDEO GAME
Super Mario Bros. from Nintendo was created by Shigeru Miyamoto, the Japanese game developer and creator of the *Donkey Kong* arcade games. Mario first appeared in *Donkey Kong* in 1982 and again in *Mario Bros.* in 1984. He has since starred in other games for the Super Nintendo, Game Boy and Virtual Boy. *Super Mario Bros. 3* has sold 15 million copies worldwide and is the best-selling video game ever.

BIGGEST CYBERSTAR
Tomb Raider, starring the fearless Lara Croft, was launched by Eidos Interactive, Europe's biggest publisher and entertainment software developer, in November 1996. The game, which was designed by Core Design, has become one of the best-selling video game titles of all time, and Lara was named one of the 50 most influential people in the computer industry by *Time Digital* magazine. In November 1997, Lara was given a makeover and some new moves for *Tomb Raider II*, which sold more than 2 million copies within two months of its launch. By March 1998 the two games had sold 6 million copies worldwide. On March 16, 1998, Eidos announced that it had entered into an agreement to license the worldwide movie rights to *Tomb Raider* with Paramount Pictures. Lara Croft has appeared on more than 80 magazine and newspaper covers around the world, including *Time Digital*'s December 1997 issue, for which she was dressed in a Santa Claus outfit.

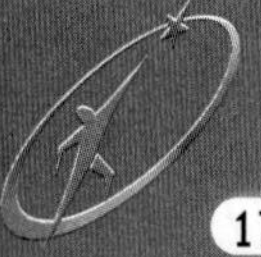

gadgets I

THINNEST SPEAKERS
New Transducers Ltd. has produced the thinnest full range speakers. They dispense with the magnets and voice coils of conventional dynamic speakers; instead, an electromagnetic exciter creates dense waves across an acoustically inert slab, making sound waves from the mixing of pressure across the slab.

BIGGEST PLASMA TV SCREEN
NEC's Hi-Vision PlasmaX PX-50V2 features a 50-inch diagonal screen incorporating plasma display technology. The set, which is designed to work with Japan's analog HDTV system, is also the world's slimmest high definition television to date: at a depth of just $3\frac{4}{5}$ inches, the system is still capable of displaying more than 1 million pixels.

SMALLEST CAMERAS
In 1998, Nintendo's Game Boy, which was launched in 1989 and has sold more than 60 million units worldwide, was reinvented as a camera and printer. The digital still camera cartridge sits on top of the Game Boy (as seen left) and can take and store up to 30 low-resolution black and white photos. The camera comes with three games that allow players to create characters using photos. The printer can then produce small prints or stickers. In 1997, the company reduced the size of the Game Boy and introduced the Game Boy Pocket, and a color version of the Game Boy is due to be launched at the end of 1998. The world's smallest pinhole video camera is the PC-21XP, sold by Supercircuits Inc. The CCD element occupies only $\frac{1}{4}$ square inch but has a 295,000-pixel array that outputs 380 video lines. It can see in low-level lighting of 0.5 lux. The overall unit measures $1\frac{15}{100}$ x $\frac{1}{2}$ inch and can run for up to five hours on one PP3 battery.

SMALLEST CELLULAR PHONE
The PHS (Personal Handyphone System), made by the Nippon Telegraph and Telephone Corp., is a wristwatch-style phone that dispenses with the conventional keypad. Numbers are selected by voice recognition circuitry within the phone. The unit weighs $2\frac{2}{5}$ ounces and measures 2 x $1\frac{1}{2}$ x $\frac{3}{5}$ inch.

SMALLEST MOBILE PHONE
The smallest GSM cellular phone is the Motorola StarTac Lite, which weighs 3 ounces but is capable of a standby time of more than 95 hours with an optional lithium ion battery. Users can hot-swap batteries, allowing them to continue talking without interruption.

SMALLEST SOLID STATE STORAGE DEVICE
The SanDisk Multimedia Card, which was developed by SanDisk and Siemens for use in portable equipment such as mobile phones and digital voice recorders, is $1\frac{1}{4}$ x $\frac{9}{10}$ x $\frac{1}{20}$ inch thick and can store up to 10 megabytes in nonvolatile memory.

SMALLEST WEARABLE PC
Seiko's RuPuter, which is slightly larger than a wristwatch, has 128 kilobytes of system memory and can exchange data with other computers by an infrared data link interface.

THINNEST LAPTOP
Mitsubishi's Pedion portable PC, which has a fully featured MMX compatible Pentium 233 processor and 3.2-gigabyte hard drive, is $\frac{7}{10}$ inch thick when folded.

SMALLEST VIDEO TRANSMITTER
The VID1 from AE Inc. allows the wireless transmission of a picture to a base station 2,000 feet away, to complement a remote camera in a covert monitoring situation. Measuring $\frac{3}{5}$ x $\frac{9}{10}$ x $\frac{3}{10}$ inch, it transmits either PAL or NTSC encoded

video at 900 MHz, reducing the need for powerful output and allowing use for up to 11 hours.

SMALLEST VIDEO RECORDER
Sony's EVO 220 Micro 8 mm weighs $1\frac{1}{2}$ pounds and measures $2\frac{3}{10}$ x $8\frac{1}{2}$ x $5\frac{7}{10}$ inches. It records up to five hours of video onto 8-mm tape.

SMALLEST PORTABLE DVD PLAYER
Panasonic's DVD-L10 weighs less than $2\frac{1}{5}$ pounds and has its own $5\frac{7}{10}$-inch LCD screen and stereo speakers. Equipped with onboard and remote controls, it can also be used as a MPEG-2 video and Dolby Digital audio source for any home theater setup. It crams all of this into a box measuring $6\frac{1}{5}$ x $6\frac{1}{5}$ x $1\frac{3}{5}$ inches deep.

SMALLEST VIDEO-CD PLAYER
The smallest video-CD player with its own screen is Panasonic's SL-DP70, which measures 5 x $1\frac{2}{5}$ x $5\frac{3}{5}$ inches. It can function for up to two hours with six AA batteries and costs about $528.

THINNEST PLASTIC WATCH
On October 1, 1997, Swiss watchmaker Swatch launched the Swatch Skin, which has a paper-thin plastic strap and a $\frac{15}{100}$-inch-thick case. It can be worn by divers down to a depth of 100 feet.

THINNEST MINIDISC RECORDER
Sony's MZ-R50 is $\frac{7}{10}$ inch thick and weighs 6 ounces. It can play for up to 22 hours with its lithium ion battery and alkaline AA cells.

SMALLEST PRINTER
Citizen's PN60 printer measures $9\frac{9}{10}$ x 2 x $2\frac{9}{10}$ inches and weighs 1 lb. $1\frac{1}{2}$ oz. It has a thermal fusion print head and produces images of up to 360 x 360 dots per inch at a rate of two pages a minute.

SMALLEST DIGITAL PRINTER
JVC's V-HT1 is the smallest digital printer able to make hard copies of digital still camera images. It produces A7 size pictures from any camera with an IRTran-P infra-red data interface.

SMALLEST SHEET-FEED SCANNER
The CanoScan 300S, which uses Canon's LED InDirect Exposure (LIDE) technology, weighs just 3 lb. 4 oz.

SMALLEST DOCUMENT SHREDDER
Piranha's PR026 measures $6\frac{1}{2}$ x $2\frac{1}{3}$ x $1\frac{1}{2}$ inches and deals with any kind of document by nibbling off slices and shredding them into slivers.

SMALLEST FAX MACHINE
Phillips' smart phone add-on connects to the Phillips PCS 1900 Digital Phone to send faxes and e-mail, access the Internet and provide other communication services. It makes the PCS 1900, at $6\frac{7}{10}$ inches in length and $5\frac{3}{5}$ ounces in weight, the smallest and lightest mobile fax.

SMALLEST BINOCULARS
The U-C 8x18 series binoculars, with 8x magnification and optics that allow focusing down to 6 ft. 7 in., weighs 5 ounces and measures 3 x $2\frac{7}{10}$ x $\frac{7}{10}$ inches.

SMALLEST AND LIGHTEST POLAROID CAMERA
In March 1998, the Polaroid Pocket Xiao, which was developed by toymaker Tomy Company Ltd. and Polaroid Corporation of Cambridge, Massachusetts, was unveiled at the Tokyo Toy Show in Japan. It measures $1\frac{7}{10}$ x $5\frac{1}{10}$ x $1\frac{1}{2}$ inches and weighs $5\frac{4}{5}$ ounces, including batteries.

SMALLEST NIGHT VISION SCOPE
The smallest scope with a built-in illuminator is the Mini Night Vision from ASL Corp. At $5\frac{1}{4}$ x $2\frac{1}{2}$ inches, it can amplify light by 15,000 times.

THINNEST PRIMARY CELL
Yuasa Exide's Power Film is a 1-mm-thick ($\frac{3}{100}$-inch) primary cell of lithium manganese internal construction used in Smart Cards and other transportable media.

SMALLEST DIGITAL CAMERA
The world's smallest digital camera with a viewfinder is the Panasonic NV-DCF2B Card Shot, which measures $3\frac{1}{2}$ x 2 x $1\frac{1}{5}$ inches. It has a 350,000-pixel CCD element allowing images up to 640 x 480 pixels to be captured in fine mode, or 320 x 240 pixels in standard mode. The two-megabyte memory can store up to 24 images in fine mode or 85 in standard mode in JPEG picture file format.

gadgets II

MOST POWERFUL GAME CONSOLE
Nintendo's N64 is the fastest and the most powerful game console in the world to date. The console has true 64-bit processing architecture and was developed in a collaboration between Nintendo of Japan and Silicon Graphics Interactive Ltd. of California. Costing $158, it has graphic manipulation capabilities that would have been present only in multimillion-dollar systems 10 years ago.

MOST POWERFUL LAPTOP
In 1998, Apple launched the PowerPC 750 RISC chip Powerbook G3 — the most powerful laptop in the world today. The Powerbook G3 looks and feels like Apple's 3400 model, but is twice as fast and has a 32-megabyte EDO DRAM memory that is upgradeable to 160 megabytes. Its power gives it a weight of 7 lb. 11 oz., making it difficult to carry in one hand.

MOST POWERFUL WEARABLE COMPUTER
The world's most powerful wearable computer is the Mentis system, which is manufactured by Teltronics Incorporated of Sarasota, Florida. The processing unit measures $7^1/_2$ x $5^1/_2$ x 1 inches and contains a fully featured Pentium-equipped multimedia system on a single board. The wearer can access the system by voice command and view the display output either via a head-mounted LCD monocle or with the assistance of an external flat LCD panel.

CHEAPEST GPS RECEIVER
The cheapest portable Global Positioning by Satellite receiver in the world today is the GPS Pioneer, which is manufactured by Magellan Systems Corporation. The Pioneer is the first GPS receiver to cost less than $100 and allows users to find their location on the planet through its ability to decode information from the NavStar network of 24 orbiting geostationary satellites.

MOST SHOCKPROOF CD PLAYER
The PCD-7900, which is manufactured by Sanyo-Fisher, is the first personal CD player in the world to incorporate a 40-second antishock memory, which compensates for errors in the disc tracking caused by external shock. The CD player has such an extensive shock-guard capability that listeners can continue to listen to the music from the original disk while they are changing discs.

INTERACTIVE CANDY
In February 1998, Hasbro Inc. introduced Sound Bites, a lollipop holder that plays tunes and noises inside the user's head. The toy is operated by the insertion of a lollipop into the Sound Bites holder. When someone bites the lollipop, a computer chip inside the holder transmits vibrations through the person's teeth directly to their inner ear, providing sounds and melodies. The music is virtually inaudible to anyone standing nearby. Sound Bites, which was co-invented by Andrew Filo, a Silicon Valley engineer, and David Capper, a toy industry entrepreneur, has four buttons that can be pressed to mix and match the sound selection. The holder takes most standard brands of lollipop. There are six versions of the toy, including three musical themes and three special effects, with cartoon noises, funny voices and space noises. For Christmas, Hasbro plans to introduce a new model that plays carols.

MOST EFFICIENT AUDIO AMPLIFIER
The Tact Millennium has a configuration known as Class D, or Pulse Width Modulation, which means that the amplifier converts almost 100% of the input power to audio power output, making it the most efficient audio amplifier in the world. It is the first Class D amplifier to be able to claim a fully digital signal path, and offers greater compatibility with new digital-only equalization equipment and effects.

MOST EXPENSIVE POWER AMPLIFIER
The AudioNote Ongaku costs $93,200, making it the world's most expensive power amplifier. The Ongaku has a valve amplifier with a Class A output configuration, giving purity of sound at the expense of electrical efficiency. The main reason for its high cost is the windings for the output transformers, which are made out of solid silver wire (silver is the most conductive metal at room temperature).

MOST EXPENSIVE HI-FI SPEAKERS
Dutch company OLS launched the Grand Enigma Reference System, a set of hi-fi speakers costing $1 million, in 1998. The 22-pound speakers are charged with 100,000 watts.

MOST EXPENSIVE PRODUCTION 35-MM SLR CAMERA
The Canon Eos 1N-RS costs $3,840, making it the most expensive production 35-mm SLR camera in the world to date. The 1N-RS has a shutter speed of $^1/_{8000}$th of a second up to 30 seconds, accepts film speeds from 25 to 5,000 ASA and can shoot up to three frames every second. Its Pentaprism viewfinder offers 100% of the view that is relayed to the film and the main body can accept any Canon EF mount lenses.

MOST EXPENSIVE MOBILE PHONE
In 1996, David Morris International of London, England designed and sold a unique mobile telephone that was made of 18-carat gold encrusted with pink and white diamonds. The price tag was a record-breaking $104,050. Other designs by the jewelers include a Game Boy made of gold and diamonds and a jellybean machine. The luxury gadgets are often purchased by royalty and other wealthy people. In 1971, David Morris International supplied all the jewelry worn by the cast of the James Bond movie *Diamonds Are Forever* (GB, 1971).

360° TV
The 360° television set was invented by Frank Gibshaw of E.S.P Electronics Inc. (pictured above with his invention) and unveiled at the International Consumer Electronics Show in Las Vegas in January 1998. The set displays the same images that are shown on regular televisions, but allows the viewer to watch from all sides of the unit. Aside from TV viewing, the potential applications of the set include video games, computer and video displays, educational presentations and movies.

FASTEST LINE MATRIX PRINTER
The world's fastest line matrix printer is the Tally T6180, which can print at speeds of up to 1,800 lines per minute. This is approximately 27% faster than its nearest rival.

MOST "INTELLIGENT" PEN
Dutch computer company LCI has developed a "smartpen" that is capable of verifying people's signatures. The smartpen's minuscule pressure pads, electronic spirit level and computer processor combine to record the pressure that is applied to it and the angle of tilt at which it is being used. The chip within the smartpen then encrypts the information and transmits it to a remote computer to be checked against a central database.

MOST EXPENSIVE CD PLAYER
A CD player with an 18-carat yellow gold case encrusted with pink pavé diamonds sold for $128,000 at David Morris International in London, England in 1996, making it the world's most expensive CD player. David Morris opened his shop in Conduit Street, Mayfair — an exclusive area of the British capital popular with wealthy socialites and movie stars — in 1969.

internet

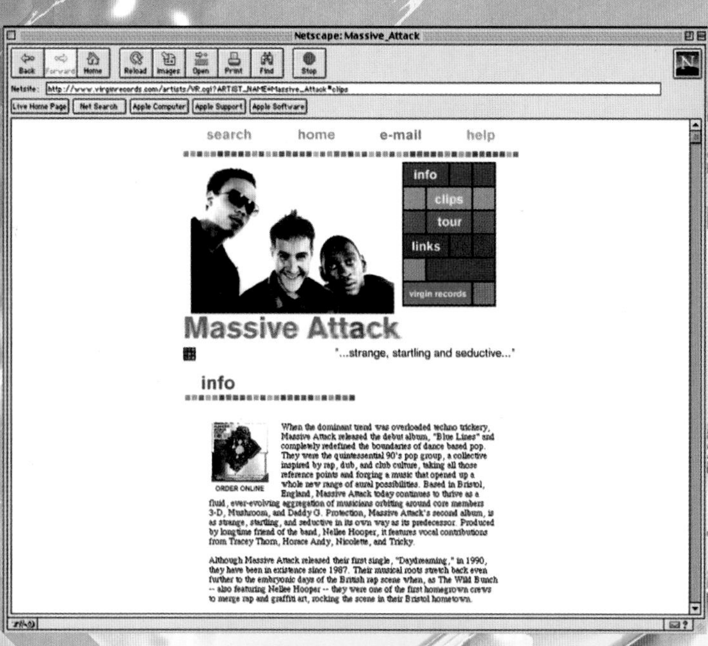

BIGGEST ALBUM RELEASE

The British band Massive Attack launched the whole of their third album *Mezzanine* (1998) online, together with a preview of the video for the first single from the album, three weeks before it was available in record stores. The site received 1,313,644 hits, and the songs were downloaded a total of 101,673 times before the album went on sale on April 20. A further 1,602,658 hits were recorded a month after the store release. Despite its availability on the Internet, *Mezzanine* went straight to No. 1 on the British album chart.

MOST ONLINE SALES

Dell Computers generates a record-breaking $3 million a day from its Web sites.

MOST SPENT ON INTERNET ADVERTISING IN A YEAR

Microsoft spent more than $13 million on advertising on the Internet in 1996, and between June 1997 and June 1998, it spent more than £600,000 ($960,000) in the United Kingdom alone.

MOST POPULAR WEB SITE

Yahoo!, a directory in which Web sites have been compiled into categories, has the biggest audience of any online service or site on the Internet. Approximately 95 million page views per day were recorded in March 1998.

MOST MENTIONED MAN ON THE INTERNET

The Internet search engine AltaVista links President Bill Clinton's name to 1,842,790 sites, making him the most mentioned man on the Internet. The word "Clinton" has a monthly average of 45,080 hits on the Yahoo! directory. "Bill Clinton" receives a further 44,080 hits.

MOST QUESTIONS RECEIVED ON AN INTERNET SITE IN 30 MINUTES

On May 17, 1997, former Beatle Sir Paul McCartney received more than 3 million questions from fans in 30 minutes during a Web event to promote his album *Flaming Pie*. On November 19, 1997, McCartney also set a record for the first ever debut performance of a classical work live on the Internet, when he performed his new work, the 75-minute symphonic poem *Standing Stones*, live from Carnegie Hall, New York City. The presentation involved radio, television, an interactive online interview and Internet audio and video broadcast across the World Wide Web. McCartney had been composing *Standing Stones* for four years.

BIGGEST SHOPPING MALL ON THE INTERNET

Internet Mall, which is situated at mecklerweb.com/imall, has a record 800 onscreen virtual stores and more than a million subscribers in the United Kingdom alone. It uses a total of 65,000 stores around the globe to create the service, which is available in more than 150 countries. The products, ranging from popcorn to car insurance, are delivered within 48 hours. Internet malls date back to 1993, when Jon Zeeff launched the Branch Mall. It had two virtual stores, Grant's Flowers and Calling Cards, and registered 400 hits in its first month. It now has 3 million visitors a month and is found at http://www.branchmall.com/.

MOST COMMERCE CONDUCTED ON THE INTERNET

In 1997, the United States saw $2 billion worth of commerce over the Internet – more than any other country.

MOST POPULAR SEARCH ENGINE

AltaVista has more than 1 billion page views and in excess of 21 million users worldwide every month. The engine works by trawling 140 million pages and 16,000 Usenet newsgroups.

MOST POPULAR SEARCH WORDS

The most frequently-used search word recorded on Yahoo is "sex," which receives an average of 1.55 million searches a month. In second place is "chat," with 414,320 searches. Other top contenders are "Netscape software," "games" and "weather."

FIRST INTERNET VERDICT

In November 1997, Judge Hiller Zobel announced that he would post his 16-page ruling on the case of 19-year-old British au pair Louise Woodward on the Internet before issuing hard copies, in order to avoid a media circus at the courthouse in Cambridge, Massachusetts. Woodward had been given a 15-year sentence after being found guilty of murdering Matthew Eappen, a baby who had been in her care. On November 10, 1997, this verdict was overturned by Judge Zobel, who reduced the sentence to 279 days and the conviction to one of involuntary manslaughter. His verdict was to be the first in legal history to be broadcast on the Internet and via e-mail before being disseminated via other channels. However, demand for the site by millions of people around the globe caused the Internet server delivering the verdict to crash, delaying the live announcement of the judgment on the Lawyer's Weekly Home Page on the World Wide Web. Pictured here, supporters of Woodward watch the announcement of the initial guilty verdict in her hometown of Elton, England.

MOST POPULAR NEWS SERVICE
CNN's seven sites have a combined average of 55 million page views per week. The sites also receive more than 3,000 user comments per day via the CNN message boards. The sites currently contain more than 210,000 pages but grow by 90–150 pages daily.

MOST POPULAR DOMAIN NAME
Of the 2.69 million domain names that were in existence worldwide by February 16, 1998, the most popular is ".com," at 1.65 million. According to NetNames Ltd., the number of domains registered grows by 7,983 a day.

BIGGEST DOMAIN OWNERSHIP
According to NetNames Ltd., the United States has a total of 1,353,550 domains, which represents 50.9% of the overall domain ownership in the world. The United Kingdom is the second largest, with 160,004, or 6%.

GREATEST NUMBER OF ACTIVE ONLINE NET ACCOUNTS
Stockbrokers Charles Schwab & Co. have more than 900,000 online accounts holding in excess of $66.6 billion in assets and accounting for more than one-third of their 99,000 daily trading operations.

BIGGEST SAVING OF PAPER THROUGH USING THE INTERNET
Federal Express has announced that it saves approximately 2 billion sheets of paper a year in the United States by tracking its shipments online.

MOST SUCCESSFUL INTERNET CRACKER
An Internet cracker (similar to a hacker) is an electronic burglar who systematically breaks into computer systems and files. One cracker is reported to have managed the biggest invasion of supposedly secure computers since the creation of the Internet. Uncharged because of the complexities of the case, he is said to have broken through every known computer system, including those used by NASA and Intel, as well as a number of nuclear weapons laboratories, government organizations and military sites. The technology used by hackers and crackers advances daily, and it is thought that Internet crime is severely under-policed. It is estimated that $300 billion a year is lost to Internet money laundering alone.

BIGGEST INTERNET CRASH
At approximately 11.30 a.m. EST on April 25, 1997, the global computer network ran into major problems, and much of the system became unusable. Human error and equipment failure had led a network in Florida to claim "ownership" of 30,000 of the Internet's 45,000 routes. Data packets were routed incorrectly and connections across the Internet failed. Some service providers took action within 15 minutes, but the problem persisted until 7.00 p.m. EST.

MOST WIRED COUNTRY
It is estimated that more than 24 million adults in the United States will be connected to the Internet by the end of 1998.

BIGGEST COMPUTER NETWORK
The number of computers using the Internet has doubled every year since 1987. In January 1997, the figure was 16.2 million, although there may be a great number of computers that are connected but hidden behind corporate firewalls designed to exclude electronic visitors, including hackers.

MOST MENTIONED WOMAN
Pamela Anderson is the most mentioned woman on the Internet. The search engine AltaVista links the star of *Baywatch* and the movie *Barb Wire* (1996) to 1,542,282 sites. She inspires an average of 172,760 hits a month on the Yahoo! search engine.

HACKING
In 1995, an advertisement on the World Wide Web for the movie *Hackers* was itself the victim of hackers. The controversial site had a hyperlink to sites that provided potentially dangerous and criminal information, including stolen credit card numbers and instructions for creating homemade bombs and printing counterfeit bills with a laser printer. The site was submitted to the FBI's National Computer Crime Squad for potential investigation, but in June 1998 it could still be accessed via the Internet.

MOST WIRED COMMUNITY
Blacksburg, Virginia claims to be the community with the most e-mail and Internet users relative to its size. According to a survey carried out in 1995, there were about 30,000 regular users of wired data communications in a population of 70,000. Of these, 20,000 users had links through the local college, Virginia Tech.

computers

BEST CHESS COMPUTER
IBM's Deep Blue was the first supercomputer to beat a human chess grandmaster in a regulation game when it played Gary Kasparov in Philadelphia in 1995. On May 11, 1997, it beat a grandmaster (Kasparov again) in a series for the first time. It won the six-match series by 3½ points to 2½.

"MOST HUMAN" COMPUTER SYSTEM
In January 1997, a computer running the program *Albert One version 1.0* was awarded the Loebner Prize for the "most human" computer system. *Albert One* is a program that a user can communicate with using human speech. The judges of the Loebner Prize put systems through a restricted version of the Turing Test, the classic test of machine intelligence.

WORST POTENTIAL BUG
The millennium bug, which will become active on January 1, 2000, could cause millions of computer systems to go haywire, including those in hospitals, banks, air traffic control centers, buildings, cars, planes and government databases. It occurs in all systems that record the year using only two figures (i.e., "99" for "1999"). Unless they are fixed, these systems will misinterpret the year 2000 as the year 1900. Pessimistic forecasters have said it will cost the world $4 trillion to fix systems containing the bug, deal with instances of it that are missed, and compensate any people that it affects.

MOST WIDESPREAD VIRUS
First detected in early 1997, the CAP computer virus infects Microsoft Word documents. It is a linked set of macros (mini programs that automate routines in Word) that change the way files are opened, closed and saved. CAP spreads by attaching itself to Word's "global template," a file that is opened whenever a document is accessed. CAP has been reported more than any other virus in history, although this may be partly because it is very difficult for non-experts to deal with.

MOST MONEY LOST DUE TO COMPUTERS
On October 19, 1987, computers contributed to the loss of $1 trillion in a rapid global stock-market crash. On the day of this catastrophe, which is now known as "Black Monday," share prices began to tumble. This caused newly-installed computer trading programs to jump into action, trading rapidly and selling shares automatically at ever-lower prices. "Black Monday" wiped 22.6% off the Dow Jones Index — the biggest drop ever recorded in stock-market history.

MOST NOTORIOUS HACKER CASE
Hacker Kevin Mitnick is alleged to have broken into several major organizations' computer systems, including those of Sun Microsystems, Motorola, and the Pentagon. Mitnick was arrested on September 16, 1996 after an FBI computer expert tracked him down. He has since been charged with software theft, wire fraud, the interception of wire communications and computer vandalism. Mitnick, the first hacker ever to have appeared on an FBI wanted poster, faces up to 12 years in prison if he is found guilty.

FASTEST COMPUTERS
The fastest general-purpose vector-parallel computer is the Cray Y-MP C90 supercomputer, which has two gigabytes of central memory and 16 CPUs (central processing units), giving a combined peak performance of 16 gigaflops.

Intel installed an even faster supercomputer in Sandia, Texas in 1996. Using 9,072 Intel Pentium Pro processors, each running at about 200 MHz, and 608 gigabytes of memory, it has a peak performance of about 1.8 teraflops.

Massively parallel computers, with enough processors, have a theoretical aggregate performance exceeding that of a C-90. The performance on real-life applications is often less, because it is harder to effectively harness the power of many small processors.

In September 1997, the US Defense Projects Research Agency (DARPA) commissioned computer researcher John McDonald to build the world's first PetOps supercomputer — a machine that can perform 1,000 trillion operations per second. DARPA gave $1 million to finance the project, which will result in the fastest computer ever commissioned. The Defense Department will use it to simulate battles and natural disasters for training purposes.

The World Supercomputing Speed Record was set in December 1994 by a team of scientists from Sandia National Laboratories and Intel Corp., who linked together two of the largest Intel Paragon parallel-processing machines. The system achieved a performance of 281 gigaflops on the Linpack benchmark. The massively parallel supercomputer also achieved 328 gigaflops running a program used for radar signature calculations. The two-Paragon system used 6,768 processors working in parallel.

FASTEST CHIPS
The Deschutes Intel P6 microarchitecture processor is the fastest PC microchip available in retail stores. A 400Mhz version of this processor with a bus speed of 66 Mhz is already on the market, and the company plans to bring out a 450Mhz chip, which will have a bus speed of 100 Mhz. In September 1997, IBM's Research and Microelectronics divisions unveiled the world's first copper-based microchip. Copper had long been recognized as a superior electrical conductor, but because it proved difficult to adapt it to semiconductor manufacturing, aluminum was used instead. The development enabled the company to shrink electronic circuitry and fit more computer logic onto each microchip. The technology is called CMOS 7S and will be used to build higher performing microprocessors for computer systems. It will also enable manufacturers to make products that need less power and less cooling and integrate more complex functions than those available on the market today, as well as being smaller and lighter. In October 1997, IBM announced the first design tools and services to help electronics providers build products using the new microchip.

BIGGEST NUMBER CRUNCHED
In April 1997, it was announced that computer scientists at Purdue University in Indiana had coordinated researchers around the world to find the two largest numbers that, multiplied together, equal a known 167-digit number, $(3^{349}-1)\div 2$. The breakthrough came after 100,000 hours of computing time. The two factors had 80 digits and 87 digits. The previous factorization record was 162 digits long.

LONGEST COMPUTER COMPUTATION FOR A YES/NO ANSWER
The 20th Fermat number, $2^{2^{20}}+1$, was tested on a CRAY-2 supercomputer in 1986 to see if it was a prime number. After 10 days of calculation, the answer was no.

LARGEST PRIME NUMBER FOUND USING A COMPUTER
On January 27, 1998, 19-year-old student Roland Clarkson discovered the prime number $2^{3,021,377}-1$. This number, which is 909,526 digits long when written out in full, was traced using software written by George Woltman and Scott Kurowski. It is the 37th known Mersenne prime. Clarkson, one of several thousand volunteers contributing to the Great Internet Mersenne Prime Search (GIMPS), found the number on his ordinary 200 MHz Pentium desktop computer.

MOST POWERFUL COMPUTER IN SPACE
The lander of the Mars *Pathfinder* is controlled by an IBM RAD6000, a radiation-hardened single-board computer that is related to the PowerPC. It has a 32-bit architecture and can carry out 22 million instructions per second. It is used to store flight software, engineering and silence data and images, and data from the rover vehicle, in 128 Mb of memory. *Pathfinder* landed on Mars in July 1997.

MOST REMOTE COMPUTER
Carrying microprocessors to control its operations and communications, the *Voyager 1* space probe was estimated to be approximately 6.7 billion miles away from the Sun at the end of 1998 — 72.5 times the distance from Earth to the Sun and far too distant for scientists to communicate with it. *Voyager 1* was launched on September 5, 1977 and was used to collect data about Jupiter and Saturn. After it passed these planets, it was left to drift out of the solar system and into deep space.

MOST PROFITABLE COMPUTER COMPANY
The Microsoft Corporation was valued at $224 billion in April 1998 and has an annual revenue in excess of $17.6 billion. The corporation produces, manufactures, sells and licenses software and online services to computer users around the world. Its chairman, Bill Gates, who currently owns about 30% of Microsoft, founded the company with Paul Allen in 1975, and it has made him the richest man in the world.

BEST-SELLING SOFTWARE
Since its release on August 24, 1995, approximately 120 million copies of the Microsoft operating system *Windows 95* have been sold. *Windows 95* is bundled with 90% of the desktop computers that are sold around the world. Only sales of MS DOS, the basic operating system that is preinstalled on almost all desktop PCs, have outstripped sales of this software.

SMALLEST CALCULATOR
Scientists at IBM Research Division's Zürich Research Laboratory in Switzerland have designed a calculating device with a diameter of less than one millionth of a millimeter ($^{39}/_{10^8}$ in). The smallest hand-held computer is the Psion Series 5 handheld computer, which weighs 12 ounces including batteries. It has a touch-type keyboard and touch-sensitive screen.

BIGGEST LAWSUIT INVOLVING A COMPUTER COMPANY
On October 20, 1997, the Justice Department filed an antitrust lawsuit against Microsoft. It objected to the fact that Microsoft bundled its own Web browser, *Internet Explorer*, with *Windows 95* software. Microsoft maintained that it had acted within the law because *Internet Explorer* is a feature of *Windows 95* itself. Microsoft won the case in June 1998, clearing the way for the release of its new operating system, *Windows 98*.

BIGGEST COMPUTERIZED BROKERAGE
The Institutional Network of Instinet Corp. was purchased by Reuters in 1987 and became the world's largest computerized brokerage, with a 1996 volume of 100 million shares per day trading via its 54,000 terminals.

FASTEST COMPUTER IN USE
A 1,328-processor CRAY T3E-900TM built by Cray Research was found to be the fastest computer in use by weather researchers at the University of Oklahoma, who used it to run storm prediction software. It is one of a small number of installed systems that can perform more than 1 trillion operations a second. Seen here is a Scarmjet computation made by a Cray supercomputer.

robots

MOST ANIMATED ROBOTS
In 1993, Steven Spielberg's company Amblin Entertainment created the most animated robots ever, for the director's movie *Jurassic Park*. The nine dinosaur species — which included a *Tyrannosaurus rex*, dilophosaurs, velociraptors and a hatchling — were made of latex, foam rubber and urethane and had dilating pupils, twitching skin and saliva-moist mouths. To turn the complex machines into actors, a miniature version of each dinosaur was manipulated to capture the performance and relay it by computer to the dinosaur robots.

A team of Belgian and British scientists led by Dr. Vassilios of Belgium is experimenting with robot technology to create dinosaurs that lie dormant and spring into life when humans appear. Sensors built into the dinosaurs' eye sockets will allow them to watch and stalk people. The team is currently perfecting the first dinosaur, an 8-ft.-2½-in. iguanodon.

BIGGEST MOVIE ROBOT
In 1993, Amblin Entertainment created an 18-foot-tall, 40-foot-long, 9,000-pound robotic *Tyrannosaurus rex* for the movie *Jurassic Park*. The biggest robot ever made for a motion picture, it was the same size as the original dinosaur.

SMALLEST ROBOT
The light-sensitive "Monsieur" microbot, developed by the Seiko Epson Corporation, Japan in 1992, measures less than 1 cm^3 (3/50 cubic inch) and weighs 1.5 g (1/20 ounce). Made from 97 separate watch parts (equivalent to two ordinary watches), it can move at 2/5 inch per second for about five minutes when charged. It won a design award at the International Contest for Hill-Climbing Micromechanisms.

MOST POPULAR ROBOT
Puma (Programmable Universal Machine for Assembly), designed by Vic Schienman in the 1970s and manufactured by Swiss company Staubli Unimation, is the most commonly used robot in university laboratories and assembly lines.

FASTEST INDUSTRIAL ROBOT
In July 1997, Japanese company Fanuc developed the LR Mate 100I high-speed conveyance robot, the axis speed of which is estimated to be 79% faster than previous models. The robot can carry objects for up to 3 km (1 mile 1,513 yd.), and can move up and down 1 inch and back and forth 12 inches in a time of 0.58 seconds — 60% faster than previous models and an industry record.

MOST ADVANCED ROBOT TOY
In January 1998, Lego unveiled MindStorms: "intelligent" plastic building blocks that can be made into "thinking" robots and brought to life through a home computer. Developed over more than 10 years by Lego, together with Professor Papert of the Massachusetts Institute of Technology, the bricks contain a microchip and sensors.

CHEAPEST ROBOT
Walkman, a 5-inch robot, was built from the wreckage of a Sony Walkman for $1.75 at the Los Alamos National Laboratory in 1996. In tests, it struggled to get free when its legs were held, without being programmed to do so and without making the same movement twice.

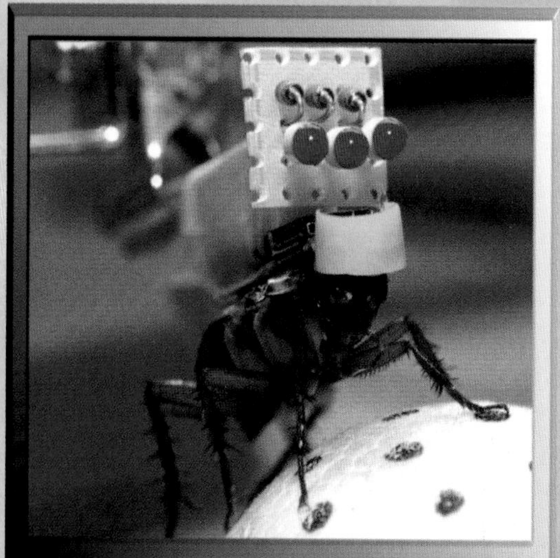

MOST BIOLOGICAL ROBOTS
In March 1998, scientists at Tsukuba and Tokyo universities, Japan created insect robots by fusing the antennae of silkmoths with wheeled robots containing electronic "brains." When the robots were lured by female moths, which secrete a sex attractant, microchips with neural networks similar to those of male moths directed the wheels of the robots towards the scent of the females. It is hoped that these prototype "cybugs," as they are known, will be of assistance in the destruction of locusts and similar pests in the future, as well as in the inspection of otherwise inaccessible areas. Japan is a major center for bio-robotics: a brown cockroach attached to a hi-tech "backpack" containing a microprocessor and electrode set is pictured here undergoing bio-robot trials in a research laboratory at Tokyo University in January 1997.

MOST AUTOMATED FACILITY
In March 1997, the Fanuc assembly plant in Yamanashi, Japan became the most automated facility in the world when a number of two-armed intelligent robots began to assemble mini-robots, resulting in a completely automated manufacturing system.

COUNTRY WITH GREATEST NUMBER OF INDUSTRIAL ROBOTS
Since 1991 approximately 325,000 robots have been installed in Japan – more than half of the 580,000 installed worldwide. For every 10,000 people employed in the Japanese manufacturing industry, there are now 265 robots in use.

BIGGEST PRODUCER OF COMMERCIAL ROBOTS
Formed in 1982, Japanese robot manufacturer Fanuc is the largest producer of commercial robots. Fanuc Robotics in the United States has more than 1,100 employees and 21,000 robots in service.

MOST DISTANT REMOTE CONTROL ON EARTH
The record for the greatest distance over which a robot has been controlled by remote control on Earth was set on July 31, 1997, when the *Nomad* robot completed a 133-mile-1,057-yd. journey over the Atacama Desert, Chile, driving 12 miles 753 yd. autonomously. It was operated from NASA's Ames Research Center in Moffett Field, California and Carnegie Mellon's Robotics Institute in Pittsburgh, Pennsylvania. The trek was part of a $1.6-million project preparing for missions to Antarctica, the Moon and Mars.

In November 1996, Professor Kevin Warwick used the Internet together with a 6-inch, 1-lb.-5-oz. robot at the cybernetics department of Reading University, England to program an identical robot at the State University of New York to move around its environment. Once they were switched on, the two robots required no remote control or human input.

MOST ADVANCED ROBOTIC ARM
In 1997, Barret Technology developed a $250,000 robotic arm with cables that act like tendons and can hold weights of 11 pounds in any position. The arm has a total of seven gearless arm and wrist joints, which are driven by brushless motors. It can throw a ball, and could also be developed for cleaning, assisting people in and out of the bathtub, opening doors and preparing meals.

MOST ADVANCED DOMESTIC ROBOT
On December 1, 1997, Electrolux unveiled a domestic robot that can clean efficiently without supervision. The miniature robot is equipped with an electronic brain and a navigational radar system that prevents it from bumping into obstacles. It is capable of cleaning up to 95% of an accessible area – this compares with an average of 75% for human beings. Although the Electrolux cannot climb stairs, it can clean an entire story of a house if the doors are left open.

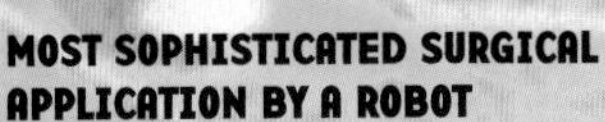

MOST SOPHISTICATED SURGICAL APPLICATION BY A ROBOT
In February 1998, Computer Motion of California unveiled *Zeus*, a robot that allows surgeons to perform heart bypasses through three incisions the width of pencils, using thin instruments that fit inside tubes in the patient's body. *Zeus* is designed to remove any shaking from the surgeon's hands. The company plans to produce a version that allows surgeons to operate over a high-speed telephone line.

MOST HUMANOID ROBOT
In 1997, Honda launched the 5-ft.-3-in. P3, seen here shaking the hand of former Chinese premier Li Peng. P3 can turn its head, step over obstacles, change direction and correct its balance if pushed, and has three-dimensional sight. Developed by 150 engineers over 11 years, at a total cost of $80 million, it could be used in nursing and for tasks that are too dangerous or strenuous for humans.

MOST DISTANT REMOTE CONTROL
In July 1997, NASA Jet Propulsion Laboratory's 2-lb.-1-oz., six-wheeled *Sojourner* rover landed on Mars. Remote-controlled from Earth, 238,854 miles away, it transmitted more than 500 images back to scientists. A new model is being developed for 2001: it will be bigger, travel farther, last a year on Mars, and store Martian surface materials for future pickup.

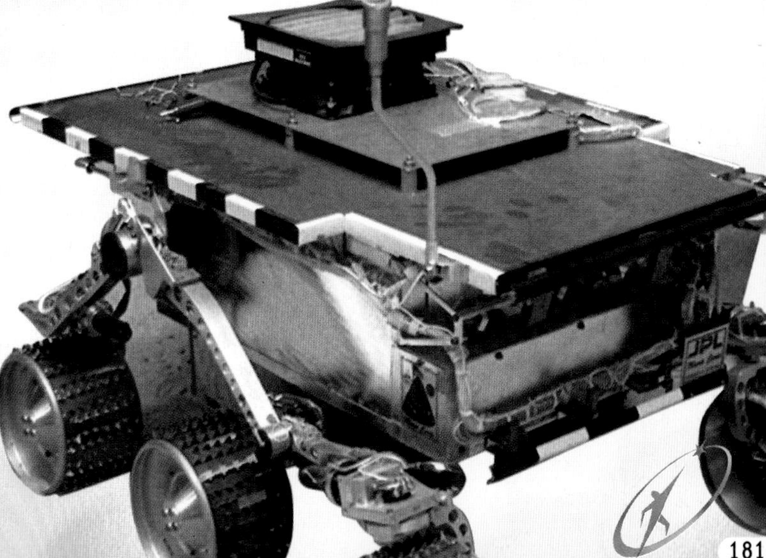

light, lasers and special effects

MOST POWERFUL TOUR LASERS
The British rock group Pink Floyd took a pair of 50-watt copper vapor lasers on their Division Bell tour, which ended in 1997. The green and red lasers, which cost a total of $400,000, were supplied by Oxford Lasers and are the most powerful and expensive lasers ever taken on a touring show.

MOST POWERFUL LASER BEAM
The world's most powerful laser beam is based at the White Sands missile base in New Mexico. The million-watt laser is driven by a rocket motor, which is fueled by a mixture of ethylene and nitrogen trifluoride. The laser beam itself is formed from microwaves at a wavelength of between 3.6 and 4.2 microns.

SMALLEST LASER
AT&T Bell Laboratories of Pasadena, California are the producers of the world's smallest laser. The laser is only 0.005 mm ($^1/_{5,000}$ in) in diameter and its reflecting disc is just 400 atoms thick. It is constructed from molecule-thick layers of indium gallium arsenide and phosphorus, over which a thin protective coatingis placed.

BRIGHTEST FLASH OF LIGHT ON EARTH
The brightest flash of light ever produced on Earth was created by research staff at the Rutherford Appleton Laboratory, Oxfordshire, England in 1996. It was produced using an ultraviolet laser called *Titania*, which has a beam that is 16$^1/_2$ inches in diameter and has a light intensity of 1,000 trillion watts, equivalent to 10 million trillion ordinary household light bulbs.

LONGEST BEAM OF ARTIFICIAL LIGHT
The longest beam of artificial light was fired by NASA scientists at a reflector placed on the Moon during the Apollo missions of the late 1960s and early 1970s. Astronauts positioned the reflector so that scientists on Earth could bounce a laser beam off it and get an accurate measurement of the distance from the Earth to the Moon (238,920 miles). On several occasions it took the scientists as many as 1,000 attempts to hit the target.

MOST POWERFUL SURFACE-TO-SPACE LASER WEAPON
The first test of a surface-to-space laser weapon occurred in October 1997. The weapon, a million-watt laser, was fired from the White Sands missile base in New Mexico and directed at a satellite that had been launched in May 1996. The satellite, which was orbiting 260 miles above the surface of Earth, was struck twice by the laser.

FASTEST LASER-POWERED SPACECRAFT
The world's fastest laser-powered spacecraft, which works by using laser beams to heat a jet of gases to extreme temperatures, was tested at White Sands missile base in November 1997. When the craft's lasers are used in conjunction with liquid hydrogen, it will be capable of speeds in excess of Mach 25 (17,000 mph).

MOST LASERS USED IN COMBAT
The greatest use of laser-guided weapons in a war zone occurred during the Gulf War on January 17, 1991. Millions of people around the world tuned in to watch live television coverage of lasers being used to guide missiles to their targets with pinpoint accuracy.

MOST MOTORISTS CAUGHT USING LASER SPEED DETECTION SYSTEM
Police in Hampshire, England set up a laser speed trap in a road construction zone on the M27 highway near Portsmouth over

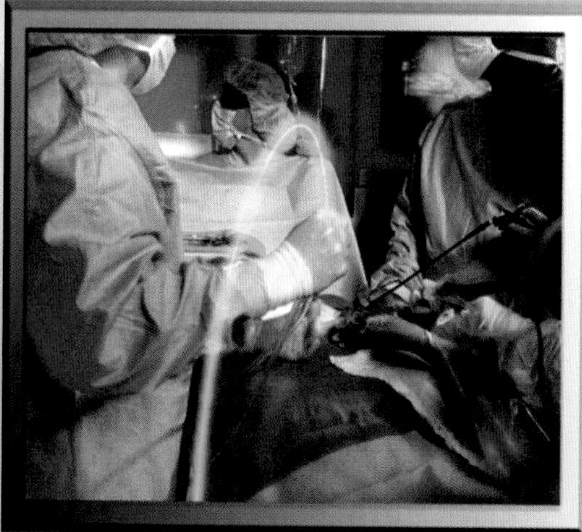

MOST SOPHISTICATED BONE-CUTTING LASER
The first practical bone-cutting laser was unveiled in 1995. Developed by surgeons at Hope Hospital, Manchester, England and physicists from the University of Manchester, it cuts through bone with precision, without damaging surrounding tissue. This makes it especially useful for brain surgeons, who need to remove the top of the skull without damaging the brain. In 1990, American Dental Technologies introduced the first dental laser, and in 1998 it unveiled an advanced laser instrument for treating ulcers and gum disease. Ophthalmologists first used high-tech laser surgery in the early 1990s. Called photorefractive keratectomy (PRK), it involves altering the eye's focusing mechanism by shaving the cornea with a laser beam. The operation stemmed from radial keratotomy (RK), corrective microsurgery first attempted in Japan in the 1950s. Slava Fyodorov, a professor of ophthalmology in Moscow, Russia, later perfected the technique. The first experiments in PRK were made at St. Thomas's Hospital, London, England and the University Eye Clinic, Berlin, Germany between 1984 and 1986.

a six-month period from December 1996 to May 1997. More than 1,900 motorists who exceeded the temporary 50-mph speed limit were caught by the laser trap, and speeding tickets with a total value of $105,000 were issued.

BIGGEST LASER PROJECTION SCREEN

The largest laser projection screen in the world is the ITV (Inflatable Tower Vision), which was built by Advanced Entertainment Technologies of California. The highly reflective inflatable nylon screen is more than 70 feet high and is supported by two inflatable cones, each 25 feet in diameter. The screen is capable of withstanding continuous wind speeds of up to 30 mph and has been seen by audiences at concerts all over the world.

MOST POWERFUL LIGHTING RIG

The most powerful lighting rig ever assembled, in terms of the amount of raw power that is needed to drive it, is generally agreed to be that used by the French rock star Johnny Halliday at the Zenith, Paris, France in December 1984. The rig drew so much power from the Paris grid that a new electricity sub-station had to be installed in order for the show to go ahead.

BIGGEST PRODUCER OF SPECIAL EFFECTS

The world's largest producer of digital special effects is Industrial Light And Magic, a division of Lucas Digital. The latter is owned by George Lucas, the director of *Star Wars* (1977). The film used spectacular computer-generated effects such as the animation of the Imperial Cruiser and the Millennium Falcon (above). The company has three times the computing power of its nearest rival and has created special effects for eight of the top 15 box office hits of all time, winning 14 Oscars and six Technical Achievement Awards along the way. The first computer-generated animation – the root of all computer-generated special effects – was created in the computer research department of the University of Utah in 1972. The animation sequence involved the recreation of a series of simple movements of a single human hand and took almost one year to produce. It laid the foundations for all subsequent computer generated special effects.

MOST POWERFUL LASER PULSE

The "Petawatt" laser at the Lawrence Livermore National Laboratory (LLNL) in California produces laser pulses of more than 1.3 quadrillion watts (1.3 petawatts) at peak power. This is more than 1,300 times the entire electrical capacity of the United States. The record was previously held by the "Nova" laser, pictured right, which is capable of generating 100 x 10^{12} watts and is also at the LLNL.

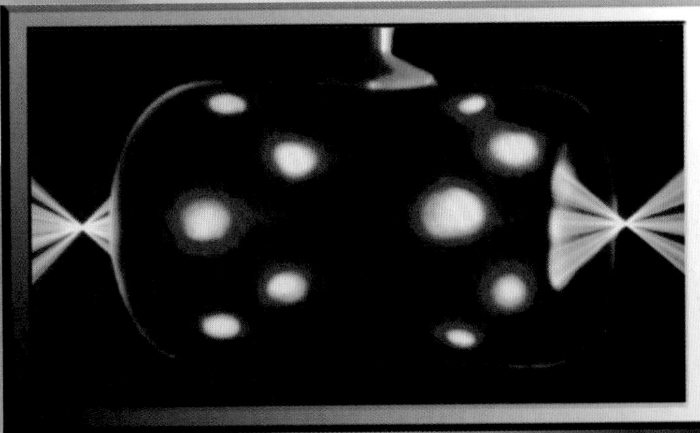

theme parks and rides

STRATOSPHERIC RIDES
The 135-story, 1,149-foot-tall Stratosphere Tower opened in Las Vegas, Nevada in April 1996 and features a host of white-knuckle attractions, including the *Let It Ride High Roller*. In May the ride was visited by 79 beauty queens, including Andrea Deak of Hungary (below left) and Miriam Ruppert of Germany (below right), who were enjoying the city's sights prior to the Miss Universe contest.

MOST EXPENSIVE THEME PARK DEVELOPMENT
Disney is reported to have spent approximately $1 billion on the design, development and realization of its Animal Kingdom in Florida. The kingdom features fantastic creatures, a safari complete with real animals and a number of rides and landscaped areas. The centerpiece of the attraction, which opened on April 22, 1998, is a Tree of Life visible from any part of the park's 500 acres.

BIGGEST THEME PARK
Disney World, near Orlando, Florida, covers 30,000 acres, making it the largest theme park in the world today. Opened on October 1, 1971, it cost approximately $400 million to develop.

MOST-VISITED THEME PARK
In 1997, Tokyo Disneyland in Japan attracted a total of 17.83 million visitors. Opened on April 15, 1983, the 114.2-acre theme park, which includes areas dedicated to the Wild West, tropical exploration, fairy tales, space travel and the future, can accommodate up to 85,000 visitors at once.

MOST FUTURISTIC PLANNED THEME PARK
Japanese construction company Obayashi plans to build a theme park in a crater on the moon by the year 2050. Lunar City will accommodate approximately 10,000 tourists from Earth. It is still on the drawing board, but Obayashi has already specified some of the attractions that might be offered. These include hang gliders and communal leisure center activities that will make the most of the moon's weak gravity.

THEME PARK WITH GREATEST NUMBER OF RIDES
Cedar Point in Ohio has a total of 56 different rides – the most of any theme park in the world today. They include classic wooden roller coasters such as *Blue Streak*, which was built in 1964, hair-raising state-of-the-art rides such as *Mantis*, built in 1996, and children's rides such as *Jr. Gemini*, built in 1978.

THEME PARK WITH GREATEST NUMBER OF ROLLER COASTERS
A record-breaking 12 roller coasters dominate the skyline at Cedar Point, Ohio, which has been nicknamed "America's Roller Coast" as a result. At its opening in 1892, the theme park had just one roller coaster, which shuttled riders around at a sedate 10 mph. Today, it has some of the tallest, fastest and most technically advanced coasters in the world. In the summer of 1997, approximately 16.8 million people rode roller coasters at Cedar Point.

FASTEST ROLLER COASTER
On January 4, 1996, *Superman The Escape*, a steel coaster installed at Six Flags Magic Mountain, California, became the world's first roller coaster to reach the psychologically significant speed of 100 mph. Riders sit in one of 15 aerodynamically-shaped cars and are accelerated to the maximum speed in a hair-raising seven seconds.

FASTEST STAND-UP ROLLER COASTER
The *Riddler's Revenge*, a steel stand-up coaster that went into service at Six Flags Magic Mountain, California on April 4, 1998, is 156 feet tall and has a top speed of 65 mph – the highest of any roller coaster in which the riders stand up.

BIGGEST THEME PARK WEDDINGS
On Valentine's Day 1997, 24 couples (including Matt Leddon and Melissa Williams, pictured far left) were married while hanging upside down aboard the *Montu* roller coaster at Busch Gardens in Tampa Bay, Florida, reciting their vows to Reverend Chris Null via headsets. The biggest ever theme park wedding took place on May 2, 1997, at the opening of *Giant Drop*, a 227-foot-high freefall tower at Six Flags Great America Gurnee, Illinois, when 144 couples were pronounced man and wife seconds before a three-second plummet towards the earth at a speed of 62 mph. Most of the wedding ceremony took place in the park's 3,200-seat stunt show arena. The couples then ascended the 22-story *Giant Drop*, where Reverend Herring completed the ceremony. The brides and grooms, who came from cities all over the United States, including Indianapolis, Grand Rapids, Milwaukee and Chicago, had been selected by radio stations to participate in the mass wedding.

It boasts six inversions (sections that turn the rider upside-down), including a 360° vertical loop with a record height of 124 feet.

HIGHEST ROLLER COASTER
With a difference of 415 feet between its peak and its base, *Superman The Escape* has the biggest drop of any roller coaster. Opened in the 25th anniversary year of Six Flags Magic Mountain, California, the ride is built on a mountainside within the park.

Fujiyama in Fujikyu Highland Park, Japan has a smaller drop than *Superman The Escape* but its tracks are raised by thousands of steel girders. With a maximum height of 239 feet, it is currently the world's tallest coaster.

TALLEST FREEFALL RIDE
The Power Tower, one of the newest rides at Cedar Point, Ohio, blasts riders 240 feet through the air at a speed of 50 mph. This attraction, which opened on May 10, 1998, is constructed around four 300-foot-high steel towers. Riders sit with their backs to these towers and with their legs dangling freely in the air.

COASTER GIVING MOST "AIRTIME"
In total, *Superman The Escape* propels riders out of their seats for a record 6.5 seconds. It begins by blasting them out of the Fortress of Solitude, a crystalline cavern. The riders experience weightlessness when they rocket to the peak of the ride, then descend backwards to its base.

LONGEST ROLLER COASTER
The Ultimate roller coaster in Lightwater Valley, North Yorkshire, England is 7,542 feet long, and the ride lasts for 5 min. 50 sec. The lift hill at the beginning of the ride is 1 mile 740 yd. long and takes riders 107 feet above the ground. Built in 1991, *The Ultimate* has steel tracks fixed to a wooden structure that winds its way through the countryside theme park.

ROLLER COASTERS WITH MOST INVERSIONS
The twisting steel coaster *Dragon Khan* takes riders upside-down eight times. The sit-down ride is the main attraction at Port Aventura, Salou, Spain. Built in 1995, the year the park opened, it has a top speed of 68 mph and a maximum height of 161 feet.

The *Monte Makaya* at Terra Encantada, Rio de Janeiro, Brazil also turns riders upside-down eight times during each complete circuit of its 2,793-ft.-4-in. steel track. Track elements include one Vertical Loop, two Cobra Rolls, a Double Corkscrew and three Zero-G-Heart Rolls.

BIGGEST DARK RIDE
Opened in August 1969, *The Haunted Mansion* in Disney World, Florida transports passengers on a journey through a dark house inhabited by 999 scary beings. Horror icon Vincent Price recites a suitably spooky poem and visitors are treated to an array of classic special effects as the action unfolds around them.

LARGEST PORTABLE THRILL RIDE
Taz's Texas Tornado has been in service at Six Flags Astroworld, Texas since March 14, 1998, but was originally assembled in Germany in 1986. The twisting steel coaster is 112 feet in total height and has a maximum speed of 60 mph. Its steepest turn is at an angle of 80°.

FIRST VERTICAL DROP RIDE
Oblivion, the world's first vertical drop ride at 87.5°, opened at Alton Towers in Staffordshire, England on March 14, 1998. The 1,222-foot ride lasts about two minutes and features a 68-mph, 180-foot drop into a pitch-black tunnel 100 feet underground. Passengers endure 4.5 *g* and on exiting the tunnel are propelled through a 90° turn. Around 5,500 bolts were used to build the ride.

space technology and rockets

HIGHEST SPEED

A speed of approximately 158,000 mph is recorded by the NASA–German *Helios A* and *Helios B* solar probes each time they reach perihelion (the point at which they are closest to the Sun) of their solar orbits.

FASTEST ESCAPE VELOCITY FROM EARTH

The ESA *Ulysses* spacecraft, powered by an IUS-PAM upper stage, achieved an escape velocity of 34,134 mph from Earth after deployment from the space shuttle *Discovery* on October 7, 1990. The craft was en route to an orbit around the poles of the Sun via a fly-by of Jupiter.

SMALLEST ROCKET

The smallest satellite launch vehicle in the world was *Pegasus*, a 49-ft.-3-in.-long three-stage booster. The original *Pegasus*, which has since been succeeded by an operational *Pegasus XL* version, was air-launched from an aircraft in 1990.

BIGGEST ROCKET

The US craft *Saturn 5* was the biggest ever rocket, at 363 feet in height with the *Apollo* spacecraft on top. It weighed 3,193 tons on the launch pad.

LARGEST SPACE TELESCOPE

The NASA Edwin P. Hubble Space Telescope weighs 12 tons and is 43 feet long, with a 7-ft.-10½-in. reflector. It was placed in orbit by a space shuttle on April 24, 1990. The telescope, which has made it possible to take photographs of space of an unprecedented quality, cost a total of $2.1 billion to construct.

MOST EXPENSIVE ROCKETS

The *Saturn 5* rocket was constructed for the *Apollo* moon landing program, which had cost approximately $25 billion by the time of the first flight to the Moon in July 1969.

Commercial customers were charged more than $120 million in total for launches to orbit communications satellites aboard the US commercial rocket *Titan*, which is no longer on the market.

MOST POWERFUL ROCKET ENGINE

Built in the former USSR by the Scientific Industrial Corporation of Power Engineering in 1980, the RD-170 has a thrust of 886 tons in open space and 814 tons at Earth's surface. It also has a turbopump rated at 190MW, and burns liquid oxygen and kerosene. It powered the four strap-on boosters of the *Energiya* booster, launched in 1987, but is now grounded due to cuts in Russia's space budget.

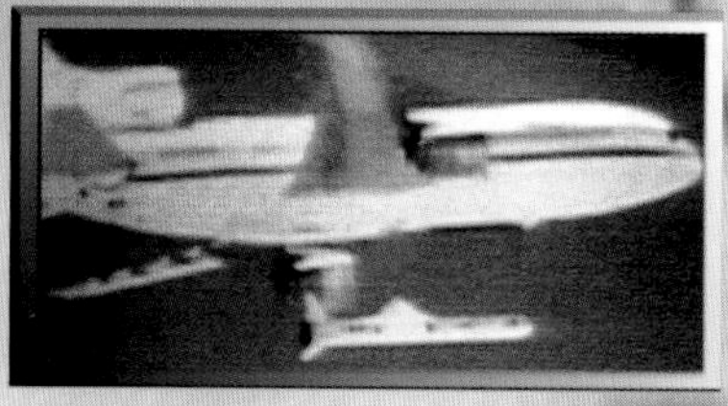

CHEAPEST SATELLITE LAUNCHER

The least expensive US satellite launcher is *Pegasus*, which was developed with a $45-million budget and costs approximately $10 million per launch. The rocket's inventor, Antonio Elias, is seen (top left) posing next to the craft in Spain in 1997. *Pegasus* was about to make history by playing a key role in the world's first ever space funeral. It took off from a Lockheed Tristar L-1011 at an altitude of 37,000 feet over the Canary Islands (bottom left) with the ashes of Timothy Leary, *Star Trek* creator Gene Roddenberry and 23 other people on board, each of whom had paid $4,800 for the space funeral. *Pegasus* represents one of the most important breakthroughs in space technology for many years because it has finally made it possible to get small satellites into orbit cheaply. A number of companies had already tried to develop small rockets that could get into space inexpensively, but without success.

MOST POWERFUL ROCKET

The NI booster, built by the former USSR, was launched from the Baikonur Cosmodrome at Tyuratam, Kazakhstan on February 21, 1969, and exploded 70 seconds after takeoff. Known as the G-1 in the West, it was the most powerful rocket of all time, with a thrust of 5,082 tons.

MOST INTELLIGENT ROCKET

The launch and flight of the space shuttle is computer-controlled and guided from nine minutes before liftoff to the craft's arrival in orbit eight minutes after launch.

MOST RELIABLE OPERATIONAL LAUNCH SYSTEMS
The space shuttle completed a total of 89 launches with one failure between April 1981 and January 1998, a 98% success rate.

The Russian *Soyuz U* series has flown a total of 781 times with 766 successes since 1973, twice recording 100 consecutive successful launches.

LEAST RELIABLE OPERATIONAL LAUNCH SYSTEM
The Russian-Ukrainian *Zenit* launcher has had 21 successful and seven failed missions since 1985, a success rate of 72%.

LARGEST ORBITING OBJECT
The largest ever object in the Earth's orbit was the Russian *Mir* space station, which docked with the space shuttle. Comprising the core, *Kvant 1* and *2*, *Kristall*, *Spektr* and *Priroda* modules, with docked *Soyuz* and *Progress* craft, it weighed more than 275 tons.

LARGEST OBJECT IN SPACE
The Italian Tethered Satellite was deployed for a distance of 12 miles from the space shuttle *STS 75 Columbia* on February 26, 1996 before the tether snapped. The satellite and the tether continued to orbit until March 19, 1996.

MOST EXPENSIVE SATELLITE
The US military communications satellite project *Milstar* has cost more than $40 billion. Two satellites have been launched, in 1994 and 1995.

SOYUZ ROCKETS
A Russian *Soyuz TM-22* rocket is pictured blasting away from the Baikonur Cosmodrome, Kazakhstan in 1995. The *Soyuz* rockets were first launched in manned flight in 1967, and since then have been major players in the Russian space program.

CHEAPEST SATELLITES
Several satellites as small as hat boxes have been built by universities and launched as "piggyback" payloads on commercial launches. They cost just $5 million to build and launch.

SATELLITES WITH LONGEST LIFE
The NASA Applications Technology Satellite *ATS 5*, which was launched on August 12, 1969, is still being used periodically for educational communications.

The US-European *International Ultraviolet Explorer*, which was launched in 1978 with an estimated operational lifetime of just three years, was shut down in 1996.

SMALLEST SATELLITE
The US satellite *Vanguard 1*, which was launched in March 1958, weighs 3 lb. 1 oz. In 1998, it was the oldest satellite still orbiting, although it is no longer operational.

BIGGEST SPACE LABORATORY
The biggest single research lab ever to have been launched is the US *Skylab*, which is 82 feet long and weighs approximately 59,000 pounds. Launched in 1973, *Skylab* also became the largest piece of space debris after it was abandoned in 1974. The laboratory reentered Earth's atmosphere in 1979.

CLOSEST APPROACH TO THE SUN BY A ROCKET
The research spacecraft *Helios B* came within a record 27 million miles of the Sun on April 16, 1976. It was carrying instrumentation belonging to the United States and West Germany.

REMOTEST MANMADE OBJECT
Voyager 1, which was launched from Cape Canaveral, Florida on September 5, 1977, was 6.5 billion miles away from the Earth on February 15, 1998, making it the remotest manmade object ever. The spacecraft's forerunner, *Pioneer 10*, became the first ever craft to leave the solar system on October 17, 1986, when it crossed the orbit of Pluto at a distance of 3.67 billion miles. *Pioneer 10* carries a plaque with messages from the Earth to any distant civilization that may find it. *Pioneer 11* and *Voyager 2* will follow these craft into interstellar space.

EXPERIMENTAL ROCKETS
The *Delta Blipper*, an experimental rocket, is seen here lifting off at White Sands Missile Range, New Mexico, in 1993. The rocket is a precursor to the *X-33*, which is being developed as a potential predecessor to a Reusable Launch Vehicle. It is hoped by New Mexico Spaceport planners that the latter will replace the space shuttle at some point in the future.

space exploration

MOST TELEVISED EVENT IN SPACE
The first moonwalk by the *Apollo 11* astronauts in July 1969 was watched on TV by an estimated 600 million people (around one-fifth of the world's population at that time).

BIGGEST SPACE BUDGET
The US manned space program is estimated to have cost more than $100 billion to the end of 1997.

REMOTEST MANMADE OBJECT
Pioneer 10, launched from Cape Canaveral on March 2, 1972, was 6.39 billion miles from Earth in July 1997. The *Pioneer* mission formally ended on March 31, 1997, but the spacecraft will continue to travel indefinitely toward the constellation Taurus.

LARGEST SPACE FUNERAL
The ashes of 24 space pioneers and enthusiasts, including the creator of *Star Trek*, Gene Roddenberry, were sent into orbit in April 1997 on board Spain's *Pegasus* rocket, at a cost of $5,000 each. Held in lipstick-sized capsules inscribed with a name and message, they will stay in orbit for 18 months to 10 years.

FURTHEST FINAL RESTING PLACE
In January 1998, one ounce of Dr. Eugene Shoemaker's ashes were launched aboard NASA's *Lunar Prospector* as it set out on a one-year mapping mission above the Moon's surface. When its power fails after about 18 months, the craft will crash to the Moon's surface with Shoemaker's remains. The scientist had said that not going to the Moon was his greatest disappointment.

MOST SPACE DEBRIS
On January 31, 1998, there were a record 2,516 payloads in orbit, along with 6,172 pieces of trackable debris.

MOST DEBRIS CREATED BY A SINGLE LAUNCH
A *Pegasus* rocket that was launched in 1994 exploded in June 1996. To date, about 700 pieces of its upper stage have been tracked.

LARGEST PIECES OF DEBRIS
Spent rocket stages form the largest pieces of space debris. A *Delta 2* third stage, for example, is 6 ft. 8 in. long and 4 ft. 1 in. in diameter.

LONGEST SPACEFLIGHTS
Russian doctor Valeriy Poliyakov was launched to the Russian *Mir 1* space station aboard *Soyuz TM15* on January 8, 1994 and landed aboard *Soyuz TM20* on March 22, 1995, after a spaceflight lasting 437 days 17 hr. 58 min. 16 sec.

The longest spaceflight by a woman was 188 days 5 hr., by Shannon Lucid (US). She was launched to the *Mir 1* space station aboard the space shuttle *STS 76 Atlantis* on March 22, 1996 and landed aboard *STS 79 Atlantis* on September 26, 1996.

SHORTEST SPACEFLIGHT
The shortest ever manned spaceflight was made by Cdr. Alan Shepard (US) aboard *Mercury-Redstone 3* on May 5, 1961. The suborbital mission lasted 15 min. 28 sec.

LONGEST LUNAR MISSION
The crew of *Apollo 17* (Capt. Eugene Cernan and Dr. Harrison Schmitt) were on the lunar surface for a record 74 hr.

LARGEST SPACE STATION CREW
The Russian *Mir* space station, launched in 1986, is shown as photographed above Africa by a shuttle crew. On June 29, 1995, a record 10 people (four Russians and six Americans) were aboard the station .

LARGEST SHUTTLE CREW
The largest crew on a single space mission was eight, commanded by Hank Hartsfield, aboard *61A Challenger*, the 22nd shuttle flight, on October 30, 1985.

59 min. during a lunar mission lasting 12 days 13 hr. 51 min. (December 7–19, 1972).

LONGEST SHUTTLE FLIGHT
Columbia's 21st mission, *STS 80*, began on November 19, 1996 and lasted 17 days 15 hr. 53 min. 26 sec. (to main gear shutdown).

MOST EXPERIENCED TRAVELER
Valeriy Poliyakov clocked up 678 days 16 hr. 33 min. 16 sec. during two space missions.

MOST SPACE JOURNEYS
Three astronauts have made six space flights each: Franklin Chang-Diaz (US), between 1986 and 1998; Story Musgrave (US), between 1983 and 1996; and Capt. John Young (US), between 1965 and 1983.

MOST PEOPLE IN SPACE AT ONCE
From March 18, 1995, a record 13 people were in space at the same time: seven Americans aboard the space shuttle *STS 67 Endeavour*, three CIS cosmonauts aboard the *Mir* space station and two cosmonauts and a US astronaut on *Soyuz TM21.*

MOST NATIONALITIES IN SPACE
Five countries had astronauts or cosmonauts in space on July 31, 1992: four Russian cosmonauts and one Frenchman were aboard *Mir*, and one Swiss, one Italian and five US astronauts were on *STS 46 Atlantis*.

On February 22, 1996, there were one Swiss, four US and two Italian astronauts on *STS 75 Columbia* and one German and

four Russian cosmonauts on board the *Mir* space station.

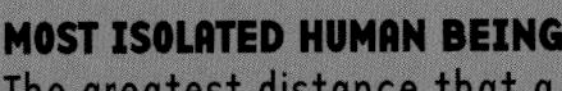

MOST ISOLATED HUMAN BEING
The greatest distance that a person has ever been from a fellow human being is 2,234 miles 1,330 yd. This was experienced by command module pilot Alfred Worden during the US *Apollo 15* lunar mission, which lasted from July 30 to August 1, 1971. David Scott and Jim Irwin were at Hadley Base exploring the Moon's surface.

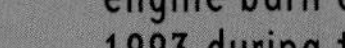

GREATEST ALTITUDES ATTAINED
The crew of *Apollo 13* (Capt. Jim Lovell Jr., Fred Haise Jr. and John Swigert) were a record 158 miles away from the Moon's surface and 248,655 miles above Earth's surface on April 15, 1970.

Kathryn Thornton (US) attained an altitude of 375 miles – the record for a woman – after an orbital engine burn on December 10, 1993 during the *STS 61 Endeavour* mission.

FASTEST SPEED ATTAINED
The top speed at which a human being has ever traveled is a record 24,791 mph, achieved by the command module of *Apollo 10* (which comprised Col. Thomas Stafford, Cdr. Eugene Cernan and Cdr. John Young) at the $75^{7}/_{10}$-mile altitude interface on its trans-Earth return flight in May 1969.

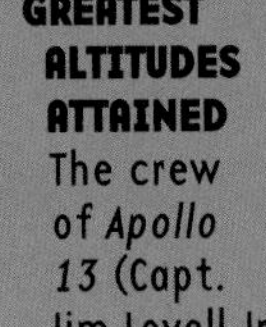

HIGHEST SPEED
The highest speed by a woman is 17,864 mph, by Kathryn Sullivan (US) at the start of reentry during the *STS 31 Discovery* shuttle mission on April 29, 1990. Kathryn Thornton may have exceeded this at the end of *STS 61 Endeavour* on December 13, 1993.

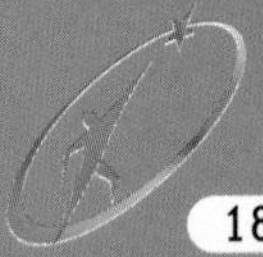

war
& disaster

war

BLOODIEST SIEGE
About 1.3–1.5 million defenders and citizens are estimated to have died in the 880-day siege of Leningrad, USSR (now St. Petersburg, Russia) by the German Army from 1941 to 1944. More than 150,000 shells and 100,000 bombs were dropped on the city. Pictured left is a World War II Russian army recruitment poster.

MOST EXPENSIVE WAR
The material cost of World War II has been estimated at $1.5 trillion – far in excess of all other wars put together.

MOST TELEVISED WAR
In terms of transmission hours, the Vietnam War is likely to remain the most televised war in history for many decades to come. In 1965, NBC screened *Actions of a Vietnamese Marine Battalion*, showing shocking action sequences, and as its ratings rocketed, CBS, ABC and foreign broadcasters rushed to put camera teams into Vietnam. It is estimated that the three major networks and their subsidiaries devoted about 10,000 hours of prime viewing time to coverage of the war between 1965 and 1975.

The collapse of Yugoslavia and associated conflicts between 1991 and 1996 eclipse Vietnam in density of TV coverage because by then it was easy for freelance journalists to travel with their own equipment and satellite dishes. During the five years of conflict, they shot and recorded millions of hours of footage, of which only a tiny percentage has been broadcast.

BIGGEST ASSAULT ON THE ENVIRONMENT DURING WAR
In January 1991, Iraqi dictator Saddam Hussein gave the order for crude Gulf oil to be pumped from Kuwait's Sea Island terminal and from seven large oil tankers. Provisional estimates put the loss at 896,000 tons. During the same campaign, Iraqi forces set fire to 600 oil wells, creating clouds of black smoke up to 7,000 feet high, enveloping warships 50 miles offshore and depositing soot as far away as the Himalayas. The last blazing well was extinguished on November 6, 1991.

MOST DEATHS CAUSED BY CHEMICAL WEAPONS IN ONE WAR
Exact figures for those wounded and killed by chemical weapons in World War I between January 1915 and November 1918 are unreliable, but at least 100,000 died and 900,000 were injured. The Russian army, equipped with inadequate respirators, sustained 56,000 fatalities and 475,000 casualties.

BIGGEST MASSACRE
The largest massacre on record took place in Nanking, China, between December 13, 1937 and the end of January 1938, when Japanese troops overran the city, which was the Nationalist Chinese capital. Estimates of the death toll vary from 20,000 by the Japanese government to 300,000 by some US and Chinese experts.

BLOODIEST MODERN BATTLES
The 142-day Battle of the Somme, which took place in northern France in 1916, is estimated to have resulted in more than 1.22 million deaths and casualties.

The losses of the German Army Group Center on the Eastern Front between June 22 and July 8, 1944 totaled 350,000 men.

The highest death toll in a battle was an estimated 1.11 million, in the Battle of Stalingrad, which ended when German forces surrendered on January 31, 1943. Only 1,515 civilians from a pre-war population of more than 500,000 survived the battle.

The final drive on Berlin by the Soviet Army and the ensuing battle for the city from April 16 to May 2, 1945 involved 3.5 million men, 52,000 guns and mortars, 7,750 tanks and 11,000 aircraft on both sides.

BLOODIEST WARS
The costliest war in terms of human life was World War II, in which the number of fatalities, including battle deaths and civilians of all countries, is an estimated 56.4 million. In Poland, 6,028,000 people were killed – 17.2% of the pre-war population.

In Paraguay's war against Brazil, Argentina and Uruguay from 1864 to 1870, Paraguay's population was reduced from 407,000 to 221,000, of whom fewer than 30,000 were adult males.

BIGGEST EVACUATION
Between May 26 and June 4, 1940, 1,200 allied craft evacuated 338,226 British and French troops from the beachhead at Dunkerque, France.

BIGGEST CIVILIAN EVACUATION
Following the Iraqi invasion of Kuwait in 1990, Air India evacuated 111,711 Indians on 488 flights over two months starting on August 13.

BIGGEST MASS SUICIDE IN WAR
About 7,000 Japanese troops committed suicide – many by

PRECISION BOMBING
High-tech bombs changed the face of warfare during the Gulf War against Iraq, and precision bombing, which was used extensively by the allied nations during their liberation of Kuwait, allowed aerial weapons to be delivered with an accuracy that exceeded all expectations. In a videotape shown to President George Bush during Operation Desert Storm, bombs exploded with pinpoint accuracy through the front door of an Iraqi Scud missile warehouse in Kuwait and into the air shaft of a building used by Iraqi president Saddam Hussein. The bombs, with names like Rockeye II Mk cluster bomb, ISCB-1 Area Denial cluster weapon and the Paveway laser-guided bomb, could be sent to the target at the press of a button, and some of the "smart" bombs could be programmed to explode their 160 "bomblets" over 24 hours to keep Iraqis from venturing within a 54-square-foot area around a target. Others had time fuses to delay the explosion. Precision-guided weapons were said to have virtually eliminated the traditional military stance, which required a 3-to-1 advantage in troop numbers before an attack could be launched.

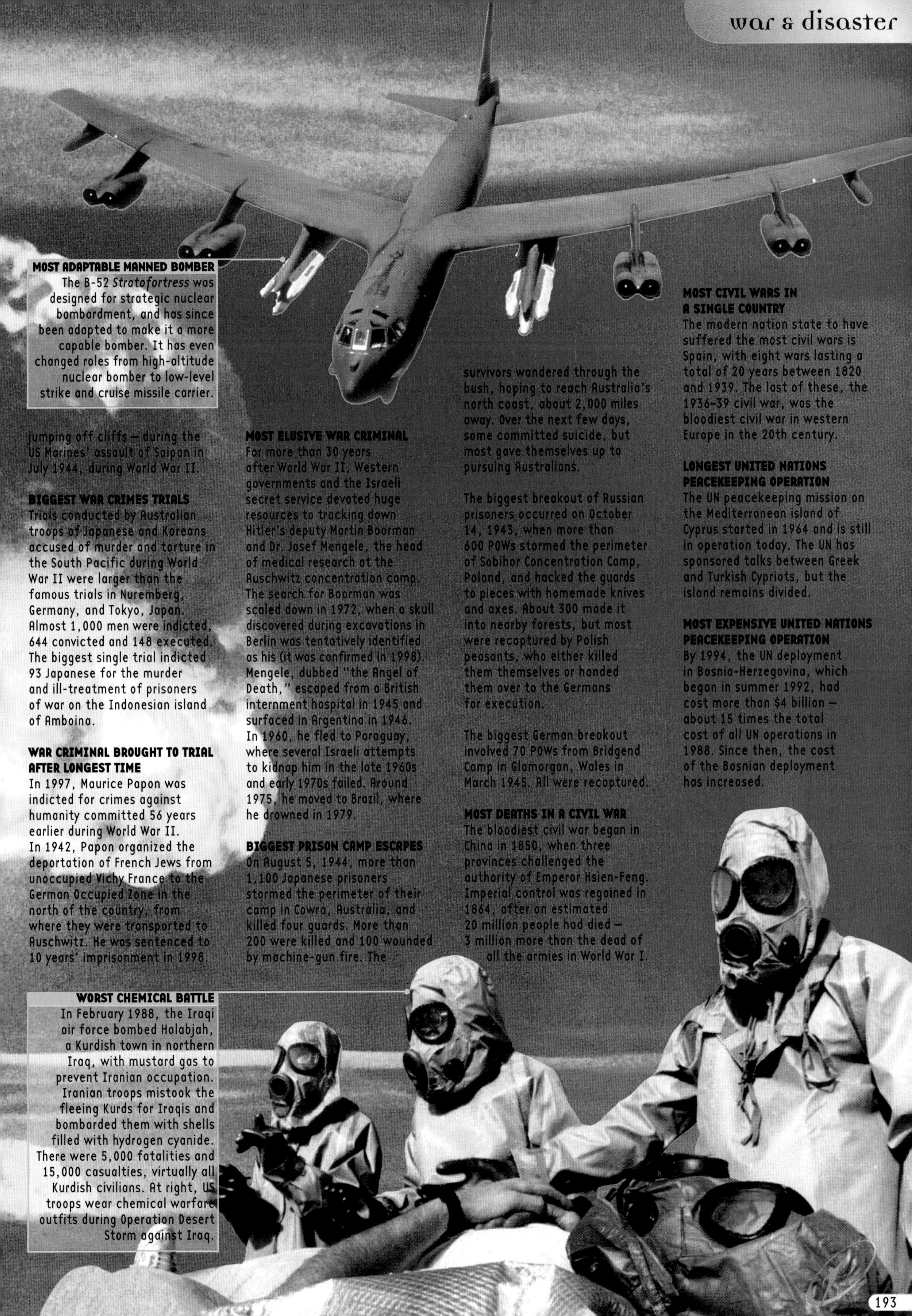

MOST ADAPTABLE MANNED BOMBER
The B-52 *Stratofortress* was designed for strategic nuclear bombardment, and has since been adapted to make it a more capable bomber. It has even changed roles from high-altitude nuclear bomber to low-level strike and cruise missile carrier.

jumping off cliffs – during the US Marines' assault of Saipan in July 1944, during World War II.

BIGGEST WAR CRIMES TRIALS
Trials conducted by Australian troops of Japanese and Koreans accused of murder and torture in the South Pacific during World War II were larger than the famous trials in Nuremberg, Germany, and Tokyo, Japan. Almost 1,000 men were indicted, 644 convicted and 148 executed. The biggest single trial indicted 93 Japanese for the murder and ill-treatment of prisoners of war on the Indonesian island of Amboina.

WAR CRIMINAL BROUGHT TO TRIAL AFTER LONGEST TIME
In 1997, Maurice Papon was indicted for crimes against humanity committed 56 years earlier during World War II. In 1942, Papon organized the deportation of French Jews from unoccupied Vichy France to the German Occupied Zone in the north of the country, from where they were transported to Auschwitz. He was sentenced to 10 years' imprisonment in 1998.

MOST ELUSIVE WAR CRIMINAL
For more than 30 years after World War II, Western governments and the Israeli secret service devoted huge resources to tracking down Hitler's deputy Martin Boorman and Dr. Josef Mengele, the head of medical research at the Auschwitz concentration camp. The search for Boorman was scaled down in 1972, when a skull discovered during excavations in Berlin was tentatively identified as his (it was confirmed in 1998). Mengele, dubbed "the Angel of Death," escaped from a British internment hospital in 1945 and surfaced in Argentina in 1946. In 1960, he fled to Paraguay, where several Israeli attempts to kidnap him in the late 1960s and early 1970s failed. Around 1975, he moved to Brazil, where he drowned in 1979.

BIGGEST PRISON CAMP ESCAPES
On August 5, 1944, more than 1,100 Japanese prisoners stormed the perimeter of their camp in Cowra, Australia, and killed four guards. More than 200 were killed and 100 wounded by machine-gun fire. The survivors wandered through the bush, hoping to reach Australia's north coast, about 2,000 miles away. Over the next few days, some committed suicide, but most gave themselves up to pursuing Australians.

The biggest breakout of Russian prisoners occurred on October 14, 1943, when more than 600 POWs stormed the perimeter of Sobihor Concentration Camp, Poland, and hacked the guards to pieces with homemade knives and axes. About 300 made it into nearby forests, but most were recaptured by Polish peasants, who either killed them themselves or handed them over to the Germans for execution.

The biggest German breakout involved 70 POWs from Bridgend Camp in Glamorgan, Wales in March 1945. All were recaptured.

MOST DEATHS IN A CIVIL WAR
The bloodiest civil war began in China in 1850, when three provinces challenged the authority of Emperor Hsien-Feng. Imperial control was regained in 1864, after an estimated 20 million people had died – 3 million more than the dead of all the armies in World War I.

MOST CIVIL WARS IN A SINGLE COUNTRY
The modern nation state to have suffered the most civil wars is Spain, with eight wars lasting a total of 20 years between 1820 and 1939. The last of these, the 1936–39 civil war, was the bloodiest civil war in western Europe in the 20th century.

LONGEST UNITED NATIONS PEACEKEEPING OPERATION
The UN peacekeeping mission on the Mediterranean island of Cyprus started in 1964 and is still in operation today. The UN has sponsored talks between Greek and Turkish Cypriots, but the island remains divided.

MOST EXPENSIVE UNITED NATIONS PEACEKEEPING OPERATION
By 1994, the UN deployment in Bosnia-Herzegovina, which began in summer 1992, had cost more than $4 billion – about 15 times the total cost of all UN operations in 1988. Since then, the cost of the Bosnian deployment has increased.

WORST CHEMICAL BATTLE
In February 1988, the Iraqi air force bombed Halabjah, a Kurdish town in northern Iraq, with mustard gas to prevent Iranian occupation. Iranian troops mistook the fleeing Kurds for Iraqis and bombarded them with shells filled with hydrogen cyanide. There were 5,000 fatalities and 15,000 casualties, virtually all Kurdish civilians. At right, US troops wear chemical warfare outfits during Operation Desert Storm against Iraq.

killing machines

BIGGEST UNMANNED AIR VEHICLE
The biggest unmanned aerial vehicle under construction is the Global Hawk, which was unveiled at Teledyne Ryan Aeronautical in San Diego, California on February 20, 1997. The aircraft, which has a 116-foot wingspan and a 14,000-mile range, will be used for aerial reconnaissance.

BIGGEST NUCLEAR WEAPONS
The most powerful ICBM (intercontinental ballistic missile) is the former USSR's SS-18 (Model 5), which is thought to be armed with 10,750-kiloton MIRVs (multiple independently targetable reentry vehicles). SS-18 ICBMs are located in Russia and Kazakhstan, although the dismantling of those in Kazakhstan has begun. START 2 (Strategic Arms Reduction Talks 2) requires the elimination of all SS-18s and other ICBMs with more than one warhead.

MOST POWERFUL THERMONUCLEAR DEVICE
A thermonuclear device with a power equivalent to that of c. 57 megatons of TNT was detonated by the former USSR in the Novaya Zemlya area in October 1961. The shockwave circled the world three times, with the first circuit taking 36 hr. 27 min. Some estimates put the power of the device at 62–90 megatons.

MOST PEOPLE KILLED IN A SINGLE CHEMICAL WARFARE ATTACK
In March 1988, an estimated 4,000 people were killed when Saddam Hussein used chemical weapons against Iraq's Kurdish minority in retaliation for its support of Iran in the Iran–Iraq War.

MOST PEOPLE KILLED BY A BOMB
The atomic bomb dropped on Hiroshima, Japan, by the US on August 6, 1945 instantly killed more than 100,000 people. A further 55,000 people died of radiation sickness within one year.

LONGEST-RANGE ATTACKS
In January 1991, seven B-52G bombers took off from Barksdale Air Force Base, Louisiana to deliver cruise missiles against Iraq just after the start of the Gulf War. Each flew 14,000 miles, refueling four times in the 35-hour round-trip. In September 1996, B-52s flew nonstop from Guam in the central Pacific to launch cruise missiles around Baghdad, Iraq.

MOST ADVANCED HELICOPTER
The Russian *Ka-52 Alligator* is one of the world's most advanced helicopters. It is a two-seat derivative of the *Ka-50 Black Shark*. The helicopter is intended primarily as a gunship and is equipped with a wide range of weapons, as well as devices that allow it to fly missions in extreme weather conditions.

MISSILES WITH GREATEST RANGE
The US *Atlas* missile entered service in 1959 and had a range of 10,360 miles – about 3,000 miles more than was necessary to hit any point in Soviet territory from launch sites in the West. The longest-range Russian missile is the SS-18, codenamed "Satan," which entered service in the early 1980s and has a range of 7,500 miles.

MOST ACCURATE HAND-PORTABLE ANTI-AIRCRAFT MISSILE
In the early 1980s, the US introduced the *Stinger*, a 5-foot-long, 22-pound missile with a range of about 3 miles and a speed of about 1,300 mph. The *Stinger's* cryogenically cooled infrared seeker distinguishes between an aircraft's infrared signature and countermeasures such as flares. It was first used by the British against Argentina in the Falklands War and by the Mujahedeen in Afghanistan.

MOST FUTURISTIC COMBAT SHIP
In October 1996, Vosper Thornycroft of Southampton, England unveiled its design for the *Sea Wraith* corvette, a combat ship designed for patrolling regional waters, with the ability to hide and deceive the enemy. The latest in stealth technology, it uses similar principles to the radar-beating technology developed by the US aircraft industry and used in the 1991 Gulf War against Iraq. The vessel is covered with materials designed to deflect signals, making the corvette difficult to track or target on radar. Its mast, radar dishes and aerials are located inside flat-sided towers to make it hard for radar to lock on. To conceal itself and its exhaust, the ship sprays a mist of water when countering infrared missiles. The ship has state-of-the-art weapons and communications systems, and its own signals are adjustable down to 1 watt of radiated energy. The first *Sea Wraith*, which has accommodation for 105 crew, will be operational in the 2000s.

MOST ADVANCED FIGHTER PLANE
The US *F22 Raptor* was developed by Lockheed Martin Aeronautical Systems, Lockheed Martin Fort Worth and Boeing in the late 1990s. Even before it went into production, it had starred in a computer game called *F-22* by Microprose (pictured below). It cost around $13.3 billion, twice as much as its European counterpart, the *Eurofighter*. It has a length of 62 ft. 1 in. and a wingspan of 44 ft. 6 in.

In the early 1990s, the US Army took delivery of the *Stinger* POST (Passive Optical Seeker Technology), which is flown to target by a programmable microprocessor. The missile can "think", and once it locks on, there is little the pilot of the target aircraft can do, other than outfly the missile, or eject.

MOST POWERFUL TORPEDO
The Russian Type 65, a 26-inch torpedo, carries a warhead of one ton of conventional explosive or a 15-kiloton nuclear warhead – slightly less explosive power than the bombs that destroyed Hiroshima and Nagasaki. It can home in acoustically on the turbulence left by the wake of a ship more than 50 miles away and can close at more than 50 knots – far in excess of the speed of the fastest surface ships.

FASTEST-FIRING MACHINE GUN
Designed for use in helicopters and armored vehicles in the late 1960s, the 7.62-mm ($^3/_{10}$-in) M 134 Minigun is the fastest-firing machine gun. Based on the multiple-barrel Gatling design, it has six barrels turned by an electric motor and fed by a 4,000-round link belt – a configuration that allows a rate of fire of 6,000 rounds per minute (about 10 times that of an ordinary machine gun).

MOST FUTURISTIC WEAPON
Developed for the "Star Wars" defense program, the electromagnetic railgun may revolutionize war on Earth. If power problems are overcome, the gun will combine the capabilities of the anti-tank and anti-aircraft gun with the machine gun. Aircraft and tanks will be ripped to pieces by a stream of small high-velocity projectiles. The bullet speed that the railgun may be capable of will require millions of kilowatts of power, at present only possible if it were linked to a high-capacity power station.

MOST REVOLUTIONARY RIFLE
In the first months of World War II, German weapons analysts began developing the *Sturmgewehr* (assault rifle), a fully automatic rifle with a level of accuracy of up to 300 yards, the distance at which most actions were fought. A light bullet in a short cartridge case meant a magazine could hold 30 rather than the usual 10 rounds. Introduced in 1943, its influence was profound: by the 1970s, virtually every army in the world was using a small arm derived from the German model.

MOST EMBARRASSING TECHNICAL FAILURE
First used in Operation Just Cause in Panama in 1989, the F117A Stealth Fighter played a key role in the penetration of Iraqi air defenses in the 1991 Gulf War. Its success depends on its radar signature, which has been much reduced by an angled fuselage and wings and by black ferrite paint that absorbs radar radiation. However, in 1997, the Pentagon reported that the paint was unstable and washed off in rain showers, making the plane visible and vulnerable because of its low speed (800 mph) and poor maneuverability.

FASTEST BOMBERS
The US variable-geometry or "swing-wing" General Dynamics FB-111A has a maximum speed of Mach 2.5, and the Russian "swing-wing" Tupolev Tu-22M, known to NATO as "Backfire," has an estimated over-target speed of Mach 2.0 but could be as fast as Mach 2.5.

FASTEST COMBAT JET
The world's fastest ever combat jet is the former Soviet Mikoyan MiG-25 fighter, the NATO codename for which is "Foxbat." The single-seat "Foxbat-A" has a wingspan of 45 ft. 9 in., is 78 ft. 2 in. long and has an estimated maximum takeoff weight of 41 tons. The reconnaissance "Foxbat-B" has been tracked by radar at about Mach 3.2 (2,110 mph).

FASTEST WARSHIP
On January 25, 1980, the 78-foot-long, 110-ton test vehicle SES-100B, a US Navy hovercraft, reached a record speed of 91.9 knots (105.4 mph).

FASTEST DESTROYER
The record for the highest speed ever attained by a destroyer is 45.25 knots (51.72 mph), by the 3,576-ton French ship *Le Terrible* in 1935. Built in Blainville, France and powered by four Yarrow small tube boilers and two Rateau geared turbines giving 100,000 shaft horsepower, the destroyer was decommissioned at the end of 1957.

SMART WEAPONS
The AGM-130 is one of a new generation of "smart" weapons being developed to destroy the chemical and biological weapons that Iraqi dictator Saddam Hussein is suspected of hiding in reinforced bunkers. Here, Frank Robbins, director of the US Air Force's Precision Strike System Program Office, stands behind an AGM-130 missile at Eglin Air Force Base, Florida in early 1998.

spying

LONGEST SPY TUNNEL
In 1955, the CIA and MI6 dug the 1,476-foot Berlin Tunnel into East Berlin to monitor Soviet and East German voice and telegraphic communications on tapped underground cables. Codenamed "Operation Gold," it was the most successful eavesdropping operation: 443,000 conversations were recorded and transcribed, and more than 50,000 reels of magnetic tape were used prior to the tunnel's discovery on April 22, 1956, following a tipoff from a KGB mole inside MI6. In November 1989, the Berlin Wall (above) came down, signaling the end of the Cold War. The wall had divided East and West Berlin since 1961.

HIGHEST-PAID SPY
KGB spy Aldrich Ames, who was a mole in the CIA for nine years, was the highest-paid spy ever. The KGB paid him $2.7 million in cash, and promised him a further $1.9 million. Ames' lavish lifestyle and free spending contributed to his discovery and arrest in 1994.

MOST EFFECTIVE SPY FAMILY
John Walker Jr. joined the KGB in 1968 and eventually recruited his brother, son and best friend. His network inflicted more strategic damage on the United States than any other spy ring. Walker was arrested in 1985 after his ex-wife tipped off the FBI.

BIGGEST SECRET STOLEN BY A SPY IN THE 20TH CENTURY
Soviet spies penetrated the US atomic program (codenamed "Manhattan Project") during World War II, and continued spying after the war. Their success allowed Soviet scientists to detonate their own nuclear weapon in August 1949.

LOWEST PRICE PAID FOR TOP SECRET MESSAGES
The KGB paid spy John Walker Jr. an estimated $1 million in total, from 1968 to his arrest on May 20, 1985, for cipher secrets that allowed the KGB to decipher over a million secret messages — roughly $1 per secret.

MOST EFFECTIVE "TRUTH SERUM"
During the Cold War, a cocktail of sodium pentothal, scopolamine, thiamin, sodium luminal, atropine sulfate and caffeine sulfate was used to create an alcohol-like disinhibition of normal behavioral restraints such as lying or deceit.

MOST EFFECTIVE SPY-TRACKING SUBSTANCE
During the Cold War, a synthesized scent of a German shepherd bitch in heat was made by East Germany's Ministry for State Security (STASI) and applied to a target's shoes or bicycle tires. Trained male German shepherds could then track the target for up to three days.

MOST OVERRATED SPY
Margaretha Zelle, better known under her stage name Mata Hari, was the world's most overrated spy. As an exotic dancer in Europe before World War I, her brief efforts to steal secrets from her lovers were amateurish and unsuccessful. Following a clumsy seduction of the German military attaché in Madrid, Spain, Mata Hari was arrested and executed as a German spy in 1917.

SMALLEST SUICIDE WEAPON
When US spy-plane pilot Francis Powers was shot down over Russia on May 1, 1960, he was carrying a grooved "needle" coated with saxitoxin (paralytic shellfish poison) hidden inside a 1 1/10-inch-long common straight pin. It could cause death from respiratory paralysis and cardiovascular collapse within minutes of injection.

MOST LETHAL POISON USED IN AN ASSASSINATION
In 1978, a weapon disguised as an umbrella was used to inject a tiny RICIN-filled pellet into the thigh of Bulgarian dissident Georgi Markov, an outspoken opponent of the Bulgarian government, in London, England. Markov died within a matter of hours. RICIN is a cytotoxin derived from the castor bean. The lethal dosage by injection is 1.36 micrograms per pound of body weight.

MOST INFORMANTS REPORTING TO AN INTELLIGENCE SERVICE
From 1985 to 1989, 260,000 people out of an adult population of 12 million were estimated to be acting as informants (*Inoffizielle Mitarbeiters* or "unofficial collaborators") for East Germany's Ministry for State Security. The density of the informer network was seven times that of Hitler's Germany. During the Cold War, the East German Intelligence Service (HVA), led by spymaster Markus Wolf, pictured here with his wife Andrea, perfected the large-scale use of "spying for love." Rigorous screening of male candidates (only 1 in 100 was accepted) produced "Romeos" who courted secretaries in NATO and the Bonn government with spectacular success, stealing both hearts and secrets. Wolf, who is now in his mid-70s, served with the Red Army in World War II before becoming a journalist for Communist publications in his occupied homeland. In 1951 he was drafted into the East German Intelligence Service, which he led for 33 years. Since German reunification in 1990, Wolf has made a living as an author and a talk-show guest.

MOST SECRET SPY PLANE
A long-range, hypersonic stealth aircraft codenamed "Aurora" and made by Lockheed's "Skunkworks" in Burbank, California is said to have a top speed of 3,800 mph, a cruise range of 5,750 miles and an operational altitude of more than 100,000 feet. The highly classified "Aurora" is the apparent successor to Lockheed's SR-71 strategic reconnaissance craft.

SMALLEST OPERATIONAL SPY SUBMARINE
The MSC (Motorized Submersible Canoe) codenamed "Sleeping Beauty" was built by the British SOE (Special Operations Executive) in World War II to transport spies or saboteurs into enemy territory. It measures just 12-ft.-8-in.-long.

DEEPEST UNDERWATER SPY OPERATION
In 1974, the CIA's "Project Jennifer" salvaged part of a Soviet submarine from a depth of 16,500 feet. It used the *Glomar Explorer*, a recovery vessel built by tycoon Howard Hughes.

DEEPEST UNDERWATER TELEPHONE TAP
A joint US Navy and National Security Agency (NSA) operation in the Sea of Okhotsk in Russia used divers from a submarine to tap into a Soviet military communications cable at a depth of 400 feet. The KGB was alerted to the tap by a former NSA employee in 1981.

SMALLEST WORLD WAR II MICRODOT
German Military Intelligence operational microdots, (1/400 photographic reductions of the original document) could be hidden in the edge of a postcard or in the spine of a book.

SMALLEST VIDEO SPY CAMERA
The Supercircuits Model PC-51XP camera can be disguised as a button or hidden in a lipstick tube. The images it takes can be beamed to a receiver more than 500 feet away using the tiny Model TXB transmitter.

MINI WEAPONRY
The Bulgarian keyring gun, with its mounted barrel attachment, is just 3 inches long and 1 inch wide, but it can fire two 36-caliber rounds and could be deadly from a distance of 20 yards.

MOST SENSITIVE SPY SATELLITE CAMERA
The CCD digital camera, which was first carried on the US KH-11 satellite, can photograph targets on Earth with a resolution of 2 inches in the visible light spectrum, including night imaging using a photomultiplier. Digital images are transmitted in "real time" to receivers on Earth, where they are relayed to the United States for analysis.

SMALLEST "BUG"
The ISG audio transmitter, codenamed "Rice Grain," is the world's smallest listening device. The 3/10-inch-by-2/10-inch cylindrical "bug" is smaller than a pharmaceutical capsule, and when attached to a telephone line, transmits the conversation on a frequency of 390–410 MHz to a listening post. It uses the telephone line for power and as an antenna.

MOST FAMOUS FICTIONAL SPY
Author Ian Fleming's spy character James Bond, the suave British Secret Service agent, is one of the most successful and widely imitated 20th-century heroes. The subject of 19 films, Bond is purportedly based on Fleming's older brother Peter, who was an officer in Special Operations Executive (SOE), a wartime espionage group.

disasters:
air, land and sea

WORST ATTACK ON TOURISTS
An attack at the Hatshepsut Temple in Luxor, Egypt left 60 tourists dead on November 17, 1997. They were shot by terrorists dressed as police. Two policemen and two Egyptian civilians also died, as well as the six attackers. More than 1,500 people have been killed in the insurgency, which has haunted Egypt's tourist industry.

MOST KILLED IN TERRORIST ATTACK
A total of 329 people were killed when a bomb exploded aboard an Air India Boeing 747 in June 1985, causing the aircraft to crash into the Atlantic Ocean.

MOST KILLED IN MASS PANIC
In 1991, 1,426 Muslim pilgrims were trampled to death in a stampede along a tunnel from Mecca to Mina, Saudi Arabia.

MOST KILLED IN SOCCER STADIUM DISASTERS
In May 1964, a total of 318 fans were killed and 500 were injured in a riot that broke out at an Olympic qualifying match between Argentina and Peru at a football stadium in Lima, Peru. The riot was sparked by a Peruvian goal that was disallowed in the last minute. It would have sent Peru to the Tokyo Olympics.

On October 21, 1982 at Luzhniki Stadium, Moscow, USSR, many supporters of Spartak Moscow were crushed to death in an icy corridor at the end of a UEFA Cup game against Dutch team Haarlem. According to official estimates, 340 people were killed.

MOST FATALITIES IN A ROLLER COASTER CRASH
In May 1972, four people were killed and seven were injured when the roller coaster at the Battersea fun fair in London, England collapsed. Of the four fatalities, three were children.

WORST SKI LIFT ACCIDENT
On March 9, 1976 a total of 42 people were killed in a ski lift disaster at the Cavalese resort in northern Italy.

WORST ELEVATOR DISASTER
An elevator operating at the gold mine Vaal Reefs, South Africa fell 1,600 feet on May 1, 1995, killing 105 workers.

WORST UNDERGROUND TRAIN DISASTER
On October 28, 1995, about 300 people were killed in a fire that broke out in an underground train in Baku, Azerbaijan.

WORST TRAIN DISASTER
On June 6, 1981, more than 800 passengers died when their train plunged off a bridge into the Bagmati River in Bihar, India.

WORST HELICOPTER DISASTER
A Russian military helicopter carrying 61 refugees was shot down near Lata, Georgia on December 14, 1992.

WORST AIR ACCIDENTS
The world's worst ever air disaster took place on March 27, 1977, when two Boeing 747s (Pan-Am and KLM) collided on the runway in Tenerife, Canary Islands, killing 583 people.

The worst air accident involving a single aircraft occurred on August 12, 1985, when JAL's Flight 123, a Boeing 747, crashed near Tokyo, Japan, killing 520 passengers and crew.

WORST SPACE DISASTERS
The worst ever disaster during actual spaceflight took place on June 29, 1971, when astronauts Georgi Dobrovolsky, Viktor Patsayev and Vladislav Volkov (all USSR), who were not wearing spacesuits, died when their *Soyuz 11* spacecraft depressurized during reentry.

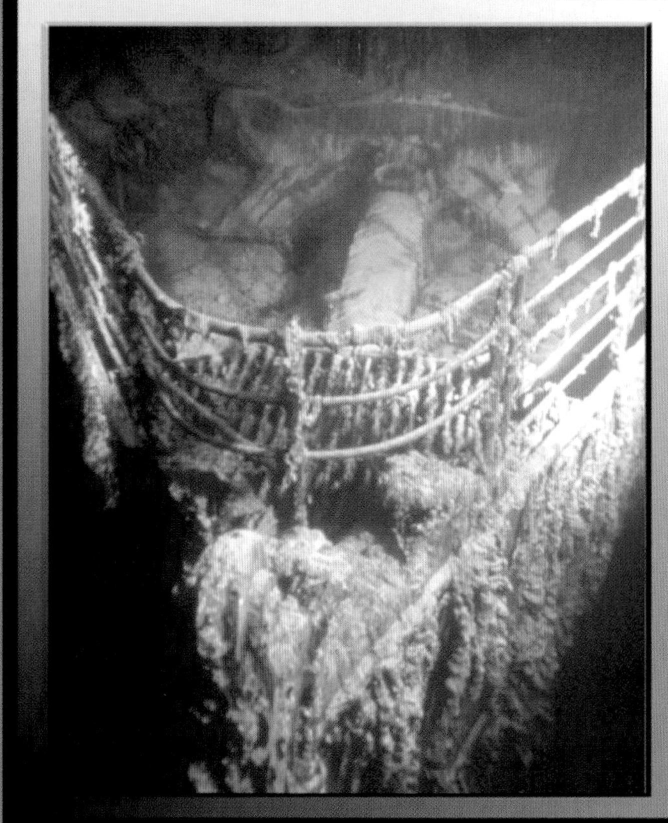

MOST ACCIDENTAL DEATHS ON A SHIP IN PEACETIME
A total of 1,513 people died when the cruise liner *Titanic* sank after hitting an iceberg 700 miles east of Halifax, Canada on April 15, 1912. Of the bodies that were subsequently recovered, 128 were never identified. The ship, which was owned by White Star Line and built by Harland & Wolff in Belfast, Northern Ireland, was believed to be unsinkable. It was described at the time as a "floating palace" – the people who traveled in the first-class accommodation paid $4,000 each for the voyage, which would be equivalent to $50,000 today. In 1985, the wreck was located by a robot submarine in an ocean canyon. Research and recovery operations carried out in 1987, 1993, 1994 and 1996 brought around 5,000 artifacts back to land, many of which can be viewed in an exhibition at the Florida International Museum. The salvage company was granted salvor-in-possession rights to the wreck in 1995. Today, just eight of the survivors of the tragedy are still alive.

The record for the greatest number of people known to have perished in any of the 207 manned spaceflights is seven (five men and two women), who were aboard *Challenger 51L* on January 28, 1986. The spacecraft broke apart under extreme aerodynamic overpressure when an explosion occurred 3 seconds after liftoff from Kennedy Space Center. The shuttle had reached an altitude of 46,000 feet.

The worst space disaster on the ground took place when an R-16 rocket exploded during fueling at the Baikonur Cosmodrome, Kazakhstan on October 24, 1960, killing 91 people.

WORST ACCIDENTAL EXPLOSION
The worst accidental explosion occurred on December 17, 1917, when the French freighter *Mont Blanc*, which was packed with 5,588 tons of explosives and combustibles, collided with another ship in Halifax Harbor, Nova Scotia, Canada, creating a blast that was felt more than 60 miles away. A total of 1,635 people died.

BIGGEST MARITIME COLLISION
The world's worst ever collision at sea occurred on December 16, 1977 when the tanker *Venoil* (330,954 dwt) struck her sister ship *Venpet* (330,869 dwt) 22 miles off the coast of southern Africa.

BIGGEST SHIPWRECK
The 321,186-dwt VLCC (very large crude carrier) *Energy Determination* blew up and broke in two in the Strait of Hormuz, Persian Gulf on December 12, 1979, causing the world's largest ever shipwreck. The ship was in ballast at the time but its hull value was $58 million.

WORST MIDAIR COLLISION
On November 12, 1996, 351 people died in a collision between a Saudi Boeing 747 scheduled flight and a Kazakh Ilushin 76 charter flight 50 miles southwest of New Delhi, India. Only the tail section of the Saudi aircraft remained intact after it plunged to the ground, where it left a 20-foot crater. Midair collisions are rare, but at the time of this accident, New Delhi airport was using the same route for arrivals and departures of civilian aircraft.

WORST FERRY DISASTER
The world's worst ferry disaster took place in the early hours of December 21, 1987, when the *Dona Paz* collided with a tanker, the *Victor*, while sailing from Tacloban to Manila, Philippines. After being engulfed in flames, both vessels sank in minutes. The *Dona Paz* officially had 1,550 passengers but may actually have had 4,000.

WORST SUBMARINE DISASTER DURING PEACETIME
On April 10, 1963, the 4,135-ton US nuclear submarine *Thresher* failed to surface while carrying out deep-diving tests in the Atlantic, 220 miles east of Cape Cod, Massachusetts. It had 112 officers and 17 civilian technicians on board. In 1964, the Navy announced that the bathyscaphe *Trieste II* had obtained pictures of large sections of the vessel's hull, which lies at a depth of 6,400 feet, but the cause of the tragedy has never been determined.

WORST ATTACK ON A BUILDING
The most people killed in a terrorist attack on a building is 168, when a bomb exploded outside the Alfred P. Murrah Federal Building in Oklahoma City, Oklahoma on April 19, 1995. The death toll included 19 children from the building's Child Day Care Center and eight federal agents. A further 850 people were injured in what is reputed to be the worst mass murder in United States history.

environmental disasters

MOST DESTRUCTIVE FIRES
The worst year in recorded history for the destruction of the natural environment was 1997, mainly because of fires that were deliberately lit to clear forest but also because of fires resulting from the droughts caused by the El Niño effect in the Pacific. The largest and most numerous fires occurred in Brazil, where they ranged along a 1,000-mile front.

WORST DEFORESTATION
It is estimated that tropical forests are being cut down at a rate equivalent to 200 football fields every minute. The country that is losing most forest in terms of area is Brazil, where about 11,600 square miles are destroyed every year. Rainforests are being felled and burned both by subsistence farmers and by big business to provide new land for pastures and cultivation.

WORST AIR POLLUTION
More than 6,300 people died from the effects of a poisonous cloud of methyl isocyanate that escaped from Union Carbide's pesticide plant near Bhopal, India on December 3, 1984. The company made a settlement of $470 million to compensate victims and their relatives.

MOST POLLUTED MAJOR CITY
Levels of sulfur dioxide, carbon monoxide and suspended atmospheric particle levels in Mexico City, the capital of Mexico, are more than double those deemed acceptable by the World Health Organization (WHO).

MOST POLLUTED TOWN
The Russian town of Dzerzhinsk, which has a population of 287,000, is home to dozens of factories producing chlorine and pesticides. In the past, chemical weapons were also made there. The Kaprolaktam plant emits 660 tons of vinyl chlorine, a carcinogenic gas, every year. Smog used to be so thick in the town that neighbors could not see one another's houses. Russia's leading authority on dioxins (toxic by-products of industrial processes or combustion) states that Dzerzhinsk, which has a life expectancy of 42 for men and 47 for women, should be evacuated.

MOST SULFUR DIOXIDE POLLUTION
The Maritsa power complex in Bulgaria releases a record 385,000 tons of the acidic gas sulfur dioxide into the Maritsa River every year. Sulfur dioxide is a pungent gas and an atmospheric pollutant with an irritating odor. It is a major cause of acid rain.

GREATEST OZONE DEPLETION
The largest "hole" in the ozone layer is above the Antarctic region. Each austral spring, a 14-mile area of ozone 1¼ times the size of the United States disappears. Above this height the ozone remains unaffected, so the gap is actually a thinning rather than a hole.

BIGGEST EMISSIONS OF GREENHOUSE GASES
The United States is home to 4% of the world's population but produces 25% of the world's emissions of carbon dioxide and other greenhouse gases.

The biggest emitter of carbon dioxide in relative terms is Luxembourg, which produces 18% more per head than the United States.

MOST ACIDIC ACID RAIN
A pH reading of 2.83 was recorded over the Great Lakes in 1982 and a reading of 1.87 was recorded in Inverpolly Forest, Scotland in 1983.

LARGEST TOXIC CLOUD
In September 1990, a fire at a factory handling beryllium in Ust Kamenogorsk, Kazakhstan released a toxic cloud that extended at least as far as the Chinese border, more than 190 miles away.

WORST NUCLEAR ACCIDENTS
The worst ever nuclear reactor disaster took place at Chernobyl No. 4 in the USSR (now Ukraine) in 1986. Contamination was experienced over 10,900 square miles and about 1.7 million people were exposed to varying levels of radiation. The official Soviet total of immediate deaths was 31, but it is not known how many of the 200,000 people involved in the cleanup operation died in the following five years. A total of 850,000 people are still living in contaminated areas.

The worst nuclear waste accident occurred at Kyshtym, Russia (then USSR) in 1957, when an overheated waste container exploded, releasing

MOST ACID RAIN DAMAGE TO FORESTS
The most damage caused to the environment by acid rain is in the Czech Republic, where 71% of forests are affected. The main causes of acid rain are the burning of coal, which disperses sulfur dioxide into the atmosphere, and emissions from cars, which are responsible for most of the nitrogen dioxides in the air. Acid rain poses a threat to the balance of sensitive ecosystems, reduces crop yields and speeds up the decay of buildings. Lakes and watercourses are also badly affected by acid rain, which disrupts the pH balance of the water and kills off wildlife. The trees that are most at risk are coniferous trees, which do not shed their needles at the end of the year if they have been exposed to a certain amount of acid rain. This interferes with the process of photosynthesis. In response to these problems, Europe has cut its sulfur dioxide emissions by 25% in the last 10 years, and in 1995, 19 countries agreed to cut their emissions by 30%.

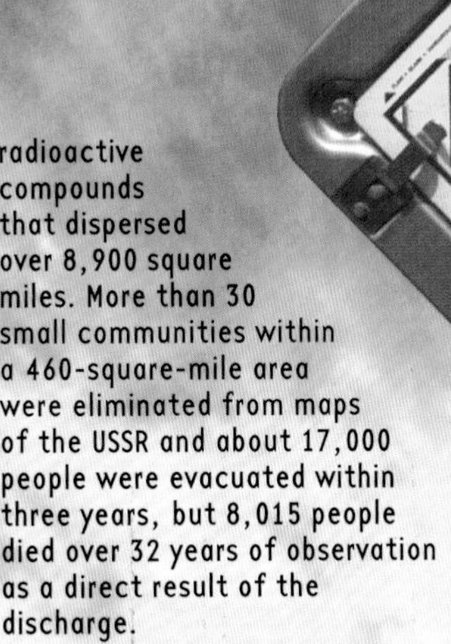

radioactive compounds that dispersed over 8,900 square miles. More than 30 small communities within a 460-square-mile area were eliminated from maps of the USSR and about 17,000 people were evacuated within three years, but 8,015 people died over 32 years of observation as a direct result of the discharge.

BIGGEST LAKE SHRINKAGE
The lake that has shrunk the most in recent times is the Aral Sea, on the border between Uzbekistan and Kazakhstan. It decreased in area from 26,300 square miles to 25,500 square miles in 1960, 13,500 square miles by 1990 and 11,000 square miles by 1994 (by which time it had divided into two smaller bodies of water). The shrinkage is mainly due to the extraction of water (for irrigation) from the major rivers that feed the sea.

WORST RIVER POLLUTION
In November 1986, firemen who were fighting a blaze at the Sandoz chemical works in Basel, Switzerland flushed 33 tons of agricultural chemicals into the River Rhine.

In August 1995, President Jagan of Guyana declared a 50-mile stretch of the Esquibo River a disaster zone after the banks of a pond holding cyanide used in gold extraction leaked into the river.

WORST MARINE POLLUTION
A plastics factory on Minimata Bay, Kyushu, Japan deposited mercury waste into the sea from 1953 to 1967. About 4,500 people were seriously harmed and different sources put the death toll at between 43 and 800.

MOST OVERFISHED WATERS
The United Nations has reported that 70% of the world's fisheries are either overfished or fished to the limit, and the problem is worsening. Countries that have reduced their fleets include Canada, Japan, Australia, New Zealand and Taiwan.

MOST DAMAGE CAUSED TO AN ISLAND BY MINING
The entire center of the 8-square-mile Pacific island-state of Nauru has been mined, producing a "lunar landscape." Only a narrow strip of coast is under vegetation. Nauru's economy depends almost entirely on the extraction and export of phosphates.

MOST OIL SPILLED IN A YEAR
The largest quantity of oil spilled into the sea in one year is 668,800 tons, in 1979. The *Atlantic Empress* produced the biggest offshore oil spill that year when it collided with the *Aegean Captain* in the Caribbean off the coast of Tobago. The *Atlantic Empress* was responsible for 315,700 tons of the spillage.

WORST COASTAL OIL DAMAGE
The *Exxon Valdez* oil tanker ran aground in Prince William Sound, Alaska in March 1989, spilling more than 33,000 tons of oil and polluting a 1,500-mile-long stretch of coast. The company was fined $5 billion and had to pay a clean-up bill of $3 billion.

WORST OIL SPILL
An oil spill beneath the Ixtoc 1 drilling rig in the Gulf of Campeche, Gulf of Mexico in June 1979 caused a 400-mile slick. The spill was halted in March 1980, after a loss of up to 550,000 tons.

MOST CONTAMINATED SPOT
Chelabinsk in Russia is the most radioactive point on the planet and has probably been so since 1940, when the Mayak weapons complex was built. Since then, there have been three nuclear disasters in the area, affecting up to 500,000 people with levels of radiation similar to those in Chernobyl. Scientists designated it the most contaminated spot in 1992 and it was closed to foreign visitors.

WORST LAND POLLUTION
From February to October 1994, thousands of tonnes of crude oil flowed across the Arctic tundra of the Komi Republic, Russia. An estimated 110,000 tons of oil were lost in a slick up to 11 miles long.

BIGGEST SOUND POLLUTION
The loudest noise occurred when the island-volcano Krakatoa, between Sumatra and Java, Indonesia, exploded in 1883. The explosion, which was heard a distance of 3,100 miles away, is estimated to have had 26 times the power of the largest ever H-bomb test and is believed to have been heard over 8% of the earth's suface.

MOST PUBLICIZED SMOG
Air pollution reached alarming levels in Kuching, Sarawak, Malaysia in 1997, and many people wore protective masks. It was due to traffic fumes and to forest fires in neighboring Indonesia. Although not the largest fires, these were the most publicized fires of 1997, covering large areas of South-east Asia with smog and hospitalizing around 40,000 people with respiratory problems.

natural disasters

MOST PEOPLE KILLED IN EARTHQUAKES
In July 1201, approximately 1.1 million people are believed to have been killed by a quake in the eastern Mediterranean. Most of the casualties were in Egypt and Syria.

The earthquake that struck the Shaanxi, Shanxi and Henan provinces of China on February 2, 1556 is believed to have killed about 830,000 people.

The highest death toll in modern times was caused by the quake in Tangshan, China on July 28, 1976. According to the first official figures, 655,237 people were killed. This was subsequently adjusted to 750,000 and then to 242,000.

MOST MATERIAL DAMAGE CAUSED BY AN EARTHQUAKE
The earthquake on Japan's Kanto plain on September 1, 1923 destroyed 575,000 homes in Tokyo and Yokohama. The official total of people killed and missing in the quake and its resultant fires was 142,807.

MOST PEOPLE KILLED IN A VOLCANIC ERUPTION
When the Tambora volcano in Sumbawa, Indonesia (then Dutch East Indies), erupted from April 5 to April 10, 1815, 92,000 people were killed, either directly or as a result of the subsequent famine.

MOST PEOPLE KILLED IN AVALANCHES
During World War I, between 40,000 and 80,000 men are believed to have been killed by avalanches that were triggered by the sound of gunfire in the Tyrolean Alps, Austria.

BIGGEST MASS BURIAL IN AN AVALANCHE
On January 11, 1954 two avalanches roared into the village of Blons near the Arlberg Pass, Austria. The first avalanche occurred at 9.36 am and the second at 7.00 pm. Of the 376 residents of the village, 111 were killed, and 29 out of 90 homes were destroyed. In the Leduc mine, 300 out of about 600 miners were buried alive.

MOST PEOPLE TRAPPED BY AVALANCHES
A total of 240 people died and more than 45,000 were trapped when a series of avalanches thundered through the Swiss, Austrian and Italian Alps on January 20, 1951. The avalanches were caused by a combination of hurricane-force winds and wet snow overlaying powder snow.

MOST PEOPLE KILLED IN LANDSLIDES
On December 16, 1920 a series of landslides triggered by a single earthquake that hit Gansu province, China killed about 180,000 people.

MOST MATERIAL DAMAGE CAUSED BY LANDSLIDES
From January 18 to January 26, 1969, a series of mudslides caused about $138 million worth of damage in southern California. The mudslides were brought about by nine days of torrential rain and a subtropical storm.

MOST PEOPLE KILLED IN A FLOOD
In October 1887, the Huang He (Yellow River) in Huayan Kou, China flooded its banks, killing about 900,000 people. Despite causing devastating seasonal floods, the Huang He suffers from water shortages and is the biggest river to dry up. In summer 1997, it ran totally dry along its lower section for more than 140 days, leaving farmland parched and threatening the harvest. The river's dry periods are getting longer, jeopardizing 17.3 million acres of crops and the livelihoods of 52 million people.

MOST PEOPLE MADE HOMELESS BY FLOODS
In September 1978, monsoon rains caused extensive river flooding in West Bengal, India, drowning 1,300 people, making 15 million people out of a population of 44 million homeless, killing 26,687 cows and destroying 1.3 million homes. The economic loss was given as $11.3 million, but unofficial estimates were up to three times that amount.

MOST PEOPLE KILLED BY A GEYSER
In August 1903, four people were killed when Waimangu geyser in New Zealand erupted. The victims were standing 90 feet from it but their bodies were found up to half a mile away. One was jammed between rocks and another was suspended in a tree.

MOST DEVASTATING ICE STORM
In January 1998, an ice storm wreaked havoc across eastern Canada and parts of the north-eastern United States, shutting

MOST PEOPLE KILLED IN A LANDSLIDE
On May 31, 1970, approximately 18,000 people were killed by a landslide on the slopes of Huascaran in the Yungay region of Peru, making it the most devastating single landslide in history. Huascaran, which is also called Nevada Huascaran, is a mountain peak of the Andes in west-central Peru. The snow-capped peak, which is 22,205 feet high, is the highest point in Peru and is a favorite destination for mountain climbers and tourists. Its slopes have been the scene of two major disasters. In 1962, a sudden thaw caused a portion of the sheer northern summit to break off, resulting in an avalanche that destroyed several villages and killed 3,500 people. The 1970 disaster occurred when an earthquake caused a landslide that buried 10 villages and most of the town of Yungay. It was one of the worst natural disasters of the 20th century in terms of the number of fatalities. On January 17, 1998 a mudslide in San Mateo, about 50 miles from Lima, Peru, blocked a major road to the capital city, but no injuries were reported. Pictured here are the remains of a truck covered in debris from the slide.

MOST PEOPLE MADE HOMELESS BY AN EARTHQUAKE
More than 1 million Guatemalans in a 3,400-square-mile area were made homeless at 3.02 am on February 4, 1976, when a giant earthquake ripped along the Montagua Fault (the boundary between the Caribbean and North American plates) and devastated their homes. The material damage was estimated at $1.4 billion and the quake is widely cited as the worst natural disaster in Central American history. In terms of material damage, it was almost matched by the 1972 Nicaraguan earthquake, which devastated Managua and caused $1.3 billion worth of material damage.

down airports and train stations, blocking roads and cutting off power to 3 million people. About 600 giant transmission towers collapsed, and five days of freezing rain coated power lines with up to 4 inches of ice – many times more weight than they could support. Two weeks later, 1 million people were still without power, and some areas remained without power for three weeks. The total cost of the damage was estimated at $650 million.

MOST DEVASTATING CYCLONE
Between 300,000 and 500,000 people are estimated to have died in the worst known cyclone, which hit East Pakistan (now Bangladesh) on November 12, 1970. Winds that reached speeds of up to 150 mph and a 50-foot-high tidal wave lashed the coast, the Ganges Delta and the offshore islands of Bhola, Hatia, Kukri Mukri, Manpura and Rangabali.

MOST PEOPLE KILLED IN A TORNADO
On April 26, 1989 approximately 1,300 people lost their lives and as many as 50,000 people were made homeless when a tornado hit the town of Shaturia in Bangladesh.

MOST MATERIAL DAMAGE CAUSED BY A TORNADO
A tornado cluster that hit the states of Iowa, Illinois, Wisconsin, Indiana, Michigan and Ohio in April 1985 killed a total of 271 people, injured thousands more and caused more than $400 million worth of damage.

MOST PEOPLE MADE HOMELESS BY A TYPHOON
Typhoon Ike hit the Philippines with 137-mph winds on September 2, 1985. It killed 1,363 people, injured 300, and made 1.12 million people homeless.

MOST PEOPLE KILLED IN A TYPHOON
Approximately 10,000 people died when a violent typhoon with winds reaching speeds of up to 100 mph struck Hong Kong on September 18, 1906.

WORST MONSOONS
Monsoons raged through Thailand in 1983, killing around 10,000 people and causing more than $396 million worth of damage. Up to 100,000 people are estimated to have contracted waterborne diseases as a result of the monsoons and around 15,000 people had to be evacuated.

MOST PEOPLE KILLED IN A DAM BURST
The Banqiao and Shimantan Dams burst almost simultaneously onto Henan province, China in August 1975, killing a total of 230,000 people.

MOST PEOPLE KILLED BY A DROUGHT
A drought in northern China between 1876 and 1879 led to the deaths of between 9 million and 13 million people.

MOST PEOPLE KILLED BY A LIGHTNING STRIKE
On December 8, 1963 a Boeing 707 jet airliner was struck by lightning near Elkton, Maryland and crashed, killing 81 passengers.

MOST KILLED IN A HAILSTORM
The worst hailstorm on record occurred in Moradabad, Uttar Pradesh, India on April 20, 1888. It claimed 246 lives. The hailstone pictured here fell near Huron, South Dakota during a severe thunderstorm in May 1998. Hailstones are usually between 1/5 inch and 1/4 inches in diameter, but stones up to 6 inches are not unknown in the Midwest.

danger zones

WORST AREA FOR PIRACY

In the last 10 years, about 1,500 acts of piracy have been reported in Southeast Asia. Most pirates operating in the region, such as these pictured in the South China Sea, are armed with submachine guns and use small speedboats to "jump" targeted vessels. Financial losses from piracy in the Pacific area are estimated to exceed $100 million a year.

MOST LIKELY PLACE IN WHICH TO DIE YOUNG

Palm Island, off Queensland, Australia, has been designated the most violent place on Earth outside a combat zone. The island's murder rate is currently 15 times higher than that of the entire state of Queensland and the life expectancy of the 3,500 inhabitants is 40 years. Palm Island also has the highest rate of youth suicide per capita in the world today: since 1994 there has been a total of 40 suicide fatalities on the island, and the community is now burying an average of one youth each day.

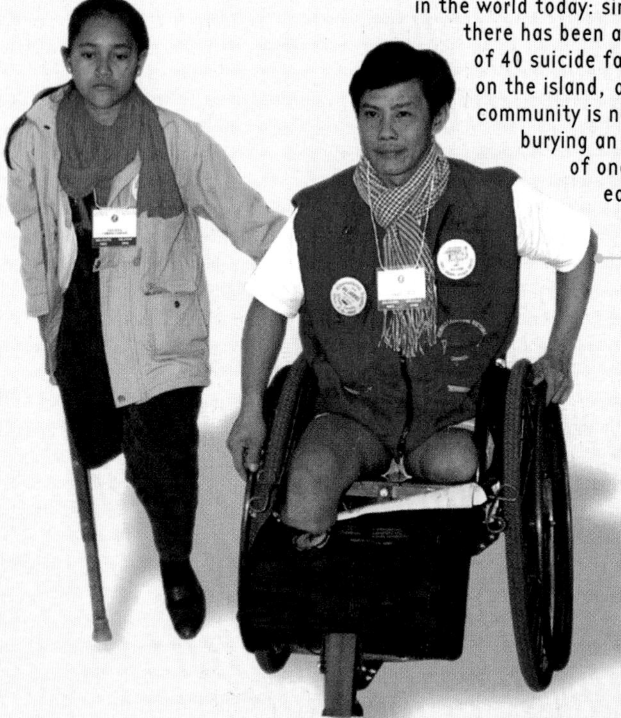

WORST AREA FOR LANDMINES

Of the 120 million landmines buried in 64 countries, about 35 million are in Afghanistan. Landmines cause an injury or fatality every 15–20 minutes, 85% of which occur in Cambodia, Afghanistan and Angola. Pictured left are Kosal Song and Tun Channareth, victims of landmines in Cambodia. Channareth accepted the Nobel Peace Prize for the International Campaign to Ban Landmines in 1997.

MOST LIKELY PLACE IN WHICH TO BE SHOT DEAD OUTSIDE WAR

There are currently more than 200 million guns in the United States, where one in four adults own a firearm and where there are estimated to be about 40,000 fatalities from guns each year. In the last 10 years, gun-related homicides in the country have risen by 18%.

MOST LIKELY PLACE IN WHICH TO BE KIDNAPPED

Of the 8,000 kidnap cases reported in 1996, 6,500 were in Latin America and more than 4,000 were in Colombia, where 10 people are kidnapped every day. The crime is alleged to be worth $200 million a year in Colombia. Only 3% of its kidnappers are convicted, compared with 95% in the United States.

MOST LIKELY PLACE IN WHICH TO BE HIT BY SPACE DEBRIS

Since the 1970s, approximately 10,000 meteorites have been discovered in Antarctica, making it the most likely place on Earth in which to be hit by space debris.

MOST LIKELY PLACES IN WHICH TO BE INVOLVED IN AN AIR CRASH

China currently accounts for 16% of all global flights and for 70% of all air accidents. Chinese pilots are reputed to average 280 flight hours a month – 180 hours more than Chinese regulations allow – because of a shortage of pilots.

The chances of dying in a plane crash in Russia are about 10 times higher than in the United States, making it one of the most dangerous countries in the world in which to fly.

The chances of being involved in an air accident in Africa are one in 50,000. This is 20 times greater than in the United States and about the same odds as being killed in a car accident.

In 1996, more than 550 people died in plane crashes in Latin America. The danger is most acute in Colombia, which is reputed to have the worst air-safety record in the Americas.

LARGEST CITY TO BE THREATENED BY AN EARTHQUAKE

Every year thousands of small tremors occur in the Tokai area southwest of Tokyo, Japan. Since a quake struck with a magnitude of 8.4 in the Tokai fault in December 1854, the Tokyo region has become an urban sprawl housing almost 30 million people, with skyscrapers, overhead expressways and millions of tons of fuel oil and poisonous chemicals stored in tanks around Tokyo Bay. At some point in the future, an earthquake will occur on the Tokai fault. It is predicted that it will be much larger than the quake that wrecked the Japanese city of Kobe in 1995.

LARGEST CITY TO BE THREATENED BY A VOLCANIC ERUPTION

Vesuvius, near Naples, Italy, is regarded as one of the most dangerous volcanoes: more than 700,000 people live on its slopes within a 6-mile radius of the summit crater, and the outskirts of Naples are within 10 miles of the vent. If enough warning can be given, the Italian government envisages an evacuation of at least 600,000 people in the event of an eruption. This would take a week, during which time Naples' outer suburbs could suffer the same fate as Pompeii.

MOST DANGEROUS PRESS BEAT
Since 1993, a total of 70 journalists have been murdered in Algeria, making it the most dangerous place in the world in which to be a journalist. On arriving in Algeria, journalists are met by a government protection team. Here firefighters are seen carrying a wounded bomb victim in Algiers, the nation's capital. The majority of the killing takes place just outside Algiers and in the Mitidja Plain. A total of 474 journalists were killed worldwide between 1987 and 1996, 128 in Europe and the republics of the former Soviet Union, 116 in the Americas, 94 in the Middle East and Africa, 85 in Asia and 51 in sub-Saharan Africa.

HIGHEST RISK OF RADIATION-RELATED ILLNESS FROM FOOD
The former Soviet republic of Belarus suffered the greatest damage from the Chernobyl disaster in 1986 — 70% of the fallout from the nuclear reactor fell on the country. In addition to radiation-related illnesses, Belarus has large areas of contaminated ground, and private plots in these areas are still being used to grow food. Almost 99% of Belarus has been contaminated to degrees above internationally accepted levels, but produce from the greater part of that land continues to be consumed.

MOST LIKELY PLACE IN WHICH TO BE EATEN BY A TIGER
In the Sundarban mangrove forests of Bangladesh and India, fatal attacks on humans by Siberian tigers (*Panthera tigris*) average around 60 a year. Siberian tigers, which can grow to a length of 13 feet, are the largest of the big cats.

MOST LIKELY PLACE IN WHICH TO BE EATEN BY A SHARK
The most likely place in the world in which to be eaten by a great white shark (*Carcharodon Carcharias*) — the species responsible for one-third of shark attacks on humans — is in the Indian Ocean, off the coasts of Indonesia and Australia. The annual tally for fatal shark attacks globally is estimated at 40, with the chances of being attacked by a shark estimated to be 300 million to one.

MOST LIKELY PLACE IN WHICH TO BE KILLED BY A SNAKE
Human beings are most likely to die of a snakebite in Sri Lanka, where an average of 800 people a year are killed by snakes.

MOST LIKELY PLACE IN WHICH TO BE KILLED BY A SCORPION
Approximately 1,000 people a year die after being stung by scorpions in Mexico. The worst year to be there was 1946, when a total of 1,933 people were killed.

GREATEST DANGER ZONE
The part of Afghanistan that is controlled by the Islamic fundamentalist Taliban movement is a dangerous place in which to dance, play music, watch videos, play soccer, read magazines, drink alcohol, fly a kite or use a paper bag. All of these are banned by the Taliban. Women are also prohibited from seeking employment or education and talking to foreigners.

arts &
media

movies I

MOST FILMED AUTHOR
A total of 309 straight or relatively straight version films have been made of plays by William Shakespeare, in addition to 41 modern versions where the storyline is loosely based on a play (such as *West Side Story*). There have also been innumerable parodies. *Hamlet* is the most popular choice, with 75 versions, followed by *Romeo and Juliet* with 51. The most recent of these was *William Shakespeare's Romeo and Juliet* (1996), starring Leonardo DiCaprio and Claire Danes.

HIGHEST BOX OFFICE GROSS
The Oscar-winning *Titanic* was released on December 19, 1997. By June 7, 1998, the epic adaptation of the tale of the doomed ship had earned over $1.7 billion worldwide.

MGM's *Gone With The Wind* (1939) took $193.6 million from 197.55 million admissions in North America – equivalent to $871.2 million today, taking into account inflation and the increased price of movie tickets.

FASTEST $100 MILLION BOX OFFICE GROSS
The Lost World: Jurassic Park made its $74-million budget back in just three days, starting on May 23, 1997, and passed the $100-million mark in 5½ days – faster than any other movie.

HIGHEST FIRST-DAY BOX OFFICE GROSS
The Lost World: Jurassic Park took $22 million from 3,281 movie theaters on May 23, 1997, beating the previous biggest single-day gross of $20 million set by *Batman Forever* on June 16, 1995.

BIGGEST LOSS
MGM's *Cutthroat Island* (1995), starring Geena Davis and directed by her then husband Renny Harlin, cost more than $100 million to produce, promote and distribute. By May 1996, it had reportedly earned back just $11 million.

MOST PROFITABLE FILM SERIES
The 18 James Bond movies, from *Dr. No* (1962) to *Tomorrow Never Dies* (1997), have grossed more than $1 billion worldwide – more than any other film series.

TOP BUDGET/BOX OFFICE RATIO
Mad Max (Australia, 1980), which starred Mel Gibson and was directed by George Miller, cost $350,000 to make and grossed $100 million in its first two years of international distribution – a budget-to-box-office ratio of 1:285.

LARGEST OPENING
Godzilla opened on May 19, 1998 on a record 7,363 screens in 3,310 theaters. The roaring reptile topped the mark previously held by *The Lost World: Jurassic Park* (1997).

LONGEST FIRST RUN
The record for the longest first run in one movie theater is 10 years 32 weeks, by *Emmanuelle* (France, 1974), starring Sylvia Kristel and directed by Just Jaeckin. It played at the Paramount City Cinema, Paris, France from 1974 to 1985, during which time it was seen by a total of 3,268,874 people.

LARGEST PUBLICITY BUDGET
Universal and its licensed merchandisers spent $68 million promoting Steven Spielberg's *Jurassic Park* (1993) in the United States alone – $8 million more than the cost of the film.

MOST EXPENSIVE FILM RIGHTS
The highest price ever paid for film rights was $9.5 million, for the Broadway musical *Annie*. The deal was announced in 1978 by Columbia, and the film was released in 1982. It was directed by John Huston and starred Albert Finney.

A contract worth $4 million plus profit-sharing was signed by New Line on July 20, 1993 for the psycho-thriller *The Long Kiss Goodnight* by 32-year-old Shane Black.

HIGHEST PAY FOR AN ACTOR
Through a percentage of the film's receipts in lieu of salary, Jack Nicholson stood to receive up to $60 million for playing the Joker in the $50-million *Batman* (1989).

HIGHEST FEES FOR A SCRIPT
Carolco Pictures paid a record $3 million to Joe Eszterhas for his speculative script for *Basic Instinct* (1992). The controversial thriller, starring Michael Douglas and Sharon Stone and directed by Paul Verhoeven, was nominated for two Oscars in 1993. It made Stone – a former model who had spent the 1980s playing minor roles – into a major star. She won awards for both Best Female Performance and Most Desirable Female at the 1993 MTV Movie Awards. Since *Basic Instinct*, her films have included *Intersection* (1993) with Richard Gere, *The Specialist* (1994) with Sylvester Stallone and *Casino* (1995) with Robert de Niro. She has become one of the most highly paid actresses in Hollywood and has her own production company, Chaos.

MOST EXPENSIVE FILMS
The movie *Titanic* (1997), starring Leonardo DiCaprio and Kate Winslet and directed by James Cameron, was due to be released in July 1997 but was delayed until December 1997 due to post-production problems. This delay added at least $20 million to the budget, making *Titanic* the most expensive movie ever made, at almost $250 million. The film went on to win a total of 11 Oscars, equaling the record that was set by *Ben-Hur* in 1959. The most expensive film ever made in terms of real costs adjusted for inflation was *Cleopatra* (1963), which starred Elizabeth Taylor and Richard Burton. The $44-million budget would equal more than $260 million in 1998 terms.

MOST SUCCESSFUL DIRECTOR
Seven of director Steven Spielberg's movies are in the all-time top 10, and collectively his films have grossed more than $2.17 billion. Spielberg won an Oscar for Best Director with *Schindler's List* (1993).

LARGEST FILM OUTPUT
India produces more feature-length films than any other country, with a peak output of 948 films in 1990. It has three major centers of production, Bombay, Calcutta and Madras, making films in 16 languages.

LARGEST FILM STUDIO COMPLEX
Universal City in Los Angeles, California covers 420 acres and has 561 buildings and 34 sound stages.

LONGEST FILM
The 85-hour *Cure for Insomnia* (1987), which was directed by John Henry Timmis IV, premiered in its entirety at the School of the Art Institute of Chicago from January 31 to February 3, 1987. Much of the film consists of L. D. Groban reading his own 4,080-page poem, interspersed with scenes of a rock band and some X-rated footage.

MOST DEATHS DURING THE PRODUCTION OF A FILM
In 1989, a fire killed more than 40 people on the set of the Indian TV movie *The Sword of Tipu Sultan*.

MOST COSTUMES IN ONE FILM
A record 32,000 costumes were worn in *Quo Vadis* (1951).

MOST COSTUME CHANGES IN ONE FILM
Madonna changed costume a record 85 times in *Evita* (1996) and wore a total of 39 hats, 45 pairs of shoes and 56 pairs of earrings. The costumes were based on Eva Perón's own clothes, many of which are kept in an Argentine bank vault. Madonna chose each pattern herself.

CHARACTERS PORTRAYED IN THE MOST FILMS
The French emperor Napoleon Bonaparte was the subject of a total of 177 films between 1897 and 1986 – a record for any historical character.

The fictional character most frequently portrayed on the big screen is Sherlock Holmes, who was created by Sir Arthur Conan Doyle. He has been portrayed by 75 actors in more than 211 films since 1900.

MOST FILMED STORY
There have been a record 95 productions of the classic fairy tale *Cinderella*, including cartoon, modern ballet, operatic, all-male, parody and pornographic versions. The first ever version was *Fairy Godmother* (UK, 1898) and the most recent version was *The Magic Riddle* (Australia, 1991).

MOST MERCHANDISING LICENSES
Warner Bros. issued 160 merchandising licenses at the time of the premiere of *Batman* (1989). It was the most successful merchandising operation in terms of license fees, adding an estimated $50 million to the $250-million box office gross. The "caped crusader" is seen here portrayed by George Clooney in *Batman and Robin* (1997).

movies II

HIGHEST EARNINGS FROM A SINGLE MOVIE
As the producer of *Star Wars* (1977), George Lucas was entitled to 40% of net profits, worth almost $50 million. In addition, Lucas held all the merchandising rights, which Fox allowed him under the contract because they could see little value in them. His cut of the estimated $4-billion revenue from retail sales of *Star Wars*-related products is undisclosed.

MOST TAKES FOR A DIALOGUE SCENE
Stanley Kubrick is reputed to have required a record 127 takes for a scene with Shelley Duvall in *The Shining* (GB, 1980). Kubrick, a notoriously demanding director, also required 85 takes for a scene with Duvall, Scatman Crothers and five-year-old Danny Lloyd, and 50–60 takes for a long tracking shot where Jack Nicholson pursues Duvall up the staircase as she brandishes a baseball bat at his face.

HIGHEST EARNINGS FROM A HORROR MOVIE
William Peter Blatty, the author and producer of *The Exorcist* (1973), earned 40% of the film's gross. The exact amount of money is not known, but the movie grossed approximately $89 million.

HIGHEST-GROSSING HORROR MOVIES
Miramax's *Scream* (1996), directed by Wes Craven and starring Drew Barrymore and Neve Campbell, cost about $15 million to make and had grossed $103 million by July 1997. *Scream II* (1997), grossed $33 million on its opening weekend and took $96 million from December 1997 to March 1998. A second sequel is due for release in 1999.

LOWEST BUDGET HORROR MOVIE
Night of the Living Dead (1968) was made on a tiny budget of about $114,000 and went on to become one of the most successful independent movies of all time. It was shot in and around director George Romero's home in Pittsburgh, Pennsylvania, over three weekends. Romero financed the project by selling $300 shares in the movie. The cast of unknowns was made up of local talent, and the film was shot by people who had previously made ads and industrial films. Two of the investors had to play minor roles due to a shortage of actors, while another — a butcher — provided blood and guts. The end result, said to be the first truly modern horror movie, was rejected by Columbia because it was not in color. It spawned two sequels and a series of Italian zombie and cannibal films in the 1970s.

In an inflation-adjusted list, *The Exorcist* (1973), directed by William Friedkin, had the highest-ever box office gross of any horror movie. If the rate of inflation and the rise in the price of theater tickets since 1973 are taken into account, the film grossed the equivalent of more than $381 million in today's terms.

HIGHEST-GROSSING SCI-FI MOVIES
Including its recent rerelease, *Star Wars* (1977) has grossed about $910 million. Taking into account the rate of inflation and the rise in the price of theater tickets, *Star Wars* has the highest box office gross of any science fiction movie.

Fox's *Independence Day* (1996), which starred Bill Pullman, Will Smith and Jeff Goldblum, grossed $811 million worldwide — the highest box office gross of a sci-fi film on its original release.

MOST EXPENSIVE SCI-FI MOVIE
Waterworld (1995), starring Kevin Costner, suffered a series of setbacks when the set broke free from its moorings in the Pacific Ocean on several occasions. This problem and other technical failures combined to made it the most expensive sci-fi movie ever, at an estimated $160 million.

MOST PROLIFIC HORROR DIRECTOR
Roger Corman directed 27 horror movies over 35 years, from *Swamp Women* (1955) to *Frankenstein Unbound* (1990). He also produced more than 100 other horror films.

MOST PROLIFIC HORROR ACTORS
Actor John Carradine starred in a record 67 horror films during his acting career, from

The Black Cat (1934) to *The Alien Within* (1991).

Christopher Lee, the British actor who rose to fame with his portrayal of Dracula, has starred in 59 movies since 1959. He was first cast by Hammer Films in *The Curse of Frankenstein* (GB, 1956) and most recently appeared in *Talos the Mummy* (GB, 1998).

MOST PORTRAYED HORROR CHARACTER
Count Dracula, who was created by Irish writer Bram Stoker in 1897, has been portrayed in more horror movies than any other character. Representations of the Count or his immediate descendants outnumber those of his closest rival, Frankenstein's monster (created by Mary Shelley in 1818), by 161 to 117.

MOST HORROR NOVELS FILMED
More than 20 of horror writer Stephen King's novels and short stories have been made into movies, including *Carrie* (1976), directed by Brian de Palma and starring Sissy Spacek, *The Shining* (GB, 1980), *Children of the Corn* (1984) and *Misery* (1990).

MOST HORROR SEQUELS
House (1986), directed by Steve Miner, was followed by *House II: The Second Story* (1987) and a further eight sequels. Many of the sequels went straight to video.

MOST SCI-FI SEQUELS
The most sequels to a US sci-fi movie is seven, for *Star Trek — The Motion Picture* (1979), directed by Robert Wise. An eighth sequel is due for release in December 1998.

MOST SECRETIVE FILM SCRIPT
George Lucas's new *Star Wars* trilogy is the most secretive project in film history. For the first prequel it was reported that Lucasfilm Ltd. gave characters bogus names, filmed scenes that were never to be used and employed different versions of the script. People who have seen the script have had to sign a confidentiality document. The first film is due to be released in May 1999.

BIGGEST HORROR FILM LINKUP
Friday the 13th (1980), which was directed by Sean S. Cunningham, had eight sequels by May 1998, and a ninth sequel, *Jason Versus Freddy*, is planned. The NewLine film will pit Jason Vorhees from *Friday the 13th* against Freddy Krueger from *A Nightmare on Elm Street* (1984), pictured below.

MOST SCI-FI SEQUELS
There have been 24 sequels to the original Japanese version of *Godzilla, King of the Monsters* (1954). The latest version, *Godzilla* (1998), had grossed $123.7 million in North America as of June 14, 1998.

movie stunts

MOST EXPENSIVE AERIAL STUNT
Simon Crane performed one of the most dangerous ever aerial stunts when he moved from one jet plane to another at an altitude of 2 miles 1,480 yd. for *Cliffhanger* (1993). The stunt was performed only once because it was so risky, and cost a record $1 million. Sylvester Stallone (left), the movie's star, is said to have offered to reduce his fee by the same amount to ensure that the stunt was included.

MOST STUNTS BY A LIVING ACTOR
Jackie Chan, the Hong Kong actor, director, producer, stunt coordinator and writer, has appeared in more than 65 movies since his debut in *Big and Little Wong Tin Bar* (Hong Kong, 1962) at the age of eight. No insurance company will underwrite Chan's productions, in which he performs all his own stunts. After a number of stuntmen were injured during the making of *Police Story* (Hong Kong, 1985), the star formed the Jackie Chan Stuntmen Association, trained the stuntmen personally and paid their medical bills out of his own pocket.

MOST STUNTS BY A SILENT MOVIE STAR
Buster Keaton starred in more than 100 movies from *The Butcher Boy* (1917) to *A Funny Thing Happened on the Way to the Forum* (1966). He is believed to have been the only star of his time to have performed all his own death-defying stunts, despite studio claims that actors such as Harold Lloyd and Douglas Fairbanks did all their own stunts.

MOST STUNTS BY AN ACTRESS
Michele Yeoh, a former Miss Malaysia, was the first actress that Jackie Chan allowed to do all her own stunts. In *Ah Lahm: The Story of a Stuntwoman* (Hong Kong, 1996) a mistimed jump off a 265-foot bridge put Yeoh in hospital for three months, but she went on to complete the movie. Her most dangerous stunt was riding a speeding motorbike on a moving train without safety nets or catch wires for *Police Story 3: Supercop* (Hong Kong, 1992). She has starred in 18 movies since 1979, achieving international fame as a Bond girl with Pierce Brosnan in *Tomorrow Never Dies* (1997).

MOST PROLIFIC STUNTMEN
Vic Armstrong has doubled for every actor playing James Bond, and in a career spanning three decades has performed stunts in more than 200 movies, including *Raiders of the Lost Ark* (1981). He has coordinated stunts for movies such as *Tomorrow Never Dies* (1997) and is married to stuntwoman Wendy Leech, whom he met when they doubled for the stars of *Superman* (1978).

Yakima Canutt performed stunts in more than 150 movies in his 15-year career. He was also a stunt double for John Wayne and Clark Gable. In 1941, he broke his ankles and began creating stunts and handling the action scenes in Hollywood movies, including the chariot race in *Ben Hur* (1959). In 1966, he was awarded an Oscar for his stunt work.

HIGHEST FREEFALL
The greatest height from which a stuntman has ever leaped in a freefall is 1,100 feet, by Dar Robinson from a ledge at the summit of the CN Tower in Toronto, Canada, for *Highpoint* (Canada, 1979). Robinson's parachute opened just 300 feet from the ground after a freefall lasting six seconds.

HIGHEST JUMP
The highest ever jump made by a movie stuntman without a parachute is 232 feet, by A. J. Bakunus while he was doubling for Burt Reynolds in the movie *Hooper* (1978). He fell onto an air mattress.

MOST STUNTS BY HOLLYWOOD ACTOR
Mel Gibson, who was born in New York City but moved to Australia at age 12, starred in the action movie *Lethal Weapon* (1987) and its three sequels. He performs his own stunts and is said to be the most daring actor in Hollywood. He is the only actor to have been credited as both leading man and a stuntman in a movie, in *Mad Max Beyond Thunderdome* (1985), pictured left, in which he starred alongside Tina Turner. Gibson made his first big screen appearance in 1977 and since then has starred in more than 30 movies.

LONGEST FIRE BURN
Nick Gillard withstood a full fire burn without air for two minutes for *Alien 3* (1992), starring Sigourney Weaver. Stuntpeople performing a full fire burn have to refrain from breathing while on fire to prevent the oxygen in their lungs from igniting. During his 20-year career, Gillard has been on fire at least 100 times and has performed and coordinated stunts in more than 15 major films including the boat and tank sequences in *Indiana Jones and the Last Crusade* (1989) and sword-work in *Robin Hood: Prince of Thieves* (1991) and *The Three Musketeers* (1993). His most recent work is as stunt coordinator on the set of George Lucas's *Star Wars: Episode I*, due to be released in 1999. Gillard has responsibility for training actors Liam Neeson and Ewan McGregor, the two Jedi Knights, in swordplay. At 12 years of age, Gillard ran away from military school to join the circus, becoming a world class horse-trick rider in the Moscow State Circus by the age of 16. His career in stunts began when he was offered work on *The Thief of Baghdad* (1978).

LONGEST LEAP IN A CAR
The world's longest ever leap made in a car that was being propelled by its own engine was performed by the stunt driver Gary Davis for the movie *Smokey and the Bandit II* (1981), starring Burt Reynolds. Davis raced a stripped-down Plymouth at a speed of 80 mph up a ramp that was butted up against the back of a double-tiered car-carrier. He flew 163 feet through the air before landing safely on the desert floor.

BIGGEST COORDINATOR OF AERIAL STUNTS
Flying Pictures of Surrey, England has planned and coordinated air stunts for more than 200 feature films, including *Cliffhanger* (1993), *GoldenEye* (1995) and *Mission Impossible* (1996), and coordinated the aerial stunts for hundreds of TV shows and ads.

HIGHEST PAY FOR A SINGLE STUNT
Dar Robinson was paid $150,000 for his freefall from Toronto's CN Tower for *Highpoint* (Canada, 1979).

BIGGEST STUNT BUDGET
More than $3 million of the $200-million budget for *Titanic* (1997) went towards the movie's stunts. In the most complex scene, 100 stuntpeople leap, fall and slide 70 feet as the ship breaks in half and rises out of the water to a 90° angle. The ship was docked in a tank filled with 20 million gallons of water.

MOST STUNT DAYS WORKED
The record for the greatest number of stunt days worked on any movie is 6,000, by the 100 stuntpeople who worked on the set of *Titanic*. The team was led by British stunt coordinator Simon Crane.

HIGHEST STUNTMAN:ACTOR RATIO
The Rookie (1990), directed by Clint Eastwood, who also starred in the movie along with Charlie Sheen and Raul Julia, featured a total of 87 stuntmen and just 37 actors.

OLDEST STUNTMAN TO STAND IN FOR CHILDREN
The only adult stuntman who stands in for children is Bobby Porter, who is 4 ft. 9 in. tall. One of Porter's most famous movies is *Annie* (1982), in which he dangled from a 20-story-high drawbridge as the stand-in for nine-year-old lead Aileen Quinn.

LONGEST BOAT JUMP
Stuntman Nick Gillard performed a record 220-foot powerboat jump over two bridges for Dick Maas's *Amsterdamned* (Netherlands, 1988), a murder mystery involving a psychopathic diver in the Dutch capital. Gillard, who has appeared in numerous *World's Greatest Stunts* videos, believes that fear is good because it keeps him on his toes.

tv and video

MOST EXPENSIVE PROGRAM

In January 1998, NBC agreed to pay $13 million for each one-hour episode of the top-rated medical drama *ER*, which stars George Clooney (right) and Julianna Margulies. It had previously paid $1.6 million per episode. The hospital drama is the number one primetime show, with a weekly audience of 32 million. The three-year deal with *ER* creators Warner Bros. will work out at $873.68 million for 22 episodes.

BIGGEST AUDIENCES

Baywatch, whose stars have included David Hasselhoff and Pamela Anderson, is the world's most widely viewed TV series, with an estimated weekly audience of more than 1.1 billion people in 142 countries.

"Goodbye, Farewell and Amen," the final episode of *M*A*S*H*, was transmitted to 77% of all US viewers on February 28, 1983. It was estimated that about 125 million people tuned in.

MOST VIEWED TRIAL

From January to October 1995, a daily average of 5.5 million US viewers watched the trial of O. J. Simpson, who was charged with the murder of his ex-wife Nicole and her friend Ronald Goldman.

LARGEST SOAP OPERA PRODUCTION

Brazil, Mexico and Puerto Rico dominate the trade in *telenovelas*, which run for an average of over 100 episodes and are supplied to stations in Latin America, Spain, Italy and Portugal.

The Brazilian network Globo is the largest and most profitable producer of *telenovelas* in Latin America. It shows soaps from 6 pm onwards each night.

MOST SUCCESSFUL *TELENOVELA*

In the 1960s, *Simply Mary* was sold to every Spanish-speaking country and once attracted more viewers than the World Cup soccer championships.

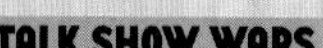

MOST SUCCESSFUL SOAP OPERA

Dallas, starring Larry Hagman and Victoria Principal, began in 1978 and by 1980 had an estimated 83 million US viewers (a then record 76% share of the TV audience) and had been seen in more than 90 countries worldwide.

LONGEST RUNNING SHOW

NBC's *Meet the Press* was first transmitted on November 6, 1947 and was shown weekly from September 12, 1948. By June 28, 1998, 2,557 shows had been aired.

LARGEST TV CONTRACT

In March 1994, talk show queen Oprah Winfrey reportedly signed a contract with the King World Corporation that guaranteed her company, Harpo, $300 million by December 31, 2000, or $46.15 million a year for 6½ years.

MOST EXPENSIVE TV DEAL

In January 1998, the National Football League (NFL) signed contracts with CBS, ABC and Fox and with the cable sportscaster ESPN totaling $17.6 billion. The contracts give each network rights to NFL games for eight years starting with the 1998–99 season. ESPN will pay the NFL $600 million per year, ABC and Fox will each pay $550 million per year, and CBS will pay $500 million per year.

BIGGEST GLOBAL TV NETWORK

CNN International news is the only global TV network. Distributed via 15 satellites, CNN and CNN International are seen by 184 million households in more than 210 countries.

MOST PROLIFIC TV PRODUCERS

Aaron Spelling has produced more than 3,784 TV episodes since 1956. Projected 24 hours a day, they would take just over four months to screen. His output includes *Starsky and Hutch*, *Dynasty* and *Beverly Hills 90210*.

TALK SHOW WARS

Jerry Springer, who once worked on Senator Robert F. Kennedy's political campaigns and became one of the youngest ever US mayors at the age of 33 in 1971, rose to international fame after being asked to launch *The Jerry Springer Show*, a one-hour talk show, in 1991. Today his controversial program is a success in the United States and is seen in more than 30 other countries around the world. In May 1996, Springer signed a contract to continue making the show for another six years, and by 1997 the show was so popular that it began to be aired twice a week. Much of its appeal lies in the fact that half of all episodes end up in fights and brawls, which are encouraged by the live studio audience. It is for this reason that the show employs several security guards for each episode. Guests who appear on the program have to sign a form stipulating that if they lie, they must pay production costs of up to $80,000. In 1998, *The Jerry Springer Show* was ranked second only to *Oprah* in the talk show ratings. The latter's host, Oprah Winfrey, is the most successful woman on TV.

MOST VISITED WEB SITES
The most visited TV series Web sites, in descending order, are those of NBC sitcoms *Seinfeld*, *Friends* and *Caroline in the City*. *Friends*, which first aired in 1994, stars Lisa Kudrow, Matthew Perry, Jennifer Aniston, David Schwimmer, Courteney Cox and Matt LeBlanc (left to right). Now in its fourth series, it is watched by about 16.5 million US viewers.

The most prolific game show producer was Mark Goodson. He produced more than 39,000 episodes of game shows, totalling 21,240 hours of airtime.

MOST EXTREME GAME SHOW
First shown in 1984, the Japanese game show *Gaman* tests the endurance of contestants who willingly put themselves in perilous situations, and face challenges ranging from starvation to dousing themselves with gasoline to experiments with live maggots.

MOST QUIZ SHOW CONTESTANTS
A record 5,000 contestants took part in Japan's *Ultra Quiz*, which was produced by Nippon Television. Competitors who correctly answered a general knowledge question had to board a plane but were required to disembark if they failed to answer a second question correctly. Those who remained aboard had to take an 800-question, two-hour exam. The two finalists faced a playoff on top of the Pan Am skyscraper in New York. Prizes included a racehorse, a helicopter and a plot of land in Nevada.

The All-Japan High-School Quiz Championship, which was televised by NTV on December 31, 1983, had a record 80,799 participants.

MOST EXPENSIVE TV RIGHTS FOR A FILM
Fox paid $82 million for the rights to Steven Spielberg's *Jurassic Park: The Lost World* in June 1997, before its international release.

MOST EXPENSIVE TV RIGHTS FOR A MINISERIES
In 1991, a group of US and European investors, led by CBS, paid $8 million for the TV rights to Alexandra Ripley's *Scarlett*, the sequel to Margaret Mitchell's *Gone With the Wind* (1939).

MOST EXPENSIVE TV MINISERIES
The 14-episode miniseries *War and Remembrance* cost $110 million to make over three years.

HIGHEST EXPENDITURE ON TV AND VIDEO PRODUCTS
The leading consumer market for video and TV products is Japan, with an average expenditure of $43.66 per person per year.

COUNTRY WITH THE MOST TV SETS
There are 227.5 million households with TV sets in China (one in six people) — almost twice as many as in the United States.

COUNTRY WITH THE MOST VCRS
A record 81% of US households (78,125,000) own at least one video recorder.

MOST SPINOFFS FROM A SERIES
Star Trek has spawned a record seven feature films and five syndicated programs: *Star Trek* (1966–69), the *Star Trek* cartoon (1973–75), *Star Trek: The Next Generation* (1987–94), *Star Trek: Deep Space Nine* (1993–present) and *Star Trek: Voyager* (1995–present). The first feature film adaptation was *Star Trek: the Motion Picture* (1980), starring William Shatner and Leonard Nimoy.

MOST RENTED VIDEO
Fox's reissue of George Lucas' *Star Wars* trilogy, featuring digitally remastered versions of *Star Wars*, *The Empire Strikes Back* and *Return of the Jedi*, has made a record $270.9 million from video rentals. Steven Spielberg's *E.T.: the Extra Terrestrial* (1982) had previously held the record for 14 years, making a total of $228.16 million.

BEST-SELLING VIDEO
Walt Disney's *The Lion King* (1994) had sold more than 55 million copies worldwide as of August 1997. The 32nd Disney animated feature, it was the first without human characters and the first based on an original story. It featured the voices of Whoopi Goldberg, Jeremy Irons and Rowan Atkinson.

FASTEST-SELLING FILM ON VIDEO
The Full Monty (1997) sold 1.8 million copies in its first week of release — almost 700,000 more than *Star Wars*, the previous record-holder in the UK. It also nearly doubled the previous record of 351,000 for UK first-day sales, held by *Independence Day*.

FASTEST VIDEO PRODUCTION
Videos of Prince Andrew and Sarah Ferguson's wedding in London, England in 1986 were made in 5 hr. 41 min. by Thames Video Collection. Live filming ended when the couple left for their honeymoon at 4:42 pm, and the first tapes were available from the Virgin Megastore, Oxford Street, London at 10:23 pm.

MOST VIDEO LIBRARIES
Bombay (Mumbai), India, has 15,000 video libraries and 500 video parlors.

books, newspapers and magazines

TOP NEWSPAPER CIRCULATIONS
Japanese newspapers have some of the highest circulation figures in the world. The newspaper with the world's highest circulation is Tokyo's *Yomiuri Shimbun*, which has a combined morning and evening circulation of 14.5 million copies daily. The most popular periodical in Japan is the countryside magazine *Le-no-Hikari*, which has an average monthly readership of 1.11 million people.

MOST TRANSLATED NOVELIST
The world's most translated novelist is Sidney Sheldon, pictured here with his wife Alexandra. Sheldon's novels, which include *Rage of Angels* (1987), have been translated into 51 languages and sold in more than 180 countries to date. He sold his first piece of writing, a poem, when he was 10 years old, and by the age of 18 was working in Hollywood as a screenwriter, going on to create such TV series as *Hart to Hart*.

BEST-SELLING BOOKS
The world's best-selling and most widely distributed book is the Bible, with an estimated 3.88 billion copies sold between 1815 and 1998.

Excluding non-copyright works such as the Bible and the Koran, the all-time best-selling book is *The Guinness Book of Records*, which was first published by Guinness Superlatives in October 1955. Global sales in 37 languages had surpassed 81 million by June 1998.

BEST-SELLING WORKS OF FICTION
Three novels have been credited with sales of about 30 million: *Valley of the Dolls* (1966, now out of print) by Jacqueline Susann, which sold 6.8 million copies in its first six months; *To Kill a Mockingbird* (1960) by Harper Lee; and *Gone With the Wind* (1936) by Margaret Mitchell.

Alistair MacLean wrote 30 novels, 28 of which sold more than 1 million copies each in the United Kingdom alone. It has been estimated that one of his novels is purchased somewhere in the world every 18 seconds.

LONGEST ON A BEST-SELLER LIST
The Road Less Traveled by M. Scott Peck had spent 694 weeks on the *New York Times* paperback best-seller list by the time it exited on April 6, 1997. More than 5 million copies of the book are in print.

TOP-SELLING AUTHORS
The top-selling fiction writer is Agatha Christie, whose 78 crime novels have sold an estimated 2 billion copies in 44 languages.

The top-selling living author is British novelist Dame Barbara Cartland, with global sales of more than 650 million for her 635 titles.

RICHEST AUTHOR
Horror novelist Stephen King is the richest author in the world, with an estimated worth of $84 million. His top-selling works include *Carrie* (1974), *The Shining* (1978), *Pet Sematary* (1983) and *Misery* (1987), all of which have been made into movies.

MOST PROLIFIC NOVELIST
Brazilian novelist José Carlos Ryoki de Alpoim Inoue had 1,046 science fiction novels, westerns and thrillers published between 1986 and 1996 — more than any other writer.

OLDEST AUTHORS
Sisters Sarah and Elizabeth Delany wrote their autobiography in 1993, when they were 103 and 102 years old respectively. In 1997, Sarah wrote the sequel, *On My Own at 107*.

MOST RECLUSIVE NOVELIST
J. D. Salinger has guarded his privacy and resisted publicity to such an extent that a book about efforts to find him has been published. *In Search of J. D. Salinger* was written by Ian Hamilton after his original biography was blocked from publication by Salinger.

TOP NEWSPAPER CIRCULATIONS
The United Kingdom has the highest newspaper circulation of any European Union country. The *Sun* has the highest circulation of any British daily newspaper, at 4.064 million, while the *News of the World* has a record Sunday circulation of 4.307 million. The most popular British periodical is *Reader's Digest*, with a circulation of 1.67 million.

MOST NEWSPAPERS
In 1995, India had more than 4,235 newspapers, most of them regional and published in different languages for a rural readership. Those with higher circulations include the daily *Malayala Manorama*, with a circulation of 800,000, and *Punjab Kesari*, a Sunday paper with a circulation of 892,000. India's most popular magazine is *India Today*, which is printed in five languages and a circulation of 970,000 for each bi-weekly edition.

BIGGEST SHORTAGE OF PRINT MATERIALS
Russia's shortage of materials, increasing taxes and high costs make it hard for daily papers to keep in constant print, and some low circulation papers appear intermittently. The highest circulation is 3.6 million, by the weekly *Argumenty y Fakty*. Russia's top-selling magazine is *Rabotmitsa*, a magazine for working women with a monthly circulation of 20.5 million.

TOP-SELLING FRENCH NEWSPAPERS AND MAGAZINES
The top-selling newspaper in France is *Ouest-France*, with a circulation of 797,091.

France's top-selling magazine is the TV listings magazine *Télé 7 Jours*, with a weekly circulation of 2.8 million.

Modes et Travaux is France's top monthly fashion magazine, with a circulation of 1.5 million.

Paris Match is France's most popular news periodical, with a circulation of 690,000.

TOP-SELLING GERMAN NEWSPAPERS AND MAGAZINES
Germany has no national papers but the regional *Zeitung* papers printed in 15 cities are Germany's most popular, with a combined circulation of 2.4 million.

The top-selling German magazine is *Hörzu*, a TV listings magazine with a circulation of 3.86 million. The top-selling non-TV listings magazine is fashion and cooking magazine *Burda Moden*, with a monthly circulation of 2.3 million.

TOP-SELLING ITALIAN NEWSPAPERS AND MAGAZINES
Italy's top circulating paper is *Corriere della Sera*, a regional paper based in Milan but with a national circulation of 720,239.

The top-selling periodical is the motoring magazine *L'Automobile*, with a circulation of 1.08 million. It is followed by Catholic magazine *Famiglia Cristiana*.

TOP-SELLING SPANISH NEWSPAPERS AND MAGAZINES
El Pais is Spain's top-selling newspaper, with a daily circulation of 1.12 million.

The TV listings magazine *TP Teleprograma* has a record circulation of 1 million.

TOP-SELLING CHINESE NEWSPAPERS AND MAGAZINES
In 1996, China had 2,235 newspapers, all state-run. *Sichuan Ribao*, which services the Chengdu region, is China's top-selling newspaper, with a circulation of 8 million.

The Biweekly review *Ban Yue Tan* is the top-selling Chinese magazine, with a circulation of 6 million.

BIGGEST ADVANCES
Tom Clancy was reportedly paid a $33.4-million advance for *The Hunt for Red October* (1984) and *Patriot Games* (1987). In 1997, he is said to have signed a $75-million, two-book deal with Penguin Putnam, Inc. In 1992, he had received the biggest known advance for one book, with a reported $14 million for the North American rights to *Without Remorse*.

TOP-SELLING US NEWSPAPERS AND MAGAZINES
The *Wall Street Journal* has a circulation of 1.84 million in the US.

The most popular periodical in the US is *Reader's Digest*, with a circulation of 16.26 million.

TOP-SELLING BRAZILIAN NEWSPAPERS AND MAGAZINES
Fôlha de Sao Paulo has a daily circulation of 558,000 and a Sunday circulation of 1.4 million.

Veja has a circulation of 800,000.

TOP-SELLING AUSTRALIAN NEWSPAPERS AND MAGAZINES
Sydney's *Sunday Telegraph* has a circulation of 705,000. The most popular daily is the *Herald Sun*, with a circulation of 675,193.

Driving magazine *The Open Road* has a circulation of 1.5 million.

BIGGEST-SELLING GAY MAGAZINE
Los Angeles-based *Advocate* magazine sells more than 2 million copies a year in the US.

TOP-SELLING SOCIETY MAGAZINE
Spain's *¡Hola!* sells 622,292 copies a week.

TOP-SELLING NEWS MAGAZINE
Time, which was launched in 1923, has a worldwide weekly circulation of 4.15 million.

TOP-SELLING STREET MAGAZINE
The *Big Issue* sells 800,000 copies a month worldwide, making it the biggest-selling street magazine. The magazine is sold by homeless people and helps 8,000–10,000 vendors a year in Los Angeles; Melbourne, Sydney and Brisbane, Australia; Cape Town, South Africa (pictured below); and the United Kingdom.

animation and comic strips

MOST CELEBRITIES FEATURED IN AN ANIMATION SERIES
The Simpsons first aired as a primetime series on January 14, 1990 and has featured a total of 120 celebrities. Guest stars have included Gillian Anderson, Magic Johnson and Elizabeth Taylor.

MOST VIDEO GAMES INSPIRED BY AN ANIMATED SERIES
Gundam, a Japanese TV series about enemies who become robots to fight one another, has inspired Robotec (which in turn inspired the toys Transformers), as well as countless Sony PlayStation spinoffs.

MOST FITS CAUSED BY A TV SHOW
In December 1997, more than 700 children in Japan were rushed to the hospital when an episode of an animated series based on the Nintendo game Pocket Monsters triggered convulsions. A total of 208 people from age three upwards were hospitalized with epilepsy-type symptoms. An explosion scene followed by five seconds of red lights flashing from the eyes of a rat-like creature called Pikachu was said by experts to be to blame for causing the fits.

MOST EXPENSIVE CELLS
One of the 150,000 color cells from Walt Disney's animated classic *Snow White* (1937) was sold in 1991 for a record $203,000. A black-and-white drawing from Walt Disney's *Orphan's Benefit* (1934) sold for $280,000 at Christie's, London, England, in 1989.

TOP FIRST-RUN GROSS
Walt Disney's *The Lion King* (1994) grossed a record $766.15 million worldwide and was screened in more than 60 countries. In 1998, the Broadway musical adaptation of the movie won the Tony Award for Best Musical. In 1995, Elton John and Tim Rice's *Can You Feel the Love Tonight*, the hit theme tune from *The Lion King*, won an Oscar for Best Original Song.

MOST EXPENSIVE ANIMATED FILM
Walt Disney's animated feature *Beauty and the Beast* (1992) cost $35 million to make. The remake of *Fantasia*, which is not scheduled to be completed for another two years, is expected to be more expensive.

MOST CONSECUTIVE OSCAR NOMINATIONS
From 1991 to 1997, Aardman Animation of Bristol, England, received six consecutive Oscar nominations for Best Short Animated Film. This is a record for any Oscar category. Three of the nominations, *The Lyp Synch* series featuring *Creature Comforts*, *The Wrong Trousers* and *A Close Shave*, which were all directed by Nick Park, went on to win Oscars.

MOST SUCCESSFUL ANIMATED FILM CHARACTER
Steamboat Willie (1928) premiered at the Colony Theater, New York City, on November 18, 1928, and marked the debut of Mickey Mouse, who went on to become the most successful cartoon character of all time.

BEST-KNOWN MANGA TITLE
The Japanese animation known as manga became a hit after its first title, *Akira*, was made into a movie and released on video in 1991. Japan produces an estimated 2.3 billion manga titles a year, which accounts for 38% of all books and magazines sold in Japan. The manga business is worth $7–9 billion in Japan alone.

LONGEST ANIMATED SERIES
Harry "Bud" Fisher's *Mutt and Jeff* began as a comic supplement to *Pathe's Weekly* on February 10, 1913, and continued as separate weekly reels from April 1, 1916, until December 1, 1926, although no titles have been traced for 1923–24. There were at least 323 films produced.

OLDEST ANIMATED FILMS IN REGULAR DISTRIBUTION
Several of the *Mutt and Jeff* films have been colorized and synchronized for video release.

LONGEST SERIES OF "TALKIES"
Max Fleisher's *Popeye The Sailor Man*, which was filmed between 1933 and 1957, consisted of 233 one-reelers and a single two-reeler. A further 220 Popeye cartoons were produced for television by King Features during the 1970s.

LONGEST AMATEUR ANIMATION
The British Film Institute has accepted a film that was produced by a British man over a period of 28 years for inclusion in its film archives. The film has 100,000 hand-painted cells and runs for 2 hr. 33 min.

MOST VALUABLE COMIC BOOK
The rarest comic book is an issue of *Detective* (No.27) in which Batman first makes an appearance. It was sold at auction for a record $85,000.

MOST FILMED COMIC STRIP CHARACTER
Zorro has been portrayed in 69 films to date. Originated by Johnston McCulley, he was also the first comic strip character to be the subject of a major feature film, *The Mark of Zorro* (1920) starring Douglas Fairbanks. The movie appeared just one year after the comic strip was printed, making Zorro the fastest comic strip character to make it from strip to the silver screen.

LONGEST-RUNNING NEWSPAPER STRIP
The "Katzenjammer Kids," created by Rudolph Dirks, was first published in the *New York Journal* in December 1897, making it the longest-running newspaper strip in the world. It is now drawn by cartoonist Hy Eisman and is syndicated to 50 newspapers by King Features Syndicate.

MOST SYNDICATED COMIC STRIP
"Peanuts" by Charles Schulz was first published in October 1950. The comic strip, featuring characters including Charlie Brown and Snoopy, now appears in 2,620 newspapers in 75 countries and 26 languages.

Ranan R. Lurie is the most widely syndicated political cartoonist in the world. As of July 1998, his work was published in 103 countries in 1,105 newspapers with a total circulation of 104 million copies.

MOST COMIC BOOKS BY A WRITER
Paul S. Newman has written more than 4,000 published stories for 360 different comic book titles, including *Superman*, *Mighty Mouse*, *Prince Valiant*, *Fat Albert*, *Tweety and Sylvester* and *The Lone Ranger*.

LONGEST SERIES
On April 26, 1998, the 200th episode of *The Simpsons* was aired on the Fox network. Now in its ninth season, *The Simpsons* is the longest-running primetime animated series and has been screened in 70 countries.

art and installations

BIGGEST OUTDOOR INSTALLATION
Desert Breath covers 25 acres and is made up of 178 cones, 89 sand cones and 89 conical depressions cut into the floor of the desert near the town of Hurghada in Egypt. It took a team of three Greek artists nine months to create, and will erode within a few years.

BIGGEST ARCHITECTURAL INSTALLATION
Tight Roaring Circle, a 39-foot-tall, 62-foot-wide inflatable play castle made of 29,333 square feet of white PVC-coated polyester, was designed by Dana Caspersen and William Forsythe and constructed in three weeks inside the Roundhouse, a circular railway turntable shed in London, England, by Southern Inflatables in 1997. Visitors were invited to interact with the structure, spurred on by low lighting, an ambient soundtrack by Joel Ryan and text by the late Japanese writer Yukio Mishima printed on the courtyard walls.

BIGGEST INSTALLATION ON THE NEW YORK SUBWAY
In December 1996, Alexander Brodsky placed four gondolas on an unused track of a downtown subway in New York City. The project, *Arts for Transit*, was funded by the New York Public Arts Fund.

MOST EXPENSIVE LANDSCAPE ARTWORK
Christo's $23-million work *The Umbrellas* (1991) involved 1,340 huge yellow umbrellas on farmland in California and a further 1,760 blue umbrellas in Japan. They were simultaneously opened by 810 workers.

BIGGEST FLOWER SCULPTURE
In 1992, artist Jeff Koons erected *Puppy*, a 40-ft.-5-in. by 18-ft. by 19-ft.-6-in. flower sculpture at the Documenta exhibition in Kassel, Germany.

LONGEST SKETCH PROJECT
Alan Whitworth has been sketching Hadrian's Wall on the border of Scotland and England for more than 12 years. His sketch will be 73 miles long when it is finished in 2007.

MOST VALUABLE PAINTING
The *Mona Lisa* (*La Gioconda*) by Leonardo da Vinci was assessed at $100 million for insurance purposes for its move to Washington, DC and New York City for exhibition in 1962–63. The insurance was not purchased because the cost of the tightest security measures was less than that of the premiums.

MOST EXPENSIVE PAINTING
Portrait of Dr. Gachet by Vincent van Gogh sold at Christie's, New York City for $82.5 million on May 15, 1990. It depicts Van Gogh's doctor and was completed weeks before the artist's suicide in 1890.

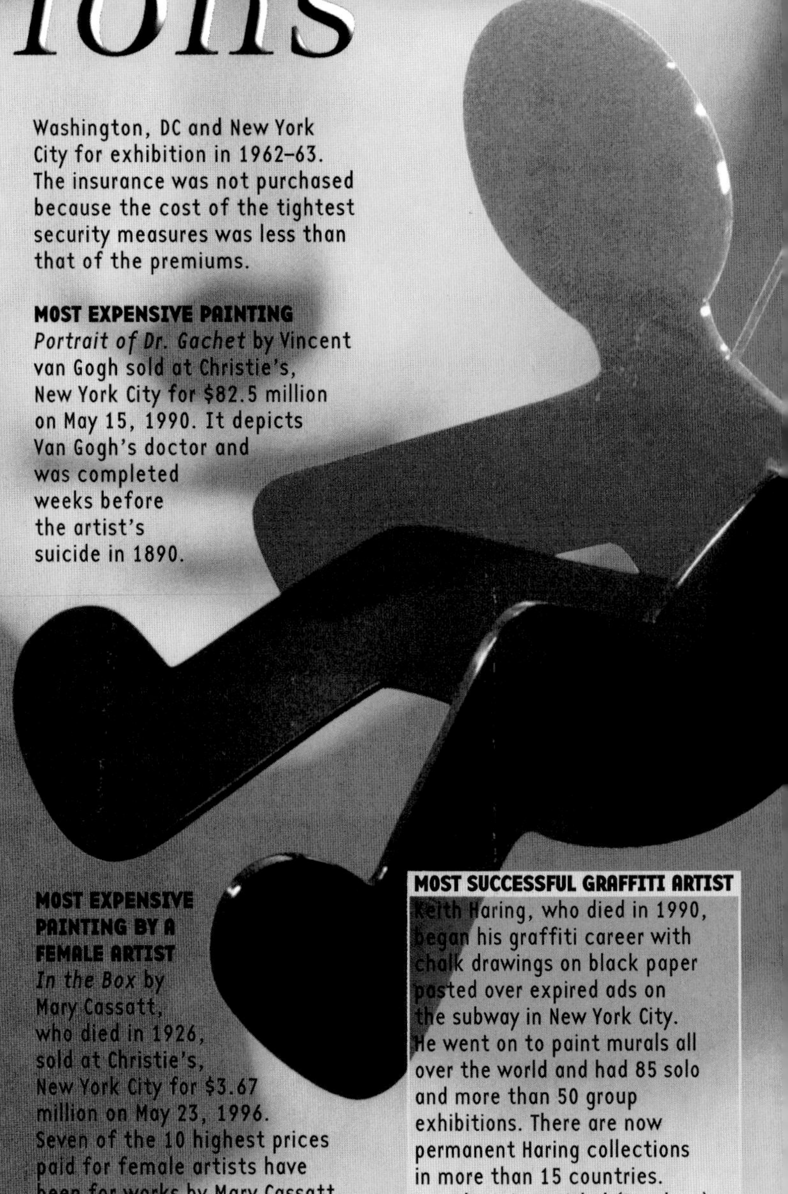

MOST EXPENSIVE PAINTING BY A FEMALE ARTIST
In the Box by Mary Cassatt, who died in 1926, sold at Christie's, New York City for $3.67 million on May 23, 1996. Seven of the 10 highest prices paid for female artists have been for works by Mary Cassatt.

MOST SUCCESSFUL GRAFFITI ARTIST
Keith Haring, who died in 1990, began his graffiti career with chalk drawings on black paper pasted over expired ads on the subway in New York City. He went on to paint murals all over the world and had 85 solo and more than 50 group exhibitions. There are now permanent Haring collections in more than 15 countries. Seen here is *Untitled (Breakers)*.

MOST SUCCESSFUL POP ARTIST
Andy Warhol has had more than 80 exhibitions worldwide since 1952 and boasts eight permanent collections in the United States, as well as one at the Moderna Museet in Stockholm, Sweden, and another at the Tate Gallery in London, England. Warhol, who began as a window dresser in Pittsburgh and designed ads for sanitary napkins after moving to New York in the 1950s, went on to become the most iconic figure in the Pop Art movement. From the age of six he was fascinated by glamour and collected film memorabilia, including magazines, movie posters and photographs. He filmed and taped much of his own life, and by his death in 1987 had captured about 6,000 hours of his life on film. Among the subjects that he painted were Campbell's soup cans, Coca-Cola bottles and Marilyn Monroe. His most expensive work, *Marilyn X100*, sold for $17.3 million – more than four times the previous price for a Warhol – at Sotheby's, New York City in May 1998.

BIGGEST LAND PORTRAIT
Crop artist Stan Herd uses his tractor to carve pictures into the landscape. His largest work to date is his 160-acre portrait of cowboy Will Rogers on the planes of southwest Kansas. His other well-known works include a sunflower still life and a portrait of Native American Saginaw Grant (right) in a 30-acre wheat field.

MOST STOLEN WORKS OF ART
The artist believed to have had the most works stolen is Picasso, with around 350 pieces missing worldwide. Also missing are nearly 270 Mirós and 250 Chagalls.

MOST VISITORS TO AN ART GALLERY IN A YEAR
In 1995, the Centre Pompidou in Paris, France had a record 6,311,526 visitors.

MOST EXPENSIVE 20TH-CENTURY PAINTING
Les Noces de Pierette by Pablo Picasso sold for $80.44 million in Paris, France in 1986.

MOST EXPENSIVE PAINTING BY AN ANONYMOUS ARTIST
Departure of the Argonauts (1487) sold at Sotheby's, London for £4.2 million ($6.7 million) on December 9, 1989.

HIGHEST PRICE PAID AT AUCTION FOR A PHOTOGRAPH
Hand With Thimble (1920), Alfred Stieglitz's photograph of one of artist Georgia O'Keeffe's hands, raised $398,500 at auction at Christie's, New York City on October 8, 1993.

MOST EXPENSIVE POSTER
A poster by Charles Rennie Mackintosh advertising an 1895 art show at the Glasgow [Scotland] Institute of Fine Arts sold for £68,200 ($105,028) at Christie's, London in February 1993.

MOST AUCTION SALES BY AN ARTIST
As of May 1997, works by Picasso had been sold at auction 3,579 times. The total value of these sales is $1.07 billion.

MOST RAISED BY A PRIVATE ART COLLECTION AT AUCTION
Victor and Sally Ganz's collection, which included works by Picasso and Johns, raised $207.04 million at Christie's, New York City in November 1997. A two-week exhibition prior to the auction had 25,000 visitors.

BIGGEST GALLERY ENDOWMENT
The J. Paul Getty Museum, Malibu, California was set up in January 1974 for $1.64 billion and has an annual budget of $100 million-plus to stock its 38 galleries with art.

MOST VISITED OUTDOOR EXHIBIT
In 1995, Christo attracted 5 million people to Berlin, Germany when he wrapped the former parliament building, the Reichstag, in 68 miles of silver polypropylene fabric. The cost of the installation was $7 million.

performance arts

HIGHEST-PAID DANCER
Michael Flatley, the Chicago-born star of *Lord of The Dance*, earns an estimated $83,215 a week for his Irish dancing. The 39-year-old dancer first found fame through dancing at the 1994 Eurovision Song Contest in Dublin, Ireland, and in *Riverdance*.

MOST CURTAIN CALLS FOR A BALLET
The record for the greatest number of curtain calls known to have been received at any ballet is 89, by Dame Margot Fonteyn and Rudolf Nureyev after a performance of *Swan Lake* at the Vienna Staatsoper, Vienna, Austria in October 1964.

LONGEST CHORUS LINES
The longest chorus lines in performing history contained up to 120 dancers, in some of the early Ziegfeld Follies, which were created by Florenz Ziegfeld, the greatest exponent of the American revue. Over the years the Ziegfeld girls included Barbara Stanwyck, Paulette Goddard and Irene Dunn.

OLDEST PROFESSIONAL CHORUS LINE
Eleven female chorus line members of the Fabulous Palm Springs Follies of Palm Springs, California make up the oldest recorded professional chorus line. Ranging from age 53 to age 85, the Fabulous Follies continuously perform 10 shows each week in front of sold-out audiences for seven months out of the year. The average age of the Follies is 67, while the aggregate stands at 737.

OLDEST PROFESSIONAL CHORUS LINE PERFORMER
Maryetta Evans, a dancer for the Fabulous Palm Springs Follies, is the oldest member of a professional chorus line, at 85. Evans performs for seven months out of the year and does splits at every performance.

BIGGEST THEATRICAL LOSSES
Side Show, a musical about real-life conjoined twins who became performers, is the third-biggest flop in Broadway history, closing after just three months in 1998. The biggest-ever theatrical loss was $7 million, by the US producers of the Royal Shakespeare Company's musical *Carrie*, which closed in May 1988 after five performances on Broadway. The musical was based on the successful Stephen King novel of 1974 and the 1976 movie starring Sissy Spacek and John Travolta.

LONGEST-RUNNING MUSICAL ON BROADWAY AND IN THE WEST END
On June 19, 1997, the musical *Cats*, which was composed by Andrew Lloyd Webber, became the longest-running musical on Broadway when it was performed at the Winter Garden Theater, New York City for the 6,138th time since October 7, 1982. The record was previously held by *A Chorus Line*, which was last staged in April 1990. By the time *Cats* took the record, more than 8.25 million people had seen the show and it had grossed $329 million on Broadway alone. In its first 15 years on Broadway, the show used a ton of yak hair for wigs, 85 gallons of shampoo and 1.5 million pounds of dry ice. The show opened at the New London Theater on Drury Lane, London, England on May 11, 1981 and became London's longest-running musical in January 1996. On June 2, 1998, it was performed in London's West End for the 7,315th time. By that date, it had grossed more than $2 billion worldwide. *Cats* has been seen by an estimated 50 million people in approximately 250 cities.

OLDEST AMATEUR CHORUS LINE PERFORMER
The oldest known amateur chorus line performer is Iris Guarino of Milton, Massachusetts at age 88. Guarino has performed as a dancer with the Ziegfield Girls of FLorida, Inc. since 1986.

HIGHEST-INSURED SHOW
The musical *Barnum*, which opened at the London [England] Palladium on June 11, 1981, was insured by its producers for the sum of $10 million. The individual insurance for the star of the show, Michael Crawford, who had to walk a high-wire and slide down a rope from the topmost box to the stage, accounted for $6 million of the total.

LONGEST CONTINUOUS THEATRICAL RUN
The Mousetrap, by Agatha Christie, opened at the Ambassadors Theater, London, England on November 25, 1952. On March 25, 1974, after a total of 8,862 performances, it moved to St. Martin's Theater next door. On June 1, 1998, the 18,944th performance took place. The box office has grossed $33.3 million from more than 9 million theater-goers.

BIGGEST ARTS FESTIVAL
Scotland's annual Edinburgh Fringe Festival began in 1947, and saw its busiest year in 1993, when 582 theater groups gave a total of 14,108 performances of 1,643 shows, August 15–September 4.

LONGEST PLAY
The longest play is *The Non-Stop Connolly Show* by John Arden, which took 26½ hours to perform in Dublin, Ireland in 1975.

SHORTEST PLAY
The world's shortest ever play is the 30-second *Breath*, which was written by Irish playwright and novelist Samuel Beckett in 1969.

MOST LEAD PERFORMANCES
Kanmi Fujiyama played the lead role in 10,288 performances by the Japanese comedy company Sochiku Shikigeki from November 1966 to June 1983.

MOST THEATRICAL ROLES
Kanzaburo Nakamura performed in 806 Kabuki titles from 1926 to 1987. Each title in this classical Japanese theatrical form lasts for 25 days, so he actually gave 20,150 performances.

MOST DURABLE UNDERSTUDY
In March 1994, 79-year-old Nancy Seabrooke retired from *The Mousetrap* after understudying the part of Mrs. Boyle for 15 years and 6,240 performances. She performed the part 72 times.

MOST FAMILY MEMBERS ON STAGE AT ONCE
A record 22 members of the Terry family (including Sir John Gielgud's mother, Kate) appeared in a Masked Dance from Shakespeare's *Much Ado About Nothing* at Ellen Terry's Jubilee Matinée in London, England on June 12, 1906.

MOST TIME SPENT IN BED TOGETHER BY A STAGE COUPLE
Jessica Tandy and Hume Cronyn were married in 1942 and spent more time in bed together than any other stage couple. They opened at the Ethel Barrymore Theater, New York City in Jan de Hartog's *The Fourposter* in October 1951, and played the bed-bound characters on Broadway and on tour for the next two years.

MOST STRUTTERS
When *A Chorus Line* broke the record as the then longest-running Broadway show ever on September 29, 1983, the show's finale featured a total of 332 top-hatted strutters.

circus stunts and feats

HIGHEST CROSSING OF THE THAMES
On September 14, 1997, Didier Pasquette (France), pictured left in front of St. Paul's Cathedral, and Jade Kindar-Martin (US) became the first tightrope walkers to cross the River Thames, London, England simultaneously in opposite directions. The 1,000-foot-long, 1-inch-thick wire was 150 feet above the river. At the point where they met, in the center of the high wire, Pasquette squatted down and Kindar-Martin stepped over him. They had planned to celebrate their meeting in the middle with a glass of champagne, but instead shook hands and threw white roses into the river in memory of Diana, Princess of Wales. The pair, who belong to French acrobatic team Les Tréteaux du Cœur Volant, then performed a series of stunts while sitting, kneeling and lying on the wire. The death-defying feat, which was accomplished without safety nets, was only the third successful crossing of the river, as well as being the highest and longest ever. Had the pair fallen, they would have plunged into 8 feet of water at about 60 mph. The first successful tightrope walk across the Thames was by another Frenchman, Charles Elleano, in 1951. A German, Franz Burbach, followed him in 1972.

HIGHEST AERIAL ACT
The highest recorded aerial act was a trapeze act, performed on August 10, 1995, by Mike Howard at an altitude of 19,600–20,300 feet. The trapeze was suspended from a hot-air balloon between Glastonbury and Street, England.

BIGGEST HUMAN MOBILE
In 1996, a record 16 performers were suspended from a crane to form a human mobile in Munich, Germany. The performers were all from the Circus of Horrors, based in Surrey, England.

LONGEST HUMAN CANNONBALL
The longest human cannonball flight was performed by Dave Smith Jr. and broadcast on the Fox television series *Guinness World Records™: Primetime.* The attempt, held in West Mifflin, Pennsylvania on May 29, 1998, also involved Smith's father, Dave Smith Sr., who held the previous record. Smith Sr. equaled his own 180-foot mark, but Smith Jr. flew 185 feet.

HIGHEST HIGH WIRE
The world's highest ever ground-supported high-wire feat took place at an altitude of 1,350 feet. It was performed by Philippe Petit of France between the towers of the World Trade Center, New York City on August 7, 1974.

GREATEST TIGHTROPE DROP
On August 4, 1989, Michel Menin of Lons-le-Saunier, France walked a record-breaking 10,335 feet on a tightrope above the French countryside.

LONGEST TIGHTROPE WALK
The world tightrope endurance record of 205 days was set by Jorge Ojeda-Guzman of Orlando, Florida, between January 1 and July 25, 1993. The tightrope wire was 36-foot-long and was suspended 35 feet above the ground. Ojeda-Guzman entertained the crowds of spectators by walking, balancing on a chair and dancing. He had a 3 x 3-foot wooden cabin at one end of the tightrope.

MOST PEOPLE JUMPED OVER ON A HIGH WIRE
On December 26, 1996, during a performance for Ringling Bros. and Barnum & Bailey Circus in Tampa, Florida, Walfer Guerrero (Colombia) jumped over a total of four people who were sitting on the high wire.

GREATEST DISTANCE COVERED BY A HUMAN ARROW
The Bulgarian artiste Vesta Gueschkova, who performed using the stage name "Airiana," was fired a record distance of 75 feet from a crossbow at Ringling Bros. and Barnum & Bailey Circus, Tampa, Florida on December 27, 1995.

MOST SWORDS SWALLOWED
Brad Byers of Moscow, Indiana swallowed eight 27-inch swords on June 26, 1998. Byers' feat was broadcast on the Fox television series *Guinness World Records™: Primetime.*

MOST PEOPLE ON ONE BICYCLE
In 1996, a record 17 people from the Shan Dong Acrobatic Troupe with Phillip Gandey's Chinese State Circus rode one bicycle.

TALLEST STILTS
Travis Wolf of Marshfield, Wisconsin mastered stilts that measured 40 ft. 10¼ in. from the ground to his ankle. He walked 26 steps without touching his safety handrail wires on March 10, 1998. Wolf broke the mark set by his father, Eddy Wolf, in 1988.

TALLEST UNICYCLE
The tallest unicycle was 101 ft. 9 in. in height. Steve McPeak rode the unicycle, with a safety wire suspended from an overhead crane, for a distance of 376 feet in Las Vegas, Nevada in October 1980.

SNAKE SITTING
The record for sitting in a bathtub with the most poisonous snakes is currently held by Jackie Bibby of Fort Worth, Texas. On June 17, 1998, Bibby sat in a tub with 35 rattlesnakes. The record was broadcast on the Fox television series *Guinness World Records™: Primetime.*

HUMAN WING SUIT
The longest air distance traveled using a wing suit is 4½ miles over Lake Elsinore, California by Adrian Nichols on May 26, 1998. Nichols' flight was measured using GPS technology. His record-breaking performance was broadcast on the Fox television series *Guinness World Records™: Primetime.*

HIGHEST-EARNING CIRCUS GROUP
Global theater group Cirque du Soleil has an annual turnover of more than $88 million. It has grown from a company started by street performers from Quebec, Canada to a multinational corporation employing 1,250 people.

BIGGEST GATHERING OF STREET/CIRCUS PERFORMERS
England's Glastonbury Festival, which attracts performers from all over the world every year, is the largest gathering of street/circus performers. In 1994, a total of 700 people juggled at one time.

MOST TARANTULA BUBBLES BLOWN
The record for blowing bubbles with a live tarantula inside the mouth is 99 in one minute. Ray Macarey of San Jose, California performed this feat on June 16, 1998. The record was broadcast on the Fox television series *Guinness World Records™: Primetime.*

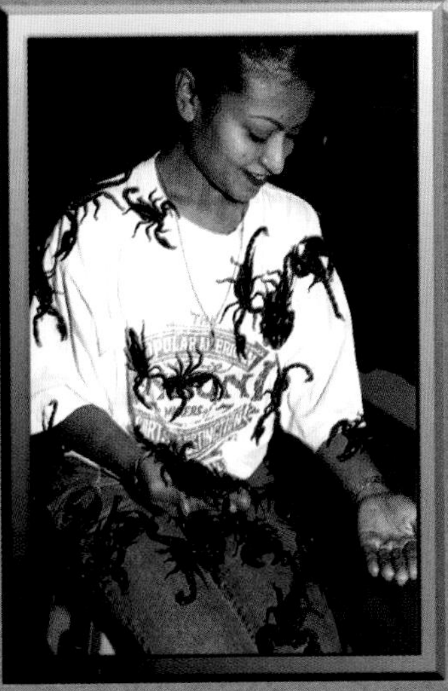

SCORPION HANDLING
Rohayo Ramli plays with hundreds of deadly scorpions in a cage at an exhibition in Seremban, in Negeri Sembilan, Malaysia, on March 21, 1998. Ramli, who used to be a dancer, began scorpion handling two years ago, having discovered that she enjoyed the feel of arachnids on her skin. People have long been fascinated by the behavior of arachnids and insects and their reactions to human contact. In June 1924, Frank Bornhofer was photographed wearing a helmet and chin strap covered in bees in Cincinnati, Ohio. The purpose of the exercise was to prove that bees rarely sting. As Bornhofer had predicted, he did not receive a single sting.

SNAKE CHARMING
The annual International Snake Charmers Competition was first held in Perlis State, Malaysia in September 1997. It attracted more than 40 snake tamers from around the world, who competed for a first prize of $2,000. Snake charmer Osman Ayub, from Langkawi Island, Perlis, Malaysia, is pictured holding a poisonous cat snake (family Colubridae) in his mouth during the first competition.

WORLD TRADE CENTER FEATS
Former professional stuntman Daniel Goodwin climbed the sheer face of the North Tower of the World Trade Center, New York City, in May 1983. Almost a decade previously, in August 1974, the 1,375-foot towers had also been the location for the world's highest ever ground-supported high-wire feat, which was performed by French trapeze artist Philippe Petit.

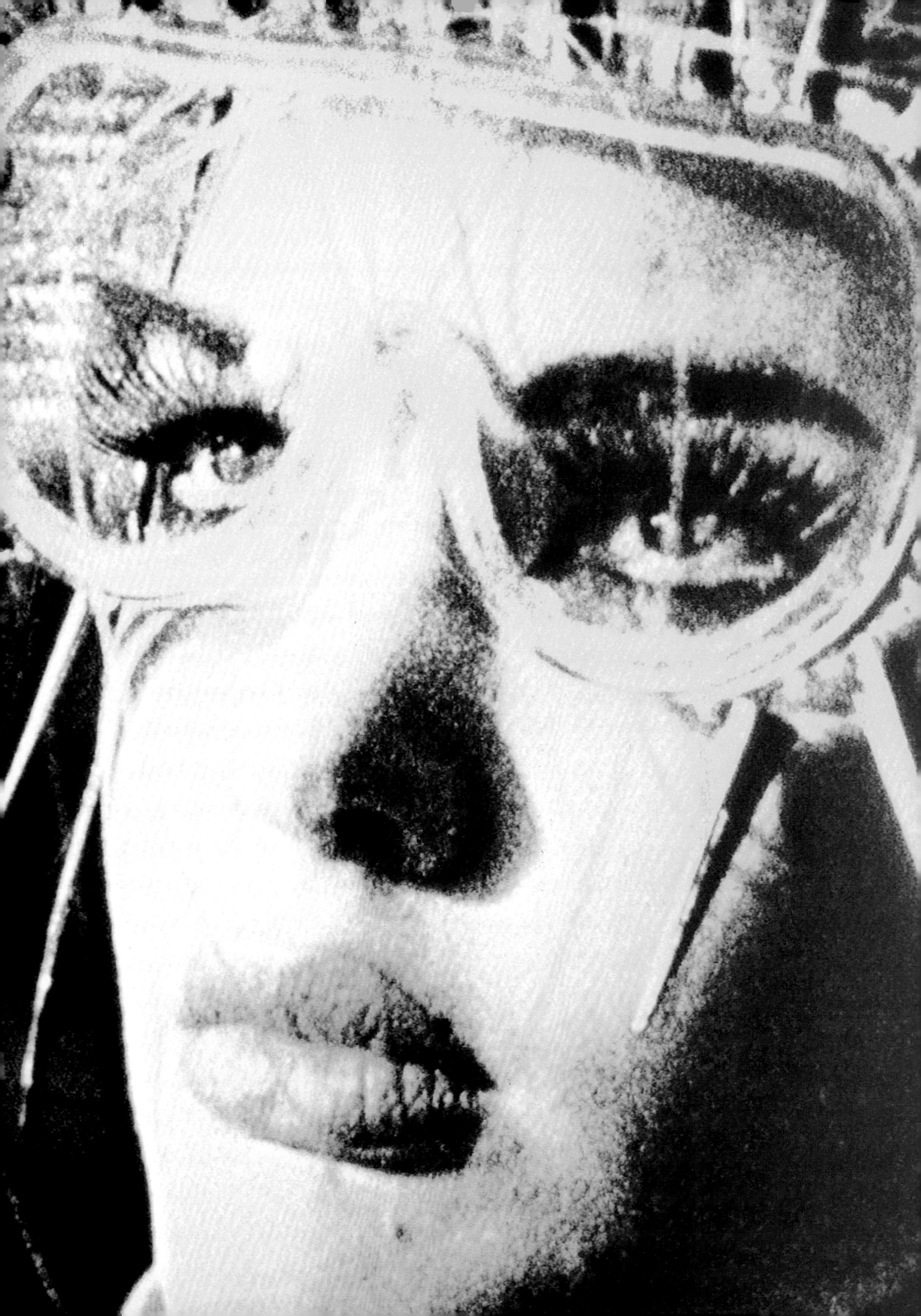

music & fashion

pop

MOST BRIT AWARDS (NON UK)
The most successful ever non-UK/US solo artist at the annual Brit Awards is the Icelandic singer/songwriter Björk, with a total of three. Björk began her recording career at the age of 11 with an eponymously-titled album of covers and went on to front the Sugarcubes in Iceland. In 1993 her album *Debut* secured her international fame.

MOST SUCCESSFUL FEMALE ARTIST
No female artist has sold more records around the world than Madonna, who has had total sales of more than 100 million. She is the most successful female artist on both the US chart, with a total of 35 Top 20 singles and 10 Top 10 albums since 1983, and the UK chart, with 45 Top 20 entries and 13 Top 10 albums (including six No. 1s – a UK chart record for any female artist).

MOST SUCCESSFUL SIBLINGS
Michael and Janet Jackson are the only siblings to have separately topped the US singles and album charts. Michael has amassed 13 No. 1 singles and four chart-topping albums and Janet has had eight No. 1 singles and three No. 1 albums.

MOST SUCCESSFUL DUOS
The most successful duo in the US is Hall & Oates, with a total of 22 Top 20 singles.

The most successful duo in the UK are the Pet Shop Boys, who have had 28 Top 20 singles.

MOST SUCCESSFUL SONGWRITER
Lionel Richie wrote at least one No. 1 hit in the US every year between 1978 and 1987.

MOST SUCCESSFUL CONCERT SERIES
Michael Jackson sold out for seven nights at Wembley Stadium, London in August 1988.

BIGGEST-SELLING ALBUM
Michael Jackson's *Thriller* (1982) has sold more than 45 million copies globally. Of these, 25 million were sold in the US, making it the biggest-selling album in the country.

Sgt. Pepper's Lonely Hearts Club Band by the Beatles has sold more than 4.3 million copies in the UK. Since it was first released in June 1967 it has re-charted on several occasions and last reached the Top 40 in April 1998.

BIGGEST-SELLING ALBUM BY A MALE SOLOIST IN THE U.K.
Michael Jackson's *Bad* (1987) has sold 3.9 million copies in the UK. His *Thriller* (1982) is the second most successful album, with sales of more than 3.3 million.

BIGGEST-SELLING ALBUM IN THE U.K. BY A FEMALE SOLOIST
The Immaculate Collection by Madonna (1990) has had UK sales of more than 2.7 million.

BIGGEST U.K. ADVANCE ORDERS
Spiceworld (1997) by the Spice Girls had record UK advance orders of 1.4 million. The global advance order was 6 million.

YOUNGEST SINGER TO TOP U.S. SINGLES CHART
Michael Jackson was 11 years five months old when he sang lead on "I Want You Back" by the Jackson Five, which reached No. 1 on the US chart in 1970.

YOUNGEST SINGER TO TOP U.K. SINGLES CHART
Jimmy Osmond was 9 years 8 months old when he reached No. 1 in 1972 with "Long Haired Lover From Liverpool."

LONGEST PERIOD AT NO. 1 ON U.S. SINGLES CHART
Mariah Carey was at No. 1 on the US chart for 26 out of 33 weeks between September 1995 and May 1996, with the singles "Fantasy" (eight weeks), "One Sweet Day" – recorded with Boyz II Men – (16 weeks) and "Always Be My Baby" (two weeks). She broke Elvis Presley's 1956 record of 25 weeks.

MOST WEEKS ON SINGLES CHART IN THE U.S.
"You Were Meant For Me/Foolish Games" by Jewel spent 65 weeks on the US chart from November 30, 1996 to February 21, 1998.

MOST CONSECUTIVE WEEKS AT NO. 1 IN THE U.S.
"One Sweet Day" by Mariah Carey & Boyz II Men spent 16 consecutive weeks at the top of the US singles chart in 1995/96. Boyz II Men feature in three of the six records to have topped the US charts for the longest time.

MOST CONSECUTIVE TOP 5 SINGLES IN THE U.S.
Madonna had a record-breaking 16 successive US Top 5 singles between 1984 and 1989 and 27 consecutive Top 20 entries between 1983 and 1992.

YOUNGEST GROUP TO EARN A PLATINUM SINGLE IN THE U.K.
"Mmmbop" by Hanson went to No. 1 in a total of 20 countries and passed the 600,000 sales mark in the UK in 1997, when the Hanson brothers' average age was 14. When the single was at No. 1 in the United States, the group's youngest member, drummer Zachary, was 11 years 6 months old – just one month older than Michael Jackson was when the Jackson Five went to the top of the US charts with "I Want You Back" in 1970. Hanson's album *Middle of Nowhere* has sold about 6 million copies worldwide and been widely acclaimed as a classic pop album. Zachary and his brothers Taylor, the band's 14-year-old vocalist and keyboard player, and Isaac, the 17-year-old guitarist, have all studied classical piano for at least five years and write a proportion of their songs. Now managed by their father, they were spotted at the South By Southwest music conference in Austin, Texas by an entertainment lawyer and Grateful Dead fanatic, Christopher Sabec, in 1994. They join a long line of youthful pop stars, including the Osmonds, the Jackson Five, Five Star, Musical Youth, Aaron Carter and Cleopatra.

MUSIC RECORDS
Because of the localized nature of the music industry, the records on the music pages are a mixture of US, British and world records.

MOST SUCCESSFUL SINGLES DEBUT IN THE U.S.
Mariah Carey's first 11 singles all reached the US Top 5. She had 13 No. 1 singles in the 1990s and has topped the chart for 58 weeks — a record bettered only by Elvis Presley and the Beatles. Carey also holds the records for the most successive US No. 1 singles by a newcomer (her first five singles reached No. 1) and for the most singles to enter at No. 1, with three by April 1998.

MOST SUCCESSIVE U.K. NO. 1 SINGLES BY A NEWCOMER
The Spice Girls reached No. 1 with their first six singles in the UK.

MOST CONSECUTIVE TOP 10 HITS IN THE U.K.
From 1984 to 1994, Madonna amassed a record 32 successive Top 10 entries in the UK.

BIGGEST-SELLING DEBUT ALBUM
Spice (1996), the debut album by the Spice Girls, is both the biggest- and fastest-selling debut album by a British act. The five-piece band, now four since the departure of Geri Halliwell ("Ginger Spice"), topped the charts in 14 countries and had worldwide sales of more than 20 million. It is also the biggest-selling debut album by any act in the UK, with certified sales of 3 million.

MOST SUCCESSFUL SINGLE BY A GERMAN ARTIST IN THE U.K.
Nena's "99 Red Balloons" topped the UK chart for three weeks in 1984. The original German version reached No. 2 in the US.

MOST SUCCESSFUL SINGLE BY A SWEDISH ARTIST IN THE U.S.
"The Sign" by Swedish group Ace of Base remained at No. 1 in the US for four weeks in 1994.

MOST TIMES AT NO. 1 BY A SINGLE
Chubby Checker's "The Twist" topped the US chart in September 1960 and January 1962, and "Bohemian Rhapsody" by Queen was No. 1 in the UK in November 1975 and December 1991.

MOST SUCCESSFUL BOY BANDS
The biggest-earning boy band ever was New Kids on the Block. The group was reported to have had gross revenues of $861 million at the peak of its career from 1989 to 1991. No US band has beaten the nine consecutive US Top 10 entries by the band between 1988 and 1990. New Kids on the Block also holds the record for the most UK Top 10 hits in a calendar year, with eight in 1990.

The greatest number of No. 1 singles on the UK chart by a British boy band is eight, by Take That between 1993 and 1996.

MOST BRIT AWARDS
The most Brit Awards won by a British performer is seven, by Annie Lennox.

The most successful US artist at the Brit Awards is The Artist (formerly known as Prince), who has won seven awards, one of which was for the music from the film *Batman* (1989).

MOST SUCCESSFULL NON UK DEBUT
Former Australian soap star Kylie Minogue's first 11 singles all reached the UK Top 5. Minogue was also the youngest female artist to top the UK album chart with *Kylie* in 1988, when she was 20 years 8 months old. It sold nearly 2 million copies in the UK. Minogue's record for the most succesful foreign UK chart debut was equaled by Boyzone in 1998.

MOST AUSTRALIAN AWARDS
The record for the greatest ever number of Aria (Australian Record Industry Association) awards won by an artist in one year is 10, by Savage Garden in 1997. They were nominated in a record 13 out of 26 categories.

LONGEST-RUNNING POP SHOW
The BBC show *Top of the Pops* was first broadcast on January 1, 1964 and featured, among other artists, the Rolling Stones and the Beatles. The program's 1,782th episode was aired on May 1, 1998.

pop classics

LONGEST CAREER ON U.S. TOP 20
Barbra Streisand first entered the US singles chart with "People" in 1964. Her most recent hit, "I Finally Found Someone" (a duet with Bryan Adams), exited 32 years 7 months later in January 1997. In 1987, she founded the Barbra Streisand Foundation for liberal causes and later founded a Streisand Chair in Cardiology and a Streisand Chair in Contemporary Gender Studies at two universities.

MOST SUCCESSFUL SOLO ARTISTS
Elvis Presley was the world's most successful solo artist of the rock era, with 18 No. 1 singles and nine No. 1 albums in the US and 17 No. 1 singles and six No. 1 albums in the UK. The first artist to reportedly sell 1 billion records, he had a record 94 chart entries in the US and 98 in the UK.

In the pre-rock era, Bing Crosby had 299 Top 20 entries in the US, including 38 No. 1s.

MOST SUCCESSFUL GROUP
The Beatles have sold around 1 billion records and cassettes and had a record 18 US No. 1 albums, and 14 UK No. 1 albums.

MOST SUCCESSFUL FAMILY GROUP IN THE U.S. AND U.K.
Between 1968 and 1998, the Bee Gees accumulated 24 Top 20 singles in the US and UK. They have also had 13 Top 20 albums in the US and 11 in the UK.

MOST SUCCESSFUL SONGWRITERS
The most US No. 1s in a calendar year is seven, by John Lennon and Paul McCartney with "I Want To Hold Your Hand," "She Loves You," "Can't Buy Me Love," "Love Me Do," "A World Without Love," "A Hard Day's Night" and "I Feel Fine" in 1964. Their songs held the top spot for 19 weeks of the year.

Barry Gibb wrote or co-wrote seven No. 1s in the 12-month period from July 30, 1976: "I Just Want To Be Your Everything," "How Deep Is Your Love," "Stayin' Alive," "Love Is Thicker Than Water," "Night Fever," "If I Can't Have You" and "Shadow Dancing."

MOST U.S. NO. 1 ALBUMS IN A YEAR
The Monkees had a record four No. 1 albums on the US chart in one year: *The Monkees*, *More Of The Monkees*, *Headquarters* and *Pisces, Aquarius, Capricorn and Jones* in 1967.

ALBUM WITH MOST WEEKS AT NO. 1 IN THE U.S. (ROCK ERA)
The soundtrack to *West Side Story* charted in May 1962 and held the top spot on the stereo album chart for 54 weeks.

ALBUM WITH MOST WEEKS AT NO. 1 IN THE U.K.
The soundtrack to *South Pacific* (1958) headed the first ever UK album chart and remained at No. 1 for 115 weeks, of which 70 were consecutive.

MOST WEEKS ON SINGLES CHART IN THE U.K.
"My Way" by Frank Sinatra entered the UK chart on 10 separate occasions and spent a total of 124 weeks there between 1969 and 1994.

MOST ENTRIES ON THE U.K. TOP 5
Frankie Laine had three entries in the UK Top 5 on November 7, 1953, with "Answer Me" at No. 2, "Hey Joe" at No. 3 and "I Believe" at No. 5.

BIGGEST CD SET BY A SOLO ARTIST
France's most consistently successful recording artist is Johnny Hallyday, who released a 40-CD, 730-track set to mark his 50th birthday in 1993. The singer, who was still scoring big hits in 1998, is reported to have sold 80 million records worldwide.

TOP FRENCH LANGUAGE ALBUM
Celine Dion's *D'eux* (1995) has sold more than 8 million globally.

MOST SUCCESSFUL SINGLE BY FRENCH ACT IN THE U.K.
"She" by Charles Aznavour headed the chart for four weeks in 1974.

MOST FRENCH ACTS ON U.K. CHART
On October 1, 1977, the UK Top 10 included "Magic Fly" by Space, "Oxygene Part IV" by Jean Michel Jarre and "Black Is Black" by La Belle Epoque.

MOST SUCCESSFUL SINGLE BY A GERMAN ACT IN THE U.S.
"Wunderland Bei Nacht" by Bert Kaempfert & His Orchestra was No. 1 for three weeks in 1961.

MOST SUCCESSFUL SINGLE BY AUSTRALIAN ACT IN THE U.K.
"Two Little Boys" by Rolf Harris was at No. 1 for six weeks in 1969.

MOST AUSTRALIAN ACTS ON THE U.S. CHART
In November 1981, "The Night Owls" by the Little River Band, "Here I Am" by Air Supply and "I've Done Everything For You" by Rick Springfield were in the US Top 10 with "Physical" by Australian-raised Olivia Newton-John.

MOST SUCCESSFUL SINGLE BY AN ITALIAN ACT IN THE U.S.
"Nel Blu Dipinto Di Blu (Volare)" by Domenico Modugno spent five weeks at No. 1 in 1958.

MOST SUCCESSFUL EUROVISION SONG CONTEST WINNERS
The 1974 Eurovision Song Contest winner, "Waterloo," launched the international career of Abba, who went on to become the most commercially successful group of the 70s and one of the biggest-selling acts of all time. They also became the most successful ever Swedish act in the UK, with a total of 19 Top 20 singles (nine of which went to No. 1) and eight No. 1 albums between 1974 and 1982. Abba split up in 1982 but experienced a revival in the early 1990s, when they topped the charts worldwide. In 1992, band members Bjorn Ulvaeus and Benny Anderson joined U2 on stage when the latter performed the Abba classic "Dancing Queen" during their *Zoo* tour. Nelson Mandela's favorite pop group, Abba had other hits including "Thank You For the Music," "Super Trouper," "Fernando," "The Winner Takes It All," "Chiquitita," "I Do, I Do, I Do, I Do, I Do," "Knowing Me Knowing You" and "Take a Chance On Me."

MOST JAMES BOND THEMES
Of the 11 James Bond themes sung by women, three have been by Shirley Bassey: "Goldfinger," "Diamonds Are Forever" and "Moonraker." Bassey also holds the record for the longest career on the UK Top 20 singles chart by a female artist, at 40 years 9 months. Born in Tiger Bay, Cardiff, Wales, she now lives in Monte Carlo.

MOST SUCCESSFUL U.K. SOLO ARTIST
Elton John, pictured at his 50th birthday party with his partner David Furnish, is the most successful British solo singer of all time in both the US and the UK. In his 30-year career, he has sold more than 150 million albums worldwide, and in the US, his 56 Top 40 hits put him second only to Elvis Presley.

MOST SUCCESSFUL SINGLE BY JAPANESE ACT IN U.S. AND U.K.
"Sukiyaki (Ue O Muite Aruko)" by Kyu Sakamoto topped the US chart for three weeks in 1963 and reached the UK Top 10.

BIGGEST-SELLING SOUNDTRACK ALBUM IN THE U.K. AND U.S.
The soundtrack of *The Bodyguard*, starring Whitney Houston and Kevin Costner, has sold a record 2.1 million copies in the UK and more than 16 million in the US since its release in 1992.

BIGGEST-SELLING MOVIE SCORE
The score of *Titanic* (1997) is the biggest- and fastest-selling movie score ever. In the US, it sold 9 million copies in 15 weeks. A No. 1 album in more than 20 countries, it was the first record containing incidental movie score music to top the UK charts. As of June 1998, it had sold close to 24 million copies worldwide.

MOST SUCCESSFUL INSTRUMENTAL ACT ON U.S. ALBUM CHART
Herb Alpert & The Tijuana Brass had a record nine successive US Top 10 albums between 1963 and 1968. On April 2, 1966 they had four albums in the US Top 10.

MOST SUCCESSFUL INSTRUMENTAL SINGLE IN THE U.S. (ROCK ERA)
"Cherry Pink And Apple Blossom White" by Perez Prado and His Orchestra topped the chart for 10 weeks in 1955.

BIGGEST-SELLING RELIGIOUS ALBUM (ROCK ERA)
Chant (*Canto Gregoriano/ Major Works of Canto Gregori*) by the Benedictine Monks Of Santo Domingo De Silos (also known as Monks Chorus Silos) from Spain sold more than 6 million copies worldwide in 1994 and reached the Top 10 in many countries, including the UK and the US.

MOST WINS IN THE EUROVISION SONG CONTEST
The most Eurovision Song Contest wins by one country is seven, by Ireland (1970, 1980, 1987, 1992, 1993, 1994, 1996). Ireland's Johnny Logan won twice, in 1980 and 1987.

BIGGEST EUROVISION HIT IN U.S.
Abba's Eurovision Song Contest winner "Waterloo" reached No. 6 on the US singles chart in 1974.

The most successful finalist is "L'Amour est Bleu," which came fourth in the 1967 contest sung by Vicky (Luxembourg). As "Love Is Blue" by Paul Mauriat and His Orchestra, the song topped the chart in 1968. It is the most successful ever single by a French act in the US.

HIGHEST POINTS IN EUROVISION SONG CONTEST
The 1997 winner, the UK entry, "Love Shine A Light" by Katrina and The Waves, scored 227 points.

MOST SUCCESSFUL JAMES BOND THEME IN THE U.S. AND U.K.
Duran Duran's "A View To A Kill" reached No. 1 in the US and No. 2 in the UK in 1985.

MOST SUCCESSFUL COVER OF A JAMES BOND THEME
The highest chart position by a James Bond cover in the UK is No. 5, by "Live And Let Die" by Guns 'N' Roses in December 1991.

LONGEST TIME TAKEN BY A JAMES BOND THEME TO BECOME A HIT
Louis Armstrong's "We Have All The Time In The World," the theme song to *On Her Majesty's Secret Service* (1969), reached No. 3 in the UK in December 1994, more than 25 years after it was originally released and 23 years after Armstrong's death.

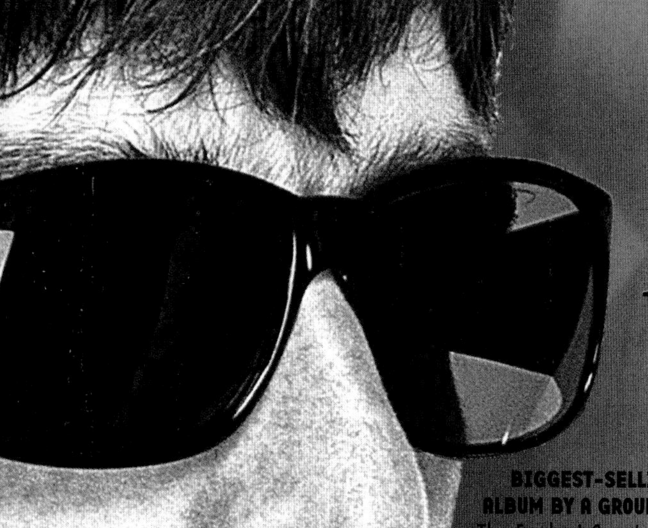

rock

BIGGEST-SELLING ALBUM BY A GROUP
The Eagles' *Greatest Hits 1971–75* is estimated to have sold more than 25 million copies worldwide. It is also the biggest-selling rock album in the US, with certified sales of 24 million.

MOST WEEKS ON U.S. ALBUM CHART
Dark Side Of The Moon by Pink Floyd entered the US chart on March 17, 1973 and is still there. It spent 741 weeks in the Top 200 and 353 weeks on the Pop Catalogue chart up to April 1998, topping the latter in its 1,075th chart week.

BIGGEST-SELLING HEAVY ROCK ALBUMS IN THE U.S.
Led Zeppelin IV (Four Symbols) by British band Led Zeppelin has sold 17 million copies since 1971.

Bruce Springsteen's *Born In The USA* (1984) is the top-selling album by a US performer in the US, with sales of 15 million.

BIGGEST-SELLING HEAVY ROCK ALBUM IN THE U.K.
Bat Out Of Hell by Meat Loaf has sold more than 2.1 million copies in the UK since 1978. It had also spent a record 472 weeks on the UK album chart by April 1998.

FASTEST-SELLING ALBUM (U.K.)
Be Here Now (1997) by Oasis sold a record 345,000 copies in the UK on its first day of release. By the third day, it had sold 700,000 copies, and within 17 days it had passed the 1 million mark. Like Oasis' first two albums, it entered the chart at No. 1, breaking the record for the most consecutive releases to enter in pole position. It also headed the charts in nine other countries in its first week of release.

BIGGEST-SELLING NON-U.K./U.S. ROCK ALBUM IN THE U.S.
Australian group AC/DC's *Back In Black* (1980) has sold more than 12 million copies in the US.

BIGGEST-SELLING NON-U.K./U.S. ROCK ALBUM IN THE U.K.
Irish group U2's *Joshua Tree* (1987) has sold 1.8 million copies in the UK.

BEST-SELLING ALBUM IN JAPAN
Japan's top-selling album of all time is *Review*, by Japanese rock band Glay. The album has sold more than 4.7 million copies in Japan alone.

MOST SUCCESSFUL POSTHUMOUS ALBUMS IN THE U.S.
Kurt Cobain and Nirvana topped the US chart with *MTV Unplugged In New York* in November 1994 and with *From The Muddy Banks Of The Wishkah* in October 1996. Cobain died in April 1994.

BIGGEST-SELLING DEBUT ALBUM
Jagged Little Pill (1995) by Canada's Alanis Morissette has sold almost 30 million copies worldwide. It is also the biggest-selling album in the US by a female artist.

MOST SUCCESSFUL ROCK SINGLE
Bryan Adams' "(Everything I Do) I Do It For You" spent a record 16 consecutive weeks at No. 1 in the UK and seven weeks at No. 1 in the US in 1991.

MOST WEEKS AT NO. 1 ON U.S. AIRPLAY CHART
"Don't Speak" by No Doubt spent 16 weeks at No. 1 on the US airplay chart in 1997 but was never available as a single so did not enter the US Top 100 sales chart.

MOST SUCCESSFUL SINGLE BY AN AUSTRALIAN ARTIST IN THE U.S.
"Down Under" by Men At Work was No. 1 for four weeks in 1983.

MOST SIMULTANEOUS "INDIE" HITS IN THE U.K.
The Smiths held the top three places on the UK indie chart on January 28, 1984.

On July 1, 1995, Oasis had six singles in the top seven of the UK indie chart.

BIGGEST ROCK CONCERT
On July 21, 1990 an estimated 200,000 people watched Roger Waters' production of Pink Floyd's *The Wall* at Potsdamer Platz on the border between East and West Berlin, Germany. It involved 600 performers.

BIGGEST CONCERT ATTENDANCES
The biggest audience at a paying concert was an estimated 195,000 people, who saw Norway's A-Ha play at the Rock in Rio festival in Brazil in 1990.

The largest paying audience for a solo performer was an estimated 180,000–184,000, for Paul McCartney at the Macaranã Stadium, Rio de Janeiro, Brazil on April 21, 1990. About 180,000 people are also believed to have watched Tina Turner's concert at the Macaranã Stadium in 1988.

The largest audience for a free concert by a solo artist was 3.5 million, to see Rod Stewart at Copacabana Beach, Rio de Janeiro, Brazil, December 31, 1994.

BIGGEST SCREEN AT A CONCERT
The largest LED (light-emitting diode) screen measures 55 feet by 170 feet and was part of the set on U2's 1997 *PopMart* tour. It showed animation and art, including material by pop artists Andy Warhol and Roy Lichtenstein.

MOST HIGHLY-PAID ROCK STARS
The Rolling Stones had an estimated gross income of $68 million in 1996–97, putting them 12th in the *Forbes* list of the world's highest-paid entertainers. The British band narrowly beat Celine Dion, who earned $65 million, and David Bowie, who earned $63 million. Formed in 1962, the Rolling Stones are the world's most enduring rock band: they had their first UK hit in 1963 with a version of Chuck Berry's "Come On" and made their debut on the US chart in 1964 with "(Tell Me) You're Coming Back." The band was still charting on both sides of the Atlantic in 1998. In 1994 and 1995, the band proved that they could still pull in the crowds when their *Voodoo Lounge* tour became the most successful tour of all time, taking an estimated $400 million in receipts. During the tour, the band, most of whom are now in their 50s, put on 62 concerts instead of the scheduled 28. Their 1997 *Bridges to Babylon* tour surpassed the *Voodoo Lounge* record, taking approximately $500 million. The band currently consists of Keith Richards, Ron Wood, Charlie Watts, Darryl Jones and frontman Mick Jagger.

MOST DEATHS AT A ROCK CONCERT
Eleven Who fans were trampled to death at the band's gig in Cincinnati, Ohio in 1979.

MOST CONTINENTS IN A DAY
Def Leppard staged shows on three continents on October 24, 1995, when they appeared in Tangiers, Morocco, London, and Vancouver.

BIGGEST ROCK COLLECTION
The Hard Rock Cafe in Philadelphia has 45,000 pieces of rock memorabilia on display, including Madonna's black bustier and Sid Vicious' vinyl trousers.

MOST EXPENSIVE ROCK ITEM
John Lennon's 1965 psychedelic Rolls-Royce *Phantom V* touring limousine was sold at Sotheby's, New York City on June 29, 1995 for $2.8 million.

BIGGEST ROCK MUSEUM
Paul Allen, the co-founder of Microsoft and the eighth richest man in the world, is donating his tens of thousands of pieces of Jimi Hendrix memorabilia to the new 130,000-square-foot Experience Music Project museum in Seattle, which will be the world's largest rock museum. A legendary guitarist, songwriter and singer, Hendrix died in 1970 at the age of 28. On September 14, 1997, more than a quarter of a century after his death, he became the first rock artist to have a prestigious English Heritage Blue Plaque placed on a building associated with him (his former house at 23 Brook Street, London, England).

MOST EXPENSIVE ROCK INSTRUMENT
The most expensive rock instrument sold at auction is an acoustic guitar owned at various times by David Bowie, George Michael and Paul McCartney, which sold for £220,000 ($369,600) at Christie's, London on May 18, 1994.

MOST VALUABLE US ROCK RECORDING
There are only two copies of Bob Dylan's *The Freewheelin' Bob Dylan* (Columbia CS-8796, in stereo), because the album was later re-pressed without four of the songs. Near-mint condition copies would be worth $20,000–30,000.

MOST IMPRESSIVE CHART ENTRY
On October 5, 1991, *Use Your Illusion II* by Guns 'N' Roses entered the US album chart at No. 1 and *Use Your Illusion I* entered at No. 2 — the most impressive entry in US chart history. In the first week, 4.2 million copies of these albums were shipped. The group also holds the record for best-selling album by a US heavy rock group: *Appetite For Destruction* (1987) has sold 14 million copies.

MOST SUCCESSFUL ROCK WIDOW
Courtney Love, who married Kurt Cobain of Nirvana in 1992, is the most successful rock widow of the 1990s. After an early acting appearance in Alex Cox's *Sid and Nancy* (1986), Love achieved rock fame with her band Hole, whose second album *Live Through This* coincided with Cobain's suicide in 1994. In 1996, she was nominated for a Golden Globe for her role in *The People vs. Larry Flynt.*

MOST ARRESTS OF A ROCK STAR
Jim Morrison of the Doors was arrested five times from 1967 to 1970, for harassment; public drunkenness (twice); indecent exposure and profanity; drunk and disorderly conduct; and interfering with personnel aboard an aircraft. Morrison died in 1971.

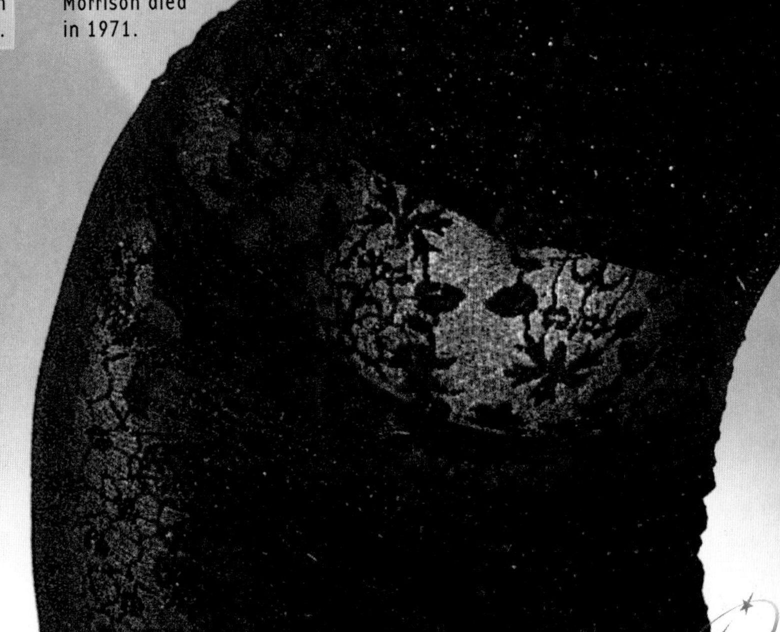

dance music

BEST-SELLING SOUNDTRACK
Saturday Night Fever (1978) is the biggest-selling movie soundtrack worldwide, with sales of more than 30 million. Of these, 11 million copies were sold in the US. The disco album featured the hits "Jive Talkin'," "Stayin' Alive," "You Should Be Dancing" and "How Deep Is Your Love" by the Bee Gees, "If I Can't Have You" by Yvonne Elliman, "More Than a Woman" by Tavares and "Disco Inferno" by the Trammps. The movie starred John Travolta, who was nominated for an Oscar for Best Actor.

BIGGEST-SELLING DANCE ALBUM IN THE U.K.
Bizarre Fruit (1994) by British group M People has sold more than 1.5 million copies in the United Kingdom – more than any other dance album. It features the hits "Sight for Sore Eyes," "Open Your Heart" and "Search for the Hero."

MOST SUCCESSFUL DANCE SINGLE IN THE U.S.
"That's The Way Love Goes" by Janet Jackson topped the singles chart in the US for a record eight weeks in 1993.

MOST SUCCESSFUL DANCE SINGLE IN THE U.K.
"Ride On Time" (1989) by Italian group Black Box shares the record for the most successful dance single in the United Kingdom with "Rhythm is a Dancer" (1992) by Snap. Both singles topped the chart for six weeks. "Ride On Time" is also the most successful single by an Italian group in the United Kingdom.

MOST SUCCESSFUL DANCE MUSIC CAREER IN THE U.K.
Prodigy has had the best run of dance hit singles in the United Kingdom, with a record 12 successive releases reaching the top 15. The British group, which is made up of Keith Flint, Leroy Thornhill, Liam Howlett and Maxim Reality (Keith Palmer) debuted with "Charly" in August 1991, and its 12th entry, the controversially titled "Smack My Bitch Up," entered the chart in November 1997.

MOST DANCE CLUB PLAY NO. 1 SINGLES IN THE U.S.
Madonna has had a total of 19 No. 1 singles on the Billboard Dance Club Play chart.

The group with the most ever No. 1s on the Billboard Dance Club Play chart is the C&C Music Factory, with eight.

The record for the most No. 1s by a male soloist on the chart is seven, by (The Artist formerly known as Prince).

TOP-SELLING DANCE ALBUM, U.S.
The soundtrack to *Purple Rain* by Prince topped the US chart for a record 24 weeks and has sold more than 13 million copies since its release in 1985. The movie, which starred Prince, was an apparently autobiographical story set in the club scene of Minneapolis. The album yielded the hits "When Doves Cry" and "Let's Go Crazy." In 1993 the singer announced that he had changed his name to

MOST SAMPLED ARTIST
James Brown, who had his first hit in 1956, has been the most influential artist in the dance field: he has been an inspiration for dance music for five decades and is the most sampled artist of all time. The stage acts of many of today's top performers, including Michael Jackson, Mick Jagger and (The Artist formerly known as Prince), owe a great deal to Brown's showstopping dance routines, in which he thrusts his hips, twists his feet and ends his act by doing the splits. Brown was born in 1933 and began his career as a performer by dancing for money in the street. At the age of 16, he was convicted of armed robbery and sent to a juvenile detention center, where he began to sing gospel music with fellow inmate Bobby Byrd. The duo formed a rock 'n' roll group called the Flames and had a million-selling debut single, "Please Please Please," in 1956, but their subsequent compositions had more of an R&B flavor. Brown's first solo album was *Live at the Apollo*, which was recorded in 1965 and sold 1 million copies. Throughout the 1970s, he used his position as one of the most popular figures in the music world to promote social issues and write songs with a strong social message.

BRITISH ACT WITH MOST U.S. DANCE CLUB PLAY NO. 1 SINGLES
The British artist with the most ever No. 1s on the Billboard Dance Club Play chart is Lisa Stansfield, with a total of seven. They include "All Around the World," which was her third UK hit, and "Change."

MOST NO. 1 HITS ON U.S. 12-INCH DANCE SINGLES CHART
Madonna has had a record 16 singles reach the top of the US 12-inch singles chart – more than double the total of the three joint runners-up, ♀ (The Artist formerly known as Prince), Janet Jackson and Michael Jackson, all of whom have had a total of seven No. 1 hits. Madonna's dance No. 1s include "Like A Prayer," "Vogue," "Into the Groove" and "Papa Don't Preach."

MOST NO. 1 U.S. 12-INCH DANCE SINGLES BY A NON-U.S. ACT
British band Soul II Soul, fronted by Jazzie B and Nellee Hooper, is the most successful non-US act on the US 12-inch singles chart, with a record four No. 1s – "Keep on Movin' " (1989), "Back to Life" (1989), "Jazzie's Groove" (1990) and "A Dream's a Dream/Courtney Blows" (1990). Hooper is also a successful dance producer and has worked with artists such as Madonna and Björk.

DANCE ACT WITH GREATEST NUMBER OF SIMULTANEOUS HITS
On April 20, 1996, all of Prodigy's 10 hit singles were in the UK Top 100. Their previous nine singles had been reissued after "Firestarter" gave them their first No. 1.

TOP-SELLING DANCE ALBUM
The biggest-selling dance album by a female artist in the US is *Janet* (1993) by Janet Jackson, which topped the chart for six weeks and sold more than 6 million copies. Born in 1966, Jackson had an eventful childhood, singing with her brothers' band, the Jackson Five, and appearing in the TV shows *Diff'rent Strokes* and *Fame*. She made her movie debut in *Poetic Justice* (1993), opposite rapper Tupac Shakur.

FASTEST-SELLING DANCE ALBUM
The fastest-selling dance album in the UK is *The Fat Of The Land* (1997) by Prodigy, which sold a record 317,000 copies in its first week. In the US, it sold more than 200,000 copies in its first week. The album entered the chart at No. 1 in a total of 20 countries, including the US, the UK, Canada, Australia, Germany, Austria and Norway. Prodigy is distinctive not only for its hardcore style of dance music, but also for the unique looks of its members – Keith Flint (left) has dyed, shaved hair and a pierced septum, while Maxim wears cat's-eye contact lenses.

hip hop rap reggae and R&B

TOP-SELLING REGGAE ALBUM

Legend (1984) by Bob Marley is the biggest-selling reggae album of all time. In the UK, where it topped the chart, it has had certified sales of 1.8 million, and in the United States it sold more than 9 million copies. Marley was awarded the Jamaican Order of Merit after his death in 1981 and is officially known as The Honorable Bob Marley.

TOP-SELLING GROUP R&B ALBUM

The biggest-selling R&B album by a group in the US is *II* (1994) by Boyz II Men, with sales of more than 12 million. The group made their chart debut in 1991, and in 1992 their "End of the Road" (from the Eddie Murphy movie *Boomerang*) beat Elvis Presley's record for the most weeks at No. 1 on the US chart, with 13. They have since broken the record twice, with "I'll Make Love to You," which was No. 1 for 14 weeks in 1994 and "One Sweet Day" (with Mariah Carey), which topped the chart for 16 weeks in 1995.

BIGGEST-SELLING HIP HOP/RAP ALBUM IN THE U.S.

Please Hammer Don't Hurt 'Em (1990) by M. C. Hammer and *Crazysexycool* (1994) by TLC share the record for the biggest-selling hip hop/rap album in the United States, with certified sales of 10 million.

MOST SUCCESSFUL HIP HOP/RAP SINGLE IN THE U.K. & U.S.

"I'll Be Missing You" by Puff Daddy & Faith Evans headed the US pop chart for 11 weeks and the UK pop chart for six weeks in 1997, and is the most successful hip hop/rap single to date.

MOST U.S. No. 1 RAP SINGLES

The artist who has had the most No. 1 singles on the Billboard Rap Chart is L. L. Cool J, with a total of eight. These included "I'm That Type of Guy," "Around the Way Girl," "Loungin' " and "Father."

The female rapper with the most No. 1 singles on the Billboard Rap Chart is MC Lyte, with four ("Cha Cha Cha," "Poor Georgie," "Ruffneck" and "Cold Rock a Party").

LABEL WITH THE MOST U.S. No. 1 RAP SINGLES

The label with the greatest number of No. 1 singles on the Billboard Rap Chart is Def Jam, with 15 as of April 1998. Def Jam acts include Public Enemy, MC Serch, Boss and L. L. Cool J.

MOST SUCCESSFUL NON-ENGLISH LANGUAGE RAP RECORDS

In 1993, "Dur Dur D'Etre Bébé" ("It's Tough to Be a Baby") by five-year-old French rapper Jordy (Jordy Lemoine) sold more than 1 million copies in France and was also a minor hit in the US.

"Da Ya Ne" by Japanese rap act East End X Yuri sold 1 million copies in Japan in 1995.

MOST SUCCESSFUL RAP PRODUCER

Sean (Puff Daddy) Coombs produced four singles that consecutively headed the US rap chart for 36 weeks in 1997. They included "Hypnotize" and "Mo Money, Mo Problems" by The Notorious B.I.G.

MOST SUCCESSFUL TRIBUTE RECORD IN THE U.K. & U.S.

"I'll Be Missing You," recorded in 1997 by Puff Daddy & Faith Evans, and featuring 112, topped the singles chart in the UK for six weeks and led the US list for 11 weeks. The record was made as a tribute to rapper The Notorious B.I.G.

MOST SUCCESSFUL REGGAE SINGLE IN THE U.S.

"Informer" by Snow and "Can't Help Falling In Love" by UB40 share the title of most successful reggae single in the US. Both recordings topped the pop chart for seven weeks in 1993.

MOST SUCCESSFUL GANGSTA RAP ACT

The world's most successful gangsta rap artist to date was 2 Pac (Tupac Shakur), who died at the age of 25 in September 1996. Four of his albums reached the US pop Top 3 and three of them (*Me Against The World*, *All Eyez on Me* and *The Don Killuminati – The 7 Day Theory*) reached No. 1. Shakur died a week after being gunned down as he was driven to a party for boxer Mike Tyson in Las Vegas. A man in a white Cadillac drew up beside his vehicle and opened fire, injuring both Shakur and his boss Suge Knight, the head of Death Row Records.

Shakur's death focused the media's attention on the sometimes brutal nature of the gangsta rap genre, in which singers boast of their violent crimes and sexual conquests. Shakur himself had been arrested for assault and battery, and in 1995 he had spent 10 months in jail for sexual assault.

BEST WEEK FOR REGGAE ON THE U.K. CHART
On March 27, 1993, for the only time in history, the top three singles on the British chart were reggae recordings. Shaggy was at No. 1 with "Oh Carolina," Snow was at No. 2 with "Informer" and Shabba Ranks was at No. 3 with "Mr. Loverman."

LONGEST TIME AT U.K. No. 1 BY POSTHUMOUS ALBUM
The record for the longest stay at the top of the UK album chart by a posthumously released album is 12 weeks, by Bob Marley's best-selling *Legend*.The album was released in 1984, three years after the artist's death in 1981 at the age of 36. Of the 11 artists who have posthumously topped the UK album chart, Otis Redding was the first, with his *Dock Of The Bay* in 1968.

MOST U.S. No. 1 R&B ALBUMS
The Temptations have had 15 No. 1 R&B albums in the US, including *With a Lot O'Soul* (1967) and *Masterpiece* (1973).

The most No. 1 R&B albums in the US by a female artist is 10, by Aretha Franklin. The list includes *I Never Loved a Man* (1967) and *Lady Soul* (1968).

The most No. 1 R&B albums in the US by a male soloist is 10, by Stevie Wonder. Among these were the albums *Fulfillingness First Finale* (1974) and *Songs in the Key Of Life* (1976).

BIGGEST-SELLING R&B ALBUM IN THE U.S. BY A FEMALE ARTIST
Whitney Houston's self-titled 1985 debut album, which has had certified sales of 12 million, is the biggest-selling R&B album in the US by a female artist. It featured "Saving All My Love for You" and "Greatest Love of All."

BIGGEST-SELLING R&B ALBUM IN THE U.K.
Bad (1987) by Michael Jackson is the biggest-selling R&B album in the UK, with certified sales of 3.9 million.

MOST SINGLES ON THE R&B CHART IN THE U.S.
The artist with the most ever singles on the US Billboard R&B chart is James Brown, with a total of 118 entries between 1956 and 1993. He has also had more Top 10 entries than any other artist, with 58. Brown's most famous hits include "Papa's Got a Brand New Bag" (1965), "I Got You (I Feel Good)" (1965), "It's a Man's Man's Man's World" (1966) and "Living in America" (1986).

The greatest number of singles on the US R&B chart by a female artist is 96, by Aretha Franklin. She also holds the record for the most Top 10 entries, with a total of 52. The greatest hits of her career include "Respect" (1967), "I Say a Little Prayer" (1968) and "Who's Zoomin' Who" (1985).

MOST No. 1 R&B HITS IN THE U.S.
Stevie Wonder and Aretha Franklin have both had a record 20 No. 1 R&B hits in the US.

MOST SUCCESSFUL R&B SINGLE IN THE U.K.
The most successful single by an R&B artist in the UK is "I Will Always Love You" by Whitney Houston, which topped the pop chart for 10 weeks in 1992.

LONGEST CAREER ON THE R&B CHART IN THE U.S.
Balladeer Nat "King" Cole, who died in 1965, made his debut on the US R&B chart on November 21, 1942, with "That Ain't Right." His last chart entry came 48 years 7 mo. later on June 29, 1991, with "Unforgettable" (a posthumously created duet with his daughter Natalie Cole).

Aretha Franklin holds the record for the longest chart career in the US by a female artist. Her first chart hit was "Today I Sing the Blues" in 1960 and her most recent was "A Rose is Still a Rose" in 1998.

YOUNGEST ARTIST TO TOP THE U.S. ALBUM CHART
The youngest artist to have ever got to No. 1 on the US album pop chart was Stevie Wonder, with *The 12 Year Old Genius* in 1963, when the singer was 13 years 3 mo. old. Wonder's most famous hits include "You Are the Sunshine of My Life" (1972) and "I Just Called to Say I Love You" (1984).

TALLEST U.S. No. 1 SINGLES ARTIST
At 6 ft. 8 in. tall, Montell Jordan is the tallest artist to have ever reached the top of the US chart. His recording of "This Is How We Do It" reached No. 1 in April 1995.

FASTEST RAPPER
Rebel X.D. of Chicago, Illinois rapped 67 syllables in 54.9 seconds at the Hair Bear Recording Studio, Alsip, Illinois on August 27, 1992. This works out at 12.2 syllables per second.

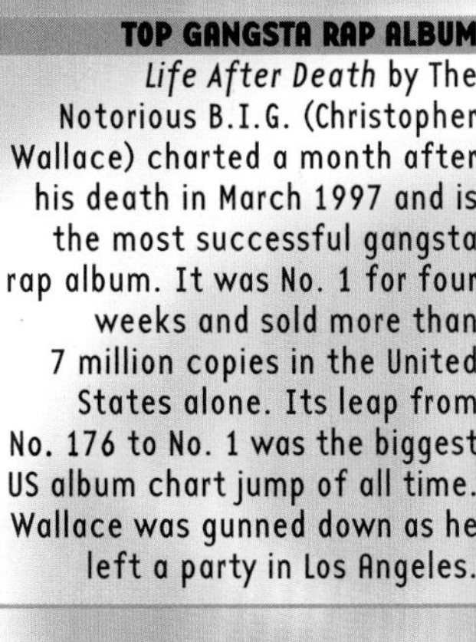

TOP GANGSTA RAP ALBUM
Life After Death by The Notorious B.I.G. (Christopher Wallace) charted a month after his death in March 1997 and is the most successful gangsta rap album. It was No. 1 for four weeks and sold more than 7 million copies in the United States alone. Its leap from No. 176 to No. 1 was the biggest US album chart jump of all time. Wallace was gunned down as he left a party in Los Angeles.

country music

MOST SUCCESSFUL COUNTRY ARTISTS IN THE UNITED STATES
Garth Brooks is the most successful country recording artist, with sales of more than 80 million albums between 1989 and 1998. His greatest hits include "If Tomorrow Never Dies" (1989), "The Dance" (1992) and "The Red Strokes" (1993).

Reba McEntire is the biggest-selling female country vocalist in the United States, with 12 platinum and six gold albums to her credit by April 1998, including *Sweet Sixteen* (1989), *Read My Mind* (1994) and *If You See Him* (1998).

HIGHEST-PAID COUNTRY SINGER
In 1997, Garth Brooks earned $26 million – more than any other country music star.

BIGGEST-SELLING COUNTRY SINGLE IN THE UNITED STATES
The only country single with certified sales of 3 million in the US is "How Do I Live" by Leann Rimes, which reached topped the charts for 32 weeks.

MOST NO. 1 COUNTRY SINGLES IN THE UNITED STATES
The most No. 1 hits on the Billboard country chart is 40, by Conway Twitty.

MOST CONSECUTIVE NO. 1 U.S. COUNTRY SINGLES
Alabama notched up a record-breaking 21 consecutive country No. 1 singles between 1980 and 1987.

MOST SINGLES ON COUNTRY CHART
On December 6, 1997, Garth Brooks had 12 tracks on the Billboard Top 75 country chart, including "Long Neck Bottle," "Two Pina Coladas" and "Cowboy Cadillac."

BIGGEST ONE-WEEK SALE OF A COUNTRY ALBUM IN THE U.S.
The Hits by Garth Brooks sold a record 907,000 copies during Christmas week 1994.

BIGGEST-SELLING COUNTRY ALBUMS IN THE U.S.
Garth Brooks' 1990 album *No Fences* sold a record total of more than 14 million copies.

The top-selling country album by a female artist in the US is *The Woman In Me* (1996) by Shania Twain, which has had certified sales of 10 million.

The best-selling country album by a group in the US is *Greatest Hits* (1986) by Alabama, with sales of 5 million.

MOST WEEKS AT NO. 1 ON ANY U.S. ALBUM CHART
No record has topped any US album chart for longer than the 8-million-selling *12 Greatest Hits* (1967) by Patsy Cline, which headed the country catalog chart in Billboard for 251 weeks (almost five years).

MOST SIMULTANEOUS ALBUM HITS IN THE UNITED STATES
On October 10, 1992, four of the Top 5 albums on the US country chart were by Garth Brooks. The albums – *The Chase, Beyond The Season, No Fences* and *Ropin' The Wind* – were all in the US Top 20 pop album chart too, and reportedly accounted for 37% of all Top 20 album sales.

MOST HIT SINGLES IN THE U.S.
The most successful group on the Billboard country chart is Alabama, with 24 chart-topping singles, including "Tennessee River" (1980), "Feels So Right" (1981) and "If You're Gonna Play In Texas" (1984).

MOST NO. 1 COUNTRY ALBUMS IN THE UNITED STATES
Willie Nelson and Merle Haggard have both had a record 15 No. 1 country albums.

The best-selling female country artist in terms of No. 1 albums in the US is Loretta Lynn, with 10, including *You Ain't Woman Enough* (1966).

The most No. 1 country albums by a group is 10, by Alabama.

TOP SELLING COMEDY ALBUM IN THE U.S.
You Might Be A Redneck If (1994), by country comedian Jeff Foxworthy, is the only comedy album to have been certified triple platinum in the US.

MOST NO. 1 SINGLES
The record for the most No. 1 hits on the Billboard country chart by a woman is 24, by Dolly Parton, from "Joshua" (1970) to "Rockin' Years" (1991) with Ricky Van Shelton. Parton has also had 56 Top 10 singles and 41 weeks in total at No. 1. In 1986, her company, Parton Enterprises, opened Dollywood, an 87-acre theme park near her birthplace in Sevier County, Tennessee.

FIRST FEMALE COUNTRY SINGER TO SELL 1 MILLION RECORDS
Tammy Wynette, who recorded more than 50 albums and sold more than 30 million records in her 25-year career, was the first female country singer to sell 1 million records. The winner of the Country Music Association's female vocalist of the year award in 1968, 1969 and 1970, she was widely known as "The First Lady of Country Music." Her signature song, "Stand By Your Man" (1968), which she wrote with her producer Billy Sherrill, was a country chart-topper, won a Grammy Award in 1969 and went on to become the UK No. 1 on its sixth reissue in 1975. Born Wynette Pugh in Itawamba County, Mississippi, Wynette changed her name in 1969, after auditioning for Billy Sherrill at Epic Records. She released her first single, "Apartment No. 9," in 1966 and went on to record 32 No. 1 country hits. Her 1969 album *Tammy's Greatest Hits* sold more copies worldwide than any other album by a female country recording artist and crossed over to the Top 40 pop lists. Wynette died at age 55 on April 6, 1998.

MOST SIMULTANEOUS ALBUM HITS IN THE U.K.
On September 24, 1964, the late Jim Reeves had a record-breaking eight entries on the UK Top 20 pop album chart – or in other words, an unprecedented 40% of the chart.

On the UK country album chart, Irish singer Daniel O'Donnell occupied six of the top seven places on November 16, 1991.

BIGGEST GAP BETWEEN POP AND COUNTRY CHART ENTRIES IN U.S.
The biggest gap between a first pop chart entry and a first country chart entry is 34 years 6 months, by the Beach Boys, whose newly-recorded version of "Little Deuce Coupe" (featuring James House) entered the country chart in August 1996.

ONLY COUNTRY/RAP/POP HIT IN THE U.S.
The only artist to have had hits on the US country, rap and pop charts is Sting. In December 1997, the pop chart veteran and former lead singer of the Police climbed the country chart with "I'm So Happy I Can't Stop Crying" (a duet with Toby Keith) and the rap chart with "Roxanne '97," the Puff Daddy remix of the 1979 Police hit.

MOST WEEKS AT NO. 1 ON ANY U.S. SINGLES CHART
On March 14, 1998, "How Do I Live," by the 15-year-old country singer Leann Rimes, spent the last of 32 weeks at the top of the country singles sales chart – the most weeks that a single has ever been at No. 1 on any US singles chart. Rimes, the first country singer to win a Grammy for Best New Artist (1997), was also the youngest performer to top either the country album or singles chart. She headed the album chart when she was 13 years 11 months old with *Blue* (1996), and the singles chart when she was 14 years 4 months old with "One Way Ticket" (1996). She is also the youngest female of all time to reach No. 1 on the US pop album chart, which she did with *Blue* when she was 13 years 11 months old. In addition to this, Rimes is the only teenage artist to have put four albums in the US pop Top 3 and the youngest US female singer to reach the UK Top 10 singles chart.

latino music

BEST-SELLING LATIN ARTISTS
Spanish vocalist Julio Iglesias is the most successful Latin music artist in the world, with reported global sales of more than 200 million albums. His album *Julio* (1983) was the first non-English language album to sell more than 2 million copies in the United States.

Cuban-born singer Gloria Estefan is the most successful female Latin artist in the world. In the United States, she has amassed eight gold albums, four of which have passed the 3-million sales mark: *Primitive Love* (1985), *Let It Loose* (1987), *Cuts Both Ways* (1989) and *Greatest Hits* (1992). In the United Kingdom, her *Anything For You* (*Let It Loose*) and *Cuts Both Ways* both sold more than 1 million copies. In 1990, Estefan was presented with a Golden Globe award for album sales of more than 5 million outside the United States. Her current total world sales are more than 35 million.

TOP-GROSSING LATIN PERFORMER
Mexican superstar Luis Miguel grossed a record $6.77 million for a series of 17 concerts at the Auditória Nacionál in Mexico City during October and November 1997, which put him into the Top 20 all-time grossing performers. The shows came soon after Miguel's debut in the US Top 20 with *Romances* – the best-selling Spanish language album of 1997.

BIGGEST-SELLING LATIN ALBUM IN THE U.S.
Julio Iglesias' *1100 Bel Air Place* (1984) is the only Latin album certified quadruple platinum in the United States.

GREATEST DOMINATION OF U.S. LATIN ALBUM CHART
Following her murder on March 31, 1995, the albums of 23-year-old Texas-born Selena (Selena Quintanilla Perez) took over the US Latin chart: on May 6, 1995 they held the top five.

TOP-SELLING MALE LATIN ARTIST
Julio Iglesias is the most successful male Latin artist on the UK album chart, with a total of six Top 20 albums: *Begin the Beguine* (1981), *Amor* (1982), *Julio* (1983), *1100 Bel Air Place* (1984), *Crazy* (1994) and *La Carretera* (1995). Iglesias learned to compose, sing and play the guitar after a near-fatal car crash ended his hopes of becoming a professional soccer player. He was signed by Discos Columbia after winning the Spanish Song Festival in 1968 and soon became a huge star throughout Europe and Latin America. He has recorded songs in French, Italian, German, Portuguese and English, as well as Spanish.

BIGGEST U.K. CHART JUMP
"Macarena," which broke the record for the biggest ever jump on the UK singles chart when it leaped from No. 74 to No. 11, was inspired by Diana Patricia Cubillan, seen above. Released in Spain in April 1993, the song became a huge success around the world, especially in Mexico and the United States. It was written and recorded by Los Del Rio (Antonio Romero and Rafael Ruiz, left), a prolific duo who had already composed 300 songs. It inspired the equally popular Macarena dance, a giant version of which was held in Key Biscayne, Florida and involved 10,000 people.

How to Macarena: Right hand forward, left hand forward, right hand on left arm, left hand on right arm, right hand on head, left hand on head, right hand on behind, left hand on behind, sway three times, jump to the left and start again.

places and were all in the pop album chart too. In a 21-month span, a record five albums by Selena reached No. 1 on the Latin chart. Selena is also the only non-UK/US act to have entered the US album chart at No. 1, with her first posthumous album, *Dreaming Of You*, on August 5, 1995.

MOST SUCCESSFUL LATIN SINGLE IN THE U.S.
"Macarena" by the Spanish duo Los Del Rio is the most successful non-UK/US Latin hit of the rock era. It topped the US chart for a total of 14 weeks in 1996 and spent 60 weeks on the Top 100 — both are records for non-US acts. It also has the distinction of having been the slowest record to get to No. 1 in the United States, reaching the top spot in its 33rd chart week. More than 4 million copies of the single were sold in the US alone, and more than 10 million were sold around the globe.

MOST SUCCESSFUL SPANISH-LANGUAGE SINGLE IN THE U.K.
The only Spanish-language record to have topped the UK chart is "Begin the Beguine (Volver a Empezar)," by Latin superstar Julio Iglesias in 1981. Iglesias was not the first Spanish act to reach the top of the UK chart: Baccara got to No. 1 in 1977 with "Yes Sir I Can Boogie."

MOST SUCCESSFUL INSTRUMENTAL SINGLE IN THE U.S.
"Cherry Pink and Apple Blossom White" by Cuban-born Perez Prado and his orchestra, which topped the US chart for 10 weeks in 1955, was the most successful instrumental single in the United States in the rock era. It was also the first Latin track to top the UK chart. Prado, known as "The King of the Mambo," also holds the record for the longest gap between hits on the UK Top 20: his "Patricia" left the Top 20 on October 24, 1958 and his "Guaglione," first released as the followup to "Patricia," returned to the chart 36 years 6 months later on May 6, 1995.

BEST-SELLING LATIN ARTIST, U.K.
Gloria Estefan has had more successful albums in the United Kingdom than any other Latin artist, with seven Top 20 entries, four of which reached the Top 3. Estefan became a global star with *Dr. Beat* in 1984. Throughout the 1990s, she has concentrated on exploring her diverse musical heritage. In 1993, she revisited classic Cuban music with *Mi Tierra*, while in 1994 her album *Hold Me, Thrill Me, Kiss Me* brought together some of her favorite rock and pop classics. In 1995, she released *Abriendo Puertas*, a Spanish-language pop/dance album drawing on different strands of Latin music.

TOP-SELLING ENGLISH-LANGUAGE RECORD ON THE U.S. LATIN CHART
The only English-language record to have ever topped the Latin chart in the United States is "My Heart Will Go On" by Celine Dion, in February 1998. The song is the theme from the Oscar-winning 1997 movie *Titanic*.

BIGGEST LATIN HIT
Puerto Rican-born performer Ricky Martin's recording of "(Un, Dos, Tres) Maria" was a hit in many countries around the world in 1997 and sold over 5 million copies. The singer, who was a member of the top Latin teen group Menudo for five years, is best known for his role as Miguel Morez on the daytime soap opera *General Hospital*. Martin also sang "La Copa de la Vida," which was the official song of the 1998 Soccer World Cup.

classical music
opera and jazz

BEST-SELLING CLASSICAL ALBUM
The Three Tenors In Concert, recorded by José Carreras, Placido Domingo, and Luciano Pavarotti for the 1990 Soccer World Cup Finals, has sold an estimated 13 million copies.

MOST GRAMMYS TO ONE ARTIST
Hungarian-born conductor Sir Georg Solti was awarded 31 Grammys (one posthumously).

BIGGEST CLASSICAL AUDIENCE
An estimated 800,000 people attended a free open-air concert by the New York Philharmonic on the Great Lawn of Central Park, New York City, on July 5, 1986.

QUIETEST PIECE
In John Cage's *4'33"*, the performer or performers sit silently on the concert platform and the "music" is any noise that comes from the audience and from outside the concert hall.

LARGEST MUSICAL PERFORMER
And God Created Great Whales (1970) by Alan Hovhaness (US) is scored for orchestra and a solo by a humpback whale (recorded).

BEST-SELLING OPERA SINGER
Luciano Pavarotti made his professional debut in 1961 and has sold about 60 million albums worldwide. His entire stage repertoire has reached disc and every recording is a bestseller.

LONGEST EVER OPERA
The Life and Times of Joseph Stalin by Robert Wilson lasted almost 13 hr. 25 min. on December 14–15, 1973 at the Brooklyn Academy of Music, New York City.

SHORTEST OPERA
The shortest published opera is *The Sands of Time* by Simon Rees and Peter Reynolds, which lasted 4 min. 9 sec. when first performed by Rhian Owen and Dominic Burns in Cardiff, Wales, in March 1993. A 3-min.-34-sec. version was directed by Peter Reynolds in London, England, in September 1993.

LONGEST OPERATIC APPLAUSE
Placido Domingo was applauded for a record 1 hr. 20 min. through a total of 101 curtain calls after a performance of *Otello* at the Vienna Staatsoper, Austria, on July 30, 1991.

MOST CURTAIN CALLS IN AN OPERA
On February 24, 1988, Luciano Pavarotti received 165 curtain calls and was applauded for 1 hr. 7 min after singing the part of Nemorino in Donizetti's *L'Elisir d'Amore* at the Deutsche Oper, Berlin, Germany.

MOST TUNELESS OPERA
Lulu (1937) by German composer Alban Berg is a modern 12-tone opera with no tunes. The composer constrained his writing by a set of mathematical rules.

LARGEST OPERA HOUSE
The Metropolitan Opera House at Lincoln Center, New York City, which was completed in September 1966 at a cost of $45.7 million, can seat and stand 4,065 people.

LOWEST NOTES
The lowest note by a human voice was sung in 1997 by Dan Britton, who produced a

HIGHEST CRITICAL ACCLAIM
Miles Davis' *Milestones* (1958) has been acclaimed as the best album in the history of jazz by more jazz writers than any other. Its only rival is *Kind of Blue*, another Miles Davis album. The trumpeter and composer was consistently voted most popular artist in all major US jazz polls from 1954 to the mid-60s, but by the 1970s he had alienated jazz purists with his adoption of rock styles.

WORST RECEPTION FOR A NEW WORK
Russian composer Igor Stravinsky's controversial ballet *The Rite of Spring* sparked violent reactions among the audience at the Théâtre des Champs-Elysées, Paris, France, at its premiere in 1913. The first few bars evoked laughter that soon escalated into full-scale riots as the audience protested against the complexity of the music, which challenged the accepted musical norms of the time. The noise made by the protesters was so loud that the dancers were unable to hear the orchestra, but Stravinsky remained unfazed by the reaction and continued with the performance. *The Rite of Spring* was eventually recognized as a masterpiece and the composer became regarded as one of the most important musical figures of the 20th century.

recognizable note that measured electronically at 16.45 Hz and is below the musical note C_0.

The lowest vocal note in the classical repertoire is in Osmin's aria in Mozart's *Die Entführung aus dem Serail*. It calls for a low D (73.4 Hz).

HIGHEST NOTE
The highest vocal note to be found in the classical repertoire is G^3, which occurs in Mozart's *Popolo di Tessaglia*.

MOST SHOCKING MODERN OPERA
Salome, seen here in a 1920s production played by Maud Allan, was the Biblical granddaughter of Herod the Great and gained notoriety when she asked for the head of John the Baptist. Her story has been retold in many works of art, including Richard Strauss' *Salome* (1905), which was banned from the New York Metropolitan Opera for 27 years after audiences were shocked by its subject matter.

LONGEST SUSTAINED NOTE
Jazz star Kenny G held an E flat on his saxophone for 45 min. 47 sec. at J & R Music World, New York City, on December 2, 1997.

LOUDEST MUSICAL INSTRUMENT
The loudest and largest musical instrument ever made is the now partially functional Auditorium Organ in Atlantic City, New Jersey. Completed in 1930, it had 1,477 stop controls and 33,112 pipes, and its volume equaled that of 25 brass bands.

GRANDEST GRAND PIANO
An 11-ft.-8-in. grand piano was made by Chas H. Challen & Son Ltd. of London, England, in 1935. Its longest bass string was 9 ft. 11 in. long.

MOST EXPENSIVE PIANO
A Steinway grand piano made *c.* 1888 was sold for $390,000 at Sotheby's, New York City, on March 26, 1980.

MOST EXPENSIVE VIOLIN
The highest price paid for a violin at auction was $1,572,850, for a 1729 Stradivarius "The Kreutzer" at Christie's, London, England, in 1998.

MOST EXPENSIVE JAZZ INSTRUMENT
A saxophone owned by Charlie Parker sold for $146,328 at Christie's, London, England, in September 1994.

BEST-SELLING JAZZ ARTIST
Saxophonist Kenny G has sold an estimated 50 million albums.

BEST-SELLING JAZZ RECORD
Kenny G's *Breathless* has sold an estimated 13 million copies.

LONGEST JAZZ CAREER
American saxophonist and pianist Benny Waters has been performing since his mid-teens and is still recording at the age of 96.

OLDEST JAZZ CLUB
The Village Vanguard cellar jazz club opened in New York City in the 1930s and has hosted mainstream jazz ever since.

BIGGEST JAZZ FESTIVAL
An 11-day multimedia extravaganza, the Festival International de Jazz de Montreal in Québec, Canada, is the world's largest jazz festival.

LONGEST PERFORMED OPERA
German composer Richard Wagner revolutionized opera in the late 19th century in works such as *Der Ring des Nibelungen*, which includes *Die Walküre* (1856), seen below. The longest frequently performed opera in the world is Wagner's *Die Meistersinger von Nürnberg* (1868). An uncut version performed by the Sadler's Wells company in London, England, in 1968 lasted 5 hr. 15 min.

clubs, parties and festivals

BIGGEST STREET FESTIVALS
Rio de Janeiro Carnival is the world's largest street festival, attracting around 2 million people each day of the festival, 300,000 of whom are tourists. In 1998, the four-day event generated more than $165 million. A seat in the Sambadrome for one of the parades costs between $300 and $600. In 1998, 14 Samba Schools contributed to the parade, each with six to eight floats and up to 5,000 elaborately dressed dancers. The Notting Hill Carnival, London, England is the biggest street festival in Europe and the world's second largest carnival, with 1 million visitors annually.

MOST POPULAR CLUBBING DESTINATION
Ibiza has a total of 740 clubs, restaurants and bars and attracts 1.5 million visitors each year.

MOST SUCCESSFUL CLUB DJ
British DJ Paul Oakenfold has sold 1 million records and owns the Perfecto music label. He is reported to earn $400,000 a year. The remixer and producer has worked with U2 and the Rolling Stones, making him the most influential DJ to have moved from club culture into the mainstream. He has worked in Australia, the US, Hong Kong, Brazil, Argentina and all over Europe, and played at private parties for Madonna, Naomi Campbell and Grace Jones.

BIGGEST TECHNO PARTY
On July 12, 1997, an estimated 1 million people congregated in the centre of Berlin, Germany for the city's ninth annual, and biggest ever, Love Parade. The ravers danced behind 38 decorated floats equipped with turbo-powered sound systems down a 4-mile boulevard starting at the Brandenburg Gate, the landmark that has become a symbol of Berlin's reunification. Parties took place in more than 130 dance clubs, as well as in parks and on Potsdamer Platz, Europe's biggest construction site. Revenue from the parade, which attracted people from around the world, was estimated at $84 million. A rival "hate parade" organized by disc jockeys who objected to the main event's "commercialism" attracted about 500 people and broke up after a few hours.

MOST SUCCESSFUL CLUB ENTERPRISE
The Ministry of Sound in London, England is reported to be worth $32 million. Since opening in 1991, the club has spawned a record company, a clothing brand and a magazine. Its record company sells 1 million records a year, mainly dance music compilations.

BIGGEST NIGHTCLUB
Gilley's Club (formerly Shelly's) on Spencer Highway, Houston, Texas, was built in 1955 and expanded to seat 6,000 people in 1971, making it the biggest club.

BIGGEST NEW YEAR'S PARTY
In 1996, more than 400,000 revellers descended on the city of Edinburgh, Scotland, Europe's most popular New Year's Eve destination. Despite raising an estimated $38 million in revenue, the city has now restricted the number of people attending to 180,000.

BIGGEST MILLENNIUM PARTY
The Times Square Business Improvement District plans a 24-hour televised entertainment production in Times Square, New York City. The millennium party will cost millions of dollars and will feature the world's biggest hologram strobe-lit spinning ball.

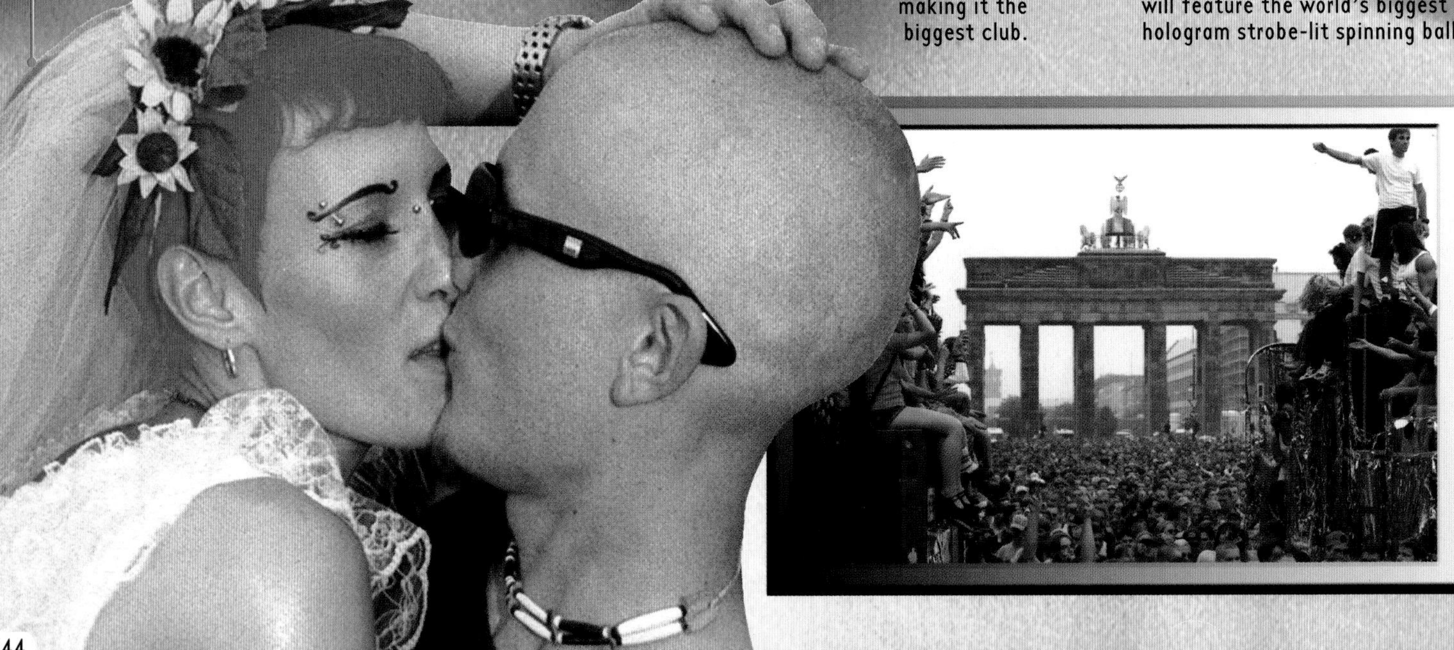

On December 31, 1999, Sydney, Australia – which is hosting the 2000 Olympic Games – will hold the world's biggest fireworks display. The event is expected to be 10 times larger than the city's bicentennial celebrations.

BIGGEST MULTICULTURAL FESTIVAL
The annual Folklorama festival in Winnipeg, Manitoba, Canada draws more than 500,000 people from all over the world. First held in 1970 to celebrate the province's 100th birthday and show the diverse cultural heritage of its people, it has grown into a two-week festival put on by 20,000 volunteers.

BIGGEST INTERNET MUSIC FESTIVAL
The 1998 Intel New York Music Festival featured more than 300 bands performing in 20 clubs in New York City. The festival web site broadcast video and audio from the clubs.

MOST PEOPLE AT A ROCK FESTIVAL
An estimated 670,000 people attended Steve Wozniak's 1983 US Festival in Devore, California. Artists included The Clash, Van Halen and David Bowie.

BIGGEST MUSIC FESTIVAL
Summerfest, held annually since 1967 on the shore of Lake Michigan in Milwaukee, Wisconsin, is billed as the world's largest music festival. In 1998, the "Big Gig" hosted over 1,000 artists on its 12 permanent stages, including Boyz II Men, Phil Collins, James Taylor and Bonnie Raitt.

BIGGEST FESTIVAL OF PERFORMANCE ART
The annual Cleveland Performance Art Festival is held in Cleveland, Ohio every May and is seen as a showcase for both emerging and established performance artists.

BIGGEST WINTER CARNIVAL
The Annual Winter Carnival in Québec City, Canada, began in 1955 but has its origins in the city's first carnival in 1894. The most popular event is the snow-sculpting demonstration. Other highlights include the canoe race, the dogsled race, a car race on ice, and snow-rolling in swimsuits. It attracts more than 500,000 people a year from all over the world and is the third biggest carnival after Rio and Notting Hill.

LARGEST SIMULTANEOUS TOAST
The greatest number of people simultaneously participating in a toast was 78,276. The Great Guinness Toast was staged on February 27, 1998 at 11.00 pm EST in pubs, restaurants and bars in 52 US metropolitan areas.

BIGGEST GAY FESTIVALS
The Gay and Lesbian Mardi Gras (pictured above) in Sydney, Australia began in 1978 and is now the world's biggest gay festival. In 1998, it was attended by 700,000 people, and a post-parade dance party attracted over 17,000 people and live performers. The biggest of the Gay Pride events takes place in San Francisco, California. One of the largest gay events in the world, it attracted 500,000 people in 1997, its 27th parade.

WOODSTOCK
Woodstock Music and Art Fair, one of the most famous music events ever, was held in Bethel, New York from August 15 to August 17, 1969 and attracted 300,000–500,000 people.

street fashion

BIGGEST-SELLING BRAND OF UNDERWEAR
The world's most popular underwear brand is made by Calvin Klein. In the 1980s, Klein capitalized on the trend among women of buying his men's underwear for themselves by launching boxer shorts for women. He even kept the fly, telling *Time* magazine that it looked sexy on women. In 1984, a record 400,000 pairs of "Calvins" (seen left on supermodel Christy Turlington) were bought, and the company made $50 million. Klein is largely responsible for popularizing designer clothing by attaching his name to the back pocket of his jeans, setting a precedent for other designers, and the Calvin Klein brand name has become one of the most recognized symbols of American fashion since it was founded by Klein and Barry Schwartz in 1968.

FASTEST-GROWING BRAND OF CLOTHING
Dockers, a brand of casual wear produced by Levi Strauss & Co., was launched in the United States in 1986, and by the early 1990s had become the fastest-growing apparel brand in US history, with the highest level of brand awareness of any casual pants. The brand was initially conceived as a comfortable alternative to jeans for middle-aged people, but the promotion, which had cost a total of $10 million within two years, propelled them to the top of the casual wear market, with sales of $6.9 billion in 1997.

BIGGEST UNDERWEAR MANUFACTURER
According to *Fortune 500 1998*, the biggest underwear manufacturer in the world is Fruit of the Loom, which is based in Chicago, Illinois. In 1997, the company had revenues of $488 million, making it the 596th largest company in the world.

BEST-SELLING BRA
The Wonderbra, made by Sara Lee, is one of the most popular bras in the world. It currently sells at a rate of more than 30,000 units a week in the United Kingdom alone, and is available in the United States, South Africa, Australia and Europe. Clients include Gwyneth Paltrow, Caprice and Kate Moss.

BIGGEST PANTYHOSE MANUFACTURER
One in every five pairs of pantyhose in the world are made by Sara Lee, making it the largest pantyhose manufacturer. The company's 31 brands also include Playtex and Wonderbra, each of which has sales of more than $100 million.

FIRST SHOE BRAND IN AN ENGLISH DICTIONARY
Dr. Martens boots, which have been manufactured since 1960, are now so famous that they warrant an entry in the *Oxford English Dictionary*. It reads as follows: "Dr. Martens (*n. phr.*) Proprietary name for a type of heavy (esp. laced) boot or shoe with a cushioned sole." The company is said to make two pairs of boots every second of the working week.

BIGGEST SELLING OWN BRAND UNDERWEAR
British department store Marks and Spencer sells 52 million pairs of its St. Michael brand of women's underpants globally each year – equivalent to 1 million pairs every week.

BIGGEST SURFWEAR MANUFACTURER
Quiksilver has annual revenues of approximately $230 million in the United States and Europe, making it the largest manufacturer of surfwear in the world to date. The company sells to more than 130 countries and sponsors hundreds of athletes, including surf champions Robbie Naish, Kelly Slater and Lisa Andersen.

FASTEST-SELLING WATCH IN HISTORY
The Swatch watch, which was invented by Swiss watchmaker Dr. Ernest Thomke and Nicholas Hayelk in 1981, had sold more than 100 million units within a period of 10 years, making it the fastest-selling brand of watch in history. In 1986, graffiti artist Keith Haring, who was famous for his work in the New York subway, was commissioned to design a series of four Swatch watches, some of which have sold at auction for more than $5,000 in the 1990s. In 1989, the company asked Italian artist Mimmo Paladino to design a watch, which was produced in limited editions of 120. Two years later, a Paladino Swatch sold at an auction in Europe for $24,000.

BEST-SELLING SUNGLASSES
Ray-Ban is one of the most widely recognized brands of sunglasses: surveys carried out in the early 1990s found that 80% of sunglass wearers in Europe, Asia and the United States could identify the name. The brand was developed by Bausch & Lomb Inc. of Rochester, New York, in response to a request from the US Army Corps, who needed an optical quality glass lens that could resist the harsh glare endured by their fighter pilots. Scientists worked through the late 1920s and early 1930s to develop the green tinted lens. The Aviator model was introduced to the public in 1936 and has become a fashion icon, along with the Wayfarer style. This was achieved through high-profile product placement in cult films such as *The Blues Brothers* (1980). The Wayfarer is the best-selling sunglass style in history, and remains one of the world's most popular styles 40 years after its launch in the early 1950s. In 1989 alone, Ray-Bans were featured in more than 110 movies, and in 1997 the Predator 2 style was prominent in *Men in Black*, starring Will Smith.

BEST-SELLING FACIAL MOISTURIZER
Oil of Ulay, which is now made by Procter & Gamble, has 28% of the world market in facial moisturizers. It was formulated by Graham Wulff of South Africa to prevent dehydration of British pilots' burn injuries during World War II. After the war, Wulff refined the product and teamed up with Shaun Adams to sell it door to door.

BIGGEST THRIFT SHOP CHAIN
Oxfam opened its first thrift shop in 1948 and now has 862 shops in the United Kingdom and Ireland, making it the biggest thrift shop chain in the world. In 1997, the company — which fights hunger, disease, exploitation and poverty worldwide — had an income of $27.36 million from its thrift shops. This is almost one third of its annual income from voluntary work.

BIGGEST SECONDHAND CLOTHING STORE
Domsey's Warehouse and Annex in Brooklyn, New York is the largest secondhand clothing store, with an area of 250,000 square feet, of which 35,000 square feet is the sales floor. The family business has been handed down through three generations and has been based in Brooklyn for 17 years. It stocks about 350,000 garments at any one time.

BIGGEST SPORTSWEAR FIRM
Sportswear giant Nike, based in Oregon, had revenue of $9.19 billion and profits of $796 million in 1997, making it the world's 198th largest company. One of its most successful lines, Nike Air training and running shoes, was inspired by Frank Rudy, a NASA engineer. Here, a model wears clothes designed by basketball player Michael Jordan and produced by Nike.

BIGGEST CLOTHING INDUSTRIES
The largest clothing industry in the world in terms of the value of the goods produced is that of the United States, which manufactured approximately $39.5 billion worth of clothing, excluding footwear, in 1996. It had about 800,000 employees in 1997.

The biggest clothing industry in terms of the number of employees is China, which had about 1.75 million people on the payroll in 1997. They made clothing (excluding footwear) worth $17.9 billion in 1996.

high fashion

MOST SPENT ON A DESIGNER CLOTHING STORE

Gianni Versace's shop on Bond Street, London is said to have cost more than any other designer store, at $21.2 million. The shop opened in 1992 and features Carrera marble, gilt and frescoes. His store in Paris, France may have cost more but the figure is undisclosed. Versace was born in Italy in 1946 and began his career working with his mother in a workshop and clothing store. He moved to Milan in 1972, and in 1978 he established his own fashion house with his brother Santo and sister Donatella. Versace is now one of the most commercially successful houses in the world, grossing $50.8 million in 1978 and $742.2 million in 1993. In July 1997, Versace was shot dead on the steps of his home in Miami, Florida. His funeral was attended by a host of top fashion luminaries and supermodels, as well as Diana, Princess of Wales, and singer Elton John.

RICHEST DESIGNER

Ralph Lauren has an estimated personal fortune of $1 billion – the highest of any designer. Born Ralph Lipschitz in New York City in 1939, Lauren began his career as a sales assistant and had his first success when he designed a collection of ties. He opened his first independent Polo shop in Beverly Hills, California, in 1971, and in 1993 launched his Polo Sport range. By 1988 his fashion house had sales of $925 million a year, compared with $7 million a year in 1974. It has supplied clothes for the Woody Allen movies *Annie Hall* (1977) and *Manhattan* (1979), and also for *The Great Gatsby* (1974), starring Robert Redford, Mia Farrow, and Patsy Kensit.

BEST-SELLING DESIGNER

The biggest-selling designer clothing brand in the world is Giorgio Armani. The Italian designer began his fashion career in 1954, doing the displays at La Rinascente department stores, before working for the design house Cerruti. In 1975, Armani sold his car and started his own fashion label. The label was hugely successful throughout the late seventies and early eighties, when his clothing began to epitomize both style and wealth. Although he does not advertise as much as his main competitors (Versace, Calvin Klein and Valentino) Armani has been a favorite of a number of celebrities, including Michelle Pfeiffer, Cindy Crawford and Richard Gere. Annual global sales of Armani clothing now exceed $320 million.

YOUNGEST INTERNATIONALLY ESTABLISHED DESIGNER

British designer Julian MacDonald got his lucky break at the age of 24 at his graduation from the Royal College Of Art in London, England, where he was spotted by Karl Lagerfeld and asked to design a knitwear range for the Chanel ready-to-wear collection. After great success in Paris, France, MacDonald presented his own collection, "Mermaids," in 1997.

FASTEST RISE TO DESIGN STARDOM

Stella McCartney, the daughter of Paul and Linda McCartney, was appointed as the new designer at Parisian fashion house Chloé in April 1997, just 18 months after graduating from Central Saint Martins College of Art and Design, London. McCartney, who replaced Karl Lagerfeld, had designed three successful lines under her own label. Supermodels Naomi Campbell and Kate Moss modeled at her graduation show. Now 26, McCartney commands a six-figure salary.

OLDEST DESIGNER

The oldest international couturier in the world is 71-year-old American designer Geoffrey Beene, who moved on to fashion after originally studying medicine.

MOST EXPENSIVE JACKET

In 1998, Naomi Campbell modeled the world's most expensive jacket for Gai Mattioli's 1998 collection. Worth $1 million, the jacket has 100-carat Burmese rubies – the biggest on the market – and 250-year-old, 36-carat emeralds as buttons.

MOST EXPENSIVE CANCELED CATWALK SHOW

Giorgio Armani's Emporio show during Paris fashion week in March 1998 was canceled by French police concerned about safety at the venue. By that time Armani had spent $300,000 on the show and

BIGGEST CATWALK WEDDING DRESS

Japanese designer Yohji Yamamoto astounded audiences at his March 1998 show in Paris, France when he unveiled a beige crinoline wedding dress with a 13-foot skirt and oversize hat. The designer wanted to add humor to his collection, and the stage was set up so that the audience could see under the dress, which is not for sale. Born in Tokyo, Japan in 1943, Yamamoto studied law before helping in his mother's dress shop and studying fashion at the famous Bunkafukuso Gaukin School. He started his own company in 1972 and in 1976 unveiled his first collection in Tokyo. Yamamoto's clothes are usually functional and understated. According to model agency chiefs, he likes to use "real-looking" women to model his collections. He also makes clothes for men, and his designs for both sexes conceal rather than emphasize the body. Yamamoto made his Paris debut in 1981, and is the only Japanese designer to have been awarded the French Chevalier de l'Ordre des Arts et des Lettres. In 1987 he opened a new headquarters in London, England, for his company, which now has an estimated annual turnover of $100 million.

a further $1 million on the after-show party, making it the most expensive fashion show never to have happened.

FASTEST DESIGN HOUSE REVAMP

Over a period of just three years Gucci's creative director Tom Ford has transformed the Italian fashion house into one of the most desired labels in the world. Gucci's annual turnover has increased from $250 million to approximately $1.2 billion in that time. One of Ford's innovations was to abandon the crossed Gs that were attached to many Gucci products for a long time. Ford himself, who started his fashion career with an internship at Chloé, has appeared in commercials for a number of companies, including McDonald's and Old Spice.

STORE THAT STOCKS THE MOST DESIGNER LABELS

The department store Saks Fifth Avenue currently stocks a total of 1,252 designer labels – more than any other store in the world. Saks' flagship store on Fifth Avenue, New York City was opened in 1924 by Horace Saks and Bernard Gimbel. There are now 41 full-line fashion specialty stores, eight fashion resort stores and seven main street stores in 23 states, and the company employs about 12,000 people.

BIGGEST-SELLING DESIGNER PERFUME

The most successful designer perfume in the world is Chanel No. 5, which sells more than 10 million bottles a year. Created in 1925, Chanel No. 5 has more than 80 ingredients. Its creator, Coco Chanel, was the first ever couturier to attach her name to a perfume. The market is now worth an estimated $7.5 billion a year, and some designers spend huge sums on advertising – Christian Lacroix, for instance, spent $40 million advertising his C'est La Vie.

MOST EXPENSIVE BRA

The Diamond Dream bra, the world's most expensive bra, was created by Harry Winston in 1997 and made by Victoria's Secret. The bra, which has a 42-carat, pear-shaped flawless diamond in the center and 100 diamonds on each side, costs $3 million. It is seen here modeled by Tyra Banks, the supermodel who rose to fame in the TV show *The Fresh Prince of Bel-Air* alongside Will Smith.

MOST VALUABLE COUTURE HOUSE

In 1998, Valentino and his business partner Giancarlo Giammetti sold the design house Valentino for a record $300 million, after running the company for 38 years. Valentino, which makes $17.3 million a year, was bought by Holding di Part. Industriali. German supermodel Claudia Schiffer is pictured here wearing a Valentino dress.

BULLS
23

sporting heroes

soccer

MOST APPEARANCES
The record for the greatest number of games played for a national team is 147, by Majed Abdullah Mohammed of Saudi Arabia from 1978 to 1994.

British goalkeeper Peter Shilton made a record 1,390 senior appearances, including a record 1,005 national league games (286 for Leicester City, 1966–74, 110 for Stoke City, 1974–77, 202 for Nottingham Forest, 1977–82, 188 for Southampton, 1982–87, 175 for Derby County, 1987–92, 34 for Plymouth Argyle, 1992–94, one for Bolton Wanderers in 1995, nine for Leyton Orient, 1996–97, one League playoff, 86 FA Cup games, 102 League Cup games, 125 internationals, 13 Under-23 games, four Football League XI games and 53 European and other club competitions).

MOST GOALS IN A GAME
The most goals scored by one player in a professional game is 16, by Stephan Stanis for Racing Club de Lens v. Aubry-Asturies in a wartime French Cup game in Lens, France, December 13, 1942.

The most goals by a player in an international game is 10, by Sofus Nielsen for Denmark v. France (17–1) in the 1908 Olympics and by Gottfried Fuchs for Germany v. Russia (16–0) in the 1912 Olympic tournament (consolation event) in Sweden.

MOST CAREER GOALS
Artur Friedenreich of Brazil scored an undocumented 1,329 goals in a 26-year professional career from 1909 to 1935.

Pelé scored a documented 1,281 goals, 1956–77.

MOST SUCCESSFUL GOALKEEPERS
The longest period that a goalkeeper has prevented goals being scored past him in professional competition is 1,275 minutes, by Abel Resino of Atletico Madrid, Spain, to March 17, 1991.

The longest period that a goalkeeper has prevented goals in international games is 1,142 minutes, by Dino Zoff (Italy), September 1972–June 1974.

HIGHEST SCORES
The highest winning margin in an international is 17, by England in its 17–0 victory over Australia in Sydney, Australia, on June 30, 1951 (not listed by England as a full international) and by Iran in its 17–0 win over the Maldives in Damascus, Syria in June 1997.

The highest score recorded in a professional game was 36, in the Scottish Cup game between Arbroath and Bon Accord on September 5, 1885. Arbroath won 36–0 on their home ground.

FASTEST GOALS
In professional soccer, the record for the fastest goal is six seconds, by Albert E. Mundy for Aldershot v. Hartlepool United in a Fourth Division game at Victoria Ground, Hartlepool, England in October 1958; by Barrie Jones for Notts County v. Torquay United in a British Third Division game in March 1962, and by Keith Smith for Crystal Palace v. Derby County in a Second Division game at the Baseball Ground, Derby, England on December 12, 1964.

The international record is three goals in 3½ minutes, by George Hall of Tottenham Hotspur for England against Ireland at Old Trafford, Manchester, England on November 16, 1938.

Maglioni is said to have scored a hat-trick in a record time of 1 min. 50 sec. while playing for Independiente against Gimnasia y Escrima de la Plata in Argentina on March 18, 1973.

RICHEST CLUB
The English Premier League's Manchester United was valued at in excess of $546.6 million in 1996, making it the richest soccer club in the world. In that same year the club had a turnover of almost $137 million. Gate receipts topped $47 million, TV rights brought in a further $19.5 million and merchandise $44.6 million. The club's nearest rivals in terms of wealth are AC Milan of Italy and Barcelona of Spain.

MOST DOCUMENTED GOALS IN A CAREER
The greatest number of documented goals scored in a career is 1,281, by the legendary Brazilian player Pelé in 1,363 games from September 7, 1956 to October 1, 1977. In 1959, Pelé had his best year, scoring 126 goals. His *milesimo* (1,000th) came during his 909th first-class game on November 19, 1969, when he scored a penalty for his club Santos at the Maracanã Stadium, Rio de Janeiro, Brazil. Pelé won his 111th and final cap for Brazil in 1971 and announced his retirement at the end of the 1974 season, but this retirement was short-lived: the next year he signed a $4.5-million contract with the New York Cosmos. He finally hung up his cleats in 1977.

MOST EXPENSIVE DEFENDER
In May 1998, Dutch defender Jaap Stam signed a contract with England's Manchester United for a record $18 million. The 26-year-old PSV Eindhoven star accepted a seven-year deal that is worth $18.3 million with bonuses. He began his professional career at 19 and made his international debut in 1996 for Holland.

BIGGEST VICTORY MARGINS IN NATIONAL SOCCER CUP FINALS
In 1935, Lausanne-Sports beat Nordstern Basel 10–0 in the Swiss Cup Final, but was defeated by the same scoreline by Grasshopper-Club (Zürich) in the 1937 Swiss Cup Final.

MOST SUCCESSIVE NATIONAL LEAGUE CHAMPIONSHIPS
Dinamo Berlin of East Germany had 10 successive championships from 1979 to 1988.

CSKA, Sofia of Bulgaria holds a European post-war record of 26 league titles, including two under the name CFKA Sredets (renamed CSKA).

LONGEST-HELD NATIONAL SOCCER LEAGUE TITLE
The Cairo club Al Ahly maintained its national soccer title from the 1948/49 season until the 1959/60 season. However, the 1952 championship was abandoned because of the Egyptian revolution and the 1955 league program also went uncompleted.

FURTHEST DISTANCE TRAVELED FOR A LEAGUE GAME
The furthest distance traveled between two clubs in the top division of a professional national soccer league is 2,979 miles, between the home stadiums of the LA Galaxy and the New England Revolution in the MLS.

BIGGEST CROWDS
The record attendance for any European Cup game is 136,505, at the semifinal between Glasgow Celtic (Scotland) and Leeds United (England) at Hampden Park, Glasgow, Scotland on April 15, 1970.

The highest recorded attendance at an amateur game was 120,000, to see North Korea v. Indonesia at the pre-Olympic Group II final at Senayan Stadium, Jakarta, Indonesia, on February 26, 1976.

BIGGEST SOCCER STADIUM
The Maracanã Municipal Stadium in Rio de Janeiro, Brazil has a normal capacity of 205,000 with seats for 155,000. It was built for the 1950 World Cup when a crowd of nearly 200,000 packed the arena for the final, which Brazil lost to Uruguay.

MOST UNDISCIPLINED GAME
On June 1, 1993, it was reported that referee William Weiler sent off 20 players in a league game between Sportivo Ameliano and General Caballero in Paraguay. Trouble flared after two Sportivo players were sent off. A 10-minute fight ensued, and Weiler dismissed a further 18 players, including the rest of the Sportivo team. The game was then abandoned.

MOST EXPENSIVE TRADE
On August 28, 1997, Real Betis (Spain) paid a world record $36 million for midfielder Denilson de Oliveira, who was 20 at the time, before immediately loaning him back to Sao Paolo. Denilson signed a 10-year contract said to be worth $127 million. He was first capped for Brazil at age 19 in November 1996, and now has his left foot insured for more than $1.6 million.

soccer: world cup

BIGGEST CROWDS
The largest ever crowd at a soccer match consisted of 199,854 people, for the 1950 World Cup match between Brazil and Uruguay at the Maracana Municipal Stadium, Rio de Janeiro, Brazil.

The record for the greatest number of spectators at a tournament is 3,587,538, for the 52 matches in the 1994 World Cup in the United States.

BUSIEST WORLD CUP HOTLINE
British Telecom estimate that 20 million callers in the United Kingdom tried to get through to the French hotline when tickets went on sale on April 22, 1998.

MOST TEAMS IN A TOURNAMENT
In 1998, 32 countries played — more than double the number that took part in the first World Cup in 1930, when a total of 18 matches were played by 13 countries. In 1998, 64 games were played.

MOST TEAM WINS
Brazil have won the World Cup a record four times (1958, 1962, 1970 and 1994).

Overall, Brazil have won a record 53 matches from 80 matches in the finals stage.

MOST TEAM APPEARANCES
Brazil have taken part in all 16 finals tournaments.

France and the USA are the only other nations to have entered every World Cup competition (the USA withdrew without playing a match in 1938).

MOST INDIVIDUAL WINS
Pelé (Brazil) is the only player to have been with a record three winning teams, in 1958, 1962 and 1970.

MOST GOALS SCORED OVERALL
Brazil have scored a record-breaking 173 goals in a total of 80 matches.

Gerd Müller (Germany) scored 10 goals in 1970 and four in 1974 for a record total of 14.

MOST GOALS IN A TOURNAMENT
A record 171 goals were scored in France in 1998.

The record for the greatest number of goals scored in one finals tournament is 27 (in five games), by Hungary in 1954.

Just Fontaine (France) scored a total of 13 goals in six matches in the final stages of the 1958 competition in Sweden.

The only players to have scored in every match in a final series are Fontaine (France),

WORLD CUP TROPHIES
Brazil are pictured above with the World Cup after victory in 1994. The first World Cup trophy — a gold statuette weighing about 3 lb — was commissioned from French sculptor Abel Lafleur by FIFA and named after the FIFA president Jules Rimet, a Frenchman who had initiated the first tournament. In 1966 the 'Jules Rimet Trophy' was stolen for the first time, in London, England. The thief, Edward Bletchley, demanded a ransom of $40,500 but was arrested when he went to collect it. He did not reveal where the cup was but it was eventually found by a dog called Pickles under a bush in his owner's back garden. The trophy was presented to Brazil — the first country to have won three World Cups — in 1970, but was stolen again and never retrieved. Since then, a copy of the original has been given to the winning team. Following the first theft a secret version of the trophy was made by London silversmiths Alexander Clarke and exhibited until 1970 around England, under heavy guard to maintain the illusion that it was the original. This trophy was auctioned by Sotheby's for $407,200 in 1997. The present trophy is the work of Italian sculptor Silvio Gazamiga, and is made of solid gold.

WORLD CUP '98
Zinedine Zidane (below) was instrumental in France's victory in the 1998 World Cup, scoring two goals in the final against Brazil. Of the 32 nations in the 1998 event, four were making their debut in the finals: South Africa, Japan, Jamaica and Croatia. Each lost at least one match, maintaining the record that no qualifier for the finals in the history of the tournament is undefeated. England, Japan, Spain and Saudi Arabia had all 22 players in their squad playing in their own domestic league.

Jaïrzinho (Brazil) and Alcide Ghiggia (Uruguay). Jaïrzinho scored seven goals in six games in 1970 and Ghiggia scored four goals in four games in 1950.

MOST GOALS IN A GAME
Iran beat the Maldives 17-0 in a qualifying match on June 2, 1997.

The highest score in the final stages was achieved by Hungary in a 10-1 win over El Salvador at Elche, Spain, on June 15, 1982.

The highest match aggregate in the finals tournament was 12, when Austria beat Switzerland 7-5 in Switzerland in June 1954.

Oleg Salenko scored five goals in Russia's 6-1 win over Cameroon in the USA on June 28, 1994.

MOST APPEARANCES
Antonio Carbajal kept goal for Mexico in five World Cup finals tournaments, in 1950, 1954, 1958, 1962 and 1966, playing 11 games in all. This record was tied by Lothar Matthäus (Germany), who played a record 25 games from 1982 to 1998. Matthäus, below right, is pictured during a challenge from Croatia's Davor Suker during Germany's quarter-final game against Croatia in Lyon, France, in July 1998. Croatia won 3–0, knocking Germany out of the tournament.

Of the nine players to have scored four goals in a match, three — Sándor Kocsis (Hungary), Just Fontaine (France) and Gerd Müller (West Germany) — have achieved one of the 35 hat-tricks scored in finals matches.

MOST GOALS IN A FINAL
Geoff Hurst scored three goals for England against West Germany on July 30, 1966.

MOST WORLD CUP FINAL MATCHES SCORED IN
Vava (Brazil) scored in 1958 and 1962, Pelé (Brazil) in 1958 and 1970, and Paul Breitner (West Germany) in 1974 and 1982.

MOST GOALS CONCEDED
The record for the greatest number of goals to have been conceded is 103 in 78 matches, by Germany.

YOUNGEST AND OLDEST PLAYERS
The youngest person to play in a finals match is Norman Whiteside, who played for Northern Ireland v. Yugoslavia at the age of 17 years 41 days in June 1982.

The youngest scorer in a finals match is Pelé, who was 17 years 239 days old when he scored for Brazil against Wales, at Gothenburg, Sweden, in 1958.

YOUNGEST SCORER IN 1998
The youngest scorer in the 1998 finals was England's Michael Owen (right), who was 18 years 191 days old when he scored against Romania at Toulouse, France, on June 22, 1998. The oldest scorer during the 1998 finals was Saudi Arabia's Youssef Al Tunian, who was 34 years 220 days old when he scored a penalty against South Africa at Bordeaux, France, on June 24, 1998.

The youngest player in the 1998 finals was Samuel Eto'o (Cameroon), who was 17 years 99 days old when he came on as a substitute v. Italy on June 17.

The oldest person to play in a finals match was Roger Milla for Cameroon v. Russia at the age of 42 years 39 days on June 28, 1994.

The oldest player in the 1998 finals was Jim Leighton, Scotland's goalkeeper, who was 39 years 334 days old in his team's final group match against Morocco at St Etienne, France, on June 23, 1998.

FASTEST GOAL
The quickest official goal in a World Cup finals match was 27 seconds, by Bryan Robson for England v. France at Bilbao, Spain, on June 16, 1982.

Based on timing from film, Vaclav Masek of Czechoslovakia scored against Mexico in 15 seconds at Viña del Mar, Chile, in 1962.

FASTEST GOAL BY A SUBSTITUTE PLAYER
Denmark's Ebbe Sand was sent on in the 59th minute of the match against Nigeria on June 28, 1998 and was on the field 16 (ball in play) seconds before he scored the fourth goal.

MOST SENDINGS OFF IN ONE GAME
The record for the greatest number of sendings off to have occurred in a single game is three, by Brazil (2) against Czechoslovakia (1) at Bordeaux, France, on June 12, 1938; Brazil (2) against Hungary (1) at Berne, Switzerland, on June 27, 1958, and Denmark (2) against South Africa (1) at Toulouse, France, on June 18, 1998.

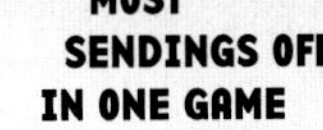

MOST UNDISCIPLINED TOURNAMENT
The worst ever World Cup tournament in terms of bookings and sendings off was France '98, with a total of 22 sendings off and 257 bookings from 64 games.

track and field

STEEPLECHASE CHAMPION
Moses Kiptanui was the first athlete to complete the 3,000-m steeplechase in less than 8 minutes. His first ambition was to play soccer, but he was directed towards track and field and began training seriously in 1989. His first breakthrough came in 1990, when he won the World junior and the African senior 1,500-m titles. He has now set up a coaching center in the mountains of his native Kenya.

FASTEST RUNNING SPEEDS
Ben Johnson (Canada) and Carl Lewis (US) both reached a peak speed of 26.95 mph (10 m in 0.83 sec.) during the 1988 Olympic Games 100-m final in Seoul, South Korea on September 24, 1988. Johnson won, but his world record was disallowed after a positive drug test.

In the women's final, Florence Griffith-Joyner (US) was timed at 0.91 sec for each 10 m from 60 m to 90 m (a speed of 24.58 mph).

MOST OLYMPIC TITLES
The most gold medals won is 10 (an absolute Olympic record), by Raymond Ewry (US): standing high, long and triple jumps in 1900, 1904, 1906 and 1908.

The most gold medals won by a woman is four, by Fanny Blankers-Koen (Netherlands) in the 100 m, 200 m, 80-m hurdles and 4 x 100-m relay, 1948; Betty Cuthbert (Australia) in the 100 m, 200 m and 4 x 100-m relay, 1956, and the 400 m, 1964; Bärbel Wöckel (East Germany) in the 200 m and 4 x 100-m relay, 1976 and 1980; and Evelyn Ashford (US) in the 100 m, 1984, and 4 x 100-m relay, 1984, 1988 and 1992.

MOST OLYMPIC MEDALS
The most medals is 12 (nine gold, three silver), by long-distance runner Paavo Nurmi (Finland) in 1920, 1924, and 1928.

The most medals by a female athlete is seven, by Shirley de la Hunty (Australia), with three gold, one silver, and three bronze in 1948, 1952, and 1956. A re-read of the photo-finish indicated that she was third, not fourth, in the 1948 200-m event, thus unofficially making her medal count eight. Irena Szewinska (Poland), the only female athlete to win a medal in four successive Games, also won seven medals (three gold, two silver, and two bronze in 1964, 1968, 1972, and 1976), as did Merlene Ottey (Jamaica), with two silver and five bronze in 1980, 1984, 1992, and 1996.

MOST WINS AT ONE GAMES
The most gold medals at one Games is five, by Paavo Nurmi (Finland) in 1924 (1,500 m, 5,000 m, 10,000-m cross-country, 3,000-m team, and cross-country team).

The most medals at individual events is four, by Alvin Kraenzlein (US) in 1900 (60 m, 110-m hurdles, 200-m hurdles, and long jump).

OLDEST AND YOUNGEST OLYMPIC CHAMPIONS
The oldest athlete was Patrick "Babe" McDonald (US), who was 42 years 26 days old when he won the 25.4-kg (56-lb.) weight throw in Belgium in August 1920.

The oldest female champion was Lia Manoliu (Romania), who was 36 years 176 days old when she won the discus in Mexico in 1968.

The youngest gold medalist was Barbara Jones (US), who was a member of the winning 4 x 100-m relay team at Helsinki, Finland, at the age of 15 years 123 days in July 1952.

RECORD-BREAKING SPRINTER
Donovan Bailey was born in Manchester, Jamaica. He began his track career running for Canada at the 1991 Pan-Am Games in Cuba, and went on to win an Olympic gold at the 1996 Summer Games in Atlanta, Georgia, setting a new 100-m world record of 9.84 seconds. Bailey also set a new indoor 50-m world record of 5.56 seconds in 1996.

The youngest male champion was Bob Mathias (US), who won the decathlon aged 17 years 263 days in London in 1948.

OLDEST AND YOUNGEST RECORD-BREAKERS
Marina Styepanova (USSR) set a 400-m hurdle record (52.94 sec) at Tashkent, USSR, in 1986, at the age of 36 years 139 days.

Wang Yan (China) set an individual women's 5,000-m walk record of 21 min. 33.8 sec. at age 14 years 334 days in China on March 9, 1986.

The youngest man to break an individual record was Thomas Ray (GB), who pole-vaulted 3.42 m (11 ft. 2¼ in.) at age 17 years 198 days on September 19, 1879.

WORLD CHAMPIONSHIPS
The most medals won is 10, by Carl Lewis (US): a record eight gold (100 m, long jump, and 4 x 100-m relay, 1983; 100 m, long jump, and 4 x 100-m relay, 1987; and 100 m and 4 x 100-m relay, 1991), a silver at long jump in 1991, and a bronze at 200 m in 1993.

The most medals won by a woman is 14, by Merlene Ottey (Jamaica), with three gold, four silver, and seven bronze from 1983 to 1997.

The most gold medals won by a woman is four, by Jackie Joyner-Kersee (US) in the long jump in 1987 and 1991 and the heptathlon in 1987 and 1993.

Sergey Bubka (Ukraine) won the same event at a record six consecutive championships in the pole vault from 1983 to 1997.

WORLD INDOOR CHAMPIONSHIPS
The most individual titles is four, by Stefka Kostadinova (Bulgaria) in the high jump in 1985, 1987, 1989 and 1993, Mikhail Shchennikov (Russia) in the 5,000-m walk in 1987, 1989, 1991, and 1993 and Sergey Bubka (Ukraine) in the pole vault in 1985, 1987, 1991, and 1995.

MOST RECORDS SET IN A DAY
Jesse Owens (US) set six world records in 45 minutes in Ann Arbor, Michigan, on May 25, 1935. He ran 100 yards in 9.4 seconds at 3:15 pm, made a 26-ft.-8¼-in. long jump at 3:25 pm, ran 220 yards in 20.3 seconds at 3:45 pm, and covered the 220-yard low hurdles in 22.6 seconds at 4 pm.

LONGEST WINNING SEQUENCES
The record winning sequence at a track event is 122, by Ed Moses (US) at the 400-m hurdles between August 1977 and June 1987.

Iolanda Balas (Romania) won a record 150 consecutive high jump competitions between 1956 and 1967.

HIGHEST JUMP ABOVE OWN HEAD
The greatest height cleared by an athlete above their own head was 1 ft. 11¼ in., by 5-ft.-8-in. Franklin Jacobs (US), who jumped 2.32 m (7 ft. 7¼ in.) in New York City on January 27, 1978.

The greatest height cleared by a female athlete above her own head was 1 ft. ¾ in., by 5-ft.-6-in. Yolanda Henry (US), who jumped 2.00 m (6 ft. 6¾ in.) in Seville, Spain, on May 30, 1990.

BEST STANDING JUMPS
The best high jump from a standing position was 1.90 m (6 ft. 2¾ in.), by Rune Almen (Sweden) in Karlstad, Sweden, on May 3, 1980.

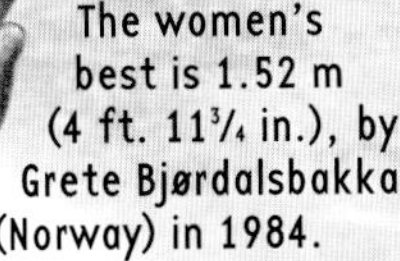

The women's best is 1.52 m (4 ft. 11¾ in.), by Grete Bjørdalsbakka (Norway) in 1984.

The best long jump was 3.71 m (12 ft. 2 in.), by Arne Tvervaag (Norway) in 1968. The best long jump by a woman was 2.92 m (9 ft. 7 in.), by Annelin Mannes (Norway) in March 1981.

FASTEST MASS RELAYS
The fastest 100 x 100-m was 19 min. 14.19 sec., by a team from Antwerp, in Belgium on September 23, 1989.

The fastest time over 100 miles by 100 runners was 7 hr. 53 min. 52.1 sec., by Baltimore Road Runners Club, Maryland, on May 17, 1981.

The greatest distance ever covered by a team of 10 runners in 24 hours is 302 miles 494 yd., by Puma Tyneside RC in Jarrow, England, in September 1994.

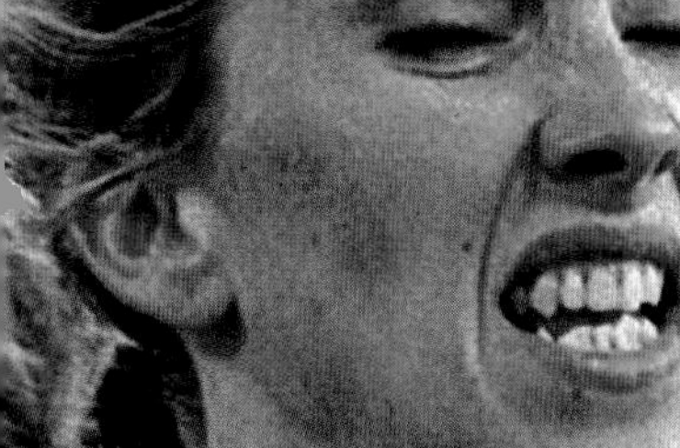

DOUBLE RECORD-BREAKER
Svetlana Masterkova (Russia) holds the 1,000-m record, after finishing in 2 min. 28.98 sec. on August 23, 1996 in Brussels, Belgium. Nine days earlier, she set a new one-mile record of 4 min. 12.56 sec. in Zürich, Switzerland. She is the first woman to hold world records at both 1,000 m and one mile since 1936.

POLE VAULTING CHAMPION
On March 21, 1998, Emma George (Australia) set a world outdoor pole vault record of 4.58 m (15 ft. ¼ in.), an improvement of ⅖ inch on the existing record, which she had set herself the week before. Five days later, on March 26, George cleared 4.55 m (14 ft. 11 in.), breaking the world indoor pole vault record by 2¾ inches. George, who is 23 years old, is a former circus performer.

golf

OLDEST US OPEN CHAMPION

Hale Irwin won the US Open at the age of 45 years 15 days on June 18, 1990. Irwin won in 1974 and 1979, but he had not been a contender for several years, and was only eligible because of a special exemption given him by the USGA. In 1997, he set the single season earnings record for the Senior PGA tour, at $2,343,364.

BRITISH OPEN

The best score in a round is 63, by Mark Hayes (US) at Turnberry, UK, in 1977, Isao Aoki (Japan) at Muirfield, UK in 1980, Greg Norman (Australia) at Turnberry, UK in 1986, Paul Broadhurst (GB) at St. Andrews, UK in 1990, Jodie Mudd (US) at Royal Birkdale, UK in 1991, Nick Faldo (GB) at Royal St. George's, UK in 1993, and Payne Stewart (US) in 1993, also at St. George's.

The best score in four rounds is 267 (66, 68, 69, 64), by Greg Norman at Royal St. George's, UK, July 15–18, 1993.

Nick Faldo completed the first 36 holes at Muirfield, UK in a record 130 strokes (66, 64), July 16–17, 1992.

US OPEN

The best score in a round is 63, by Johnny Miller (US) on the 6,921-yard, par-71 Oakmont Country Club course, Pennsylvania in June 1973, and by Jack Nicklaus (US) and Tom Weiskopf (US) at Baltusrol Country Club (7,015 yards), Springfield, New Jersey, both on June 12, 1980.

The best score over two rounds is 134, by Jack Nicklaus (63, 71) at Baltusrol in 1980, Chen Tze-Chung of (Taiwan; 65, 69) at Oakland Hills, Michigan in 1985, and Lee Janzen of the (US; 67, 67) at Baltusrol in June 1993.

The best score over four rounds is 272, by Jack Nicklaus (63, 71, 70, 68) at Baltusrol in June 1980 and Lee Janzen (67, 67, 69, 69) at Baltusrol in June 1993.

THE MASTERS

The lowest score in a round is 63, by Nick Price (Zimbabwe) in 1986 and Greg Norman in 1996.

The best score over two rounds is 131 (65, 66), by Raymond Floyd (US) in 1976.

PGA CHAMPIONSHIP

The best score in any round is 63, by Bruce Crampton (Australia) at Firestone, Akron, Ohio, in 1975; Raymond Floyd at Southern Hills, Tulsa, Oklahoma, in 1982; Gary Player (South Africa) at Shoal Creek, Birmingham, Alabama, in 1984; Vijay Singh (Fiji) at Inverness Club, Toledo, Ohio, in 1993; and Michael Bradley (US) and Brad Faxon (US) at Riviera Country Club, Pacific Palisades, California in 1995.

The record aggregate is 267 by Steve Elkington (Australia), with 68, 67, 68, 64, and Colin Montgomerie (GB), with 68, 67, 67, 65, at Riviera Country Club, Pacific Palisades in 1995. Elkington won in a playoff.

WORLD CUP

The US has won the World Cup 21 times between 1955 and 1995.

The lowest aggregate score for 144 holes is 536, by the US (Fredrick Couples and Davis Love III) at Dorado, Puerto Rico, November 10–13, 1994.

The lowest ever individual score was 265, by Fred Couples on the same occasion.

Arnold Palmer and Jack Nicklaus have been on a record six winning teams, Palmer in 1960, 1962–64, and 1966–67, and Nicklaus in 1963–64, 1966–67, 1971 and 1973.

Jack Nicklaus has taken the individual title a record three times (1963–64, 1971).

WALKER CUP

The US has won the Walker Cup a record 31 times.

Jay Sigel (US) won a record 18 matches from 1977 to 1993.

Joseph Carr (GB and Ireland) played in 10 contests, 1947–67.

MOST TOURNAMENT WINS

Byron Nelson (US) won a record 18 tournaments and an unofficial tournament in a year, including a record 11 consecutive wins, from March 8 to August 4, 1945.

After turning professional in 1934, Sam Snead won a record 81 official US tour events.

The LPGA tour record is 88, by Kathy Whitworth (US), 1959–91.

The most career victories in European Order of Merit tournaments is 55, by Severiano Ballesteros (Spain), 1974–95.

BIGGEST WINNING MARGIN

The greatest margin of victory in a major tournament is 21 strokes, by Jerry Pate (US), who won the 1981 Colombian Open with 262.

Charlotte Pitcairn Leitch won the Canadian Ladies' Open in 1921 by the biggest margin for a major title: 17 up and 15 to play.

EUROPEAN VICTORY IN THE RYDER CUP

The Ryder Cup, golf's most prized team trophy, began in 1927 at the instigation of wealthy British seed merchant Samuel Ryder. The idea was the result of a match between professionals from Great Britain and the US at Wentworth, Surrey, England the previous year. The biennial event was originally contested between the US and Great Britain (Great Britain and Ireland 1973–77). In 1979, the British team was expanded to include European players, a reflection of the rapidly growing European Tour, although it was not until 1985 that a European side gained victory in the event. Prior to this, Britain had won only three times (1929, 1933 and 1957), while the US had won 21 times. Since 1985, however, Europe has won a further four times and interest has grown in the event. In 1997, it was held outside the British Isles and the US for the first time, at Valderrama, Spain. Europe (seen left), captained by Spaniard Severiano Ballesteros, secured victory by 14.5 to 13.5 points.

YOUNGEST AND OLDEST NATIONAL CHAMPIONS
Thuashni Selvaratnam won the Sri Lankan Ladies' Amateur Open Golf Championship at age 12 in 1989.

Isa Goldschmid won the Italian Women's Championship at the age of 50 in 1976.

MOST HOLES
Eric Freeman (US) played 467 holes, using a cart, at Glen Head Country Club, New York in 12 hours in 1997. The nine-hole course is 3,272 yards long.

Ian Colston played 401 holes in 24 hours at Bendigo GC, Victoria, Australia (par-73, 6,061 yards) in 1971.

Steve Hylton played 1,128 holes in a week at Mason Rudolph GC (6,060 yards), Clarksville, Tennessee in August 1980.

VARE TROPHY WINNER
Annika Sörenstam (Sweden) began playing golf at age 12, winning the World Amateur Championship in 1991. She began her professional career at 23 on the WPG European Tour (1993). She became the first foreign-born player to win the LPGA's Vare Trophy for low scoring average. Sörenstam was the first player in seven years to win six events in one season and is the eighth woman to have been player of the year more than once.

LONGEST CARRY
The record for the longest carry below an altitude of 1,000 m (3,281 feet) is 365 yards, by Karl Woodward (GB) at the Boca Raton Country Club, Florida, 1996.

LONGEST PUTT
The longest known holed putt in a major tournament is 110 feet, by Jack Nicklaus in the 1964 Tournament of Champions, and Nick Price in the 1992 PGA Championship.

MOST BALLS HIT IN ONE HOUR
The most balls driven in one hour, over 100 yards and into a target area, is 2,146, by Sean Murphy of Canada at Swifts Practice Range, Carlisle, England on June 30, 1995.

YOUNGEST MASTERS CHAMPION
Tiger Woods holds the record for the best score in four rounds in the Masters, with 270 (70, 66, 65, 69) in 1997, the year in which he became the youngest player to win the Masters. Born in 1975, Woods swung his first golf club at the age of 11 months. He turned professional on August 26, 1996, and became the first player to record five consecutive top-10 finishes on a US tour.

LONGEST STRAIGHT HOLE ACHIEVED IN ONE SHOT
The longest straight hole ever holed in one shot was the 10th (447 yards) at Miracle Hills GC, Omaha, Nebraska, by Robert Mitera on October 7, 1965. Mitera stood 5 ft. 6 in. tall and weighed 165 pounds. He was a two-handicap player who normally drove 245 yards. A 50-mph gust carried his shot over a 290-yard dropoff.

LONGEST "DOG-LEG" HOLE
The record for the longest "dog-leg" hole achieved in one stroke is the 496-yard 17th by Shaun Lynch at Teign Valley GC, England on July 24, 1995.

LONGEST HOLE BY A BLIND GOLFER
On May 9, 1997 Kenneth E. Schreiber aced the 135-yard 12th hole at Beacon Woods Golf Club, Bayonet Point, Florida. It is the longest hole-in-one achieved by a legally blind person.

tennis

MOST GRAND SLAM WINS
The most singles championships in grand slam tournaments is 24, by Margaret Court (Australia): 11 Australian, five US, five French and three Wimbledon, 1960–73.

The record for the most men's singles championships in grand slam tournaments is 12, by Roy Emerson (Australia): six Australian and two each French, US and Wimbledon, 1961–67.

The most grand slam tournament wins by a doubles partnership is 20, by Althea Brough (US) and Margaret Du Pont (US): 12 US, five Wimbledon and three French 1942–57; and Martina Navrátilová and Pam Shriver (both US): seven Australian, five Wimbledon, four French and four US, 1981–89.

Pam Shriver and Martina Navrátilová (both US) won a record eight successive grand slam tournament women's doubles titles and 109 successive matches in all events from April 1983 to July 1985.

Six successive grand slam tournaments were won by Maureen Connolly (US) in 1953, Margaret Court (Australia) in 1970 and Martina Navrátilová (US) from 1983 to 1984.

MOST WIMBLEDON WINS
Billie-Jean King (US) won a record 20 women's titles between 1961 and 1979: six singles, 10 women's doubles and four mixed doubles.

Martina Navrátilová (US) has won a record nine women's singles titles in 1978–79, 1982–87 and 1990.

Elizabeth Ryan (US) won a record 19 women's doubles titles (12 women's, seven mixed), 1914–34.

The most titles by a man is 13, by Hugh Doherty (GB) with five singles titles (1902–06) and a record eight men's doubles (1897–1901 and 1903–05), partnered by his brother Reginald.

YOUNGEST FRENCH OPEN WINNER
Michael Chang (US) won the men's singles title at the age of 17 years 109 days in 1989, becoming the youngest ever grand slam champion, and also the first US man to win the French Open since 1955. The French Championships were first held in 1891, but remained closed to players who did not belong to a French club until 1925. They have been held at the Stade Roland Garros since 1928.

The most men's singles wins since the Challenge Round was abolished in 1922 is five, by Björn Borg (Sweden), 1976–80.

The most men's mixed doubles titles is four, by Elias Seixas (US) from 1953 to 1956; Ken Fletcher (Australia) in 1963, 1965, 1966 and 1968; and Owen Davidson (Australia) in 1967, 1971, 1973 and 1974.

OLDEST AND YOUNGEST WIMBLEDON CHAMPIONS
Margaret Du Pont (US) was 44 years 125 days old when she won the mixed doubles in 1962.

Arthur Gore (GB) won the men's singles at the age of 41 years 182 days in 1909.

Lottie Dod (GB) was 15 years 285 days old when she won the women's singles in 1887.

The youngest seed was Jennifer Capriati (US), who was 14 years 89 days old at her first match in 1990. She won, making her the youngest ever Wimbledon winner.

MOST US OPEN WINS
Margaret Du Pont (US) won 25 titles from 1941 to 1960: a record 13 women's doubles (12 with Althea Brough, US), nine mixed doubles and three singles.

The most women's singles titles is eight, by Molla Mallory (US), 1915–18, 1920–22, and 1926.

The most men's titles is 16, by Bill Tilden (US), including seven singles (1920–25, 1929). Seven singles titles were also won by Richard Sears (US), 1881–87, and William Larned (US), 1901–02, 1907–11.

YOUNGEST AND OLDEST US OPEN WINNERS
Vincent Richards (US) was 15 years 139 days old when he won the men's doubles in 1918.

The youngest singles champion was Tracy Austin (US), who was 16 years 271 days old when she won the 1979 women's title.

The youngest men's singles champion was Pete Sampras (US), who was 19 years 28 days old when he won the title in 1990.

The oldest ever champion was Margaret Du Pont (US), who won the mixed doubles title at the age of 42 years 166 days in 1960.

The oldest ever singles champion was William Larned (US), who won at the age of 38 years 242 days in 1911.

YOUNGEST MAN TO WIN WIMBLEDON SINGLES TITLE
German tennis star Boris Becker became the first unseeded player and the youngest ever winner of the Wimbledon men's singles title at the age of 17 years 227 days in 1985. He retained the title the following year, and in 1989, having won the US Open for the first time, took home his third Wimbledon title. Becker was beaten by Michael Stich in the 1991 Wimbledon finals, having lost to Stefan Edberg in the 1988 and 1990 finals. In 1997 he announced his retirement from Wimbledon and the other grand slam tennis tournaments after being beaten by Pete Sampras in the quarter-finals. At that time, Becker had more than 40 career titles to his name and had won at least two titles every year for 12 consecutive years. In 1998, he came out of semi-retirement, reaching the quarter-finals at Monte Carlo in April and representing his country in the World Team Cup in Dusseldorf, Germany in May.

MOST AUSTRALIAN OPEN WINS
Margaret Court (Australia) won 21 titles: 11 women's singles (1960–66, 1969–71 and 1973), eight women's doubles, and two mixed doubles.

Roy Emerson (Australia) won six men's singles (1961, 1963–67).

Thelma Long (Australia) won a record 12 women's doubles and four mixed doubles for a record total of 16 doubles titles.

Adrian Quist (Australia) won 10 consecutive men's doubles (1936–40 and 1946–50) and three men's singles.

YOUNGEST AND OLDEST AUSTRALIAN OPEN WINNERS
Rodney Heath (Australia) was 17 when he won the men's singles in 1905.

The oldest champion was Norman Brookes (Australia), who was 46 years 2 months old when he won the 1924 men's doubles.

Ken Rosewal (Australia) won the men's singles at the age of 37 years 62 days in 1972.

MOST FRENCH OPEN WINS
Margaret Court (Australia) won a record 13 titles from 1962–73: five singles, four women's doubles and four mixed doubles.

The men's record is nine, by Henri Cochet (France), with four singles, three men's doubles and two mixed doubles, 1926–30.

The singles record is seven by Chris Evert (US): 1974–75, 1979–80, 1983 and 1985–86.

Björn Borg (Sweden) won six men's singles from 1974 to 1975, and 1978 to 1981.

OLDEST AND YOUNGEST FRENCH OPEN CHAMPIONSHIPS
Elizabeth Ryan (US) won the 1934 women's doubles at the age of 42 years 88 days.

The oldest singles champion was Andrés Gimeno (Spain), at the age of 34 years 301 days in 1972.

The youngest doubles champions were the 1981 mixed doubles winners Andrea Jaeger and Jimmy Arias (both US). Jaeger was 15 years 339 days old and Arias 16 years 296 days old.

The youngest women's singles winner is Monica Seles (then Yugoslavia, now US), who won at age 16 years 169 days in 1990.

MOST WINS IN THE ATP TOUR CHAMPIONSHIP
Ivan Lendl (Czechoslovakia/US) won five titles: 1981, 1982, 1985 1986 and 1987.

Seven doubles titles were won by John McEnroe and Peter Fleming (both US) from 1978 to 1984.

MOST DAVIS CUP WINS
The US has won the Davis Cup 31 times from 1900 to 1997.

LONGEST GRAND SLAM MATCH
The 1992 semi-final of the US Championships between Stefan Edberg (Sweden) and Michael Chang (US) lasted a total of 5 hr 26 min. Edberg won 6–7, 7–5, 7–6, 5–7, 6–4.

FASTEST SERVE
The fastest service timed with modern equipment was 149 mph, by Greg Rusedski (GB) during the Newsweek Championships Cup at Indian Wells, California on March 14, 1998. The record for the fastest timed women's service was set by Brenda Schultz-McCarthy (Netherlands) during the Australian Championships on January 22, 1996, and stands at 121.8 mph.

YOUNGEST WIMBLEDON CHAMP
The youngest ever Wimbledon champion is Martina Hingis (Switzerland), who was 15 years 282 days old when she won the women's doubles in 1996. In 1997, Hingis also became the youngest ever winner of the women's singles title at the Australian Open, at the age of 16 years 117 days.

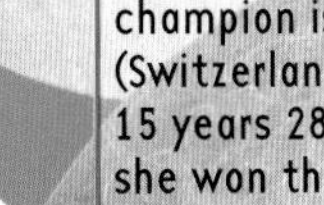

national football league (NFL)

LARGEST TV AUDIENCE
Around 138.5 million viewers in the United States and a further 800 million worldwide watched Super Bowl XXX between the Dallas Cowboys and the Pittsburgh Steelers on January 28, 1996.

LARGEST CROWDS
The largest crowd in any NFL game was 112,376 during the America Bowl, a pre-season game between the Dallas Cowboys and the Houston Oilers at Azteca Stadium, Mexico City, Mexico on August 15, 1994.

On January 20, 1980, 103,985 spectators watched Super Bowl XIV, between the Pittsburgh Steelers and the LA Rams at the Rose Bowl, Pasadena, California.

MOST SUPER BOWL WINS
The greatest number of team wins is five, by the San Francisco 49ers (XVI, XIX, XXIII, XXIV and XXIX) and by the Dallas Cowboys (VI, XXI, XXVII, XXVIII and XXX).

The most wins by an individual player is five, by Charles Hayley for the San Francisco 49ers (XXIII and XXIV) and the Dallas Cowboys (XXVII, XXVIII and XXX).

Chuck Noll has the most wins by a coach. He led the Pittsburgh Steelers to four Super Bowl titles: IX, X, XIII and XIV.

MOST SUPER BOWL APPEARANCES BY A COACH
Don Shula has been the head coach of six Super Bowl teams: the Baltimore Colts (III) and the Miami Dolphins (VI, VII, VIII, XVII and XIX). He won two games and lost four.

HIGHEST SUPER BOWL SCORES
The highest team score was set by the San Francisco 49ers when they beat the Denver Broncos 55–10 in New Orleans, Louisiana on January 28, 1990. This was also the highest victory margin.

In Super Bowl XXIX, the San Francisco 49ers set the record for the highest aggregate score, beating the San Diego Chargers 49–26.

MOST NFL TITLES
The Green Bay Packers have won 12 NFL championships: 1929–31, 1936, 1939, 1944, 1961–62, 1965, and Super Bowls I, II and XXXI (1966, 1967 and 1996 seasons).

MOST CONSECUTIVE NFL WINS
The Chicago Bears had the most consecutive NFL victories, winning 17 games in succession from 1933 to 1934.

LONGEST UNBEATEN NFL RUN
The most consecutive games without defeat is 25, by Canton, with 22 wins and 3 ties, 1921–23.

MOST NFL WINS IN A SEASON
The most wins in a season is 15, by the San Francisco 49ers in 1984 and the Chicago Bears in 1985.

The Miami Dolphins won all their games in the 1972 season (14 regular season matches and three playoff games, including the Super Bowl).

HIGHEST NFL SCORES
The highest individual team score in a regular season game is 72, by the Washington Redskins against the New York Giants (who scored 41) on November 27, 1966. This was also the highest aggregate score for a match.

In the NFL Championship game on December 8, 1940, the Chicago Bears beat the Washington Redskins 73–0 – the highest individual team score in a post-season game and the largest margin of victory in any game.

MOST NFL GAMES PLAYED
George Blanda played in 340 games in a record 26 seasons in the NFL (Chicago Bears 1949, 1950–58, Baltimore Colts 1950, Houston Oilers 1960–66 and Oakland Raiders 1967–75).

MOST EXPENSIVE TV ADVERTISING SLOT
A 30-second advertising slot for Super Bowl XXXII, between the Denver Broncos and the Green Bay Packers on January 25, 1998, cost a record $1.3 million – four times the cost of a normal advertising slot at a similar time. It is estimated that 45% of US homes tune in to the annual Super Bowl, and a single 30-second slot is estimated to reach about 100 million viewers. There were more than 30 advertisers for the 1998 Super Bowl, including Pizza Hut (top picture), Pepsi (bottom picture), Doritos, Intel and Coca-Cola, and all 58 spots are reported to have been sold two months before the game.

LONGEST RUN FROM SCRIMMAGE
Tony Dorsett scored on a touchdown run of 99 yards for the Dallas Cowboys against the Minnesota Vikings on January 3, 1983. Dorsett, the winner of the 1976 Heisman Trophy, is the leading rusher in the Cowboys' history and is third on the all-time rushers list, with 12,739 yards.

MOST SUCCESSFUL NFL COACH
The record for the greatest number of games won as coach is 347, by Don Shula for the Baltimore Colts (1963–69) and the Miami Dolphins (1970–95).

MOST NFL GAMES LOST
The Tampa Bay Buccaneers lost a record 26 consecutive games from 1976 to 1977.

LONGEST NFL PASS COMPLETION
A pass completion of 99 yards has been achieved on eight occasions and has always resulted in a touchdown. The most recent 99-yard pass was from Brett Favre to Robert Brooks of the Green Bay Packers against the Chicago Bears on September 11, 1995.

LONGEST NFL FIELD GOAL
The longest field goal kicked is 63 yards, by Tom Dempsey of the New Orleans Saints against the Detroit Lions, November 8, 1970.

LONGEST NFL PUNT
Steve O'Neal kicked a punt of 98 yards for the New York Jets against the Denver Broncos on September 21, 1969.

LONGEST NFL PUNT RETURN
The longest return is 103 yards, by Robert Bailey for the Los Angeles Rams against the New Orleans Saints, October 23, 1994.

LONGEST INTERCEPTION RETURNS IN AN NFL GAME
The longest recorded return for a touchdown by a team is 104 yards. It was achieved by James Willis and Troy Vincent for the Philadelphia Eagles in a game against the Dallas Cowboys on November 3, 1996. Willis returned the ball 14 yards and lateraled it to Vincent, who returned it for the remaining 90 yards.

The longest interception return for a touchdown by an individual player is 103 yards. The record was set by Venice Glenn for the San Diego Chargers in a game against the Denver Broncos on November 29, 1987. It was equaled by Louis Oliver for the Miami Dolphins against the Buffalo Bills, on October 4, 1992.

LONGEST NFL KICKOFF RETURN
The record for the longest ever NFL kickoff return for a touchdown is 106 yards, by three players: Al Carmichael for the Green Bay Packers against the Chicago Bears on October 7, 1956; Noland Smith for the Kansas City Chiefs against the Denver Broncos on December 17, 1967; and Roy Green for the St. Louis Cardinals against the Dallas Cowboys on October 21, 1979.

BIGGEST CONTRACT
In July 1997, Packers quarterback Brett Favre signed what is believed to be the NFL's biggest contract. It is estimated that the two-time NFL MVP's contract is to average $6–6.5 million per year for seven years and includes a $12 million signing bonus.

olympics

SUMMER OLYMPICS
The next Summer Games will take place in Sydney, Australia, in 2000. More than 30 disciplines will be contested, including, for the first time, trampolining, and triathlon. At the first modern Games in 1896, nine sports were contested: athletics, cycling, fencing, gymnastics, shooting, swimming, tennis, weightlifting, and wrestling.

LONGEST LIVE BROADCAST
The French-language, state-owned Swiss TV station Suisse 4 broadcast the 1996 Olympic Games in Atlanta, Georgia, nonstop for 16 days 22 hr. 45 min., July 19–August 5, 1996.

MOST GAMES COMPETED
Five countries have competed at all 24 Summer Games: Australia, France, Greece, Great Britain, and Switzerland (the latter only competed in the Equestrian events in Stockholm, Sweden, in 1956 and did not attend the Games in Melbourne, Australia). France, Great Britain, and Switzerland have also competed at every Winter Games.

MOST PARTICIPANTS
The most competitors at a Summer Games is 10,744 (7,060 men, 3,684 women), at Atlanta in 1996.

The most competitors at a single Winter Games is 1,801 (1,412 men and 489 women) at Albertville, France, in 1992.

A record 72 countries competed at the 1998 Winter Games at Nagano, Japan.

MOST GOLD MEDALS
The most individual gold medals by a male competitor in the modern Games is 10, by Raymond Ewry (US) in track and field from 1900 to 1908.

The record for the greatest number of individual gold medals ever won by a female competitor is seven, by Vera Caslavska-Odlozil (Czechoslovakia) in gymnastics: three in 1964 and four (one shared) in 1968.

Swimmer Mark Spitz (US) won a record seven golds (including three for relay) at a single celebration, at Munich, Germany, in 1972.

The record for the greatest number of gold medals won in individual events at one celebration is five, by speed skater Eric Heiden (US) at Lake Placid, New York, in 1980.

The greatest number of consecutive individual titles won in the same event is four, by Alfred Oerter (US) in the discus (1956–68) and Carl Lewis (US) in the long jump (1984–96).

Raymond Ewry (US) won both the standing long jump and the standing high jump at four games in succession (1900, 1904, 1906, and 1908). This includes the official Intercalated Games of 1906.

Paul Elvstrøm (Denmark) won four successive gold medals at monotype yachting events from 1948 to 1960, but there was a class change (1948 Firefly class, 1952–60 Finn class).

British rower Steven Redgrave won four consecutive gold medals as a member of the coxed fours in 1984 and the coxless pairs in 1988, 1992, and 1996.

MOST MEDALS
Gymnast Larisa Latynina (USSR) won a record 18 medals from 1956 to 1964. The men's record is 15, by gymnast Nikolay Andrianov (USSR) from 1972 to 1980.

The most medals won at one celebration is eight, by gymnast Aleksandr Dityatin (USSR) in 1980.

WOMEN'S ICE HOCKEY
The 1998 Winter Olympics at Nagano, Japan, was the first Games to feature women's hockey, with four countries competing for medals. The Olympics represented a great breakthrough for women's hockey, and it is hoped that the event will help the sport to attract the kind of serious financial backing that is enjoyed by men's hockey. However, the current lack of support is regarded as a major hindrance to the women's game. In Canada, for example, female players currently have to rely on monthly stipends provided by Sport Canada, ranging from $800 for A-card athletes to $400 for less experienced players. Despite this, women's hockey is increasingly popular – the number of women and girls registered with USA Hockey has quadrupled since the 1990 Women's World Championship, while the total number participating in the sport in the United States is an estimated 23,000 or more. The most prominent American player is Cammi Granato, who had an endorsement deal with Nike for the Olympics. She scored the first ever women's Olympic hockey goal, against China.

LUGEING
Stefan Krausse and Jan Behrendt from Germany are pictured in action on their way to winning a second Olympic gold and completing a German clean sweep at the 1998 Winter Games at Nagano, Japan. German lugers have dominated the sport at the Olympics, winning 21 out of a possible 30 gold medals since the introduction of lugeing to the Games in 1964.

MOST GAMES ENTERED
Yachtsman Hubert Raudaschl (Austria) competed in nine Games from 1964 to 1996. Fencer Kerstin Palm (Sweden) holds the women's record, with seven Games (1964–88).

LONGEST OLYMPIC CAREERS
The longest Olympic career is 40 years, by Ivan Osiier (Denmark), fencing (1908–32, 1948), Magnus Konow (Norway), yachting, (1908–20, 1928, 1936–48), Paul Elvstrøm (Denmark), yachting (1948–60, 1968–72, 1984–88), and Durward Knowles (Great Britain 1948, then Bahamas), yachting (1948–72, 1988). The longest Olympic career by a woman is 28 years, by Anne Ransehousen (US), in dressage (1960, 1964, 1988), and Christilot Hanson-Boylen (Canada) in dressage (1964–76, 1984, 1992).

MOST MEDALS ★
SUMMER GAMES (1896–1996)

USA 2,015:
833 gold, 634 silver, 548 bronze
Soviet Union[1] 1,234:
485 gold, 395 silver, 354 bronze
Great Britain 635:
177 gold, 233 silver, 225 bronze
France 562:
176 gold, 181 silver, 205 bronze
Germany[2] 516:
151 gold, 181 silver, 184 bronze
Sweden 459:
134 gold, 152 silver, 173 bronze
Italy 444:
166 gold, 136 silver, 142 bronze
Hungary 425:
142 gold, 128 silver, 155 bronze
GDR (East Germany)[3] 410:
153 gold, 130 silver, 127 bronze
Australia 294:
87 gold, 85 silver, 122 bronze
Finland 292:
99 gold, 80 silver, 113 bronze
Japan 280:
93 gold, 89 silver, 98 bronze
Romania 239:
63 gold, 77 silver, 99 bronze
Poland 227:
50 gold, 67 silver, 110 bronze
Canada 217:
49 gold, 77 silver, 91 bronze
FRG (West Germany)[4] 200:
56 gold, 64 silver, 80 bronze
Netherlands 187:
49 gold, 57 silver, 81 bronze
Bulgaria 182:
43 gold, 76 silver, 63 bronze
Switzerland 174:
46 gold, 68 silver, 60 bronze
China 164:
52 gold, 63 silver, 49 bronze

This excludes medals that were won in Official Art competitions from 1912 to 1948.

WINTER GAMES (1924–98)

Norway 239:
83 gold, 87 silver, 69 bronze
Soviet Union[1] 217:
87 gold, 63 silver, 67 bronze
USA 159:
59 gold, 59 silver, 41 bronze
Austria 145:
39 gold, 53 silver, 53 bronze
Finland 135:
38 gold, 49 silver, 48 bronze
GDR[3] 110:
39 gold, 36 silver, 35 bronze
Germany[2] 106:
46 gold, 38 silver, 32 bronze
Sweden 102:
39 gold, 28 silver, 35 bronze
Switzerland 92:
29 gold, 31 silver, 32 bronze
Canada 79:
25 gold, 25 silver, 29 bronze
Italy 77:
27 gold, 27 silver, 23 bronze
Netherlands 61:
19 gold, 23 silver, 19 bronze
France 61:
18 gold, 17 silver, 26 bronze
Russia[6] 42:
21 gold, 14 silver, 7 bronze
FRG (West Germany)[4] 39:
11 gold, 15 silver, 13 bronze
Japan 29:
8 gold, 9 silver, 12 bronze
Czechoslovakia[6] 26:
2 gold, 8 silver, 16 bronze
Great Britain 24:
7 gold, 4 silver, 13 bronze
Korea 16:
9 gold, 3 silver, 4 bronze
China 15:
0 gold, 10 silver, 5 bronze

SPEED SKATING
Gianni Romme (Netherlands) won both the 5,000-m and the 10,000-m gold medals in world record times at the 1998 Winter Games. Speed skating is one of the sports that was contested at the first Winter Olympics, held at Chamonix, France, in 1924. Technical innovations such as aerodynamically-designed suits and "clap" skates have lowered times considerably since the first Games.

★ Totals are for all the leading nations for all Summer and Winter Olympic disiplines and include events which have now been discontinued.

[1] Includes CIS (Unified team) 1992
[2] Germany 1896–1964 and 1992–94
[3] GDR (East Germany) 1968–88
[4] FRG (West Germany) 1968–88
[5] Includes Bohemia
[6] Includes Czarist Russia

paralympics

FASTEST 100-M BREASTSTROKE
Kaspar Engel of Germany celebrates after setting a world record in the men's 100-m breaststroke at the Atlanta Paralympics on August 24, 1996. His time was 1:31.50.

FASTEST 100-M ICE SLED
Norway's Anne Mette Samdal set a world record in the women's 100-m ice sled speed race at the Winter Paralympic Games in Nagano, Japan on March 7, 1998. Her time was 15.69 seconds. The 26-year-old bank clerk also won gold in the 500-m race in a Paralympic record time of 1:17.26 on the same day. The 1998 Winter Paralympics were the largest ever, with around 1,200 athletes and officials from more than 32 countries.

BIGGEST PARALYMPICS
A record 4,912 athletes from a record 104 countries competed in the Summer Paralympics in Atlanta, Georgia in 1996.

MOST WORLD RECORDS BY A MALE TRACK ATHLETE
Spain's Javier Conde, an amputee, set eight records in track events at the Barcelona Paralympics, Spain, in 1992, and the marathon record in Atlanta.

MOST WORLD RECORDS BY A FEMALE TRACK ATHLETE
Rima Batalova (USSR/Russia), a blind athlete, holds six records in track events. The last was set in an 800-m class in Atlanta.

MOST WORLD RECORDS BY A MALE FIELD ATHLETE
Wheelchair athlete Stephanus Lombaard of South Africa set three records in shot put and javelin between 1994 and 1996.

MOST WORLD RECORDS BY A FEMALE FIELD ATHLETE
Maria Buggenhagen (Germany) set four wheelchair records in shot put and discus from 1992 to 1996, when she set a shot put record in Atlanta.

MOST WORLD RECORDS BY MALE SWIMMERS
Duane Kale (New Zealand) and Alwin De Groot (Netherlands) set four world records in Atlanta.

MOST WORLD RECORDS BY A FEMALE SWIMMER
Beatrice Hess of France set six records in Atlanta.

MEN'S TEAM ARCHERY: STANDING
The record for the 3 x 72 archery event was set by Poland, with 1.73 points in Atlanta.

The 27 + 27 event record was set by South Korea, with 457 points in Atlanta.

The record for the 27 event is 232 points, which was set by South Korea in Atlanta.

WOMEN'S TEAM ARCHERY, OPEN
The record for the 3 x 72 archery event was set by Italy, with 1.58 points in Atlanta.

The 27 + 27 record is 438 points, by Italy in Atlanta.

The record for the 27 archery event was set by Italy, with 220 points in Atlanta.

MEN'S 100 M
The fastest 100 m by a blind man is 10.96 seconds, by A. Managaro (Italy) in Valencia, Spain, in 1995.

The record for the fastest 100 m by a male athlete with cerebral palsy is 11.79 sec, by Hoon Son (South Korea) in Seoul, South Korea, on October 17, 1988.

The fastest 100 m by a male amputee is 10.72 seconds, by Ajibola Adeoye (Nigeria) in Barcelona on September 5, 1992.

The best 100 m by a male athlete in a wheelchair is 14.45 seconds, by David Holding (GB) in Atlanta.

WOMEN'S 100 M
The best 100 m by a blind woman is 12.43 seconds, by R. Takbulatova (USSR) in Bulgaria in 1983.

The fastest 100 m by a female athlete with cerebral palsy is 14.56 seconds, by Alison Quinn (Australia) in Berlin, Germany in July 1994.

The record for the 100 m by a female amputee is 12.51 seconds, by Petra Buddelmeyer (Germany) in Belgium, in May 1957.

MEN'S 1,500 M
The fastest 1,500 m by a blind man is 3:55.00, by Noel Thatcher (GB) in Leeds, England in 1991.

The record for the 1,500 m by a male athlete with cerebral palsy is 4:19.90, by Ross Davis (US) in a wheelchair in Hartford, Connecticut in August 1996.

The fastest 1,500 m by a male amputee is 3:58.53, by Javier Conde (Spain) in Barcelona.

WOMEN'S 1,500 M
The fastest 1,500 m by a blind female athlete is 4:37.02, by Rima Batalova (Russia) in Berlin, Germany in July 1994.

The record for the 1,500 m by a woman with cerebral palsy is 5:20.50, by Linda Mastandrea (US) in a wheelchair in Hartford, Connecticut on August 5, 1995.

The fastest 1,500 m by a female amputee is 6:09.43, by Britta Brockskothon (Germany) in Hasselt, Belgium in May 1987.

The fastest 1,500 m by a woman in a wheelchair is 3:30.45, by Louise Sauvage (Australia) in Atlanta.

MOST SUCCESSFUL WHEELCHAIR TENNIS PLAYER
Ricky Molier of the Netherlands was ranked No. 1 on the International Wheelchair Tennis Federation Tour for the 1996 and 1997 seasons and was the Paralympic champion in Atlanta, Georgia in 1996. The 1997 season reinforced his dominance: he won almost 50% of Tour events, including the British, Austrian, Swiss, Czech, Polish, French and Finnish opens, and the Sportement and USTA nationals. The major difference between standard tennis and the wheelchair version is that the ball is allowed to bounce twice before it has to be returned in the latter, although it is often returned after just one bounce in top-level wheelchair tennis. Due to the nature of the game, a full-blown backhand can be difficult and is usually sliced. Spin plays a more prominent part in wheelchair tennis than in standard tennis, but that is not to say that it lacks speed and power – Ricky Molier's serve has been clocked at speeds in excess of 100 mph.

MEN'S HIGH JUMP
The best high jump by a blind man is 2.02 m (6 ft. 7½ in.), by Olaf Mehlmann (Germany) in 1994.

The best high jump by a male amputee is 1.96 m (6 ft. 5 in.), by Arnold Boldt (Canada) in Arnhem, Netherlands, on June 17, 1980.

WOMEN'S HIGH JUMP
The best high jump by a blind woman is 1.80 m (5 ft. 11 in.), by Maria Runyan (US) in 1995.

FASTEST 1,500 M, WHEELCHAIR
The record for the 1,500 m by a male athlete in a wheelchair is 3:02.00, by Swiss sportsman Franz Nietlispach (seen below left) at Zürich, Switzerland, on August 14, 1996. Nietlispach is seen here in the men's 1,500-m wheelchair final at Barcelona, Spain, in 1992, where he came second to Claude Issorat of France (right).

The best high jump by a female amputee is 1.66 m (5 ft. 5 in.), by Petra Buddelmeyer (Germany) in New York on June 24, 1986.

MEN'S LONG JUMP
The best long jump by a blind man is 7.23 m (23 ft. 8½ in.), by Enrique Cepeda (Cuba) in Argentina, 1995.

The longest jump by a male athlete with cerebral palsy is 5.92 m (19 ft. 5 in.), by Darren Thrupp (Australia) in China, 1994.

The best long jump by a male amputee is 6.75 m (22 ft. 2 in.), by Ruben Alvarez (Spain) in Atlanta.

WOMEN'S LONG JUMP
The best jump by a blind woman is 6.11 m (20 ft.), by Purification Ortiz (Spain) in Spain in 1995.

The best long jump by a woman with cerebral palsy is 4.49 m (14 ft. 8¾ in.), by A. Grigalluniene (Lithuania) in Atlanta.

The record for the long jump by a female amputee is 5.70 m (18 ft. 8¼ in.), by Irina Leontiouk (Belarus) in Atlanta.

MEN'S SWIMMING
The fastest 100-m butterfly by a male swimmer is 1:02.44, by Jody Cundy (GB) in Atlanta.

The fastest 100-m freestyle by a man is 56.40 sec, by Alwin Houtsma (Netherlands) in Atlanta.

The fastest 100-m freestyle by a severely disabled male swimmer is 1:31.35, by Ricardo Oribe (Spain) in Atlanta.

The fastest 100-m freestyle by a very severely disabled male swimmer is 2:41.94, by James Anderson (GB) in Atlanta.

The fastest 100-m backstroke by a male swimmer is 1:04.10, by Alwin DeGroot (Netherlands) in Atlanta.

The record for the fastest 100-m backstroke by a blind male swimmer is 1:04.80, by Walter Wu (Canada) in Atlanta.

WOMEN'S SWIMMING
The fastest 100-m butterfly by a woman is 1:08.88, by Gemma Dashwood (Australia) in Atlanta.

The fastest 100-m freestyle by a woman is 1:08.16, by Joyce Luncher (US) in Atlanta.

The fastest 100-m freestyle by a severely disabled female swimmer is 1:36.23, by Mayumi Narita (Japan) in Atlanta.

The fastest 100-m freestyle by a very severely disabled female swimmer is 3:09.00, by Betiana Basualdo (Argentina) in Atlanta.

The record for the 100-m backstroke by a female swimmer is 1:26.41, by Kristin Hakonard (Iceland) in Atlanta.

basketball

SPORTS ICON
Widely regarded as basketball's greatest ever player, Michael Jordan holds many NBA records, including highest career average for players exceeding 10,000 points and highest career scoring average for the playoffs. Jordan's rise to superstardom began in 1984, when he was drafted by the Chicago Bulls. He won the first of his five NBA MVP crowns in 1988 and took his sixth NBA Finals MVP title in 1998. Jordan's success, however, transcends the court. He has signed lucrative endorsement deals with a host of well known companies, including Coke, Gatorade and McDonald's, but his biggest contract, with Nike, has made him a celebrity icon and arguably the world's most famous athlete. Jordan reportedly receives $12 million a year for the deal with Nike, whose Air Jordan sneakers sell for up to $2,000 second-hand. He is also co-chairman of P.L.A.Y, a $10-million Nike-sponsored initiative to provide recreational facilities for children. In addition, he owns a restaurant, has hosted *Saturday Night Live* and has appeared in the movie *Space Jam*. He was described by one commentator as "the ultimate sports icon of the generation."

MOST OLYMPIC TITLES
The United States has won 11 men's Olympic titles. From 1936 to 1972, they won 63 consecutive matches, until they lost 50–51 to the USSR in the disputed final in Munich. Since then, they have won a further 37 matches and had another loss to the USSR (in 1988).

The women's title has been won a record three times by the USSR in 1976, 1980 and 1992 (by the Unified team from the republics of the ex-USSR) and the United States in 1984, 1988 and 1996.

MOST WORLD TITLES
The record for most men's World Championships titles is three, by the USSR (1967, 1974 and 1982), Yugoslavia (1970, 1978 and 1990), and by the United States (1954, 1986 and 1994).

The USSR has won six women's World Championships titles (1959, 1964, 1967, 1971, 1975 and 1983).

HIGHEST INTERNATIONAL SCORE
In a senior international match, Iraq scored 251 against Yemen, who scored 33, at the Asian Games in New Delhi, India in 1982.

MOST TITLES: NBA
The Boston Celtics have won 16 NBA titles: in 1957, from 1959 to 1966, and in 1968, 1969, 1974, 1976, 1981, 1984 and 1986.

HIGHEST SCORES: NBA
The highest aggregate score in a game was 370, when the Detroit Pistons beat the Denver Nuggets 186–184 in Denver, Colorado on December 13, 1983. Three overtimes were played after a 145–145 tie in regulation time.

The highest ever aggregate score in regulation time was 320, when the Golden State Warriors beat the Denver Nuggets 162–158 in Denver on November 2, 1990.

The highest-scoring individual was Wilt Chamberlain, who scored a record 100 points for Philadelphia against New York in Hershey, Pennsylvania on March 2, 1962. This included a record 36 field goals and 28 free throws from 32 attempts, as well as a record 59 points in one half.

Chamberlain's free-throw record was equaled by Adrian Dantley for Utah against Houston in Las Vegas, Nevada in January 1984.

MOST SEASON WINS: NBA
The Chicago Bulls had 72 NBA wins in the 1995–96 season, a record number of NBA wins within a single season.

MOST GAMES: NBA
Robert Parish played 1,611 regular season

TALLEST NBA PLAYER
Gheorghe Muresan of the Washington Wizards is 7 ft. 7 in. tall. Nicknamed Ghitza ("Little Gheorghe"), Muresan was born in Transylvania, Romania in 1971 and made his pro debut in 1994. His height is due to a pituitary gland condition.

YOUNGEST PLAYERS
On November 5, 1996, Kobe Bryant of the Los Angeles Lakers became the youngest NBA player at the age of 18 years 63 days. He played for six minutes and missed with his only shot attempt. His record was broken one month later by Jermaine O'Neal of the Portland Trail Blazers. O'Neal played for a mere three minutes and was successful with his only shot, scoring two points on his debut.

games over 21 seasons for the Golden State Warriors (1976–80), the Boston Celtics (1980–94), the Charlotte Hornets (1994–96) and the Chicago Bulls (1996–97).

The record for the greatest number of complete games played in a single season is 79, by Wilt Chamberlain for Philadelphia in 1961/62. During this period he was on court for a record total of 3,882 minutes.

MOST POINTS: NBA
Kareem Abdul-Jabbar scored a record total of 38,387 points during his career, which works out at an average of 24.6 points per game. This included a total of 15,837 field goals in regular season games and 2,356 field goals in playoff games.

The highest career average for players exceeding 10,000 points is 31.5, by Michael Jordan, who scored a total of 29,277 points in 930 games for the Chicago Bulls from 1984 to 1998.

The highest career average for playoffs is 33.4, by Michael Jordan, who scored 5,987 points in 179 games from 1984 to 1998. Jordan has earned more from endorsement deals than any other basketball player.

GREATEST WINNING MARGIN: NBA
A record winning margin of 68 points was achieved when the Cleveland Cavaliers beat the Miami Heat 148–80 on December 17, 1991.

BEST WINNING STREAK: NBA
The Los Angeles Lakers won a record 33 games in succession from November 5, 1971 to January 7, 1972.

YOUNGEST PLAYER: NBA
Jermaine O'Neal was 18 years 53 days old when he made his debut for the Portland Trail Blazers against the Denver Nuggets on December 5, 1996.

OLDEST REGULAR PLAYER: NBA
Robert Parish of the Chicago Bulls was 43 years 286 days old at the end of the 1996/97 season on June 13, 1997, making him the oldest regular player in the NBA.

TALLEST EVER PLAYER
The tallest ever player is thought to be Suleiman Ali Nashnush, who was reputed to be 8 ft. ¼ in. tall when he played for the Libyan team in 1962.

HIGHEST ATTENDANCE
The biggest ever crowd was 80,000, for the final of the European Cup Winners' Cup between AEK Athens and Slavia Prague in Athens, Greece, on April 4, 1968.

HIGHEST VERTICAL DUNK
Sean Williams and Michael Wilson, both of the Harlem Globetrotters, dunked a basketball at a rim height of 11 ft. 8 in. at Disney-MGM Studios, Orlando, Florida on September 16, 1996.

LONGEST GOAL
Christopher Eddy scored a 90-ft.-2¼-in. field goal for Fairview High School against Iroquois High School in Erie, Pennsylvania on February 25, 1989. The shot was made as time expired in overtime and won the game 51–50 for Fairview.

TOP SHOOTING SPEEDS
Jeff Liles scored 231 goals out of 240 attempts in 10 minutes using one ball and one rebounder at Southern Nazarene University, Bethany, Oklahoma on June 11, 1992. He also scored 231 goals out of 241 attempts on June 16, 1992.

In 24 hours (September 29–30, 1990) Fred Newman scored 20,371 free throws from a total of 22,049 taken (a success rate of 92.39%) at Caltech, Pasadena, California. Ted St. Martin scored a record 5,221 consecutive free throws in Jacksonville, Florida on April 28, 1996.

Jeff Liles of Joplin, Missouri scored 53 points (29 baskets out of 33 attempts) in one minute from seven positions on May 8, 1997 at the YMCA in Carthage, Missouri.

LONGEST DRIBBLE
Ashrita Furman dribbled a basketball 96 miles 1,003 yd. in 24 hours without traveling at Victory Field Track, Forest Park, Queens, New York, May 17–18, 1997.

MOST BALLS SPUN
On December 20, 1997, Michael Kettman of St. Augustine, Florida balanced and spun 20 balls across his body for a total of five seconds.

baseball

OUTSTANDING PITCHER
Roger Clemens of the Toronto Blue Jays is one of three pitchers to have won the Cy Young Award, along with Steve Carlton and Greg Maddux. Clemens won the award in 1986, 1987, 1991 and 1997. He is also one of two pitchers to have struck out 20 batters in a 9-inning game, on April 29, 1986 and September 18, 1996; Chicago Cubs rookie sensation Kerry Wood performed the same feat on May 6, 1998.

BIGGEST CONTRACTS
The top baseball contracts (based on the average annual salary for the duration of the contract) are for $11.5 million. They were signed by pitchers Greg Maddux of the Atlanta Braves in August 1997 and Pedro Martinez of the Boston Red Sox in December 1997. Maddux's contract is worth $57.5 million over five years and Martinez's is worth $69 million over six years. Martinez has the option for a seventh year, however, which could bring the total value of the contract to $90 million — an average of $12.85 million per year.

MOST SPECTATORS
An estimated 114,000 spectators watched a demonstration game between Australia and an American Services team during the Olympic Games in Melbourne, Australia, on December 1, 1956.

HIGHEST BATTING AVERAGE (CAREER)
Ty Cobb, Detroit Tigers (AL), 1905–26; Philadelphia Athletics (AL), 1927–28 holds the all-time mark for highest batting average at .367. Cobb compiled his record from 4,191 hits in 11,429 at-bats.

MOST HITS (CAREER)
The career record for the most hits is 4,256, by Pete Rose, Cincinnati Reds (NL), 1963–78, 1984–86; Philadelphia Phillies (NL), 1979–83; Montreal Expos (NL), 1984. Rose compiled his record hits total in 14,053 at-bats.

MOST HOME RUNS (CAREER)
Hank Aaron holds the major league career record with 755 home runs — 733 for the Milwaukee/Atlanta Braves (NL) 1954–74, and 22 for the Milwaukee Brewers (AL) 1975–76.

MOST RBI'S (CAREER)
The career record for the most RBI's is 2,297, by Hank Aaron, Milwaukee/Atlanta Braves (NL), 1954–74; Milwaukee Brewers (AL), 1975–76.

MOST RUNS SCORED (CAREER)
The career record for the most runs scored is 2,245, by Ty Cobb, Detroit Tigers (AL), 1905–26; Philadelphia Athletics (AL), 1927–28.

MOST TOTAL BASES (CAREER)
The career record for total bases is 6,856, by Hank Aaron, Milwaukee/Atlanta Braves (NL), 1954–74; Milwaukee Brewers (AL), 1975–76. Aaron's record includes 2,294 singles, 624 doubles, 98 triples and 755 home runs.

MOST GRAND SLAMS (CAREER)
Lou Gehrig of the New York Yankees (AL) hit 23 grand slams from 1923 to 1939.

MOST WALKS (CAREER)
The career record for the most walks is 2,056, by Babe Ruth, Boston Red Sox (AL), 1914–19; New York Yankees (AL), 1920–34; Boston Braves (NL), 1935.

MOST GAMES PLAYED
The record for the most games played is 3,562, by Pete Rose, Cincinnati Reds (NL), 1963–78, 1984–86; Philadelphia Phillies (NL), 1979–83; Montreal Expos (NL), 1984.

MOST WINS (CAREER)
The career record for the most wins is 511, by Cy Young, Cleveland Spiders (NL), 1890–98; St. Louis Cardinals (NL),

BIGGEST REPLICA BAT
The world's biggest ever replica baseball bat is 120 feet in height and weighs 68,000 pounds. Here it is seen being placed in front of bat manufacturer Hillerich & Bradsby's new headquarters in Louisville, Kentucky in October 1995. The bat is modeled on the "R43" bat made for Babe Ruth. In the spring of 1927, Ruth strode into the Hillerich & Bradsby plant and asked them to make him some bats. He hit his then record of 60 home runs with the resulting bats that year. The largest actual baseball bat, made from a solid cypress log, is 12 ft. 2 in. long, has a diameter of 11¹/₄ inches at the handle and 14 inches at the barrel, and weighs 280 pounds. The bat, completed in 1996, was made by Thomas Timm, his father Russ, and his son Joshua of Custom Woodcrafter in Summerville, South Carolina.

1899–1900; Boston Red Sox (AL), 1901–08; Cleveland Indians (AL), 1909–11; Boston Braves (NL), 1911.

MOST STRIKEOUTS (CAREER)
The record for the most strikeouts is 5,714, by Nolan Ryan, New York Mets (NL), 1966–71; California Angels (AL), 1972–79; Houston Astros (NL), 1980–88; Texas Rangers (AL), 1989–93.

MOST INNINGS PITCHED (CAREER)
The career record for the most innings pitched is 7,356, by Cy Young, Cleveland Spiders (NL), 1890–98; St. Louis Cardinals (NL), 1899–1900; Boston Red Sox (AL), 1901–08; Cleveland Indians (AL), 1909–11; Boston Braves (NL), 1911.

MOST SAVES (CAREER)
The career record for the most saves is 478, by Lee Smith, Chicago Cubs (NL), 1980–87; Boston Red Sox (AL), 1988–90; St. Louis Cardinals (NL), 1990–93; New York Yankees (AL), 1993; Baltimore Orioles (AL), 1994; California Angels (AL), 1995–96; Cincinnati Reds (NL), 1996; and Montreal Expos (NL), 1997.

MOST NO-HITTERS (CAREER)
The career record for the most no-hitters is seven, by Nolan Ryan: California Angels v. Kansas City Royals (3–0), May 15, 1973; California Angels v. Detroit Tigers (6–0), July 15, 1973; California Angels v. Minnesota Twins (4–0), September 28, 1974; California Angels v. Baltimore Orioles (1–0), June 1, 1975; Houston Astros v. Los Angeles Dodgers (5–0), September 26, 1981; Texas Rangers v. Oakland Athletics (5–0), June 11, 1990; and Texas Rangers v. Toronto Blue Jays (3–0), May 1, 1991.

MOST GAMES PITCHED (CAREER)
The career record for the most games pitched is 1,070, by Hoyt Wilhelm, New York Giants (NL), 1952–56; St. Louis Cardinals (NL), 1957; Cleveland Indians (AL), 1957–58; Baltimore Orioles (AL), 1958–62; Chicago White Sox (AL), 1963–68; California Angels (AL), 1969; Atlanta Braves (NL), 1969–70; Chicago Cubs (NL), 1970; Atlanta Braves (NL), 1971; Los Angeles Dodgers (NL), 1971–72.

LONGEST GAME (ELAPSED TIME)
The Chicago White Sox (AL) played the longest major league ballgame in elapsed time, 8 hr. 6 min., beating the Milwaukee Brewers, 7–6, in the 25th inning on May 9, 1984 in Chicago. The game started on Tuesday night and was still tied at 3–3 when the 1 a.m. curfew caused suspension until Wednesday night.

LONGEST GAME (MOST INNINGS)
The most innings in a major league game was 26, when the Brooklyn Dodgers (NL) and the Boston Braves (NL) played to a 1–1 tie on May 1, 1920.

SHORTEST GAME (ELAPSED TIME)
In the shortest major league game, the New York Giants (NL) beat the Philadelphia Phillies (NL), 6–1, in nine innings in 51 minutes on September 28, 1919.

LONGEST 9-INNING GAME (ELAPSED TIME)
The Baltimore Orioles (AL) played for 4 hr. 22 min., beating the New York Yankees 13–9 on September 5, 1997.

MOST WORLD SERIES WINS
The New York Yankees hold the record for the most wins in the World Series, with 23 victories. One of the team's newest recruits is Orlando "El Duque" Hernandez, a former Cuban star pitcher who signed a $6.6-million, four-year contract in 1998. Before signing with the Yankees, Hernandez made about $8 a month in Cuba.

BIGGEST CONTRACT
In August 1997, pitcher Greg Maddux signed a record-breaking contract worth $11.5 million a year when he re-signed with the Atlanta Braves. His record was equaled later that year by Pedro Martinez, who was acquired by the Boston Red Sox. Maddux is also one of three players to have won four Cy Young Awards (1992, 1993, 1994 and 1995).

auto sports

MOST WINS AT LE MANS
Porsche cars have won Le Mans, France a record 16 times (1970–71, 1976–77, 1979, 1981–87, 1994 and 1996–98). These wins represent just a fraction of their successes in the International Sports Car World Championships: with well over 100 wins, the German company is the world's most successful sports car manufacturer. Porsche won the Manufacturers' World title 13 times between 1969 and 1985.

GRAND PRIX

MOST SUCCESSFUL DRIVERS
The World Drivers' Championship has been won five times by Juan-Manuel Fangio (Argentina), in 1951 and from 1954 to 1957. When Fangio retired in 1958, he had won 24 Grand Prix races (two shared) from 51 starts.

Alain Prost (France) had 51 wins from a total of 199 races between 1980 and 1993. During his career, he gained a record 798.5 Grand Prix points.

The most pole positions is 65, by the late Ayrton Senna (Brazil) from 161 races (41 wins) between 1985 and 1994.

The most Grand Prix starts is 256, by Ricardo Patrese (Italy) from 1977 to 1993.

The most Grand Prix wins in a year is nine, by Nigel Mansell (GB) in 1992 and by Michael Schumacher (Germany) in 1995.

MOST SUCCESSFUL MANUFACTURERS
Williams has won a record nine World Championships (1980–81, 1986–87, 1992–94 and 1996–97).

McLaren won 15 of the 16 Grand Prix in the 1988 season: Ayrton Senna had eight wins and three seconds and Alain Prost had seven wins and seven seconds.

Excluding the Indianapolis 500 race (then included in the World Drivers' Championship), Ferrari won all seven races in 1952 and the first eight (of nine) in 1953.

FASTEST RACE
Peter Gethin (GB) averaged a speed of 150.759 mph in a BRM in the 1971 Italian Grand Prix at Monza.

FASTEST QUALIFYING LAP
Keke Rosberg (Finland) set a record of 1 min. 5.59 sec. in a Williams-Honda in the 1985 British Grand Prix at Silverstone, England. His average speed was 160.817 mph.

CLOSEST FINISHES
Peter Gethin (GB) beat Ronnie Peterson (Sweden) by 0.01 seconds in the 1971 Italian Grand Prix.

Ayrton Senna (Brazil) beat Nigel Mansell (GB) by a margin of 0.014 seconds in the 1986 Spanish Grand Prix at Jerez de la Frontera.

INDIANAPOLIS 500

MOST SUCCESSFUL DRIVERS
Three drivers have had four wins: A. J. Foyt Jr. (US) in 1961, 1964, 1967 and 1977; Al Unser Sr. (US) in 1970, 1971, 1978 and 1987; and Rick Mears (US) in 1979, 1984, 1988 and 1991.

Rick Mears has started from pole position a record six times (1979, 1982, 1986, 1988–89 and 1991.

A. J. Foyt Jr. started in a record 35 races from 1958 to 1992.

FASTEST RACE
Arie Luyendyk (Netherlands) won in 2 hr. 41 min. 18.404 sec., driving a Lola-Chevrolet on May 27, 1990. His average speed was 185.981 mph.

FASTEST QUALIFYING LAPS
The highest average speed for the four qualifying laps is 236.986 mph, by Arie Luyendyk (Netherlands) in a Reynard-Ford-Cosworth on May 12, 1996. This included a one-lap record of 237.498 mph. On May 9, 1996 Luyendyk also set the unofficial track record of 239.260 mph.

BIGGEST PRIZES
The record for the largest ever prize fund is $8.72 million, in 1998.

The biggest individual prize was $1.57 million, won by Arie Luyendyk (Netherlands) in 1997.

LE MANS

GREATEST DISTANCE COVERED
Dr. Helmut Marko (Austria) and Gijs van Lennep (Netherlands) covered 3,315 miles 363 yd. in a 4,907 cc flat-12 Porsche 917K Group 5 sports car from June 12 to June 13, 1971.

The greatest distance covered on the current circuit is 3,313 miles 264 yd., by Jan Lammers (Netherlands), Johnny Dumfries and Andy Wallace (both GB) in a Jaguar XJR-9 from June 11 to June 12, 1988. Their average speed was 138.047 mph.

FASTEST LAPS
The fastest ever race lap is 3 min. 21.27 sec, by Alain Ferté (France) in a Jaguar XJR-9 on June 10, 1989. His average speed over the 8-mile-728-yd. lap was 150.429 mph.

Hans Stück (West Germany) set the record for the fastest ever practice lap speed on June 14, 1985, reaching a speed of 156.377 mph.

MOST GRAND PRIX WINS
In 1995, German driver Michael Schumacher, pictured left celebrating his victory in the Monaco Grand Prix in 1997, equaled Nigel Mansell's record nine Grand Prix wins in a year, which was set in 1992. Now 28 years old, Schumacher is one of the world's best racing drivers: he won two World Championships when he was driving for Benetton (1994 and 1995) and clinched a $56-million, two-year deal with Ferrari in 1996, although he has yet to win a championship with the manufacturer. In the same year, he earned approximately $60 million, making him one of the wealthiest sportsmen in the world. Michael's younger brother Ralph began Formula 1 racing in 1997, after a career in Formula 3000. He signed a three-year contract with Jordan–Peugeot and earns an estimated $8 million a year, but he has yet to win a race.

MOST WINS
The most wins by one driver is six, by Jacky Ickx (Belgium): 1969, 1975–77 and 1981–82.

RALLYING

LONGEST RALLIES
The Singapore Airlines London–Sydney Rally covered 19,329 miles from Covent Garden, London, England to Sydney Opera House, Sydney, Australia. It was won by Andrew Cowan, Colin Malkin and Michael Broad in a Mercedes 280E in 1977.

The longest annual rally is the Safari Rally, first run through Kenya, Tanzania and Uganda but now restricted to Kenya. The 17th Safari in 1971 covered 3,874 miles. The race has been won a record five times by Shekhar Mehta (Kenya), in 1973 and from 1979 to 1982.

MOST MONTE CARLO WINS
The Monte Carlo Rally has been won four times by Sandro Munari (Italy), in 1972, 1975, 1976 and 1977, and Walter Röhrl (West Germany), with co-driver Christian Geistdorfer, in 1980 and from 1982 to 1984.

SMALLEST CAR TO WIN MONTE CARLO RALLY
An 851-cc Saab driven by Erik Carlsson and Gunnar Häggbom and by Carlsson and Gunnar Palm (all Sweden) won the Monte Carlo Rally in 1962 and 1963.

MOST RAC RALLY WINS
Hannu Mikkola (Finland), with co-driver Arne Hertz (Sweden), has had four wins, in a Ford Escort in 1978 and 1979 and an Audi Quattro in 1981 and 1982.

MOST WORLD CHAMPIONSHIP WINS
The World Drivers' Championships has been won four times by Juha Kankkunen (Finland), in 1986, 1987, 1991 and 1993.

The record for the most wins in World Championship races is 21, by Juha Kankkunen (Finland) and Carlos Sainz (Spain).

The most wins in a season is six, by Didier Auriol (France) in 1992.

Lancia won a record-breaking total of 11 Manufacturers' World Championships between 1972 and 1992.

FASTEST RACE
The Busch Clash race, over a distance of 50 miles on a 2½-mile-long, 31° banked track at Daytona, Florida, is the world's fastest race. In 1987, Bill Elliott averaged a speed of 197.802 mph in a Ford Thunderbird. Elliott won a record 11 races in 1985, and has been voted the Most Popular Driver in the NASCAR Winston Cup series 12 times.

BEST RACE TIMES

FASTEST CIRCUIT
The record for the highest ever average lap speed on any closed circuit in the world is 250.958 mph. It was achieved by Dr. Hans Liebold (Germany) when he lapped the 7-mile-1,496-yd. high-speed track at Nardo, Italy in a Mercedes-Benz C111-IV experimental coupe in a time of 1 min. 52.67 sec. on May 5, 1979. The car was powered by a V8 engine with two KKK turbochargers, with an output of 500 hp at 6,200 rpm.

FASTEST 500-MILE RACE
Al Unser Jr. (US) set the world record for any 500-mile race on August 9, 1990, when he won the Michigan 500 at an average speed of 189.7 mph.

MOST GRAND PRIX WINS
The greatest number of Grand Prix race victories by a manufacturer is 115, by Ferrari, following the 1998 Canadian Grand Prix. Pictured here is the new Ferrari F300, which first raced in 1998. Ferrari has won the Manufacturers' World title eight times, although their last success was in 1983. They had their first Grand Prix success in July 1951 at Silverstone, England and dominated the next two seasons. The first Manufacturers' championship was contested in 1958, and Ferrari's first success came in 1961. That year they won five of the eight races, but their final success was marked by the tragic death of German driver Wolfgang von Trips, who was killed along with 14 spectators when his Ferrari crashed at the Italian Grand Prix.

swimming and diving

SWIMMING

MOST OLYMPIC MEDALS

The most individual gold medals is five, by Krisztina Egerszegi (Hungary) with the 100-m backstroke in 1992, the 200-m backstroke in 1988, 1992 and 1996 and the 400-m medley in 1992.

The most individual gold medals by a man is four by: Charles Daniels (US) in the 100-m freestyle, 1906 and 1908, the 220-yd. freestyle, 1904, and the 440-yd. freestyle, 1904; Roland Matthes (East Germany) in the 100-m and 200-m backstroke, 1968 and 1972; Tamás Daryni (Hungary) in the 200-m and 400-m medley, 1988 and 1992; Aleksandr Popov (Russia) in the 50-m and 100-m freestyle, 1992 and 1996; and Mark Spitz (see below).

The most gold medals by a woman is six, by Kristin Otto (East Germany) at Seoul, South Korea, in 1988: 100-m freestyle, backstroke and butterfly, 50-m freestyle, 4 x 100-m freestyle and 4 x 100-m medley.

The most Olympic golds won by a swimmer is nine, by Mark Spitz (US) in the 100-m and 200-m freestyle in 1972, the 100-m and 200-m butterfly in 1972, the 4 x 100-m freestyle in 1968 and 1972, the 4 x 200-m freestyle in 1968 and 1972 and the 4 x 100-m medley in 1972. In all but one (the 1968 4 x 200-m freestyle) he set a world record.

FASTEST MALE SWIMMER

Tom Jager (US) had an average speed of 5.37 mph over 50 yards in a 25-yard pool in Nashville, Tennessee on March 23, 1990. His time was 19.05 seconds. If Jager, winner of two Olympic golds, a silver and a bronze, were able to maintain this pace indefinitely, he would be able to halve the record time for crossing the English Channel (7 hr. 17 min.).

Mark Spitz won a record total of 11 medals: a silver (100-m butterfly) and a bronze (100-m freestyle) in 1968 as well as his nine golds. This record was equalled by Matt Biondi (US), with a gold in 1984, five gold, one silver and one bronze in 1988, and two golds and a silver in 1992.

Spitz's record of seven medals at a single Games (1972) was also equalled by Matt Biondi in 1988.

The most medals won by a woman is eight, by Dawn Fraser (Australia) with four gold and four silver from 1956 to 1964, Kornelia Ender (East Germany) with four gold and four silver from 1972 to 1976, and Shirley Babashoff (US) with two gold and six silver from 1972 to 1976.

MOST WINS IN ONE EVENT

Two swimmers have won the same event on three occasions: Dawn Fraser (Australia) in the 100-m freestyle (1956, 1960, 1964) and Krisztina Egerszegi (Hungary) in the 200-m backstroke (1988, 1992, 1996).

MOST MEDALS IN THE WORLD CHAMPIONSHIPS

Michael Gross (West Germany) won 13 World Championship medals (five gold, five silver and three bronze) from 1982 to 1990.

The most medals by a woman is 10, by Kornelia Ender (eight gold and two silver in 1973 and 1975).

The most gold medals by a man is six (two individual and four relay) by James Montgomery (US) in 1973 and 1975.

The most medals at a single championship is seven, by Matt Biondi (US) with three gold, one silver and three bronze in 1986.

MOST WORLD RECORDS

The most world records set by a man is 32, by Arne Borg (Sweden) between 1921 and 1929.

The most world records set by a woman is 42, by Ragnhild Hveger (Denmark) from 1936 to 1942.

The most world records set by a man in currently recognized events (metric distances in 50-m pools) is 26, by Mark Spitz (US) from 1967 to 1972.

The greatest number of world records set by a woman in currently recognized events is 23, by Kornelia Ender (East Germany) from 1973 to 1976.

FASTEST FEMALE SWIMMER

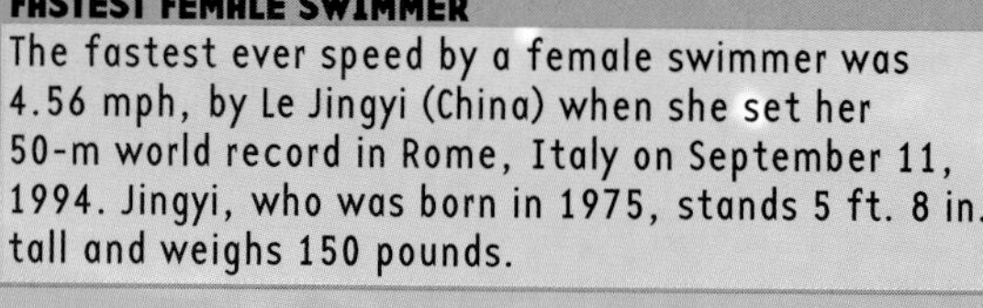

The fastest ever speed by a female swimmer was 4.56 mph, by Le Jingyi (China) when she set her 50-m world record in Rome, Italy on September 11, 1994. Jingyi, who was born in 1975, stands 5 ft. 8 in. tall and weighs 150 pounds.

The most world records set in one pool is 86, in the North Sydney pool, Australia, between 1955 and 1978. This includes 48 imperial distance records.

LONGEST SWIMS
Fred Newton swam 21,826 miles down the Mississippi River, between Ford Dam (near Minneapolis, Minnesota) and Carrollton Ave., New Orleans, Louisiana, from July 6 to December 29, 1930. He was in the water for 742 hours.

The greatest distance swum in 24 hours is 63 miles 559 yd., by Anders Forvass (Sweden) at the 25-m Linköping public swimming pool, Sweden, October 28–39, 1989.

The greatest distance swum by a woman in 24 hours is 59 miles 771 yd., by Kelly Driffield at the 50-m Mingara Leisure Center pool, Tumbi Umbi, Australia, in June 1997.

The greatest distance swum underwater is 49 miles 68 yd. in 24 hours, by Paul Cryne (GB) and Samir Sawan al Awami (Qatar) from Doha to Umm Said, Qatar and back again in 1985.

The greatest distance swum underwater by a relay team is 94 miles 774 yd., by six people in a pool in Czechoslovakia (now Czech Republic), October 17–18, 1987.

LONGEST RELAYS
The 20-strong New Zealand national relay team swam a record 113 miles 1,040 yd. in Lower Hutt, New Zealand, in a time of 24 hours, December 9–10, 1983.

The 24-hour club record by a team of five is 100 miles 1,045 yd., by the Portsmouth Northsea SC at the Victoria Swimming Center, Portsmouth, England, March 4–5, 1993.

DIVING

MOST OLYMPIC MEDALS
The greatest number of Olympic medals ever won by a diver is five, by Klaus Dibiasi (Italy) with three gold and two silver from 1964 to 1976, and by Greg Louganis (US) with four gold and one silver in 1976, 1984 and 1988. Dibiasi is also the only diver to have ever won the same event (highboard) at three successive Olympic Games (1968, 1972 and 1976).

The record for the greatest number of highboard and springboard doubles wins is two, by Patricia McCormick (US) in 1952 and 1956 and by Greg Louganis (US) in 1984 and 1988.

MOST WORLD TITLES
Greg Louganis has won a record five world titles (highboard in 1978 and both highboard and springboard in 1982 and 1986, as well as four Olympic gold medals in 1984 and 1988).

HIGHEST DIVING SCORES
Diver Greg Louganis achieved record scores at the 1984 Olympic Games in Los Angeles, California, with 754.41 points for the 11-dive springboard event and 710.91 for the highboard. Louganis, who has won an unprecedented 47 national titles during his career, revealed his HIV-positive status after the 1988 Summer Olympics in Seoul, where he injured his head while diving.

The record for the greatest number of gold medals ever to have been won in a single event since the inaugural World Championship in 1973 is three, by Philip Boggs (US) in the springboard in 1973, 1975 and 1978. Boggs also won the 1976 Olympic springboard title.

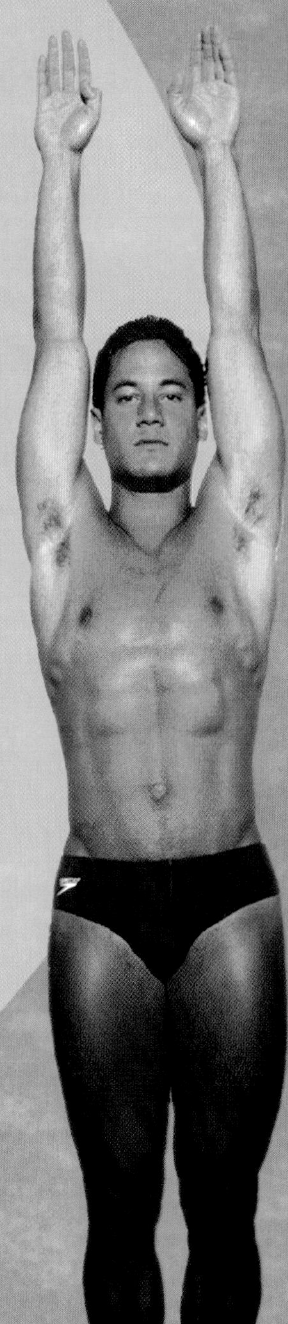

skiing

HIGHEST SCORING JUMP
Chinese skier Xu Nannan performs her jump during the women's aerials qualification round at the 1998 Winter Olympics in Nagano, Japan. A former gymnast, Nannan was in a highly advantageous position after the qualifying round, which she led. She remained on form and executed the highest scoring jump of the competition but went on to win silver rather than gold.

MOST WORLD ALPINE CHAMPIONSHIP TITLES
The most titles won by a man in the World Alpine Championship is seven, by Toni Sailer (Austria), who won all four (giant slalom, slalom, downhill and the non-Olympic Alpine combination) in 1956 and the downhill, giant slalom and combined in 1958.

The record for the most titles by a woman is 12, by Christl Cranz (Germany), who won seven individual (four slalom, 1934 and 1937–39, and three downhill, 1935, 1937 and 1939) and five combined (1934–35 and 1937–39). Cranz also won the gold medal for the combined in the 1936 Olympics.

MOST WORLD NORDIC CHAMPIONSHIP TITLES
The most titles won by a woman is 17, by Yelena Välbe (Russia), with 10 individual titles and seven relay titles from 1989 to 1998.

The most titles by a jumper is five, by Birger Ruud (Norway) in 1931 and 1932 and from 1935 to 1937. Ruud is the only person to have won Olympic events in the Alpine and Nordic disciplines: the ski-jumping and the Alpine downhill in 1936.

MOST WORLD NORDIC CHAMPIONSHIP MEDALS
The most medals won is 23, by Raisa Smetanina (USSR, later CIS), including seven golds (1974–92).

FASTEST OLYMPIC DOWNHILL SPEED
The record for the highest ever average speed achieved in the Olympic downhill race is 66.64 mph, by French skier Jean-Luc Cretier at the 1998 Nagano Winter Olympics. A jubilant Cretier is pictured here seconds after receiving his medal for men's downhill alpine skiing on February 15. He had been competing at the highest level for a total of 11 years but had so far failed to win a single race or medal. He announced his retirement at the end of the season.

MOST WORLD CUP WINS
The record for the greatest number of individual event wins is 86 (46 giant slalom and 40 slalom) from a total of 287 races, by Ingemar Stenmark (Sweden) from 1974 to 1989. This included a men's record of 13 wins in one season (1978/79). Of these, 10 were part of a record 14 successive giant slalom wins, March 18, 1978–January 21, 1980.

Franz Klammer (Austria) won 25 downhill races, 1974–84.

Annemarie Moser (Austria) won a women's record 62 individual events from 1970 to 1979. She also had a record 11 consecutive downhill wins from 1972 to 1974.

Vreni Schneider (Switzerland) won a record total of 13 events (and one combined event), including all seven slalom events, in 1988/89.

MOST WORLD NORDIC TITLES
The most titles won by any skier (including Olympics) is 18, by Bjørn Daehlie (Norway), who won 12 individual and six relay from 1991 to 1998. At the 1998 Nagano Olympics, Daehlie become the most successful individual in the history of the Winter Games when he won an eighth gold medal. He plans to add to his Olympic victories at the 2002 Games in Salt Lake City, Utah.

MOST FREESTYLE TITLES
Edgar Grospiron (France) has won a record three titles (moguls in 1989 and 1991 and aerials in 1995). He also won an Olympic title in 1992.

The record for the most men's overall titles in the World Cup is five, by Eric Laboureix (France) from 1986 to 1988 and in 1990 and 1991.

The most women's overall titles in the World Cup is 10, by Connie Kissling (Switzerland) from 1983 to 1992.

LONGEST SKI-JUMPS
The longest ski-jump recorded in a World Cup event is 669 feet, by Andreas Goldberger (Austria) in Harrachov, Czech Republic, on March 9, 1996.

The longest ski-jump by a woman is 367 feet, by Eva Ganster (Austria) in Bischofshofen, Austria, on January 7, 1994.

The longest ever dry ski-jump was 302 feet, by Hubert Schwarz (West Germany) in Berchtesgarten, Germany, on June 30, 1981.

HIGHEST SPEEDS
The official world speed record is 150.028 mph, by Jeffrey Hamilton (US) in Vars, France on April 14, 1995.

The official women's record is 140.864 mph, by Karine Dubouchet (France) in Les Arcs, France on April 20, 1996.

The highest speed reached in a World Cup downhill is 69.8 mph, by Armin Assinger (Austria) in Sierra Nevada, Spain on March 15, 1993.

The record time for a 50-km (31-mile) race in a major championship is 1 hr. 54 min. 46 sec., by Aleksey Prokurorov (Russia) in Thunder Bay, Canada in 1994. His average speed was 16.24 mph.

The record for the fastest speed ever attained by a person skiing on one leg is 115.306 mph, by Patrick Knaff (France) in 1988.

LONGEST RACES
The longest Nordic ski race is the 55-mi.-528-yd. annual Vasaloppet in Sweden. There were 10,934 starters in 1977.

The longest downhill race is the 9-mi.-1,408-yd. Inferno from the top of the Schilthorn to Lauterbrunnen, Switzerland. The record time is 13 min. 53.4 sec., by Urs von Allmen (Switzerland) in 1991.

LARGEST RACE
The Finlandia Ski Race is 46 mi. 1,056 yd. long, from Hämeenlinna to Lahti, Finland. In February 1984, it had 13,226 starters and 12,909 finishers.

LONGEST ALL-DOWNHILL SKI RUN
The Weissfluhjoch-Küblis Parsenn skiing course near Davos, Switzerland is a record 7 mi. 1,056 yd. long.

GREATEST DISTANCE COVERED
Seppo-Juhani Savolainen (Finland) covered 258 mi. 352 yd. in 24 hours in Saariselkä, Finland, April 8–9, 1988.

The women's 24-hour record is 205 miles, by Sisko Kainulaisen (Finland) in Jyväskylä, Finland, March 23–24, 1985.

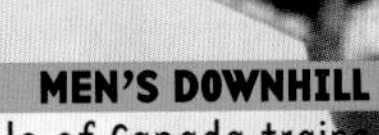

MEN'S DOWNHILL
Brian Stemmle of Canada trains for the men's downhill at the Nagano Winter Olympics. The men's downhill is the Blue Riband event of the Winter Olympics and is always eventful: 1998 was no exception. The race was delayed on numerous occasions due to heavy snow and eventually took place on February 13, which was a Friday. It proved unlucky for some – 13 skiers failed to finish.

ice hockey

MOST OLYMPIC AND WORLD TITLES
The USSR won 22 world titles (including the Olympic titles of 1956, 1964 and 1968) from 1954 to 1990 and one title as Russia in 1993. They won a further five Olympic titles in 1972, 1976, 1984, 1988 and 1992 (as the CIS, with an all-Russian team) for an Olympic record of eight.

Canada won the first four world championships for women (1990, 1992, 1994 and 1997) without losing a single game.

ICE HOCKEY COMPETITIONS
World ice hockey championships were first held for amateur players in 1920 in conjunction with the Olympic Games, which were also considered world championships up to 1968. Since 1976, world championships have also been open to professional players. Women's ice hockey was first introduced to the Olympic Games in 1998. The winner was the US, who beat Canada in the final.

MOST HIGHLY-PAID PLAYER
Sergey Federov (Russia) of the Detroit Red Wings is reported to have earned the record sum of $20 million for the 1997/98 season, making him the highest-paid ice hockey player ever. His basic salary was $2 million; the rest was made up of bonuses. Federov led the Red Wings to consecutive Stanley Cup victories in 1997 and 1998.

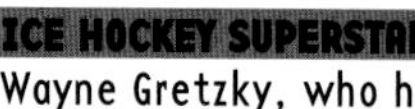

ICE HOCKEY SUPERSTAR
Wayne Gretzky, who has played for the Edmonton Oilers, the Los Angeles Kings, the St. Louis Blues and the New York Rangers, is the most successful ice hockey player today, earning an estimated $6.5 million (£3.9 million) a year. He holds numerous Stanley Cup records: most points (382), most goals (122) and most assists (260), as well as most points in a season, with 47 (16 goals and a record 31 assists) in 1985. He also holds the NHL scoring records for the regular season and play-off games, with 837 goals and 1,771 assists for a record 2,608 points from 1,253 games. In 1981/82 he scored a record 92 goals in a season for the Edmonton Oilers and in all his 1981/82 games (including Stanley Cup play-offs and matches for Canada in the world championship) he scored 238 points (103 goals and 135 assists). In 1985/86 he scored an NHL record of 215 points, including a record 163 assists. Born in Canada in 1961, Gretzky began his professional career in 1978. Nicknamed "the Great One", he is now regarded by many as the greatest ice hockey player of all time. He is pictured here on the pages of the 1998 *Sports Illustrated* swimsuit edition with his wife, actress Janet Jones.

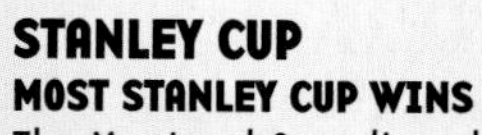

STANLEY CUP

MOST STANLEY CUP WINS
The Montreal Canadiens have won the Stanley Cup a record 24 times: 1916, 1924, 1930–31, 1944, 1946, 1953, 1956–60, 1965–66, 1968–69, 1971, 1973, 1976–79, 1986, 1993.

Henri Richard played on a record 11 winning teams for the Canadiens from 1956 to 1973.

Two coaches have led teams to eight Stanley Cup titles: Toe Blake, Montreal Canadiens, 1956–60, 1965–66, 1968; and Scotty Bowman, Montreal Canadiens, Pittsburgh Penguins, Detroit Red Wings, 1973, 1976–79, 1992, 1997–98.

MOST CONSECUTIVE WINS
The Montreal Canadiens won the Stanley Cup for five consecutive years, 1956–60.

MOST GOALS (GAME)
Five goals in a Stanley Cup game were scored by five players: Newsy Lalonde, Montreal Canadiens v. Ottawa Senators, March 1, 1919; Maurice Richard, Montreal Canadiens v. Toronto Maple Leafs, March 23, 1944; Darryl Sittler, Toronto Maple Leafs v. Philadelphia Flyers, April 22, 1976; Reggie Leach, Philadelphia Flyers v. Boston Bruins, May 6, 1976; and Mario Lemieux, Pittsburgh Penguins v. Philadelphia Flyers, April 25, 1989.

MOST GOALS (SEASON)
The record for the most single-season goals (19) is held by Reggie Leach of the Philadelphia Flyers in 1976 and Jari Kurri of the Edmonton Oilers in 1985.

MOST GOALS (CAREER)
Wayne Gretzky (Edmonton Oilers, Los Angeles Kings, St. Louis Blues, New York Rangers) holds the record for the most goals scored in one career with 122, 1979–97.

MOST ASSISTS (GAME)
Six assists were achieved by Mikko Leinonen for the New York Rangers (7) v. Philadelphia Flyers (3), on April 8, 1982; and Wayne Gretzky, Edmonton Oilers (13) v. Los Angeles Kings (3), April 9, 1987.

MOST ASSISTS (SEASON)
The most assists attained in a season in the NHL is 31, in the 1988 season by Wayne Gretzky for the Edmonton Oilers.

MOST ASSISTS (CAREER)
Wayne Gretzky (Edmonton Oilers, Los Angeles Kings, St. Louis Blues, New York Rangers) holds the career record of 260 assists from 1979 to 1997.

MOST POINTS (GAME)
The most points in one game is eight, by Patrik Sundstrom (Sweden) for the New Jersey Devils (10) v. Washington Capitals (4), April 22, 1988, and by Mario Lemieux for the Pittsburgh Penguins (10) v. Philadelphia Flyers (7) on April 25, 1989.

MOST POINTS (SEASON)
The most points scored in a season in the NHL is 47, in the 1985 season by Wayne Gretzky for the Edmonton Oilers.

MOST POINTS (CAREER)
Wayne Gretzky (Edmonton Oilers, Los Angeles Kings, St. Louis Blues, New York Rangers) scored a record 382 points, 1979–97.

MOST SHUTOUTS, GOALIE (SEASON)
The most shutouts by a goalie in a season is four, achieved by eight players on nine occasions: Clint Benedict, Montreal Maroons, 1926 and 1928; Dave Kerr, New York Rangers, 1937; Frank McCool, Toronto Maple Leafs, 1945; Terry Sawchuk, Detroit Tigers, 1952; Bernie Parent, Philadelphia Flyers, 1975; Ken Dyrden, Montreal Canadiens, 1977; Mike Richter, New York Rangers, 1994; and Kirk McLean, Vancouver Canucks, 1994.

MOST SHUTOUTS, GOALIE (CAREER)
Clint Benedict (Ottawa Senators, Montreal Maroons) holds the mark for career shutouts by a goaltender at 15, 1917–30.

NHL REGULAR SEASON

MOST WINS
The Detroit Red Wings won 62 games during the 1995–96 season. In 82 games, the Red Wings won 62, lost 13 and tied 7.

HIGHEST WINNING PERCENTAGE
The 1929–30 Boston Bruins set an NHL record .875 winning percentage. The Bruins' record was 38 wins, 5 losses and 1 tie.

MOST POINTS, WINS AND TIES
The Montreal Canadiens accumulated 132 points during their record-setting campaign of 1976–77, when they won a record 60 games.

LONGEST WINNING STREAK
The Pittsburgh Penguins won 17 consecutive games, March 9 through April 10, 1993.

LONGEST UNDEFEATED STREAK
The longest undefeated streak during one season is 35 games by the Philadelphia Flyers. The Flyers won 25 games and tied 10 from October 14, 1979 to January 6, 1980.

STANLEY CUP
The Stanley Cup was first presented in 1893 by Lord Stanley of Preston, then the governor-general of Canada. From 1894 onwards, the contest was played out by amateur teams for the Canadian Championship. This lasted until 1910, when it became the award for the winners of the professional league playoffs.

powerboats and jetskiing

POWERBOATS

FASTEST WATER SPEEDS, OFFICIAL

The official world water speed record is 317.6 mph, by Kenneth Warby in an unlimited hydroplane on Blowering Dam Lake, New South Wales, Australia, on October 8, 1978.

The official world water speed record by a woman is 197 mph, and was set by Mary Rife in Flint, Texas in 1977.

FASTEST WATER SPEEDS, UNOFFICIAL

Kenneth Warby achieved an unofficial record speed of 345.48 mph in his unlimited hydroplane *Spirit of Australia* on Blowering Dam Lake, Australia on November 20, 1977.

Mary Rife set a women's unofficial record speed of 206.72 mph in her blown fuel hydro *Proud Mary* in Tulsa, Oklahoma on July 23, 1977.

FASTEST SPEED IN AN ELECTRIC POWERBOAT

David Mischke set the APBA electric powerboat speed record of 70.6 mph in a 14-foot outboard hydroplane with a 48-volt motor at the Kilometer Speed Trials in Oregon on October 14, 1995.

FASTEST CIRCUIT RACING

In 1997, Guido Cappellini (Italy) achieved a Formula 1 speed of 132.97 mph in a DAC/Mercury. Formula 1 boats must be at least 15 ft. 8 in. long, weigh no more than 860 pounds, and have a maximum engine capacity of 2 liters.

In 1996, L. Norman (Sweden) set the record Formula 2 speed of 108.08 mph in a Molgard/Mercury. Formula 2 boats must be no longer than 15 ft. 8 in., weigh at least 860 pounds, and have a maximum engine capacity of 2 liters.

In 1995, P. Sandown (Hungary) set the Formula 3 speed record of 105.82 mph in a Hungasv/Johnson. Formula 3 boats must be no longer than 12 ft. 9 in., weigh at least 551 pounds, and have an engine capacity of no more than 850cc.

Andy Chesman (Great Britain) attained a Formula 500 record speed of 101.5 mph in 1996. The boat used was a Fort/Konig. Formula 500 boats must be at least 12 ft. 8 in. long, weigh at least 286 lb. 9 oz., and have an engine capacity of no more than 500cc.

FASTEST SPEEDS IN OFFSHORE RACING

In 1994, Tom Gentry (US) set the offshore Class 1 speed record of 157.43 mph in a 40-foot Skater with twin Mercury V8 engines. Class 1 boats are 39–48 feet long, weigh no less than 9,920 pounds and have a top engine capacity of 16 liters.

Charles Burnett III (Great Britain) set the offshore Class 2 speed record of 137.32 mph in a 28-foot Skater with triple Mercury 2.5 EFI outboards in 1996. Class 2 boats are 32–39 feet long, with a minimum

POWERBOATING

Powerboating began in 1863, when Frenchman Jean Lenoir installed a gasoline engine on a boat. Competitive racing started around 1900 and the first major race was between Calais, France and Dover, England in 1903. The American Power Boat Association (APBA) was formed the same year and held its first Gold Cup on the Hudson River, New York in 1904. The Cowes to Torquay [England] race was instituted in 1961. It was originally run from Cowes to Torquay, but from 1968 also included the return journey.

FASTEST TRANS-ATLANTIC CROSSINGS

In 1989, Tom Gentry (second from left, with Virgin boss Richard Branson, far left) set the trans-Atlantic speed record in *Gentry Eagle*, then the world's fastest motoryacht, crossing the ocean in 2 days 14 hr. 7 min. 47 sec. In 1992, the Italian-owned *Destriero* broke his record, crossing in 58 hr. 34 min. 4 sec. The voyage marked the 500th anniversary of Columbus's arrival in the Americas. When the record fell, Gentry set out to win it back, but in 1994 he went into a coma after a boating accident. He died in 1998.

weight of 6,063 pounds and an engine capacity of no more than 8 liters.

In 1995, Bo Warelius of Finland attained a record Class 3 speed of 113.11 mph in a 28-foot Skater with twin Mercury 2.5 EFI outboards. Class 3 boats are 25–33 feet long, weigh no less than 3,528 pounds and have a maximum engine capacity of 6 liters.

HIGHEST APBA GOLD CUP AVERAGE SPEED
The highest ever average speed in the APBA Gold Cup race is 149.160 mph, by Chip Hanauer (US) piloting *Miss Budweiser* in 1995.

MOST APBA GOLD CUP WINS
The most wins by a driver is 10, by Chip Hanauer: 1982–88, 1992, 1993 and 1995.

Bornie Little, the owner of *Miss Budweiser* (registered at Hydroplane Inc.), holds the record for the most wins by an owner, at 10: in 1969 (driven by Bill Sterett Sr.), in 1970, 1973, 1980 and 1981 (driven by Dean Chenoweth), in 1989 and 1990 (driven by Tom D'eath), in 1992, 1993 and 1995 (driven by Chip Hanauer) and in 1997 (driven by Dave Villwock).

Chip Hanauer has had a record seven successive victories, winning the APBA Gold Cup from 1982 to 1988.

MOST COWES TO TORQUAY WINS
The most wins in the 199-mile race from Cowes to Torquay, England is four, by Renato della Valle (Italy), 1982–85.

FASTEST COWES TO TORQUAY SPEED
The highest ever average speed in the race was 85.89 mph, by Fabio Fuzzi (Italy) piloting *Cesa* in 1988.

LONGEST RACES
The longest ever offshore race was the Port Richborough London to Monte Carlo Marathon Offshore international event, which covered 2,947 miles in 14 stages from June 10 to June 25, 1972. The race was won by *H.T.S.* (Great Britain), piloted by Mike Bellamy, Eddie Chater and Jim Brooker in 71 hr. 35 min. 56 sec. – an average speed of 41.15 mph.

The longest circuit race is the 24-hour race on the River Seine at Rouen, France, which has been held annually since 1962.

JETSKIING

LONGEST JETSKI JOURNEY
In 1993, Gary Frick (US) traveled a record 5,040 miles along the US coastline on a stand-up Kawasaki 650sx Jet Ski. He left Lubec, Maine on May 8 and arrived in Seattle, Washington on September 16.

FASTEST SPEED ON A SOLO BIKE
In 1994, D. Condemine (France) attained a record-breaking speed of 43.09 mph on a Solo Yamaha bike. A solo bike is the original type of jetski with a pivoting handbole.

POWERBOATING CHAMPION
La Gran Argentina, piloted by Daniel Scioili (Argentina) and throttleman Jorge Bordas, won the 1997 UIM Class Three (6 liter) World Offshore Championships, securing success in home waters off the coast of Buenos Aires. It was a fourth consecutive world title for Scioili, who was partnered by Fabio Buzzi of Italy when they won the Superboat Vee class world championship at the Key West World offshore powerboat race in 1996 .

FASTEST SPEED ON A SPORT BIKE
In 1997, Ray Purkiss (Great Britain) set the record speed for a sport bike when he attained a speed of 56.68 mph on a Sport Yamaha bike. A sport bike is a two-seater jetski.

FASTEST SPEED ON A RUNABOUT
In 1997, Steve Longbottom (Great Britain) attained a record-breaking speed of 61.38 mph on a Runabout Bombardier bike. A Runabout is a three-seater jetski.

JET-SKIING
Jet-skiing was developed by Clayton Jacobsen (US) in the early 1960s. He loved the excitement of moto-cross and water-skiing and dreamed of combining the two. He spent the 1960s refining his craft, and in 1971, presented his idea to Kawasaki, the Japanese motorcycle manufacturer. In 1973, the first commercially available jet-skis were produced. Since then, jet-skiing has evolved into a highly competitive sport with a global following.

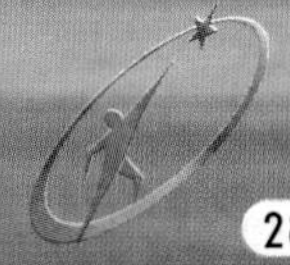

wrestling boxing and martial arts

BIGGEST *YOKOZUNA*
Hawaiian-born sumo wrestler Chad Rowan, alias Akebono, is pictured lifting his opponent Tochinowaka during a bout. The tallest and heaviest *yokozuna* in sumo history, Akebono is 6 ft. 8 in. tall and weighs 501 pounds. In January 1993, he became the first foreign *rikishi* ever to be promoted to the rank of *yokozuna,* and in 1996 he became a Japanese citizen.

SUMO

MOST SUCCESSFUL WRESTLERS

Yokozuna (grand champion) Sadji Akiyoshi, alias Futabayama, holds the all-time record of 69 consecutive wins (1937–39).

Yokozuna Koki Naya, alias Taiho (meaning "Great Bird"), won the Emperor's Cup a record 32 times to his retirement in 1971.

The *ozeki* Tameemon Torokichi, alias Raiden, won 254 bouts and lost only 10 in 21 years, giving him the highest ever winning percentage of 96.2.

MOST WINS

Yokozuna Mitsugu Akimoto, alias Chiyonofuji, won the Kyushu Basho (one of the six annual tournaments) for eight successive years (1981–88). He also holds the record for the most career wins (1,045) and the most *Makunouchi* (top division) wins (807).

In 1978, Toshimitsu Ogata (Kitanoumi) won 82 of the 90 bouts that the top *rikishi* fight each year. In 1974, at the age of 21 years 2 months, he became the youngest ever man to become a *yokozuna*.

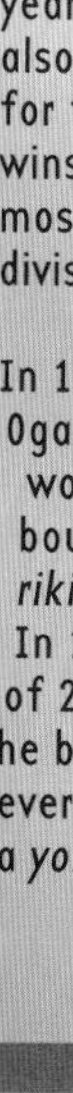

BIGGEST PAY-PER-VIEW TV AUDIENCE
In July 1997, Mike Tyson was fined $3 million and had his boxing license revoked for a year after biting a chunk out of the ear of his opponent, Evander Holyfield, during the World Boxing Association heavyweight championship fight on June 28. After the incident, the chunk of ear was found on the canvas by Mitch Libonati, an employee of the MGM Grand Hotel, who is said to have wrapped it up in a latex glove and taken it to Holyfield's dressing room. Holyfield was then rushed to the hospital, where the piece was reattached. The fight was watched by the biggest pay-per-view audience in boxing history, while celebrities such as Whitney Houston and Robert de Niro were among 16,000 spectators who paid up to $1,440 to watch the fight live.

MOST TOP-DIVISION BOUTS

Jesse Kuhaulua (Takamiyama) (US) fought 1,231 consecutive bouts (1981). He was the first non-Japanese to win an official top-division tournament, in 1972.

The most consecutive bouts in all six divisions is 1,631, by Yukio Shoji, alias Aobajo (1964–86).

The most career bouts is 1,891, by Kenji Hatano (Oshio) from 1962 to 1988.

WRESTLING

MOST OLYMPIC TITLES

Three titles were won by: Carl Westergren (Sweden) in 1920, 1924 and 1932; Ivar Johansson (Sweden) in 1932 (two) and 1936; Aleksandr Medved (USSR) in 1964, 1968 and 1972; and Aleksandr Karelin (Russia) in 1988, 1992 and 1996.

MOST OLYMPIC MEDALS

Four Olympic medals were won by: Eino Leino (Finland) at

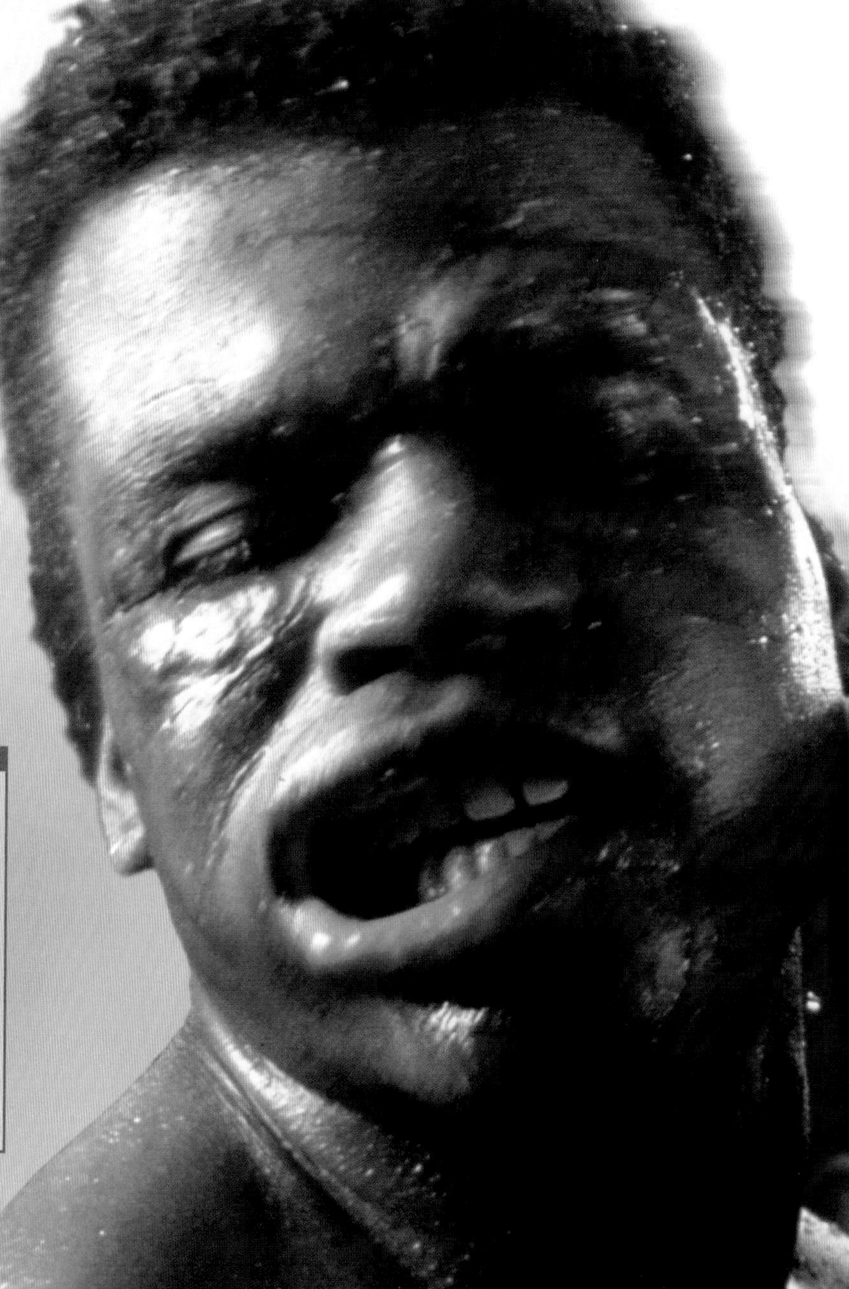

freestyle from 1920 to 1932; Imre Polyák (Hungary) at Greco-Roman from 1952 to 1964; and Bruce Baumgartner (US) at freestyle from 1984 to 1996.

MOST WORLD TITLES
Freestyler Aleksandr Medved (USSR) won a record 10 titles at three weight categories (1962–64 and 1966–72).

LONGEST BOUT
The longest recorded bout lasted 11 hr. 40 min., when Martin Klein (Estonia representing Russia) beat Alfred Asikáinen (Finland) for the Greco-Roman 75-kg "A" event silver medal in the 1912 Olympics.

BOXING

SHORTEST FIGHT
The shortest world title fight lasted 20 seconds, when Gerald McClellan (US) beat Jay Bell in a WBC middleweight bout in Puerto Rico on August 7, 1993.

MOST KNOCKOUTS
The most finishes classed as "knockouts" in a career is 145 (129 in professional bouts), by Archie Moore (US), 1936–63.

LONGEST REIGNS
Joe Louis (US) was the heavyweight champion for 11 years 252 days, from 1937 to his retirement in 1949. This record stands for all divisions.

Rocky Marciano (US) is the only world champion at any weight to have won every fight of his entire professional career (49 fights), from 1947 to 1955.

LONGEST FIGHT
The longest world title fight under Queensberry Rules was between lightweights Joe Gans and Oscar Nelson (both US) in Goldfield, Nevada on September 3, 1906. It was terminated in the 42nd round when Gans was declared the winner on a foul.

JUDO

MOST TITLES
Yasuhiro Yamashita (Japan) won four world titles and one Olympic title: the Over 95 kg in 1979, 1981 and 1983, the Open in 1981 and the Olympic Open in 1984. He retired undefeated after 203 successive wins (1977–85).

Four world titles were also won by Shozo Fujii (Japan) in the Under 80 kg in 1971, 1973 and 1975 and the Under 78 kg in 1979 and by Naoya Ogawa (Japan) in the Open in 1987, 1989 and 1991 and the Over 95 kg in 1989.

MOST WOMEN'S TITLES
Ingrid Berghmans (Belgium) has won a record six women's world titles: the Open in 1980, 1982, 1984 and 1986 and the Under 72 kg in 1984 and 1989. She has also won four silver medals and a bronze. She won the Olympic 72-kg title in 1988, when women's judo was introduced as a demonstration sport.

KARATE

MOST WORLD TITLES
Great Britain has won a record six world titles at the Kumite team event (1975, 1982, 1984, 1986, 1988 and 1990).

The record for the most men's individual kumite titles is two, by: Pat McKay (GB) at the Under 80 kg in 1982 and 1984; Emmanuel Pinda (France) at the Open in 1984 and the Over 80 kg in 1988; Thierry Masci (France) at the Under 70 kg in 1986 and 1988; and José Manuel Egea (Spain) at the Under 80 kg in 1990 and 1992.

A record four women's kumite titles have been won by Guus van Mourik (Netherlands) at the Over 60 kg in 1982, 1984, 1986 and 1988.

The most men's individual kata titles is three, by Tsuguo Sakumoto (Japan) in 1984, 1986 and 1988.

The record for the greatest number of individual kata titles in women's competition is three, by Mie Nakayama (Japan) in 1982, 1984 and 1986 and by Yuki Mimura (Japan) in 1988, 1990 and 1992.

BOXING RULES
In 1867, the sport of boxing came under the Queensberry Rules, which were formulated for John Sholto Douglas, the eighth Marquess of Queensberry. The rules stipulated the wearing of gloves (earlier contests had been fought by bareknuckled boxers). The first champion under the Queensberry Rules was the heavyweight James Corbett, in 1892.

gymnastics and weightlifting

GYMNASTICS

MOST MEN'S WORLD TITLES

The most individual men's titles is 13, by Vitaliy Scherbo (Belarus) between 1992 and 1995. He also won a team gold medal in 1992.

Boris Shakhlin (USSR) won a record 10 individual titles and three team titles between 1954 and 1964.

The USSR won the team title a record 13 times (eight World Championships and five Olympics) between 1952 and 1992.

MOST WOMEN'S WORLD TITLES

The record for the most titles won in the World Championships (including Olympic Games) is 18 (12 individual, six team), by Larisa Latynina (USSR) between 1954 and 1964.

The USSR won the team title on a record 21 occasions (11 World Championships and 10 Olympics).

YOUNGEST WORLD TITLE WINNERS

Aurelia Dobre (Romania) won the women's overall world title at the age of 14 years 352 days in Rotterdam, Netherlands on October 23, 1987.

In 1990, Daniela Silivas (Romania) revealed that she was born a year later than she had previously claimed and was in fact 14 years 185 days old when she won the gold medal for balance beam in 1985.

The youngest male world champion was Dmitriy Bilozerchev (USSR), who was 16 years 315 days old when he competed in Budapest, Hungary on October 28, 1983.

MOST MEN'S OLYMPIC TITLES

The men's team title has been won five times by Japan (1960, 1964, 1968, 1972 and 1976) and the USSR/Unified Team (1952, 1956, 1980, 1988 and 1992).

The greatest number of men's individual gold medals is six, by Boris Shakhlin (USSR) — one in 1956, four (two shared) in 1960 and one in 1964 — and by Nikolay Andrianov (USSR) — one in 1972, four in 1976 and one in 1980.

MOST MEN'S OLYMPIC MEDALS

Male gymnast Nikolay Andrianov (USSR) won a record 15 Olympic medals (seven gold, five silver and three bronze), from 1972 to 1980.

Aleksandr Dityatin (USSR) won a record eight medals at one Games, in Moscow, Russia (then USSR) in 1980. He won a medal in all eight categories (three gold, four silver and one bronze).

MOST WOMEN'S OLYMPIC TITLES

The USSR won the Olympic women's title a record 10 times (from 1952 to 1980 and in 1988 and 1992). The last title was won by the Unified team from the republics of the former USSR.

Vera Caslavska-Odlozil (Czechoslovakia) holds the record for the most individual gold medals: three in 1964 and four (one shared) in 1968.

MOST WOMEN'S OLYMPIC MEDALS

Larisa Latynina (USSR) won six individual gold medals and three team golds from 1956 to 1964. She also won five silver and four bronze medals, making an Olympic record total of 18.

YOUNGEST COMPETITOR

Pasakevi "Voula" Kouna (Greece) was just 9 years 299 days old at the start of the Balkan Games in Serres, Greece in 1981.

MOST WORLD CUP TITLES

Male gymnasts Li Ning (China), Nikolay Andrianov (USSR) and Aleksandr Dityatin (USSR) and female gymnast Maria Filatova (USSR) have each won two World Cup overall titles.

FASTEST SOMERSAULTS

On April 30, 1986, Ashrita Furman performed 8,341 forward rolls in 10 hr. 30 min. over 12 miles 390 yd. from Lexington to Charleston, Massachusetts.

On July 21, 1996, Ashrita Furman somersaulted 1 mile in 19 min. 38 sec., in Edgewater Park, Cleveland, Ohio.

Vitaliy Scherbo (Belarus) backwards somersaulted 50 m (54 yd.) in just 10.22 seconds at Makuhar Messe Event Hall, Chiba, Japan on August 31, 1995.

MOST TITLES

Alexei Nemov is seen performing on the parallel bars for the USSR. The former Soviet Union was the most successful nation in men's gymnastics, winning 13 world titles. Russia continued the success, taking the Olympic title in 1996.

RHYTHMIC SPORTIVE GYMNASTICS

MOST WORLD TITLES
The most overall individual world titles is three, by Maria Gigova (Bulgaria) in 1969, 1971 and 1973 (shared) and by Maria Petrova (Bulgaria) in 1993, 1994 and 1995 (shared).

Bianka Panova (Bulgaria) won all four apparatus gold medals (all with maximum scores) and a team gold in 1987.

Bulgaria has won a record nine team titles in rhythmic sportive gymnastics: 1969, 1971, 1981, 1983, 1985, 1987, 1989 (shared), 1993 and 1995.

PERFECT SCORES IN GREATEST NUMBER OF DISCIPLINES
At the 1988 Olympics in Seoul, South Korea, Marina Lobach (USSR) won the rhythmic gymnastic title with perfect scores in all six disciplines.

TRAMPOLINING

MOST TITLES
The most men's trampolining titles is five, by Aleksandr Moskalenko (Russia): three individual from 1990 to 1994 and two pairs from 1992 to 1994.

Brett Austine (Australia) also won three individual men's trampolining titles (double mini from 1982 to 1986).

Judy Wills (US) has won a record nine women's titles: five individual from 1964 to 1968 (a record), two pairs in 1966 and 1967 and two tumbling in 1965 and 1966.

WEIGHTLIFTING

MOST MEN'S TITLES
Naim Suleymanoğlü (Turkey) won 10 world titles (including Olympic Games) in 1985, 1986, 1988, 1989 and from 1991 to 1996.

Naim Suleymanoğlü has won three Olympic golds: the 60 kg in 1988 and 1992 and the 64 kg in 1996.

MOST MEN'S MEDALS
Norbert Schemansky (US) won a record four Olympic medals: gold for middle-heavyweight in 1952, silver for heavyweight in 1948 and bronze for heavyweight in 1960 and 1964.

MOST WOMEN'S GOLD MEDALS
Li Hongyun (China) won 13 medals in the 60/64-kg class from 1992 to 1996.

YOUNGEST AND OLDEST WORLD RECORD HOLDERS
Naim Suleimanov (Bulgaria) set world records for clean and jerk (160 kg or 352½ lb.) and total (285 kg or 628½ lb.) in the 56-kg class at the age of 16 years 62 days in Allentown, New Jersey on March 26, 1983. Suleimanov changed his name to Suleymanoğlü and now competes for Turkey.

Norbert Schemansky (US) was 37 years 333 days old when he snatched 164.2 kg (362 lb.) in the then unlimited heavyweight class in Detroit, Michigan in 1962.

RHYTHMIC SPORTIVE GYMNASTICS
An Olympic sport since 1984, rhythmic sportive gymnastics (seen left and far left) is popular throughout the world.

POWERLIFTING

MOST WORLD TITLES
The most men's world titles is 17, by Hideaki Inaba (Japan) at 52 kg from 1974 to 1983 and 1985 to 1991.

The most women's powerlifting titles is six, by Beverley Francis (Australia) at 75 kg in 1980 and 1982 and 82.5 kg in 1981 and from 1983 to 1985, and Sisi Dolman (Netherlands) at 52 kg in 1985 and 1986 and from 1988 to 1991.

BEST TIMED LIFTS
A world deadlifting record of 3.14 million kg (6.92 million lb.) was set by a team of 10 people at the Pontefract Sports and Leisure Center, West Yorkshire, England, May 3–4, 1997.

The individual deadlift record is held by Chris Lawton, who lifted 450,095 kg (992,288 lb.) at Barnsdale Country Club, Rutland, England, April 5–6, 1997.

A bench press record of 4.5 million kg (9.95 million lb.) was set by a team of nine men at the Pulse 8 Fitness Studio in Reading, England, May 31–June 1, 1997.

An individual bench press record of 815,434 kg (1.8 million lb.) was set by Glen Tenove (US) in 12 hours in Irvine, California on December 17, 1994.

A squat record of 2.17 million kg (4.78 million lb.) was set by a team of 10 men at St. Albans Weightlifting Club and Ware Boys Club, Hertfordshire, England, July 20–21, 1986.

WOMEN'S WEIGHTLIFTING
China's Chen Yanqing sets a new world record lift of 131.5 kg (290 lb.) during the women's 54-kg class at the World Weightlifting Championships in Chang Mai, Thailand. Women's weightlifting will become an Olympic sport for the first time at the Sydney Olympics in 2000. There will be 74 women lifters competing at the Sydney Games, compared with 176 men, and there will be seven body weight classes for female lifters, ranging from 48 kg to 75 kg plus.

bike sports

CYCLING

MOST OLYMPIC TITLES
The most gold medals won is three, by Paul Masson (France) in 1896, Francisco Verri (Italy) in 1906, Robert Charpentier (France) in 1936 and Daniel Morelon (France) in 1968 (two) and 1972. Morelon also won a silver medal in 1976 and a bronze medal in 1964.

Marcus Hurley (US) won four events in the "unofficial" 1904 cycling program.

MOST WORLD CHAMPIONSHIP TITLES
The most wins at one event is 10, by Koichi Nakano (Japan) in the professional sprint from 1977 to 1986.

The most wins at a men's amateur event is seven, by Daniel Morelon (France) in the sprint (1966, 1967, 1969–71, 1973 and 1975) and Leon Meredith (GB) in the 100-km motor paced (1904–05, 1907–09, 1911 and 1913).

MOST WOMEN'S WORLD TITLES
The most women's titles is 10, by Jeannie Longo (France) in pursuit (1986 and 1988–89), road (1985–87, 1989 and 1995), points (1989) and the time-trial (1995 and 1996). In addition to her world titles, Longo has set numerous world records, including the current 1-hour mark, and in 1996, she won an Olympic gold medal.

MOST TOUR DE FRANCE WINS
The greatest ever number of wins in the annual Tour de France race is five, by Jacques Anquetil (France) in 1957 and from 1961 to 1964; Eddy Merckx (Belgium) from 1969 to 1972 and in 1974; Bernard Hinault (France) from 1978 to 1979, 1981 to 1982 and in 1985; and Miguel Induráin (Spain) from 1991 to 1995.

CLOSEST TOUR DE FRANCE RACE
The closest race took place in 1989, when Greg LeMond (US) beat Laurent Fignon (France) by just eight seconds, after 2,030 miles over 23 days. LeMond's time was 87 hr. 38 min. 35 sec.

MOST CYCLO-CROSS TITLES
The most World Championship titles is eight, by Eric De Vlaeminck of Belgium, who won the Amateur and Open in 1966 and six professional titles from 1968 to 1973.

LONGEST ONE-DAY CYCLING RACE
The longest single-day "massed start" road race in the world is the 342–385-mile event from Bordeaux to Paris, France. Paced over all or part of the route, the highest average speed was 29.32 mph, by Herman van Springel (Belgium) in 1981. He covered 363 miles 176 yd. in 13 hr. 35 min. 18 sec.

HIGHEST CYCLING ALTITUDE
Canadians Bruce Bell, Philip Whelan and Suzanne MacFadyen cycled at a record altitude of 22,834 feet on the peak of Mt. Aconcagua, Argentina, on January 25, 1991. This achievement was equaled by Mozart Hastenreiter Catão (Brazil) on March 11, 1993 and by Tim Sumner and Jonathon Green (Great Britain) on January 6, 1994.

MOTORCYCLES

FASTEST MOTORCYCLE CIRCUITS
The highest ever average lap speed attained on any closed circuit on a motorcycle is 160.288 mph, by Yvon du Hamel (Canada) on a modified 903cc four-cylinder Kawasaki Z1 at the 31° banked 2-mile-880-yd- Daytona International Speedway, Daytona, Florida, in March 1973. His lap time was 56.149 sec.

The fastest ever road circuit was Francorchamps, near Spa, Belgium. At 8 miles 1,250 yd. in length, it was lapped in 3 min. 50.3 sec. — an average speed of 137.150 mph — by Barry Sheene (Great Britain) on a 495cc four-cylinder Suzuki during the Belgian Grand Prix on July 3, 1977. Sheene set a record time of 38 min. 58.5 sec. for the 10-lap race, giving him an average speed of 135.068 mph over the course.

MOST MOTO-CROSS WINS
Moto-cross first began as an organized sport during the 1920s in the United Kingdom. It gained international status after World War II with the inauguration of the Moto-Cross des Nations. Joël Robert (Belgium) won a record six 250cc Moto-Cross World Championships, in 1964 and from 1968 to 1972. Between April 25, 1964 and June 18, 1972, he also won a record 50 250cc Grand Prix.

LONGEST MOTORCYCLE CIRCUIT
The 37-mile-284-yd. "Mountain" circuit on the Isle of Man has hosted the principal TT races since 1911 (with minor amendments in 1920). It has 264 curves and corners and is the longest circuit used for any motorcycle race.

MOST SUCCESSFUL MOTORCYCLISTS
The most World Championship titles won is 15, by Giacomo Agostini (Italy): seven at 350cc from 1968 to 1974 and eight at 500cc from 1966 to 1972 and in 1975. Agostini is also the only man to have won two World Championships in five consecutive years (350cc and 500cc titles from 1968 to 1972).

Giacomo Agostini won 122 races (68 at 500cc and 54 at 350cc) in the World Championship series between April 24, 1965 and September 25, 1977, including a record-breaking 19 in 1970. This season total was equaled by Mike Hailwood (GB) in 1966.

Angel Roldan Nieto (Spain) won a record seven 125cc titles (1971–72, 1979 and 1981–84) and a record six titles at 50cc (1969–70, 1972 and 1975–77).

Phil Read (GB) won a record four 250cc titles, in 1964, 1965, 1968 and 1971.

Switzerland's Rolf Biland won a record seven world side-car titles from 1978 to 1979, in 1981 and 1983 and from 1992 to 1994.

The greatest number of career wins in any one class is 79, by Rolf Biland at the side-car.

MOST TOURIST TROPHY WINS
The record for the greatest number of victories in the Isle of Man TT races is 23, by Joey Dunlop (Ireland) between 1977 and 1998.

The most events won in the Isle of Man TT races in one year is four (Formula 1, Junior, Senior and Production), by Phillip McCallen (Ireland) in 1996.

HIGHEST TOURIST TROPHY SPEEDS
The Isle of Man TT circuit record is 123.61 mph, by Carl Fogarty on June 12, 1992.

On June 12, 1992, Steve Hislop set the race record of 1 hr. 51 min. 59.6 sec — an average speed of 121.28 mph — when he won the Senior TT on a Norton.

The record for the fastest average women's speed around the "Mountain" circuit is 112.65 mph, by Sandra Barnett (GB) in the Junior TT on June 4, 1997.

MOST TRIALS WINS
Jordi Tarrès (Spain) won six World Trials Championships, in 1987, from 1989 to 1991 and from 1993 to 1994.

FASTEST TOUR DE FRANCE SPEED
The fastest average speed in the Tour de France was 24.547 mph, by Miguel Induráin (Spain) in 1992. Induráin is the winner of five consecutive Tour de France races, and also won both the Giro d'Italia and the Tour de France in 1992 and again in 1993. He retired at the end of 1996, never having won the Vuelta a España, the major tour of his native country.

horse sports

HORSE RACING

MOST SUCCESSFUL RACE CAREER

Chorisbar won 197 out of 324 races in Puerto Rico between 1937 and 1947.

Lenoxbar won a record 46 races from 56 starts in one year, in Puerto Rico in 1940.

HIGHEST RACE SPEEDS

The record for the highest known race speed is 43.26 mph – 440 yards in 20.8 seconds – by *Big Racket* in Mexico City, Mexico, on February 5, 1945 and by *Onion Roll* at Thistledown, Cleveland, Ohio on September 27, 1993.

The highest speed over a distance of 1 mile 880 yd. is 37.82 mph, by three-year-old *Hawkster* at Santa Anita Park, Arcadia, California on October 14, 1989. Carrying 121 pounds, *Hawkster* finished in 2 min. 22.8 sec.

OLDEST WINNERS

The oldest horses ever to have won at flat racing were the 18-year-olds *Revenge*, in Shrewsbury, England on September 23, 1790; *Marksman*, in Ashford, England on September 4, 1826; and *Jorrocks*, in Bathurst, Australia on February 28, 1851.

Wild Aster was 18 when it won three hurdle races in six days in March 1919 and *Sonny Somers* was 18 when it won two steeplechases in February 1980.

MOST SUCCESSFUL JOCKEYS

Bill Shoemaker (US), whose racing weight was 97 pounds at 4 ft. 11 in., rode a record 8,833 winners from a total of 40,350 mounts between 1949 and 1990.

The most races won in a year is 598 from 2,312 rides, by Kent Desormeaux (US) in 1989.

Chris McCarron (US) earned a career record of $213,851,293 from 1974 through 1997.

The most money won in a year is $28.4 million, by Yutaka Take in Japan in 1993.

MOST WINS

Chris Antley (US) rode nine winners in one day on October 31, 1987 – four in the afternoon at Aqueduct, New York, and five in the evening at The Meadowlands, New Jersey.

The most winners ridden on one card is eight by six riders, most recently (and from the fewest rides) by Pat Day (US) from nine rides at Arlington International, Illinois on September 13, 1989.

The longest winning streak is 12, by Sir Gordon Richards (GB) (one race in Nottingham, England on October 3, six races out of six at Chepstow, England on October 4 and the first five races on October 5 at Chepstow, in 1933) and by Pieter Stroebel (Rhodesia) at Bulawayo, Southern Rhodesia (now Zimbabwe), from June 7 to July 7, 1958.

MOST SUCCESSFUL OWNERS

The most lifetime wins by an owner is 4,775, by Marion Van Berg (US) in North America over 35 years from 1936 to 1971.

The most wins in a year is 494, by Dan Lasater (US) in 1974.

MOST SUCCESSFUL TRAINERS

The most career wins is 7,200, by Dale Baird (US), 1962–97.

Jack Van Berg (US) had a record 496 wins in a year, in 1976.

MOST RUNNERS

The record for the greatest number of horses in a race is 66 in the Grand National, Aintree, England on March 22, 1929.

The record for the turf is 58, in the Lincolnshire Handicap, Lincoln, England, March 13, 1948.

LONGEST TURF RACE

The Queen Alexandra Stakes, held at Ascot, England in June each year, is run over a record 2¾ miles.

SHOW JUMPING

MOST OLYMPIC WINS

The most team wins in the Prix des Nations is seven, by Germany (as West Germany from 1968 to 1990) in 1936, 1956, 1960, 1964, 1972, 1988 and 1996.

The record for the most individual gold medals is two, by Pierre Jonquères d'Oriola (France) in 1952 and 1964.

The greatest number of Olympic gold medals is five, by Hans Winkler (West Germany): four team in 1956, 1960, 1964 and 1972 and the individual Grand Prix in 1956. He also won team silver in 1976 and team bronze in 1968, making a record seven medals overall.

LOWEST SCORE AT OLYMPICS

The record for the lowest score obtained by a winner is no faults, by: Frantisek Ventura (Czechoslovakia) on *Eliot* in 1928; Alwin Schockemöhle (West Germany) on *Warwick Rex* in 1976; and Ludger Beerbaum (Germany) on *Classic Touch* in 1992.

MOST WORLD CHAMPIONSHIP WINS

The record for the greatest number of team wins is three, by France in 1982, 1986 and 1990.

The most men's titles is two, by Hans Winkler (West Germany) in 1954 and 1955 and Raimondo d'Inzeo (Italy) in 1956 and 1960.

The record for the greatest number of women's titles is two, by Jane Tissot (France) on *Rocket* in 1970 and 1974.

MOST WORLD CUP WINS

Hugo Simon (Austria) won three times, in 1979, 1996 and 1997.

OLDEST CONTESTED RACE

The oldest contested horse race is the *Palio*, which is contested by 10 of the 17 *contrade* (parishes) of the city of Siena, Italy to confirm who is the strongest. Traditionally believed to have begun in the 13th century, it has been run twice yearly (on July 2 and August 16) since 1701, except during wartime. During the three days preceding the *Palio*, the horses are kept under guard and each jockey is held incommunicado. On the day itself, the contestants march into town under their banners. The course winds through the town's maze of streets, making the event highly dangerous, and many horses have been killed during the race. The jockeys are very well paid, currently earning more than $416,100 to ride with the *Palio* (a banner depicting the Virgin Mary) for the *contrade*. The most successful *contrade* is Oca (Goose) with 59 victories. An edict passed by Benito Mussolini in 1935 gave the Sienese exclusive control of the word "*Palio*," preventing towns in any other part of Italy from holding similar events.

HIGHEST JUMP
The official Fédération Equestre Internationale high-jump record is 8 ft. 1¼ in., by *Huasó*, ridden by Capt. Alberto Morales (Chile) at Viña del Mar, Santiago, Chile on February 15, 1949.

LONGEST JUMP
The record for a long jump over water is 27 ft. 6¾ in. by *Something*, ridden by André Ferreira (South Africa) in Johannesburg, South Africa on April 25, 1975.

THREE DAY EVENTING

MOST OLYMPIC WINS
Charles Pahud de Mortanges (Netherlands) won a record four Olympic gold medals: team in 1924 and 1928 and individual (riding *Marcroix*) in 1928 and 1932, when he also won a team silver medal.

MOST WORLD CHAMPIONSHIP WINS
Bruce Davidson (US) has won two titles, on *Irish Cap* in 1974 and *Might Tango* in 1978.

DRESSAGE

MOST OLYMPIC WINS
Germany (as West Germany from 1968 to 1990) has won a record nine team gold medals: 1928, 1936, 1964, 1968, 1976, 1984, 1988, 1992 and 1996.

A record two individual gold Olympic medals were won by Henri St. Cyr (Sweden) in 1952 and 1956 and by Nicole Uphoff (Germany) in 1988 and 1992.

Dr. Reiner Klimke (West Germany) won a record six Olympic golds (team from 1964 to 1988 and individual in 1984). He also won individual bronze in 1976.

MOST WORLD CHAMPIONSHIP WINS
Germany (as West Germany from 1968 to 1990) has had a record seven team wins (1966, 1974, 1978, 1982, 1986, 1990, 1994).

A record two world titles were won by Dr Reiner Klimke (West Germany), on *Mehmed* in 1974 and *Ahlerich* in 1982.

MOST WORLD CUP WINS
The record for the most wins is two, by Christine Stückelberger (Switzerland) on *Gauguin de Lully* in 1987 and 1988, Monica Theodorescu (Greece) on *Ganimedes Tecrent* in 1993 and 1994, and Anky van Grunsven (Netherlands) on *Camelion Bonfire* in 1995 and 1996.

CARRIAGE DRIVING

MOST WORLD CHAMPIONSHIP WINS
The most team titles is three, by Great Britain (1972, 1974 and 1980), Hungary (1976, 1978 and 1984), Netherlands (1982, 1986 and 1988) and Germany (1992, 1994 and 1996).

A record two individual titles have been won by György Bárdos (Hungary) in 1978 and 1980, Tjeerd Velstra (Netherlands) in 1982 and 1986 and Ijsbrand Chardon (Netherlands) in 1988 and 1992.

HORSE RACING
Jockeys urge their horse on to the winning post at a horse race in Hong Kong. Horsemanship was an important part of the Hittite culture of Turkey, dating from 1400 BC. In 648 BC, the 33rd ancient Olympic Games in Greece featured horse racing. Since then, it has spread across the globe and has become both a multi-million-dollar industry and a popular sport.

POLO

HIGHEST HANDICAP
The highest handicap based on six 7½-minute "chukkas" is 10 goals (introduced in the US in 1891 and in the United Kingdom and Argentina in 1910). A total of 56 players have received 10-goal handicaps: for the 1998 season there are eight 10-goal handicap players in the UK.

HIGHEST SCORE
The most goals in an international match was 30, when Argentina beat the United States 21–9 at Long Island, New York in 1936.

ROYAL ASCOT
Gold Cup day at Royal Ascot sees thousands of women donning hats of all shapes and sizes. In the Royal Enclosure, morning dress must be worn by the gentlemen and hats worn by the ladies. This famous race day spectacle was immortalized in the hit movie and musical *My Fair Lady*.

cricket

MOST CAREER GAMES PLAYED
Mohammad Azharuddin of India has played 282 games, including 90 test matches, from the start of his career in 1985 to 1998. He has also made the most career catches by a fielder, at 134, and scored 100 in his first three test matches. In 1996, Azharuddin was relieved of his captaincy of the Indian team, and in 1997 he was dropped altogether, but he was reinstated as captain in 1998.

HIGHEST TEAM INNINGS
Victoria scored 1,107 runs in 10 hr. 30 min. v. New South Wales in an Australian Sheffield Shield match in Melbourne in 1926.

The Test record is 952 for six, by Sri Lanka v. India in Colombo, Sri Lanka, August 4–6, 1997.

LOWEST TEAM INNINGS
The traditional first-class record is 12, by Oxford University (a man short) v. Marylebone Cricket Club in Oxford, England in 1877, and Northamptonshire v. Gloucestershire in Gloucester, England in June 1907.

"The Bs" scored six in their second innings against England in London in 1810.

The Test match record is 26, by New Zealand v. England in Auckland, New Zealand, in 1955.

HIGHEST INDIVIDUAL INNINGS
Brian Lara scored 501 not out in 7 hr. 54 min. for Warwickshire against Durham at Edgbaston, England in June 1994. His innings included the most runs in a day (390) and the most runs from strokes worth four or more (308: 62 fours and 10 sixes).

The Test record is also held by Brian Lara, with 375 in 12 hr. 48 min. for the West Indies against England in St. John's, Antigua, in April 1994.

MOST SIXES IN AN INNINGS
Andrew Symonds hit 16 in an innings of 254 not out for Gloucestershire v. Glamorgan in a County Championship match in Abergavenny, Wales in August 1995. He added four in his second innings of 76, for a record match total of 20.

Chris Cairns hit a record 14 sixes in a limited-overs international, in his 157 (from 89 deliveries) for New Zealand against Kenya in Nairobi on September 7, 1997.

MOST WICKETS IN A MATCH
Jim Laker took 19 wickets for 90 runs (9–37 and 10–53) for England v. Australia at Old Trafford, England in July 1956.

MOST WICKETS IN AN INNINGS
Alfred Freeman of Kent, England took all 10 wickets in an innings on a record three occasions, against Lancashire in 1929 and 1931 and against Essex in 1930.

The fewest runs scored off a bowler taking all 10 wickets is 10, off Hedley Verity for Yorkshire v. Nottinghamshire in Leeds, England in 1932.

John Wisden bowled out all 10 for North against South at Lord's, London, England in 1850.

FASTEST BOWLER
The highest electronically measured speed for a bowled ball is 99.7 mph, bowled by Jeffrey Thomson of Australia against the West Indies in December 1975.

MOST CATCHES
The greatest number of catches in an innings is seven, by Michael Stewart for Surrey against Northamptonshire in Northampton, England on June 7, 1957, and by Anthony Brown for Gloucestershire against Nottinghamshire at Trent Bridge, Nottingham, England on July 26, 1966.

MOST CATCHES IN A MATCH
Walter Hammond held 10 catches for Gloucestershire against Surrey in Cheltenham, England, August 16–17, 1928.

MOST CATCHES IN A TEST MATCH
Seven catches were made by Greg Chappell for Australia v. England in Perth, Australia in 1974, Yajurvindra Singh for India v. England in Bangalore, India in 1977, and Hashan Prasantha Tillekeratne for Sri Lanka v. New Zealand in Colombo, Sri Lanka, December 7–9, 1992.

MOST DISMISSALS
The most dismissals in an innings is nine, by Tahir Rashid (eight catches and a stumping) for Habib Bank against Pakistan Automobile Corporation in Gujranwala, Pakistan, in November 1992, and by Wayne James (seven catches and two stumpings) for Matabeleland against Mashonaland Country Districts in Bulawayo, Zimbabwe, in April 1996.

The most stumpings in an innings is six, by Hugo Yarnold for Worcestershire against Scotland at Broughty Ferry, Dundee, Scotland on July 2, 1951.

The most dismissals in a match is 13, by Wayne James (11 catches, two stumpings) for Matabeleland v. Mashonaland Country Districts in Bulawayo, Zimbabwe, April 19–21, 1996. The record of 11 catches has been equaled on six other occasions.

The most stumpings in a match is nine, by Frederick Huish for Kent v. Surrey at The Oval, London, England in 1911.

SHORTEST TEST MATCH IN TERMS OF BALLS BOWLED
The shortest ever Test, in terms of the number of balls bowled, was the First Test of the West Indies–England series in 1998. Only 10.1 overs were possible during England's first innings at Sabina Park in Kingston, Jamaica, on January 29. For the first time in Test history, play was abandoned not because of the weather but because the pitch was deemed too dangerous. Faced by the quick bowling of the West Indies opening pair, Curtly Ambrose and Courtney Walsh, England struggled to 17–3. Such was the spiteful nature of the wicket that England's physiotherapist, Wayne Morton, was called on to treat the batsmen six times for blows to hands and body. No player sustained broken bones, but the team captains and match umpires decided to halt play following Morton's sixth visit. The details of the match have been noted in the record books, so the West Indies fast bowler Nixon McLean, who was making his Test debut, "played" but never bowled a ball. Bookmakers William Hill paid out to every customer who had backed Alec Stewart to be the highest-scoring batsman. Stewart scored possibly the lowest highest total ever, with nine.

MOST SIXES IN A TEST INNINGS
Wasim Akram hit a record 12 sixes in his 257 not out for Pakistan against Zimbabwe at Sheikhupura, Pakistan, from October 18 to October 20, 1996. Akram also holds the record for the greatest number of wickets taken in a career, with a total of 356 in 247 matches – an average of 22.79 – between 1985 and 1998.

MOST DISMISSALS IN TESTS
The record in an innings is seven (all caught), by Wasim Bari for Pakistan v. New Zealand in Auckland in February 1979, Bob Taylor for England v. India in Bombay in February 1980, and Ian Smith for New Zealand v. Sri Lanka in Hamilton, New Zealand in February 1991.

The record in a match is 11, all caught, by Jack Russell for England v. South Africa in Johannesburg, South Africa, November 30–December 3, 1995.

MOST TEST APPEARANCES
Allan Border of Australia played a record 156 Test matches between 1979 and 1994.

SHORTEST MATCH
The shortest playing time was during the first Test between England and Australia in Nottingham, England in June 1926. There were 50 minutes of play, in which 17.2 overs were bowled and England scored 32–0.

MOST CAREER RUNS SCORED
Desmond Haynes of the West Indies scored a total of 8,648 runs in 238 matches (an average of 41.37 a match) from 1977 to 1994. This total includes a record 17 centuries.

MOST CAREER DISMISSALS
Ian Healy of Australia made 234 (195 caught, 39 stumped) in 168 matches from 1988 to 1997.

The highest innings score between Test-playing nations in a one day international is 371–9, by Pakistan against Sri Lanka in Nairobi, Kenya, in October 1996.

The lowest completed innings total in a one day international is 43, by Pakistan against the West Indies at Newlands, Cape Town, South Africa on February 25, 1993.

LONGEST MATCH
The 1939 England v. South Africa test in South Africa was stopped after 10 days because the ship taking the England team home was due to leave. The total playing time was 43 hr. 16 min. and a record Test match aggregate of 1,981 runs was scored.

HIGHEST AND LOWEST INNINGS IN A MATCH
The record for the highest innings score in a one day international is 398–5. It was set by Sri Lanka against Kenya in a World Cup match played at Kandy, Sri Lanka, on March 6, 1996.

MOST FEARED BOWLER
Shane Warne is Australia's most effective spinner, and one of cricket's most talented bowlers ever. Born in 1969, Warne made his international debut against New Zealand at Wellington in March 1993. He is master of the "googley" and has invented his own lethal variations of many deliveries. In 1993, he bowled the "ball of the century" in the Ashes against Mike Gatting at Old Trafford, England.

street and beach sports

HIGHEST JUMP ON IN-LINE SKATES

The first in-line skates date back to the 1100s, when Arctic dwellers made skates by attaching animal bones to their boots in order to improve ice travel. The first modern-day skates were made in 1960 by the Chicago Skate Company. The highest ever jump on in-line skates was 8 ft. 11 in., by Randolph Sandoz (Switzerland) in Amsterdam, Netherlands, on December 15, 1996.

STREET LUGE

TOP SPEED

On May 29, 1998 Tom Mason of Van Nuys, California set an official world record for street luge when he achieved a speed of 81.28 mph at Mount Whitney, California. Mason, who took up street luge in 1995, set the record on a 23-pound board and was timed by Bob Pererya from the street luge sanctioning body RAIL (Road Racing Association for International Luge).

MOST STREET LUGE TITLES

Michael Sherlock (US), known as "Biker," began competing in 1995. He won the EDI series race in 1996 and in 1997, and has won three gold medals at the ESPN Summer X Games – for Mass Luge in 1996 and for Mass Luge and Dual Luge in 1997. In 1997, he also took the silver medal for Super Mass Luge at the ESPN Summer X Games.

SKATEBOARDING

TOP SPEEDS

The highest speed recorded on a skateboard is 78.37 mph by Roger Hickey (US) on a course near Los Angeles, California on March 15, 1990. He was in a prone position.

The stand-up speed record is 55.43 mph, by Roger Hickey in San Demas, California on July 3, 1990.

Eleftherios Argiropoulos covered 271 miles 510 yd. in 36 hr. 33 min. 17 sec. in Ekali, Greece, November 4–5, 1993.

IN-LINE SKATING AND ROLLER HOCKEY

BIGGEST CASH PRIZE

The Ultimate In-line Challenge offers a record cash purse of $60,000. The competition is presented by Rollerblade and races include 20-km and 1,500-m sprints.

FASTEST ROAD TIMES

Eddy Matzger (US) skated 21 miles 1,126 yd. in an hour at Long Beach, California in February 1991.

Jonathan Seutter (US) holds the 12-hour road record, covering a distance of 177 miles 1,109 yd. at Long Beach, California, on February 2, 1991.

Kimberly Ames (US) set the 24-hour road record when she skated 283 miles 123 yd. in Portland, Oregon on October 2, 1994.

LONGEST DISTANCE SKATED

In March 1996, Fabrice Gropaiz of France began a 19,000-mile round-the-world trek on skates, setting out from San Francisco. In August, he skated into Mexico after crossing the United States, and by early 1997, he was skating across Europe. In October 1997, he skated from Paris, France, to St. Petersburg, Russia, where he stopped due to freezing road conditions and to raise more funds. In April 1998, Gropaiz crossed Australia before returning to Russia, where the roads were now skateable.

HIGHEST MOUNTAIN SKATED

In January 1998, Eddy Matzger and Dave Cooper (both US) skated up and down the Murango Route of Mt. Kilimanjaro, the highest peak in Africa. It took them six days to complete the 3-mile-1,162-yd. climb. Conditions allowed them to roll about 30% of the time.

MOST ROLLER HOCKEY WORLD CHAMPIONSHIP VICTORIES

Portugal won 14 titles between 1947 and 1993.

FASTEST "ROCKET" STREET LUGER

On May 15, 1998, Billy Copeland, a machine press operator from Ashland City, Tennessee, set a world speed record for "Rocket" street luge when he held a jet-assisted speed of 70 mph over 150 feet of level ground on Granite Road in Kern County, California. He began the 2¼-mile course on an incline, and when he reached a speed of about 65 mph, he ignited the rockets that were attached with steel to the back of the 7-foot-long street luge to achieve the record speed on level ground. Copeland's speed was clocked using a radar speed gun, and his attempt was broadcast on the Fox television series *Guinness World Records™: Primetime*. Copeland has been street lugeing as a hobby since 1992 and claims to have unofficially reached speeds of more than 80 mph since he began attaching the rockets to his board. The eight Aerotech G64 White Lightning rocket motors can be fired in pairs or all at once. He was inspired to try out the rockets by a Mountain Dew ad that featured street lugers in California, having realized that the hills around his home town were not steep enough to enable him to reach speeds of more than 60 mph.

HIGHEST SKATEBOARD JUMPS
World skateboarding championships have been staged intermittently since 1966, and the sport is popular around the world. The skateboarding high-jump record is 5 ft. 5³/₄ in., by Trevor Baxter of Burgess Hill, England, in Grenoble, France, on September 14, 1982. The high air-jump record from a half pipe is 11 ft. 10 in., by Sergie Ventura (US).

VOLLEYBALL

MOST WORLD TITLES

The USSR has won a record six titles (1949, 1952, 1960, 1962, 1978 and 1982).

The greatest number of women's titles is five, by the USSR (1952, 1956, 1960, 1970 and 1990).

MOST OLYMPIC TITLES

The USSR has won a record three men's titles (1964, 1968, 1980).

The most women's titles is four, by the USSR (1968, 1972, 1980 and 1988).

MOST OLYMPIC MEDALS

The record for the greatest number of Olympic medals won by a volleyball player is four, by Inna Valeryevna Ryskal (USSR), who won women's silver medals in 1964 and 1976 and gold medals in 1968 and 1972.

The greatest number of Olympic medals won by male volleyballers is three, by Yuriy Mikhailovich Poyarkov (USSR), who won gold medals in 1964 and 1968 and a bronze in 1972, Katsutoshi Nekoda (Japan), who won gold in 1972, silver in 1968 and bronze in 1964, and Steve Timmons (US), who won gold in 1984 and 1988 and bronze in 1992.

BEACH VOLLEYBALL

HIGHEST-EARNING PLAYERS

Karch Kiraly of San Clemente, California left the indoor volleyball circuit after leading the US indoor team to victory in the 1984 and 1988 Olympic Games. He became a five-time MVP on the US professional circuit and the first beach volleyball player to amass winnings of more than $2 million. Kiraly is the highest-earning beach volleyballer of all time, having earned $2,784,889 by June 30, 1998.

Karolyn Kirby of San Diego, California is the highest-earning woman in beach volleyball today, with total winnings of more than $650,000. She has earned a record $110,000 in 30 grand slam events, including a record 25 appearances in the final four. Kirby has finished in first place on the WPVA (Women's Professional Volleyball Association) tour 61 times.

SAND YACHTING

HIGHEST SPEEDS

The official world record for a sand yacht is 66.48 mph, by Christian-Yves Nau (France) in *Mobil* at Le Touquet, France, on March 22, 1981. The wind speed reached 75 mph.

A speed of 88.4 mph was attained by Nord Embroden (US) in *Midnight at the Oasis* at Superior Dry Lake, California on April 15, 1976.

LONGEST SAND RACE

The Transat des Sables, which was held in the desert in Mauritania from March 8 to March 18, 1997, was the longest and toughest sand race ever. It was organized by the French Federation of Sand & Land Yachting and the French Ministry of Sport, and was competed by sand yachts, kite yachts and speed-sails. Yachters had to cover 60–120 miles daily, which required 6–8 hours of sailing every day.

MOST BEACH VOLLEYBALL WINS
Beach volleyball made its Olympic debut at the 1996 Summer Games in Atlanta, Georgia. The world's most successful beach volleyballer is Sinjin Smith (US), who won his first career open in 1977 and has gone on to win a record 139 times. He has been a beach volleyball pro for 21 years and was the second player to earn $1 million, in 1992.

snow and ice sports

SNOWBOARDING

MOST WORLD CUP TITLES

The record for the most World Cup titles won is 11, by Karine Ruby (France): the overall from 1996 to 1998, the slalom from 1996 to 1998, the giant slalom from 1995 to 1998 and the snowboard cross in 1997.

The most men's World Cup titles won is three, by Mike Jacoby (US): the overall in 1996 and the giant slalom in 1995 and 1996.

MOST WORLD CHAMPIONSHIP TITLES WON

The most World Championship titles (including Olympics) is three, by Karine Ruby (France): the giant slalom in 1996 and 1998 (Olympic) and the snowboard cross in 1997. No man has won more than one title.

SKI-BOB

HIGHEST SPEED

The record for the highest speed ever attained on a ski-bob is 103.1 mph, by Erich Brenter (Austria) in Cervinia, Italy in 1964.

MOST WORLD TITLES

The most World Championship titles by a man is three, by Walter Kronseil (Austria) from 1988 to 1990.

The record for the most individual World Championship combined titles is four, by Petra Tschach-Wlezcek (Austria) from 1988 to 1991.

CRESTA RUN

MOST CRESTA RUN WINS

The most wins in the Grand National is eight, by the 1948 Olympic champion Nino Bibbia (Italy) from 1960 to 1964 and in 1966, 1968 and 1973, and by Franco Gansser (Switzerland) in 1981, from 1983 to 1986, from 1988 to 1989, and in 1991.

The most wins in the Curzon Cup is eight, by Nino Bibbia (1950, 1957–58, 1960, 1962–64, 1969).

FASTEST CRESTA RUN TIMES

The record for the fastest ever time on the 3,977-foot-long Cresta Run course, which has a drop of 514 feet, is 50.41 seconds, by Christian Bertschinger (Switzerland) on February 23, 1992. His average speed was 53.79 mph.

On January 15, 1995, Johannes Badrutt (Switzerland) set a record of 41.27 seconds from Junction, at an altitude of 2,920 feet.

SNOWBOARDING CHAMPION

Far right, Canada's Ross Rebagliati celebrates victory in the men's giant slalom at the Nagano Olympics. Rebagliati was born in 1971 and lives in Vancouver, British Columbia. Prior to his success in the Olympics, he had only ever won one giant slalom race in the World Championships or World Cup series. Behind him stands Thomas Prugger of Italy, who finished just 0.02 seconds behind Rebagliati to receive the silver medal.

BOBSLED

MOST TITLES AND MEDALS

The world four-man bobsled title has been won a record 20 times by Switzerland (1924, 1936, 1939, 1947, 1954–57, 1971–73, 1975, 1982–83, 1986–90 and 1993). This total includes a record five Olympic victories (1924, 1936, 1956, 1972 and 1988).

Switzerland has won the two-man title a record 17 times (1935, 1947–50, 1953, 1955, 1977–80, 1982–83, 1987, 1990, 1992 and 1994). This total includes a record four Olympic successes (in 1948, 1980, 1992 and 1994).

Eugenio Monti was a member of 11 world championship crews from 1957 to 1968 (eight two-man and three four-man).

SNOWBOARDING WORLD CUP

Mike Jacoby (US) holds the record for most combined points in the FIS World Cup, with a total score of 1,243.22 in 1996. In the same year, Karine Ruby (France) set the women's record with a score of 1,760.60. Ruby also holds the record for most World Championship titles, with three.

The record for the greatest number of Olympic gold medals won by an individual is three, by Meinhard Nehmer and Bernhard Germeshausen (both of the GDR) in the 1976 two-man and the 1976 and 1980 four-man events.

The greatest number of medals won is seven (one gold, five silver, one bronze), by Bogdan Musiol (GDR, later Germany) from 1980 to 1992.

LUGEING

MOST TITLES

The record for the most World Championship lugeing titles won (including Olympics) is six, by Georg Hackl (GDR/Germany): single-seater in 1989, 1990, 1992, 1994, 1997 and 1998.

Stefan Krausee and Jan Behrendt (both GDR/Germany) have won a record six two-seater titles (1989, 1991–93, 1995 and 1998).

Margit Schumann (GDR) has won a record five women's titles, from 1973 to 1975 and in 1976 (Olympic) and 1977.

Steffi Walter (GDR) has won a record two Olympic single-seater luge titles, at the women's event in 1984 and 1988.

FASTEST SPEED

The record for the highest photo-timed speed is 85.38 mph, by Asle Strand (Norway) at Tandådalens Linbana, Sälen, Sweden on May 1, 1982.

ICE-YACHTING

HIGHEST SPEED

The highest officially recorded speed by an ice-yacht is 143 mph, by John Buckstaff in a Class A stern-steerer on Lake Winnebago, Wisconsin in 1938. Such a speed is possible in a wind of 72 mph.

LARGEST ICE-YACHT

Icicle, an ice-yacht built for Comm. John Roosevelt for racing on the Hudson River, New York in 1869, was 68 ft. 11 in. long and carried 1,070 square feet of canvas.

WINTER X GAMES

The Winter X Games, the world's largest extreme sports extravaganza, was launched by ESPN in 1997. It features ice climbing, in which competitors scale a 66-foot-high manmade frozen waterfall; snow mountain bike racing; free skiing; skiboarding; snowboarding; and snowcross. Competitors from the United States, Russia, Australia, South Korea, Germany and Sweden competed in the 1998 Winter X Games at Crested Butte in Colorado.

MOST ICE CLIMBING MEDALS

The most ice climbing medals won is three, by Will Gadd (US): the bronze difficulty medal in 1997 and the gold speed and gold difficulty medals in 1998.

MOST MEDALS FOR SNOW MOUNTAIN BIKING

The most snow mountain biking medals is three, by Cheri Elliott (US): the 1997 gold speed medal and the 1998 silver speed and silver difficulty medals.

FASTEST SPEED ON A SNOW MOUNTAIN BIKE

The fastest speed recorded on a snow mountain bike at the Winter X Games is 73 mph, by Jan Karpie (US).

SNOWBOARDING COMPETITIONS

Klas Vangen (Norway) is seen training for the snowboard halfpipe in preparation for the 1998 Winter Olympics. Snowboarding is now part of the Fédération Internationale de Ski. A World Cup series began in 1995 and World Championships were inaugurated the following year. Competitions are held in halfpipe, slalom, parallel slalom, giant slalom and snowboard cross.

water sports

SURFING

Surfing, which evolved from the Polynesian practice of standing in canoes, took off in the 1950s and is now an international sport with an established world tour.

HIGHEST EARNINGS IN A SEASON

Kelly Slater (US) earned a record $208,200 in the 1997 season. Slater turned professional at the age of 19, after winning about 200 amateur competitions, and became the youngest ever world champion at the age of 20 in 1992. *Black and White*, a video released in 1990, showed him redefining surfing's traditional maneuvers. He has since won three more world titles, in 1994, 1995, and 1996.

The women's record for the highest earnings is $55,510, by US surfer Lisa Andersen in 1996.

HIGHEST CAREER EARNINGS

Kelly Slater had earned a record $654,495 by the end of the 1997 season. In 1991, the surfer was the subject of a fierce sponsorship bidding war between the major surfwear companies. It was eventually won by Quiksilver, the world's biggest surfwear manufacturer.

The women's career record is $270,275, by Pam Burridge (Australia) to the end of the 1997 season.

MOST WORLD PROFESSIONAL SERIES TITLES

The men's title has been won five times, by Mark Richards (Australia) in 1975 and from 1979 to 1982.

The women's professional title has been won four times by: Frieda Zamba (US), 1984–86 and 1988, and by Wendy Botha (Australia, formerly South Africa), 1987, 1989, 1991, and 1992.

MOST WORLD AMATEUR CHAMPIONSHIP TITLES

The most titles is three, by Michael Novakov (Australia) in the Kneeboard event in 1982, 1984, and 1986.

The most titles by a woman is two, by Joyce Hoffman (US) in 1965 and 1966 and Sharon Weber (US) in 1970 and 1972.

WATER-SKIING

MOST WATER-SKIING TITLES

The US won the team championship on 17 successive occasions from 1957 to 1989.

The World Overall Championships have been won five times by Patrice Martin (France), in 1989, 1991, 1993, 1995 and 1997.

The record for the most women's titles in the World Overall Championships is three, by Willa McGuire (US) in 1949, 1950 and 1955, and Liz Allan-Shetter (US) in 1965, 1969 and 1975.

SURFING BIGGEST SURFING COMPETITION

The G-Shock US Open of Surfing, which takes place at Huntington Beach, California, is generally regarded as the biggest surfing competition in the world today. The competition, which forms part of the world qualifying series, has attracted approximately 200,000 spectators every year since it started in 1994, and has about 700 competitors. The total prize money is $155,000. Out of this, $100,000 goes to the winner of the men's surfing contest, and $15,000 goes to the winner of the women's surfing contest.

HIGHEST WAVES

Waimea Bay, Hawaii, is said to provide the most consistently high waves, which often reach the normal rideable limit of 30–35 feet. In 1998, K2, the ski and snowboard manufacturer, announced that it was launching a new K2 Surf line of clothing, and with it the inaugural K2 "Big Wave Challenge," which offered a $50,000 prize for the rider of the biggest wave of the winter. The challenge, which attracted surfers from around the world, was won by 26-year-old Taylor Knox of Carlsbad, California. His winning ride (pictured left) took place at Todos Santos, an isolated surf spot off the Mexican coast, on a wave just under 50 feet in height. Knox, who was rated No. 9 in the world at the end of 1997, has been competing on the surfing pro tour since 1992 and now travels on the world pro tour for elite surfers. The coasts of Mexico offer some of the world's top surfing spots: the longest sea wave rides experienced cover approximately 1 mile and are possible four to six times a year when rideable surfing waves break in Matanchen Bay near San Blas, Nayarit, Mexico.

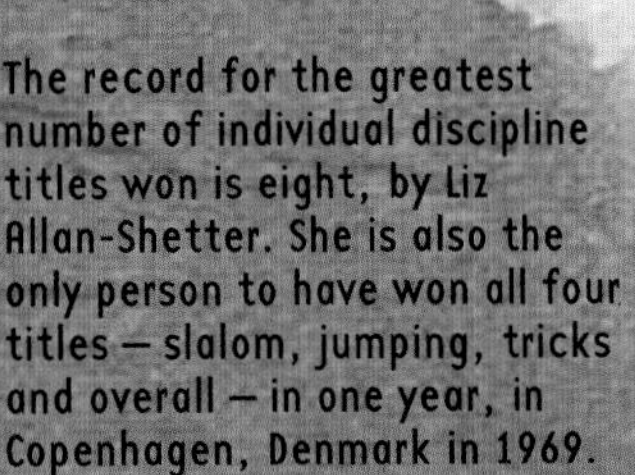

The record for the greatest number of individual discipline titles won is eight, by Liz Allan-Shetter. She is also the only person to have won all four titles — slalom, jumping, tricks and overall — in one year, in Copenhagen, Denmark in 1969.

The most World Barefoot Championship Overall titles is four, by Kim Lampard (Australia) in 1980, 1982, 1985 and 1986.

The greatest number of men's World Barefoot Championship Overall titles is three, by Brett Wing (Australia) in 1978, 1980, and 1982.

The World Barefoot Championship team title has been won a record five times by Australia, in 1978, 1980, 1982, 1985, and 1986.

HIGHEST SPEED

The highest speed known to have been attained by any water-skier is 143.08 mph, by Christopher Massey (Australia) on the Hawkesbury River, Windsor, Australia, on March 6, 1983. His drag boat driver was Stanley Sainty.

Donna Patterson Brice (US) set a women's record of 111.11 mph at Long Beach, California, on August 21, 1977.

The official barefoot speed record is 135.74 mph, by Scott Pellaton (US) over a 440-yard course in Chandler, California, in November 1989.

MOST WATER-SKIERS TOWED BY ONE BOAT

On October 18, 1986 a record-breaking 100 skiers were towed on double skis over a nautical mile by the cruiser *Reef Cat* at Cairns, Queensland, Australia. This feat, which was organized by the Cairns and District Powerboating and Ski Club, was then replicated by 100 skiers on single skis.

CANOEING

MOST OLYMPIC MEDALS

Gert Fredriksson (Sweden) won a record six Olympic gold medals from 1948 to 1960. He also won a silver and a bronze, for a record total of eight medals.

The most gold medals won by a woman is five, by Birgit Schmidt (East Germany) from 1980 to 1996. Schmidt also won three silvers, to equal Fredriksson's total of eight medals.

MOST WORLD AND OLYMPIC TITLES

A record 25 world titles (including Olympic titles) were won by Birgit Schmidt from 1979 to 1996.

The men's record is 13, by Gert Fredriksson from 1948 to 1960, Rüdiger Helm (East Germany), 1976–83, and Ivan Patzaichin (Romania), 1968–84.

HIGHEST SPEEDS

At the 1995 World Championships, the Hungarian four won the 200-m title in a time of 31.227 seconds, at an average speed of 14.32 mph.

On August 4, 1992 the German four-man kayak Olympic champions at Barcelona, Spain, covered 1,000 m in 2 min. 52.17 sec. — an average speed of 12.98 mph.

BIGGEST CANOE RAFT

On August 17, 1996, a raft made up of 649 kayaks and canoes free-floated for 30 seconds, held together by participants' hands only, on the Rock River, Byron, Illinois. The feat was organized by the United States Canoe Association.

WHITE WATER RAFTING AND KAYAKING

MOST SUCCESSFUL NATION IN WHITE WATER RAFTING

Slovenia has been the overall world champion at every World Rafting Challenge Championship (1995, 1996 and 1997). In each championship, it gained first place in all three elements (raft sprint, raft slalom and raft down river) except for the raft down river in 1996, which was won by South Africa.

MOST SUCCESSFUL NATIONS IN WHITE WATER KAYAKING

The most successful nations to date are Croatia (who won the World Championship in 1996) and Zimbabwe (who won the title in 1997). White water kayaking has been part of the World Rafting Challenge Championship since 1996.

BOARDSAILING

Boardsailing was introduced to the Olympic Games in 1984. The first gold was won by Stephan van den Berg (Netherlands), who also won a record five world titles from 1979 to 1983. The fastest overall speed by a boardsailer is 45.34 knots (52.21 mph), by Thierry Bielak (France) at Camargue, France, in 1993. The women's record is 40.36 knots (46.44 mph), by Babethe Coquelle of France at Tarifa, Spain, on July 7, 1995.

TOUGHEST WHITE WATER RIVER

The Kali Gandaki River in central Nepal — a popular course for whitewater rafting — winds through remote canyons and deep gorges filled with intense rapids and is classified as 6+, making it the most difficult whitewater river regularly rafted (rivers are graded 1 to 6 in terms of difficulty). The World Rafting Challenge Championship is staged annually in Zimbabwe.

high sports

BIGGEST MASS BUNGEE JUMP
On October 19, 1997, 16 women made the world's largest ever mass bungee jump at Offenbach am Main, Germany. They jumped from a specially constructed platform 170 ft. 1,056 yd. in height and were tied together by six ropes, each 32 ft. 1,408 yd. in length, joined one behind the other. The event was organized by Sky Bungee Jumping and Sky Veranstaltungen from Munich, Germany.

LOWEST PARACHUTE ESCAPE
Terence Spencer (Great Britain) made the lowest ever escape, at 30–40 feet over Wismar Bay in the Baltic Sea in 1945.

BIGGEST CANOPY STACK BY PARACHUTISTS
The world's largest canopy stack, held for 37.54 seconds over Davis, California, involved a total of 46 people from a number of countries. It took place on on October 12, 1994.

BIGGEST PARACHUTE FREEFALL FORMATIONS
The biggest official freefall formation involved a total of 200 people from 10 countries over Myrtle Beach, South Carolina on October 23, 1992. It was held for 6.47 seconds from 3 miles 229 yd.

The unofficial freefall record is 297 people from a total of 26 countries, who held a formation from 4 miles 70 yd. over Anapa, Russia on September 27, 1996.

Elvira Fomitcheva (USSR) made the longest ever delayed parachute drop by a woman, falling 9 miles 352 yd. over Odessa, USSR (now Ukraine), on October 26, 1977.

LONGEST BUNGEE JUMP
A record 820-foot-long bungee was used by Gregory Riffi during a jump from a helicopter above the Loire Valley, France in February 1992. Riffi's cord stretched to a length of 2,000 feet during the jump.

HIGHEST BASE JUMP BY PARACHUTISTS
Dr. Glenn Singleman and Nicholas Feteris jumped from a 3-mile-1,102-yd. ledge on the Great Trango Tower, Kashmir on August 26, 1992.

MOST JUMPS BY A SKYSURFER
Eric Fradet from Le Tignet, France, has logged more than 14,700 jumps during his skysurfing career.

LOWEST MID-AIR RESCUE BY A PARACHUTIST
On October 16, 1988, Eddie Turner saved Frank Farnan, who was unconscious after being injured in a collision while jumping out of an aircraft at 2 miles 792 yd. Turner pulled Farnan's ripcord at 1,800 feet over Clewiston, Florida.

LONGEST UPSIDE-DOWN FLIGHT
The longest inverted flight was 4 hr. 38 min. 10 sec., by Joann Osterud from Vancouver to Vanderhoof, Canada in July 1991.

HIGHEST BALLOON SKYWALK
The highest altitude at which anyone has completed a balloon skywalk is 18,800 feet. Mike Howard performed the feat, which was broadcast on the Fox TV series *Guinness World Records™: Primetime*. The 32-year-old Briton walked between two hot air balloons connected by a metal beam, using only a pole to balance with, and without the aid of safety ropes.

LONGEST PARACHUTE FALL
William Rankin fell for a record 40 minutes, due to thermals, in North Carolina on July 26, 1956.

LONGEST DELAYED DROPS BY PARACHUTE
Joseph Kittinger fell 16 miles from a balloon at 19 miles 872 yd. at Tularosa, New Mexico on August 16, 1960.

HIGHEST PARACHUTE ESCAPE
Flight Lieutenant J. de Salis and Flying Officer P. Lowe (both Great Britain) escaped from a plane at 10 miles 1,108 yd. over Derby, England in 1958.

MOST LOOPS DURING FLIGHT
On August 9, 1986, David Childs performed 2,368 inside loops in a Bellanca Decathlon over North Pole, Alaska.

Joann Osterud made 208 outside loops in a Supernova Hyperbipe over North Bend, Oregon on July 13, 1989.

HIGHEST TOY BALLOON FLIGHT

In September 1987, British daredevil Ian Ashpole set a world altitude record for toy balloon flight when he reached a height of 1 mile 1,575 yd. over Ross-on-Wye, England. Ashpole was lifted to the target altitude by the hot-air balloon *Mercier*. When he reached the desired height, he cut himself free from the hot-air balloon, then one by one from the 400 helium-filled toy balloons that suspended him in midair. Once freed from all the balloons, each of which was 2 feet in diameter, he began freefalling at approximately 90 mph before parachuting to the ground.

SKYSURFING

The skysurfing World Championships were first staged in 1997 in Turkey. The men's title was won by Oliver Furrer and the women's by Vivian Wegrath (both Switzerland).

LONGEST DISTANCE COVERED IN AN ULTRALIGHT
The greatest ever distance covered in a straight line was 1,011 miles 845 yd., by Wilhelm Lischak (Austria) from Volsau, Austria, to Brest, France, on June 8, 1988.

GREATEST ALTITUDE ACHIEVED IN AN ULTRALIGHT
The record for the greatest altitude ever reached in a ultralight is 6 miles 70 yd., by Serge Zin (France) over Saint Auban, France in 1994.

LONGEST HANG GLIDES
The record for the greatest straight line and declared goal distance is 307 miles 1,056 yd., by Larry Tudor (US) from Rock Springs, Wyoming on July 1,1994.

The greatest distance by a woman is 208 miles 1,165 yd., by Kari Castle (US) over Owens Valley, California on July 22, 1991.

GREATEST HEIGHT GAINS BY HANG GLIDERS
Larry Tudor gained 2 miles 1,232 yd. over Owens Valley, California, in 1985.

The greatest height gain by a woman was 2 miles 822 yd., by British hang glider Judy Leden over Kuruman, South Africa, on December 1, 1992.

LONGEST PARAGLIDING FLIGHTS
The men's record is 176 miles 722 yd., by Alex François Louw (South Africa) from Kuruman, South Africa on December 31, 1992.

The greatest distance flown by a woman is 177 miles 169 yd., by British paraglider Kat Thurston from Kuruman, South Africa, on December 25, 1995.

The greatest distance flown on a tandem paraglider is 124 miles 493 yd., by Britons Richard and Guy Westgate, from Kuruman, South Africa, on December 23, 1995 and January 1, 1996 respectively.

GREATEST HEIGHT GAINS BY PARAGLIDERS
The height gain record is 2 miles 1,426 yd., by British paraglider Robby Whittal at Brandvlei, South Africa, on January 6, 1993.

The women's height gain record is 2 miles 1,209 yd., by Kat Thurston (GB) at Kuruman, South Africa on January 1, 1996.

The height gain record on a tandem paraglider is 2 miles 1,271 yd., by Richard and Guy Westgate at Kuruman, South Africa, on December 23, 1995 and January 1, 1996 respectively.

HIGHEST DIVES
The highest ever dive into a lake was made by Harry Froboess of Switzerland, who jumped 394 feet into Lake Constance from the airship *Hindenburg* on June 22, 1936.

The highest dive from a diving board was 176 ft. 10 in., by Olivier Favre of Switzerland at Villers-le-Lac, France, on August 30, 1987.

The highest dive from a diving board by a woman was 120 ft. 9 in., by Lucy Wardle (US) at Ocean Park, Hong Kong on April 6, 1985.

The highest regularly performed headfirst dives are made by professional divers from a height of 87 ft. 6 in. from La Quebrada ("the break in the rocks") in Acapulco, Mexico. The base rocks, which are 21 feet out from the takeoff point, necessitate an outward leap of 27 feet. The water is 12 feet deep.

BUNGEE JUMPING

Bungee jumping originated on Pentecost Island in the South Pacific, where for thousands of years, people have climbed towers 50–80 feet tall, attached vines to their ankles, and jumped headfirst toward the ground. In 1970, photographer and author Kal Muller visited the island and became the first foreigner to attempt the plunge. The first commercial operation opened in 1988 in Ohakune, New Zealand.

mountain sports

LARGEST VERTICAL FACES
The Trango Towers, which are situated next to the Baltoro Glacier on the approach to K2, the Gasherbrums and Broad Peak in Kashmir, are home to the largest vertical faces in the world. The Great Trango Tower's three summits are all over 19,700 feet in altitude, with the main summit at 20,625 feet. The latter was climbed for the first time in 1977, two years after the area was opened for climbing after being closed for many years.

MOST SUCCESSFUL MOUNTAINEER
Reinhold Messner (Italy) has scaled all 14 of the world's mountains that are more than 26,250 feet in altitude, without oxygen. In 1982, Messner also became the first person to have climbed the three highest mountains when he ascended Kanchenjunga, having previously climbed Mt. Everest and K2.

FIRST ASCENT OF SEVEN SUMMITS
The first person to climb the highest mountain on all seven continents, including Kosciusko in Australia, was Richards Bass (US), who scaled the last of the peaks with his conquest of Mt. Everest in 1985.

Ngga Pulu (formerly Carstensz Pyramid) on Irian Jaya, Indonesia is the highest mountain in Australasia (New Zealand, New Guinea, Tasmania, the Pacific Islands and Australia). The first person to scale the highest peak on every continent including Australasia was Patrick Morrow (Canada), who completed his conquest on May 7, 1986.

FASTEST SEVEN-SUMMIT ASCENT
In 1990, New Zealanders Gary Ball, Peter Hillary (son of Sir Edmund Hillary) and Andy Hall completed an ascent of the seven summits in a record time of seven months.

MOST EUROPEAN SUMMITS
British climber Eamon Fullen has climbed the highest summits in 44 European countries. He began with Elbrus in Russia, Europe's highest point, in August 1992, and is set to complete the ascent of the final three peaks by August 1998.

FIRST ASCENT OF MT EVEREST
The summit of Mt. Everest (29,029 feet in altitude) was first reached in May 1953 by Edmund Hillary (New Zealand) and Tenzing Norgay (Nepal), in an expedition led by Henry Hunt (GB).

FIRST SOLO ASCENT OF MT. EVEREST
The first person to make the entire climb solo was Reinhold Messner (Italy), in August 1980.

FIRST SOLO ASCENT OF MT. EVEREST BY A WOMAN
In May 1994, 33-year-old Alison Hargreaves (GB) became the first woman to reach the summit of Mt. Everest alone and without oxygen tanks. In August 1995, having reached the summit of K2, Hargreaves was one of seven climbers who were swept to their death during the descent.

MOST ASCENTS OF MT. EVEREST
Sherpa Ang Rita has scaled Mt. Everest a record 10 times (in 1983, 1984, 1985, 1987, 1988, 1990, 1992, 1993, 1995 and 1996), each time without the use of bottled oxygen.

MOST PEOPLE ON MT. EVEREST
The Mount Everest International Peace Climb, a team of US, Soviet and Chinese climbers led by James Whittaker (US), succeeded in putting a record 10 people on the summit of Mt. Everest on May 7–10, 1990.

MOST PEOPLE TO REACH MT. EVEREST SUMMIT IN ONE DAY
On May 10, 1993, 40 climbers (32 men and eight women) from nine expeditions and 10 different countries (United States, Canada, Australia, United Kingdom, Russia, New Zealand, Finland, Lithuania, India and Nepal) reached the summit of Mt. Everest.

MOST GENERATIONS OF A FAMILY TO CLIMB MT EVEREST
Tashi Wangchuk Tenzing, a travel agent from Sydney, Australia, climbed the world's highest mountain in May 1997, reaching the summit almost 44 years after his grandfather Tenzing Norgay made the first ever ascent of Mt. Everest with Edmund Hillary in 1953. At the peak, Tashi, who is a devout Buddhist, left a 6-inch-tall statue of the Buddha. A record three generations of the Tenzing family have now climbed the mountain, and Tashi is the first grandson of an Everest conqueror to reach the peak (Sir Edmund Hillary's son Peter was the first son of an Everest mountaineer to reach the summit). Tashi, who made the ascent in just under nine hours, first tried to climb Mt. Everest in 1993 to mark the 40th anniversary of his grandfather's climb, but the attempt came to a tragic end when his uncle, Lobsang, who was climbing with him, died. Now that he has achieved his goal, Tashi has no plans to scale the mountain again, although 90% of the 700-plus people from 43 different countries who have climbed Mt. Everest have attempted to repeat the experience.

FASTEST TIME FROM EVEREST BASE CAMP TO KATHMANDU
Hélène Diamantides and Alison Wright (both GB) traveled from Everest base camp to Kathmandu, Nepal in a time of 3 days 10 hr. 8 min., from October 8 to October 10, 1987. They covered 180 miles, climbed 32,000 ft, and descended 46,000 ft.

HIGHEST BIVOUAC
Mark Whetu (New Zealand) and Michael Rheinberger (Australia) reached the summit of Mt. Everest on May 26, 1994 and bivouacked just 66 feet below the summit that night. Rheinberger died the next day during the descent.

MOST SUCCESSFUL SKI DOWN MT. EVEREST
In September 1992, Pierre Tardivel (France) skied 10,500 feet from the South Summit of Mt. Everest to base camp in three hours of jump turns. Tardivel has notched up more than 60 first descents, mostly in the Alps.

DEADLIEST YEAR ON MT. EVEREST
In 1996, 15 of the 98 people who reached the summit of Mt. Everest died during the descent.

BIGGEST CLIMBING WALL
The 16,404-foot Rupal Face on the southern side of the Nanga Pardat, Pakistan is the biggest climbing wall in the world. The equivalent of two-and-a-half Eigers guard the 26,600-foot summit of Nanga Pardat, also known as the "Naked Mountain."

MOST DIFFICULT FREE CLIMB
The world's most difficult free climb is reputed to be Action Direkt in the Frankenjua, Germany, which has a 9A rating. The climb has earned its reputation because of its overhang and small holds. Action Direkt was first climbed by Wolfgang Gullich in 1994.

FASTEST RACES: MT. CAMEROON
Reginald Esuke (Cameroon) descended from the summit of Mt. Cameroon (13,435 feet) to Buea Stadium (3,002 feet) in a time of 1 hr. 2 min. 15 sec. on January 24, 1988. This equals a vertical rate of 167.5 feet per minute.

Timothy Leku Lekunze (Cameroon) set a record time of 3 hr. 46 min. 34 sec. for the race to the summit of Mt. Cameroon and back in 1987. The temperature varied between 95°F at the foot and 32°F at the summit.

The fastest ever ascent of Mt. Cameroon was 2 hr. 25 min. 20 sec., by Jack Maitland (GB) in 1988.

The fastest ascent of Mt. Cameroon in a women's race was 4 hr. 42 min. 31 sec., by Fabiola Rueda (Colombia) in 1989.

FASTEST RACES: BEN NEVIS (SCOTLAND)
The record time for the race from Fort William Town park to the summit of Ben Nevis (4,418 ft) and return is 1 hr. 25 min. 34 sec., by Kenneth Stuart (GB) on September 1, 1984.

The women's record is 1 hr. 43 min. 25 sec., by Pauline Haworth (GB), September 1, 1984.

FASTEST RACES: SNOWDON (WALES)
The record for the fastest time from Llanberis to the summit of Snowdon (3,560 feet) is 1 hr. 2 min. 29 sec., by Kenneth Stuart in 1985.

The best women's time is 1 hr. 12 min. 48 sec., by Carol Greenwood (GB) in 1993.

ABSEILING
Abseiling, or rappeling, the descent of a steep slope or vertical drop by a rope secured from above, gets its name from the German verb *abseilen*, which means to descend by a rope. Abseiling is not only a recreational activity; it is also practiced in army training and rescue operations. The record for the greatest overall distance covered by abseilers is 3,627 feet, by a team of four British Royal Marines, each of whom abseiled down the Boulby Potash Mine, Cleveland, England from 25 feet below ground level to the shaft bottom on November 2, 1993.

MOUNTAIN CLIMBING
Mountaineering began as a sport in the 18th century, when Swiss scientist Horace-Bénédict de Saussure offered a prize to the first person to scale Mont Blanc. The prize was not claimed until 20 years later in 1786. The 19th century saw an emphasis on the climbing of alpine and other European mountains, but climbers were expected to not only scale the peaks but to reach them by ever more demanding routes. The worldwide spread of mountaineering continued from the end of the 19th century, when attention turned towards the Himalayas, particularly Mt. Everest, which was eventually scaled in 1953.

marathons and endurance

MOST MARATHONS RUN
Horst Preisler (Germany) ran a total of 631 races of 26 miles 385 yd. or longer from 1974 to May 29, 1996.

Henri Girault (France) ran a total of 330 100-km races – an IAAF recognized distance – from 1979 to June 1996 and has completed a run on every continent except Antarctica.

FASTEST HALF MARATHON
The best time on a properly measured course is 59 min. 17 sec., by Paul Tergat (Kenya) in Milan, Italy on April 4, 1998.

OLDEST MARATHON FINISHERS
Dimitrion Yordanidis (Greece) was 98 when he raced in Athens, Greece in October 1976. His time was 7 hr. 33 min.

The oldest woman to complete a marathon was Thelma Pitt-Turner (New Zealand), who was 82 when she raced in New Zealand in August 1985. Her time was 7 hr. 58 min.

LONGEST RUNNING RACE
The world's longest ever race covered a distance of 3,665 miles from New York City to Los Angeles in 1929. Finnish-born Johnny Salo won in 79 days and an elapsed time of 525 hr. 57 min. 20 sec., averaging 6.97 mph.

PENTATHLON: MOST WORLD TITLES
András Balczó (Hungary) won six individual titles: 1963, 1965–67, 1969 and 1972 (Olympic) and seven team titles (five world and two Olympic, 1960–70).

The USSR won 14 world and four Olympic team titles.

Hungary has also won a record four Olympic team titles.

The most women's titles is three, by Eva Fjellerup (Denmark), with individual titles in 1990, 1991 and 1993.

Poland has won a record seven women's world team titles (1985, 1988–92, 1995).

MOST OLYMPIC TITLES
The record for the greatest number of Olympic gold medals won is three, by András Balczó of Hungary (team in 1960 and 1968 and individual in 1972).

The record for the most individual championships won is two, by Lars Hall (Sweden) in 1952 and 1956.

MOST OLYMPIC MEDALS
Pavel Serafimovich Lednyev (USSR) won a record seven medals (two team gold, one team silver, one individual silver and three individual bronze) from 1968 to 1980.

FASTEST FEMALE IRONMAN
The record for the fastest Hawaii Ironman time by a woman is 8 hr. 55 min. 28 sec., by Paula Newby-Fraser (Zimbabwe) in 1992. Newby-Fraser also holds the record for the fastest time by a woman for any official Ironman course, at 8 hr. 55 min., in Roth, Germany on July 12, 1992, and for the greatest number of race wins by a woman, with eight (1986, 1988, 1989, 1991 to 1994 and 1996). Surprisingly, Newby-Fraser has never won the official World Championships.

FASTEST MARATHON
The fastest ever marathon (26 miles 385 yd.) was 2 hr. 6 min. 50 sec., by Belayneh Dinsamo (Ethiopia) in Rotterdam, Netherlands on April 17, 1988. Dinsamo bettered the previous world record, which had been set at Rotterdam three years earlier by Carlos Lopes of Portugal, by 22 seconds.

RECORD-BREAKING RUNNER
Haile Gebrselassie has broken 14 world records since 1994, making him one of the greatest distance runners of all time. The 5-ft.-4-in.-tall athlete is soon to be immortalized in a Disney biographical movie tracing his life from his humble beginnings as one of 10 children from a poor district in Ethiopia to victory at the Olympics in 1996. The 24-year-old has won two Mercedes in competitions, but they remain unused because he has not yet learned to drive. His sponsorship deal with Adidas will bring him $1 million over five years.

BIATHLON: MOST TITLES
Frank Ullrich (East Germany) won a record six individual world titles: four at 10 km, 1978–81, including the 1980 Olympics, and two at 20 km in 1982 and 1983.

Aleksandr Tikhonov was in a record 10 winning Soviet relay teams (1968–80) and won four individual titles.

The most individual World Championship titles is three, by Anne-Elinor Elvebakk (Norway): 10 km in 1988 and 7.5 km from 1989 to 1990.

Kaya Parve (USSR) won six titles: two individual and four relay from 1984 to 1986 and in 1988.

The most men's Olympic individual titles is two, by Magnar Solberg (Norway) in 1968 and 1972 and Frank-Peter Rötsch (East Germany) at both 10 km and 20 km in 1988.

Aleksandr Tikhonov (USSR) won four relay golds (1968–80) and a silver in the 20 km in 1968.

The most women's titles is two, by Anfissa Restzova of Russia: 7.5 km in 1992 and 4 x 7.5-km in 1994, and by Myriam Bédard of Canada: 7.5 km and 15 km in 1994.

The Biathlon World Cup was won four times by Frank Ullrich (East Germany) (1978, 1980–82) and Franz Rötsch (also East Germany) (1984, 1985, 1987, 1988).

TRIATHLON: BEST IRONMAN TIMES
The fastest time for the Hawaii Ironman, which consists of a 2-mile 440-yd. swim, a 112-mile cycle ride and a full marathon of 26 miles 385 yd., is 8 hr. 4 min. 8 sec., by Luc van Lierde (Belgium) in 1996.

The fastest ever time over the Ironman distances is 7 hr. 50 min. 27 sec., by Luc van Lierde (Belgium) in Roth, Germany on July 13, 1997.

The most wins in the men's race is six, by Dave Scott (US): 1980, 1982–84 and 1986–87; and by Mark Allen: 1989–93 and 1995.

TRIATHLON: MOST WORLD CHAMPIONSHIP WINS
The World Championship consists of a 40 km (24-mile-1,496-yd.) cycle, a 10-km (6-mile-370-yd.) run, and a 1,500-m (4,921-ft.-3-in.) swim. Simon Lessing (UK) has won three (1992, 1995 and 1996).

The most wins in the women's event is two, by Michelle Jones (Australia) in 1992 and 1993 and Karen Smyers (US) in 1990 and 1995.

Prior to 1989, a race held annually in Nice, France was regarded as the unofficial World Championship. Mark Allen (US) won 10 titles from 1982 to 1986 and from 1989 to 1993.

Paula Newby-Fraser (Zimbabwe) had four women's wins, 1989–92.

TRIATHLON: BEST WORLD CHAMPIONSHIP TIMES
The best men's time is 5 hr. 46 min. 10 sec., by Mark Allen (US) in 1986.

The best women's time is 6 hr. 27 min. 6 sec., by Erin Baker (New Zealand) in 1988.

STAMINA: MOST PUSH-UPS
The most push-ups in 24 hours is 46,001, by Charles Servizio, in Fontana, California in 1993.

The most one-arm push-ups in five hours is 8,794, by Paddy Doyle (Great Britain) in 1996.

The most fingertip push-ups in five hours is 8,200, by Terry Cole in Walthamstow, London, England in 1996.

STAMINA: MOST SQUAT THRUSTS
Paul Wai Man Chung did 3,552 in an hour in Hong Kong in 1992.

STAMINA: MOST BURPEES
The most burpees in an hour is 1,840, by Paddy Doyle in February 1994.

FASTEST WOMEN'S MARATHON
The fastest women's half marathon is 66 min. 40 sec., by Ingrid Kristiansen (Norway) in Sandnes, Norway on April 5, 1987. Kristiansen had held the full marathon world record for nearly 14 years, until it was bettered by Tegla Loraipe (Kenya) in Rotterdam, Netherlands on April 19, 1998 in a time of 2 hr. 20 min. 7 sec.

sports reference

The following pages contain more than 800 sports records. This section includes many sports that are not covered in the Sporting Heroes chapter.

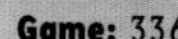

nfl

NFL Regular Season Records
POINTS
Career: 2,002
George Blanda, Chicago Bears, Baltimore Colts, Houston Oilers, Oakland Raiders, 1949–75
Season: 176
Paul Hornung, Green Bay Packers, 1960
Game: 40
Ernie Nevers, Chicago Cardinals v. Chicago Bears, November 28, 1929
TOUCHDOWNS
Career: 166
Jerry Rice, San Francisco 49ers, 1985–97
Season: 25
Emmitt Smith, Dallas Cowboys, 1995
Game: 6
Ernie Nevers, Chicago Cardinals v. Chicago Bears, November 28, 1929
William Jones, Cleveland Browns v. Chicago Bears, November 25, 1951
Gale Sayers, Chicago Bears v. San Francisco 49ers, December 12, 1965
YARDS GAINED RUSHING
Career: 16,726
Walter Payton, Chicago Bears, 1975–87
Season: 2,105
Eric Dickerson, Los Angeles Rams, 1984
Game: 275
Walter Payton, Chicago Bears v. Minnesota Vikings, November 20, 1977
YARDS GAINED RECEIVING
Career: 16,455
Jerry Rice, San Francisco 49ers, 1985–97
Season: 1,848
Jerry Rice, San Francisco 49ers, 1995
Game: 336
Willie Anderson, Los Angeles Rams v. New Orleans Saints, November 26, 1989
COMBINED NET YARDS GAINED
Career: 21,803
Walter Payton, Chicago Bears, 1975–87
Season: 2,535
Lionel James, San Diego Chargers, 1985
Game: 404
Glyn Milburn, Denver Broncos v. Seattle Seahawks, December 10, 1995
YARDS GAINED PASSING
Career: 55,416
Dan Marino, Miami Dolphins, 1983–97
Season: 5,084
Dan Marino, Miami Dolphins, 1984
Game: 554
Norm Van Brocklin, Los Angeles Rams v. New York Yanks, September 28, 1951
PASS COMPLETIONS
Career: 4,453
Dan Marino, Miami Dolphins, 1983–97
Season: 404
Warren Moon, Houston Oilers, 1991
Game: 45
Drew Bledsoe, New England Patriots v. Minnesota Vikings, November 13, 1994
PASS RECEPTIONS
Career: 1,057
Jerry Rice, San Francisco 49ers, 1985–97
Season: 123
Herman Moore, Detroit Lions, 1995
Game: 18
Tom Fears, Los Angeles Rams v. Green Bay Packers, December 3, 1950
TOUCHDOWN PASSES
Career: 385
Dan Marino, Miami Dolphins, 1983–97
Season: 48
Dan Marino, Miami Dolphins, 1984
Game: 7
Sid Luckman, Chicago Bears v. New York Giants, November 14, 1943
Adrian Burk, Philadelphia Eagles v. Washington Redskins, October 17, 1954
George Blanda, Houston Oilers v. New York Titans, November 19, 1961
Y. A. Tittle, New York Giants v. Washington Redskins, October 28, 1962
Joe Kapp, Minnesota Vikings v. Baltimore Colts, September 28, 1969
FIELD GOALS
Career: 385
Gary Anderson, Pittsburgh Steelers, Philadelphia Eagles, San Francisco 49ers, 1982–97
Season: 37
John Kasay, Carolina Panthers, 1996
Game: 7
Jim Bakken, St. Louis Cardinals v. Pittsburgh Steelers, September 24, 1967
Rich Karlis, Minnesota Vikings v. Los Angeles Rams, November 5, 1989
Chris Boniol, Dallas Cowboys v. Green Bay Packers, November 18, 1996

Terrell Davis of the Denver Broncos was voted the Most Valuable Player of Super Bowl XXXII, having scored a record-equaling three touchdowns. Denver won the Super Bowl for the first time in five attempts, defeating reigning champions Green Bay 31–24.

Jack Tragis proudly displays his record-breaking Pacific halibut, which he landed off the coast of Alaska. The side shown is the characteristically white "blind" side of the flat fish. The eyes are found on the other side, which is normally brown, dark green or black.

Super Bowl Game & Career Records
POINTS
Game: 18
Roger Craig (San Francisco 49ers), 1985
Jerry Rice (San Francisco 49ers), 1990 and 1995
Ricky Watters (San Francisco 49ers), 1995
Terrell Davis (Denver Broncos), 1998
Career: 42
Jerry Rice, 1989–90, 1995
TOUCHDOWNS
Game: 3
Roger Craig, 1985
Jerry Rice, 1990 and 1995
Ricky Watters, 1990
Terrell Davis, 1998
Career: 7
Jerry Rice, 1989–90, 1995
TOUCHDOWN PASSES
Game: 6
Steve Young (San Francisco 49ers), 1995
Career: 11
Joe Montana (San Francisco 49ers), 1982, 1985, 1989–90
YARDS GAINED PASSING
Game: 357
Joe Montana, 1989
Career: 1,142
Joe Montana, 1982, 1985, 1989–90
YARDS GAINED RECEIVING
Game: 215
Jerry Rice, 1989
Career: 512
Jerry Rice, 1989–90, 1995
YARDS GAINED RUSHING
Game: 204
Timmy Smith (Washington Redskins), 1988
Career: 354
Franco Harris (Pittsburgh Steelers), 1975–76, 1979–80
PASS COMPLETIONS
Game: 31
Jim Kelly (Buffalo Bills), 1994
Career: 83
Joe Montana, 1982, 1985, 1989–90
PASS RECEPTIONS
Game: 11
Dan Ross (Cincinnati Bengals), 1982
Jerry Rice, 1989
Career: 28
Jerry Rice, 1989–90, 1995
FIELD GOALS
Game: 4
Don Chandler (Green Bay Packers), 1968
Ray Wersching (San Francisco 49ers), 1982
Career: 5
Ray Wersching, 1982, 1985
MOST VALUABLE PLAYER
Joe Montana, 1982, 1985, 1990

fishing

World Fishing Records
FRESHWATER AND SALTWATER
A selection of All-Tackle records ratified by the International Game Fish Association as of January 1998.
Barracuda, Great: 85 lb.
John W. Helfrich, Christmas Island, Kiribati, April 11, 1992
Bass, Striped: 78 lb. 8 oz.
Albert R. McReynolds, Atlantic City, New Jersey, September 21, 1982

Catfish, Flathead: 91 lb. 4 oz.
Mike Rogers, Lake Lewisville, Texas, March 28, 1982
Cod, Atlantic: 98 lb. 2 oz.
Alphonse J. Bielevich, Isle of Shoals, New Hampshire, June 8, 1969
Conger: 133 lb. 4 oz.
Vic Evans, Berry Head, England, June 5, 1995
Halibut, Pacific: 459 lb.
Jack Tragis, Dutch Harbor, Alaska, June 11, 1996
Mackerel, King: 90 lb.
Norton I. Thornton, Key West, Florida, February 16, 1976
Marlin, Black: 1,560 lb.
Alfred C. Glassell Jr., Cabo Blanco, Peru, August 4, 1953
Pike, Northern: 55 lb. 1 oz.
Lothar Louis, Lake of Grefeern, Germany, October 16, 1986
Sailfish (Pacific): 221 lb.
C. W. Stewart, Santa Cruz Island, Ecuador, February 12, 1947
Salmon, Atlantic: 79 lb. 2 oz.
Henrik Henriksen, Tana River, Norway, 1928
Shark, Hammerhead: 991 lb.
Allen Ogle, Sarasota, Florida, May 30, 1982
Shark, Porbeagle: 507 lb.
Christopher Bennett, Pentland Firth, UK, March 9, 1993
Shark, Thresher: 802 lb.
Dianne North, Tutukaka, New Zealand, February 8, 1981
Shark, White: 2,664 lb.
Alfred Dean, Ceduna, South Australia, April 21, 1959
Sturgeon, White: 468 lb.
Joey Pallotta III, Benicia, California, July 9, 1983
Swordfish: 1,182 lb.
L. Marron, Iquique, Chile, May 7, 1953
Trout, Brook: 14 lb. 8 oz.
Dr W. J. Cook, Nipigon River, Ontario, Canada, July 1916
Trout, Brown: 40 lb. 4 oz.
Howard L. Collins, Heber Springs, Arkansas, May 9, 1992
Trout, Lake: 66 lb. 8 oz.
Rodney Harback, Great Bear Lake, NWT, Canada, July 19, 1991
Trout, Rainbow: 42 lb. 2 oz.
David Robert White, Bell Island, Alaska, June 22, 1970
Tuna, Bluefin: 1,496 lb.
Ken Fraser, Aulds Cove, Nova Scotia, Canada, October 26, 1979
Tuna, Yellowfin: 388 lb. 12 oz.
Curt Wiesenhutter, San Benedicto Island, Mexico, April 1, 1977
Wahoo: 158.8 lb.
Keith Winter, Loreto, Baja California, Mexico, June 10, 1996

archery

World Archery Records
Men (Single FITA rounds)
FITA: Oh Kyo-moon (South Korea) scored 1,368 points from a possible 1,440 in 1995
90 m: Vladimir Yesheyev (USSR) scored 330 points from a possible 360 in 1990
70 m: Jackson Fear (Australia) scored 345 points from a possible 360 in 1997
50 m: Kim Kyung-ho (South Korea) scored 351 points from a possible 360 in 1997
30 m: Han Seuong-hoon (South Korea) scored 360 points from a possible 360 in 1994
Team: South Korea (Oh Kyo-moon, Lee Kyung-chul, Kim Jae-pak) scored 4,053 points from a possible 4,320 in 1995
Women (Single FITA rounds)
FITA: Kim Jung-rye (South Korea) scored 1,377 points from a possible 1,440 in 1995
70 m: Chung Chang-sook (South Korea) scored 341 points from a possible 360 in 1997
60 m: He Ying (China) scored 349 points from a possible 360 in 1995
50 m: Kim Moon-sun (South Korea) scored 345 points from a possible 360 in 1996
30 m: Joanne Edens (GB) scored 357 points from a possible 360 in 1990
Team: South Korea (Kim Soo-nyung, Lee Eun-kyung, Cho Yuon-jeong) scored 4,094 points from a possible 4,320 in 1992
INDOOR (18 M)
Men
Magnus Pettersson (Sweden) scored 596 points from a possible 600 in 1995
Women
Lina Herasymenko (Ukraine) scored 591 points from a possible 600 in 1996
INDOOR (25 M)
Men
Magnus Pettersson (Sweden) scored 593 points from a possible 600 in 1993
Women
Petra Ericsson (Sweden) scored 592 points from a possible 600 in 1991

Kim Kyung-wook of South Korea winning the 1996 Olympic individual women's gold. South Korea is one of the dominant forces in archery; since 1984 no other nation has won an Olympic gold in women's events.

track and field

World Track and Field Records
Men
World outdoor records for the men's events scheduled by the International Amateur Athletic Federation. Fully automatic electric timing is mandatory for events up to 400 meters.
Running
100 m: 9.84
Donovan Bailey (Canada)
Atlanta, Georgia, July 27, 1996
200 m: 19.32
Michael Johnson (US)
Atlanta, Georgia, August 1, 1996
400 m: 43.29
Butch Reynolds Jr. (US) Zürich, Switzerland, August 17, 1988
800 m: 1:41.11
Wilson Kipketer (Denmark)
Cologne, Germany, August 24, 1997
1,000 m: 2:12.18
Sebastian Coe (GB)
Oslo, Norway, July 11, 1981
1,500 m: 3:27.37
Noureddine Morceli (Algeria)
Nice, France, July 12, 1995
1 mile: 3:44.39
Noureddine Morceli (Algeria)
Rieti, Italy, September 5, 1993
2,000 m: 4:47.88
Noureddine Morceli (Algeria)
Paris, France, July 3, 1995
3,000 m: 7:20.67
Daniel Komen (Kenya)
Rieti, Italy, September 1, 1996
5,000 m: 12:39.36
Haile Gebrselassie (Ethiopia)
Helsinki, Finland, June 13, 1998
10,000 m: 26:22.75
Haile Gebrselassie (Ethiopia)
Hengelo, Netherlands, June 1, 1998
20,000 m: 56:55.6
Arturo Barrios (Mexico, now US)
La Flèche, France, March 30, 1991
25,000 m: 1:13:55.8
Toshihiko Seko (Japan)
Christchurch, New Zealand, March 22, 1981
30,000 m: 1:29:18.8
Toshihiko Seko (Japan)
Christchurch, New Zealand, March 22, 1981
1 hour: 21,101 m
Arturo Barrios (Mexico, now US)
La Flèche, France, March 30, 1991
110-m hurdles: 12.91
Colin Ray Jackson (GB)
Stuttgart, Germany, August 20, 1993
400-m hurdles: 46.78
Kevin Curtis Young (US)
Barcelona, Spain, August 6, 1992
3,000-m steeplechase: 7:55.72
Bernard Barmasai (Kenya)
Cologne, Germany, August 24, 1997
4 x 100-m: 37.40
US (Michael Marsh, Leroy Burrell, Dennis A. Mitchell, Carl Lewis)
Barcelona, Spain, August 8, 1992
and: US (John A. Drummond Jr., Andre Cason, Dennis A. Mitchell, Leroy Burrell)
Stuttgart, Germany, August 21, 1993
4 x 200-m: 1:18.68
Santa Monica Track Club (US) (Michael Marsh, Leroy Burrell, Floyd Wayne Heard, Carl Lewis)
Walnut, California, April 17, 1994
4 x 400-m: 2:54.29
US (Andrew Valmon, Quincy Watts, Butch Reynolds, Michael Johnson)
Stuttgart, Germany, August 21, 1993
4 x 800-m: 7:03.89
Great Britain (Peter Elliott, Garry Peter Cook, Steve Cram, Sebastian Coe)
Crystal Palace, London, August 30, 1982
4 x 1,500-m: 14:38.8
West Germany (Thomas Wessinghage, Harald Hudak, Michael Lederer, Karl Fleschen)
Cologne, Germany, August 17, 1977
Field Events
High Jump: 2.45 m (8 ft. 1/2 in.)
Javier Sotomayor (Cuba)
Salamanca, Spain, July 27, 1993
Pole Vault: 6.14 m (20 ft. 1 3/4 in.)
Sergey Nazarovich Bubka (Ukraine)
Sestriere, Italy, July 1, 1994
(Record set at high altitude. The best mark at low altitude is 6.13 m (20 ft. 1 1/4 in.) by Sergey Bubka in Tokyo, Japan, on September 19, 1992.)
Long Jump: 8.95 m (29 ft. 4 1/2 in.)
Mike Powell (US)
Tokyo, Japan, August 30, 1991
Triple Jump: 18.29 m (60 ft. 1/4 in.)
Jonathan Edwards (GB) Gothenburg, Sweden, August 7, 1995
Shot: 23.12 m (75 ft. 10 1/4 in.)
Randy Barnes (US)
Los Angeles, California, May 20, 1990

Michael Johnson winning the 1996 200-m Olympic title in a record time of 19.32 seconds. With this record, he surpassed the longest-standing track and field record of the time, Pietro Mennea's 19.79 seconds, achieved in February 1979.

Discus: 74.08 m (243 ft.)
Jürgen Schult (East Germany)
Neubrandenburg, Germany, June 6, 1986
Hammer: 86.74 m (284 ft. 7 in.)
Yuriy Georgiyevich Sedykh (USSR, now Russia), Stuttgart, Germany, August 30, 1986
Javelin: 98.48 m (323 ft. 1 in.)
Jan Zelezny (Czech Republic)
Jena, Germany, May 25, 1996
Decathlon: 8,891 points
Dan O'Brien (US)
Talence, France, September 4–5, 1992
Day 1: 100 m: 10.43 sec.; long jump: 8.08 m (26 ft. $6\frac{1}{4}$ in); shot: 16.69 m (54 ft. $9\frac{1}{4}$ in); high jump: 2.07 m (6ft $9\frac{1}{2}$ in); 400 m: 48.51 sec.
Day 2: 110-m hurdles: 13.98 sec.; discus: 48.56 m (159 ft. 4 in); pole vault: 5.00 m (16 ft. $4\frac{1}{4}$ in); javelin 62.58 m (205 ft. 4 in); 1,500 m: 4:42.10

WOMEN'S WORLD RECORDS

World outdoor records for the women's events scheduled by the International Amateur Athletic Federation. Fully automatic electric timing is mandatory for all events up to 400 meters.

10,000 m: 29:31.78
Wang Junxia (China)
Beijing, China, September 8, 1993
20,000 m: 1:06:48.8
Izumi Maki (Japan)
Amagasaki, Japan, September 20, 1993
25,000 m: 1:29:29.2
Karolina Szabo (Hungary)
Budapest, Hungary, April 23, 1988
30,000 m: 1:47:05.6
Karolina Szabo (Hungary)
Budapest, Hungary, April 23, 1988
1 hour : 18,084 m
Silvana Cruciata (Italy)
Rome, Italy, May 4, 1981
100-m hurdles: 12.21
Yordanka Donkova (Bulgaria)
Stara Zagora, Bulgaria, August 20, 1988
400-m hurdles: 52.61
Kim Batten (US)
Gothenburg, Sweden, August 11, 1995
4 x 100-m: 41.37
East Germany (Silke Gladisch, Sabine Rieger, Ingrid Auerswald, Marlies Göhr)
Canberra, Australia, October 6, 1985
4 x 200-m: 1:28.15
East Germany (Marlies Göhr, Romy Müller, Bärbel Wöckel, Marita Koch)
Jena, Germany, August 9, 1980
4 x 400-m: 3:15.17
USSR (Tatyana Ledovskaya, Irina

Potsdam, Germany, September 9, 1988
Heptathlon: 7,291 points
Jacqueline Joyner-Kersee (US)
Seoul, South Korea, September 23–24, 1988
100-m hurdles: 12.69 sec.; high jump: 1.86 m (6 ft. $1\frac{1}{4}$ in); shot: 15.80 m (51 ft. 10 in); 200 m: 22.56 sec.; long jump: 7.27 m (23 ft. $10\frac{1}{4}$ in); javelin: 45.66 m (149 ft. 10 in); 800 m: 2 min. 8.51 sec.

MEN'S INDOOR RUNNING RECORDS

Track performances around a turn must be made on a track of circumference no longer than 200 meters.

50 m: 5.56
Donovan Bailey (Canada)
Reno, Nevada, February 9, 1996
(Set at high altitude. Best at low altitude: 5.61 sec., Manfred Kokot [East Germany], Berlin, Germany, February 4, 1973 and James Sanford [US], San Diego, California, February 20, 1981.)
60 m: 6.39
Maurice Greene (US)
Madrid, Spain, February 3, 1998
200 m: 19.92
Frank Fredericks (Namibia)
Liévin, France, February 18, 1996
400 m: 44.63
Michael Johnson (US)

Karsten Just, Thomas Schönlebe)
Seville, Spain, March 10, 1991
5,000-m walk: 18:07.08
Mikhail Shchennikov (Russia)
Moscow, Russia, February 14, 1995

Field Events

High Jump: 2.43 m (7 ft. $11\frac{1}{2}$ in)
Javier Sotomayor (Cuba)
Budapest, Hungary, March 4, 1989
Pole Vault: 6.15 m (20 ft. $2\frac{1}{4}$ in)
Sergey Nazarovich Bubka (Ukraine)
Donyetsk, Ukraine, February 21, 1993
Long Jump: 8.79 m (28 ft. $10\frac{1}{4}$ in)
Carl Lewis (US)
New York, January 27, 1984
Triple Jump: 17.83 m (58 ft. 6 in)
Elliecer Urrutia (Cuba)
Sindelfingen, Germany, March 1, 1997
Shot: 22.6674 m (4 ft. $\frac{1}{4}$ in)
Randy Barnes (US)
Los Angeles, California, January 20, 1989
Heptathlon: 6,476 points
Dan O'Brien (US)
Toronto, Canada, March 13–14, 1993
60 m: 6.67 sec.; long jump: 7.84 m (25 ft. 8 in); shot: 16.02 m (52 ft. 6 in); high jump: 2.13 m (7 ft.); 60-m hurdles: 7.85 sec.; pole vault 5.20 m (17 ft.); 1,000 m: 2:57.96

SERGEY BUBKA OF UKRAINE HAS DOMINATED POLE VAULTING FOR OVER 15 YEARS, SETTING NUMEROUS WORLD RECORDS, BOTH INDOORS AND OUT. HE IS THE ONLY ATHLETE, MALE OR FEMALE, TO HAVE WON THE SAME EVENT AT ALL SIX TRACK AND FIELD WORLD CHAMPIONSHIPS.

ASHIA HANSEN OF GREAT BRITAIN SETTING A NEW WOMEN'S INDOOR TRIPLE JUMP WORLD RECORD OF 15.16 M DURING THE EUROPEAN INDOOR CHAMPIONSHIPS IN VALENCIA, SPAIN.

Running

100 m: 10.49
Florence Griffith Joyner (US)
Indianapolis, Indiana, July 16, 1988
200 m: 21.34
Florence Griffith Joyner (US)
Seoul, South Korea, September 29, 1988
400 m: 47.60
Marita Koch (East Germany)
Canberra, Australia, October 6, 1985
800 m: 1:53.28
Jarmila Kratochvílová (Czechoslovakia)
Munich, Germany, July 26, 1983
1,000 m: 2:28.98
Svetlana Masterkova (Russia)
Brussels, Belgium, August 23, 1996
1,500 m: 3:50.46
Qu Yunxia (China)
Beijing, China, September 11, 1993
1 mile: 4:12.56
Svetlana Masterkova (Russia)
Zürich, Switzerland, August 14, 1996
2,000 m: 5:25.36
Sonia O'Sullivan (Ireland)
Edinburgh, Scotland, July 8, 1994
3,000 m: 8:06.11
Wang Junxia (China)
Beijing, China, September 13, 1993
5,000 m: 14:28.09
Jiang Bo (China)
Beijing, China, October 23, 1997

Nazarova, Maria Pinigina, Olga Bryzgina)
Seoul, South Korea, October 1, 1988
4 x 800-m: 7:50.17
USSR (Nadezhda Olizarenko, Lyubov Gurina, Lyudmila Borisova, Irina Podyalovskaya)
Moscow, USSR, August 5, 1984

Field Events

High Jump: 2.09 m (6 ft. $10\frac{1}{4}$ in.)
Stefka Kostadinova (Bulgaria)
Rome, Italy, August 30, 1987
Pole Vault: 4.59 m (15 ft. $\frac{3}{4}$ in.)
Emma George (Australia)
Brisbane, Australia, March 21, 1998
Long Jump: 7.52 m (24 ft. $8\frac{1}{4}$ in.)
Galina Chistyakova (USSR)
Leningrad, USSR, June 11, 1988
Triple Jump: 15.50 m (50 ft. $10\frac{1}{4}$ in.)
Inessa Kravets (Ukraine)
Gothenburg, Sweden, August 10, 1995
Shot: 22.6374 m (74 ft. 3 in.)
Natalya Venedictovna Lisovskaya (USSR)
Moscow, USSR, June 7, 1987
Discus: 76.80 m (252 ft.)
Gabriele Reinsch (East Germany)
Neubrandenburg, Germany, July 9, 1988
Hammer: 73.10 m (239 ft. 10 in.)
Olga Kuzenkova (Russia)
Munich, Germany, June 22, 1997
Javelin: 80.00 m (262 ft. 5 in.)
Petra Felke (East Germany)

Atlanta, Georgia, March 4, 1995
800 m: 1:42.67
Wilson Kipketer (Denmark)
Paris, France, March 9, 1997
1,000 m: 2:15.26
Noureddine Morceli (Algeria)
Birmingham, England, February 22, 1992
1,500 m: 3:31.18
Hicham El Gerrouj (Morocco)
Stuttgart, Germany, February 2, 1997
1 mile: 3:48.45
Hicham El Gerrouj (Morocco)
Ghent, Belgium, February 12, 1997
3,000 m: 7:24.90
Daniel Komen (Kenya)
Budapest, Hungary, February 6, 1998
5,000 m: 12.51.48
Daniel Komen (Kenya)
Stockholm, Sweden, February 19, 1998
50-m hurdles: 6.25
Mark McKoy (Canada)
Kobe, Japan, March 5 ,1986
60-m hurdles: 7.30
Colin Jackson (GB)
Sindelfingen, Germany, March 6, 1994
4 x 200-m: 1:22.11
United Kingdom (Linford Christie, Darren Braithwaite, Ade Mafe, John Regis)
Glasgow, Scotland, March 3, 1991
4 x 400-m: 3:03.05
Germany (Rico Lieder, Jens Carlowitz,

WOMEN'S INDOOR RUNNING RECORDS

50 m: 5.96
Irina Privalova (Russia)
Madrid, Spain, February 9, 1995
60 m: 6.92
Irina Privalova (Russia)
Madrid, Spain, February 9, 1995
200 m: 21.87
Merlene Ottey (Jamaica)
Liévin, France, February 13, 1993
400 m: 49.59
Jarmila Kratochvílová (Czechoslovakia)
Milan, Italy, March 7, 1982
800 m: 1:56.36
Maria Lurdes Mutola (Mozambique)
Liévin, France, February 22, 1998
1,000 m: 2:31.23
Maria Lurdes Mutola (Mozambique)
Stockholm, Sweden, February 25, 1996
1,500 m: 4:00.27
Doina Melinte (Romania)
East Rutherford, New Jersey, February 9, 1990
1 mile: 4:17.14
Doina Melinte (Romania)
East Rutherford, New Jersey, February 9, 1990
3,000 m: 8:33.82
Helly van Hulst (Netherlands)
Budapest, Hungary, March 4, 1989

5,000 m: 15:03.17
Elizabeth McColgan (GB)
Birmingham, England, February 22, 1992
50 m hurdles: 6.58
Cornelia Oschkenat (East Germany)
Berlin, Germany, February 20, 1988
60 m hurdles: 7.69
Lyudmila Narozhilenko (Russia)
Chelyabinsk, Russia, February 4, 1993
4 x 200 m: 1:32.55
S. C. Eintracht Hamm (West Germany)
(Helga Arendt, Silke-Beate Knoll, Mechthild Kluth, Gisela Kinzel)
Dortmund, Germany, February 19, 1988
4 x 400 m: 3:26.84
Russia (Tatyana Chebykina, Olga Goncharenko, Olga Kotlyarova, Tatyana Alekseyeva)
Paris, France, March 9, 1997
3,000 m walk: 11:44.00
Alina Ivanova (Ukraine)
Moscow, Russia, February 7, 1992
FIELD EVENTS
High jump: 2.07 m (6 ft. $9\frac{1}{2}$ in)
Heike Henkel (Germany)
Karlsruhe, Germany, February 9, 1992
Pole vault: 4.55 m (14 ft. 11 in)
Emma George (Australia)
Adelaide, Australia, March 26, 1998
Long jump: 7.37 m (24 ft. $2\frac{1}{4}$ in)
Heike Drechsler (East Germany)

SPRINTER MAURICE GREEN (US), WINNER OF THE 1997 100-M WORLD CHAMPIONSHIP TITLE, CONTINUED HIS GOOD FORM INTO THE 1997/98 INDOOR SEASON, SETTING A NEW 60-M WORLD RECORD IN MADRID IN FEBRUARY.

Vienna, Austria, February 13, 1988
Triple jump: 15.16 m (49 ft. $8\frac{3}{4}$ in)
Ashia Hansen (GB)
Valencia, Spain, February 28, 1998
Shot: 22.50 m (73 ft. 10 in)
Helena Fibingerová (Czechoslovakia)
Jablonec, Czechoslovakia, February 19, 1977
Pentathlon: 4,991 points
Irina Belova (Russia)
Berlin, Germany, February 14–15, 1992
60-m hurdles: 8.22 sec.; high jump: 1.93 m (6 ft. $3\frac{1}{4}$ in); shot: 13.25 m (50 ft. $5\frac{1}{2}$ in); long jump: 6.67 m (21 ft. 10 in); 800 m: 2:10.26
u=unratified

badminton

World Badminton Records
World Championships
The most wins at the men's World Team Badminton Championships for the Thomas Cup (instituted 1948) is 10, by Indonesia (1958, 1961, 1964, 1970, 1973, 1976, 1979, 1984, 1994 and 1996).
The most wins at the women's World Team Badminton Championships for the Uber Cup (instituted 1956) is five by: Japan (1966, 1969, 1972, 1978 and 1981); and China (1984, 1986, 1988, 1990 and 1992).

baseball

MAJOR LEAGUES
BATTING RECORDS
Average
Career: .367
Ty Cobb (Detroit AL, Philadelphia AL), 1905–28.
Season: .438
Hugh Duffy (Boston NL), 1894.
Runs
Career: 2,245
Ty Cobb, 1905–28.
Season: 196
Billy Hamilton (Philadelphia NL), 1894.
Home runs
Career: 755
Hank Aaron (Milwaukee NL, Atlanta NL, Milwaukee AL), 1954–76.
Season: 61
Roger Maris (New York AL), 1961.
Runs batted in
Career: 2,297
Hank Aaron, 1954–76.
Season: 190
Hack Wilson (Chicago NL), 1930.
Game: 12
James Bottomley (St. Louis NL), September16 , 1924; Mark Whiten (St. Louis NL), September 7, 1993.
Inning: 7
Edward Cartwright (St. Louis AL), September 23, 1890.
Base hits
Career: 4,256
Pete Rose (Cincinnati NL, Philadelphia NL, Montreal NL, Cincinnati NL), 1963–86.
Season: 257
George (St. Louis AL), 1920.
Total bases
Career: 6,856
Hank Aaron, 1954–76.
Season: 457
Babe Ruth (New York AL), 1921.
Consecutive hits: 12
Pinky Higgins (Boston AL), June 19–21, 1938; Moose Dropo (Detroit AL), July 14–15, 1952.
Consecutive games batted safely: 56
Joe DiMaggio (New York AL), May 15–July 16, 1941.
Stolen bases
Career: 1,259 (as of June 17, 1998)
Rickey Henderson (Oakland AL, New York AL, Oakland AL, Toronto AL, Oakland AL, San Diego NL, Anaheim AL, Oakland AL), 1979–98.
Season: 130
Rickey Henderson (Oakland AL), 1982.
Consecutive games played: 2,549
Cal Ripken Jr. (Baltimore AL), May 30, 1982–June 17, 1998.
PITCHING
Games won
Career: 511
Cy Young (Cleveland NL, St. Louis NL, Boston AL, Cleveland AL, Boston NL), 1890–1911.
Season: 60
"Old Hoss" Radbourn (Providence NL), 1884.
Consecutive games won: 24
Carl Hubbell (New York NL), 1936–37.
Shutouts
Career: 110
Walter Johnson (Washington AL), 1907–27.

CAL RIPKEN HAS PLAYED IN EVERY GAME FOR THE BALTIMORE ORIOLES FOR NEARLY 16 YEARS, PLAYING A STAGGERING TOTAL OF MORE THAN 2,500 GAMES.

Season: 16
George Bradley (St. Louis NL), 1876; Grover Alexander (Philadelphia NL), 1916.
Strikeouts
Career: 5,714
Nolan Ryan (New York NL, California AL, Houston NL, Texas AL), 1966–93.
Season: 383
Nolan Ryan (California AL), 1973. (513 Matt Kilroy (Baltimore AA), 1886).
Game (9 innings)**:** 20
Roger Clemens (Boston AL) v. Seattle, April 29, 1986 and v. Detroit, September 18, 1996.
Kerry Wood (Chicago NL) v. Houston, May 6, 1998
No-hit games
Career: 7
Nolan Ryan, 1973–91.
Earned run average
Season: 0.96 Dutch Leonard (222 inns) (Boston AL), 1914;
1.12 Bob Gibson (305 inns) (St. Louis NL), 1968.
WORLD SERIES RECORDS
Most series played: 14
Yogi Berra (New York, AL), 1947–63
Most series played by pitcher: 11
Whitey Ford (New York, AL), 1950–64
Most home runs in a game: 3
Babe Ruth (New York, AL), October 6, 1926 and 9 October 1928; and Reggie Jackson (New York, AL), October 18, 1977
Runs batted in: 6
Bobby Richardson (New York, AL), October 8, 1960
Strikeouts: 17
Bob Gibson (St. Louis, NL), October 2, 1968
Perfect game: (9 innings)
Don Larson (New York, AL) v. Brooklyn, October 8, 1956
AL - American League
NL - National League

canoeing

Most titles, World and Olympic
Including Olympics, 26 world titles have been won by Birgit Schmidt (East Germany/Germany), 1979–96. The men's record is 13 by Gert Fredriksson, 1948–60, Rüdiger Helm (East Germany), 1976–83, and Ivan Patzaichin (Romania), 1968–84.
Highest speed
The German four-man kayak Olympic champions in 1992 in Barcelona, Spain, covered 1000 m in 2 min. 52.17 sec.
Canoe raft
A raft of 649 kayaks and canoes, organized by the United States Canoe Association, was held together by hands only, while free floating for 30 seconds, on the Rock River, Byron, Illinois, on August 17, 1996.

cricket

Individual Cricket Records
FIRST-CLASS (FC) AND TEST CAREER
BATTING
Most runs: FC 61,237
Sir Jack Hobbs (1882–1963) (av. 50.65) Surrey/England, 1905–34
Test: 11,174 Allan Border (av. 50.56) Australia (156 Tests), 1978–94
Most centuries: FC 197
Sir Jack Hobbs (in 1,315 innings), Surrey/England, 1905–34
Test: 34 Sunil Gavaskar (in 214 innings), India, 1971–87

Highest average: FC 95.14
Sir Donald Bradman, NSW/South Australia/Australia, 1927–49 (28,067 runs in 338 innings, including 43 not outs)
Test: 99.94
Sir Donald Bradman (6,996 runs in 80 innings), Australia (52 Tests), 1928–48
Bowling
Most wickets: FC 4,187
Wilfred Rhodes (av. 16.71), Yorkshire/England, 1898–1930
Test: 434
Kapil Dev Nikhanj (av. 29.62), India (131 Tests), 1978–94
Lowest average: Test 10.75
George Lohmann (112 wickets), England (18 Tests), 1886–96
(min. 25 wickets)
Wicket-keeping
Most dismissals: FC 1,649
Robert Taylor, Derbyshire/England, 1960–88
Test: 355
Rodney Marsh, Australia (96 Tests), 1970–84
Most catches: FC 1,473
Robert Taylor, Derbyshire/England, 1960–88
Test: 343
Rodney Marsh, Australia, 1970–84

Wicket-keeping
Most dismissals: 28
Rodney Marsh (all caught), Australia v. England (5), 1982/83
Most stumpings: 9
Percy Sherwell, South Africa v. Australia (5), 1910/11
Fielding
Most catches: 15
Jack Gregory, Australia v. England (5), 1920/21
All-round
400 runs/30 wickets 475/34, George Giffen (1859–1927), Australia v. England (5), 1894/95

cycling

World Cycling Records
These records are those recognized by the Union Cycliste Internationale (UCI). From January 1, 1993, their list no longer distinguished between those set by professionals and by amateurs, indoor and outdoor records, or records set at altitude and sea level.

Bordeaux, France, April 29, 1995
Unpaced flying start
200 m: 10.831
Olga Slyusareva (Russia)
Moscow, Russia, April 25, 1993
500 m: 29.655
Erika Salumäe (USSR)
Moscow, USSR, August 6, 1987

darts

24-Hour Scoring Records
Men
(8 players): 1,722,249
Broken Hill Darts Club in Broken Hill, NSW, Australia, 28–29 September 1985.
Women
(8 players): 830,737
By a team from the Cornwall Inn, Killurin, Ireland, August 1–2, 1997.
Individual: 567,145
Kenny Fellowes , The Prince of Wales, Cashes Green, England, September 28–29, 1996.
Bulls and 25s: (8 players) 526,750 by a team at the George Inn, Morden, England, July 1–2, 1994.

soccer

International Soccer Competitions
Most Wins
NATIONAL LEVEL
Olympic Games (1896)
(unofficial until 1908): 3
Great Britain 1900, 1908, 1912
Hungary, 1952, 1964, 1968
S. American Championships (1910)
(Copa America since 1975): 15
Argentina, 1910, 1921, 1925, 1927, 1929, 1937, 1941, 1945–47, 1955, 1957, 1959, 1991, 1993
Asian Cup (1956): 3
Iran, 1968, 1972, 1976
Saudi Arabia 1984, 1988, 1996
African Cup of Nations (1957): 4
Ghana, 1963, 1965, 1978, 1982
Egypt, 1957, 1959, 1986, 1998
European Championships (1958): 3
West Germany/Germany, 1972, 1980, 1996
Club level
World Club Championship (1960): 3
Peñarol (Uruguay), 1961, 1966, 1982
Nacional (Uruguay), 1971, 1980, 1988
Milan (Italy), 1969, 1989, 1990

CHRIS BOARDMAN IN ACTION IN THE 1996 WORLD INDOOR CHAMPIONSHIPS, DURING WHICH HE BETTERED THE WORLD RECORD TIME FOR THE 4,000 M INDIVIDUAL PURSUIT BY MORE THAN NINE SECONDS.

RONALDO PLAYING FOR BARCELONA DURING THE 1997 EUROPEAN CUP WINNERS' CUP FINAL AGAINST AJAX, BEFORE HIS RECORD-BREAKING TRADE TO INTER MILAN. BARCELONA WON 1–0, WINNING FOR A RECORD FOURTH TIME.

Most stumpings: FC 418
Leslie Ames, Kent/England, 1926–51
Test: 52
William Oldfield, Australia (54 Tests), 1920–37
Fielding
Most catches: FC 1,018
Frank Woolley, Kent/England, 1906–38
Test: 156
Allan Border, Australia (156 Tests), 1978–94
TEST SERIES
Batting
Most runs: 974
Sir Donald Bradman (av. 139.14), Australia v. England (5), 1930
Most centuries: 5
Sir Clyde Leopold Walcott, West Indies v. Australia (5), 1954/55
Highest average: 563.00
Walter Hammond, England v. New Zealand (2), 1932/33
(563 runs, 2 inns, 1 not out)
Bowling
Most wickets: 49
Sydney Barnes (av. 10.93), England v. South Africa (4), 1913/14
Lowest average: 5.80
George Alfred Lohmann (35 wickets), England v. South Africa (3), 1895/96
(min. 20 wickets)

Men
Unpaced standing start
1 km: 1:00.613
Shane Kelly (Australia)
Bogotá, Colombia, September 26, 1995
4 km: 4:11.114
Chris Boardman (GB)
Manchester, England, August 29, 1996
4 km team: 4:00.958
Italy
Manchester, England, August 31, 1996
1 hour (kms): 55.291
Tony Rominger (Switzerland)
Bordeaux, France, November 6, 1994
Unpaced flying start
200 m: 9.865
Curtis Harnett (Canada)
Bogotá, Colombia, September 28, 1995
500 m: 26.649
Aleksandr Kiritchenko (USSR)
Moscow, USSR, October 29, 1988
Women
Unpaced standing start
500 m: 33.438
Galina Yenyukhina (Russia)
Moscow, Russia, April 29, 1993
3 km: 3:30.974
Marion Clignet (France)
Manchester, England, August 31, 1996
1 hour (kms): 47.112
Catherine Marsal (France)

10-Hour Scoring Records
Most trebles: 3,056 (from 7,992 darts)
Paul Taylor, Woodhouse Tavern, London, England, October 19, 1985.
Most doubles: 3,265 (from 8,451 darts)
Paul Taylor, Lord Brooke, London, England, September 5, 1987.
Highest score: 465,919
(retrieving own darts)
Jon Archer and Neil Rankin, Royal Oak, Cossington, England, November 17, 1990.
Bulls (individual) 1,321: Jim Damore, Parkside Pub, Chicago, Illinois, June 29, 1996
6-Hour Scoring Records
Men: 210,172
Russell Locke, Hugglescote Working Men's Club, Coalville, England, September 10, 1989.
Women: 99,725
Karen Knightly, Lord Clyde, London, England, March 17, 1991.
Million and One Up
Men: (8 players) 36,583 darts
Team at Buzzy's Pub and Grub, Lynn, Massachusetts, October 19–20, 1991.
Women: (8 players) 70,019 darts
"Delinquents" team, Top George, Combe Martin, England, September 11–13, 1987.

Europe
UEFA Cup (1955): 3
Barcelona (Spain), 1958, 1960, 1966
European Cup (1956): 7
Real Madrid, 1956–60, 1966, 1998
Cup Winners Cup (1960): 4
Barcelona, 1979, 1982, 1989, 1997
South America
Copa Libertadores (1960): 7
Independiente (Argentina), 1964–65, 1972–75, 1984
Africa
Cup of Champion Clubs (1964): 4
Zamalek (Egypt), 1984, 1986, 1993, 1996
Cup Winners Cup (1975): 4
Al Alhy Cairo (Egypt), 1984–86, 1993

soaring

World Soaring Single-Seater Records
Straight Distance: 1;460.8 km
(907 miles 1,232 yd.)
Hans-Werner Grosse (West Germany)
Lübeck, Germany, to Biarritz, France, April 25, 1972

Declared Goal Distance: 1,383 km (859 miles 704 yd.)
Gérard Herbaud (France), Vinon, France, to Fes, Morocco, April 17, 1992
Jean Nöel Herbaud (France), Vinon, France, to Fes, Morocco, April 17, 1992
Goal and Return: 1,646.68 km (1,023 miles 352 yd.)
Thomas L. Knauff (US)
Williamsport, Pennsylvania to Knoxville, Tennessee, April 25, 1983
Absolute Altitude: 14,938 m (49,009 ft.)
Robert R. Harris (US)
California, February 17, 1986
Height Gain: 12,894 m (42,303 ft.)
Paul F. Bikle (US)
Mojave, California, February 25, 1961
SPEED OVER TRIANGULAR COURSE
100 km: 217.41 km/h (135.09 mph)
James Payne (US)
California, March 4, 1997
300 km: 176.99 km/h (109.97 mph)
Beat Bünzli (Switzerland)
Bitterwasser, Namibia, November 14, 1985
500 km: 171.7 km/h (106.7 mph)
Hans-Werner Grosse (West Germany)
Mount Newman, Australia, December 31, 1990
750 km: 161.33 km/h (100.24 mph)
Hans-Werner Grosse (West Germany)
Alice Springs, Australia, January 10, 1988
1,250 km: 143.46 km/h (89.14 mph)
Hans-Werner Grosse (West Germany)
Alice Springs, Australia, January 10, 1987

golf

World Golf Records
Most Major Golf Titles
The British Open: 6
Harry Vardon 1896, 1898–89, 1903, '11, '14
The British Amateur: 8
John Ball 1888, '90, '92, '94, '99, 1907, '10, '12
US Open: 4
Willie Anderson 1901, '03–05
Bobby Jones Jr. 1923, '26, '29–30
Ben Hogan 1948, '50–51, '53
Jack Nicklaus 1962, '67, '72, '80
US Amateur: 5
Bobby Jones Jr.: 1924–25, '27–28, '30
PGA Championship: 5
Walter Hagan 1921, '24–27
Jack Nicklaus 1963, '71, '73, '75, '80
The Masters: 6
Jack Nicklaus 1963, '65–66, '72, '75, '86
US Women's Open: 4
Betsy Earle-Rawls 1951, '53, '57, '60
Mickey Wright 1958–59, '61, '64
US Women's Amateur: 6
Glenna Collett Vare 1922, '25, '28–30, '35
British Women's: 4
Charlotte Pitcairn Leitch 1914, '20–21, '26
Joyce Wethered 1922, '24–25, '29
Note: Jack Nicklaus is the only golfer to have won five different major titles (British Open, US Open, Masters, PGA and US Amateur titles) twice and a record 20 overall (1959–86).
In 1930, Bobby Jones achieved a unique "Grand Slam" of the US and British Open and Amateur titles.

Jack Nicklaus has won an unprecedented number of Majors. Despite the fact that his primary occupation is now course design, his success in playing the game continues, illustrated by his finishing 6th at the 1998 Masters.

hang gliding

Hang Gliding World Records
The Fédération Aéronautique Internationale recognizes world records for rigidwing, flexwing and multiplace flexwing. These records are the greatest in each category.
Greatest distance in straight line: 495 km (307 miles 880 yd.), Larry Tudor (US), from Rock Springs, Wyoming to Stoneham, Colorado, June 30, 1994.
Height gain: 4.343 km (14,250 ft.), Larry Tudor (US), Horseshoe Meadows, California, August 4, 1985.
Greatest distance (woman): 335.8 km (208 miles 1,056 yd.), Kari Castle (US), over Lone Pine, California, July 22, 1991.
Height gain (woman): 3.97 km (13,025 ft.), Judy Leden (GB) Kuruman, South Africa, December 1, 1992.
World Championships
The World Team Championships (officially instituted 1976) have been won most often by Great Britain (1981, 1985, 1989 and 1991).

field hockey

World Field Hockey Records
World Cup
The most women's wins is five by the Netherlands, 1974, 1978, 1983, 1986 and 1990. The most men's wins is four by Pakistan, 1971, 1978, 1982 and 1994.
Most Olympic medals
India was Olympic champion from the reintroduction of Olympic hockey in 1928 until 1960. They had their eighth win in 1980. Of the six Indians who have won three Olympic team gold medals, two have also won a silver medal – Leslie Walter Claudius, in 1948, 1952, 1956 and 1960 (silver), and Udham Singh, in 1952, 1956, 1964 and 1960 (silver).
Most Olympic titles
A women's tournament was added in 1980, and Australia has won twice – in 1988 and 1996.
Champions' Trophy
The most wins is six, by Australia, 1983–85, 1989–90 and 1993. The first women's Champions' Trophy was held in 1987, Australia has won four times, 1991, 1993, 1995 and 1997.

The Australian hockey team defending their goal during the 1996 Olympics tournament, where they became the first nation to win the women's hockey Olympic gold twice, having previously won in 1988.

horse racing

Major Race Records
Derby (1780) (UK)
Record time: 2 min. 32.31 sec.
Lammtarra 1995
Most wins (jockey): 9
Lester Piggott 1954, '57, '60, '68, '70, '72, '76, '77, '83
Most wins (trainer): 7
Robert Robson 1793, 1802, '09, '10, '15, '17, '23
John Porter 1868, '82, '83, '86, '90, '91, '99
Fred Darling 1922, '25, '26, '31, '38, '40, '41
Most wins (owner): 5
Earl of Egremont 1782, '34, 1804, '05, '07, '26
Aga Khan III 1930, '35, '36, '48, '52
2000 GUINEAS (1809) (UK)
Record time: 1 min. 35.08 sec.
Mister Baileys 1994
Most wins (jockey): 9
Jem Robinson 1825, '28, '31, '33, '34, '35, '36, '47, '48
Most wins (trainer): 7
John Scott 1842, '43, '49, '53, '56, '60, '62
Most wins (owner): 5
Duke of Grafton 1820, '21, '22, '26, '27
Earl of Jersey 1831, '34, '35, '36, '37
1000 GUINEAS (1814) (UK)
Record time: 1 min. 36.71 sec.
Las Meninas 1994
Most wins (jockey): 7
George Fordham 1859, '61, '65, '68, '69, '81, '83
Most wins (trainer): 9
Robert Robson 1818, '19, '20, '21, '22, '23, '25, '26, '27
Most wins (owner): 8
Duke of Grafton 1819, '20, '21, '22, '23, '25, '26, '27
OAKS (1779) (UK)
Record time: 2 min. 34.19 sec.
Intrepidity 1993
Most wins (jockey): 9
Frank Buckle 1797, '98, '99, 1802, '03, '05, '17, '18, '23
Most wins (trainer): 12
Robert Robson 1802, '04, '05, '07, '08, '09, '13, '15, '18, '22, '23, '25
Most wins (owner): 6
Duke of Grafton 1813, '15, '22, '23, '28, '31
ST. LEGER (UK)
Record time: 3 min. 01.6 sec.
Coronach 1926 and *Windsor Lad* 1934
Most wins (jockey): 9
Bill Scott 1821, '25, '28, '29, '38, '39, '40, '41, '46
Most wins (trainer): 16
John Scott 1827, '28, '29, '32, '34, '38, '39, '40, '41, '45, '51, '53, '56, '57, '59, '62
Most wins (owner): 7
9th Duke of Hamilton 1786, '87, '88, '92, 1808, '09, '14
KING GEORGE VI AND QUEEN ELIZABETH DIAMOND STAKES (UK)
Record time: 2 min. 26.98 sec. *Grundy* 1975
Most wins (jockey): 7
Lester Piggott 1965, '66, '69, '70, '74, '77, '84
Most wins (trainer): 5
Dick Hern 1972, '79, '80, '85, '89
Most wins (owner): 3
Sheikh Mohammed 1990, '93, '94
PRIX DE L'ARC DE TRIOMPHE (France)
Record time: 2 min. 24.6 sec.
Peintre Célèbre 1997
Most wins (jockey): 4
Jacques Doyasbère 1942, '44, '50, '51
Frédéric Head 1966, '72, '76, '79
Yves St.-Martin 1970, '74, '82, '84
Pat Eddery 1980, '85, '86, '87

Most wins (trainer): 4
Charles Semblat 1942, '44, '46, '49
Alec Head 1952, '59, '76, '81
François Mathet 1950, '51, '70, '82
Most wins (owner): 6
M. Boussac 1936, '37, '42, '44, '46, '49
VRC MELBOURNE CUP (Australia)
Record time: 3 min. 16.3 sec.
Kingston Rule 1990
Most wins (jockey): 4
Bobby Lewis 1902, '15, '19, '27
Harry White 1974, '75, '78, '79
Most wins (trainer): 10
Bart Cummings 1965, '66, '67, '74, '75, '77, '79, '90, '91, '96
Most wins (owner): 4
Etienne de Mestre 1861, '62, '67, '78
KENTUCKY DERBY
Record time: 1 min. 59.4 sec.
Secretariat 1973
Most wins (jockey): 5
Eddie Arcaro 1938, '41, '45, '48, '52
Bill Hartack 1957, '60, '62, '64, '69
Most wins (trainer): 6
Ben Jones 1938, '41, '44, '48, '49, '52
Most wins (owner): 8
Calumet Farm 1941, '44, '48, '49, '52, '57, '58, '68
IRISH DERBY (Ireland)
Record time: 2 min. 25.60 sec.
St. Jovite 1992
Most wins (jockey): 6
Morny Wing 1921, '23, '30, '38, '42, '46
Most wins (trainer): 6
Vincent O'Brien 1953, '57, '70, '77, '84, '85
Most wins (owner): 5
Aga Khan III 1925, '32, '40, '48, '49
JUMPING
GRAND NATIONAL (UK)
Record time: 8 min. 47.8 sec.
Mr. Frisk 1990
Most wins (jockey): 5
George Stevens 1856, '63, '64, '69, '70
Most wins (trainer): 4
Fred Rimell 1956, '61, '70, '76
Most wins (owner): 3
James Machell 1873, '74, '76
Sir Charles Assheton-Smith 1893, 1912, '13
Noel Le Mare 1973, '74, '77
CHELTENHAM GOLD CUP (UK)
Record time: 6 min. 23.4 sec.
Silver Fame 1951
Most wins (jockey): 4
Pat Taaffe 1964, '65, '66, '68
Most wins (trainer): 5
Tom Dreaper 1946, '64, '65, '66, '68
Most wins (owner): 7
Dorothy Paget 1932, '33, '34, '35, '36, '40, '52
CHAMPION HURDLE (UK)
Record time: 3 min. 48.4 sec.
Make A Stand 1997

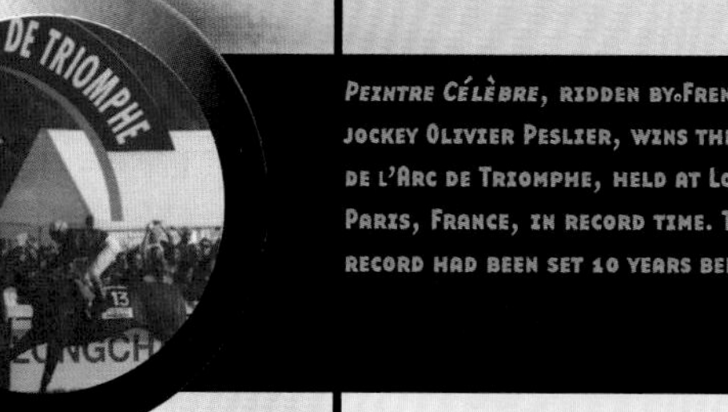

Peintre Célèbre, ridden by French jockey Olivier Peslier, wins the 1997 Prix de l'Arc de Triomphe, held at Longchamps, Paris, France, in record time. The previous record had been set 10 years before.

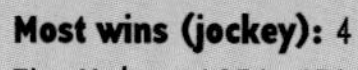

Most wins (jockey): 4
Tim Molony 1951, '52, '53, '54
Most wins (trainer): 5
Peter Easterby 1967, '76, '77, '80, '81
Most wins (owner): 4
Dorothy Paget 1932, '33, '40, '46

hurling

World Hurling Records
Most titles
The greatest number of All-Ireland Championships won by one team is 27 by Cork between 1890 and 1990.
Most appearances
The most appearances in All-Ireland finals is 10, shared by Christy Ring (Cork and Munster), John Doyle (Tipperary) and Frank Cummings (Kilkenny). Ring and Doyle also share the record of All-Ireland medals won, with eight each. Ring's appearances on the winning side were in 1941–44, 46 and 52–54, while Doyle's were in 1949–51, 58, 61–62 and 64–65. Ring also played in a record 22 interprovincial finals (1942–63) and was on the winning side 18 times.

World Gaelic Football Records
All-Ireland Championships
The greatest number of All-Ireland Championships won by one team is 31 by Kerry between 1903 and 1997. The greatest number of successive wins is four by Wexford (1915–18) and Kerry twice (1929–32, 1978–81).
The highest team score in a final was when Dublin, 27 (5 goals, 12 points), beat Armagh, 15 (3 goals, 6 points), on September 25, 1977.
The highest combined score was 45 points when Cork (26) beat Galway (19) in 1973.

lacrosse

World Lacrosse Records
Most World titles
The US has won six of the seven World Championships, in 1967, 1974, 1982, 1986, 1990 and 1994. Canada won the other world title in 1978 beating the US 17–16 after extra time – this was the first tied international match.

World Championships/World Cup/Women
The first World Cup was held in 1982, replacing the World Championships which had been held three times since 1969. The US has won four times, in 1974, 1982, 1989 and 1993.
Highest scores/Men
The highest score in a World Cup match is Scotland's 34–3 win over Germany in Manchester, England on July 25, 1994. In the World Cup Premier Division, the record score is the United States' 33–2 win over Japan in Manchester, England, on July 21, 1994.
Highest score/Women
The highest score by an international team was by Great Britain and Ireland with their 40–0 defeat of Long Island during their 1967 tour of the US.

powerlifting

World Powerlifting Records
(All weights in kilograms)
Men
52 kg
Squat: 277.5
Andrzej Stanaszek (Poland), 1997
Bench press: 177.5
Andrzej Stanaszek, 1994
Deadlift: 256
E. S. Bhaskaran (India), 1993
Total: 592.5
Andrzej Stanaszek, 1996
56 kg
Squat: 287.5
Magnus Carlsson (Sweden), 1996
Bench press:187.5
Magnus Carlsson, 1996
Deadlift: 289.5
Lamar Gant (US), 1982
Total: 637.5
Hu Chun-hsing (Taipei), 1997
60 kg
Squat: 295.5
Magnus Carlsson, 1994
Bench press: 185
Magnus Carlsson, 1997
Deadlift: 310
Lamar Gant,1988
Total: 707.5
Joe Bradley, 1982
67.5 kg
Squat: 303
Wade Hooper (US), 1997
Bench press: 200.5
Aleksey Sivokon (Kazakhstan), 1997
Deadlift: 316
Daniel Austin (US), 1991
Total: 765
Aleksey Sivokon, 1994
75 kg
Squat: 328
Ausby Alexander (US), 1989
Bench press: 217.5
James Rouse (US), 1980
Deadlift: 337.5
Daniel Austin, 1994
Total: 850
Rick Gaugler (US), 1982
82.5 kg
Squat: 379.5
Mike Bridges (US), 1982
Bench press: 240
Mike Bridges, 1981
Deadlift: 357.5
Veli Kumpuniemi (Finland), 1980
Total: 952.5
Mike Bridges, 1982
90 kg
Squat: 375
Fred Hatfield (US), 1980
Bench press:255
Mike MacDonald (US), 1980
Deadlift: 372.5
Walter Thomas (US), 1982
Total: 937.5
Mike Bridges, 1980
100 kg
Squat: 423
Ed Coan (US), 1994
Bench press: 261.5
Mike MacDonald, 1977
Deadlift: 390
Ed Coan, 1993
Total: 1035
Ed Coan, 1994
110 kg
Squat: 415
Kirk Karwoski (US), 1994
Bench press: 270
Jeffrey Magruder (US), 1982
Deadlift: 395
John Kuc (US), 1980
Total: 1,000
John Kuc, 1980
125 kg
Squat: 455
Kirk Karwoski, 1995
Bench press: 278.5
Tom Hardman (US), 1982
Deadlift: 387.5
Lars Norén (Sweden), 1987
Total: 1,045
Kirk Karwoski, 1995
125+ kg
Squat: 447.5
Shane Hamman (US), 1994
Bench press: 322.5

Lacrosse is the modern version of the Native American game of baggataway, played long before the arrival of Columbus. Europeans in Canada began playing the game in the 1840s, and in 1867 it became Canada's national game.

James Henderson (US), 1997
Deadlift: 406
Lars Norén, 1988
Total: 1,100
Bill Kazmaier (US), 1981
Women
44 kg
Squat: 162.5
Raija Koskinen (Finland), 1997
Bench press: 85
Svetlana Tesleva (Russia), 1996
Deadlift: 165.5
Anna-Liisa Prinkkala (Finland), 1998
Total: 397.5
Raija Koskinen, 1997
48 kg
Squat: 171
Raija Koskinen, 1997
Bench press: 100
Marlina (Indonesia), 1997
Deadlift: 182.5
Majic Jones (US), 1984
Total: 415
Yelena Yamkich (Russia), 1997
52 kg
Squat: 182.5
Oksana Belova (Russia), 1997
Bench press: 107.5
Anna Olsson (Sweden), 1997
Deadlift: 197.5
Diana Rowell (US) 1984
Total: 475
Oksana Belova, 1997
56 kg
Squat: 191.5
Carrie Boudreau (US), 1995
Bench press: 122.5
Valentina Nelubova (Russia), 1997
Deadlift: 222.5
Carrie Boudreau, 1995
Total: 522.5
Carrie Boudreau, 1995
60 kg
Squat: 210
Beate Amdahl (Norway), 1993
Bench press: 118
Helena Heiniluoma (Finland), 1996
Deadlift: 213.5
Ingeborg Marx (Belgium), 1997
Total: 525
Ingeborg Marx, 1997
67.5 kg
Squat: 230
Ruthi Shafer (US), 1984
Bench press: 120
Vicki Steenrod (US), 1990
Deadlift: 244
Ruthi Shafer, 1984
Total: 572.5
Lisa Sjöstrand (Sweden), 1997

75 kg
Squat: 245
Anne Sigrid Stiklestad (Norway), 1997
Bench press: 145.5
Marina Zhguleva (Russia), 1997
Deadlift: 252.5
Yelena Sukhoruk, 1995
Total: 605
Yelena Sukhoruk, 1995
82.5 kg
Squat: 242.5
Anne Sigrid Stiklestad (Norway), 1997
Bench press: 151
Natalia Rumyantseva (Russia), 1997
Deadlift: 257.5
Cathy Millen (New Zealand), 1993
Total: 637.5
Cathy Millen, 1993
90 kg
Squat: 260
Cathy Millen, 1994
Bench press: 162.5
Cathy Millen, 1994
Deadlift: 260
Cathy Millen, 1994
Total: 682.5
Cathy Millen, 1994
90+kg
Squat: 277.5
Juanita Trujillo (US), 1994
Bench press: 175
Chao Chen-yeh (Taipei), 1997
Deadlift: 262.5
Katrina Robertson (Australia), 1997
Total: 657.5
Lee Chia-sui (Taipei), 1997

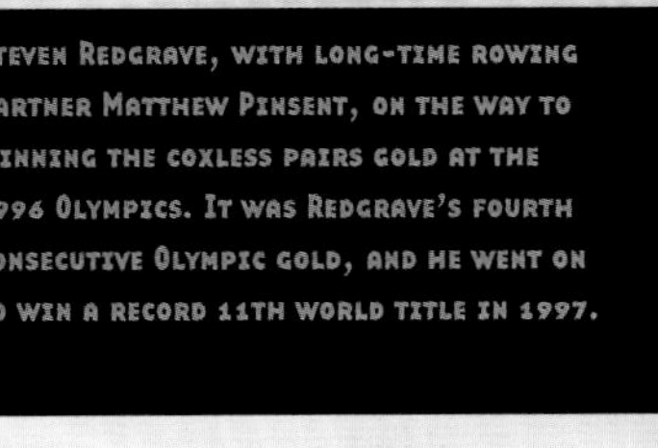

Steven Redgrave, with long-time rowing partner Matthew Pinsent, on the way to winning the coxless pairs gold at the 1996 Olympics. It was Redgrave's fourth consecutive Olympic gold, and he went on to win a record 11th world title in 1997.

rowing

World Rowing Records
World Championships
World Rowing Championships distinct from the Olympic Games were first held in 1962, at first four yearly, but from 1974 annually, except in Olympic years. The most gold medals won at World Championships and Olympic Games is 11 by Steven Redgrave who, in addition to his four Olympic successes, won world titles at coxed pairs 1986, coxless pairs 1987–88, 1991–96, coxless fours 1984 1997. Francesco Esposito (Italy) has won nine titles at lightweight events, coxless pairs, 1980–84, 1988, 1994 and coxless fours, 1990, 1992. At women's events Yelena Tereshina has won a record seven golds, all eights for the USSR, 1978–79, 1981–83 and 1985–86.
The most wins at single sculls is five by: Peter-Michael Kolbe (West Germany), 1975, 1978, 1981, 1983 and 1986; Pertti Karppinen (Finland), 1976, 1979–80 and 1984–85 and three Olympic 1976, 1980 and 1984; Thomas Lange (East Germany/Germany), 1987, 1989 and 1991 and two Olympics 1988 and 1992; and in the women's events by Christine Hahn (née Scheiblich; East Germany), 1974–75, 1977–78 (and the 1976 Olympic title).
Most Olympic golds
The most golds is four by Steven Redgrave (GB), coxed fours (1984), coxless pairs (1988, 1992 and 1996).
Most Olympic golds
The most by women is three, by Canadian pair Kathleen Heddle and Marnie McBean, coxless pairs 1992, eights 1992 and double sculls 1996.
Highest speed
The record time for 2,000 m (1 mile 427 yd.) on non-tidal water is 5 min. 23.90 sec. (22.22 km/h or 13.80 mph) by the Dutch National team (eight) in Duisburg, Germany, on 19 May 1996.
Highest speed
The women's record time for 2,000 m on non-tidal water is 5 min. 58.50 sec. (20.08 km/h or 12.48 mph) by Romania in Duisburg, Germany on May 18, 1996.
Highest speed
The single sculls record is 6 min. 37.03 sec. (18.13 km/h or 11.26 mph) by Juri Jaanson (Estonia) in Lucerne, Switzerland on July 9, 1995.
Highest speed
The single sculls record is 7 min. 17.09 sec. (16.47 km/h or 10.23 mph), Silken Laumann (Canada) in Lucerne, Switzerland, on July 17, 1994.

rugby

World Rugby Records
Rugby League
World Cup
The World Cup competition was first held in 1954. Australia has the most wins, with seven, (1957, 1968, 1970, 1977, 1988, 1992 and 1995) as well as a win in the International Championship of 1975.
International match
The highest score in an international match is Australia's 86–6 defeat of South Africa in Gateshead, England, on October 10, 1995.
Individual international records
The most points scored in a game is 32 by: Andrew Johns (Australia) (2 tries, 12 goals) v. Fiji in Newcastle, NSW, Australia on July 12, 1996 and Bobby Goulding (GB) (3 tries, 10 goals) v. Fiji in Nadi, Fiji, on October 5, 1996.
Jim Sullivan (Wigan) played in most internationals (60 for Wales and Great Britain, 1921–39), kicked most goals (160) and scored most points (329).
Rugby Union Titles
On the three occasions the World Cup has been held, 1987, 1991 and 1995, the winners have been New Zealand, Australia and South Africa respectively.
Highest team score
New Zealand beat Japan 145–17 in Bloemfontein, South Africa, on June 4, 1995. During this match New Zealand scored a record 21 tries.
Most international appearances
Philippe Sella (France) has played in 111 internationals for France, 1982–95.
Internationals
The highest score in any full international is when Hong Kong beat Singapore 164–13 in a World Cup qualifying match in Kuala Lumpur, Malaysia, on October 27, 1994.
The highest aggregate score for any international match between the Four Home Unions is 82, when England beat Wales by 82 points (7 goals, 1 drop goal and 6 tries) to zero in Blackheath, England, on February 19, 1881. (There was no point scoring in 1881.) The highest aggregate score under the modern points system between two of the eight major nations is 93, when New Zealand beat Scotland 62–31 in Dunedin, New Zealand, on June 15, 1996. The highest score by an overseas side in an international in the British Isles is 68 points by South Africa v. Scotland (10) at Murrayfield, Edinburgh, on December 6, 1997.

Percy Montgomery of South Africa on his way to scoring the first try in his team's 68–10 demolition of Scotland, the heaviest defeat in an international by an overseas side in the British Isles.

shooting

Shooting – Individual World Records
In 1986, the International Shooting Union (UIT) introduced new regulations for major championships and world records. Now the leading competitors undertake an additional round with a target subdivided to tenths of a point for rifle and pistol shooting, and an extra 25, 40 or 50 (depending

on category) shots for trap and skeet. Harder targets have since been introduced and the listing below shows the world records, as recognized by the UIT, for the 15 Olympic shooting disciplines, the score for the number of shots specified is in brackets plus the score in the additional round.

Men

Free Rifle 50 m 3 x 40 Shots
1,287.9 (1,186+101.9)
Rajmond Debevec (Slovenia)
Munich, Germany, August 29, 1992

Free Rifle 50 m 60 Shots Prone
704.8 (600 + 104.8)
Christian Klees (Germany)
Atlanta, Georgia, July 25, 1996

Air Rifle 10 m 60 Shots
700.2 (596 + 104.2)
Leif Steinar Rolland (Norway)
Munich, Germany, May 20, 1997

Free Pistol 50 m 60 Shots
675.3 (580 + 95.3)
Taniu Kiriakov (Bulgaria)
Hiroshima, Japan, April 21, 1995

Rapid-Fire Pistol 25 m 60 Shots
699.7 (596 + 107.5)
Ralf Schumann (Germany)
Barcelona, Spain, June 8, 1994

Air Pistol 10 m 60 Shots
695.1 (593 + 102.1)
Sergey Pyzhyanov (USSR)
Munich, Germany, October 13, 1989

Running Target 10 m 30/30 Shots
687.9 (586 + 101.9)
Ling Yang (China)
Milan, Italy, June 6, 1996

Skeet 125 Targets
150 (125 + 25)
Marcello Tittarelli (Italy)
Suhl, Germany, June 11, 1996
Ennio Falco (Italy)
Lonato, Italy, May 13, 1997

Trap 125 Targets
150 (125 + 25)
Jan Henrik Heinrich (Germany)
Lonato, Italy, June 5, 1996
Andrea Benelli (Italy)
Suhl, Germany, June 11, 1996

Double Trap 150 Targets
191 (143 + 48)
Joshua Lakatos (US)
Barcelona, Spain, June 15, 1993

Women

Standard Rifle

50 m 3 x 20 Shots
689.7 (592 + 97.7)
Vessela Letcheva (Bulgaria)
Munich, Germany, June 15, 1995

Air Rifle 10 m 40 Shots
501.5 (398 + 103.5)
Vessela Letcheva (Bulgaria)
Havana, Cuba, April 12, 1996

Sport Pistol

25 m 60 shots
696.2 (594 + 102.2)
Diana Jorgova (Bulgaria)
Milan, Italy, May 31, 1994

Air Pistol 10 m 40 Shots
492.7 (392 + 100.7)
Jasna Sekaric (Yugoslavia)
Nafels, Switzerland, September 22, 1996

Double Trap 120 Targets
149 (113 + 36)
Deborah Gelisio (Italy)
Nicosia, Cyprus, June 19, 1995

CHRISTIAN KLEES ON HIS WAY TO WINNING OLYMPIC GOLD AT THE 1996 GAMES IN THE 50-M FREE RIFLE PRONE EVENT. HAVING SCORED A PERFECT 600 IN THE CLASSIFICATION ROUND, HE WENT ON TO SCORE 104.8 IN THE FINAL ROUND TO SET A WORLD RECORD.

skating

World Speed Skating Records

Men

500 m: 34.82
Hiroyasu Shimizu (Japan)
Calgary, Canada, March 28, 1998

1,000 m: 1:09.60
Sylvain Bouchard (Canada)
Calgary, Canada, December 29, 1997

1,500 m: 1:46.43
Ådne Søndrål (Norway)
Calgary, Canada, March 28, 1998

3,000 m: 3:48.91
Bart Veldkamp (Netherlands)
Calgary, Canada, March 21, 1998

5,000 m:
Gianni Romme (Netherlands)
Calgary, Canada, March 27, 1998

10,000 m: 13:08.71
Gianni Romme (Netherlands)
Calgary, Canada, March 29, 1998

Women

500: 37.55
Catriona Le May Doan (Canada)
Calgary, Canada, December 29, 1997

1,000 m: 1:14.96
Christine Witty (US)
Calgary, Canada, March 28, 1998

1,500: 1:56.93
Anni Friesinger (Germany)
Calgary, Canada, March 29, 1998

3,000 m: 4:01.67
Gunda Niemann-Stirnemann (Germany)
Calgary, Canada, March 27, 1998

5,000: 6:58.63
Gunda Niemann-Stirnemann (Germany)
Calgary, Canada, March 28, 1998

WORLD RECORDS – SHORT TRACK

Men

500 m: 41.938
Nicola Franceschina (Italy)
Bormio, Italy, March 29, 1998

1,000 m: 1:28.23
Marc Gagnon (Canada)
Seoul, South Korea, April 4, 1997

1,500 m: 2:15.50
Kai Feng (China)
Habin, China, November 11, 1997

3,000 m: 4:53.23
Lee Seung-chan (South Korea)
Beijing, China, November 23, 1997

5,000 m relay: 7:00.042
South Korea
Nagano, Japan, March 30, 1997

Women

500 m: 44.867
Isabelle Charset (Canada)
Nagano, Japan, March 29, 1997

1,000 m: 1:31.991
Yang Yang (China)
Nagano, Japan, February 21, 1998

1,500 m: 2:25.17
Kim Yun-mi (South Korea)
Harbin, China, December 2, 1995

3,000 m: 5:02.19
Chun Lee-kyung (South Korea)
Gyovik, Norway, March 19, 1995

3,000-m relay: 4:16.26
South Korea
Nagano, Japan, February 17, 1998

CANADIAN SKATER CATRIONA LE MAY DOAN WINNING THE 500-M RACE DURING THE ICE SPEED WORLD CHAMPIONSHIPS IN BERLIN, GERMANY, WHERE SHE SET A NEW TRACK RECORD. LE MAY DOAN ALSO HOLDS THE WORLD RECORD FOR 500 M, WITH A TIME OF 37.55 SECONDS.

Most Olympic titles/Men
The most Olympic gold medals won by a man is five by: Clas Thunberg (Finland) (including one tied) in 1924 and 1928; and Eric Heiden (US), uniquely at one Games in Lake Placid, New York in 1980. The most medals is seven by Clas Thunberg, who additionally won one silver and one tied bronze; and Ivar Ballangrud (Norway), four gold, two silver and a bronze, 1928–36.

Most Olympic titles/Women
The most Olympic gold medals won in speed skating is six by Lidiya Pavlovna Skoblikova (USSR), in 1960 (two) and 1964 (four). The most medals is eight by Karin Kania (East Germany), three gold, four silver and a bronze, 1980–88.

Most world titles/Men
The greatest number of world overall titles (instituted 1893) won by any skater is five; by Oscar Mathisen (Norway) in 1908–09 and 1912–14; and by Clas Thunberg in 1923, 1925, 1928–29 and 1931. A record six men's sprint overall titles have been won by Igor Zhelezovskiy (USSR/Belarus), 1985–86, 1989 and 1991–93.

The record score achieved for the world overall title is 153.367 points by Ids Postma (Netherlands) in Heerenven, Netherlands, on March 13–15, 1998.

Most world titles/Women
The most titles won in the women's events (instituted 1936) is seven by Gunda Neimann-Stirnemann (Germany), 1991–93 and 1995–98.
The record low women's score is 163.02 points by Gunda Neimann-Stirnemann (Germany), in Heerenven, Netherlands, on March 13–15, 1998.

FIGURE SKATING

Most world titles – Individual
The greatest number of men's individual world figure skating titles (instituted 1896) is 10 by Ulrich Salchow (Sweden), 1901–05 and 1907–11.
The women's record (instituted 1906) is also 10 individual titles by Sonja Henie between 1927 and 1936.

Most world titles – Pairs
Irina Rodnina won 10 pairs titles (instituted 1908), four with Aleksey Nikolayevich Ulanov, 1969–72, and six with her husband Aleksandr Gennadyevich Zaitsev, 1973–78.
The most ice dance titles (instituted 1952) won is six, by Lyudmila Alekseyevna Pakhomova and her husband Aleksandr Georgiyevich Gorshkov (USSR), 1970–74 and 1976. They also won the first ever Olympic ice dance title in 1976.

Triple Crown
Karl Schäfer (Austria) and Sonja Henie achieved double "Grand Slams," both in the years 1932 and 1936. This feat was repeated by Katarina Witt (East Germany) in 1984 and 1988.

skiing

World Skiing Records

Most Olympic Skiing Titles

Men

ALPINE: 3
Toni Sailer (Austria)
Downhill, slalom, giant slalom, 1956
Jean-Claude Killy (France)

Downhill, slalom, giant slalom, 1968, Alberto Tomba (Italy)*
Slalom, giant slalom, 1988; giant slalom, 1992
NORDIC: 8
Bjørn Dæhlie (Norway)
15 km, 50 km, 4 x 10-km 1992; 10 km, 15 km 1994
10 km, 50 km, 4 x 10-km 1998
JUMPING: 4
Matti Nykänen (Finland) 70-m hill 1988; 90-m hill 1984, 1988; Team 1988
Women
ALPINE: 3
Vreni Schneider (Switzerland)*
Giant slalom, slalom 1988; slalom 1994
Katja Seizinger (Germany)*
Downhill 1994; combined, downhill 1998
Deborah Campagnoni (Italy)
Super giant slalom 1992; giant slalom 1994; giant slalom 1998
NORDIC: 6
Lyubov Yegorova (Russia)
10 km, 15 km, 4 x 5-km 1992; 5 km, 10 km, 4 x 5-km 1994
***Most medals**
12 (men), Bjørn Dæhlie (Norway) also won four silver in Nordic events, 1992–98. 10 (women), Raisa Smetanina (USSR/CIS), four gold, five silver and one bronze in Nordic events, 1976–92.

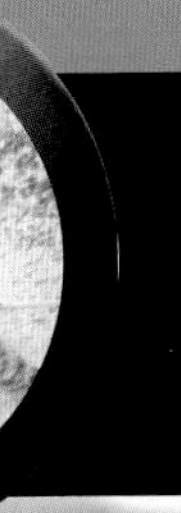

KATJA SEIZINGER HAD A SUCCESSFUL 1997/98 SEASON, WINNING THE SUPER GIANT SLALOM WORLD CUP TITLE FOR A RECORD FIFTH TIME, AND TWO GOLDS AND A BRONZE AT THE 1998 WINTER OLYMPICS. HER OVERALL TOTALS OF THREE GOLDS AND FIVE MEDALS ARE BOTH RECORDS.

In Alpine skiing, the record is five: Alberto Tomba won silver in the 1992 and 1994 slalom; Vreni Schneider won silver in the combined and bronze in the giant slalom in 1994; Katja Seizinger won bronze in the 1992 and 1998 super giant slalom; and Kjetil André Aamodt (Norway) won one gold (super giant slalom 1992), two silver (downhill, combined 1994) and two bronze (giant slalom 1992, super giant slalom 1994).

Most World Cup Titles
ALPINE SKIING (instituted 1967)
Men
Overall: 5
Marc Girardelli (Luxembourg), 1985–86, 1989, 1991, 1993
Downhill: 5
Franz Klammer (Austria), 1975–78, 1983
Slalom: 8
Ingemar Stenmark (Sweden), 1975–81, 1983
Giant Slalom: 7
Ingemar Stenmark (Sweden), 1975–76, 1978–81, 1984
Super Giant Slalom: 4
Pirmin Zurbriggen (Switzerland) 1987–90
Two men have won four titles in one year: Jean-Claude Killy (France) won all four possible disciplines (downhill, slalom, giant slalom and overall) in 1967; and Pirmin Zurbriggen (Switzerland) won four of the five possible disciplines (downhill, giant slalom, super giant slalom [added 1986] and overall) in 1987.
Women
Overall: 6
Annemarie Moser-Pröll (Austria), 1971–75, 1979
Downhill: 7
Annemarie Moser-Pröll, 1971–75, 1978–79
Slalom: 6
Vreni Schneider (Switzerland) 1989–90, 1992–95
Giant Slalom: 5
Vreni Schneider (Switzerland), 1986–7, 1989, 1991, 1995
Super Giant Slalom: 5
Katja Seizinger (Germany), 1993–96, 1998
NORDIC SKIING (instituted 1981)
Men
Jumping: 4
Matti Nykänen (Finland), 1983, 1985–86, 1988
Cross-country: 5
Gunde Svan (Sweden), 1984–86, 1988–89
Bjørn Dæhlie (Norway), 1992–93, 1995–97
Women
Cross Country: 4
Yelena Välbe (USSR/Russia), 1989, 1991–92, 1995

squash

World Squash Records
World Championships
The most men's world team titles is six by: Australia 1967, 1969, 1971, 1973, 1989 and 1991; and Pakistan 1977, 1981, 1983, 1985, 1987 and 1993.
The women's title has been won four times by, England, 1985, 1987, 1989 and 1990 (Great Britain won in 1979) and Australia, 1981, 1983, 1992 and 1994.
Jansher Khan (Pakistan) has won eight World Open (instituted 1976) titles, 1987, 1989–90, 1992–96. Jahangir Khan (Pakistan) won six World Open titles, 1981–85 and 1988, and the International Squash Rackets Federation world individual title (formerly World Amateur, instituted 1967) in 1979, 1983 and 1985. Geoffrey B. Hunt (Australia) won four World Open titles, 1976–77 and 1979–80 and three World Amateur, 1967, 1969 and 1971.
The most women's World Open titles is four by Susan Devoy (New Zealand), 1985, 1987, 1990 and 1992.

swimming

World Swimming Records
WORLD RECORDS
(set in 50-m pools)
Men
Freestyle
50 m: 21.81
Tom Jager (US)
Nashville, Tennessee, March 24, 1990
100 m: 48.21
Aleksandr Popov (Russia)
Monte Carlo, June 18, 1994
200 m: 1:46.69
Giorgio Lamberti (Italy)
Bonn, Germany, August 15, 1989
400 m: 3:43.80
Kieren Perkins (Australia)
Rome, Italy, September 9, 1994
800 m: 7:46.00
Kieren Perkins (Australia)
Victoria, Canada, August 24, 1994
1,500 m: 14:41.66
Kieren Perkins (Australia)
Victoria, Canada, August 24, 1994
4 x 100 m: 3:15.11
US (David Fox, Joe Hudepohl, Jon Olsen, Gary Hall Jr.)
Atlanta, Georgia, August 12, 1995
4 x 200-m: 7:11.95
CIS (Dmitriy Lepikov, Vladimir Pyechenko, Venyamin Tayanovich, Yevgeniy Sadovyi)
Barcelona, Spain, July 27, 1992
Breaststroke
100 m: 1:00.60
Frédéric Deburghgraeve (Belgium)
Atlanta, Georgia, July 20, 1996
200 m: 2:10.16
Michael Barrowman (US)
Barcelona, Spain, July 29, 1992
Butterfly
100 m: 52.15
Michael Klim (Australia)
Australia, October 9, 1997
200 m: 1:55.22
Denis Pankratov (Russia)
Canet-en-Roussillon, France, June 14, 1995
Backstroke
100 m: 53.86
Jeff Rouse (US)
Barcelona, Spain, July 31, 1992
200 m: 1:56.57
Martin López-Zubero (Spain)
Tuscaloosa, Alabama, November 23, 1991
Medley
200 m: 1:58.16
Jani Nikanor Sievinen (Finland) Rome, Italy, September 11, 1994
400 m: 4:12.30
Tom Dolan (US), Rome, Italy, September 6, 1994
4 x 100-m: 3:34.84
US (Gary Hall Jr., Mark Henderson, Jeremy Linn, Jeff Rouse)
Atlanta, Georgia, July 26, 1996
Women
Freestyle
50 m: 24.51
Le Jingyi (China)
Rome, Italy, September 11, 1994
100 m: 54.01
Le Jingyi (China)
Rome, Italy, September 5, 1994
200 m: 1:56.78
Franziska van Almsick (Germany)
Rome, Italy, September 6, 1994
400 m: 4:03.8
Janet Evans (US)
Seoul, South Korea, September 22, 1988
800 m: 8:16.22
Janet Evans
Tokyo, Japan, August 20, 1989
1,500 m: 15:52.10
Janet Evans
Orlando, Florida, March 26, 1988

MARK WARNECKE OF GERMANY, HOLDER OF THE SHORT-COURSE WORLD RECORD FOR 50-M BREASTSTROKE, HAS SET THE RECORD TIME OF 26.97 SECONDS FOR THE EVENT ON NO FEWER THAN THREE OCCASIONS.

4 x 100-m: 3:37.91
China (Le Jingyi, Shan Ying, Le Ying, Lu Bin)
Rome, Italy, September 7, 1994
4 x 200-m: 7:55.47
East Germany (Manuela Stellmach, Astrid Strauss, Anke Möhring, Heike Friedrich)
Strasbourg, France, August 18, 1987
Breaststroke
100 m: 1:07.02
Penny Heyns (South Africa) Atlanta, Georgia, July 21, 1996
200 m: 2:24.76
Rebecca Brown (Australia)
Brisbane, Australia, March 16, 1994
Butterfly
100 m: 57.93
Mary T. Meagher (US)
Brown Deer, Wisconsin, August 16, 1981
200 m: 2:05.96
Mary T. Meagher (US)
Brown Deer, Wisconsin, August 13, 1981
Backstroke
100 m: 1:00.16
He Cihong (China)
Rome, Italy, September 10, 1994
200 m: 2:06.62
Krisztina Egerszegi (Hungary)
Athens, Greece, August 25, 1991

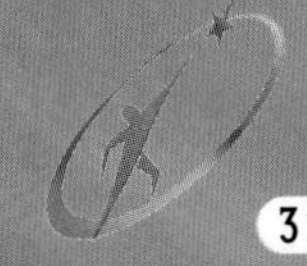

Medley
200 m: 2:09.72
Wu Yanyan (China)
Shanghai, China, October 17, 1997
400 m: 4:34.79
Chen Yan (China)
Shanghai, China, October 17, 1997
4 x 100-m: 4:01.67
China (He Cihong, Dai Guohong, Liu Limin, Le Jingyi)
Rome, Italy, September 10, 1994

Short-Course Swimming World Records
(set in 25-m pools)

Men
Freestyle
50 m: 21.50
Aleksandr Popov (Russia)
Desenzano, Italy, March 13, 1994
100 m: 46.74
Aleksandr Popov (Russia)
Gelsenkirchen, Germany, March 19, 1994
200 m: 1:43.64
Giorgio Lamberti (Italy)
Bonn, Germany, February 11, 1990
400 m: 3:40.46
Danyon Loader (New Zealand)
Sheffield, England, February 11, 1995
800 m: 7:34.90
Kieren Perkins (Australia)
Sydney, Australia, July 25, 1993
1,500 m: 14:26.52
Kieren Perkins (Australia)
Auckland, New Zealand, July 15, 1993
4 x 50-m: 1:27.62
Sweden
Stavanger, Norway, December 2, 1994
4 x 100-m: 3:12.11
Brazil
Palma de Mallorca, Spain, December 5, 1993
4 x 200-m: 7:02.74
Australia
Gothenburg, Sweden, April 18, 1997
Backstroke
50 m: 24.25
Chris Renaud (Canada)
St. Catharine's, Canada, February 28, 1997
100 m: 51.43
Jeff Rouse (US)
Sheffield, England, April 12, 1993
200 m: 1:52.51
Martin Lopez-Zubero (Spain)
Gainesville, Florida, April 10, 1991
Breaststroke
50 m: 26.97
Mark Warnecke (Germany)
Paris, France, February 8, 1997
Sydney, Australia, January 22, 1998
Paris, France, March 28, 1998
100 m: 59.02
Frédéric Deburghgraeve (Belgium)
Bastogne, Belgium, February 17, 1996
200 m: 2:07.79
Adrey Korneev (Russia)
Paris, France, March 28, 1998
Butterfly
50 m: 23.35
Denis Pankratov (Russia)
Paris, France, February 8, 1997
100 m: 51.07
Michael Klim (Australia)
Sydney, Australia, January 22, 1998
200 m: 1:51.76
James Hickman (GB)
Paris, France, March 28, 1998
Medley
100 m: 53.10
Jani Sievinen (Finland)
Malmö, Sweden, January 30, 1996
200 m: 1:54.65
Jani Sievinen
Kuopio, Finland, January 21, 1994
400 m: 4:05.41
Marcel Wouda (Netherlands)
Paris, France, February 8, 1997
4 x 50-m: 1:36.69
Auburn Aquatics
Auburn, New York, April 9, 1996
4 x 100-m: 3:30.66
Australia
Gothenburg, Sweden, April 17, 1997

James Hickman (GB), center, in the yellow cap, starts the 100-m butterfly in Sheffield, England, one of the World Cup short course series venues for the 1997/98 season. Hickman dominated longer distance butterfly events in the season and set a new 200-m world record in the final World Cup meet in Paris, France.

Women
Freestyle
50 m: 24.23
Le Jingyi (China)
Palma de Mallorca, Spain, December 3, 1993
100 m: 53.01
Le Jingyi (China)
Palma de Mallorca, Spain, December 2, 1993
200 m: 1:54.17
Claudia Poll (Costa Rica)
Gothenburg, Sweden, April 18, 1997
400 m: 4:00.03
Claudia Poll
Gothenburg, Sweden, April 19, 1997
800 m: 8:15.34
Astrid Strauss (East Germany)
Bonn, Germany, February 6, 1987
1,500 m: 15:43.31
Petra Schneider (East Germany)
Gainesville, Florida, January 10, 1982
4 x 50-m: 1:40.63
Germany
Espoo, Finland, November 22, 1992
4 x 100-m: 3:34.55
China
Gothenburg, Sweden, April 19, 1997
4 x 200-m: 7:51.92
China
Gothenburg, Sweden, April 17, 1997
Backstroke
50 m: 27.64
Bai Xiuyu (China)
Desenzano, Italy, March 12, 1994
100 m: 58.50
Angel Martino (US)
Palma de Mallorca, Spain, December 3, 1993
200 m: 2:06.09
He Cihong (China)
Mallorca, Spain, December 5, 1993
Breaststroke
50 m: 30.77
Han Xue (China)
Gelsenkirchen, Germany, February 2, 1997
100 m: 1:05.70
Samantha Riley (Australia)
Rio de Janeiro, Brazil, December 2, 1995
200 m: 2:20.85
Samantha Riley
Rio de Janeiro, Brazil, December 1, 1995
Butterfly
50 m: 26.48
Jenny Thompson (US)
Toronto, Canada, November 29, 1997
100 m: 57.79
Jenny Thompson
Gothenburg, Sweden, April 19, 1997
200 m: 2:05.65
Mary T. Meagher (US)
Gainesville, Florida, January 2, 1981
Medley
100 m: 1:00.60
Hu Xiaowen (China)
Beijing, China, November 29, 1997
200 m: 2:07.79
Allison Wagner (US)
Mallorca, Spain, December 5, 1993
400 m: 4:29.00
Dai Gouhong (China)
Mallorca, Spain, December 2, 1993
4 x 50-m: 1:52.44
Germany
Espoo, Finland, November 21, 1992
4 x 100-m: 3:57.73
China
Mallorca, Spain, December 5, 1993

water skiing

World Water Skiing Records
Slalom
Men: 1 buoy on 9.75-m (32-ft.) line
Jeff Rogers (US)
Charleston, South Carolina, on August 31, 1997.
Women: 1 buoy on 10.25-m (34-ft.) line
Kristi Overton Johnson (US)
West Palm Beach, Florida, September 14, 1996
TRICKS
Men: 11,680 points
Cory Pickos (US)
Zachary, Louisiana, May 10, 1997
Women: 8,580 points
Tawn Larsen (US)
Groveland, Florida, July 4, 1992.
JUMPING
Men: 67.8 m (222 ft.)
Bruce Neville (Australia)
Orangeville, Canada, July 27, 1997
John Swanson (US)
Bow Hill, Washington, September 13, 1997
Women: 50.5 m (165 ft.)
Brenda Nichols Baldwin (US)
Okahumpka, Florida, April 27, 1997.

Of the three disciplines in water skiing, jumping is considered the most exciting. In 1997, the first jump in excess of 50 meters by a woman was achieved when Brenda Nichols Baldwin leaped to 50.5 m in April. The men's first 50 m-plus jump was made in 1970 by American Mike Suyderhoud.

weightlifting

World Weightlifting Records
From January 1, 1993, the International Weightlifting Federation (IWF) introduced modified bodyweight categories, thereby making the then world records redundant. This is the current list for the new weight categories (as of December 31, 1997).
Bodyweight 54 kg (119 lb.)
Snatch: 132.5 kg (292 lb.)
Halil Mutlu (Turkey)
Atlanta, Georgia, July 20, 1996
Jerk: 160.5 kg (353 3/4 lb.)
Lan Shizang (China)
Chiang Mai, Thailand, December 6, 1997
Total: 290 kg (639 1/4 lb.)
Halil Mutlu
Istanbul, Turkey, November 18, 1994
Bodyweight 59 kg (130 lb.)
Snatch: 140 kg (308 1/2 lb.)
Hafiz Suleymanoğlü (Turkey)
Warsaw, Poland, May 3, 1995
Jerk: 170 kg (374 3/4 lb.)
Nikolai Peshalov (Bulgaria)
Warsaw, Poland, May 3, 1995
Total: 307.5 kg (677 3/4 lb.)
Tang Ningsheng (China)
Atlanta, Georgia, July 21, 1996

Bodyweight 64 kg (141 lb.)
Snatch: 150 kg (330½ lb.)
Wang Guohua (China)
Pusan, South Korea, May 12, 1997
Jerk: 187.5 kg (413¼ lb.)
Valerios Leonidis (Greece)
Atlanta, Georgia, July 22, 1996
Total: 335 kg (738½ lb.)
Naim Suleymanoğlü (Turkey; formerly Naim Suleimanov or Neum Shalamanov of Bulgaria), Atlanta, Georgia, July 22, 1996
Bodyweight 70 kg (154¼ lb.)
Snatch: 163 kg (359¼ lb.)
Wan Jianhui (China)
Guangzhou, China, July 9, 1997
Jerk: 195.5 kg (429¾ lb.)
Zhan Xugang (China)
Chiang Mai, Thailand, December 9, 1997
Total: 357.5 kg (788 lb.)
Zhan Xugang
Atlanta, Georgia, July 23, 1996
Bodyweight 76 kg (167½ lb.)
Snatch: 170 kg (374¾ lb.)
Ruslan Savchenko (Ukraine)
Melbourne, Australia, November 16, 1993
Jerk: 208 kg (458½ lb.)
Pablo Lara (Cuba)
Szekszárd, Hungary, April 20, 1996
Total: 372.5 kg (821 lb.)
Pablo Lara
Szekszárd, Hungary, April 20, 1996

Bodyweight 108 kg (238 lb.)
Snatch: 200 kg (440¾ lb.)
Timur Taimazov (Ukraine)
Istanbul, Turkey, November 26, 1994
Jerk: 236 kg (520½ lb.)
Timur Taimazov
Atlanta, Georgia, July 29, 1996
Total: 435 kg (959 lb.)
Timur Taimazov
Istanbul, Turkey, November 26, 1994
Bodyweight Over 108 kg
Snatch: 205 kg (451¾ lb.)
Aleksandr Kurlovich (Belarus)
Istanbul, Turkey, November 27, 1994
Jerk: 262.5 kg (578½ lb.)
Andrey Chemerkin (Russia)
Chiang Mai, Thailand, December 14, 1997
Total: 462.5 kg (1,019½ lb.)
Andrey Chemerkin
Chiang Mai, Thailand, December 14, 1997

Bodyweight 59 kg (130 lb.)
Snatch: 100 kg (220¼ lb.)
Zou Feie (China)
Pusan, South Korea, May 13, 1997
Jerk: 125 kg (275½ lb.)
Suta Khassaraporn (Thailand)
Jakarta, Thailand, October 13, 1997
Total: 220 kg (485 lb.)
Chen Xiaomin (China)
Hiroshima, Japan, October 4, 1994
Bodyweight 64 kg (141 lb.)
Snatch: 107.5 kg (237 lb.)
Chen Xiaomin
Guangzhou, China, July 10, 1997
Jerk: 130.5 kg (287½ lb.)
Shi Lihua (China)
Lahti, Finland, August 9, 1997
Total: 235 kg (518 lb.)
Li Hongyun (China)
Istanbul, Turkey, November 22, 1994
Bodyweight 70 kg (154¼ lb.)
Snatch: 105.5 kg (232½ lb.)
Xiang Fenglan (China)
Chiang Mai, Thailand, December 11, 1997
Jerk: 131 kg (288¾ lb.)
Xiang Fenglan
Chiang Mai, Thailand, December 11, 1997
Total: 235 kg (518 lb.)
Xiang Fenglan
Chiang Mai, Thailand, December 11, 1997

yachting

World Yachting Records
Olympic Titles
The first sportsman ever to win individual gold medals in four successive Olympic Games was Paul Elvstrøm (Denmark) in the Firefly class in 1948 and the Finn class in 1952, 1956 and 1960.
Elvstrøm also won eight other world titles in a total of six classes.
AMERICA'S CUP
There have been 29 challenges since August 8, 1870, with the US winning on every occasion except 1983 (to Australia) and 1995 (to New Zealand).
In individual races sailed, US boats have won 81 races. Non-US challengers have won 13 races.
Most appearances in the America's Cup
Dennis Conner, six appearances since 1974

ZHAN XUGANG OF CHINA AT THE 1996 OLYMPICS IN ATLANTA, WHERE HE SET WORLD RECORDS IN SNATCH, JERK AND TOTAL. HIS TOTAL RECORD REMAINED THE BEST MARK WHEN THE GOVERNING BODY RESTRUCTURED THE CATEGORIES AND CONSIGNED THE RECORDS AS OF DECEMBER 31, 1997 TO THE ARCHIVES.

THE UNITED STATES COMPETING DURING THE AMERICA'S CUP. AMERICAN SAILORS HAVE DOMINATED THE COMPETITION THROUGHOUT ITS HISTORY, LOSING ONLY TWO CHALLENGES SINCE THE FIRST WAS MADE IN 1870.

Bodyweight 83 kg (183 lb.)
Snatch: 180 kg (396¾ lb.)
Pyrros Dimas (Greece)
Atlanta, Georgia, July 26, 1996
Jerk: 214 kg (471¾ lb.)
Zhang Yong (China)
Guangzhou, China, July 12, 1997
Total: 392.5 kg (865¼ lb.)
Pyrros Dimas, Atlanta, Georgia, July 26, 1996
Bodyweight 91 kg (200½ lb.)
Snatch: 187.5 kg (413¼ lb.)
Aleksey Petrov (Russia)
Atlanta, Georgia, July 27, 1996
Jerk: 228.5 kg (503¾ lb.)
Akakide Kakhiasvilis (Greece)
Warsaw, Poland, May 6 1995
Total: 412.5 kg (909¼ lb.)
Aleksey Petrov (Russia)
Sokolov, Czech Republic, May 7, 1994
Bodyweight 99 kg (218¼ lb.)
Snatch: 192.5 kg (424¼ lb.)
Sergey Syrtsov (Russia)
Istanbul, Turkey, November 25, 1994
Jerk: 235 kg (518 lb.)
Akakide Kakhiasvilis (Greece)
Atlanta, Georgia, July 28, 1996
Total: 420 kg (925¾ lb.)
Akakide Kakhiasvilis
Atlanta, Georgia, July 28, 1996

WOMEN'S WEIGHTLIFTING RECORDS
Bodyweight 46 kg (101¼ lb.)
Snatch: 81.5 kg (179½ lb.)
Jiang Yinsu (China)
Pusan, South Korea, May 11, 1997
Jerk: 105.5 kg (232½ lb.)
Xing Fen (China)
Guangzhou, China, July 8 1997
Total: 185 kg (407¾ lb.)
Guang Hong (China)
Yachiyo, Japan, April 4, 1996
Bodyweight 50 kg (110¼ lb.)
Snatch: 88 kg (194 lb.)
Jiang Baoyu (China)
Pusan, South Korea, July 3, 1995
Jerk: 110.5 kg (243½ lb.)
Liu Xiuhua (China)
Hiroshima, Japan, October 3, 1994
Total: 197.5 kg (435¼ lb.)
Liu Xiuhua
Hiroshima, Japan, October 3, 1994
Bodyweight 54 kg (119 lb.)
Snatch: 93.5 kg (206 lb.)
Yang Xia (China)
Guangzhou, China, July 9, 1997
Jerk: 117.5 kg (259 lb.)
Mengh Xiajuan (China)
Chiang Mai, Thailand, December 8, 1997
Total: 207.5 kg (457¼ lb.)
Yang Xia (China)
Guangzhou, China, July 9, 1997

Bodyweight 76 kg (167½ lb.)
Snatch: 107.5 kg (237 lb.)
Hua Ju (China)
Chiang Mai, Thailand, December 12, 1997
Jerk: 140.5 kg (309¾ lb.)
Hua Ju
Chiang Mai, Thailand, December 12, 1997
Total: 247.5 kg (545½ lb.)
Hua Ju
Chiang Mai, Thailand, December 12, 1997
Bodyweight 83 kg (183 lb.)
Snatch: 117.5 kg (259 lb.)
Tang Weifang (China)
Chiang Mai, Thailand, December 13, 1997
Jerk: 143 kg (315¼ lb.)
Tang Weifang
Chiang Mai, Thailand, December 13, 1997
Total: 260 kg (573 lb.)
Tang Weifang
Chiang Mai, Thailand, December 13, 1997
Bodyweight over 83 kg (183 lb.)
Snatch: 112.5 kg (248 lb.)
Wang Yanmei (China)
Guangzhou, China, July 14, 1997
Jerk: 155 kg (341½ lb.)
Li Yajuan (China)
Melbourne, Australia, November 20, 1993
Total: 260 kg (573 lb.)
Li Yajuan
Melbourne, Australia, November 20, 1993

Admiral's Cup
The ocean racing team series to have had the most participating nations (three boats allowed to each nation) is the Admiral's Cup, organized by the Royal Ocean Racing Club.
A record 19 nations competed in 1975, 1977 and 1979.
Britain has had a record nine wins.
Highest speeds
Men
The highest speed reached under sail on water by any craft over a 500-m timed run is 46.52 knots (86.21 km/h or 53.57 mph) by trifoiler *Yellow Pages Endeavour* piloted by Simon McKeon and Tim Daddo, both of Australia, at Sandy Point near Melbourne, Australia, on October 26, 1993.
Highest speeds
Women
The highest speed reached under sail on water by any craft over a 500-m timed run is by Elisabeth Coquelle (France), with 40.38 knots (74.83 km/h or 46.5 mph) in Tarifa, Spain, on July 7, 1995.

index

C

PHOTO CREDITS

ADVERTISING ARCHIVES: 44, 45 (x2), 246. **ALLSPORT:** 284 Simon Bruty, 303 Bob Martin. **ALPHA:** 57 Angeli, 73 Angeli. **ASSOCIATED PRESS:** 6 Itsuo Inouye, 6 Kevorn Djansezian, 7 Mark Fallander, 12 Michel Euler, 12&13 Reed Saxon, 15 Nelson Machin/ABC, 16 Fred Jewel, 16 Antonio Calanni, 17 Jytte Nielsen, 17 Steve Stevett, 23 Giovanni Diffidenti, 23 Jacqueline Arzt, 26 Max Nash, 27 Alexander Zemlianichenko, 27 Ron Edmonds, 28 Damian Dovarganes, 32 Mike Fiala, 33 Jonathan Exley/ABC, 35 Anatoly Maltsev, 35 Emil Wamsteker, 36 Stuart Ramson, 37 Sotheby's, 37 Gino Domenico, 38 Lennox McLendon (x2), 38 EFE, 40 Lionel Cironneau, 42 Sakchai Lalit, 44, 46 John Moore, 48 Katsumi Kasahara, 49 David J. Coulson, 49 Jack Dempsey, 50, 51 Ed Reinke, 53 Green Tree Financial Corp, 53 Noemi Bruzak, 58 Susan Goldman, 60 Michael Lipchitz, 61 Sven Kaestner, 62 Michel Lipchitz, 67 Mark Lennihan, 69 Marty Lederhandler, 72 Bill Waugh, 73 Bill Sikes (x2), 76 Lennox McLendon, 77 Jeff Scheid, 78 Chris Brandis, 78 Jalil Bounhar, 79 Rob Orchiston, 79 David Thompson, 81, 80 A.F. Singer/CBS, 84 Pat Roque, 85, 86, 87 Adam Stoltman, 88 Farmers Museum (x2), 89 Eric Draper, 90 Saurabh Das, 91 Joan Esteve/EFE, 92 Barry Sweet, 96 Jean-Marc Bouju, 97 Liu Hong Shing, 98 Bernhard Kunz, 101 Tassanee Vejpongsa, 102 Mohamed El-Dakhakhny, 103 Michael Kardis, 106 Lacy Atkins, 109 Long Photography, 112 Damon Winter, 117 Ueno Zoo, 118 Sherwin Crasto, 122 Barry Sweet, 128 Michael Caulfield, 132 Minnesota Pollution Control Agency, 133 Craig Line, 134 LM Otero, 136 Lou Krasky, 136 Michel Springler, 137 Pierre Thielemans, 137 Tad Motoyama, 138 Charles Dharapak, 138 Susan Ragan, 143, 144 Jack Smith, 144 Mata Kokkali, 156 Eric Draper, 156 Santiago Lyon, 158 Dusan Vranic, 160 Marty Lederhandler, 161 Chrysler Corp, 161 Donald Stampfli, 163 Sergei Karpukhin, 165 Murad Sezer, 166 Peter Cosgrove, 166 Mauel Podio/EFE, 167 Guilo Broglio, 173 Katsumi Kasahara, 174 Michael Schmelling, 175 Lennox McLendon, 177, 177 Michael Probst, 178 Adam Nadel, 178 IBM, 180 Katsumi Kasahara, 181 Itsuo Inouye, 181 Michael Tweed, 184 Lennox McLendon (x2), 184 Jim Tuten/Busch Gardens, 186 NASA, 186 EFE, 186 Silvina Frydlewsky, 187 White Sands Missile Range, 187, 193 Win McNamee, 194 Denis Poroy, 194, 195 Manuel Chavez, 196 Lionel Cironneau, 196 Heinz Ducklau, 197 Dimitar Deinov, 198 Peter Lauth/Keystone, 198 Undersea Imaging Intl, 199 Ajit Kumar, 199 David Longstreath, 201 Bernama, 202 Martin Mejia, 203 Doug Dreyer, 204 Jonathan Hayward/CP, 205, 205 Zaheeruddin Abdullah, 211, 214, 216 Katsumi Kasahara, 216 Susan Goldman, 220 Richard Drew, 220-21 Whitney Museum of Modern Art, 224 Joan Marcus, 224 Nigel Teare, 224 John Parkin, 225 Mark Fallander, 225, 235 Kevorn Djansezian, 238, 239 Michael Caulfield, 240 Jose Caruci, 241 Diego Giudice, 241 Thomas Kienzle, 244 Sven Kaestner, 244 Jan Bauer, 247 Kathy Willens, 248 Laurent Rebours, 248 Michel Euler, 249 Michel Lipchitz, 250-51 Kirthmon Dozier, 254/255 & 256 Remy de la Mauviniere, 256 Denis Paquin, 257 Keystone, 257 News Ltd, 258 Susan Sterner, 258 Laurent Rebours, 259 David Longstreath, 260 Brian K. Diggs, 260 Thomas Kienzle, 261 Kevork Djansezian, 261 Steve Holland, 262 (x3), 263 Doug Mills, 264 Eric Draper, 264 Alexander Zemlianichenko, 265 Beth A. Keiser, 265 Lynne Sladky, 266 John Bazemore, 266 Tsugufumi Matsumoto, 267 Denis Paquin, 268 Michael Conroy, 268 Tannen Maury, 269 Mark J. Terrill, 270 Frank Gunn, 270 Drew Murphy, 271 John Bazemore, 271 Bill Sikes, 272 Laurent Rebours, 272 Lionel Cironneau, 273 Luca Bruno, 273 David Graham, 274 Tom Strattman, 274 David Longstreath, 276 Paul Sakuma (x2), 277 Claudio Scaccini, 277 Luca Bruno, 278 Tom Pidgeon, 278 *Sports Illustrated*, 280 Andy Newman, 282 Itsuo Inouye, 282 Jack Smith, 284 Chitose Suzuki, 285 Fabrice Coffrini, 285, 286 Jozef Klamar, 288 Pietro Cinotti, 289 Louisa Buller, 289 Vincent Yu, 290 Pavel Rahman, 291 Rick Rycroft, 293 Chien-Min Chung, 293 Kevork Djansezian, 294 Robert F. Bukaty (x2), 295 Robert F. Bukaty, 296, 300 Bonod Joshi, 302 Peter Dejong, 302 Tony Cheng, 302 Denis Paquin, 304, 305 (x2), 306 (x2), 307 (x2), 308 (x2), 309 (x2), 310 (x2), 311, 312 (x2), 314, 315. **BILDERBERG ARCHIVE:** 221. **BOOMERANG:** 112 Steve Haworth/Zuma. **COMSTOCK:** 221 Dr G. Gerster. **CORBIS:** 10, 18, 18 Mitchell Gerber, 24 Bettmann, 24 Tim Page, 28 & 29 Neal Preston, 41 James Marshall, 47 Nevada Wier, 47 Gina Glover, 48 Kelly Mooney, 59 Kevin Fleming, 63 Kelly Mooney, 66 The Purcell Team, 66 Arne Hodalic, 71 Mitchell Gerber, 72 Hulton-Deutsch Collection, 74 Chris Taylor, 75 Gunter Marx, 76 Reinhard Eisele, 86 Tim Wright, 88 Christopher Cormack, 90 UPI, 93 UPI/Bettmann, 93 Wolfgang Kaehler, 98-99 Science Pictures, 99 Mary Clark/Cordaiy, 106/107 Science Pictures, 110 Dave G. Houser, 111, 132 Anthony Bannister/ABPL, 132/133 Steve Austin/Papilio, 150 Bob Rowan, 150 Kit Kittle, 151 Owen Franken, 154 Earl Kowall, 155 Eye Ubiquitous, 156 Roger Ressmeyer, 162 George Hall, 163 Museum of Flight, 164 George Hall, 179 NASA, 182 Neal Preston, 192 Bettmann, 192 US Department of Defense, 192-93 U.S. Department of Energy, 193 US Department of Defense, 197 Gianni Dagli Orti, 200 Eva Miessler/Ecoscene, 201 Tim Wright, 202-03 Roger Ressmeyer, 203 The Purcell Team, 217 Kevin Fleming, 234 David Reed, 239 Neal Preston, 239 Pat O'Hara, 240 Neal Preston, 242 Erich Auerbach, 242 UPI/Bettmann, 243 Hulton-Deutsch Collection, 244 Stephanie Maze, 245 Richard Glover, 245 Peter Finger, 254 Christian Liewig, 275 Neal Preston (x3), 281 Michelle Chaplow, 292, 296 Tony Arruza, 297 Patrick Ward, 301 Robert Holmes, 300&301 Galen Rowell, 314, 315, 336 Hulton-Deutsch Collection. **EMPICS:** 252, 252, 253, 253 Leo Vogelzang, 254 Tony Marshall, 255 Michael Steele, 259, 286 Mathew Ashton, 287 Presse Sport, 291, 311, 313, 313 Steve Mitchell. **FSP:** 70 David Atlan, 71 Ponomareff, 91 Pete Souza/Gamma/Liason, 97 Ferry/Gamma/Liason, 101 Kumar Ajit/Gamma/Liason. **GARDEN PICTURE LIBRARY:** 142 JS Sira, 142 C. Fairweather, 143 John Glover, 143 JS Sira. **IDOLS:** 19 George Bodnar, 228 Barry Marsden, 229 William Rutten, 232 Barry Marsden, 233 Gene Kirkland, 235 Sergey Sergeyev, 236 Y. Lenquette/Vision. **IMAGE BANK:** 8-9 Daniel Arsenault, 30 Henry Sims, 30-31 Derek Berwin, 32-33 Andy Caulfield, 38-39 C. Van Der Lende, 39 Mitchell Funk, 46 Andy Caulfield, 61 D. Roundtree, 62 Anthony Johnson, 65 D. W. Hamilton, 73 Larry Keenan, 80 Flip Chalfant, 82-83 Tomek Sikora, 85 Bardos&Bardos, 86 Mahaux, 98 Derek Berwin, 106 Garry Gay, 107 Benn Mitchell, 107, 114-15 Derek Berwin, 116 & 118 Joseph Van Os, 123 Derek Berwin, 125 James Carmichael, 125 Joseph van Os, 126 Derek Berwin, 127, 127 Grant V. Faint, 128 Luis Castaneda, 129 P. Goetgeluck, 130 Alain Chambon, 130-31 Luis Castaneda, 140 Grant V. Faint, 135 A. Boccaccio, 145 F. Ruggeri, 146 Steve Bronstein, 147 Andre Gallant, 151 White/Packert, 154 Pete Turner, 154-55 Frans Lemmens, 157, 164 Pete Turner, 167 Terje Rakke, 168 Steve Dunwell, 168-69 T. Anderson, 180-81 Stephen Marks, 182, 190-91 H. De Lespinasse, 212-13 Gary Russ, 226-27 Tomek Sikora, 262-63 Yellow Dog Prds, 278 Terje Rakke, 279 M. Tcherevkoff, 282-83 Jay Silverman, 297 Tom King, 299, 299 Terje Rakke, 304-05 Peter Holst, 306-07 Steve Satshek, 308-09 Terje Rakke, 310-11 David Madison, 312-13 Stephen Marks, 314-15 John Banagan. **IMAGES:** 118 & 119 *National Geographic*, 122 & 124 *National Geographic*. **JOHN CONNOR PRESS:** 57. **KATZ:** 15 Mark Selinger/Outline, 20 Dana Lixenberg/Outline, 21 Andrew Eccles/Outline, 21 Darryl Estrine. **KOBAL:** 25, 210 (x2), 211 (x2), 212, 213 (x2). **LFI:** 228 David Fisher, 230, 230 Ted Hawes, 236, 236 Nick Elgar, 237 Gregg De Guire, 240 David Fisher. **NASA:** Cover, endpapers, 146, 148 (x2), 149 (x3), 188 (x2), 189 (x2). **NETWORK:** 204 Mike Goldwater. **OXFORD SCIENTIFIC FILMS:** 116 Keren Su, 117 Richard Packwood, 120 & 121 Norbet Wu, 129 Mantis, 141 Kjell Sandved. **PA NEWS:** 20 Neil Munns, 22 (x2), 22 Michael Stephens, 23, 45 Sean Dempsey, 51, 63 Manuel Moura/EPA, 78 Chas Breton/Western Daily Press, 81, 105, 124 Hoang Dinh Nam/AFP, 139 EPA, 145 Roslin Institute, 160 Renault, 161 Honda, 162, 163, 185 Rui Vieira, 194, 225, 229 Lousia Buller, 231 Neil Munns (x2), 234 Sean Dempsey, 290 Rebecca Naden. **PLANET EARTH:** 121 James D Watt, 123 Paulo De Oliveira, 134 Chris Huxley, 141 Robert A. Jureit. **POPPERFOTO:** 131 Reuters. **PPCM:** 176. **RETNA:** 232 King Collection, 232 David Atlas, 233 Baron Wolman, 233 Andy Earl. **REX FEATURES:** 11 (x2), 24 Kirk Weddle/Sipa Press, 25 Brian Rasic, 39 Sipa Press, 41 Ralph Merlino, 52 Terry Richards/Sun/Sipa Press, 52 Sipa Press, 63 Nils Jorgenson, 100 Shakhverdiev/Sipa Press, 108 Sipa Press, 108 Ben Simmons/Sipa Press, 109 Dave Hogan, 111 Greg Williams, 113 Ian Waldie, 175 Charles Ommanney (x2), 298 MAMP/Sipa Press. **SCIENCE PHOTO LIBRARY:** 104 NIBSC, 105 A. Gragera/Latin Stock. **SOLO:** 20 (x5). **SPLASH:** 10 Rupert Thorpe. **SYGMA:** 68 Alberto Pizzoli, 74 Steve Liss, 103. **TONY STONE:** 30 Tony Garcia, 152-53 Susan Werner, 243 Jon Riley. **WELLCOME TRUST:** 104, 132 (x2). **OTHER:** 6 & 246 Baush & Lomb, 217 *The Big Issue*, 64 Kevin Brown, 77 Saloo Choudhury, 42 Coca-Cola Corporation, 159 Combidrive Ltd, 336 Diageo PLC, 218 Disney, 69 Herb Ferguson, 58 Kevin Rubio & Shant Jordan/Pat Perez of TheForce.net (x3), 7 & 54-55 Ron Tom/Fox Television, 99 Prof. Brimal C. Ghosh, 266 Gordon Gillespie, 170 GT Interactive, 14 Harpo Inc, 28 *Hello!* magazine, 157 Ian Lambot/Foster and Partners, 180 Lego, 43 Levi Strauss & Co, 136 Peter Lomas, 113 Grace Martin, 159 McLaren Cars Ltd, 197 MGM, 172 NEC, 172 Nintendo Corporation, 68 Garry Norman, 173 Panasonic, 43 Pepsi Corporation, 280 & 281 Dag Pike, 32 Residensea, 139 Sharon Robinson, 298 Rudolf Rupperath, 70 Robert Schumann, 65 Sean Shannon, 34 The Collection of Mr & Mrs Bernard C. Solomon, 11 Spelling Productions, 173 Swatch, 172 Transducers Inc, 14 20th Century Fox, 183 20th Century Fox, 208 & 209 20th Century Fox, 219 Matt Groenig/20th Century Fox, 249 Victoria's Secret, 176 Virgin Records, 158 Volkswagen, 209 Warner Bros, 19 Mario Testino/Wea.

ACKNOWLEDGMENTS

Founder Editor: Norris McWhirter • Guinness Publishing Ltd would like to thank the following organizations and individuals: Andrew Adams • Duncan Anderson • Sarah Angliss • John Arblaster • Belinda Archer • Richard Balkwill • Howard Bass • BBC • Dennis Bird • Paul Boyd • Richard Braddish • Ben Brandstätter • Robert Brook • Christie's • Hilary Curtis at The World • Andrea Davies at the Tate Gallery, London • Peter Dredge at the Royal Yachting Association • Clive Everton • Adrian Firth • Michael Flynn • Foreign and Commonwealth Office • Paulette Foyle • Tim Furniss • Max Glaskin • Dr Martin Godfrey • Simon Gold • Dave Golder • Stan Greenberg • Guinness *Rockopedia*® Team • Capt. Elwyn Hartley Edwards • Ron Hildebrant • Ron Hill • Duncan Hislop • Sir Peter Johnson • Ove Karlsson • Matthew Keating at *The Guardian* • Nicky King • Tara King • Fiona Leahy • Caroline Lucas • Vincent Lucas • Dave McAleer • Chris McHugh • Chris Mason • Keith Melton • Andrzej Michalski • Andy Milroy • The Natural History Museum • Barry Norman • Antonio Pasolini • Natalie Pecht • John Randall • Jo Renshaw • Chris Rhys • Ellen Root • Irvin Saxton • Dr Karl Shuker • Tony Shuker • David Singmaster • Karen Smith • Sotheby's • Gerry Spencer • Kurt Steffick • Martin Stone • Sian Stott at *Hello!* • Jackie Swanson • Steve Trew • Juhani Virola • Jonathan Wall • Professor Kevin Warwick at Reading University • John Watson • Lt. Col. Digby Willoughby • Hugh Wrampling •

getting into the book

COLLECTIONS
Interest in big collections, such as the world's biggest collection of Barbie dolls, seen right, is evident from the many requests from collectors received by *The Guinness Book of Records*. To be considered for inclusion, collections should be clearly "themed" or contain broadly similar, but different, items. Duplicates do not count.

OPEN TO THE PUBLIC
Ashrita Furman, one of the world's most prolific record-breakers, is pictured here breaking the record for balancing glasses. Most record attempts, especially those staged to raise money for charity, are widely publicized and attract large numbers of spectators. Few challenges could be as public as those broadcast on the Fox television series *Guinness World Records™: Primetime*, but all attempts do require independent witness verification.

SPORTS RECORDS
The Guinness Book of Records is the final arbiter for all the records in this book. However, in the case of sports (and certain similar) records, verification lies with the official world governing body of each sport. For example, records in track and field events, such as the javelin, are provided by the International Amateur Athletic Federation (IAAF).

GETTING INTO THE BOOK
The Guinness Book of Records features many people who have accomplished extraordinary feats. Do you think you have what it takes to become a Guinness record-breaker? If you think you would like to break, or establish, a record, you are on the way to getting into the book.

I CAN DO THAT
Not everyone can break the 100-m track record, walk the high wire at a record altitude or become the world's youngest 300 bowler. But everyone can set or break a record, as an individual or as part of a team.

One option might be to start a large and unusual collection. This need not entail great expense: among current record-breaking collections are four-leaf clovers and lightbulbs. Nor would you have to be a professional dancer to take part in an attempt on the world line dance record. Even the most sedentary could participate in a record-breaking event – by joining in the biggest gathering of couples kissing simultaneously, for instance. Another way of getting into the book could be to devise your own record category.

DOCUMENTATION
Each and every record claim must be accompanied by detailed documentation. Two independent witness statements are the minimum requirement, and your witnesses should be people of some standing in the local community: a doctor, lawyer, elected official, police officer, or official of a professional or athletic organization, for example. Certain records may also require the judgment of an expert, such as a surveyor or a public health official. Neither witness may be related to you. Witnesses should not only be able to confirm that they have seen the successful progress and completion of the record attempt, but also that the guidelines have been followed. *The Guinness Book of Records* is unable to supply personnel to witness attempts but reserves the right to do so.

Many record attempts also require a logbook or some form of similar documentation. The requirements are specified in the guidelines. Video footage is required as part of the documentation of every record. Photographs are also required. Newspaper clippings are useful additional evidence.

APPLY EARLY
Whatever record category you decide to attempt, it is important to contact us early. If your proposal is accepted as a new category, we may have to draw up new guidelines with the assistance of experts. So please allow both Guinness and yourself plenty of time for preparation. You should also check with us shortly before the attempt in order to make sure that the record has not recently been broken.

BIGGEST AND SMALLEST
The smallest street-legal car pictured here is one of many tiny items that hold world records. All minuscule and gigantic items should be perfectly scaled-down or scaled-up versions of the real thing. They must be made from the correct materials and be fully functional.

GUIDELINES

Specific guidelines have been drawn up for almost all human achievement challenges, from window cleaning and bed making to stamp licking and cow-pat tossing. The six categories for which the most requests are received are ladder climbing, longest paper chain, longest paper clip chain, human centipede, darts and line dancing. The following guidelines for the longest paper clip chain give an idea of the regulations and standards that record-challengers can expect:

1. The maximum length of each paper clip used is 1½ inches.
2. The maximum number of people who may make the chain is 60, and the time limit is 24 hours (in one 24-hour period – not, for example, eight hours one day, eight the next and eight on a third day).
3. The chain must be one single chain, with each clip hooked into one end of another clip.

The current world record for the longest paper clip chain is 16 miles 978 yd. It was made by 60 members of Nanyang Technological University, Hall of Residence 8, Singapore, in 24 hours from July 25 to July 26, 1997.

MARATHONS

Marathons, from unicycling to musical feats, are traditionally identified with *The Guinness Book of Records*. Continuous challenges of more than 24 hours operate under strict safety guidelines. Expert advice as well as consultation with *The Guinness Book of Records* should be sought before trying them.

PHOTOGRAPHIC EVIDENCE

Susan Montgomery Williams is pictured below breaking the record for the blowing the biggest bubble-gum bubble. Detailed documentation is necessary to establish any record claim. For all categories, video and photographic evidence is now required.

NEW CATEGORIES

Every mailbag brings us a host of suggestions for new record categories, and we try to find ways of encouraging and accepting as many of these ideas as possible. What we are looking for in a new category is a challenge that is interesting, requires skill, is safe, is measurable, and – most importantly – is likely to attract subsequent challenges from other people.

GETTING IN TOUCH

To contact *The Guinness Book of Records*, write to us at:
Guinness Media, Inc.
6 Landmark Square
Stamford, CT 06901
Alternatively, you can e-mail us at infousa@guinnessrecords.com.

WILL IT BE IN THE BOOK?

Not all new records appear in the book. With many thousands of records on the *Guinness Book of Records* database, the book is a selection of the subjects and categories that we believe are of the most interest to our readers. More records will be available on our Web site.

TAKING CARE

Safety precautions are an important factor in record guidelines. All record attempts are undertaken at the sole risk of the competitor. Guinness Publishing Ltd. cannot be held responsible for any (potential) liability whatsoever arising out of any such attempt, whether to the claimant or any third party.

GUIDELINES

For most human endeavor categories, *The Guinness Book of Records* has specific guidelines to ensure that all contestants are attempting a record under exactly the same conditions as previous and subsequent challengers. Only in this way can we compare achievements.

In 1759 Arthur Guinness founded the Guinness Brewery at St. James' Gate, Dublin, and by 1833 the brewery was the largest in Ireland. Arthur Guinness Son & Co. Ltd. became a limited liability company in London in 1886, and by the 1930s Guinness had two breweries in Britain producing its special porter stout. The slogans "Guinness is good for you," "Guinness for strength" and "My Goodness, My Guinness" appeared everywhere. Guinness was the only beer on sale in every public house, yet Guinness did not actually own any of the pubs — except for the Castle Inn on its hop farms in Bodiam, England. Thus the company was always on the lookout for promotional ideas.

While at a shooting party in Co. Wexford, Ireland in 1951, Sir Hugh Beaver, the company's managing director, was involved in a dispute as to whether the golden plover was Europe's fastest game bird. Again in 1954, an argument arose as to whether grouse were faster than golden plover. Sir Hugh realized that such questions could arise among people in pubs and a book that provided answers for debates such as these would be of great use to licensees.

Chris Chataway, the record-breaking British track star was then an underbrewer at Guinness' Park Royal Brewery. He recommended the ideal people to produce the book — the twins Norris and Ross McWhirter, whom he had met through track and field events. The McWhirter brothers were then running a fact-finding agency in Fleet Street, London.

They were commissioned to compile what became *The Guinness Book of Records* and, after a busy year of research, the first copy of the 198-page book was bound on August 27, 1955. It was an instant success and became Britain's No. 1 best-seller before Christmas.

The Guinness Book of Records English language edition is now published in 40 different countries with another 37 editions in foreign languages. Sales of all editions passed 50 million in 1984, 75 million in 1994 and will reach the 100 million mark early in the next millennium.